DESIGN OF MACHINE ELEMENTS-II

M.H. Annaiah
Professor
Department of Mechanical Engineering
M.S. Ramaiah Institute of Technology
Bangalore, Karnataka

PUBLISHING FOR ONE WORLD

NEW AGE INTERNATIONAL (P) LIMITED, PUBLISHERS

New Delhi • Bangalore • Chennai • Cochin • Guwahati • Hyderabad
Jalandhar • Kolkata • Lucknow • Mumbai • Ranchi
Visit us at www.newagepublishers.com

Published by New Age International (P) Ltd., Publishers
First Edition: 2010
Reprint: 2012

BRANCHES

- **Bangalore** 37/10, 8th Cross (Near Hanuman Temple), Azad Nagar, Chamarajpet, Bangalore-560 018
  Tel.: (080) 26756823, Telefax: 26756820, E-mail: bangalore@newagepublishers.com
- **Chennai** 26, Damodaran Street, T. Nagar, Chennai-600 017
  Tel.: (044) 24353401, Telefax: 24351463, E-mail: chennai@newagepublishers.com
- **Cochin** CC-39/1016, Carrier Station Road, Ernakulam South, Cochin-682 016
  Tel.: (0484) 2377004, Telefax: 4051303, E-mail: cochin@newagepublishers.com
- **Guwahati** Hemsen Complex, Mohd. Shah Road, Paltan Bazar, Near Starline Hotel, Guwahati-781 008
  Tel.: (0361) 2513881, Telefax: 2543669, E-mail: guwahati@newagepublishers.com
- **Hyderabad** 105, 1st Floor, Madhiray Kaveri Tower, 3-2-19, Azam Jahi Road, Nimboliadda, Hyderabad-500 027
  Tel.: (040) 24652456, Telefax: 24652457, E-mail: hyderabad@newagepublishers.com
- **Kolkata** RDB Chambers (Formerly Lotus Cinema) 106A, 1st Floor, S.N. Banerjee Road, Kolkata-700 014
  Tel.: (033) 22273773, Telefax: 22275247, E-mail: kolkata@newagepublishers.com
- **Lucknow** 16-A, Jopling Road, Lucknow-226 001
  Tel.: (0522) 2209578, 4045297, Telefax: 2204098, E-mail: lucknow@newagepublishers.com
- **Mumbai** 142C, Victor House, Ground Floor, N.M. Joshi Marg, Lower Parel, Mumbai-400 013
  Tel.: (022) 24927869, Telefax: 24915415, E-mail: mumbai@newagepublishers.com
- **New Delhi** 22, Golden House, Daryaganj, New Delhi-110 002
  Tel.: (011) 23262368, 23262370, Telefax: 43551305, E-mail: sales@newagepublishers.com

ISBN : 978-81-224-2838-4

C-12-07-6431

Printed in India at Ajit Printers, Delhi.
Typeset at In-house.

PUBLISHING FOR ONE WORLD
NEW AGE INTERNATIONAL (P) LIMITED, PUBLISHERS
7/30 A, Daryaganj, New Delhi-110002
Visit us at **www.newagepublishers.com**

Preface

Design of Machine Elements (also known as Machine Design) is a coarse subject for students pursuing Mechanical Engineering course in India and abroad. This subject, a second course in Machine Design is dealt in detail in eight chapters.

Chapter 1 deals with design of curved beam, wherein various cross-sections used in crane hooks are explained using graded examples.

Design of thin cylindrical shells, thick and thin cylinders are dealt in chapter 2.

Chapter 3 deals with the design of various types of springs such as helical springs, nested springs, laminated springs (*i.e.*, automobile springs) etc.

Design of spur, bevel, helical and worm gears are dealt in chapters 4 and 5.

Chapters 6, 7 and 8 deal with the design of various clutches and brakes, lubrication and bearings, belt, rope and chain drives.

The book contains 152 worked examples and 71 exercise problems for practice.

M.H. Annaiah

Acknowledgement

I wish to acknowledge V.H. family members for the encouragement and support given to me while writing this book.

Thanks are due to my Guru Prof. Dr. K. Lingaiah, former Principal, Dean, Professor (P.G. studies), UVCE, Bangalore and author of Machine Design Data Handbook for giving permission to use equations and tables from his handbook.

I thank members of Gokula Education Foundation, the founders of M.S. Ramaiah Group of Institutions for providing a conducive environment while writing this book.

Thanks are due to M/s New Age International Publishers Pvt. Ltd., New Delhi and Mr. Sudarshan, Branch Manager, for publishing this textbook.

M.H. Annaiah

Contents

CHAPTER

1 Design of Curved Beams

NOTATIONS AND SYMBOLS USED

σ = Stress, MPa.

σ_d = Direct stress, tensile or compressive, MPa.

σ_i = Stress at inner fibre, MPa.

σ_o = Stress at outer fibre, MPa.

σ_{bi} = Normal stress due to bending at inner fibre, MPa.

σ_{bo} = Normal stress due to bending at outer fibre, MPa.

M_b = Bending moment for critical section, N-mm.

c_i = Distance of neutral axis from inner fibre, mm.

c_o = Distance of neutral axis from outer fibre, mm.

e = Eccentricity, mm.

r_i = Distance of inner fibre from centre of curvature, mm.

r_o = Distance of outer fibre from centre of curvature, mm.

r_c = Distance of centroidal axis from centre of curvature, mm.

r_n = Distance of neutral axis from centre of curvature, mm.

d = Diameter of circular rod used in curved beam, mm.

h = Depth of curved beam [square, rectangular, trapezoidal or I-section], mm.

τ_{max} = Maximum shear stress, MPa.

A = Area of cross-section of member, (curved beam), mm^2.

P = Load on member, N.

INTRODUCTION

Machine frames having curved portions are frequently subjected to bending or axial loads or to a combination of bending and axial loads. With the reduction in the radius of curved portion, the stress due to curvature become greater and the results of the equations of straight beams when used becomes less satisfactory. For relatively small radii of curvature, the actual stresses may be several times greater than the value obtained for straight beams. It has been found from the results of Photoelastic experiments that in case of curved beams, the neutral surface does not coincide with centroidal axis but instead shifted towards the centre of curvature. It has also been found that the stresses in the fibres of a curved beam are not proportional to the distances of the fibres from the neutral surfaces, as is assumed for a straight beam.

Differences between Straight and Curved Beams

	Straight beam	*Curved beam*
1.	The neutral axis of beam coincides with centroidal axis.	The neutral axis is shifted towards the centre of curvature by a distance called eccentricity *i.e.* the neutral axis lies between centroidal axis and centre of curvature.
2.	The variation of normal stress due to bending is linear, tensile at the inner fibre and compressive at the outer fibre with zero value at the centroidal axis.	The variation of normal stress due to bending across section is non-linear and is hyperbolic.

Derivation of Expression to Determine Stress at any Point on the Fibres of a Curved Beam

Consider a curved beam with r_c, as the radius of centroidal axis, r_n, the radius of neutral surface, r_i, the radius of inner fibre, r_o, the radius of outer fibre having thickness 'h' subjected to bending moment M_b.

Let AB and CD be the two adjacent cross-sections separated from each other by a small angle $d\phi$.

Because of M_b the section CD rotates through a small angle $d\alpha$. The unit deformation of any fibre at a distance y from neutral surface is

Deformation $$\in = \frac{\delta}{l} = \frac{y d\alpha}{(r_n - y)d\phi} \qquad \text{... (1.1)}$$

The unit stress on this fibre is,

Stress = Strain × Young's modulus of material of beam

$$\sigma = \in E = \frac{E y d\alpha}{(r_n - y)d\phi} \qquad \text{... (1.2)}$$

For equilibrium, the summation of the forces acting on the cross sectional area must be zero.

i.e., $$\int \sigma dA = 0$$

or $$\int \frac{E\ y d\alpha\ dA}{(r_n - y)d\phi} = 0$$

$$E\frac{d\alpha}{d\phi}\int \frac{y dA}{r_n - y} = 0 \qquad \text{... (1.3)}$$

Also the external moment M_b applied is resisted by internal moment. From equation 1.2 we have,

$$\int y(\sigma dA) = M$$

i.e.,
$$\int \frac{E\, y^2 d\alpha dA}{(r_n - y)d\phi} = M$$

$$E\frac{d\alpha}{d\phi}\int \frac{y^2 dA}{(r_n - y)} = M \qquad \text{... (1.4)}$$

i.e.,
$$M = \frac{Ed\alpha}{d\phi}\left[\int(-y)dA + r_n \int \frac{ydA}{(r_n - y)}\right] \qquad \text{... (1.5)}$$

Note: *In equation 1.5, the first integral is the moment of cross sectional area with respect to neutral surface and the second integral is zero from equation 1.3.*

Therefore,
$$M = \left[E\frac{d\alpha}{d\phi}\right]Ae \qquad \text{... (1.6)}$$

Here 'e' represents the distance between the centroidal axis and neutral axis.

i.e.,
$$e = r_c - r_n$$

Rearranging terms in equation 1.6, we get

$$\frac{d\alpha}{d\phi} = \frac{M}{AeE} \qquad \text{... (1.7)}$$

Substituting $\frac{d\alpha}{d\phi} = \frac{M}{AeE}$ in equation 1.2,

Stress $\sigma = \frac{Ey}{(r_n - y)}\frac{d\alpha}{d\phi}$ becomes

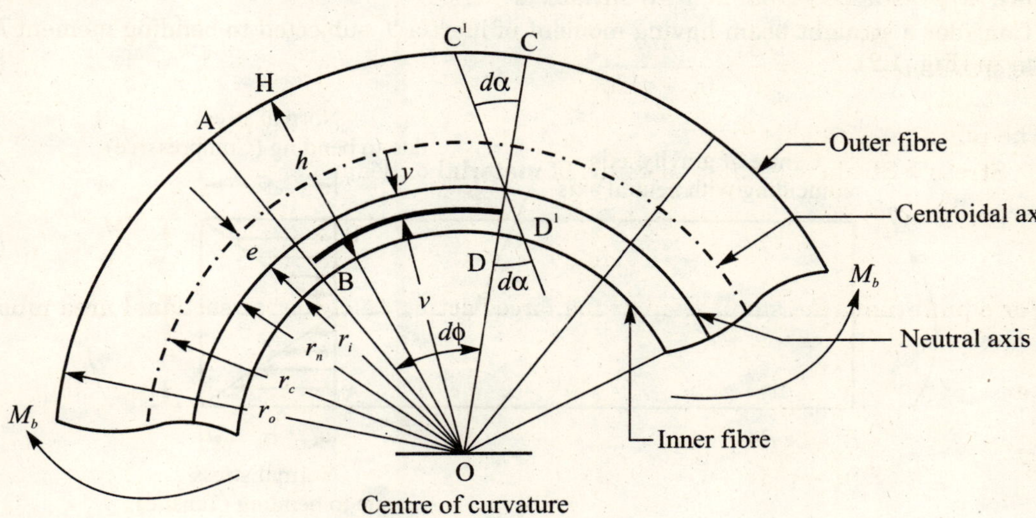

Figure: 1.1

$$= \frac{Ey}{(r_n - y)} \frac{M}{AeE}$$

i.e.,
$$\sigma = \frac{My}{(r_n - y)Ae} \qquad \text{... (1.8)}$$

From figure 1.1,

$$r_n = v + y$$

or
$$y = r_n - v$$

Therefore, from equation 1.3

$$\int \frac{ydA}{(r_n - y)} = \int \frac{(r_n - v)dA}{(r_n - y)}$$

$$= r_n \int \frac{dA}{v} - \int dA = 0$$

$$= r_n \int \frac{dA}{V} - A = 0$$

or
$$r_n = \frac{A}{\int \frac{dA}{v}} \qquad \text{...(1.9)}$$

Note: *Since $e = r_c - r_n$, equation 1.9 can be used to determine 'e'. Knowing the value of 'e', equation 1.8 is used to determine the stress σ.*

Straight and Curved Beams

(a) Straight beam

Consider a straight beam having moment of inertia 'I' subjected to bending moment M_b as shown in (Fig. 1.2).

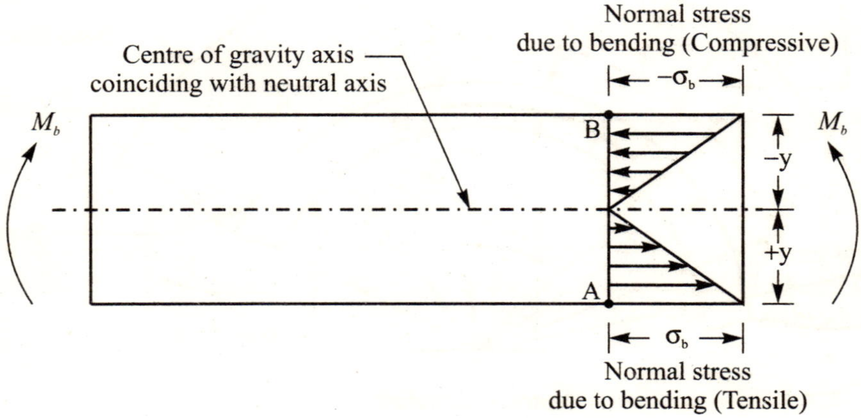

Figure: 1.2

From fundamental equation of bending,

$$\frac{M_b}{I} = \frac{\sigma_b}{y} = \frac{E}{R} \quad ; \quad \frac{M_b}{I} = \frac{\sigma_b}{y}$$

i.e., Bending stress $\sigma_b = \frac{M_b}{I} y$

For a given beam, M_b and 'I' are constant and hence $\sigma_b \propto y$, *i.e.,* the variation of bending stress is linear and is directly proportional to its distance from centre of gravity axis which coincides with neutral axis. The maximum bending (tensile) stress σ_b tensile at A and compressive at B are equal in magnitude at 'A' and 'B' as shown in the Fig. 1.2.

(b) *Curved beam*

Figure 1.3 shows a curved beam subjected to bending moment M_b.

Let r_i = Distance of inner fibre from centre of curvature, C

r_o = Distance of outer fibre from centre of curvature

r_c = Distance of centroidal axis (CG axis) from centre of curvature

r_n = Distance of neutral axis from centre of curvature

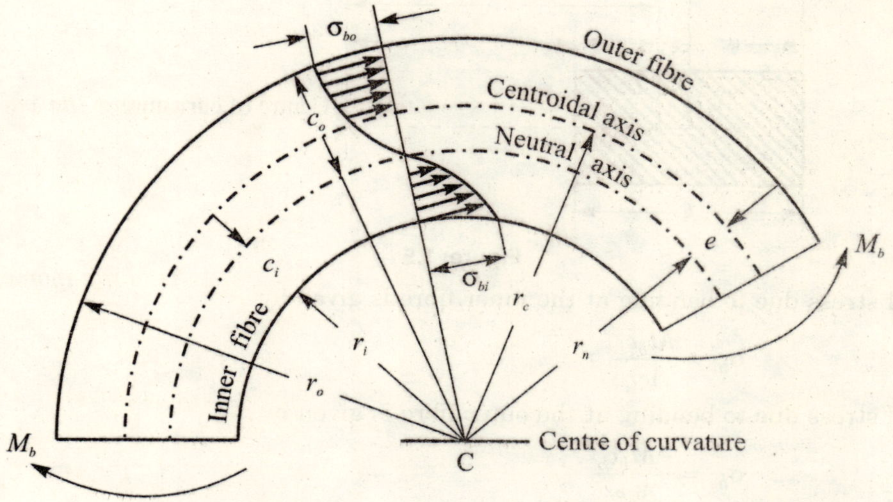

Figure: 1.3

The neutral axis is shifted towards the centre of curvature by a distance called eccentricity 'e'. The value 'e' should be computed very accurately since a small variation in the value of 'e' causes a large variation in the values of stress.

i.e., $e = r_c - r_n$

c_i = Distance between neutral axis and inner fibre = $r_n - r_i$

c_o = Distance between outer fibre and neutral axis = $r_o - r_n$

Note: *1.* If the cross-section is circular with diameter 'd', then, $d = c_i + c_o$ (Refer figure 1.4)

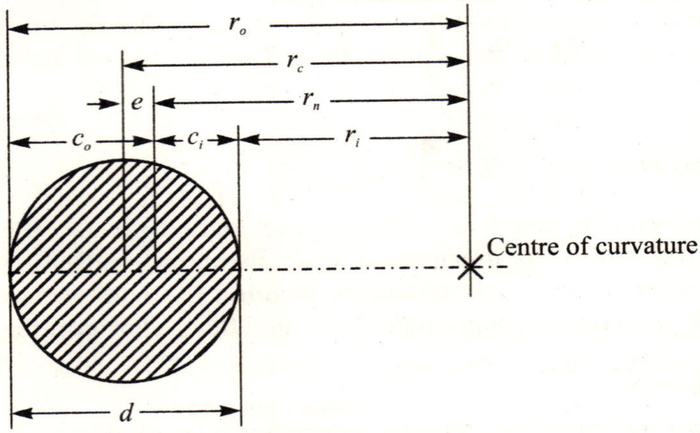

Figure: 1.4

2. If the cross-section is rectangular, then
$h = c_i + c_o$ [Refer Fig. 1.5]

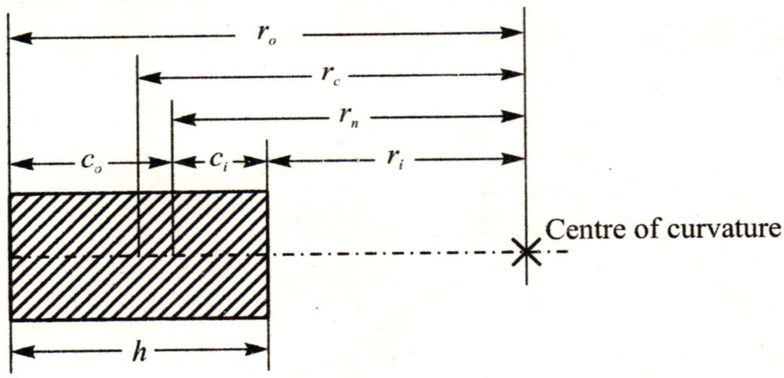

Figure: 1.5

Normal stress due to bending at the inner fibre is given by

$$\sigma_{bi} = \frac{M_b c_i}{Aer_i} \quad \text{...E(25-55)}$$

Normal stress due to bending at the outer fibre is given by

$$\sigma_{bo} = \frac{-M_b c_o}{Aer_o} \quad \text{...E(25-54)}$$

Where, A = Area of cross-section of member.

VARIATION OF BENDING STRESS

If the cross-section of curved beam is symmetrical such as circular, rectangular or '*T*' section with equal flanges, and subjected to tensile load, the maximum bending stress occurs at the inner fibre and minimum stress at the outer fibre. If the cross-section of beam is unsymmetrical such as beam of '*T*' section with unequal flanges, Then the maximum bending stress may occur at the inner or outer fibre. When the section is subjected to axial load along with bending load, the axial stress must be added algebraically to the bending stress.

CROSS-SECTION OF CURVED BEAMS

The general cross-sections used for curved beam are (i) Circular (ii) Rectangular (iii) Trapezoidal (iv) I-section with equal or unequal flanges (v) T-section and (vi) Tubular section with rectangular cross-section. [Refer Fig. 1.6]

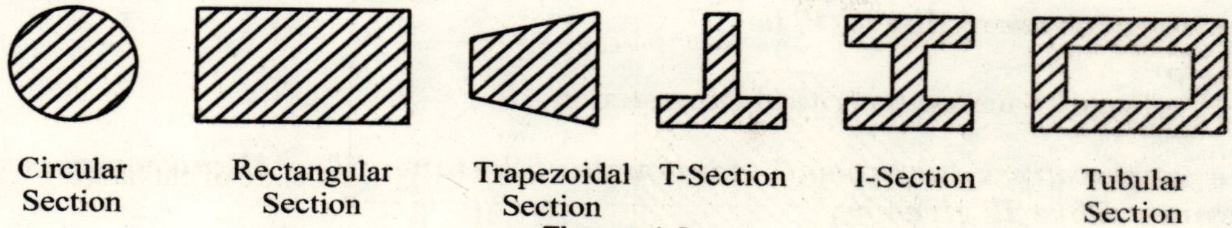

Figure: 1.6

For the values of the distance of neutral axis from centre of curvature (r_n) and the distance between inner fibre and neutral axis *i.e.,* eccentricity 'e' refer table T (25-2 MDH)

Table - (25-2 MDH)

Section	*Radius of neutral surface, r_n*	
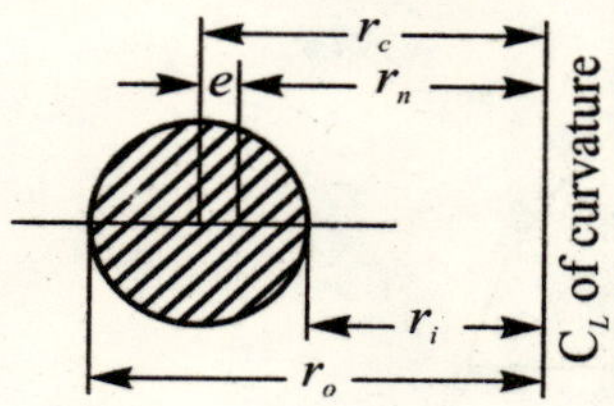	$r_n = \dfrac{\left(\sqrt{r_o} + \sqrt{r_i}\right)^2}{4}$	(25-60)
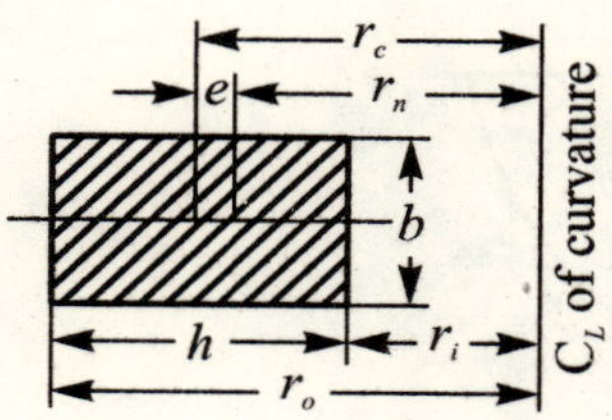	$r_n = \dfrac{h}{\ln\left(\dfrac{r_o}{r_i}\right)}$	(25-61)
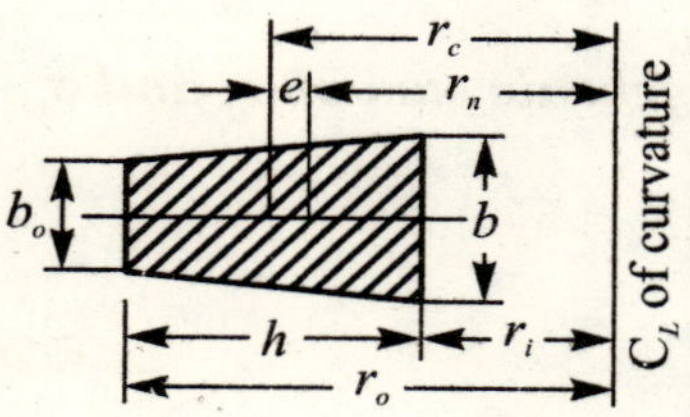	$r_n = \dfrac{\frac{1}{2}h(b_i + b_o)}{\dfrac{b_i r_o - b_o r_i}{h}\ln\left(\dfrac{r_o}{r_i}\right) - (b_i - b_o)}$ if $b_o = 0$, this section reduces to triangle	(25-62)
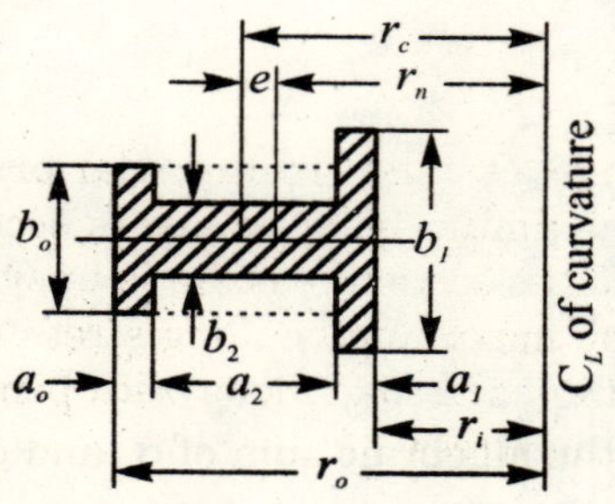	$r_n = \dfrac{A}{b_i \ln\dfrac{r_i + a_i}{r_i} + b_2 \ln\dfrac{r_o - a_o}{r_i + a_i} + b_o \ln\dfrac{r_o}{r_o - a_o}}$ if $a_o = 0$ this section reduces to a $\perp$ section, r_n is the same for a box section in dotted lines with each side panel $\frac{1}{2}b_2$ thick.	(25-63)

The concept of curved beam with variation of stress at the critical cross-section is better understood by studying the following examples.

Example (A) : Consider a beam of circular section of diameter 'd' subjected to a tensile load 'P'.

(i) The direct stress σ_d due to 'P' is

$$\sigma_d = \frac{P}{A} \text{ (tensile) across the critical cross-section } AB.$$

(ii) The normal stress due to bending is tensile at the inner fibre 'A' and compressive at the outer fibre 'B' given by,

$$\sigma_{bi} = \sigma)_{b\ at\ A} = \frac{M_b c_i}{Ae r_i} \text{(tensile)}$$

$$\sigma_{bo} = \sigma)_{b\ at\ B} = \frac{-M_b c_o}{Ae r_o} \text{(compressive)}$$

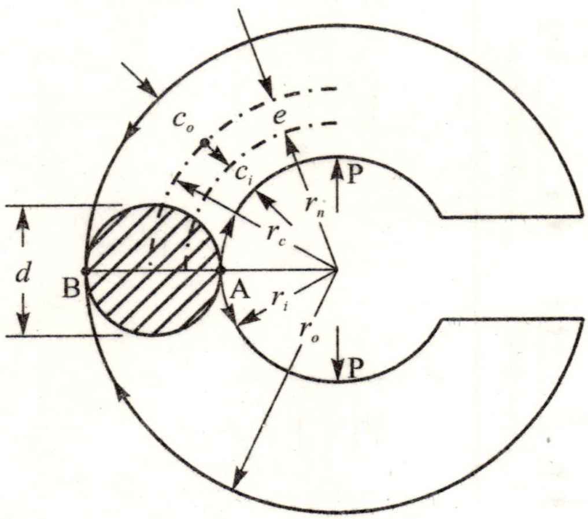

Figure: 1.7

(iii) The resultant stress σ_i at the inner fibre 'A' is the algebraic sum of σ_d and σ_{bi}

Therefore, $\sigma_i)_{at\ A} = \sigma_d + \sigma_{bi}$

$$= \frac{P}{A} + \frac{M_b c_i}{Ae r_i} \text{(tensile)} \qquad \text{... E(25-59)}$$

Where, $M_b = P r_c;$

$$A = \text{Area of cross-section} = \frac{\pi d^2}{4}$$

Therefore, $\sigma_i)_{at\ A} = \frac{P}{A} + \frac{(P r_c) c_i}{Ae r_i}$

Similarly the resultant stress σ_o at the outer fibre 'B' is the algebraic sum of σ_d and σ_{bo}

$$\sigma_o)_{at\ B} = \sigma_d + \sigma_{bo}$$

i.e., $$= \frac{P}{A} - \frac{(M_b)c_o}{Aer_o} \quad \text{... E(25-58)}$$

$$\sigma_o)_{at\ B} = \frac{P}{A} - \frac{(Pr_c)c_o}{Aer_o} (compressive)$$

Example (B): when the direction of load 'P' shown in figure-1.7 is reversed, the outer fibre of critical section AB is subjected to tension and the inner fibre to compression. [Refer figure-1.8]

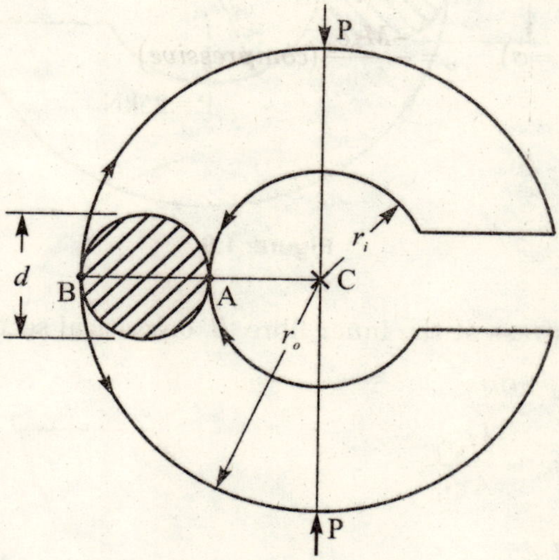

Figure:1.8

(i) The direct stress σ_d due to load 'P' is

$\sigma_d = -P/A$ (compressive) across-section AB

(ii) The normal stress due to bending at the inner fibre 'A' is

$$\sigma_{bi} = \sigma_b)_{at\ A} = -\frac{M_b c_i}{Aer_i} (compressive)$$

(iii) The normal stress due to bending at the outer fibre 'B' is

$$\sigma_{bo} = \sigma_b)_{at\ B} = +\frac{M_b c_o}{Aer_o} (tensile)$$

(iv) The resultant stress at the inner fibre 'A' is the algebraic sum of σ_d and σ_{bi}

$$\sigma_A = \sigma_i = \sigma_d + \sigma_{bi} = \frac{-P}{A} - \frac{M_b c_i}{Aer_i} (compressive)$$

Similarly, (v) the resultant stress at the outer fibre is the algebraic sum of σ_d and σ_{bo}

$$\sigma_B = \sigma_o = \sigma_d + \sigma_{bo} = \frac{-P}{A} + \frac{M_b c_o}{Aer_o} (tensile) \qquad \text{Where, } M_b = Pr_c.$$

***Example 1.1:* An open ring is made from 100 mm diameter rod. The inside diameter of ring is 120 mm. A load of 25 kN is applied as shown in figure-1.9. Determine the value of maximum shear stress induced in the ring and its location.**

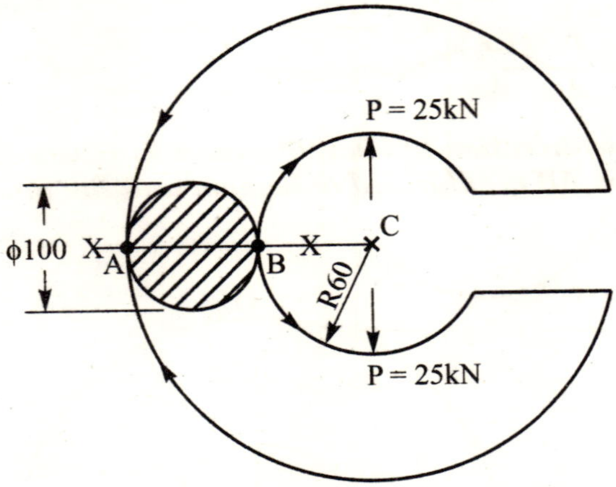

Figure: 1.9

Solution:

Due to load 'P', the stress at the inner fibre 'B' on critical section X-X is,

$$\sigma_B = \sigma_i = \sigma_d + \sigma_{bi},$$

$$\sigma_d = \frac{P}{A}; \quad \sigma_{bi} = \frac{M_b c_i}{Aer_i};$$

i.e.,
$$\sigma_B = \frac{P}{A} + \frac{M_b c_i}{Aer_i} \qquad \text{... E(25-59)} \quad (1.10)$$

Similarly the stress at 'A', the outer fibre of critical section is

$$\sigma_A = \sigma_o = \sigma_d + \sigma_{bo}$$

Where, $\sigma_{bo} = \dfrac{-M_b c_o}{Aer_o}$

$$\sigma_A = \frac{P}{A} - \frac{M_b c_o}{Aer_o} \qquad \text{... E(25-58)} \quad (1.11)$$

Note: *In equations (1.10) and (1.11),*

$\dfrac{P}{A}$ = Direct stress. It is tensile in nature at the critical section.

Where, P = Load = 25 kN = 25×10^3 N

A = Area of cross-section $= \dfrac{\pi}{4}d^2 = \dfrac{\pi}{4}(100)^2 = 7853.98 \text{ mm}^2$

M_b = Bending moment for the critical section = Pr_c

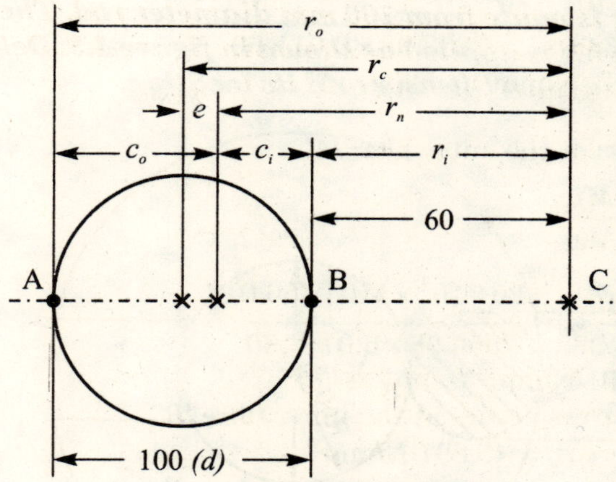

Figure: 1.10

From figure 1.10,

r_i = Distance of inner fibre 'B' from centre of curvature 'C' = 60 mm.

r_o = Distance of outer fibre 'A' from centre of curvature 'C'

$= r_i + d = 60 + 100 = 160$ mm

r_c = Distance of centroidal axis from centre of curvature 'C'

$$= r_i + \frac{d}{2} = 60 + \frac{100}{2} = 110 \text{ mm}$$

r_n = Distance of neutral axis from 'C', the centre curvature for circular cross-section,

$$= \frac{\left(\sqrt{r_o} + \sqrt{r_i}\right)^2}{4} = \frac{\left(\sqrt{160} + \sqrt{60}\right)^2}{4} = 103.99 \text{ mm} \qquad \text{... E(25-60)}$$

c_i = Distance of inner fibre 'B' from neutral axis

$= r_n - r_i$

$= 103.99 - 60 = 43.99$ mm

c_o = Distance of outer fibre 'A' from neutral axis

$= r_o - r_n$

$= 160 - 103.99 = 56.01$ mm

Note: *For circular section,*

$d = c_i + c_o$

For rectangular section,

$h = c_i + c_o$

e = Distance between neutral axis and centroidal axis

$= r_c - r_n$

$= 110 - 103.99 = 6.01$ mm

Now, σ_i = Stress at inner fibre B

$$= \frac{P}{A} + \frac{M_b c_i}{A e r_i} \qquad \text{... E(25-59)}$$

$$= \frac{25\times10^3}{7853.98} + \frac{\left[\left(25\times10^3\right)\times110\right]\times43.99}{7853.98\times6.01\times60}$$

$$= 45.897 \text{ N/mm}^2 \text{ (tensile)}$$

Similarly,

σ_o = Stress at the outer fiber '*A*'

$$= \frac{P}{A} - \frac{M_b c_o}{Aer_o} \quad \text{... E(25-58)}$$

$$= \frac{25\times10^3}{7853.98} - \frac{\left[25\times10^3\times110\right]\times56.01}{7853.98\times6.01\times160}$$

$$= -17.21 \text{ N/mm}^2 \text{ (compressive)}$$

Maximum tensile stress occurs at the inner fibre '*B*'.

Its value is, $\sigma_{tensile} = \sigma_i = 45.897 \text{ N/mm}^2$

Maximum shear stress also occurs at '*B*' and its value is

$$\tau_{max} = \frac{\sigma_{tensile}}{2}$$

$$= \frac{\sigma_B}{2} = \frac{45.897}{2} = 22.945 \text{N/mm}^2$$

Example 1.2: An open ring is formed from a 100 mm bar. The inside diameter of ring is 120 mm and a load of 25 kN is applied as shown in figure-1.11. Determine the value of stresses and their nature at the extreme ends of critical section. (Similar to VTU, July 2007)

Solution:

Due to compressive load '*P*', tensile stress occurs at '*A*' and compressive stress at '*B*'.

$$\sigma_{\text{tensile at A}} = \sigma_A = \sigma_d + \sigma_{bo}$$

$$= -\frac{P}{A} + \frac{M_b c_o}{Aer_o}$$

$$\sigma_{\text{compression at B}} = -\frac{P}{A} - \frac{M_b c_i}{Aer_i}$$

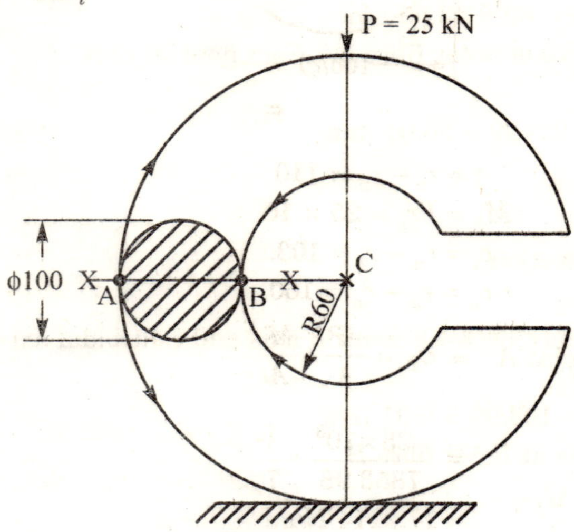

Figure: 1.11

Where, $P = 25 \times 10^3$ N

$$A = \text{Area of cross-section} = \frac{\pi}{4}(d^2)$$

$$= \frac{\pi}{4}(100)^2 = 7853.98 \text{ mm}^2$$

For the given beam, *i.e.,* from figure-1.12

$$r_i = 60 \text{ mm}$$

$$r_c = r_i + \frac{d}{2} = 60 + \frac{100}{2} = 110 \text{ mm}$$

$$r_o = r_i + d$$

$$= 60 + 100 = 160 \text{ mm}$$

$$r_n = \frac{\left(\sqrt{r_o} + \sqrt{r_i}\right)^2}{4} \quad \text{... E(25-60)}$$

$$= \frac{\left(\sqrt{160} + \sqrt{60}\right)^2}{4}$$

$$= 103.99 \text{ mm}$$

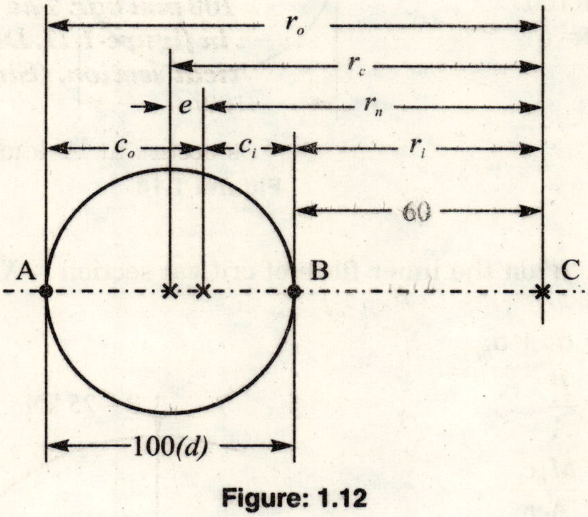

Figure: 1.12

Eccentricity $e = r_c - r_n = 110 - 103.99 = 6.01$ mm

$$M_b = Pr_c = 25 \times 10^3 \times 110 = 27.5 \times 10^5 \text{ N-mm}$$

$$c_i = r_n - r_i = 103.99 - 60 = 43.99 \text{ mm}$$

$$c_o = r_o - r_n = 160 - 103.99 = 56.01 \text{ mm}$$

Stress at point A $= \sigma_A = \dfrac{-P}{A} + \dfrac{M_b c_o}{A e r_o}$

$$= \frac{-25\times10^3}{7853.98} + \frac{(27.5\times10^5)\times56.01}{7853.98\times6.01\times160}$$

$$= 17.2114 \text{ N/mm}^2 \text{ (\textit{tensile})}$$

$$\text{Stress at point } B = \sigma_B = \frac{-P}{A} - \frac{M_b c_i}{Aer_o}$$

$$= \frac{-25\times10^3}{7853.98} - \frac{\left(27.5\times10^5\right)\times43.99}{7853.98\times6.01\times60}$$

$$= -\,45.8972 \text{ N/mm}^2 \text{ (compressive)}$$

Example 1.3: A load of 15 kN is applied to an offset bar shown in figure-1.13. Determine the offset 'X' limiting the maximum tensile stress in the bar to 80 N/mm². Calculate the value of maximum shear stress and state where it occurs.

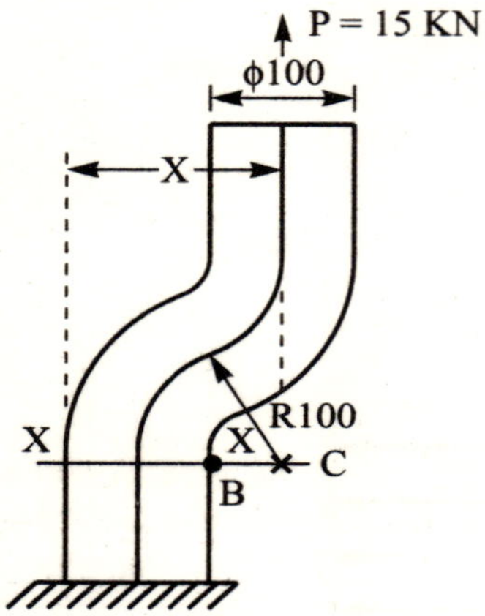

Figure: 1.13

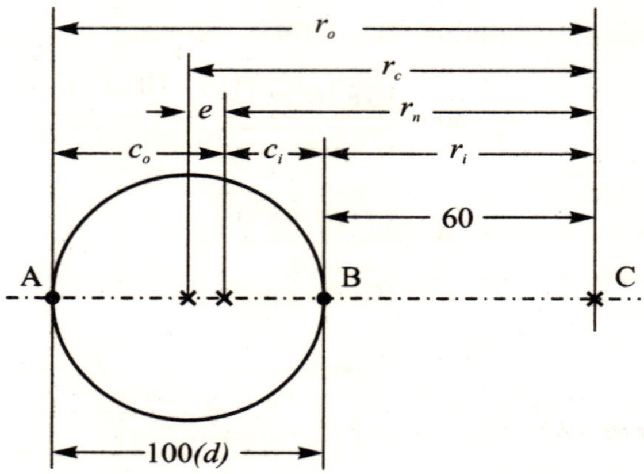

Figure: 1.14

Solution:

Due to load P, the point 'B' on the inner fibre of critical section X-X is subjected to maximum tensile stress given by

$$\sigma_B = \sigma_d + \sigma_{bi}$$

Where,

$$\sigma_d = \frac{P}{A}$$

$$\sigma_{bi} = \frac{M_b c_i}{Aer_i} \quad \text{... E(25-55)}$$

Therefore,

$$\sigma_B = \frac{P}{A} + \frac{M_b c_i}{Aer_i} \quad \text{... E(25.59) (1)}$$

For the given bar, (refer figure-1.14)

$$r_c = 100 \text{ mm}$$

$$r_i = r_c - \frac{d}{2} = 100 - \frac{100}{2} = 50 \text{ mm}$$

$$r_o = r_c + \frac{d}{2} = 100 + \frac{100}{2} = 150 \text{ mm}$$

$$r_n = \frac{\left(\sqrt{r_o} + \sqrt{r_i}\right)^2}{4} \quad \text{... E(25-60)}$$

$$= \frac{\left(\sqrt{150} + \sqrt{50}\right)^2}{4} = 93.3 \text{ mm}$$

$$e = r_c - r_n = 100 - 93.3 = 6.7 \text{ mm}$$

$$c_i = r_n - r_i = 93.3 - 50 = 43.3 \text{ mm}$$

$$c_o = r_o - r_n = 150 - 93.3 = 56.7 \text{ mm}$$

$$\sigma_B = \sigma_i = 80 \text{N/mm}^2 \text{ (given)}$$

$$M_b = P \times X = \left(15 \times 10^3\right) X \text{ N-mm}$$

Substituting in Equation (1),

$$80 = \frac{15 \times 10^3}{7853.98} + \frac{\left(15 \times 10^3 X\right) 43.3}{7853.98 \times 6.7 \times 50}$$

Therefore, offset $X = 316.34$ mm

The maximum offset X that can be allowed = 316.34 mm.

The maximum shear stress at the B, the inner fibre is given by

$$\tau_{max} = \frac{\sigma_i}{2} = \frac{\sigma_t}{2} = \frac{80}{2} = 40 \text{N/mm}^2 .$$

Example 1.4: A crane hook of circular cross-section shown in figure-1.15 is to carry a tensile load of 2 kN. Determine the maximum tensile stress induced in the member and state where it occurs.

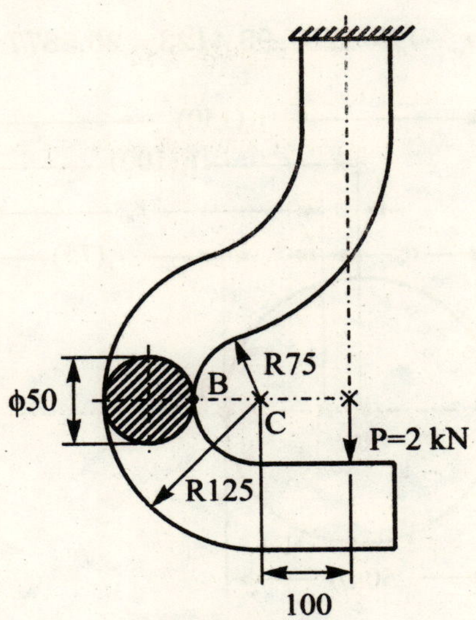

Figure: 1.15

Solution:

Due to load P, the point B at inner fibre of critical section is subjected to maximum tensile stress given by

$$\sigma_{tensile} = \frac{P}{A} + \frac{M_b c_i}{A e r_i} \qquad \text{... E(25-59)}$$

Where, P = Load on member = 2 kN = 2000 N

$$A = \text{Area of cross-section} = \frac{\pi}{4}\left(d^2\right) = \frac{\pi}{4}(50)^2 = 1963.5 \text{ mm}^2$$

$$M_b = P\left(r_c + 100\right) \text{ N-mm}$$

$$r_c = r_i + \frac{d}{2} = 75 + \frac{50}{2} = 100 \text{ mm}$$

Therefore, $M_b = (2000)(100 + 100) = 4 \times 10^5$ N-mm

To compute dimensions r_n, c_i, c_0, e, etc.

From figure 1.16,

$$r_i = 75 \text{ mm}, \quad r_c = 100 \text{ mm}$$

$$r_o = r_c + \frac{d}{2} = 125 \text{ mm}$$

$$r_n = \frac{\left(\sqrt{r_o} + \sqrt{r_i}\right)^2}{4} \qquad \text{... E(25-60)}$$

$$= \frac{\left(\sqrt{125} + \sqrt{75}\right)^2}{4} = 98.4123 \text{ mm}$$

Eccentricity, $e = r_c - r_n = 100 - 98.4123 = 1.5877$ mm

$$c_i = r_n - r_i = 98.4123 - 75 = 23.4123 \text{ mm}$$

$$c_o = r_o - r_n = 125 - 98.4123 = 26.5877 \text{ mm}$$

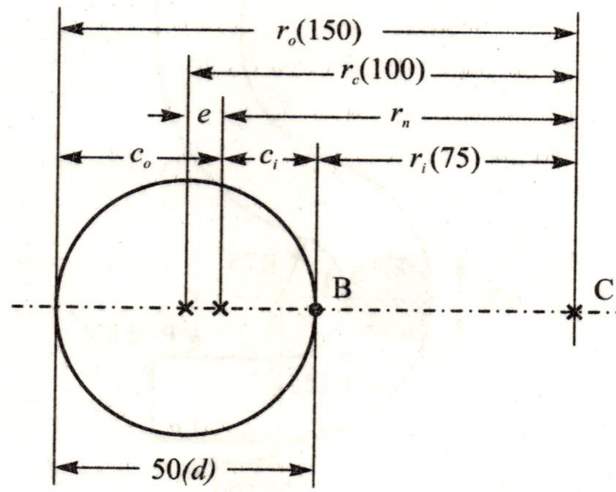

Figure: 1.16

Note: $c_o + c_i = d$

Substituting in the formula,

$$\sigma_{\text{tensile}} = \frac{P}{A} + \frac{M_b c_i}{A e r_i},$$

We get, $$\sigma_{tensile} = \frac{2\times10^3}{1963.5} + \frac{(4\times10^5)\times23.4123}{1963.5\times1.5877\times75}$$
$$= 41.072 \text{ N/mm}^2$$

Example 1.5: An open 'S' link made from 40 mm diameter rod is loaded as shown in figure-1.17. Determine the values of maximum tensile and shear stresses. Also mention where they occur.

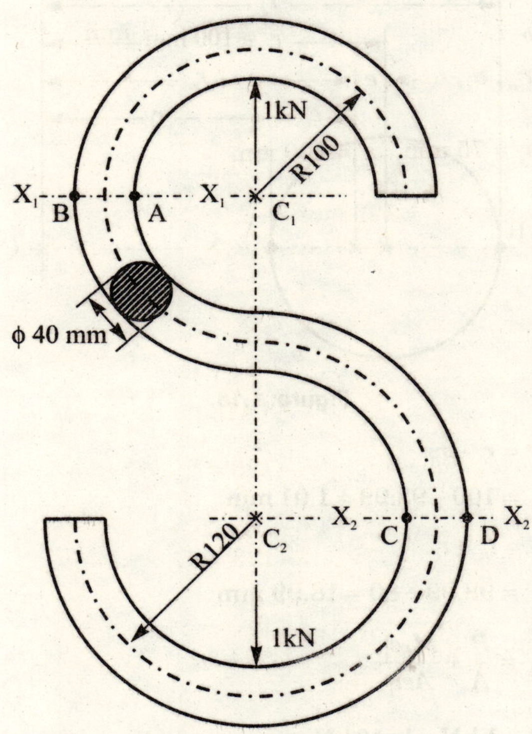

Figure: 1.17

Solution:

Due to load 1 kN, the point 'A' on section $X_1 - X_1$ and point 'C' on section $X_2 - X_2$ are subjected to tensile stresses.

Consider section $X_1 - X_1$

From figure 1.18,

$$r_i = r_c - \frac{d}{2}$$

$$r_c = 100 \text{ mm}, \; d = 40 \text{ mm}$$

$$r_o = 100 - \frac{d}{2}$$

$$= 100 - \frac{40}{2} = 80 \text{ mm}$$

$$r_n = \frac{\left(\sqrt{r_o} + \sqrt{r_i}\right)^2}{4}$$

$$= \frac{\left(\sqrt{120} + \sqrt{80}\right)^2}{4} = 98.99 \text{ mm}$$

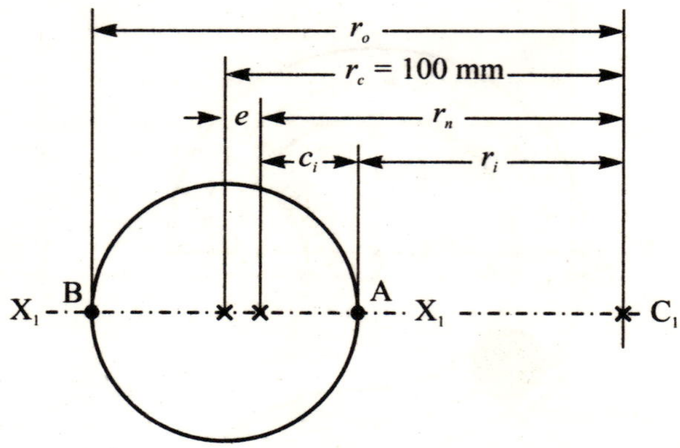

Figure: 1.18

Therefore, $e = r_c - r_n$

$= 100 - 98.99 = 1.01$ mm

$c_i = r_n - r_i$

$= 98.99 - 80 = 18.99$ mm

Therefore, $\sigma_{\text{tensile at A}} = \dfrac{P}{A} + \dfrac{M_b c_i}{A e r_i}$

Where, $P = 1 \text{ kN} = 1 \times 10^3$ N

Area of cross section $A = \dfrac{\pi d^2}{4}$

$= \dfrac{\pi}{4}(40)^2 = 1256.64 \text{ mm}^2$

Bending moment $M_b = P \times r_c$

$= 1 \times 10^3 \times 100 = 1 \times 10^5$ N-mm

Therefore, $\sigma_{\text{tensile at A}} = \dfrac{1 \times 10^3}{1256.64} + \dfrac{1 \times 10^5 \times 18.99}{1256.64 \times 1.01 \times 80}$

$= 0.795773 + 18.10263$

$= 19.4984 \text{ N/mm}^2$ (*tensile*)

Considering the lower portion of S-link,

At point C on section X_2–X_2, the tensile stress induced in the member is given by

$$\sigma_{\text{tensile at C}} = \frac{P}{A} + \frac{M_b c_i}{A e r_i} \qquad \text{... E(25-59)}$$

Note: *In the above equation M_b, c_i, e and r_i refer to the values at the lower portion of link.*

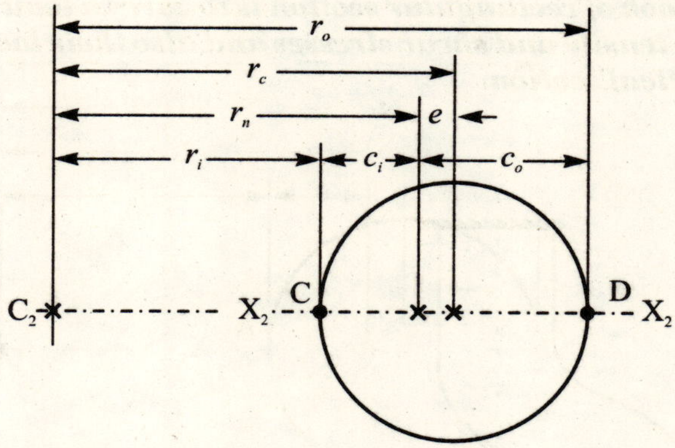

For the lower portion of link,

$$r_c = 120 \text{ mm}, \; d = 40 \text{ mm}$$

$$r_i = r_c - \frac{d}{2} = 120 - \frac{40}{2} = 100 \text{ mm}$$

$$r_o = r_c + \frac{d}{2} = 120 + \frac{40}{2} = 140 \text{ mm}$$

$$r_n = \frac{\left(\sqrt{r_o} + \sqrt{r_i}\right)^2}{4} = \frac{\left(\sqrt{140} + \sqrt{100}\right)^2}{4} = 119.161 \text{ mm}$$

$$e = r_c - r_n = 120 - 119.161 = 0.839 \text{ mm}$$

$$c_i = r_n - r_i = 119.161 - 100 = 19.161 \text{ mm}$$

Therefore, $\sigma_{\text{tensile at C}} = \dfrac{P}{A} + \dfrac{M_b c_i}{A e r_i}$

Where, $M_b = P r_c$

$$= 1 \times 10^3 \times 120$$

$$= 120 \times 10^3 \; N\text{-mm}$$

$$\sigma_{\text{tensile at C}} = \frac{1 \times 10^3}{1256.64} + \frac{\left(120 \times 10^3\right) \times 19.161}{1256.64 \times 0.839 \times 100}$$

$$= 22.604 \text{ N/mm}^2 \text{ (tensile)}$$

Therefore, maximum tensile stress occurs at C, the inner fibre of the lower portion of link on section X_2–X_2 and is given by,

$$\sigma_{\text{tensile at C}} = \sigma_{\max} = 22.604 \text{ N/mm}^2$$

The maximum shear stress also occurs at C and its magnitude is

$$\tau_{max} = \frac{\sigma_{max}}{2}$$

$$= \frac{22.604}{2} = 11.302\,\text{N/mm}^2$$

Example 1.6 : A crane hook of rectangular section is to carry a load of 100kN. Determine the values of maximum tensile and shear stresses and also their location. Plot the stress distribution for the critical section.

Solution:

From figure 1.19,

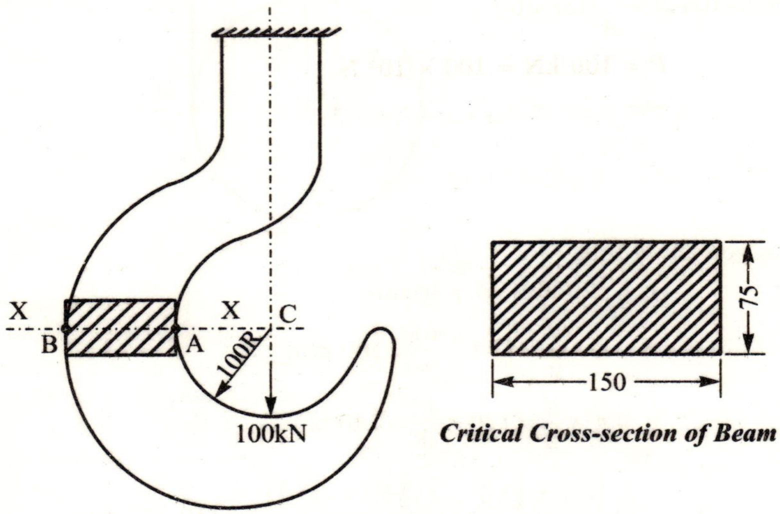

Figure: 1.19

$$r_i = 100 \text{ mm}, \; h = 150 \text{ mm}$$

$$r_c = r_i + \bar{x} = 100 + \frac{150}{2} = 175 \text{ mm}$$

$$r_o = r_i + h = 100 + 150 = 250 \text{ mm}$$

To find r_n, the distance of neutral axis from centre of curvature.

For rectangular cross-section,

$$r_n = \frac{h}{\ln\left(\frac{r_o}{r_i}\right)} \quad \text{... E(25-61)}$$

Therefore,
$$r_n = \frac{150}{\ln\left(\frac{250}{100}\right)} = 163.7 \text{ mm}$$

Now, $e = r_c - r_n = 175 - 163.7 = 11.3$ mm

$$c_i = r_n - r_i = 163.7 - 100 = 63.7 \text{ mm}$$

$$c_o = h - c_i \text{ or } (r_o - r_n)$$

$$c_o = 150 - 63.7 = 86.3 \text{ mm}$$

To find the stress at the critical cross-section.

For the critical section *X-X*,

(*a*) σ_d = Direct tensile stress $= \frac{P}{A}$ (tensile)

Where, $P = 100 \text{ kN} = 100 \times 10^3$ N

A = area of cross-section = bh

$$= 75 \times 150 = 11250 \text{ mm}^2$$

Therefore, $\sigma_d = \frac{100 \times 10^3}{11250} = 8.89 \text{ N/mm}^2$

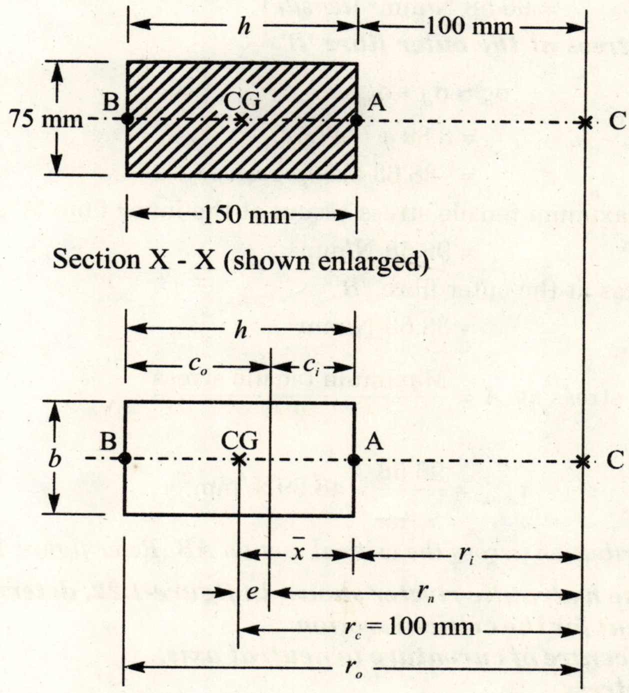

Figure: 1.20

(b) Normal stress due to bending at the extreme fibres (σ_{bi} and σ_{bo})

For the inner fibre,

$$\sigma_{bi} = \frac{M_b c_i}{Aer_i} \qquad \text{... E(25-55)}$$

For the outer fibre,

$$\sigma_{bo} = \frac{-M_b c_o}{Aer_o} \qquad \text{... E(25-54)}$$

Where, bending moment $M_b = Pr_c = 100 \times 10^3 \times 175 = 175 \times 10^5$ N-mm

Therefore, $$\sigma_{bi} = \frac{175 \times 10^5 \times 63.7}{11250 \times 11.3 \times 100} = 87.69\,\text{N/mm}^2$$

$$\sigma_{bo} = \frac{-175 \times 10^5 \times 86.3}{11250 \times 11.3 \times 250} = -47.52\,\text{N/mm}^2$$

(c) The resultant stress (combined stress) at the inner fibre 'A'

$$\sigma_i = \sigma_d + \sigma_{bi}$$
$$= 8.89 + 87.69$$
$$= 96.58 \text{ N/mm}^2 \ (tensile)$$

The resultant stress at the outer fibre 'B'

$$\sigma_o = \sigma_d + \sigma_{bo}$$
$$= 8.89 + (-47.52)$$
$$= -38.63 \ (compressive)$$

Therefore, the maximum tensile stress occurs at the inner fibre 'A' and its magnitude is

$$= 96.58 \text{ N/mm}^2$$

Compressive stress at the outer fibre, 'B'

$$= 38.63 \text{ N/mm}^2$$

$$\text{Maximum shear stress at } A = \frac{\text{Maximum tensile stress}}{2}$$

i.e., $$\tau_{max} = \frac{96.58}{2} = 48.29\,\text{N/mm}^2$$

(d) Plot of stress distribution across the critical section AB (Refer figure 1.21)

Example 1.7: For the hydraulic riveter shown in figure-1.22, determine,

(i) Bending moment for the critical section.
(ii) Distance from centre of curvature to neutral axis.
(iii) Direct tensile stress.
(iv) Maximum tensile stress and its location.
(v) Maximum shear stress and its location.
(vi) Plot the variation of stress across the critical section.

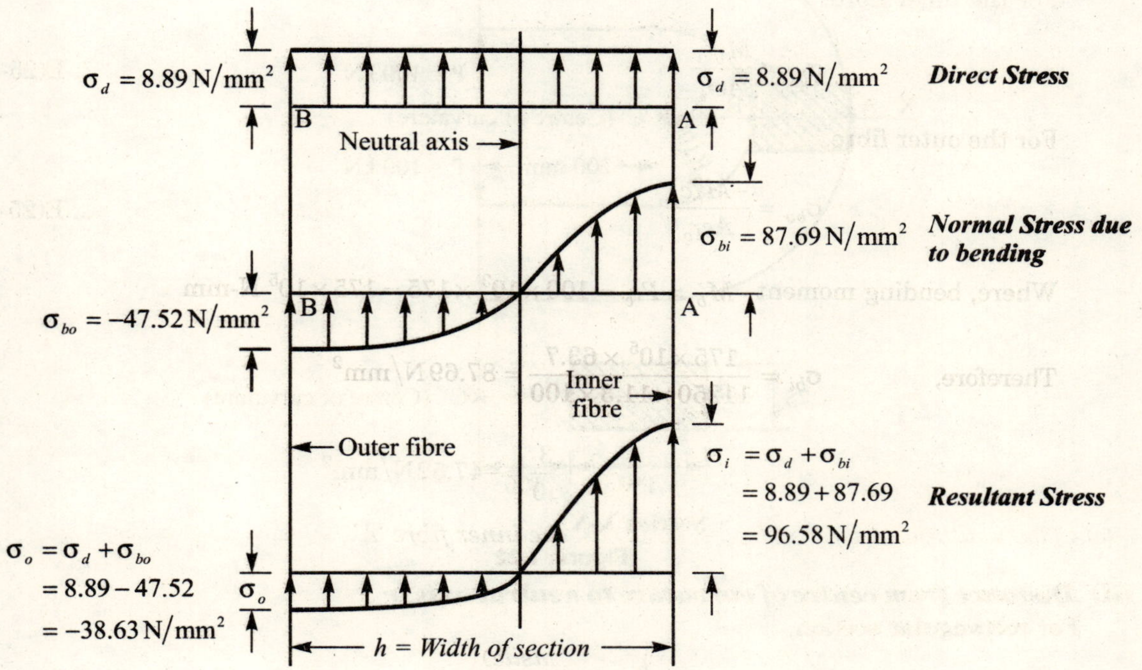

Figure: 1.21

Solution:

(i) Bending moment for the critical section (M_b)

For the critical section *X-X*,

Bending moment,

$$M_b = P\,[r_c + 200] \text{ from figure-1.23.}$$

$$r_c = r_i + \frac{h}{2}$$

$$= 100 + \frac{150}{2} = 175 \text{ mm}$$

Therefore, $M_b = P[r_c + 200]$

$$= 100 \times 10^3\,[175 + 200]$$

Where, $P = 100 \times 10^3 \text{N}$

$$M_b = 375 \times 10^5 \text{ N-mm}$$

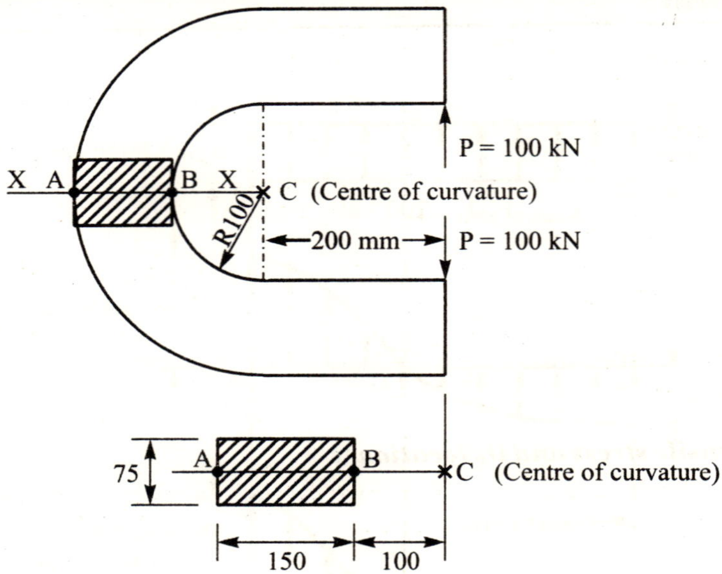

Section X-X

Figure: 1.22

(ii) Distance from centre of curvature to neutral axis (r_n)

For rectangular section,

$$r_n = \frac{h}{\ln\left(\frac{r_o}{r_i}\right)} \qquad \text{... E(25-61)}$$

Here $r_i = 100$ mm, $r_o = 100 + 150 = 250$ mm

$$r_n = \frac{150}{\ln\left(\frac{250}{100}\right)} = 163.7 \text{ mm}$$

Therefore, the distance from centre of curvature to neutral axis is $r_n = 163.7$ mm

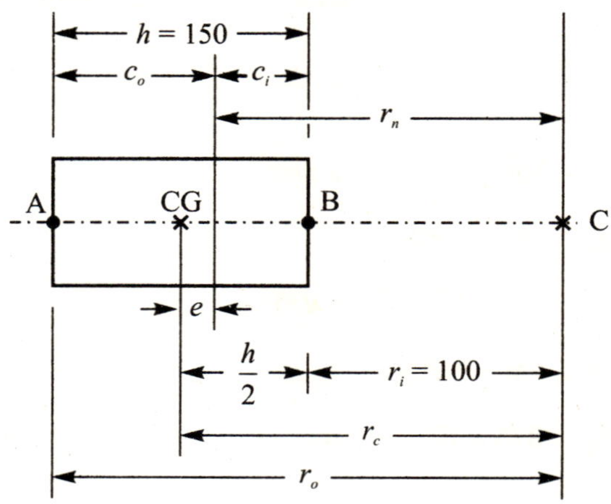

Figure: 1.23

(iii) Direct tensile stress

Direct tensile stress $\sigma_d = \dfrac{P}{A}$

Where,

$$P = 100 \text{ kN} = 100 \times 10^3 \text{ N}$$

$$A = bh = 75 \times 150 = 11250 \text{ mm}^2$$

Therefore, direct tensile stress $= \dfrac{P}{A} = \dfrac{100 \times 10^3}{11250} = 8.89 \text{N/mm}^2$

(iv) Maximum tensile stress and its location

Note : *For the crane hooks, irrespective of the cross-section, maximum tensile stress occurs at the inner fibre i.e., at B in the cross-section X-X of beam and is given by*

$$\sigma_{\text{tensile(max)}} = \frac{P}{A} + \frac{M_b c_i}{A e r_i} \quad \text{... E(25-59)}$$

For the given section,

$$c_i = r_n - r_i = 163.7 - 100 = 63.7 \text{ mm}$$

$$e = r_c - r_n = 175 - 163.7 = 11.3 \text{ mm}$$

$$c_o = h - c_i = 150 - 63.7 = 86.3 \text{ mm}$$

Therefore, $\sigma_{\text{tensile(max)}} = \dfrac{100 \times 10^3}{11250} + \dfrac{375 \times 10^5 \times 63.7}{11250 \times 11.3 \times 100} = 196.8 \text{N/mm}^2$

(v) Maximum shear stress and its location

Maximum shear stress occurs at point where maximum tensile stress occurs. Therefore maximum shear stress occurs at B, the inner fibre of the beam and its value is given by

$$\tau_{\max} = \text{Maximum shear stress} = \frac{\sigma_{\text{tensile(max)}}}{2}$$

$$= \frac{196.8}{2} = 98.4 \text{N/mm}^2$$

(vi) Plot of variation of stress across the critical section

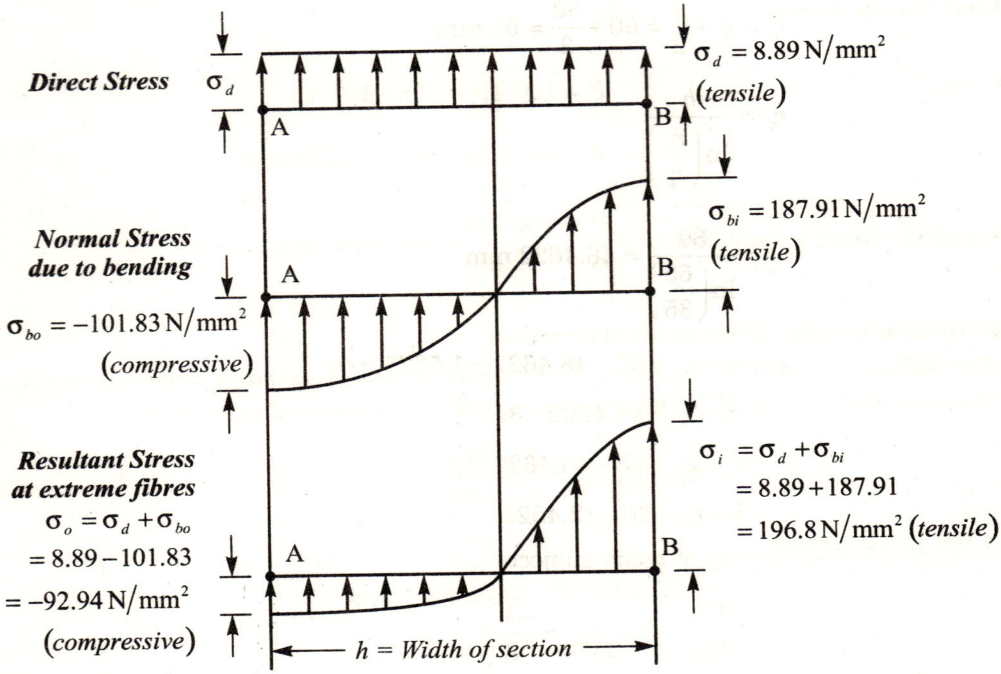

Figure: 1.24

Example 1.8: Determine the numerical value of $\sigma_{o\,max}/\sigma_{i\,max}$ for a curved beam in pure bending for a square beam 30 mm × 30 mm, if the radius of curvature of centroidal axis is 50 mm.

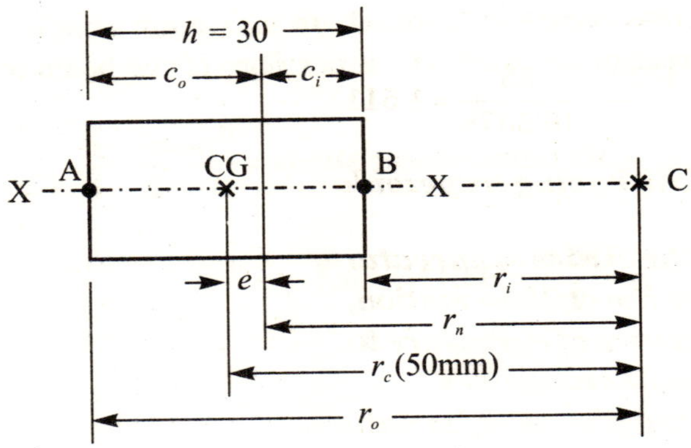

Figure: 1.25

Solution:

For the given cross-section,

$$r_c = 50\text{ mm (given)},\ h = 30\text{ mm}$$

$$r_i = r_c - \frac{h}{2} = 50 - \frac{30}{2} = 35 \text{ mm}$$

$$r_o = r_c + \frac{h}{2} = 50 + \frac{30}{2} = 65 \text{ mm}$$

$$r_n = \frac{h}{\ln\left(\frac{r_o}{r_i}\right)} \quad \text{... E(25-61)}$$

$$= \frac{30}{\ln\left(\frac{65}{35}\right)} = 48.4622 \text{ mm}$$

Eccentricity, $e = r_c - r_n = 50 - 48.4622 = 1.5378$ mm

$$c_i = r_n - r_i = 48.4622 - 35 = 13.4622 \text{ mm}$$

$$c_o = r_o - r_n = 65 - 48.4622 = 16.5378 \text{ mm}$$

Note: *Also,* $c_o = h - c_i = 30 - 13.4622 = 16.5378$ mm

Assuming the cross-section of beam subjected to pure bending,

$$\sigma_{bi} = \frac{M_b c_i}{A e r_i} \text{ and } \sigma_{bo} = \frac{-M_b c_o}{A e r_o}$$

Considering only the magnitude of bending stress,

$$\frac{\sigma_{bi}}{\sigma_{bo}} = \frac{M_b c_i}{A e r_i} \div \frac{M_b c_o}{A e r_o}$$

$$= \frac{c_i}{r_i} \times \frac{r_o}{c_o}$$

$$= \frac{13.4622}{35} \times \frac{65}{16.5378} = 1.5118$$

Example 1.9: A crane hook having trapezoidal section is loaded as shown in figure-1.26. Determine,

(a) The distance from the centre of curvature to the centroidal axis.

(b) Bending moment for the critical section, X-X.

(c) Distance from the centre of curvature to the neutral axis.

(d) Area of cross-section at section X-X.

(e) Stress at 'B', the inner fibre and its nature.

(f) Stress at 'A', the outer fibre and its nature.

(g) Maximum shear stress and its location.

(h) Plot the stress distribution across the critical section.

(Similar to VTU June/July 2008)

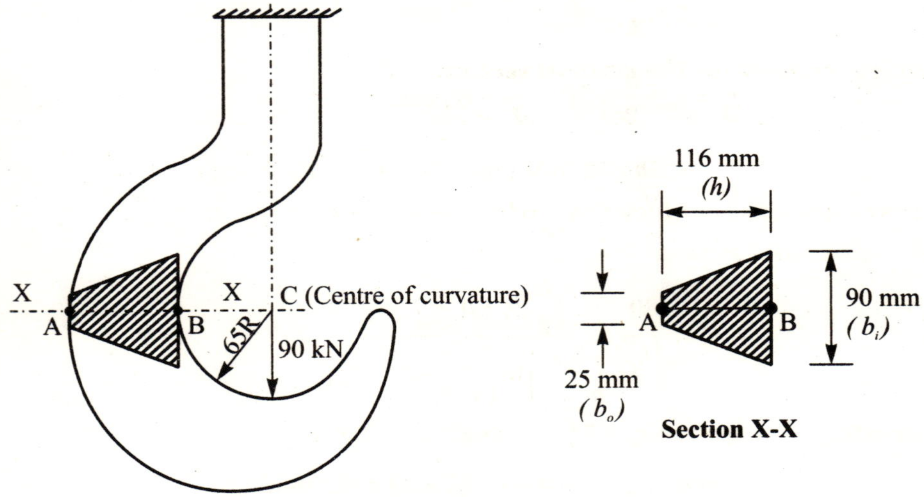

Figure: 1.26

Solution:

From figure 1.26 and 1.27,

$$r_i = 65 \text{ mm}$$

$$r_o = r_i + h = 65 + 116 = 181 \text{ mm}$$

$\bar{x}$ = Distance of C.G. of section from the inner fibre '*B*' is

$$\bar{x} = \frac{h}{3}\left[\frac{b_i + 2b_o}{b_i + b_o}\right] = \frac{116}{3}\left[\frac{90 + 2 \times 25}{90 + 25}\right] = 47.07 \text{ mm}$$

Therefore, $r_c = r_i + \bar{x} = 65 + 47.07 = 112.07$ mm

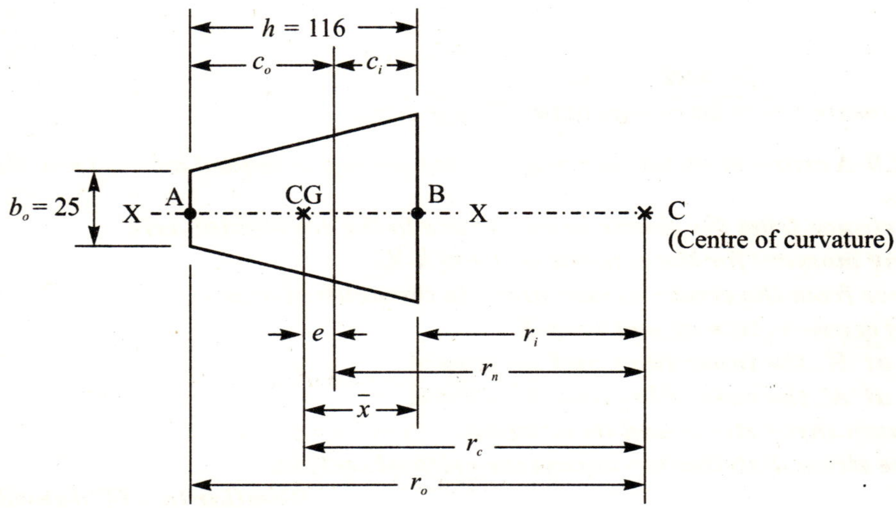

Figure: 1.27

(a) The distance from the centre of curvature to the centroidal axis

$$r_c = 112.07 \text{ mm}$$

(b) Bending moment for the critical section, (M_b)

$$M_b = Pr_c = \left(90 \times 10^3\right) \times 112.07$$

$$= 10086300 \text{ N-mm} = 100.863 \times 10^5 \text{ N-mm}$$

(c) Distance from the centre of curvature to the neutral axis (r_n)

Note: *For trapezoidal section,*

$$r_n = \frac{\frac{h}{2}(b_i + b_o)}{\left(\frac{b_i r_o - b_o r_i}{h}\right)\ln\left(\frac{r_o}{r_i}\right) - (b_i - b_o)} \quad \text{... E(25-62)}$$

$$= \frac{\frac{116}{2}(90 + 25)}{\left(\frac{90 \times 181 - 25 \times 65}{116}\right)\ln\left(\frac{181}{65}\right) - (90 - 25)}$$

$$= 103.4583 \text{ mm}$$

(d) Area of cross-section at section X-X

Area of trapezium at *X-X*

$$A = \frac{1}{2}\text{height} \times \text{sum of parallel sides}$$

$$= \frac{h}{2}(\text{sum of parallel sides})$$

$$= \frac{h}{2}[b_i + b_o]$$

$$= \frac{116}{2}[90 + 25] = 6670 \text{ mm}^2$$

(e) Maximum tensile stress at point 'B' is given by,

$$\sigma_{\text{tensile at B}} = \frac{P}{A} + \frac{M_b c_i}{A e r_i}$$

Where, $P = load = 90 \text{ kN} = 90 \times 10^3 \text{N}$

$A = 6670 \text{ mm}^2$

To find dimensions c_i and e

$$c_i = r_n - r_i = 103.4583 - 65 = 38.4583 \text{ mm}$$

$$e = r_c - r_n = 112.07 - 103.4583 = 8.6117 \text{ mm}$$

$$c_o = h - c_i = 116 - 38.4583 = 77.5417 \text{ mm}$$

Since, $h = c_i + c_o$ and $c_o = h - c_i$

Therefore, $\sigma_{\text{tensile at B}} = \dfrac{90\times10^3}{6670} + \dfrac{10086300\times38.4583}{6670\times8.6117\times65}$

$$= 117.39 \text{ N/mm}^2 \text{ (tensile)}$$

(f) Compressive stress at 'A'

$$\sigma_{\text{compressive at A}} = \frac{P}{A} - \frac{M_b c_o}{Aer_o}$$

$$= \frac{90\times10^3}{6670} - \frac{10086300\times77.5417}{6670\times8.6117\times181}$$

$$= -61.73 \text{ N/mm}^2 \text{ (compressive)}$$

(g) Maximum shear stress $(\tau_{\max})$

$$\tau_{\max} = \frac{\sigma_{\text{tensile at B}}}{2} = \frac{117.39}{2} = 58.695 \text{ N/mm}^2$$

Note: *Maximum shear stress occurs at 'B' where the maximum tensile stress occurs.*

(h) To plot the stress distribution across the critical cross-section X-X

(*a*) Direct stress due to $P = \sigma_d = \dfrac{P}{A}$ (tensile)

Where, $P = 90\times10^3$ N

$A = 6670 \text{ mm}^2$

$$\sigma_d = \frac{P}{A} = \frac{90\times10^3}{6670} = 13.4933 \text{ N/mm}^2$$

$$= 13.4933 \text{ N/mm}^2 \text{ (tensile)}$$

Note: *Normal stress due to bending at the inner and outer fibres* $(\sigma_{bi}$ *and* $\sigma_{bo})$

At the inner fibre, i.e. at B

$$\sigma_{bi} = \frac{M_b c_i}{Aer_i}$$

$$= \frac{10086300\times38.4583}{6670\times8.6117\times65}$$

$$= 103.8948 \text{ N/mm}^2 \text{ (tensile)}$$

At the outer fibre i.e., at 'A',

$$\sigma_{bo} = \frac{-M_b c_o}{Aer_o}$$

$$= \frac{-10086300 \times 77.5417}{6670 \times 8.6117 \times 181}$$

$$= -75.227 \text{ N/mm}^2 \text{ (compressive)}$$

Resultant stress at inner fibre 'B' (Refer figure-1.28)

$$\sigma_i = \sigma_d + \sigma_{bi}$$

$$= 13.4932 + 103.8948 = 117.3880 \approx 117.39 \text{ N/mm}^2 \text{ (tensile)}$$

Resultant stress at outer fibre 'A'

$$\sigma_o = \sigma_d - \sigma_{bo}$$

$$= 13.8948 - 75.227 = -61.33 \text{ N/mm}^2 \text{ (compressive)}$$

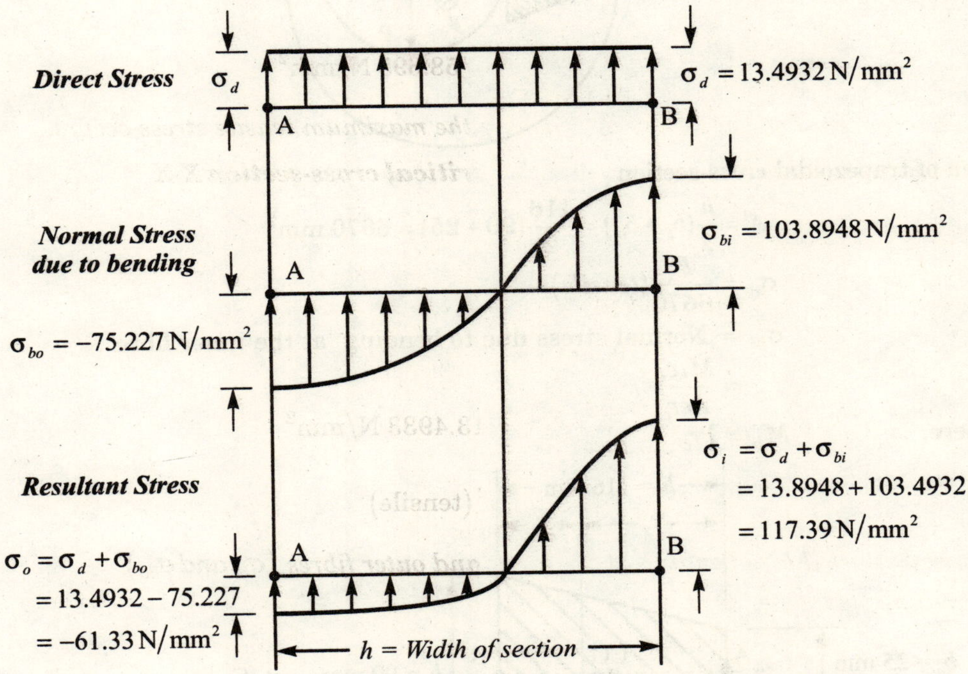

Figure: 1.28 : Stress distribution across the critical cross-section

Example 1.10: A crane hook of trapezoidal section shown in figure-1.29 is subjected to a load 'P'. Determine 'P' such that the maximum tensile stress in the hook is limited to 117.39 N/mm². ***(VTU, Dec 2007/Jan 2008)***

Solution:

Due to load P, maximum tensile stress occurs at the inner fibre 'B' of critical section and is given by

$$\sigma_i = \sigma_{\text{tensile at } B} = \sigma_d + \sigma_{bi}$$

Where, σ_d = Direct stress (tensile) $= \dfrac{P}{A}$

P = Load (to be determined)

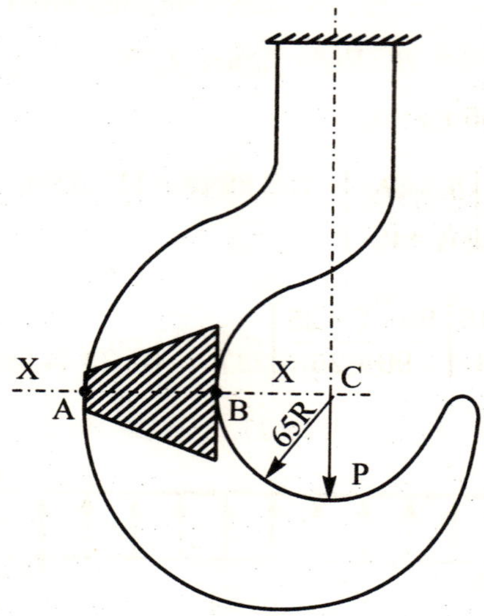

Area of trapezoidal cross-section

$$A = \frac{h}{2}(b_i + b_o) = \frac{116}{2}(90 + 25) = 6670 \text{ mm}^2$$

$$\sigma_d = \frac{P}{6670}(tensile)$$

σ_{bi} = Normal stress due to bending at the inner fibre

$$= \frac{M_b c_i}{Aer_i}$$

Where, $M_b = Pr_c$

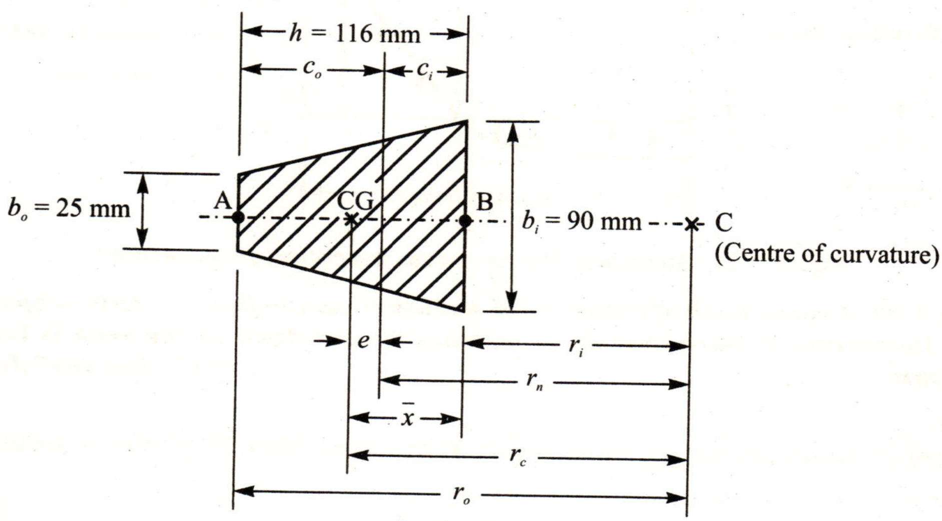

Section X-X

Figure: 1.29

To find the dimensions r_n, r_c, c_i and e.

Here $r_i = 65$ mm and $r_o = r_i + h = 65 + 116 = 181$ mm

From figure 1.29,

$$r_c = r_i + \bar{x}$$

$$= 65 + \bar{x}$$

Where,
$$\bar{x} = \frac{h}{3}\left[\frac{b_i + 2b_o}{b_i + b_o}\right]$$

$$= \frac{116}{3}\left[\frac{90 + 2 \times 25}{90 + 25}\right] = 47.07 \text{ mm}$$

Therefore, $r_c = 65 + 47.07 = 112.07$ mm

For trapezoidal section,

$$r_n = \frac{\frac{h}{2}(b_i + b_o)}{\left(\frac{b_i r_o - b_o r_i}{h}\right)\ln\left(\frac{r_o}{r_i}\right) - (b_i - b_o)} \quad \text{... E(25-62)}$$

$$= \frac{\frac{116}{2}(90 + 25)}{\left(\frac{90 \times 181 - 25 \times 65}{116}\right)\ln\left(\frac{181}{65}\right) - (90 - 25)}$$

$$= 103.4583 \text{ mm}$$

Eccentricity, $e = r_c - r_n = 112.07 - 103.4583 = 8.6117$ mm

$$c_i = r_n - r_i = 103.4583 - 65 = 38.4583 \text{ mm}$$

Therefore,
$$\sigma_{bi} = \frac{M_b c_i}{A e r_i} = \frac{P \times 112.07 \times 38.4583}{6670 \times 8.6117 \times 65} = 1.1544 \times 10^{-3} P$$

Hence,
$$\sigma_i = \frac{P}{6670} + 1.1544 \times 10^{-3} P = 117.39 \text{ (given)}$$

$$P = 90000 \text{ N}$$

Therefore, the maximum load the crane hook can lift = 90000 N = 90 kN

Example 1.11: A crane hook having trapezoidal section as shown in figure-1.30 has its inner fibre 100 mm from the centre of curvature. The load axis is 75 mm from the inner fibre. Determine the values of stresses at the inner and outer fibres when it carries a load of 10 kN.

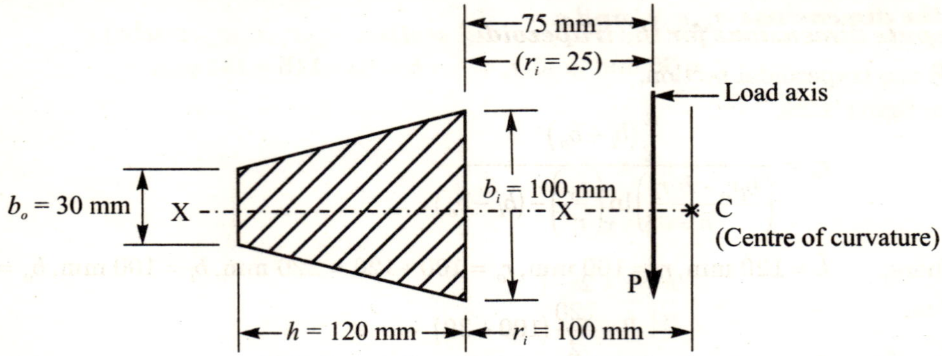

Solution:

The critical section of crane hook is *X-X*. The maximum tensile stress occurs at the inner fibre '*B*' and compressive stress at the outer fibre '*A*'.

Maximum tensile stress at the inner fibre '*B*' is

$$\sigma_i = \sigma_d + \sigma_{bi}$$

$$\sigma_i = \frac{P}{A} + \frac{M_b c_i}{Aer_i}$$

Where $P = \text{Load} = 10 \text{ kN} = 10 \times 10^3 \text{N}$

$$A = \frac{h}{2}(b_i + b_o) \text{ (i.e., area of trapezium)}$$

$$= \frac{120}{2}(100 + 30) = 7800 \text{ mm}^2$$

$$M_b = P(r_i - 25)$$

(Because the load axis is shifted towards the inner fibre by 25 mm).

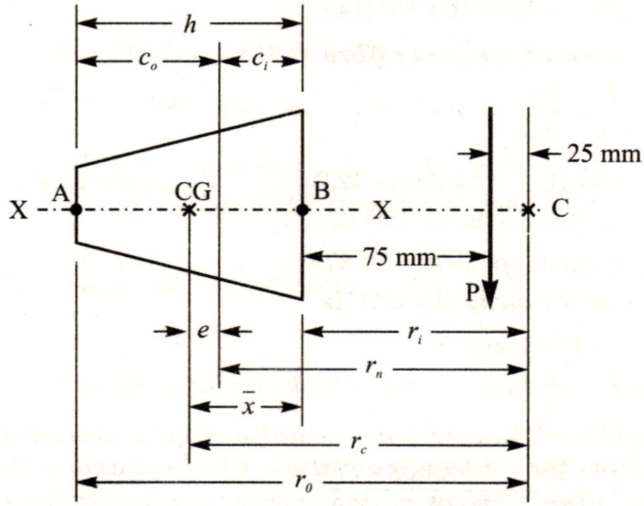

Figure: 1.30

To compute dimensions for the trapezoidal section $(r_n, r_c, c_i, c_o, \text{and } e)$

For the trapezoidal section,

$$r_n = \frac{\frac{h}{2}(b_i + b_o)}{\left(\frac{b_i r_o - b_o r_i}{h}\right)\ln\left(\frac{r_o}{r_i}\right) - (b_i - b_o)} \quad \text{... E(25-62)}$$

Where, $h = 120$ mm, $r_i = 100$ mm, $r_o = 100 + 120 = 220$ mm, $b_i = 100$ mm, $b_o = 30$ mm

Therefore, $$r_n = \frac{\frac{120}{2}(100+30)}{\left(\frac{100\times 220 - 30\times 100}{120}\right)\ln\left(\frac{220}{100}\right) - (100-30)}$$

$= 142.2236$ mm

$$r_c = r_i + \bar{x}$$

Where, $$\bar{x} = \frac{h}{3}\left(\frac{b_i + 2b_o}{b_i + b_o}\right)$$

$$= \frac{120}{3}\left(\frac{100 + 2\times 30}{100+30}\right)$$

$= 49.2308$ mm

Therefore, $r_c = 100 + 49.2308 = 149.2308$ mm

$$c_i = r_n - r_i = 142.2236 - 100 = 42.2236 \text{ mm}$$

$$c_o = h - c_i = r_o - r_n = 220 - 142.2236 = 77.7764 \text{ mm}$$

$$e = r_c - r_n = 149.2308 - 142.2236 = 7.0072 \text{ mm}$$

$$M_b = P(r_c - 25) = 10\times 10^3 (149.2308 - 25) = 1242308 \text{ N-mm}$$

Maximum tensile stress at the inner fibre 'B' is given by

$$\sigma_i = \frac{P}{A} + \frac{M_b c_i}{Aer_i} \quad \text{... E(25-59)}$$

$$= \frac{10\times 1C^3}{7800} + \frac{1242308\times 42.2236}{7800\times 7.0072\times 100}$$

$$\sigma_i = 1.28205 + 9.5972 = 10.8793 \text{ N/mm}^2 \ (\textit{tensile})$$

Compressive stress at the outer fibre 'A' is

$$\sigma_o = \sigma_d + \sigma_{bo}$$

$$= \frac{P}{A} - \frac{M_b c_o}{Aer_o} \quad \text{... E(25-58)}$$

$$= \frac{10\times 10^3}{7800} - \frac{1242308\times 77.7764}{7800\times 7.0072\times 220}$$

$$\sigma_o = -6.75349 \text{ N/mm}^2 \ (\textit{compressive})$$

Example 1.12: In a curved beam having trapezoidal section, shown in figure 1.31 all dimensions excepting b_o are known. Determine the value of b_o such that the normal stresses due to bending at the extreme fibres are numerically equal. If the cross-section is subjected to a bending moment of 40 N-m, determine the value of bending stress at the extreme fibres.

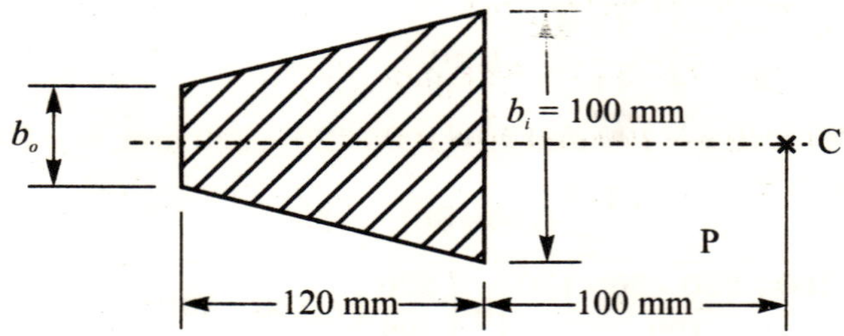

Figure: 1.31

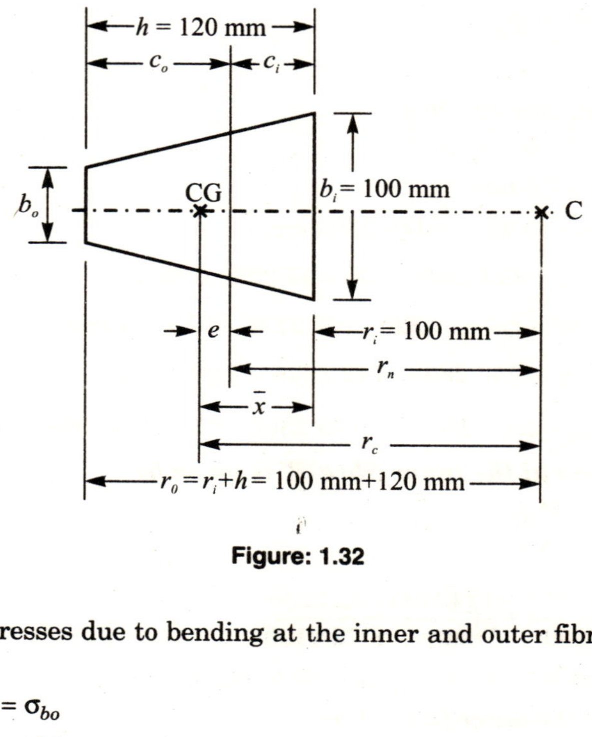

Figure: 1.32

Solution:

As per data, normal stresses due to bending at the inner and outer fibres are numerically the same.

i.e., $$\sigma_{bi} = \sigma_{bo}$$

or $$\frac{M_b c_i}{Aer_i} = \frac{M_b c_o}{Aer_o}$$

$$\frac{c_i}{r_i} = \frac{c_o}{r_o}$$

i.e., $$\frac{r_o}{r_i} = \frac{c_o}{c_i}$$

$$\frac{c_o}{c_i} = \frac{r_o}{r_i} \qquad \text{...(1)}$$

From figure 1.32,

$$r_i = 100 \text{ mm}, \; h = 120 \text{ mm}$$

$$r_o = 100 + 120 = 220 \text{ mm}$$

Therefore, $\frac{r_o}{r_i} = \frac{220}{100} = 2.2$

Substituting in equation 1,

$$\frac{c_o}{c_i} = 2.2$$

i.e., $c_o = 2.2c_i$ ...(2)

Also, $h = c_i + c_o$ (from figure 1.32)

Substituting $c_o = 2.2c_i$ in equation-2,

$$120 = c_i + 2.2c_i = 3.2c_i$$

Therefore, $c_i = \frac{120}{3.2} = 37.5$ mm

To find b$_o$

$$c_i = r_n - r_i$$

i.e., $37.5 = r_n - 100$

Therefore, $r_n = 137.5$ mm

For the trapezoidal section,

$$r_n = \frac{\frac{h}{2}(b_i + b_o)}{\left(\frac{b_i r_o - b_o r_i}{h}\right)\ln\left(\frac{r_o}{r_i}\right) - (b_i - b_o)} \qquad \text{... E(25-62)}$$

Substituting the values we get,

$$137.5 = \frac{\frac{120}{2}(100 + b_o)}{\left(\frac{100 \times 220 - b_o \times 100}{120}\right)\ln\left(\frac{220}{100}\right) - (100 - b_o)}$$

$$= \frac{60(100 + b_o)}{(183.33 - 0.833b_o) \times (0.78846) - (100 - b_o)}$$

$$= \frac{6000 + 60b_o}{(183.33 - 0.833b_o) \times (0.78846) - (100 - b_o)}$$

i.e., $b_o = 9.79$ mm

To compute normal stress due to bending at the extreme fibres

$$\sigma_{bi} = \frac{M_b c_i}{A e r_i}$$

Where, $M_b = 40 \text{ N-m} = 40 \times 10^3 \text{N-mm}$

$c_i = 37.5 \text{ mm}$

$$A = \frac{h}{2}(b_i + b_o)$$

$$= \frac{120}{2}[100 + 9.79] = 6587.4 \text{ mm}^2$$

Where, $\bar{x}$ = distance of CG from inner fibre

$$\bar{x} = \frac{h}{3}\left[\frac{b_i + 2b_o}{b_i + b_o}\right]$$

$$= \frac{120}{3}\left[\frac{100 + 2 \times 9.79}{100 + 9.79}\right]$$

$$\bar{x} = 43.57 \text{ mm}$$

Therefore, $e = (100 + 43.57) - 137.5 = 6.07 \text{ mm}$

$$\sigma_{bi} = \frac{(40 \times 10^3) \times 37.5}{6587.4 \times 6.07 \times 100}$$

$$\sigma_{bi} = 0.375 \text{N/mm}^2 = \sigma_{bo} \text{ (from data)}$$

Example 1.13: Compute the combined stresses at the inner and outer fibres in the critical section of a crane hook which is required to lift loads upto 25 kN. The hook has trapezoidal section with parallel sides 60 mm and 30 mm, the distance between them being 90 mm. The inner radius of hook is 100 mm. The load line is nearer to the inner surface of the hook by 25 mm than the centre of curvature at the critical section.

(VTU, Dec 06/Jan 07)

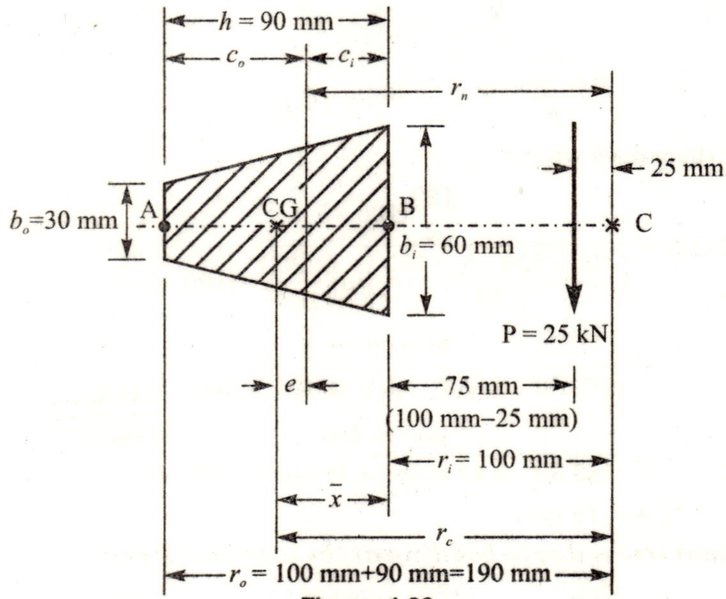

Figure: 1.33

Solution:

Due to load, the inner fibre of the critical section AB at B is subjected to maximum tensile stress given by,

$$\sigma_i = \sigma_{max} = \sigma_d + \sigma_{bi}$$

$$\sigma_{tensile} = \frac{P}{A} + \frac{M_b c_i}{A e r_i} \quad \text{... E(25-59)}$$

Where, P = Load to be lifted $= 25$ kN $= 25 \times 10^3$ N

A = Area of trapezoidal section.

$$A = \frac{h}{2}(b_i + b_o) = \frac{90}{2}(60 + 30) = 4050 \text{ mm}^2$$

$$M_b = P(r_c - 25)$$

To calculate r_c, r_n, c_i and e

$$r_c = r_i + \bar{x}$$

Where,

$$\bar{x} = \frac{h}{3}\left[\frac{b_i + 2b_o}{b_i + b_o}\right]$$

$$= \frac{90}{3}\left[\frac{60 + 2(30)}{60 + 30}\right] = 40 \text{ mm}$$

Therefore, $r_c = 100 + 40 = 140$ mm

For the trapezoidal section,

$$r_n = \frac{\frac{h}{2}(b_i + b_o)}{\left(\frac{b_i r_o - b_o r_i}{h}\right)\ln\left(\frac{r_o}{r_i}\right) - (b_i - b_o)} \quad \text{... E(25-62)}$$

$$= \frac{\frac{90}{2}(60 + 30)}{\left(\frac{60 \times 190 - 30 \times 100}{90}\right)\ln\left(\frac{190}{100}\right) - (60 - 30)}$$

$= 135.4227$ mm

i.e.,

$$e = r_c - r_n = 140 - 135.4227 = 4.5773 \text{ mm}$$

$$c_i = r_n - r_i = 135.4227 - 100 = 35.4227 \text{ mm}$$

Therefore,

$$\sigma_i = \sigma_{max(tensile)} = \frac{25 \times 10^3}{4050} + \frac{2875000 \times 35.4227}{4050 \times 4.5773 \times 100}$$

Similarly, the stress at the outer fibre 'A' is

$$\sigma_o = \sigma_{(compressive)} = \frac{P}{A} - \frac{M_b c_o}{A e r_o} \quad \text{... E(25-58)}$$

Where,

$$c_o = r_o - r_n = 190 - 135.4227 = 54.5773 \text{ mm}$$

$$\text{Therefore, } \sigma_{(compressive)} = \frac{25\times10^3}{4050} - \frac{2875000\times54.5773}{4050\times4.5773\times190}$$

$$= -38.3755 \text{ N/mm}^2$$

Example 1.14: The crane hook of trapezoidal cross-section with circular centre line of used to carry a load of 90 kN. The face 90 mm side is the concave side of beam and has a radius of curvature of 70 mm. The depth of beam is 115 mm and the other parallel side of the section 25 mm. Determine the maximum stress induced in the section and compare the same that found using straight beam formula.

Solution:

Due to load P = 90 kN, the maximum tensile stress is induced at the inner fibre B given by,

$$\sigma_i = \sigma_{i\ at\ B} = \frac{P}{A} + \frac{M_b c_i}{A e r_i}$$

To find c_i, c_o, r_n, r_c and e

$$r_c = r_i + \bar{x}$$

Where,

$$\bar{x} = \frac{h}{3}\left(\frac{b_i + 2b_o}{b_i + b_o}\right)$$

$$= \frac{115}{3}\left(\frac{90 + 2\times25}{90+25}\right) = 46.6667 \text{ mm}$$

$$r_c = r_i + \bar{x}\text{, i.e., } r_c = 70 + 46.6667 = 116.6667 \text{ mm}$$

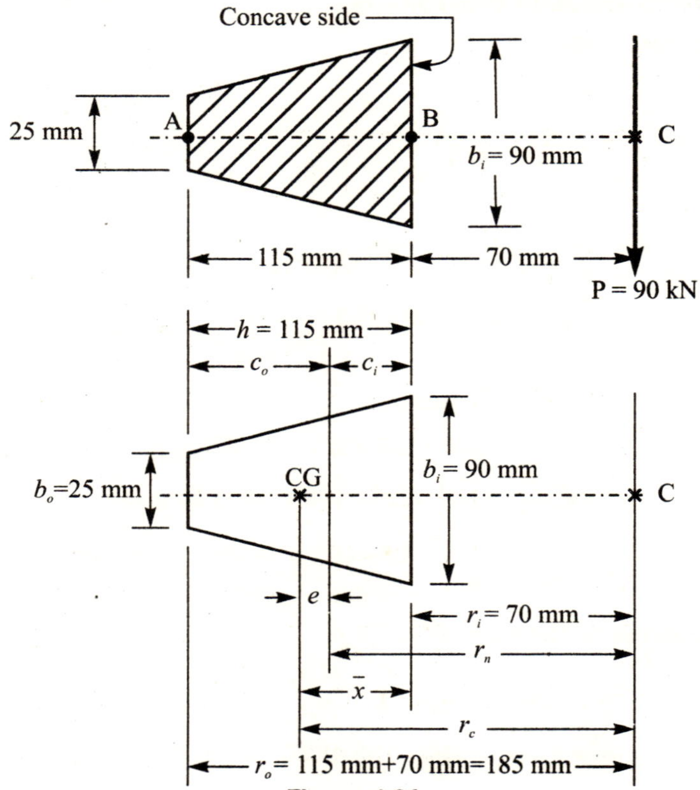

Figure: 1.34

For the trapezoidal section,

$$r_n = \frac{\frac{h}{2}(b_i + b_o)}{\left(\frac{b_i r_o - b_o r_i}{h}\right)\ln\frac{r_o}{r_i} - (b_i - b_o)} \qquad \text{... E(25-62)}$$

$$= \frac{\frac{115}{2}(90+25)}{\left(\frac{90\times185 - 25\times70}{115}\right)\ln\left(\frac{185}{70}\right) - (90-25)} = 108.5452 \text{ mm}$$

$$e = r_c - r_n = 116.6667 - 108.5452 = 8.1215 \text{ mm}$$

$$c_i = r_n - r_i = 108.5452 - 70 = 38.5452 \text{ mm}$$

$$M_b = Pr_c = 90\times10^3 \times 116.6667 = 10500003 \text{ N-mm}$$

$$A = \frac{h}{2}(b_i + b_o) = \frac{115}{2}(90+25) = 6612.5 \text{ mm}^2$$

Therefore,
$$\sigma_i = \frac{90\times10^3}{6612.5} + \frac{10500003\times38.5452}{6612.5\times8.1215\times70}$$
$$= 121.2719 \text{ N/mm}^2$$

For a straight beam subjected to bending

$$\frac{M_b}{I} = \frac{\sigma_b}{y} = \frac{E}{R}$$

Therefore, $\sigma_b = \frac{M_b}{I}y = \frac{M_b}{z_b}$; because $Z_b = \frac{I}{y}$

For trapezoidal section,

$$z_b = \frac{\left(6b^2 + 6bb_o + b_o^{\,2}\right)h^2}{12(3b + b_o)}$$

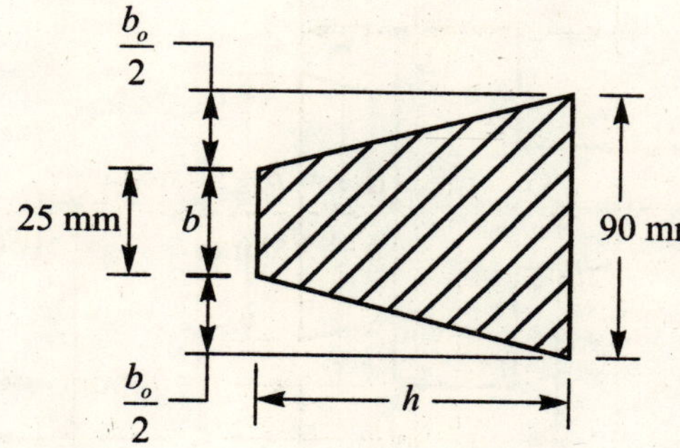

Here, $b = 25 \text{ mm}$, $h = 115 \text{ mm}$, $b_o = 90 - b = 90 - 25 = 65 \text{ mm}$

Therefore,
$$z_b = \frac{\left[6(25)^2 + 6\times25\times65 + (65)^2\right]115^2}{12(3\times25 + 65)}$$

$$= 139531.62 \text{ mm}^2$$

$$\sigma_b = \frac{10500003}{139531.62} = 75.2518 \text{ N/mm}^2$$

Therefore, $$\frac{(\sigma_i)\text{curved beam}}{(\sigma_b)\text{straight beam}} = \frac{121.2719 \text{ N/mm}^2}{75.2518 \text{ N/mm}^2} = 1.6116$$

Example 1.15: Determine the maximum stresses in the external fibres of the frame of T-section shown in figure-1.35.

Solution:

Due to load P = 500 kN, point B on critical section is subjected to maximum tensile stress and point A is subjected to compressive stress. The maximum shear stress occurs at point B where the magnitude of stress is maximum.

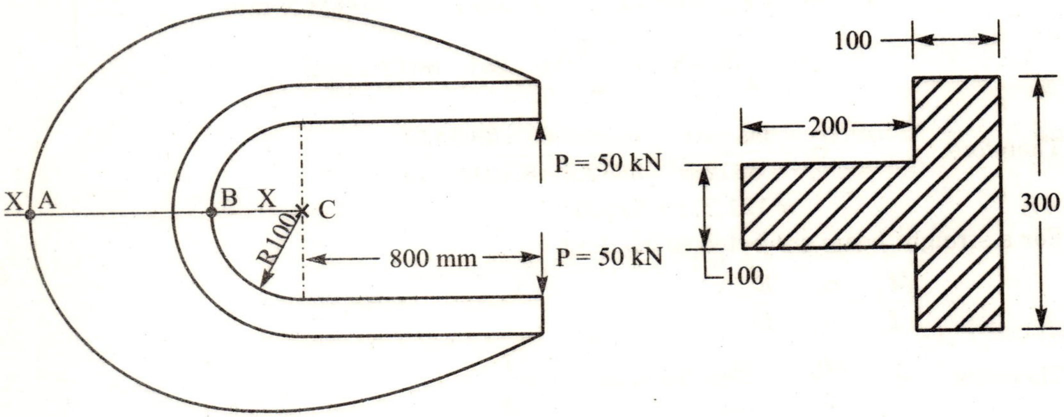

Figure: 1.35

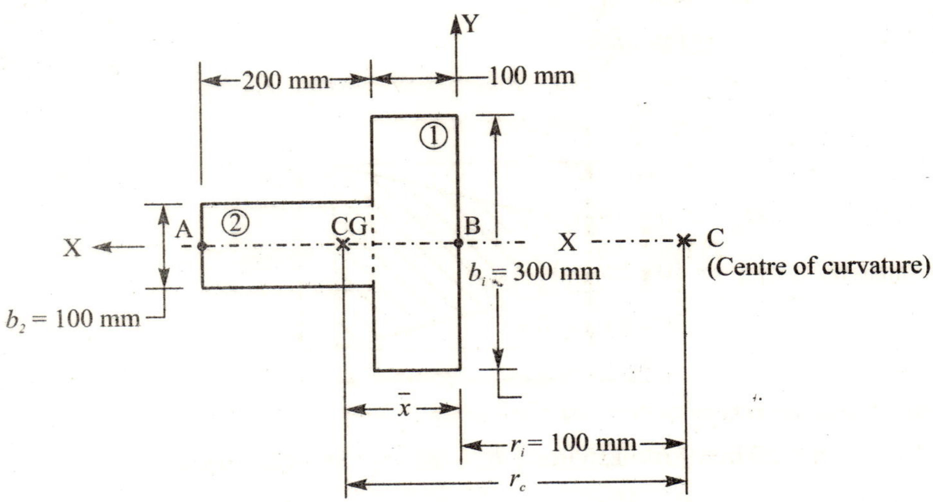

Figure: 1.36

Consider the critical cross-section *X-X* of beam (Fig. 1.36)

Here $r_i = 100$ mm , $r_o = r_i + 300 = 100 + 300 = 400$ mm , $r_c = r_i + \bar{x}$

Where, $\bar{x} = \dfrac{a_1 x_1 + a_2 x_2}{a_1 + a_2}$

$$a_1 = 100 \times 300 = 3 \times 10^4 \text{ mm}^2$$

$$a_2 = 100 \times 200 = 2 \times 10^4 \text{ mm}^2$$

$$x_1 = \frac{100}{2} = 50 \text{ mm}$$

$$x_2 = 100 + \frac{200}{2} = 200 \text{ mm}$$

$$\bar{x} = \frac{3 \times 10^4 \times 50 + 2 \times 10^4 \times 200}{3 \times 10^4 + 2 \times 10^4} = 110 \text{ mm}$$

Therefore, $r_c = 100 + 110 = 210$ mm

To find r_n, the distance of neutral axis from centre of curvature 'c'

For *T*-section from equation (25-62), substituting $a_o = 0$,

$$r_n = \frac{A}{b_i \ln\left(\frac{r_i + a_i}{r_i}\right) + b_2 \ln\left(\frac{r_o}{r_i + a_i}\right)} \quad \text{... E(25-62)}$$

Where, $A = a_1 + a_2 = 3 \times 10^4 + 2 \times 10^4 = 5 \times 10^4 \text{ mm}^2$

$b_i = 300$ mm, $a_i = 100$ mm, $b_2 = 100$ mm, $r_i = 100$ mm, $r_o = 400$ mm

Therefore, $r_n = \dfrac{5 \times 10^4}{300 \ln\left(\frac{100 + 100}{100}\right) + 100 \ln\left(\frac{400}{100 + 100}\right)}$

$= 180.3369$ mm

and $e = r_c - r_n = 210 - 180.3369 = 29.6631$ mm

$$c_i = r_n - r_i = 180.3369 - 100 = 80.3369 \text{ mm}$$

$$c_o = h - c_i = 300 - 80.3369 = 219.6631 \text{ mm}$$

$$M_b = P(r_c + 800)$$

$$= 50 \times 10^3 (r_c + 800)$$

$$= 50 \times 10^3 (210 + 800)$$

$$= 505 \times 10^5 \text{ N-mm}$$

The maximum tensile stress occurs at the inner fibre B and is given by,

$$\sigma_i = \sigma_d + \sigma_{bi}$$

$$= \frac{P}{A} + \frac{M_b c_i}{A e r_i} \quad \text{... E(25-59)}$$

$$= \frac{50\times10^3}{5\times10^4} + \frac{\left(505\times10^5\right)\times80.3369}{5\times10^4\times29.6631\times100}$$

$= 1 + 27.3539$

$= 28.3539$ N/mm² *(tensile)*

Compressive stress at the outer fibre A is

$$\sigma_o = \sigma_d + \sigma_{bo}$$

$$= \frac{P}{A} - \frac{M_b c_o}{Aer_o} \qquad \text{... E(25-58)}$$

$$= \frac{50\times10^3}{5\times10^4} - \frac{\left(505\times10^5\right)\times219.6631}{5\times10^4\times29.6631\times400}$$

$= 1 - 18.6983$

$= - 17.6983$ N/mm² *(compressive)*

The magnitude of maximum stress 28.3539 N/mm² *(at the inner fibre)*

Therefore, maximum shear stress τ_{max} occurs at B and its value is

$$\tau_{max} = \frac{28.3539}{2} = 14.1769 \text{ N/mm}^2$$

Therefore, $\tau_{max} = 14.1769 \text{ N/mm}^2$ *and occurs at the inner fibre B*

Example 1.16: Determine the value of 'P' in the frame shown in figure -1.37 such that the maximum stress induced in frame is limited to 80 MPa.

Solution:

Due to P, maximum tensile stress is produced at the inner fibre B on section X-X given by

$$\sigma_{max} = \sigma_{tensile} = \sigma_d + \sigma_i = \frac{P}{A} + \frac{M_b c_i}{Aer_i} \qquad \text{... E(25-29)}$$

Where, $P =$ Load in N, $A =$ Area of cross-section

$A = 40 \times 80 + 60 \times 40 = 5600$ mm²

$$M_b = P\left[r_c + 120\right]$$

(Because the load axis is away from centre of curvature by a distance of 120 mm)

To compute r_c, r_n, e, c_i

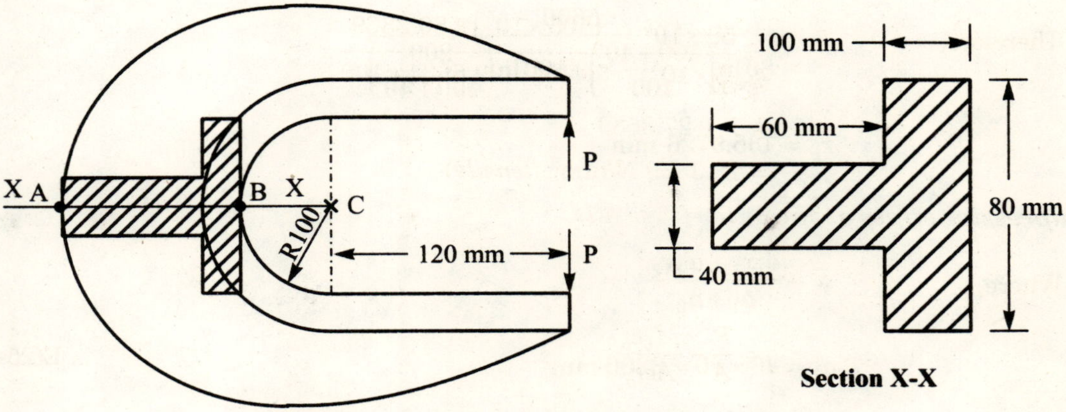

Figure: 1.37

For the *I*-section,

$$r_n = \frac{A}{b_i \ln\left(\frac{r_i + a_i}{r_i}\right) + b_2 \ln\left(\frac{r_o - a_o}{r_i + a_i}\right) b_o \ln\left(\frac{r_o}{r_o - a_o}\right)} \quad \text{... E(22-80)}$$

Note: *For T-section, put* $a_o = 0$

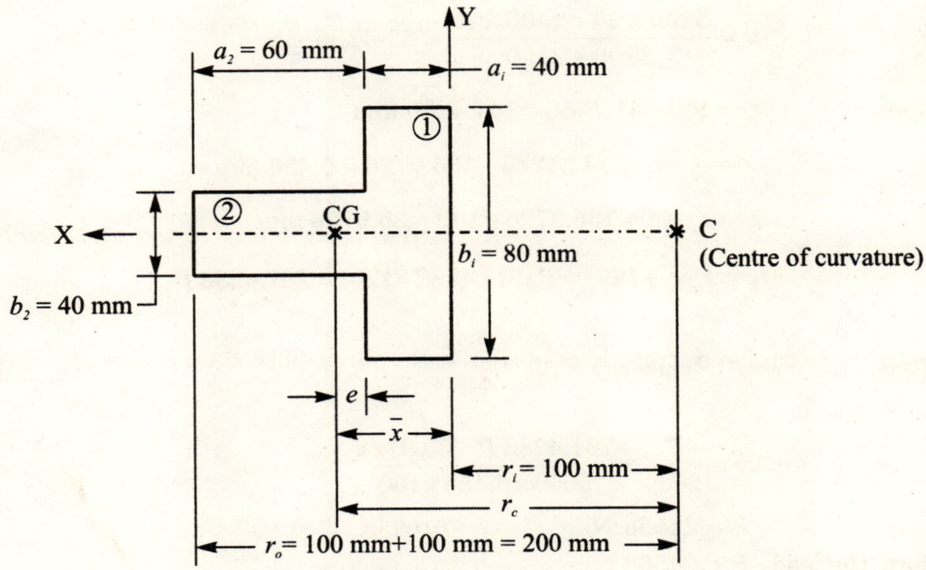

Figure: 1.38

Therefore, $$r_n = \frac{A}{b_i \ln\left(\frac{r_i + a_i}{r_i}\right) + b_2 \ln\left(\frac{r_o}{r_i + a_i}\right)}$$

Where, r_i = 100 mm, r_o = 200 mm, b_i = 80 mm, b_2 = 100 mm, a_i = 40 mm,

Therefore, $$r_n = \frac{5600}{80\ln\left(\frac{100+40}{100}\right)+100\ln\left(\frac{200}{100+40}\right)}$$

$$r_n = 135.9726 \text{ mm}$$

$$r_c = r_i + \bar{x}$$

Where, $$\bar{x} = \frac{a_1x_1 + a_2x_2}{a_1 + a_2}$$

$$a_1 = 40 \times 80 = 3200 \text{ mm}^2$$

$$a_2 = 60 \times 40 = 2400 \text{ mm}^2$$

$$x_1 = \frac{40}{2} = 20 \text{ mm}$$

$$x_2 = 40 + \frac{60}{2} = 70 \text{ mm}$$

Hence, $$\bar{x} = \frac{3200 \times 20 + 2400 \times 70}{3200 + 2400} = 41.4286 \text{ mm}$$

Therefore, $$r_c = 100 + 41.4286 = 141.4286 \text{ mm}$$

$$e = r_c - r_n = 141.1286 - 135.9726 = 5.456 \text{ mm}$$

$$c_i = r_n - r_i = 135.9726 - 100 = 35.9726 \text{ mm}$$

$$M_b = P(r_c + 120) = P(141.4286 + 120) = 261.4286\, P$$

Therefore, $$\sigma_{max} = \sigma_{\text{tensile at A}} = \frac{P}{A} + \frac{M_b c_i}{Aer_i} \qquad \text{... E(25-59)}$$

i.e., $$80 = \frac{P}{5600} + \frac{261.4286\, P \times 35.9726}{5600 \times 5.456 \times 100}$$

$$P = 24566 \text{ N}$$

Therefore, the load $P = 24566$ N

$$P = 24.566 \text{ kN.}$$

Example 1.17:* *A curved beam having T-section (shown in figure-1.39) subjected to pure bending. Find a proper value't', so that extreme fibre stress are numerically equal. If this section is subjected to a couple which develops a maximum fibre stress of 50 N/mm², determine the magnitude of this couple.

Solution:

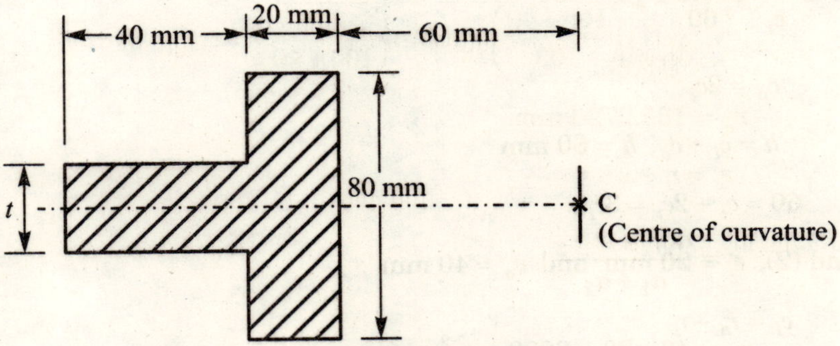

Figure: 1.39

From data, *extreme fibre stress due to bending are numerically equal.*

Therefore, $\sigma_{bi} = \sigma_{bo}$

$$\frac{M_b c_i}{Aer_i} = \frac{M_b c_o}{Aer_o}$$

Therefore, $\frac{c_i}{c_o} = \frac{r_i}{r_o}$ or $\frac{c_o}{c_i} = \frac{r_o}{r_i}$

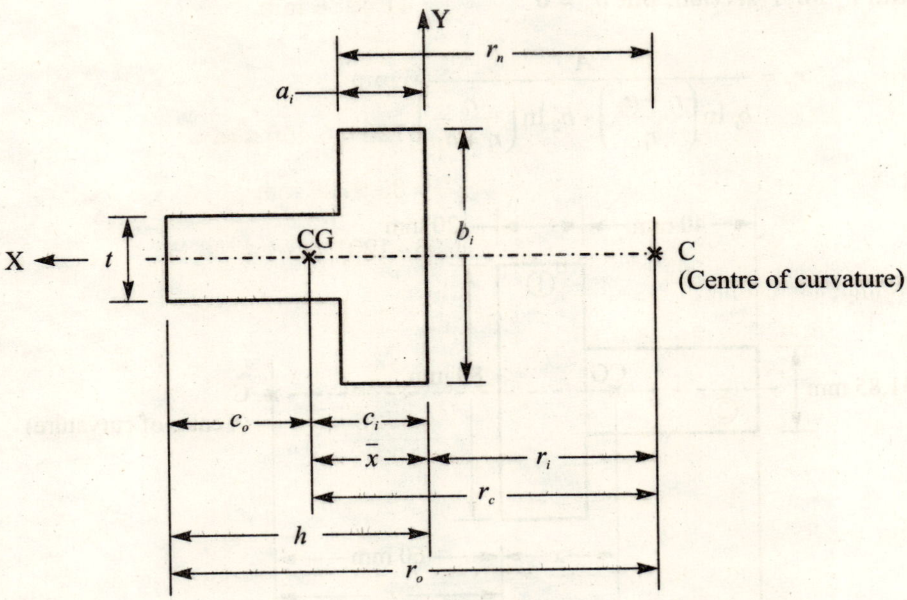

Figure: 1.40

From figures 1.39 and 1.40,

$$r_i = 60 \text{ mm},$$

$$r_o = r_i + h$$

$$= 60 + 60 = 120 \text{ mm}$$

Therefore, $\frac{c_o}{c_i} = \frac{120}{60} = 2$

i.e., $c_o = 2c_i$ ....(1)

Also, $h = c_i + c_o,\ h = 60$ mm .... (2)

Therefore, $60 = c_i + 2c_i = 3c_i$

From (1) and (2), $c_i = 20$ mm and $c_o = 40$ mm

But, $c_i = r_n - r_i$

$20 = r_n - 60$

Therefore, $r_n = 80$ mm

For an *I*-section,

$$r_n = \frac{A}{b_i \ln\left(\frac{r_i + a_i}{r_i}\right) + b_2 \ln\left(\frac{r_o - a_o}{r_i + a_i}\right) b_o \ln\left(\frac{r_o}{r_o - a_o}\right)} \quad \text{... E(25-63)}$$

To obtain r_n for *T*-section, put $a_o = 0$

i.e.,

$$r_n = \frac{A}{b_i \ln\left(\frac{r_i + a_i}{r_i}\right) + b_2 \ln\left(\frac{r_o}{r_i + a_i}\right)}$$

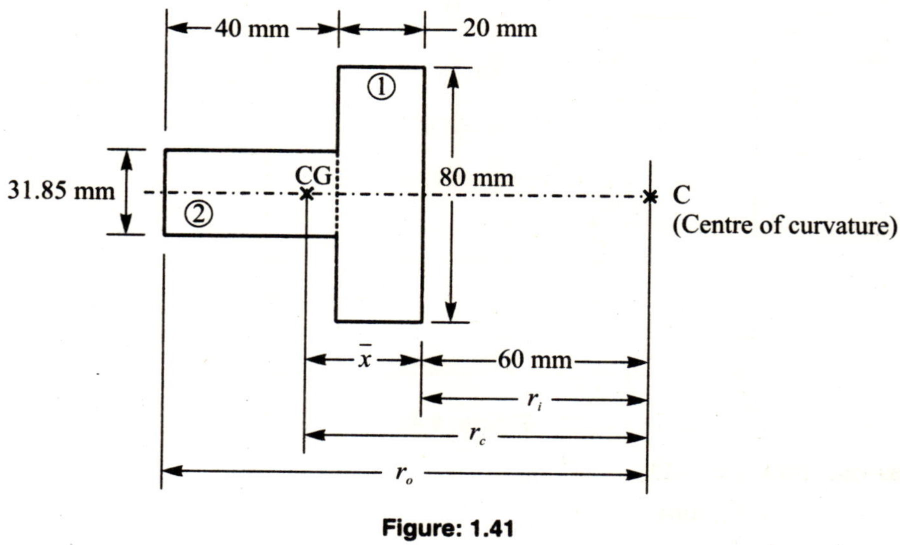

Figure: 1.41

From figure, $A = 80 \times 20 + 40 \times t$

$$A = 1600 + 40t$$

$$b_i = 80 \text{ mm};\ r_i = 60 \text{ mm};\ a_i = 20 \text{ mm};\ b_2 = t;\ r_o = 120 \text{ mm}$$

Therefore,
$$r_n = \frac{1600 + 40t}{80 \ln\left(\frac{60+20}{60}\right) + t \ln \frac{120}{60+20}}$$

$$80 = \frac{1600 + 40t}{23.01 + t\,(0.4055)}$$

i.e., $t = 31.85$ mm

With $t = 31.85$ mm, the cross-section of beam has dimensions as shown in figure-1.41

To find extreme fibre stresses

From figure, $r_i = 60$ mm, $r_o = 120$ mm

$$r_c = r_i + \bar{x}$$

Where,
$$\bar{x} = \frac{a_1 x_1 + a_2 x_2}{a_1 + a_2}$$

$$a_1 = 20 \times 80 = 1600 \text{ mm}^2$$

$$a_2 = 40 \times t = 40 \times 31.85 = 1274 \text{ mm}^2$$

$$x_1 = 10 \text{ mm},\ x_2 = 40 \text{ mm}$$

$$\bar{x} = \frac{1600 \times 10 + 1274 \times 40}{1600 + 1274} = 23.29 \text{ mm}$$

$$r_c = 60 + 23.29 = 83.29 \text{ mm}$$

$$e = r_c - r_n = 83.29 - 80 = 3.29 \text{ mm}$$

$$A = a_1 + a_2 = 1600 + 1274 = 2874 \text{ mm}^2$$

Extreme fibre stress due to bending

$$\sigma_{bi} = \frac{M_b c_i}{A e r_i}$$

i.e.,
$$50 = \frac{M_b \times 20}{2874 \times 3.29 \times 60}$$

Therefore couple $M_b = 1452807$ N-mm

$= 1452.807$ N-m

Example 1.18: For the curved beam shown in figure-1.42 determine,

(i) Bending moment for the critical section.

(ii) Distance from centre of curvature to centroidal axis.

(iii) Distance between centroidal axis and neutral axis.

(iv) Maximum tensile stress and its location.

(v) Maximum compressive stress and its location.

(vi) Maximum shear stress and its location.

(vii) Plot the distribution of stress across the critical section.

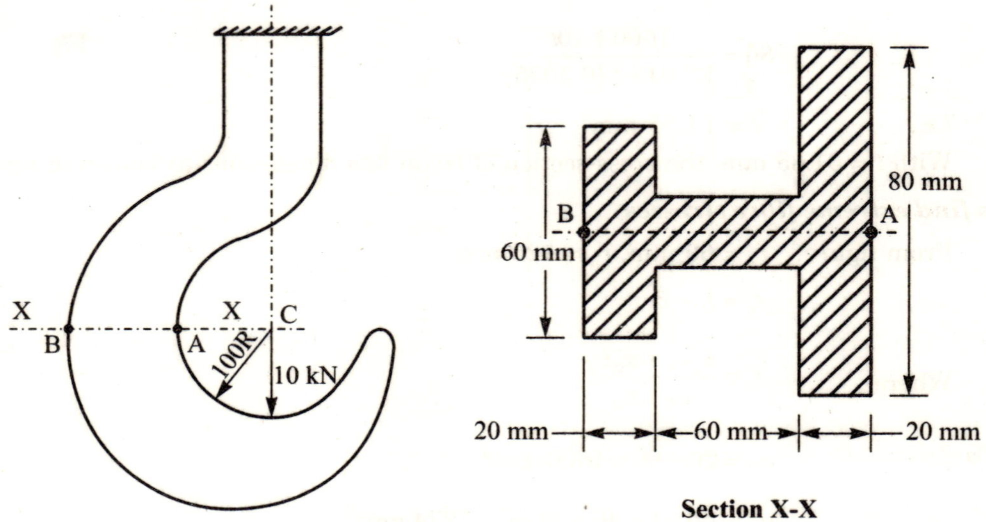

Figure: 1.42

Solution:

For the *I*-section,

$$r_n = \frac{A}{b_i \ln\left(\frac{r_i + a_i}{r_i}\right) + b_2 \ln\left(\frac{r_o - a_o}{r_i + a_i}\right) + b_o \ln\left(\frac{r_o}{r_o - a_o}\right)} \quad \text{... E(25-63)}$$

$$A = 80 \times 20 + 60 \times 20 + 60 \times 20 = 4000 \text{ mm}^2$$

$$r_i = 100 \text{ mm}, r_o = 200 \text{ mm}, a_i = 20 \text{ mm}, a_o = 20 \text{ mm},$$

$$b_i = 80 \text{ mm}, b_2 = 20 \text{ mm}, b_o = 60 \text{ mm}$$

Therefore,

$$r_n = \frac{4000}{80 \ln\left(\frac{100+20}{100}\right) + 20 \ln\left(\frac{200-20}{100+20}\right) + 60 \ln\left(\frac{200}{200-20}\right)}$$

$$= 137.8519 \text{ mm}$$

$$r_c = r_i + \bar{x} = 100 + \bar{x}$$

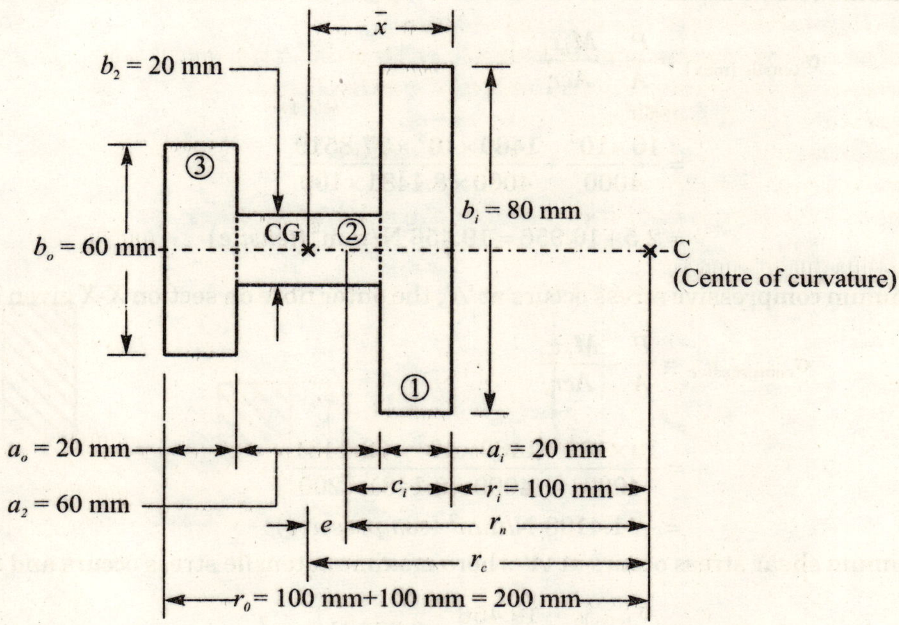

Figure: 1.43

To find $\bar{x}$, the distance of CG of critical section from the inner fibre

$$\bar{x} = \frac{a_1x_1 + a_2x_2 + a_3x_3}{a_1 + a_2 + a_3}$$

Where, $a_1 = 80 \times 20 = 1600 \text{ mm}^2$, $a_2 = 60 \times 20 = 1200 \text{ mm}^2$, $a_3 = 60 \times 20 = 1200 \text{ mm}^2$

$$x_1 = \frac{20}{2} = 10 \text{ mm}; \quad x_2 = 20 + \frac{60}{2} = 50 \text{ mm}; \quad x_3 = 80 + \frac{20}{2} = 90 \text{ mm}$$

Therefore, $$\bar{x} = \frac{1600 \times 10 + 1200 \times 50 + 1200 \times 90}{4000} = 46 \text{ mm}$$

Note: $$a_1 + a_2 + a_3 = A = 4000 \text{ mm}^2$$

Therefore, $$r_c = 100 + 46 = 146 \text{ mm}$$

$$e = r_c - r_n = 146 - 137.8519 = 8.1481 \text{ mm}$$

$$c_i = r_n - r_i = 137.8519 - 100 = 37.8519 \text{ mm}$$

$$c_o = r_o - r_n = 200 - 137.8519 = 62.1481 \text{ mm}$$

(*i*) Bending moment for the critical section is

$$M_b = Pr_c = 10 \times 10^3 \times 146 = 1460 \times 10^3 \text{ N-mm}$$

(*ii*) Distance from centre of curvature to centroidal axis is

$$r_c = 146 \text{ mm}$$

(*iii*) Distance between centroidal axis and neutral axis is

$$e = r_c - r_n = 146 - 137.8419 = 8.1481 \text{ mm}$$

(*iv*) Maximum tensile stress occurs at the inner fibre '*B*' on section *X-X* and is given by

$$\sigma_{\text{tensile (max)}} = \frac{P}{A} + \frac{M_b c_i}{Aer_i} \qquad \text{... E(25-59)}$$

$$= \frac{10 \times 10^3}{4000} + \frac{1460 \times 10^3 \times 37.8519}{4000 \times 8.1481 \times 100}$$

$$= 2.5 + 16.956 = 19.456 \text{ N/mm}^2 \ (tensile)$$

(*v*) Maximum compressive stress occurs at '*A*', the outer fibre on section *X-X* given by

$$\sigma_{\text{compressive}} = \frac{P}{A} - \frac{M_b c_o}{Aer_o} \qquad \text{... E(25-58)}$$

$$= \frac{10 \times 10^3}{4000} - \frac{1460 \times 10^3 \times 62.1481}{4000 \times 8.1481 \times 200}$$

$$= -11.4198 \text{ N/mm}^2 \ (compressive)$$

(*vi*) Maximum shear stress occurs at '*A*' where maximum tensile stress occurs and its value is

$$\tau_{\max} = \frac{\sigma_{\text{tensile}}}{2} = \frac{19.456}{2} = 9.728 \text{ N/mm}^2$$

(*vii*) Plot of stress distribution across the critical cross-section *AB*

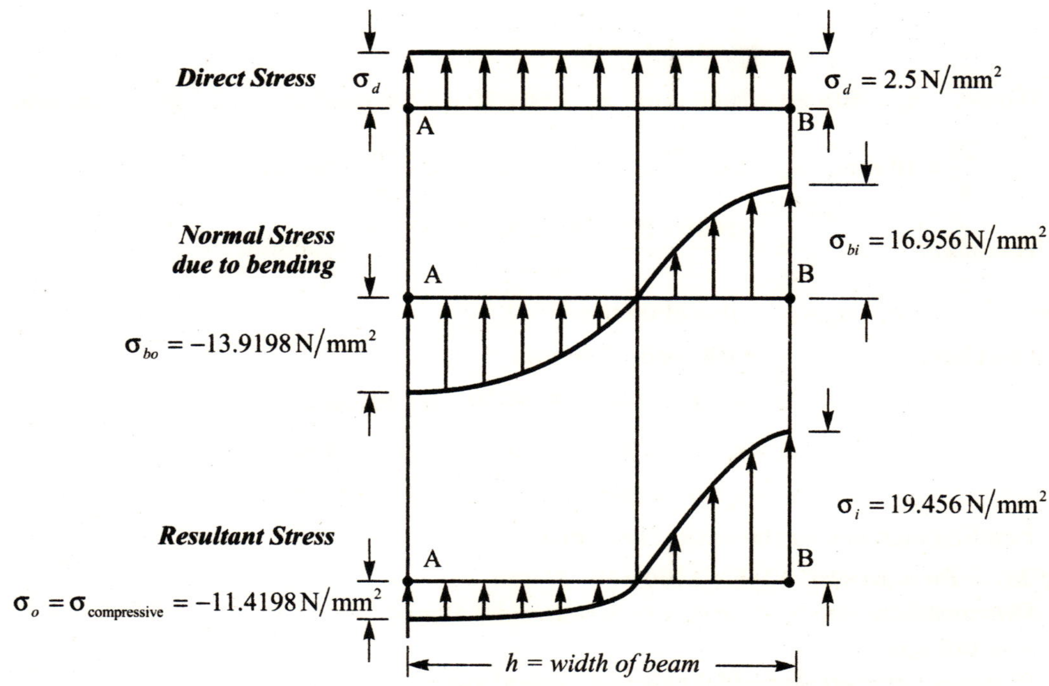

Figure: 1.44

Where, $\sigma_d = \frac{P}{A}(tensile) = \frac{10 \times 10^3}{4000} = 2.5 \text{ N/mm}^2$

$$\sigma_{bi} = \frac{M_b c_i}{Aer_i} = 16.956 \text{ N/mm}^2$$

$$\sigma_{bo} = \frac{-M_b c_o}{Aer_o} = -11.4198 \text{ N/mm}^2$$

Example 1.19: Determine F the maximum load the crane hook of I-section shown in figure-1.45 can carry limiting the maximum stress in the hook to 19.5 N/mm².

Solution:

The maximum tensile stress at the inner fibre '*B*' for the critical section *X-X* is given by

$$\sigma_{tensile(max)} = \sigma_d + \sigma_{bi} = \frac{F}{A} + \frac{M_b c_i}{Aer_i} \quad \text{... E(25.59)}$$

Where, F = Load, the crane hook can carry, in N

A = Area of cross-section, mm²

$= 20 \times 80 + 60 \times 20 + 60 \times 20 = 4000 \text{ mm}^2$

$M_b = Fr_c$

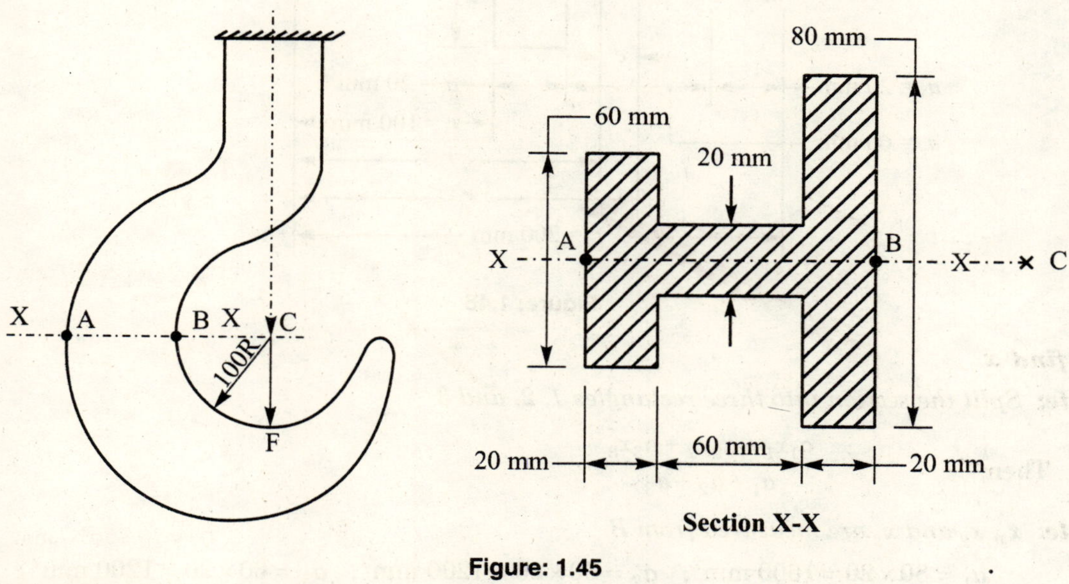

Figure: 1.45

To find dimensions r_c, r_n, e and c_i

For *I*-section,

$$r_n = \frac{A}{b_i \ln\left(\frac{r_i + a_i}{r_i}\right) + b_2 \ln\left(\frac{r_o - a_o}{r_i + a_i}\right) + b_o \ln\left(\frac{r_o}{r_o - a_o}\right)} \quad \text{... E(25-63)}$$

Here, $A = 4000 \text{ mm}^2, r_i = 100 \text{ mm}, r_o = 200 \text{ mm}, a_i = 20 \text{ mm}, a_o = 20 \text{ mm}$,

$b_i = 80 \text{ mm}, b_2 = 20 \text{ mm}, b_o = 60 \text{ mm}$

Therefore,
$$r_n = \frac{4000}{80 \ln\left(\frac{100+20}{100}\right) + 20 \ln\left(\frac{200-20}{100+20}\right) + 60 \ln\left(\frac{200}{200-20}\right)}$$

$$r_n = 137.8519 \text{ mm}$$

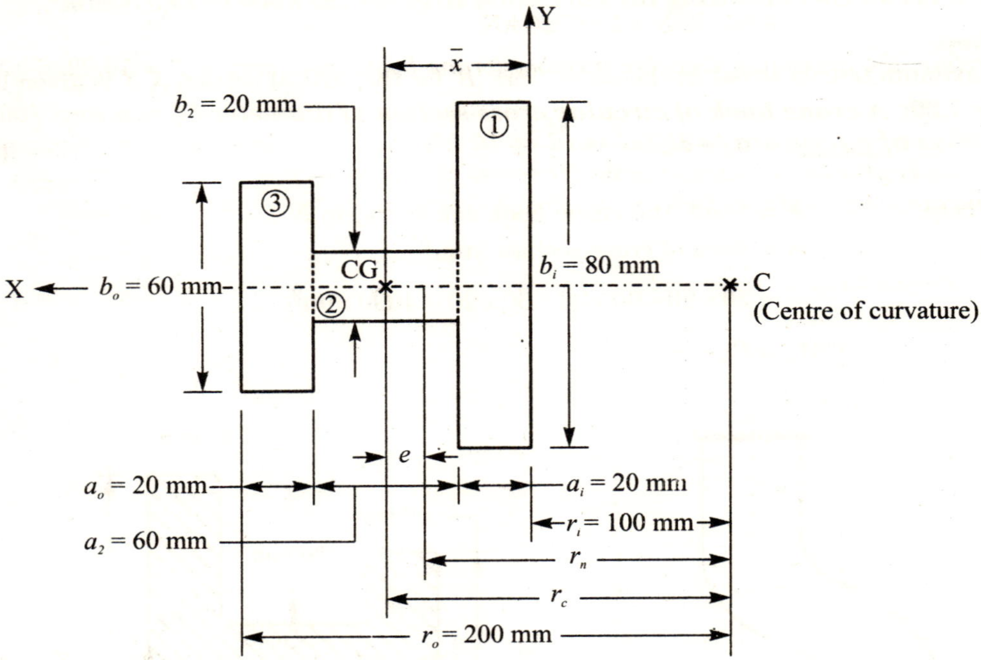

Figure: 1.46

To find $\bar{x}$

Note: *Split the section into three rectangles 1, 2, and 3*

Then,
$$\bar{x} = \frac{a_1x_1 + a_2x_2 + a_3x_3}{a_1 + a_2 + a_3}$$

Note: *x_1, x_2 and x_3 are measured from B*

$$a_1 = 80 \times 20 = 1600 \text{ mm}^2, \quad a_2 = 60 \times 20 = 1200 \text{ mm}^2, \quad a_3 = 60 \times 20 = 1200 \text{ mm}^2,$$

$$x_1 = \frac{20}{2} = 10 \text{ mm}, \quad x_2 = 20 + \frac{60}{2} = 50 \text{ mm}, \quad x_3 = 80 + \frac{20}{2} = 90 \text{ mm}$$

Therefore,
$$\bar{x} = \frac{1600 \times 10 + 1200 \times 50 + 1200 \times 90}{4000} = 46 \text{ mm}$$

Therefore, $r_c = 100 + 46 = 146$ mm

$$A = a_1 + a_2 + a_3 = 4000 \text{ mm}^2$$

$$e = r_c - r_n = 146 - 137.8519 = 8.1481 \text{ mm}$$

$$c_i = r_n - r_i = 137.8519 - 100 = 37.8519 \text{ mm}$$

Now, $M_b = F \times r_c = F \times 146 = 146F$

Therefore, $\sigma_{tensile} = \dfrac{F}{A} + \dfrac{M_b c_i}{A e r_i} = \dfrac{F}{4000} + \dfrac{146F \times 37.8519}{4000 \times 88.1481 \times 100} = 19.5$ (given)

$$F = 10022.62 \text{ N} = 10.0226 \text{ kN}$$

Therefore, the maximum load the member (crane hook) can carry is $F = 10.0226$ kN

Example 1.20: A crane hook of circular cross-section of diameter 50 mm and 100 mm inner radius of curvature to lift a load of 10 kN is to be replaced by a rectangular section. The replaced rectangular section has the same inner radius of curvature as that of the circular section. Determine the dimensions of the replaced section.

Solution:

Consider the circular cross-section of beam

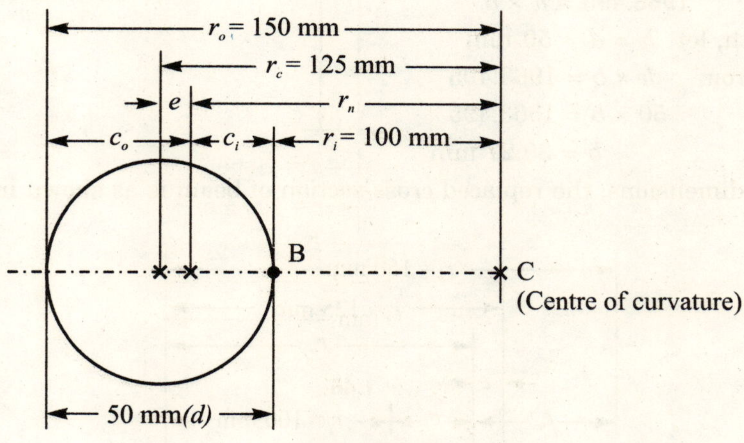

Figure: 1.47

For the circular cross-section shown, $r_i = 100$ mm, $r_o = 150$ mm, $r_c = 125$ mm

$$r_n = \frac{\left(\sqrt{r_i} + \sqrt{r_o}\right)^2}{4} \quad \text{... E(25-60)}$$

$$= \frac{\left(\sqrt{100} + \sqrt{150}\right)^2}{4} = 123.7372 \text{ mm}$$

$$e = r_c - r_n = 125 - 123.7372 = 1.2628 \text{ mm}$$

$$c_i = r_n - r_i = 123.7372 - 100 = 23.7372 \text{ mm}$$

$$M_b = Pr_c = \left(10 \times 10^3\right) \times 125 = 125 \times 10^4 \text{ N-mm}$$

A = Area of cross-section

$$A = \frac{\pi d^2}{4} = \frac{\pi(50)^2}{4} = 1963.495 \text{ mm}^2$$

Therefore, σ_i = Maximum tensile stress at the inner fibre is given by,

$$\sigma_i = \frac{P}{A} + \frac{M_b c_i}{Aer_i} \qquad \text{... E(25-59)}$$

$$= \frac{10 \times 10^3}{1963.495} + \frac{125 \times 10^4 \times 23.7372}{1963.495 \times 1.2628 \times 100}$$

$$= 124.76 \text{ N/mm}^2$$

Note: *When the circular section is replaced by rectangular section, the stress at the inner fibre of replaced section should be equal to that of stress at the inner fibre of circular section.*

Trial 1: *Considering rectangular section,*

Let 'h' and 'b' be the depth and width of section.

Equating Area of circular cross-section to Area of rectangular section,

$$1963.495 = h \times b$$

To start with, let $h = d = 50$ mm

Therefore, from $h \times b = 1963.495$

$$50 \times b = 1963.495$$

i.e., $b = 39.27$ mm

With these dimensions, the replaced cross-section of beam is as shown in Fig. 1.48

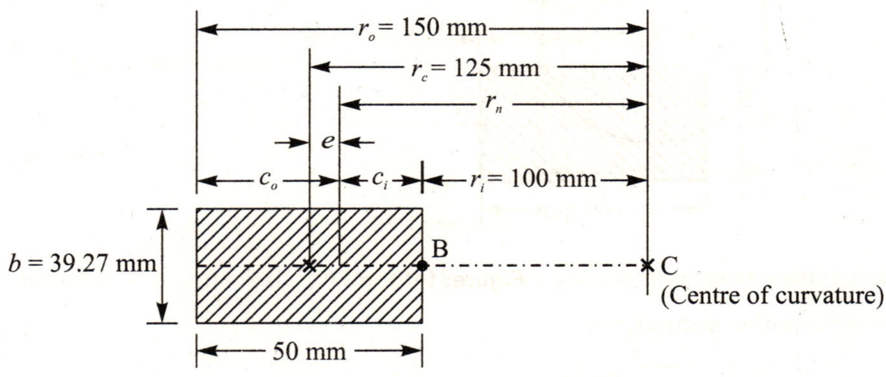

Figure: 1.48

For the rectangular section,

$$r_n = \frac{h}{\ln\left(\frac{r_o}{r_i}\right)} \qquad \text{... E(25-60)}$$

$$= \frac{50}{\ln\left(\frac{150}{100}\right)} = \frac{50}{0.4054651} = 123.3152 \text{ mm}$$

$$e = r_c - r_n = 125 - 123.3152 = 1.6848 \text{ mm}$$

$$c_i = r_n - r_i = 123.3152 - 100 = 23.3152 \text{ mm}$$

$$M_b = Pr_c = \left(10 \times 10^3\right) \times 125 = 125 \times 10^4 \text{ N-mm}$$

Therefore, maximum tensile stress at the inner fibre 'A' is

$$\sigma_{\text{tensile(max)}} = \frac{P}{A} + \frac{M_b c_i}{A e r_i}$$

$$= \frac{10 \times 10^3}{1963.495} + \frac{125 \times 10^4 \times 23.3152}{1963.495 \times 1.6848 \times 100}$$

Therefore, $\sigma_{\text{tensile(max)}} = 93.192 \text{ N/mm}^2$

Trial 2: *Change width to 60 mm and with this change,*

$$b = \frac{A}{h} = \frac{1963.495}{60} = 32.73 \text{ mm}$$

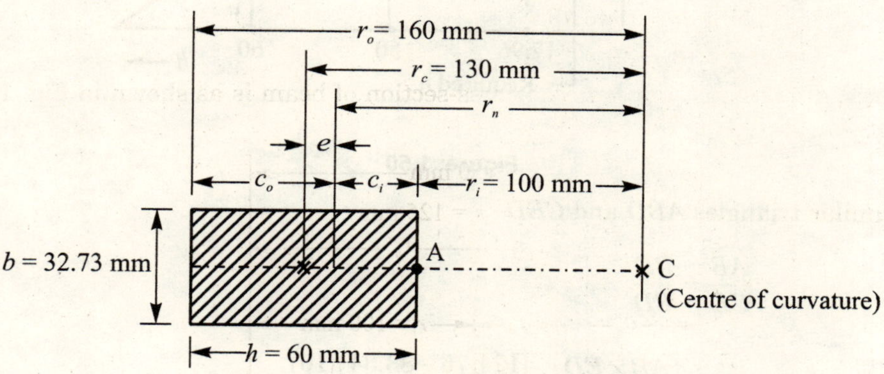

Figure: 1.49

For this rectangular section,

$$r_n = \frac{h}{\ln\left(\frac{r_o}{r_i}\right)} = \frac{60}{\ln\left(\frac{160}{100}\right)} = 127.6596 \text{ mm}$$

$$e = r_c - r_n = 130 - 127.6596 = 2.3404 \text{ mm}$$

$$c_i = r_n - r_i = 127.6596 - 100 = 27.6596 \text{ mm}$$

$$M_b = P \times r_c = \left(10 \times 10^3\right) \times 130 = 130 \times 10^4 \text{ N-mm}$$

Therefore, the maximum tensile stress at the inner fibre '*A*' is

$$\sigma_{tensile(max)} = \frac{P}{A} + \frac{M_b c_i}{A e r_i} \quad \text{... E(25-59)}$$

$$= \frac{10 \times 10^3}{1963.495} + \frac{130 \times 10^4 \times 27.6596}{1963.495 \times 2.3404 \times 100}$$

$$= 83.34 \text{ N/mm}^2$$

Plot a graph of 'h' versus the tensile stress $\sigma_{tensile}$ and obtain the required thickness.

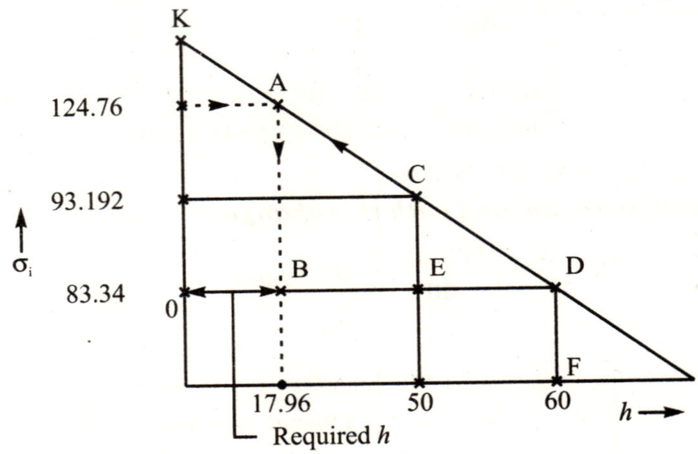

Figure: 1.50

From similar triangles *ABD* and *CED*

$$\frac{AB}{CE} = \frac{BD}{ED}$$

Therefore, $$BD = \frac{AB \times ED}{CE} = \frac{(124.76 - 83.34)(10)}{(93.192 - 83.34)} = 42.04 \text{ mm}$$

Therefore,. $$OB = \text{required width} = OD - BD = 60 - 42.04 = 17.96 \text{ mm}$$

$$b = \frac{A}{h} = \frac{1963.495}{17.96}$$

The dimensions of replaced rectangular section are, width b = 109.33 mm and h = 17.96 mm

Example 1.21: A link is made of round steel rod of diameter 30 mm having inside radius 30 mm is shown in figure 1.51. The straight portion of the link is 60 mm long. What load the link can take assuming maximum stress in the link to be 80 N/mm²?

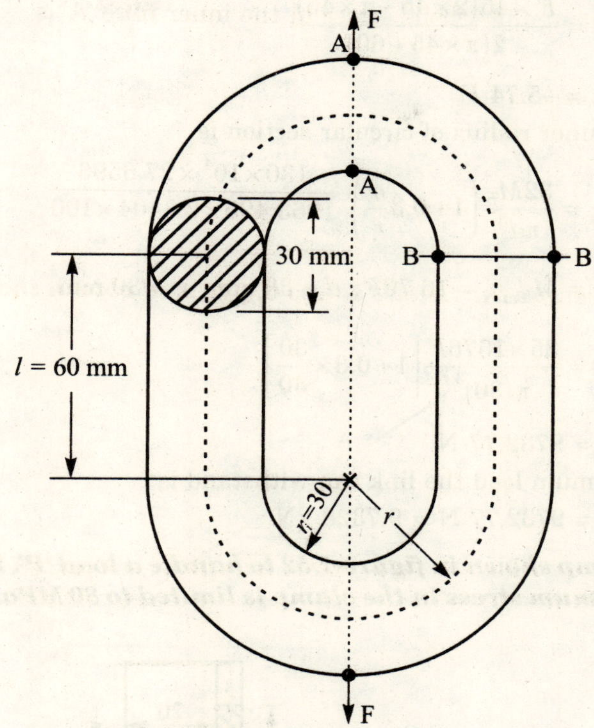

Figure: 1.51

Solution:

The moment M_{bA} at the point of application of load is

$$M_{bA} = \frac{Fr(2r+l)}{2(\pi r + l)} \quad \text{... E(25-76)}$$

For the given link,

$$r = 30 + \frac{30}{2} = 45 \text{ mm}$$

$$l = 60 \text{ mm}$$

Therefore, $$M_{bA} = \frac{F \times 45(2 \times 45 + 60)}{2(\pi \times 45 + 60)}$$

$$= \frac{6750F}{402.74} = 16.76\,F$$

The moment M_{bB} at the section 90° away from the point of application of load is

$$M_{bB} = \frac{Fr(2r - \pi r)}{2(\pi r + l)} \quad \text{... E(25-77)}$$

$$= \frac{F \times 45(2\times 45 - \pi \times 45)}{2(\pi \times 45 + 60)}$$

$$= -5.74\ F$$

The stress at the inner radius of circular section is

$$\sigma_i = \frac{32M_b}{\pi d^3}\left(1 + 0.3\frac{d}{r_i}\right) \qquad \text{... E(25-66)}$$

Where, $M_b = M_{b\max} = 16.76F;\ d = 30\ \text{mm};\ r_i = 30\ \text{mm}$

Therefore, $$80 = \frac{35 \times 1676F}{\pi(30)^3}\left[1 + 0.3 \times \frac{30}{30}\right]$$

Therefore, $F = 9732.77$ N

Therefore the maximum load the link can withstand is

$$F = 9732.77\ \text{N} = 9.7328\ \text{kN}$$

Example 1.22: A C-clamp shown in figure-1.52 to handle a load 'P'. Determine the value 'P' such that the maximum stress in the clamp is limited to 80 MPa.

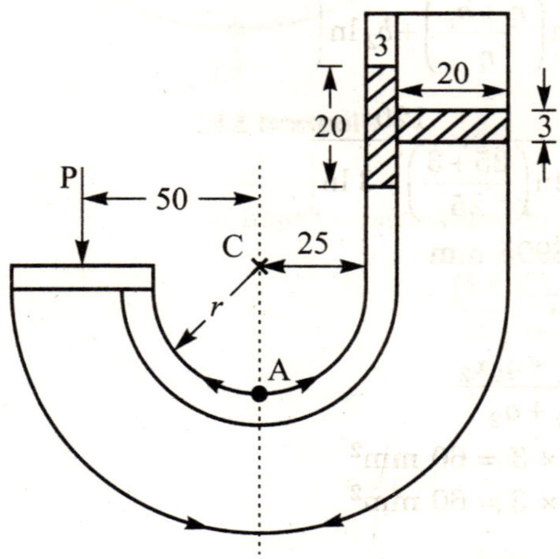

Figure: 1.52

Solution:-

For the C-clamp, maximum tensile stress occurring at 'A', the inner fibre is given by,

$$\sigma_{\max} = \sigma_{\text{tensile}} = \frac{P}{A} + \frac{M_b c_i}{A e r_i}$$

Where, P = Load in N

A = Area of cross-section

$= 20 \times 3 + 20 \times 3 = 120\ \text{mm}^2$

To find dimensions r_n, r_c, c_i and e

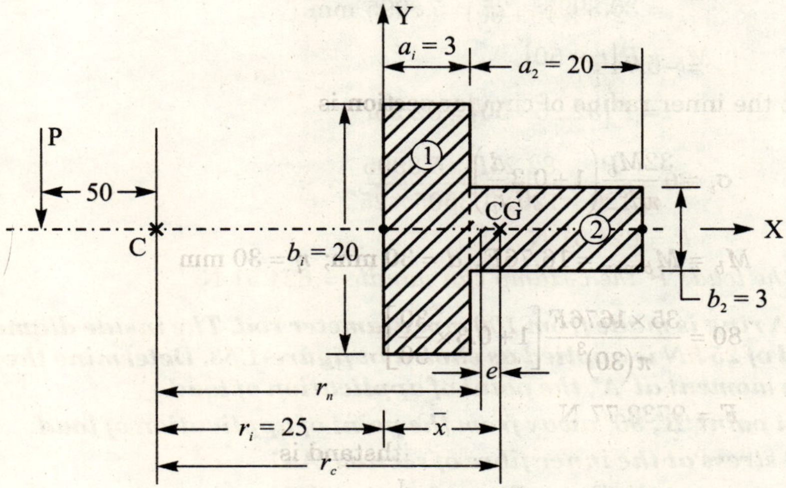

For the *I*-section put $a_o = 0$ in equation E(22-80), of *I*-section

Therefore,
$$r_n = \frac{A}{b_i \ln\left(\frac{r_i + a_i}{r_i}\right) + b_2 \ln\left(\frac{r_o}{r_o + a_i}\right)}$$

$$= \frac{120}{20 \ln\left(\frac{25+3}{25}\right) + 3 \ln\left(\frac{48}{25+3}\right)}$$

$$= 30.8995 \text{ mm}$$

$$r_c = r_i + \bar{x}$$

Where,
$$\bar{x} = \frac{a_1 x_1 + a_2 x_2}{a_1 + a_2}$$

$$a_1 = 20 \times 3 = 60 \text{ mm}^2$$
$$a_2 = 20 \times 3 = 60 \text{ mm}^2$$

$$x_1 = \frac{3}{2} = 1.5 \text{ mm}$$

$$x_2 = 3 + \frac{20}{2} = 13 \text{ mm}$$

Therefore,
$$\bar{x} = \frac{60 \times 15 + 60 \times 13}{60 + 60} = 7.25 \text{ mm}$$

$$r_c = 25 + 7.25 = 60 \text{ mm}^2$$
$$= 32.25 \text{ mm}$$

$$e = r_c - r_n$$
$$= 32.25 - 30.8995 = 1.3505 \text{ mm}$$

$$c_i = r_n - r_i$$
$$= 30.8995 - 25 = 5.8995 \text{ mm}$$

Therefore, $M_b = P\left[r_c + 50\right]$

$$= P\left[32.25 + 50\right] = 82.25P$$

$$80 = \frac{P}{120} + \frac{82.25P \times 5.8995}{120 \times 1.3505 \times 25}$$

Therefore, $P = 624.51$ N

Therefore, the load, 'P' the c-clamp can handle = 624.51 N

Example 1.23: A ring is made from 100 mm diameter rod. The inside diameter of ring is 120 mm. A load of 25 kN is applied as shown in figure-1.53. Determine the values of

(i) Maximum moment at 'A', the point of application of load.

(ii) Moment at point 'B', 90° away from the point of application of load.

(iii) Resultant stress at the inner fibre of section 'AA'

(iv) Resultant stress at the inner fibre of section 'BB'

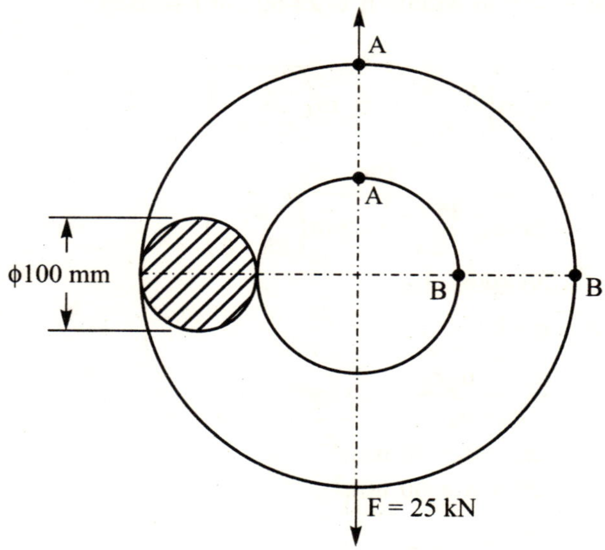

Figure: 1.53

Solution:

(i) Maximum moment for circular ring at the point of application of load, A

$$M_{b\max} = \pm\frac{Fr}{\pi} = \mp 0.318Fr \qquad \text{... E(25-68)}$$

Where, (–ve) negative sign is used for tensile load.

(+ve) positive sign is used for compressive load.

Therefore, $M_{b\max} = -\ 0.318Fr$

Where, $r = r_c = r_i + \frac{d}{2}$

$= 60 + \frac{100}{2} = 110$ mm

Therefore, $M_{b\max} = -0.318 \times (25 \times 10^3) 110$

$= -874500$ N-mm

(ii) Moment at a point 90° away from point of application of load is

$M_b = \pm 0.182\ Fr$ ... E(25-69)

Where, (–ve) negative sign is used for compressive load.

(+ve) positive sign is used for tensile load.

Therefore, $M_b = \pm 0.182\ Fr$

$= 0.182 \times 25 \times 10^3 \times 110$

$= 500500$ N-mm

(iii) Resultant stress at inner fibre of section AA is

$$\sigma_r = \sigma_d + \frac{M_b c_i}{A e r_i}$$

Where, $M_b = -874500$ N-mm

For the circular cross-section

$$r_n = \frac{\left(\sqrt{r_o} + \sqrt{r_i}\right)^2}{4} \quad \text{... E(22-77)}$$

Where, $r_o = r_i + d = 60 + 100 = 160$ mm

$r_i = 60$ mm

$r_c = r_i + \frac{d}{2} = 60 + \frac{100}{2} = 110$ mm

Therefore, $r_n = \frac{\left(\sqrt{160} + \sqrt{60}\right)^2}{4} = 103.99$ mm

$e = r_c - r_n = 110 - 103.99 = 6.01$ mm

$c_i = r_n - r_i = 103.99 - 60 = 43.99$ mm

$A = \frac{\pi d^2}{4} = \frac{\pi}{4}(100)^2 = 7853.95\ \text{mm}^2$

$\sigma_d = 0$ at A

Therefore, $\sigma_r)_{\text{at inner fibre } A} = -\frac{M_b c_i}{A e r_i}$

$$= -\frac{874500 \times 43.99}{7853.98 \times 6.01 \times 60}$$

$$= -13.85 \text{ N/mm}^2 \text{ (compressive)}$$

(iv) Resultant stress at inner fibre of section BB is

$$\sigma_r = \sigma_d + \sigma_{bi})_{at\ BB}$$

$$= \frac{F}{2A} + \frac{M_b)_{at\ BB} \times c_i}{Aer_i}$$

$$= \frac{25 \times 10^3}{2 \times 7853.98} + \frac{500500 \times 43.99}{7853.98 \times 6.01 \times 60}$$

$$= 1.5916 + 7.774$$

$$= 9.3656 \text{ N/mm}^2 \text{ (tensile)}$$

EXERCISE

1. The central horizontal section of a crane hook is a symmetrical trapezium 100 mm deep, the inner width being 60 mm and outer width being 40 mm. The hook carries a tensile load of 25 kN. The inner radius of hook is 75 mm. The load line is nearer to the inner surface of the hook by 25 mm than the centre of curvature at the critical cross-section. Determine the maximum tensile, compressive and shear stress induced in the cross-section.
2. The parallel sides of the trapezoidal cross-section of a crane hook of capacity 50 kN are 100 mm and 60 mm, the depth of section being 120 mm. The radius of curvature of inner fibre is 150 mm. Determine the normal stresses at the extreme fibres and plot them along the critical cross-section.
3. The section of a crane hook is a trapezium whose inner and outer sides are 80 mm and 40 mm respectively. The depth of section is 100 mm. The centre of curvature of section is at a distance of 120 mm from the inner side of section and the load line is 110 mm from the same point. Determine the load carrying capacity of hook, if the maximum stress is not to exceed 80 MPa.
4. A closed ring made out of 7.5 mm diameter rod and has inside diameter of 100 mm and is subjected to a diametral compressive load of 20 kN. Calculate the values of stress (Maximum compressive and shear stress) and indicate their locations.
5. Compute the values of extreme fibre stresses in the critical cross-section of a hook which is required to lift load upto 25 kN. The hook has trapezoidal cross section with parallel sides measuring 60 mm and 300 mm, the distance between them being 90 mm. The inner radius of hook is 100 mm, the load line is nearer to the inner surface of hook by 25 mm than the centre of curvature at the critical section.
6. (*a*) Explain why curved beams have to be analyzed for stresses specially when we already have straight beam equations for determining stresses.

   (*b*) The curved beam shown in figure is subjected to a load of 50 kN. Determine the stresses at the inner and outer fibres. Plot the stress distribution. ***(VTU, July 2006)***

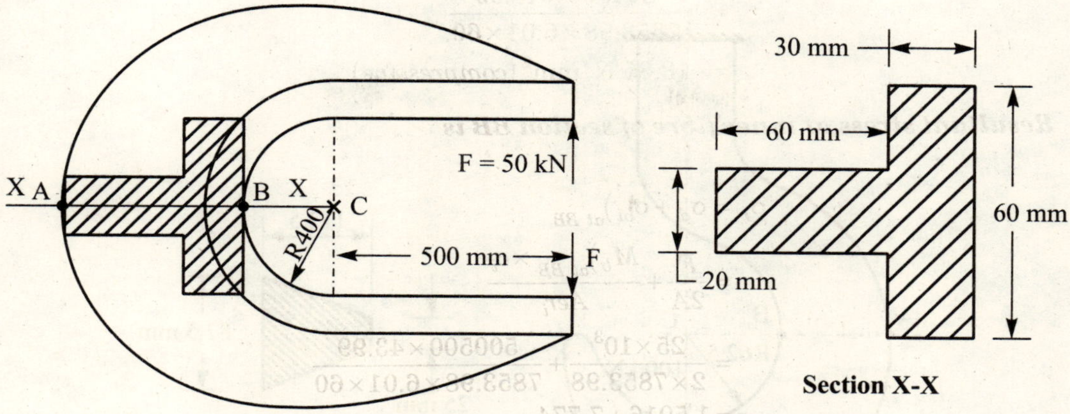

7. Calculate the stresses at point A and B for a circular beam shown in figure when subjected to a compressive load of 6 kN.

(VTU, July 2007)

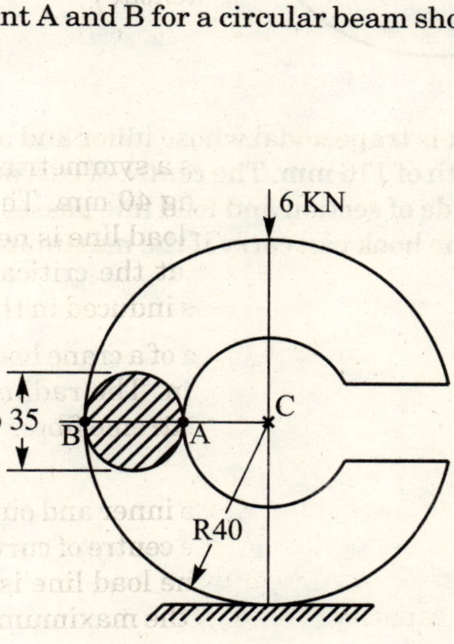

8. (*a*) Differentiate between a straight beam and a curved beam with stress distribution in each of the beam.

   (*b*) For the crane hook of trapezoidal section shown in figure, determine stresses in the outer, inner, CG and also at the neutral fibre and draw the stress distribution across the section AB.

(VTU, June / July 2008)

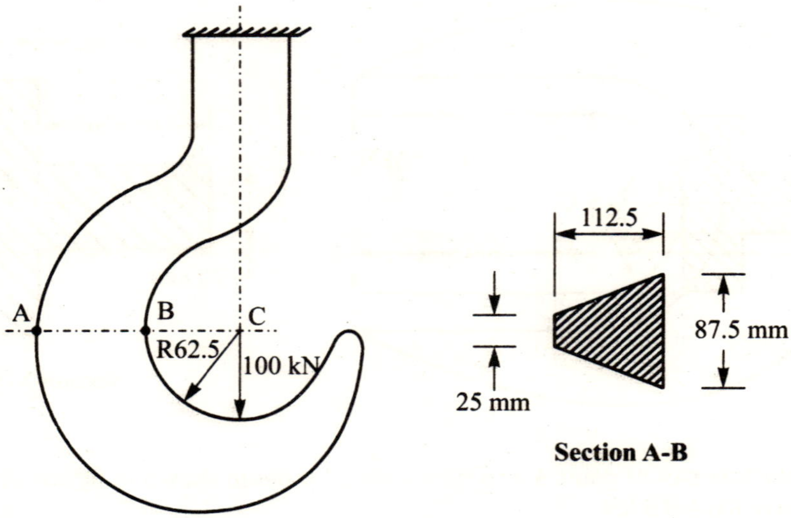

9. The section of a crane hook is trapezoidal whose inner and outer sides are 90 mm and 25 mm respectively and has a depth of 116 mm. The centre of curvature of the section is at a distance of 65 mm from the inner side of section and load line passes through the centre of curvature. Find the maximum load the hook can carry if the maximum stress does not exceed 70 MPa.

(VTU, Dec 07 / Jan 08)

CHAPTER

2 Cylinders and Cylinder Heads

THIN CYLINDRICAL SHELLS

A cylindrical shell is considered to be thin if the ratio of the thickness of the shell to its diameter is less than $\frac{1}{10}$ to $\frac{1}{15}$. They find application in water pipes, liquid storage tanks, boilers and some components of airplanes, etc.

THIN CYLINDRICAL SHELLS UNDER INTERNAL FLUID PRESSURE

Consider a thin cylindrical shell of radius *r,* thickness *t,* and length *L* subjected to an internal fluid pressure of *p* N/mm^2.

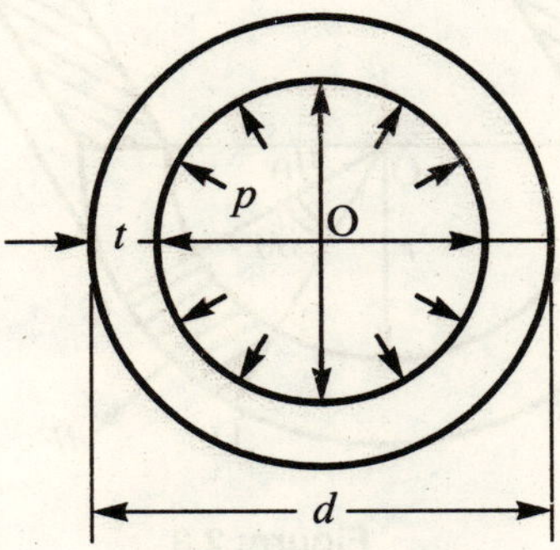

Figure: 2.1

For the purpose of analysis let us take two elements *AB* and *CD* of cylinder symmetrically placed on XX subtending angle $\delta\theta$ at the centre of the cylinder *O*. Let dF be the force acting on each element as shown in Fig. 2.2.

Then, $dF = Area\ dF = Area\ of\ element \times Intensity\ of\ pressure$

$= (r\delta\theta)\ Lp$

$$dF = prL\delta\theta \quad \text{... (1)}$$

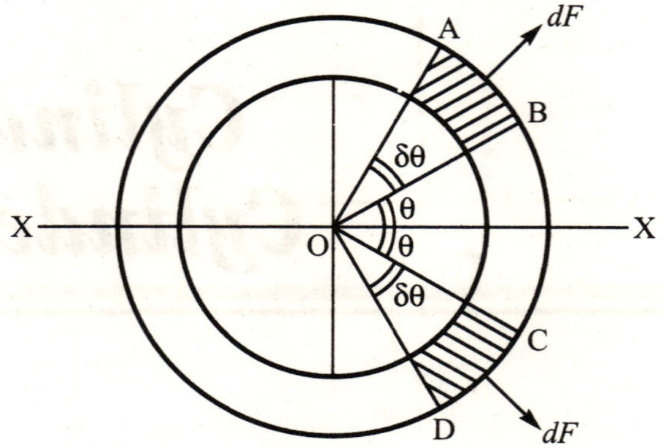

Figure: 2.2

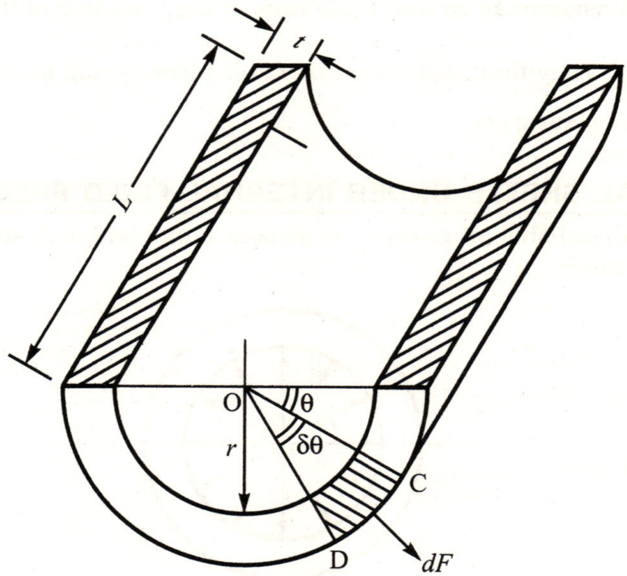

Figure: 2.3

Resolving the forces dF along and normal to XX we get,

Along XX, horizontal force $= dF \cos\theta + dF \cos\theta$

$= 2dF \cos\theta$ ... (2)

When forces dF are resolved normal to XX, the vertical components get cancelled.

Therefore, substituting dF in equation (2) yields

Horizontal force $= 2pLr\ \delta\theta \times \cos\theta$

$= pLd \cos\theta\delta\theta$

Since, $2r = d =$ Diameter of cylinder

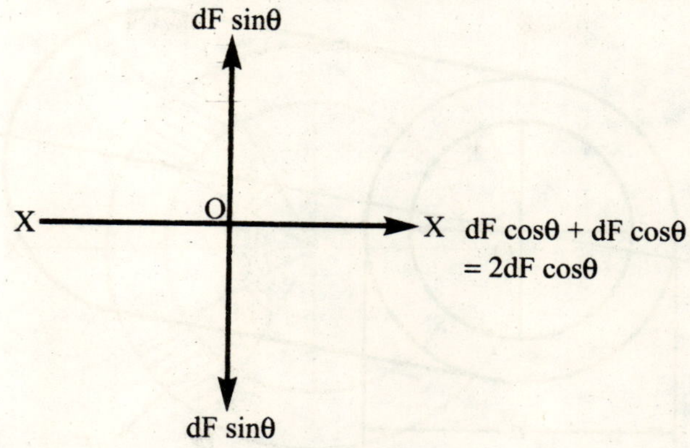

Figure: 2.4

Therefore, total horizontal force $= \int_0^{\pi/2} pLd \cos\theta\delta\theta$

i.e., Bursting force $= pLd \int_0^{\pi/2} \cos\theta\delta\theta$

$$= pLd[\sin\theta]_0^{\pi/2}$$

Bursting force $= pLd$

If σ_h is the hoop stress due to fluid pressure, it is obtained by dividing the bursting force by the projected area of the cylinder.

$$\sigma_h = \text{Circumferential stress} = \frac{pLd}{(tl)+(tl)}$$

$$= \frac{pLd}{2tL} = \frac{pd}{2t}$$

Therefore, $$\sigma_h = \frac{pd}{2t} \quad \text{... (1)}$$

LONGITUDINAL STRESS

If σ_L is the longitudinal stress, then tearing force is resisted by bursting force as shown in Fig. 2.5

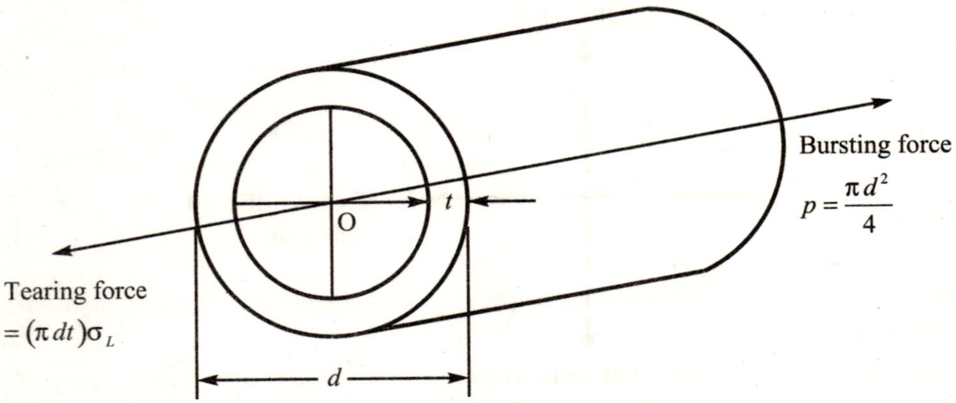

Figure: 2.5

Here, Tearing force = $(\pi dt)\sigma_L$

And, Bursting force = $p\left(\frac{\pi d^2}{4}\right)$

Equating the above forces, we get

$$\left(\frac{\pi d^2}{4}\right)p = (\pi dt)\sigma_L$$

Therefore,
$$\frac{pd}{4t} = \sigma_L$$

$$\sigma_L = \frac{pd}{4t} \quad \text{... (2)}$$

From equations (1) and (2) we see that longitudinal stress σ_L is one half the circumferential stress or hoop stress.

If η_1 and η_2 are the efficiencies of circumferential and longitudinal joints then

$$\sigma_h = \frac{pd}{2t\eta_1}$$

$$\sigma_L = \frac{pd}{4t\eta_2}$$

MAXIMUM SHEAR STRESS

If σ_h and σ_L are hoop stress and longitudinal stresses due to p, then

Maximum shear stress, $$\tau_{max} = \frac{\sigma_h - \sigma_L}{2}$$

$$= \frac{\frac{pd}{2t} - \frac{pd}{4t}}{2}$$

$$= \frac{pd}{4t} \times \frac{1}{2} = \frac{pd}{8t}$$

Therefore, $$\tau_{max} = \frac{pd}{8t}$$

Expression for change in volume of a thin cylindrical shell subjected to fluid pressure 'p':

Consider a thin cylinder of diameter 'd' and thickness 't' subjected to a fluid pressure p N/mm^2. Because of 'p', we know that there exists both σ_h and σ_L. Let e_h and e_L be the hoop strain and longitudinal strain due to σ_h and σ_L respectively.

We have, $$e_h = \frac{\sigma_h}{E} - \frac{\mu\sigma_L}{E}$$

$$e_h = \frac{1}{E}\left(\sigma_h - \frac{\sigma_L}{m}\right); \quad \text{Since} \quad \mu = \frac{1}{m}$$

$$= \frac{1}{E}\left(\frac{pd}{2t} - \frac{pd}{4tm}\right)$$

$$e_h = \frac{pd}{2tE}\left(1 - \frac{1}{2m}\right) \qquad \dots (1)$$

Similarly, longitudinal strain,

$$e_L = \frac{\sigma_L}{E} - \mu\frac{\sigma_h}{E}$$

$$= \frac{1}{E}(\sigma_L - \mu\sigma_h)$$

$$= \frac{1}{E}\left(\sigma_L - \frac{1}{m}\sigma_h\right)$$

$$= \frac{1}{E}\left(\frac{pd}{4t} - \frac{1}{m}\frac{pd}{2t}\right)$$

$$= \frac{pd}{2tE}\left(\frac{1}{2} - \frac{1}{m}\right)$$

Therefore, $$e_L = \frac{pd}{2tE}\left(\frac{1}{2} - \frac{1}{m}\right) \qquad \dots (2)$$

But, $$e_h = \frac{\text{Change in diameter}}{\text{Original diameter}} = \frac{\delta d}{d} \qquad \dots (3)$$

$$e_L = \frac{\text{Change in length}}{\text{Original length}} = \frac{\delta l}{l} \qquad \dots (4)$$

Using equations (3) and (4) either change in diameter or change in length can be computed. Due to fluid pressure, let diameter 'd' increase to ($d + \delta d$) and length increase to ($l + \delta l$)

Then, *Change in volume = Final volume – Original volume*

$$dv = \frac{\pi}{4}(d+\delta d)^2(l+\delta l) - \frac{\pi}{4}d^2 l$$

$$= \frac{\pi}{4}\left[(d+\delta d)^2(l+\delta l) - d^2 l\right]$$

$$= \frac{\pi}{4}\left[\left\{d^2 + 2d \times \delta d + \delta d^2\right\}\left\{l + \delta l\right\} - d^2 l\right]$$

$$= \frac{\pi}{4}\left[\begin{matrix} d^2 l + 2d \times \delta d \times l + l \times \delta d^2 + d^2 \times \delta l \\ +2d \times \delta d \times \delta l + \delta l \times \delta d^2 - d^2 l \end{matrix}\right]$$

Neglecting higher powers δd and product ($\delta d \times \delta l$) we get,

Change in volume,

$$dv = \frac{\pi}{4}\left[2dl \times \delta d + d^2 \times \delta l\right]$$

$$= \frac{\pi}{4}d^2\left[2l \times \frac{\delta d}{d} + \delta l\right]$$

$$= \frac{\pi}{4}d^2 l\left[2\frac{\delta d}{d} + \frac{\delta l}{l}\right]$$

$$= V\left[2e_h + e_L\right]$$

Since, $\frac{\delta d}{d} = e_h, \quad \frac{\delta l}{l} = e_L$

Therefore, Change in volume $= V\left[2e_h + e_L\right]$

$$\frac{\text{Change in volume}}{V} = \frac{\text{Change in volume}}{\text{Original volume}} = \text{Volumetric strain}$$

Therefore, Volumetric strain $= \frac{dv}{V} = 2e_h + e_L$

But, $e_h = \frac{pd}{2tE}\left(1 - \frac{1}{2m}\right)$ and $e_L = \frac{pd}{2tE}\left(\frac{1}{2} - \frac{1}{m}\right)$

Substituting e_h and e_L we get,

$$\frac{dv}{V} = 2\left(\frac{pd}{2tE}\right)\left(1 - \frac{1}{2m}\right) + \frac{pd}{2tE}\left(\frac{1}{2} - \frac{1}{m}\right)$$

$$= \frac{pd}{2tE}\left[2 - \frac{1}{m} + \frac{1}{2} - \frac{1}{m}\right]$$

$$= \frac{pd}{2tE}\left[2\frac{1}{2} - \frac{2}{m}\right]$$

$$= \frac{pd}{2tE}\left[\frac{5}{2} - \frac{2}{m}\right]$$

Therefore, Volumetric strain of the cylindrical shell

$$= \frac{dv}{V} = \frac{pd}{2tE}\left[\frac{5}{2} - \frac{2}{m}\right]$$

THIN SPHERICAL SHELL

Expression for Stress

Let a thin spherical shell of radius 'r' and thickness 't' be subjected to an internal fluid pressure of p N/mm^2 as shown in Fig. 2.6.

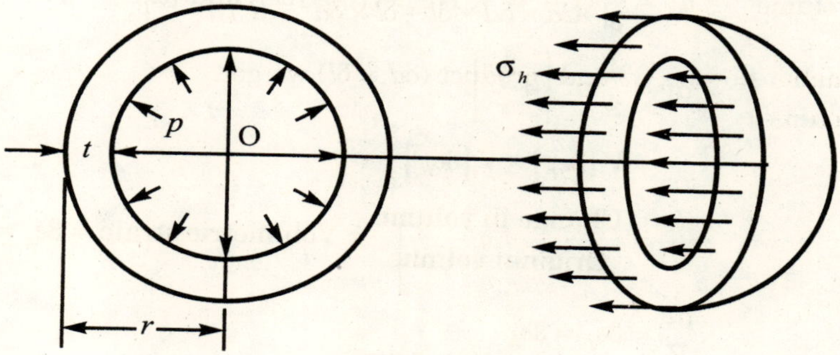

Figure: 2.6

$$\text{Area resisting fluid pressure} = \frac{\pi d^2}{4}$$

$$\text{Total fluid pressure} = \left(\frac{\pi d^2}{4}\right)p$$

This fluid pressure is resisted by $(\pi dt)\sigma_h$

Therefore, $$\left(\frac{\pi d^2}{4}\right)p = (\pi dt)\sigma_h$$

$$\sigma_h = \frac{pd}{4t}$$

Because of symmetry,

$$\sigma_h = \sigma_L = \frac{pd}{4t}$$

If η is the efficiency of riveted joint, then

$$\sigma_h = \sigma_L = \frac{pd}{4t\eta}$$

Expression for change in volume of a thin spherical shell

Consider a thin spherical shell of radius 'r' and thickness 't' subjected to a fluid pressure of p N/mm^2. Let the radius of the sphere change to $(r + \delta r)$

Then, *Change in volume = Final volume – Initial volume*

i.e.,
$$dv = \frac{4}{3}\pi(r+\delta r)^3 - \frac{4}{3}\pi r^3$$
$$= \frac{4}{3}\pi\left[(r+\delta r)^3 - r^3\right]$$
$$= \frac{4}{3}\pi\left[r^3 + (\delta r)^3 + 3r\delta r(r+\delta r) - r^3\right]$$
$$= \frac{4}{3}\pi\left[r^3 + (\delta r)^3 + 3r^2\delta r + 3r(\delta r)^2 - r^3\right]$$

Change in volume $= dv = \frac{4}{3}\pi\left[3r^2\delta r\right]$, Neglecting $(\delta r)^3$ and $(\delta r)^2$

$$dv = \frac{4}{3}\pi r^3\left[3\frac{\delta r}{r}\right]$$
$$= V[3e_r] = V[3e_h]$$

Therefore, $$\frac{dv}{V} = \frac{\text{Change in volume}}{\text{Original volume}} = \text{Volumetric strain} = 3e_r = 3e_h$$

$$\frac{dv}{V} = 3e_r = 3e_h$$

In case of spherical shells,

$$e_h = e_L = e_r = \frac{\sigma_h}{E} - \frac{\sigma_L}{E} \times \frac{1}{m}$$
$$= \frac{\sigma_h}{E}\left[1 - \frac{1}{m}\right]$$
$$= \frac{pd}{4tE}\left[1 - \frac{1}{m}\right]$$

Therefore, $$\frac{dv}{V} = 3e_h$$
$$= 3\frac{pd}{4tE}\left(1 - \frac{1}{m}\right); \qquad \text{Because, } \sigma_h = \frac{pd}{4t}$$
$$\frac{dv}{V} = \frac{3pd}{4tE}\left(1 - \frac{1}{m}\right)$$

Stress in cylindrical vessels with spherical ends

Consider a cylindrical vessel of length 'l' and thickness 't_1' with hemispherical ends of radius 'r' and thickness 't_2' as shown in figure-7 subjected to a fluid pressure of p N/mm^2. Due to fluid pressure, strains are produced in both cylinder and hemispherical ends and assuming that there is no distortion, a relation between the thickness t_1 and t_2 can be obtained for a given value of Poisson's ratio μ.

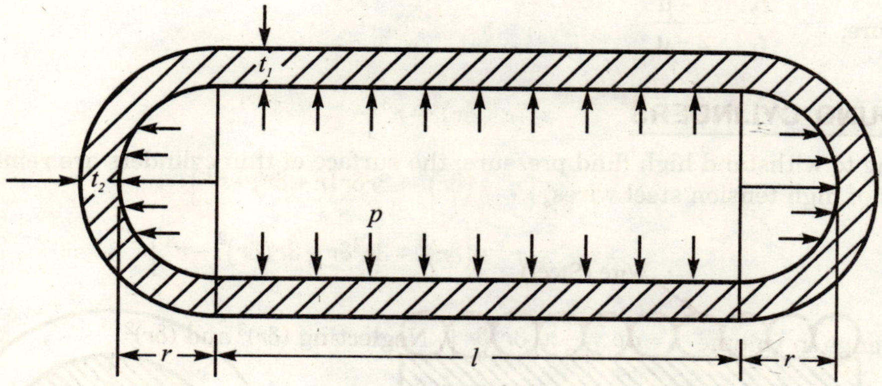

Figure: 2.7

Now consider cylinder

For cylinder, we have,

$$\sigma_h = \frac{pd}{2t_1} \text{ and } \sigma_L = \frac{pd}{4t_1}$$

The corresponding strains are given by,

$$e_h = \frac{pd}{2t_1E}\left(1 - \frac{1}{2m}\right)$$

And $$e_L = \frac{pd}{2t_1E}\left(\frac{1}{2} - \frac{1}{m}\right)$$

Similarly for hemispherical ends we have,

$$\sigma_h = \frac{pd}{4t_2}$$

And $$e_h = \frac{pd}{4t_2E}\left(1 - \frac{1}{m}\right)$$

Since there is no distortion,

Strain in cylindrical portion = Strain in spherical ends

Therefore, $$\frac{pd}{2t_1E}\left(1 - \frac{1}{2m}\right) = \frac{pd}{4t_2E}\left(1 - \frac{1}{m}\right)$$

$$\frac{1}{t_1}\left(1 - \frac{1}{2m}\right) = \frac{1}{2t_2}\left(1 - \frac{1}{m}\right)$$

Therefore, $$\frac{t_2}{t_1} = \frac{\left(1 - \frac{1}{m}\right)}{\left(2 - \frac{1}{m}\right)} = \left(\frac{1-\mu}{2-\mu}\right); \ \mu = \frac{1}{m}$$

Therefore, $$\frac{t_2}{t_1} = \frac{1-\mu}{2-\mu}$$

WIRE WOUND CYLINDERS

Many a time to withstand high fluid pressure, the surface of thin cylinders are reinforced with close layers of high tension steel wires.

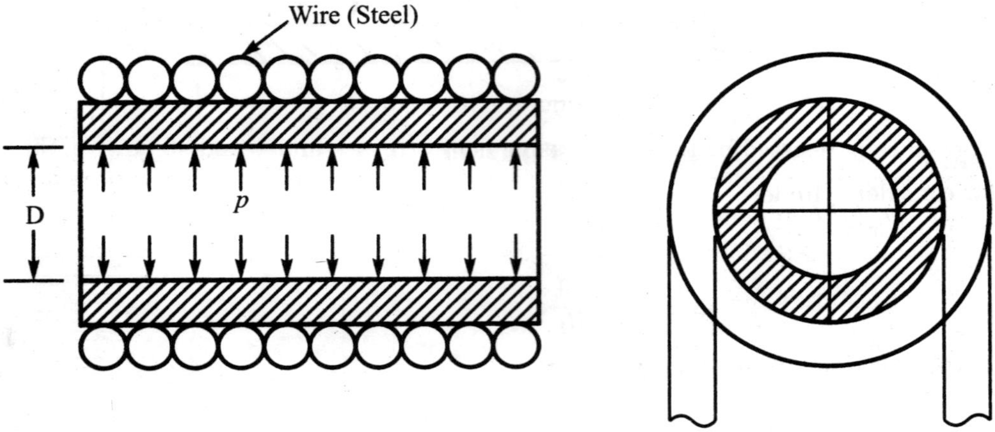

Figure: 2.8

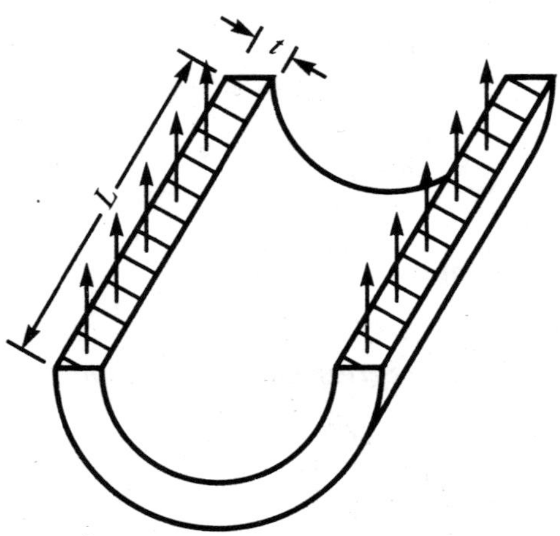

Figure: 2.9

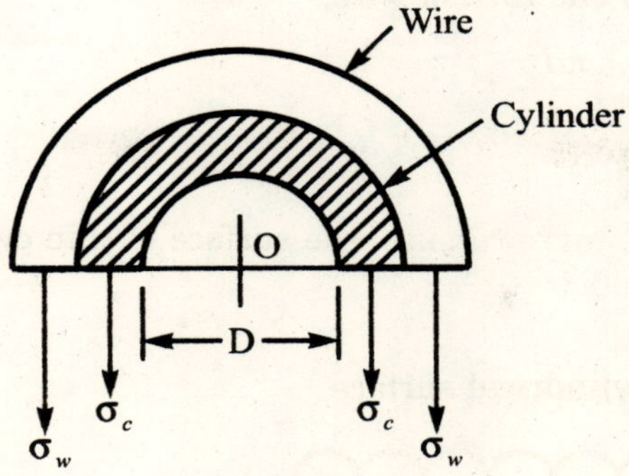

Figure: 2.10

The fluid pressure is resisted by the compressive hoop stress cylinder and steel wire. Since the wire and surface of the cylinder are intact, the strains in them are assumed to be constant.

Let, D be the diameter of the cylinder.

t be the thickness and 'l' be the length of cylinder.

And d_w the diameter of steel wire.

σ_w be the initial tensile stress in wire.

σ_c be the initial compressive stress in cylinder (before admitting fluid under pressure).

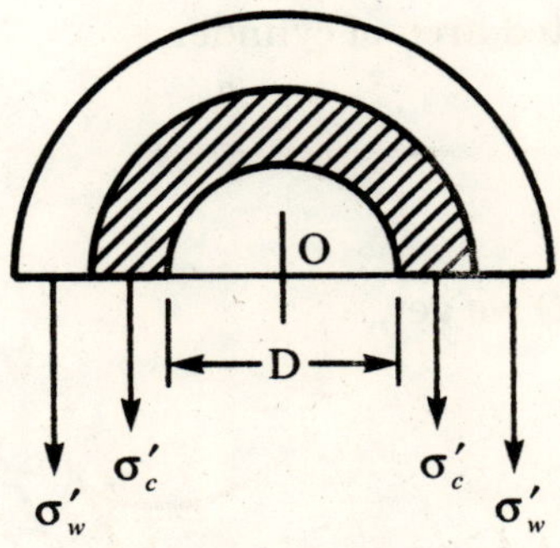

Figure: 2.11

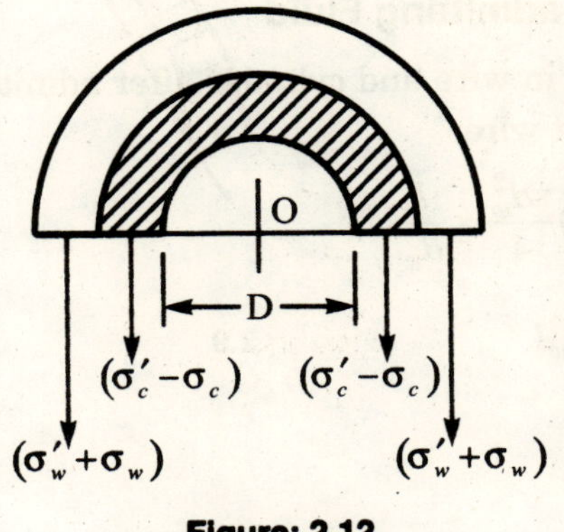

Figure: 2.12

Compressive force due to one turn of wire,

$$= (\sigma_w + \sigma_w)\frac{\pi d_w^2}{4}$$

$$= 2\sigma_w \frac{\pi d_w^2}{4}$$

$$= \frac{\pi d_w^2}{2}\sigma_w$$

Number of coils on the cylindrical surface

$$= n = \frac{l}{d_w}$$

Therefore, Total compressive force

$$= n\left(\frac{\pi d_w^2}{2}\right)\sigma_w$$

$$= \frac{\pi l d_w^2}{2d_w}\sigma_w \quad \text{... (1)}$$

$$= \frac{\pi d_w l}{2}\sigma_w$$

The resisting force in cylinder

$$= \sigma_c \times \text{Projected area of cylinder}$$

$$= \sigma_c (tl + tl)$$

$$= \sigma_c (2tl) \quad \text{... (2)}$$

$$= 2\sigma_c tl$$

Equating equations (1) and (2) we get,

$$\frac{\pi d_w l}{2}\sigma_w = 2\sigma_c tl$$

Therefore, $\dfrac{\sigma_w}{\sigma_c} = \dfrac{4t}{\pi d_w}$ ... (3)

Analysis for Stresses after admitting Fluid

Let σ'_w and σ'_c be the stresses in wire and cylinder after admitting fluid.

Then, the resisting force of wire

$$= (\sigma'_w + \sigma'_w)\frac{\pi d_w^2}{4} \times \frac{l}{d_w}$$

$$= \frac{2\sigma'_w}{4d_w} \times \pi d_w^2 l$$

$$= \frac{\pi d_w \sigma'_w l}{2}$$

Bursting force = pDl

Resisting force of cylinder = $2tl\ \sigma'_c$

Resisting force of cylinder + Resisting force of wire = Bursting force of fluid

Therefore, $2tl\sigma'_c + \dfrac{\pi d_w \sigma'_w l}{2} = pDl$

Therefore, $2t\sigma'_c + \dfrac{\pi d_w \sigma'_w}{2} = pD$

Multiplying by 2 throughout we get

$$2pD = 4t\sigma'_c + \pi d_w \sigma'_w \quad \text{... (4)}$$

As mentioned earlier, the strain in cylinder = Strain in wire.

Therefore, $\dfrac{\sigma'_c}{E_{cyl}} - \mu \dfrac{\sigma_h}{E_{cyl}} = \dfrac{\sigma'_w}{E_{wire}}$

But, $\sigma_h = \dfrac{pD}{4t}$

Therefore, $\dfrac{\sigma'_c}{E_{cyl}} - \dfrac{\mu pD}{4tE_{cyl}} = \dfrac{\sigma'_w}{E_{wire}}$

i.e., $\dfrac{1}{E_{cyl}}\left[\sigma'_c - \dfrac{1}{m}\dfrac{pD}{4t}\right] = \dfrac{\sigma'_w}{E_{wire}}$

Therefore, $\sigma'_w = \dfrac{E_{wire}\left[\sigma'_c - \dfrac{pD}{4tm}\right]}{E_{cyl}}$

$$\sigma'_w = \frac{E_{wire}}{E_{cyl}}\left[\sigma'_c - \frac{pD}{4tm}\right] \quad \text{... (5)}$$

Using equations 3, 4 and 5 and knowing the dimensions of wire and cylinder, Young's modulii of materials (wire and cylinder) the final stresses can be computed as shown

Final stress in wire $= (\sigma_w + \sigma'_w)$

Final stress in cylinder $= (\sigma'_c + \sigma_c)$

THICK CYLINDERS AND SHELLS

Lame's Equations for Thick Cylinders

In case of thin cylinders, both hoop stress and longitudinal stress are assumed to be fairly uniform and in case of thick cylinders, the longitudinal strain is assumed to be almost uniform throughout the length. The hoop stress varies from a maximum at the inner surface to a minimum at the outer surface of the cylinder.

Assumptions made in deriving Lame's Equations

In deriving Lame's equations for thick cylinders, the following assumptions are made

(i) *The material of the cylinder is homogeneous and isotropic.*

(ii) *The longitudinal strain is fairly equal along the length and*

(iii) *The properties are tested within the elastic limit of material.*

Derivation of Lame's Equations

For the purpose of analysis of hoop stress and radial stress, consider a thick cylinder of inner radius '*x*' and thickness *dx* subjected to internal pressure p_x and external pressure $p_x + \delta p_x$. Let σ_h be the hoop stress induced (figure-2.13)

If e_L is the longitudinal strain, then

$$e_L = \frac{\sigma_L}{E} - \mu\frac{\sigma_h}{E} + \frac{\mu}{E}p_x$$

Where, μ = Poisson's ratio $= \dfrac{1}{m}$

δ_L = Longitudinal stress

$$= \frac{\sigma_L}{E} - \frac{\mu}{E}(\sigma_h - p_x)$$

Let $(\sigma_h - p_x) = 2a$ = constant

Therefore, $$e_L = \frac{\sigma_L}{E} - \frac{\mu}{E}(2a)$$

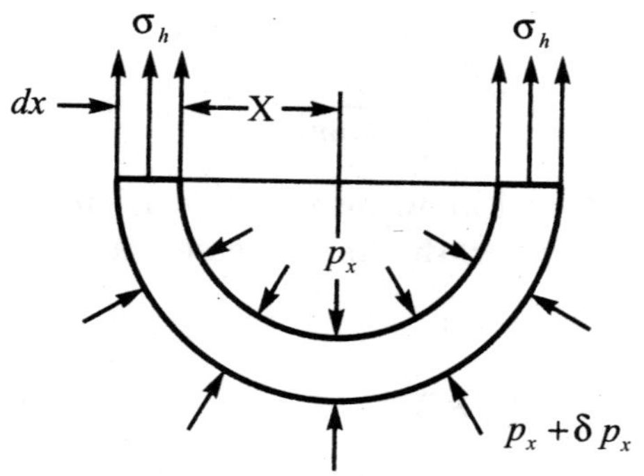

Figure: 2.13

Considering the equilibrium of an unit length of cylinder with the forces shown in Fig. 2.14, we have,

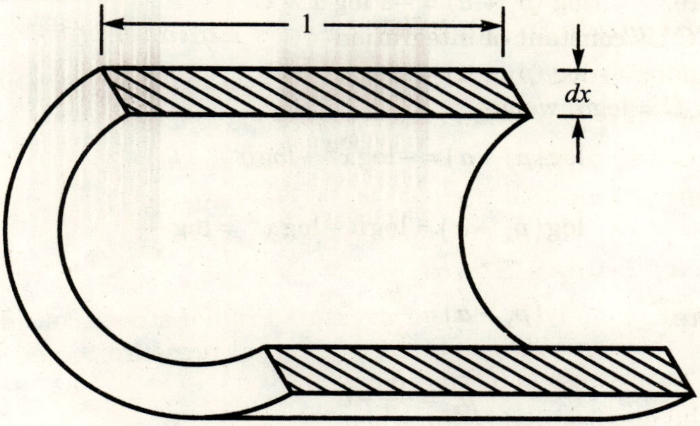

Figure: 2.14

$$(p_x + \delta p_x)(2)(x + \delta x) + 2\sigma_h(\delta_x + 1) - p_x(x + \delta x) = 0$$

i.e.,
$$2(p_x + \delta p_x)(x + \delta x) + 2\sigma_h(\delta_x) - p_x(x + \delta x) = 0$$

$$(p_x + \delta p_x)(x + \delta x) + \sigma_h(\delta_x) - p_x(x + \delta x) = 0$$

$$p_x x + p_x \delta x + x\delta p_x + \delta p_x \delta x + \sigma_h \delta x - x p_x - p_x \delta x = 0$$

Neglecting $\delta p_x \, \delta x$

$$x\frac{\delta p_x}{\delta x} + p_x + \sigma_h = 0$$

But
$$\sigma_h - p_x = 2a$$

Therefore, substituting for σ_h we get,

$$x\frac{\delta p_x}{\delta x} + p_x + (2a + p_x) = 0$$

i.e.,
$$x\frac{\delta p_x}{\delta x} + 2a + 2p_x = 0$$

i.e.,
$$x\frac{\delta p_x}{\delta x} + 2(p_x + a) = 0$$

Transferring 2 $(p_x + a)$ to the R.H.S. we get,

$$x\frac{\delta p_x}{\delta x} = -2(p_x + a)$$

On rearranging the terms we get

$$x\frac{\delta p_x}{(p_x + a)} = -2\delta x$$

i.e.,
$$\frac{\delta p_x}{(p_x + a)} = -2\frac{\delta x}{x}$$

Integrating, we get

$$\int \frac{\delta p_x}{(p_x + a)} = -2\int \frac{\delta x}{x}$$

Therefore, $\log (p_x + a) = -2 \log x + C$

Where 'C' is constant of integration

$$\log (p_x + a) = -\log x^2 + C$$

Taking $C = \log b$, we get

$$\log(p_x + a) = -\log x^2 + \log b$$

$$\log(p_x + a) = \log b - \log x^2 = \log \frac{b}{x^2}$$

Therefore, $(p_x + a) = \dfrac{b}{x^2}$

or $$p_x = \frac{b}{x^2} - a \quad \text{... (1)}$$

Also, $\sigma_h - p_x = 2a$

Therefore,
$$\sigma_h = 2a + p_x$$
$$= 2a + \left(\frac{b}{x^2} - a\right)$$
$$= a + \frac{b}{x^2}$$
$$\sigma_h = \frac{b}{x^2} + a \quad \text{... (2)}$$

Equations (1) and (2) are known as Lame's equations.

Equation (1) gives radial stress and equation (2) gives hoop stress. The constants of Lame's equation (a) and (b) can be obtained from boundary conditions.

Case (i): When external pressure = 0, and internal pressure = p_r

Consider a thick cylinder of inner and outer radii respectively 'r' and R.

We have Lame's equations,

$$p_x = \frac{b}{x^2} - a$$

And $$\sigma_x = \frac{b}{x^2} + a$$

$$p_x \big]_{x=r} = \frac{b}{r^2} - a = p_r$$

Therefore, $$\frac{b}{r^2} - a = p_r \quad \text{... (1)}$$

Similarly $p_x \big]_{x=R} = \dfrac{b}{R^2} - a = p_R = 0$

Therefore, $$\frac{b}{R^2} - a = 0 \quad \text{... (2)}$$

Subtracting equation (2) from equation (1),

$$p_r - 0 = \frac{b}{r^2} - \frac{b}{R^2} = b\left[\frac{R^2 - r^2}{R^2 r^2}\right]$$

Therefore, $$p_r = b\left[\frac{R^2 - r^2}{R^2 r^2}\right]$$

And $$b = \frac{p_r R^2 r^2}{\left(R^2 - r^2\right)}$$

Substituting in p_x we get

$$p_x = \frac{p_r R^2 r^2}{\left(R^2 - r^2\right)} \times \frac{1}{x^2} - a$$

$$p_x \Big]_{x=R} = External\ pressure = 0 = \frac{p_r R^2 r^2}{\left(R^2 - r^2\right)} \times \frac{1}{R^2} - a$$

Therefore, $$a = \frac{p_r r^2}{\left(R^2 - r^2\right)}$$

Substituting 'a' and 'b' in σ_x we get

Hoop stress, $$\sigma_x = \frac{b}{x^2} + a$$

$$= \frac{p_r R^2 r^2}{\left(R^2 - r^2\right)} \times \frac{1}{x^2} + \frac{p_r r^2}{\left(R^2 - r^2\right)}$$

$$= \frac{p_r r^2}{\left(R^2 - r^2\right)}\left[\frac{R^2}{x^2} + 1\right]$$

Maximum hoop stress occurs at the inner surface *i.e.,* at $x = r$

Therefore, $$\sigma_r = \sigma_x \Big]_{x=r} = \frac{p_r r^2}{\left(R^2 - r^2\right)}\left[\frac{R^2}{r^2} + 1\right]$$

$$= \frac{p_r r^2}{\left(R^2 - r^2\right)}\left[\frac{R^2 + r^2}{r^2}\right] = p_r\left[\frac{R^2 + r^2}{R^2 - r^2}\right]$$

Therefore maximum hoop stress

$$= p_r\left[\frac{R^2 + r^2}{R^2 - r^2}\right]$$

Case (ii): When external pressure = p_R and internal pressure = 0.

From, $$p_x = \frac{b}{x^2} - a$$

$$p_x\Big]_{x=r} = \frac{b}{r^2} - a = 0 \qquad \text{... (1)}$$

And $$p_x\Big]_{x=R} = \frac{b}{R^2} - a = p_r \qquad \text{... (2)}$$

Subtracting equation (2) from equation (1)

$$p_r - 0 = \frac{b}{R^2} - \frac{b}{r^2} = b\left[\frac{r^2 - R^2}{R^2 r^2}\right]$$

Therefore, $$p_r = b\left[\frac{r^2 - R^2}{R^2 r^2}\right]$$

Therefore, $$b = \frac{p_r R^2 r^2}{\left(r^2 - R^2\right)}$$

Also from equation (1), $\frac{b}{r^2} = a$

Therefore, $$a = \frac{1}{r^2} b$$

$$= \frac{1}{r^2}\left[\frac{p_r R^2 r^2}{r^2 - R^2}\right] = \frac{p_R R^2}{\left(r^2 - R^2\right)}$$

Substituting 'a' and 'b' in σ_x we get,

Hoop stress $$= \sigma_x = \frac{b}{x^2} + a$$

$$= \frac{p_R R^2 r^2}{\left(r^2 - R^2\right)} \frac{1}{x^2} + \frac{p_R R^2}{\left(r^2 - R^2\right)}$$

$$= \frac{p_R R^2 r^2}{\left(r^2 - R^2\right)}\left[\frac{r^2}{x^2} + 1\right]$$

Hoop stress is maximum at the inner surface *i.e.*, at $x = r$

Therefore, $$\sigma_x\Big]_{x=r} = \frac{p_R R^2}{\left(r^2 - R^2\right)}\left[\frac{r^2}{r^2} + 1\right] \frac{2 p_R R^2}{\left(r^2 - R^2\right)}$$

Therefore, $$\sigma_x\Big]_{x=r} = \frac{2 p_R R^2}{\left(r^2 - R^2\right)}$$

Since $R > r$, the hoop stress is negative *i.e.,* when the cylinder is subjected to only external pressure, compressive hoop stress is induced in the cylinder.

Case (iii): When internal pressure = p_r and external pressure = p_R

We have, $$p_x = \frac{b}{x} - a,$$

$$p_x\big]_{x=r} = \frac{b}{r^2} - a = p_r \quad \text{... (1)}$$

And $$p_x\big]_{x=R} = \frac{b}{R^2} - a = p_R \quad \text{... (2)}$$

Subtracting equation (1) from (2),

$$p_R - p_r = \frac{b}{R^2} - \frac{b}{r^2}$$

$$= b\left[\frac{1}{R^2} - \frac{1}{r^2}\right] = b\left[\frac{r^2 - R^2}{r^2 R^2}\right]$$

Therefore, $$p_r - p_R = b\left[\frac{R^2 - r^2}{R^2 r^2}\right]$$

Therefore, $$b = (p_r - p_R) \times \frac{R^2 r^2}{(R^2 - r^2)}$$

Now p_x becomes,

$$p_x = \frac{b}{x^2} - a$$

$$p_x = \frac{R^2 r^2 (p_r - p_r)}{(R^2 - r^2)} \frac{1}{x^2} - a$$

$$p_x\big]_{x=R} = p_R = \frac{R^2 r^2}{(R^2 - r^2)} [p_r - p_R] \frac{1}{R^2} - a$$

$$P_R = \frac{(p_r - p_R) r^2}{(R^2 - r^2)} - a$$

Therefore, $$a = \frac{(p_r - p_R) r^2}{(R^2 - r^2)} - p_R$$

Substituting '*a*' and '*b*' in

$$\sigma_x = \frac{b}{x^2} + a, \text{we get}$$

$$\sigma_x = \frac{R^2 r^2 (p_r - p_R)}{(R^2 - r^2)x^2} + \frac{(p_r - p_R) r^2}{(R^2 - r^2)} - p_R$$

$$\sigma_x \Big]_{x=r} = \sigma_r = \frac{R^2 r^2 (p_r - p_R)}{(R^2 - r^2) r^2} + \frac{(p_r - p_R) r^2}{(R^2 - r^2)} - p_R$$

$$= \frac{(p_r - p_R) R^2}{(R^2 - r^2)} + \frac{(p_r - p_R) r^2}{(R^2 - r^2)} - p_R$$

$$= \frac{(p_r - p_R)}{(R^2 - r^2)} \left[R^2 + r^2\right] - p_R$$

$$= \frac{(p_r - p_R)(R^2 + r^2) - p_R (R^2 - r^2)}{(R^2 - r^2)}$$

$$\sigma_r = \frac{p_r (R^2 + r^2) - 2 p_R R^2}{(R^2 - r^2)}$$

σ_r is positive when $p_r\ (R^2 + r^2) > 2p_R R^2$

i.e., when $\dfrac{(R^2 + r^2)}{R^2} > \dfrac{2p_R}{p_r}$

Autofrettage (Self-hooping)

This method is used to increase the resistance of thick walled cylinders to internal pressure. The principle of autofrettage in brief is as follows:

The stresses induced in the cylinder is a function of internal pressure. With the increase in internal pressure, the stresses go on increasing with maximum stresses occurring at the inner surface and minimum at the outer periphery and the variation is parabolic. At a time when the stresses in the cylinder are beyond elastic limit, and if the stresses are further increased, the strain increases rapidly. Now if the internal pressure is released, the outer surface which is still elastic exerts compressive hoop stress on the inner surface and tensile stress at the outer surface. For any subsequent rise in internal pressure, the external compressive stresses have to be nullified before any tensile circumferential stress is developed. Obviously a greater internal pressure is required to stress the material to the proportional limit than initial pressure.

Example 2.1: A compound tube 500 mm internal diameter and 50 mm thick is shrunk on another tube 500 mm outer diameter and 50 mm thick. The pressure at the junction is 10 N/mm^2. If this compound tube is subjected to an internal fluid pressure of 10 N/mm^2, determine variation of hoop stress along the cross-section of the compound tube.

Solution:

The hoop stress is the algebraic sum of

(*i*) Stress due to shrinking of one tube over the other and

(*ii*) Stress induced due to the fluid pressure.

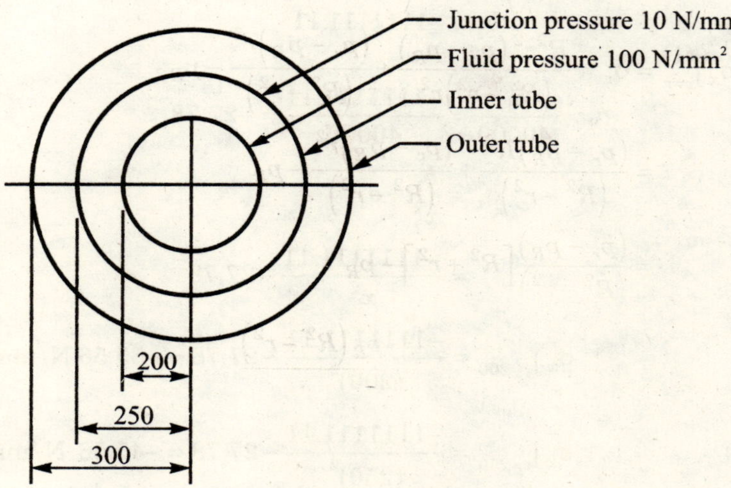

Case (i): Stress due to shrinking of one tube over the other

When the outer tube is shrunk on the inner tube

$$p_x\,\big]_{x=200\text{ mm}} = 0$$

$$p_x\,\big]_{x=250\text{ mm}} = \text{Junction pressure} = 10\ \text{N/mm}^2$$

$$p_x\,\big]_{x=300\text{ mm}} = 0 \text{ as no external pressure is applied}$$

From, $$p_x = \frac{b}{x^2} - a,$$

$$p_x\,\big]_{x=200} = \frac{b_1}{(200)^2} - a_1 = 0$$

Where a_1 and b_1 are constants of Lame's equation for inner tube

Therefore, $$\frac{b_1}{40000} - a_1 = 0 \qquad \dots (1)$$

Similarly, $$p_x\,\big]_{x=250} = \frac{b_1}{(250)^2} - a_1 = 10$$

Therefore, $$\frac{b_1}{62500} - a_1 = 10 \qquad \dots (2)$$

From equations (1) and (2),

$$\left(\frac{b_1}{62500}-a_1\right)-\left(\frac{b_1}{40000}-a_1\right)=10-0=10$$

i.e., $$b_1\left[\frac{1}{62500}-\frac{1}{40000}\right]=10$$

Therefore, $b_1 = -1111111.11$

From equation (1),

$$a_1=\frac{b_1}{40000}=\frac{-1111111.11}{40000}=-27.78$$

Therefore, $$\sigma_x=\frac{b_1}{x^2}+a_1$$

$$=\frac{-1111111.11}{x^2}-27.78$$

Therefore, $$\sigma_x\big]_{x=200}=\frac{-1111111.11}{(200)^2}-27.78=-55.56\ \text{N/mm}^2$$

$$\sigma_x\big]_{x=250}=\frac{-1111111.11}{(250)^2}-27.78=-45.56\ \text{N/mm}^2$$

Similarly, for the outer tube if a_2 and b_2 are Lame's constants.

$$p_x=\frac{b_2}{x^2}-a_2$$

$$p_x\big]_{x=250}=\frac{b_2}{(250)^2}-a_2=10$$

Therefore, $$\frac{b_2}{62500}-a_2=10 \quad \text{... (3)}$$

$$p_x\big]_{x=300}=\frac{b_2}{(300)^2}-a_2=0$$

Therefore, $$\frac{b_2}{90000}-a_2=0 \quad \text{... (4)}$$

From equations (3) and (4),

$$\left(\frac{b_2}{62500}-a_2\right)-\left(\frac{b_2}{90000}-a_2\right)=10-0=10$$

$$b_2\left[\frac{1}{62500}-\frac{1}{90000}\right]=10$$

Therefore, $$b_2\left[\frac{90000-62500}{62500\times 90000}\right]=10$$

Therefore, $b_2 = 2045454.545$

And $$a_2 = \frac{b_2}{90000} = \frac{2045454.545}{90000} = 22.73$$

Substituting a_2 and b_2 in σ_x we get,

$$\sigma_x = \frac{2045454.545}{x^2} + 22.73$$

$$\sigma_x \big]_{x=250} = \frac{2045454.545}{(250)^2} + 22.73 = 55.55 \text{ N/mm}^2$$

$$\sigma_x \big]_{x=300} = \frac{2045454.545}{(300)^2} + 22.73 = 45.46 \text{ N/mm}^2$$

Case (ii): When it is subjected to an internal fluid pressure of 100 N/mm², the compound tube can be considered as a hollow tube of 200 mm inner radius and 300 mm external radius.

Lame's equation becomes,

$$p_x \big]_{x=200} = \frac{b}{(200)^2} - a = 100$$

Therefore, $$\frac{b}{40000} - a = 100 \qquad \text{... (5)}$$

And $$p_x \big]_{x=300} = \frac{b}{(300)^2} - a = 0$$

Therefore, $$\frac{b}{90000} - a = 0 \qquad \text{... (6)}$$

From equations (5) and (6),

$$\left(\frac{b}{40000} - a\right) - \left(\frac{b}{90000} - a\right) = 100 - 0 = 100$$

Therefore, $$b\left[\frac{1}{40000} - \frac{1}{90000}\right] = 100$$

Therefore, $$b\left[\frac{90000 - 40000}{40000 \times 90000}\right] = 100$$

Therefore, $b = 7200000$

$$a = \frac{b}{90000}$$

$$= \frac{7200000}{90000} = 80$$

Now, $$\sigma_x = \frac{7200000}{x^2} + 80$$

$$\sigma_x\Big]_{x=200} = \frac{7200000}{(200)^2} + 80 = 260 \text{ N/mm}^2$$

$$\sigma_x\Big]_{x=300} = \frac{7200000}{(300)^2} + 80 = 160 \text{ N/mm}^2$$

$$\sigma_x\Big]_{x=200} = -55.55 + 260 = 204.45 \text{ N/mm}^2$$

$$\sigma_x\Big]_{x=250} = -45.56 + 55.45 = 9.89 \text{ N/mm}^2$$

$$\sigma_x\Big]_{x=300} = -45.56 + 160 = 114.44 \text{ N/mm}^2$$

Example 2.2: A thick spherical shell 80 mm diameter is required to withstand an internal pressure of 30 N/mm². Determine the necessary thickness of shell if the permissible tensile stress is 80 N/mm².

Solution:

For a thick spherical shell, we have Lame's equation

$$p_x = \frac{2b}{x^3} - a$$

And $$\sigma_x = \frac{b}{x^3} + a$$

Where, a and b are Lame's constants.

From the data,

$$p_x\Big]_{x=40} = 30 = \frac{2b}{(40)^3} - a$$

Therefore, $$30 = \frac{2b}{(40)^3} - a \quad \text{... (1)}$$

And $$\sigma_x\Big]_{x=40} = \frac{b}{(40)^3} + a = 80$$

Therefore, $$\frac{b}{(40)^3} + a = 80 \quad \text{... (2)}$$

Adding equations (1) and (2) we get,

$$\left[\frac{2b}{(40)^3} - a + \frac{b}{(40)^3} + a\right] = 80 + 30 = 110$$

$$(2b + b)\frac{1}{(40)^3} = 110$$

Therefore, $$b = 2346666.67$$

$$a = 80 - \frac{b}{(40)^3} \text{ from equation (2)}$$

$$= 80 - \frac{2346666.67}{64000} = 43.33$$

At the outer surface, $p_r = 0$

Therefore, $$p_x\big]_{x=r} = p_r = \frac{2b}{x^3} - a$$

Where, r is the outer radius of shell.

Therefore, $$0 = \frac{2 \times 2346666.67}{r^3} - 43.33$$

$$r = 47.668 \text{ mm}$$

Therefore thickness of shell = Outer radius – Inner radius

$$= 47.668 - \frac{80}{2}$$

$$= 7.668 \text{ mm}$$

Example 2.3: Calculate the thickness of cylindrical shell of internal diameter 250 mm required to withstand a fluid pressure of 50 N/mm² assuming the permissible circumferential stress as180 N/mm².

Solution:

We have, $$p_x = \frac{b}{x^2} - a$$

And $$\sigma_x = \frac{b}{x^2} + a$$

Considering fluid pressure,

$$p_x\big]_{x=125} = 50 = \frac{b}{(125)^2} - a$$

Therefore, $$50 = \frac{b}{(125)^2} - a \quad \text{... (1)}$$

From hoop stress consideration,

Maximum hoop stress occurs at x = 125 mm *i.e.,* at the inner surface

Therefore, $$180 = \frac{b}{(125)^2} + a \quad \text{... (2)}$$

Adding equations (1) and (2)

$$50 + 180 = \frac{b}{(125)^2} + \frac{b}{(125)^2}$$

Therefore, $$2b = (230)\,(125)^2$$

$$b = 1796875$$

$$a = 180 - \frac{b}{(125)^2}$$

$$= 180 - \frac{1796875}{(125)^2}$$

$$a = 65$$

$$p_x = \frac{1796875}{x^2} -- 65$$

$$p_x \rfloor_{x=r} = 0 = \frac{1796875}{r^2} - 65$$

Therefore, $$r^2 = \frac{1796875}{65}$$

Where, r is the outer radius of shell.

$$r = 166.3 \text{ mm}$$

Therefore, Thickness of shell = Outer radius – Inner radius

= 166.3 – 125

Thickness of shell = 41.3 mm

Example 2.4: The cylinder head of a steam engine is held in position by 10 bolts. The diameter of the cylinder is 400 mm and the maximum pressure of steam stem in cylinder is 1 MPa. A copper gasket is used to make the joint leak proof. Determine the standard size of bolt required by taking the design tensile stress for bolt material equal to 90 MPa.

Solution:

The maximum tensile load F_f is given by

$$F_f = KF_a + F_i \qquad \text{... E(18-4)}$$

Where, F_a = External load on each bolt in kN.

D_i = Inside diameter of cylinder in mm.

P_f = Steam pressure in N/mm²

$$P_f = \frac{Steam\ load}{Number\ of\ bolts} = \frac{\frac{\pi}{4}\left(D_i^2\right)p_f}{10}$$

$$= \frac{\frac{\pi}{4}(400)^2 \times 1}{10} = 12566.37 \text{ N}$$

$$= 12.5664 \text{ kN}$$

F_i = Initial tightening load

$= 2804.69\, d$ ... E(18-5a)

d, the outside diameter of bolt in meter.

K = Gasket factor.

For copper gasket, $K = 0.4$ ... T(18-1)

Therefore, $F_f = 0.4 \times 12.5664 + 2804.69d$

$F_f = 5.02656 + 2804.69d$

Equating F_f to $\frac{\pi}{4} d_c^2 \sigma_t$,

$$F_f = \frac{\pi}{4} d_c^2 \sigma_t \text{ ; } \sigma_t \text{ in kN/m}^2$$

i.e., $(5.02656 + 2804.69d) = \frac{\pi}{4} d_c^2 (90000)$

Assuming $d_c = 0.8d,$

And using $\sigma_t = 90 \text{ N/mm}^2 = 90000 \text{ kN/m}^2$ (given)

$$5.02656 + 2804.69d = \frac{\pi}{4}(0.8d)^2 \times 90000$$

$$20.106 + 11218.76d = 180955.74d^2$$

i.e., $d^2 - 0.062d - 0.001 = 0$

Hence, $d = 0.06357$ metre

$= 63.57$ mm $= 64$ mm

Refer table (18-7) and obtain the standard size of ISO metric screw threads corresponding to $d = 72$ mm, pitch = 6 mm.

Example 2.5: The cylinder of a stationary engine is 120 mm in diameter and is held to the crank case by M12 × 1.75 Cr – Ni steel bolts. The maximum gas pressure in the cylinder is 3.5 MPa. Assume the ultimate strength of this steel as 800 MPa and yield stress as 600 MPa. Determine the number of bolts required. Take gasket factor = 0.75.

(VTU, July/August 2003).

Solution:

The bolts are subjected to fluctuating axial loads and the Soderberg's equation for fluctuating axial loading is

$$\frac{\sigma_a}{\sigma_{-1d}} + \frac{\sigma_m}{\sigma_{yd}} = 1 \qquad \text{... E(5-40)}$$

To find σ_a

$$\sigma_a = \text{Stress amplitude} = \frac{F_a}{A}$$

Where, $F_a = \text{Load amplitude} = \frac{F_{max} - F_{min}}{2}$

To find F_{max} and F_{min}

$$F_{max} = F_f = KF_a + F_i$$

Where, K = Gasket factor = 0.75

F_a = External load on each bolt

$$= \frac{\text{Gas load}}{\text{Number of bolts}} = \frac{\frac{\pi}{4}(D_i^2) p_f}{i}$$

$$= \frac{\frac{\pi}{4}(120)^2 \times 35}{i} = \frac{39584.1}{i} \text{ N}$$

$$F_a = \frac{39.5841}{i} \text{ kN}$$

$$F_i = \text{Initial tightening load} = 2804.69d \quad \text{... E(18-5a)}$$

Where, d = Outside diameter of bolt in metre

$$F_i = 2804.69\text{d}$$

$$= 2804.69 \times \frac{12}{1000} \text{ kN} = 33.656 \text{ kN}$$

Note: *M12 × 1.75 bolts have,*

$$d = 12 \text{ mm} = \frac{12}{1000} \text{ metre}$$

Therefore, $$F_{max} = 0.75\left(\frac{39.5841}{i}\right) + 33.656$$

$$F_{max} = \frac{29.69}{i} + 33.656 \text{ kN}$$

$$F_{min} = F_i = 33.656 \text{ kN}$$

Therefore, $$F_a = \frac{F_{max} - F_{min}}{2}$$

$$= \frac{\left(\frac{29.69}{i} + 33.656\right) - 33.656}{2}$$

$$F_a = \frac{14.845}{i}$$

Therefore, $$\sigma_a = \frac{F_a}{A} = \frac{14.845}{Ai}$$

$$A = A_c = \frac{\pi}{4} d_c^2$$

For d = 12 mm,

$$A_c = A = 84.3 \text{ mm}^2$$

Therefore, $$\sigma_a = \frac{14.845}{84.3i}$$

$$= \frac{0.1761}{i}$$

To find F_m

Mean load $$F_m = \frac{F_{max} + F_{min}}{2}$$

$$= \frac{\left(\frac{29.69}{i} + 33.656\right) + 33.656}{2}$$

$$F_m = \frac{14.845}{i} + 33.656$$

Therefore,
$$\sigma_m = \frac{\frac{14.845}{i} + 33.656}{A}$$

$$= \frac{\frac{14.845}{i} + 33.656}{84.3}$$

$$= \frac{0.1761}{i} + 0.3992$$

To find σ_{-1d}

$$\sigma_{-1d} = \frac{\sigma_{-1}}{n_{-1d}}$$

Where,
$$\sigma_{-1d} = 0.5\ \sigma_u$$
$$= 0.5 \times 800 = 400 \text{ MPa}$$
$$= 400 \times 10^3 \text{ kN/m}^2$$
$$n_{-1d} = K_{sz} K_{sr} K_l n_{-1a}$$

Where,
$$K_{sz} = \text{Size factor} = 0.85$$
$$K_{sr} = \text{Surface factor}$$
$$= \frac{1}{e_{sr}}$$
$$K_l = \text{Load factor} = 0.7 \text{ for axial loading}$$
$$n_{-1a} = \text{Factor of safety} = 2$$
$$= 0.85 \times \frac{1}{e_{sr}} \times 0.7 \times 2$$

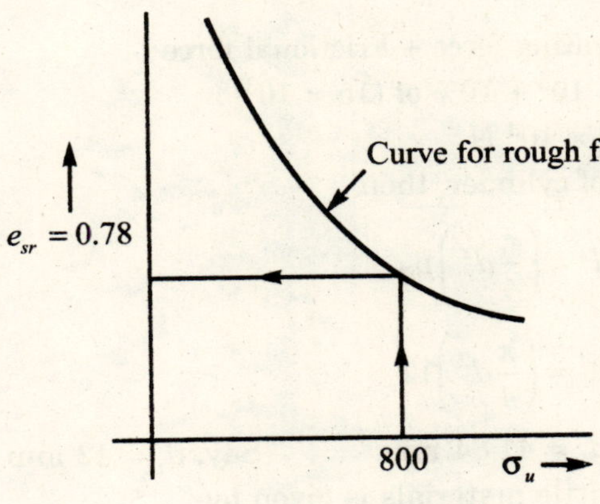

Therefore, $$n_{-1d} = 0.85 \times \frac{1}{0.75} \times 0.7 \times 2 = 1.5256$$

And $$\sigma_{-1d} = \frac{400 \times 10^3}{1.5256} = 262191.9245 \text{ kN/m}^2$$

To find σ_{yd}

$$\sigma_{yd} = \frac{\sigma_y}{n_{yd}}$$

Where, $$\sigma_y = 600 \text{ MPa} = 600 \times 103 \text{ N/m}^2$$

$$n_{yd} = K_{sz}\ K_{\sigma_a}\ n_{ya}$$

$$= 0.85 \times 1 \times 2 = 1.7$$

Therefore, $$\sigma_{yd} = \frac{600 \times 10^3}{1.7} = 352941.18 \text{ kN/m}^2$$

Substituting in Soderberg's equation we get,

$$\frac{\frac{0.1761}{i}}{262191.9245} + \frac{\left(\frac{0.1761}{i} + 0.3992\right)}{352941.18} = 1$$

$$\frac{6.7165 \times 10^{-7}}{i} + \frac{4.9895 \times 10^{-7}}{i} + 1.1311 \times 10^{-6} = 1$$

$$\frac{11.706}{i} = 1 - 1.311 \times 10^{-6}$$

$$\frac{11.706}{i} = 0.99999$$

$$i = 12 \text{ bolts.}$$

Example 2.6: In a hydraulic cylinder made of cast iron, the piston rod exerts an operating force of 15 kN. The frictional forces may be taken as 10% of the operating force. The pressure in cylinder is 12 MPa. Taking ultimate strength of cast iron as 210 MPa, determine the dimensions of cylinder based on factor of safety = 5.

Solution:

Total force on piston = Operating force + Frictional force

$$= 15 \times 10^3 + 10\% \text{ of } (15 \times 10^3)$$

$$P = 16.5 \times 10^3 \text{ N}$$

If d_i is the inside diameter of cylinder, then

$$P = \left(\frac{\pi}{4} d_i^2\right) p_i$$

i.e., $$16.5 \times 10^3 = \left(\frac{\pi}{4} d_i^2\right) 12$$

Therefore, $d_i = 41.84$ mm; Say, $d_i = 42$ mm

The wall thickness 'h' for brittle materials is given by

$$h = \frac{d_i}{2}\left(\sqrt{\frac{\sigma_\theta + p_i}{\sigma_\theta - p_i}} - 1\right) \qquad \text{... E(7-24)}$$

Where, $d_i = 42$ mm

$$\sigma_\theta = \frac{210}{5} = 42 \text{ MPa}$$

$p_i = 12$ MPa

Therefore,
$$h = \frac{42}{2}\left(\sqrt{\frac{42+12}{42-12}} - 1\right)$$
$$= 7.1745 \text{ mm}$$

Adopt $h = 8$ mm

Example 2.7: A cylindrical tank of 300 mm diameter is required to sustain gas pressure of 20 MPa. Determine the thickness of cylinder taking 40C8 as the material of tank. Use factor of safety 5 and Poisson's ratio = 0.3.

Solution:

The thickness of closed end cylinder using Clavarinio's equation is given by

$$h = \frac{d_i}{2}\left[\sqrt{\frac{\sigma'_\theta + (1-2\gamma)p_i}{\sigma'_\theta - (1+\gamma)p_i}} - 1\right] \qquad \text{... E(7-28)}$$

Where, $d_i = 300$ mm

σ'_θ = Permissible stress

For 40C8 steel, $\sigma_{ut} = 600$ MPa ... T(1-25)

Factor of safety = 5

Therefore,
$$\sigma'_\theta = \frac{\sigma_{ut}}{5} = \frac{600}{5} = 120 \text{ MPa}$$

p_i = Internal pressure = 20 MPa

γ = Poisson's ratio = 0.3

Therefore,
$$h = \frac{300}{2}\left[\sqrt{\frac{120+(1-2\times 0.3)20}{120-(1+0.3)20}} - 1\right]$$

$$h = 25 \text{ mm}$$

Example 2.8: A circular plate ma de of steel and of diameter 200 mm with thickness 10 mm is subjected to a load inducing a pressure of 4 MPa. Taking E = 201 kN/mm², Poisson's ratio = 0.3, determine

- ***(i) The maximum stress, its location and maximum deflection when the edges of the plate are supported.***
- ***(ii) The maximum stress, its location and maximum deflection when the edge of the plate is fixed.***

Solution:

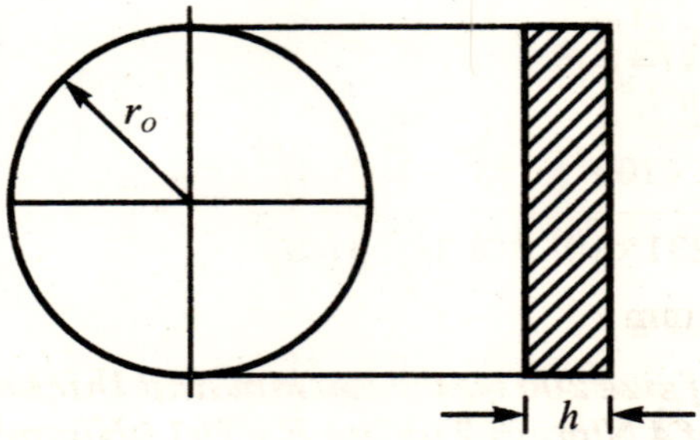

$$r_o = \frac{d}{2} = \frac{200}{2} = 100 \text{ mm}$$

$$h = 10 \text{ mm}$$

Case (i): When the edges of the plate are supported

The maximum stress,

$$\sigma_{max} = \sigma_r = \sigma_o \text{ is given by,}$$

$$\sigma_{max} = \frac{-3F(3m+1)}{8\pi m h^2}$$

Where, F = Total load on plate

$$= \pi r_o^2 p$$

$$= \pi\ (100)^2\ 4$$

$$= 4\pi \times 10^4 \text{ N}$$

$$m = \frac{1}{\gamma} = \frac{1}{0.3} = 3.33$$

Therefore, $$\sigma_{max} = \frac{-3 \times 4\pi \times 10^4 (3 \times 3.33 + 1)}{8\pi \times 0.33 \times 10^2} = -495.5 \text{ N/mm}^2$$

Note: *This stress occurs at the centre of plate.*

The maximum deflection of plate, y_{max} is given by,

$$y_{max} = \frac{3F(m-1)(5m+1)r_o^2}{16\pi E m^2 h^3}$$

Where, E = 201 kN/mm^2

$$= 201 \times 10^3 \text{ N/mm}^2$$

$$y_{max} = \frac{3 \times 4\pi \times 10^4 (3.33 - 1)(5 \times 3.33 + 1)(100)^2}{16\pi \times 201 \times 10^3 \times (3.33)^2 \times 10^3} = 1.534 \text{ mm}$$

Case (ii): When the edges of the plate are fixed

$$\sigma_{max} = \sigma_r = \frac{3F}{4\pi h^2}$$

$$= \frac{3 \times 4\pi \times 100^2}{4\pi (10)^2} = 300 \text{ MPa}$$

Note: The maximum stress occurs at the edge of the plate

$$y_{max} = \frac{3F(m^2-1)r_o^2}{16\pi E m^2 h^3}$$

$$= \frac{3\times 4\pi\times 100^2(3.33^2-1)(100)^2}{16\pi\times 201\times 10^3\times(3.33)^2\times(10)^3}$$

$$y_{max} = 0.3358 \text{ mm}$$

Example 2.9: A rectangular steel plate of size 200 mm × 100 mm and thickness 10 mm is subjected to a load causing a pressure of 4 N/mm². Taking E = 201 kN/mm², determine

(i) The maximum stress induced in the plate, its location and maximum deflection when the all edges of the plate are supported.

(ii) The maximum stress induced, its location and maximum deflection when all the edges of the plate are fixed.

Solution:

Case (i): When all the edges of the plate are supported

$$\sigma_{max} = \sigma_b = \frac{-0.75b^2 p}{h^2\left[1+1.61\frac{b^3}{a^3}\right]} \quad \text{Where, } p = 4 \text{ N/mm}^2$$

$$= \frac{0.75\times 100^2\times 4}{10^2\left[1+1.61\times\frac{100^3}{200^3}\right]} = 249.74 \text{ N/mm}^2$$

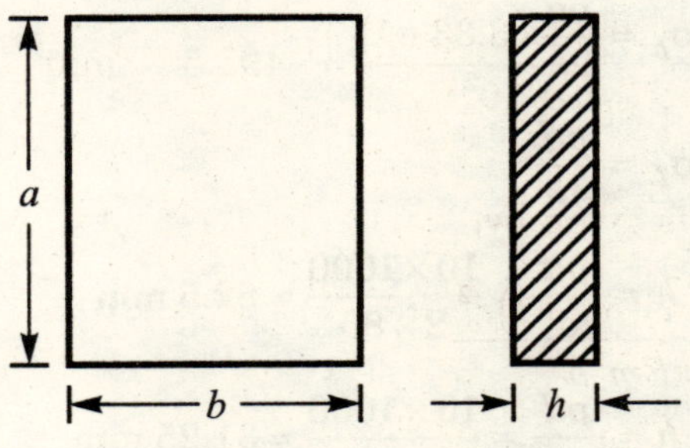

$a = 200$ mm.

$b = 100$ mm

$h = 10$ mm.

Note: *This maximum stress occurs at the centre of the plate.*

The maximum deflection is given by,

$$y_{max} = \frac{0.1422b^4 p}{Eh^3\left[1+2.21\frac{b^3}{a^3}\right]}$$

$$= \frac{0.1422\times 100^4\times 4}{201\times 10^3\times 10^3\left[1+2.21\times\frac{100^3}{200^3}\right]}$$

$$= 0.5543 \text{ mm}$$

Case (ii): When all the edges of the plate are fixed

The maximum stress in plate is given by,

$$\sigma_{max} = \sigma_b = \frac{0.5b^2 p}{h^2\left[1+0.623\dfrac{b^6}{a^6}\right]}$$

$$= \frac{0.5\times 100^2 \times 4}{10^2\left[1+0.623\times\dfrac{100^6}{200^6}\right]} = 495.18\,\text{N/mm}^2$$

Note: *The maximum stress occurs at the centre of long edge.*

The maximum deflection of plate is given by,

$$y_{max} = \frac{0.0284b^4 p}{Eh^3\left[1+1.056\dfrac{b^5}{a^5}\right]}$$

$$= \frac{0.0284\times 100^4 \times 4}{201\times 10^3\times 10^3\left[1+1.056\times\dfrac{100^5}{200^5}\right]} = 0.1368 \text{ mm}$$

Example 2.10: Determine the thickness of a cylindrical shell of 1 metre diameter to withstand fluid pressure of 10 N/mm² assuming the permissible tensile stress for the material of boiler as 80 N/mm².

Solution:

Hoop stress $\sigma_h = \dfrac{pd}{2h}$ ... (i)

Longitudinal stress $\sigma_L = \dfrac{pd}{4h}$ ... (ii)

From equation (i) $h = \dfrac{pd}{2\sigma_h} = \dfrac{10\times 1000}{2\times 80} = 62.5$ mm

From equation (ii) $h = \dfrac{pd}{4\sigma_h} = \dfrac{10\times 1000}{4\times 80} = 31.25$ mm

Therefore, adopt thickness of shell $h = 62.5$ mm.

Example 2.11: Calculate the permissible fluid pressure a cylindrical shell of 50 mm thickness and 600 mm diameter can withstand assuming the permissible stress equal to 55 N/mm².

Solution:

From, $\sigma_h = \dfrac{pd}{2h},\ p = \dfrac{2h\sigma_h}{d}$ ... (i)

Similarly, $\sigma_L = \dfrac{pd}{4h},\ p = \dfrac{4h\sigma_L}{d}$ ... (ii)

From the above analysis we find that the fluid pressure '*p*' based on hoop stress is less than that of longitudinal stress and hence the design based on

$$p = \frac{2h\sigma_h}{d}$$

$$= \frac{2 \times 50 \times 55}{600} = 9.17 \text{N/mm}^2$$

Example 2.12: A boiler is made from 10 mm thick plate is 1 metre in diameter and subjected to a fluid pressure 1 N/mm². Assuming the permissible tensile stress as 80 N/mm², determine the circumferential efficiency of the joint.

Solution:

We have hoop stress (circumferential stress),

$$\sigma_h = \frac{pd}{2\eta h}$$

Where, η = Efficiency of the joint

Therefore, $$\eta = \frac{pd}{2h\sigma_h}$$

$$= \frac{1 \times 1000}{2 \times 80 \times 10} = 0.625 = 62.5\%$$

Example 2.13: A pipe carrying water is 1 metre in diameter and has a head of 50 metre. Assuming specific weight of water as 10 kN/m³, permissible tensile stress as 20 N/mm², calculate the thickness of pipe required.

Solution:

Pressure of water in pipe = Specific weight of water × Head

$= (10 \times 10^3) 50$

$= 50 \times 10^4 \text{ N/m}^2 = 50 \times 10^{-2} \text{ N/mm}^2$

From, $$\sigma_h = \frac{pd}{2h}$$

$$h = \frac{pd}{2\sigma_h}$$

$$= \frac{(50 \times 10^{-2})1000}{2 \times 20} = 12.5 \text{ mm}$$

Example 2.14: A thin cylindrical shell of 1 metre diameter is subjected to internal pressure of 1 N/mm². Find the thickness of shell required if the ultimate tensile strength of plate is 40 N/mm², use factor of safety = 4.

Solution:

Hoop stress, $$\sigma_h = \frac{pd}{2h}$$

Therefore, $$h = \frac{pd}{2\sigma_h}$$

Where, $$\sigma_h = \frac{\text{Tensile strength}}{f.o.s} = \frac{400}{4} = 100 \text{ N/mm}^2$$

$$p = 1 \text{ N/mm}^2, \; d = 1 \text{ m} = 1000 \text{ mm}$$

$$h = \text{Thickness of shell} = \frac{1 \times 1000}{2 \times 100} = 5 \text{ mm}$$

Example 2.15: Calculate the increase in volume of a boiler shell 2.5 metre long and 1 metre in diameter when subjected to an internal pressure of 2 N/mm². The wall thickness is such that the maximum tensile stress is 22 N/mm² under the pressure. Use E = 20 × 104 N/mm² and γ = 0.28.

Solution:

Change in volume of a thin cylindrical shell is given by

$$dv = v(2e_h + e_L) \qquad \text{... (i)}$$

Where, $$v = \text{Initial volume} = \frac{\pi}{4} d^2 L$$

$$= \frac{\pi}{4}(1000)^2 \times (2.5 \times 10^3)$$

$$= 1.963 \times 10^9 \text{ mm}^3$$

To find e_h, hoop strain or circumferential strain

$$e_h = \frac{\sigma_h}{E} - \frac{\sigma_L}{mE}$$

$$= \frac{1}{E}\left[\sigma_h - \frac{\sigma_L}{m}\right]$$

$$= \frac{1}{E}[\sigma_h - \gamma\sigma_L]$$

$$= \frac{1}{20 \times 10^4}\left[22 - 0.28 \times \frac{22}{2}\right]$$

$$e_h = 1.098 \times 10^{-4}$$

Note: $$\sigma_h = 2\sigma_L$$

Longitudinal strain,

$$e_L = \frac{\sigma_L}{E} - \frac{\sigma_h}{mE}$$

$$= \frac{1}{E}[\sigma_L - \gamma\sigma_h]$$

$$= \frac{1}{20 \times 10^4}\left[\frac{\sigma_h}{2} - \gamma\sigma_h\right]$$

$$= \frac{\sigma_h}{20 \times 10^4}\left[\frac{1}{2} - \gamma\right] = \frac{22}{20 \times 10^4}\left[\frac{1}{2} - 0.28\right]$$

$$e_L = 0.242 \times 10^{-4}$$

Therefore change in volume from equation (*i*) is

$$dv = 1.963\times10^{9}\left[2\times1.098\times10^{-4} + 0.242\times10^{-4}\right]$$

$$= 478579.4 \text{ mm}^3$$

Example 2.16: Calculate the maximum permissible gas pressure a spherical tank 1 metre diameter and 100 mm thick can withstand assuming working stress for the material of tank as 80 N/m m².

Solution:

For a thin spherical pressure used,

$$\text{Permissible stress} = \frac{pr}{2h}$$

Where, r = Radius of spherical tank

$$= \frac{1000}{2} = 500 \text{ mm}$$

h = Thickness of shell = 100 mm

Therefore,
$$80 = \frac{p\times500}{2\times100}$$

$$p = 32 \text{ N/mm}^2$$

Example 2.17: Calculate the change in volume of a spherical shell 1.2 metre and 10 mm thick when it is subjected to a fluid pressure of 20 N/mm². Use E = 20 × 10⁵ N/mm² and γ = 0.3.

Solution:

For a thin spherical shell change in volume is given by

$$\text{Change in volume} = v\times\frac{3pd}{4hE}(1-\gamma)$$

Where, v = Volume of sphere = $\frac{4}{3}\pi r^3$

$$= \frac{4}{3}\pi(600)^3 = 9.048\times10^{8} \text{ mm}^3$$

Therefore,
$$dv = \frac{9.048\times10^{8}\times3\times20\times(1200)}{4\times10\times2\times10^{5}}[1-0.3]$$

$$dv = 57\times10^{6} \text{ mm}^3$$

Example 2.18: A cylindrical vessel 500 mm inside diameter, 15 mm thick and 2000 mm long with spherical ends is subjected to an internal pressure 20 N/mm². Calculate the change in volume of Vessel using E = 2 × 10⁵ N/mm² and γ = 0.28.

Solution:

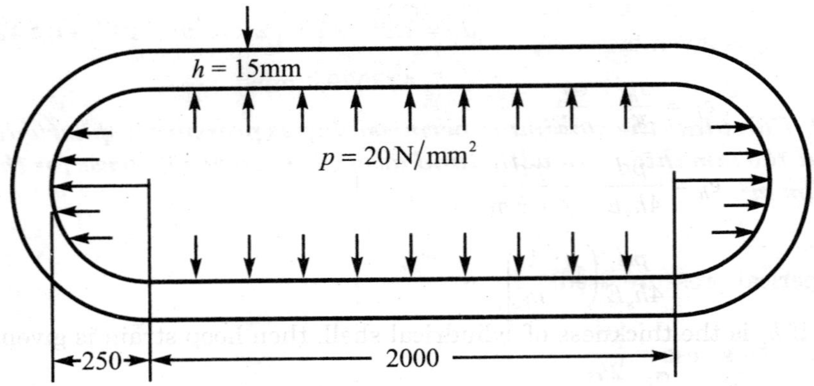

Change in volume of the vessel = Change in volume of spherical portion + Change in volume of cylindrical portion of shell ... (1)

Change in volume of spherical portion of shell

$$= \frac{4\pi r^3}{3} \times \frac{3pd}{4hE}(1-\gamma)$$

$$= \frac{4}{3}\pi(250)^3 \frac{3\times 20\times 500}{4\times 15\times 2\times 10^5}(1-0.28)$$

$$= 117809.73 \text{ mm}^3$$

Change in volume of cylindrical shell is

$$= \frac{pd}{2hE}\left(\frac{5}{2}-2\gamma\right)v$$

$$= \frac{pd}{2hE}\left(\frac{5}{2}-2\gamma\right)\left(\frac{\pi d^2}{4}l\right)$$

$$= \frac{20\times 500}{2\times 15\times 2\times 10^5}\left[\frac{5}{2}-2\times 0.28\right]\left[\frac{\pi}{4}\times 500^2\times 2000\right]$$

$$= 1269727 \text{ mm}^3$$

Substituting in equation (1)

Change in volume = 117809.73 + 1269727

$= 1387536.8 \text{ mm}^3$

Example 2.19: A cylindrical shell with hemispherical ends is 2 metre in diameter and 10 mm thick is subjected to an internal fluid pressure of 25 N/mm². Calculate the thickness of the hemispherical ends assuming the same strain in hemispherical and cylindrical portions. Take $\frac{1}{m} = 0.3$.

Solution:

Let h_s be the thickness of hemispherical ends

Hoop strain e_h is given by,

$$e_h = \frac{\sigma_h}{E} - \frac{\sigma_L}{mE}$$

Therefore,
$$e_h = \frac{pd}{4h_sE} - \frac{pd}{4h_sEm}$$

$$= \frac{pd}{4h_sE}\left(1 - \frac{1}{m}\right) \quad \text{... (1)}$$

Similarly if h_c is the thickness of cylindrical shell, then hoop strain is given by,

$$\left.e_h\right)_{cyl} = \frac{\sigma_h}{E} - \frac{\sigma_L}{mE}$$

$$= \frac{pd}{2h_cE} - \frac{pd}{4h_cEm}$$

$$= \frac{pd}{4h_cE}\left(2 - \frac{1}{m}\right) \quad \text{... (2)}$$

Equating equations (1) and (2)

$$\frac{pd}{4h_sE}\left(1 - \frac{1}{m}\right) = \frac{pd}{4h_cE}\left(2 - \frac{1}{m}\right)$$

Therefore,
$$\frac{h_c}{h_s} = \frac{\left(2 - \frac{1}{m}\right)}{\left(1 - \frac{1}{m}\right)} = \frac{2 - 0.3}{1 - 0.3} = 2.4286$$

Therefore,
$$h_s = \frac{h_c}{2.4286}$$

$$= \frac{10}{2.4286} = 4.118 \text{ mm}$$

Therefore, thickness of hemispherical ends = 4.118 mm.

Example 2.20: A thick cylindrical pipe of 400 mm internal diameter and 100 mm thick is subjected to an internal fluid pressure of 10 N/mm². Calculate the maximum and minimum intensities of circumferential stress and plot these along the thickness of pipe.

Solution:

Lame's equation for thick cylinders are given by,

$$P_x = \frac{b}{x^2} - a \quad \text{... } (i)$$

And
$$\sigma_x = \frac{b}{x^2} + a \quad \text{... } (ii)$$

Where a and b are Lame's constants.

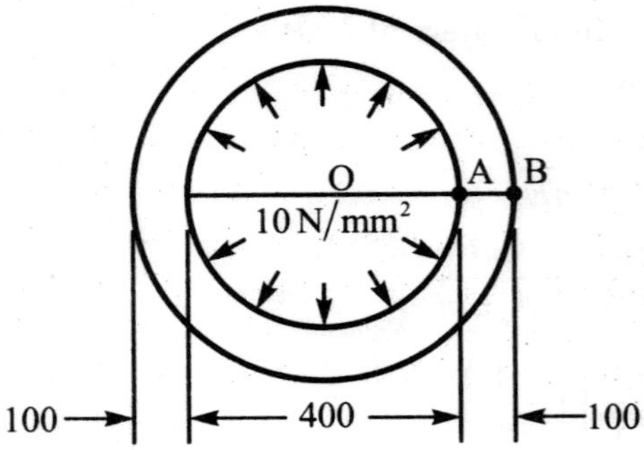

At the inside surface (at A) where x = 200 mm,,

Note: *x is measured from centre of cylinder, O.*

Therefore, $$P_x\Big]_{at\,x=200} = \frac{b}{(200)^2} - a = 10$$

Therefore, $$\frac{b}{40000} - a = 10 \qquad \text{... }(i)$$

At the outer surface (at B) where x = 200 + 100 = 300 mm

$$P_x\Big]_{at\,x=300} = \frac{b}{(300)^2} - a = 0$$

[Since no pressure is applied at the outer surface]

Therefore, $$\frac{b}{90000} - a = 0 \qquad \text{...}(ii)$$

Subtracting equation (*ii*) from equation (*i*),

$$\left(\frac{b}{40000} - a\right) - \left(\frac{b}{90000} - a\right) = 10 - 0 = 10$$

i.e., $$\frac{b}{40000} - \frac{b}{90000} = 10$$

Therefore, $b = 72 \times 10^4$

Substituting the values of b in equation (*i*)

$$\frac{b}{40000} - a = 10$$

Therefore, $$\frac{72 \times 10^4}{40000} - a = 10$$

Therefore, $a = 8$

Substituting the values of a and b in equations (*i*) and (*ii*)

$$P_x = \frac{72 \times 10^4}{x^2} - 8 \qquad \text{... }(iii)$$

$$\sigma_x = \frac{72 \times 10^4}{x^2} + 8 \qquad \text{... }(iv)$$

From equation (*iii*)

$$P_x\Big]_{at\,x=250} = \frac{72\times10^4}{(250)^2} - 8 = 6.88 \text{ N/mm}^2$$

From equation (*iv*)

$$\sigma_x\Big]_{at\,x=250} = \frac{72\times10^4}{(250)^2} + 8 = 19.52 \text{ N/mm}^2$$

$$P_x\Big]_{at\,x=200} = \frac{72\times10^4}{(200)^2} + 8 = 26 \text{ N/mm}^2$$

$$P_x\Big]_{at\,x=300} = \frac{72\times10^4}{(300)^2} + 8 = 16 \text{ N/mm}^2$$

Plot of Stress

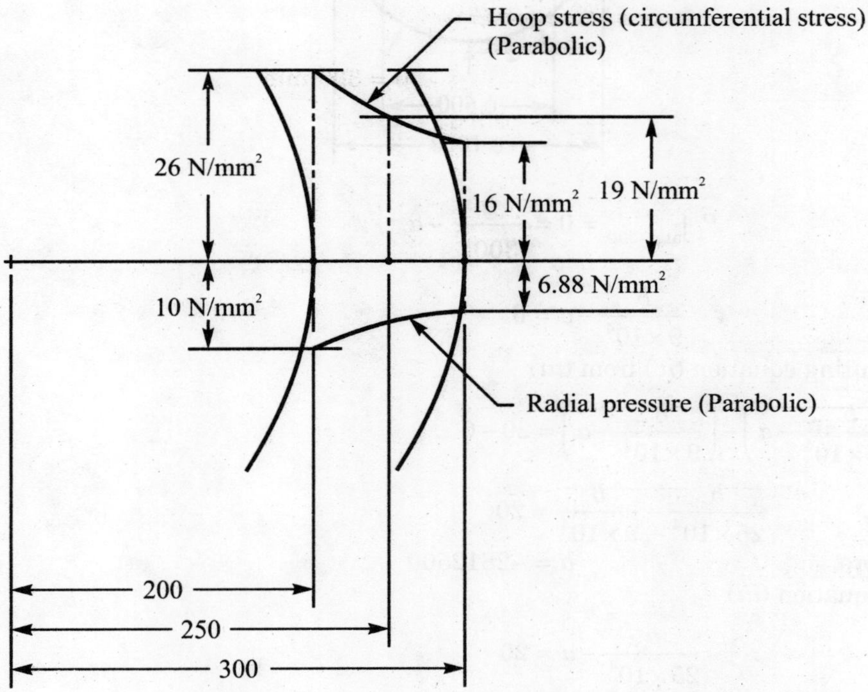

Example 2.21: A thick pipe 600 mm internal diameter and 1000 mm external diameter is subjected to an external fluid pressure of 20 MPa. Determine the maximum and minimum hoop stress and plot these values along the cross-section of pipe.

Solution:

Lame's equation for thick cylinders is

$$P_x = \frac{b}{x^2} - a \qquad \text{... } (i)$$

And $$\sigma_x = \frac{b}{x^2} + a \qquad \text{... (ii)}$$

$$P_x\Big]_{x=500} = \frac{b}{(500)^2} - a = 20$$

Therefore, $$\frac{b}{25\times10^4} - a = 20 \qquad \text{... (iii)}$$

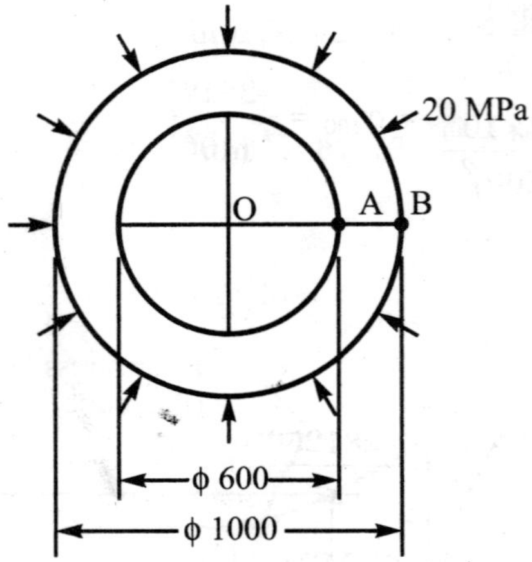

At A, $$P_x\Big]_{\text{at } x=300} = 0 = \frac{b}{(300)^2} - a$$

i.e., $$\frac{b}{9\times10^4} - a = 0 \qquad \text{... (iv)}$$

Substituting equation (*iv*) from (*iii*)

$$\left(\frac{b}{25\times10^4} - a\right) - \left(\frac{b}{9\times10^4} - a\right) = 20 - 0$$

i.e., $$\frac{b}{25\times10^4} - \frac{b}{9\times10^4} = 20$$

Therefore, $$b = -2812500$$

From equation (*iii*)

$$\frac{b}{25\times10^4} - a = 20$$

i.e., $$\frac{-2812500}{25\times10^4} - a = 20$$

Therefore, $$a = -31.25$$

From equation (*i*)

$$p_x = \frac{-2812500}{x^2} + 31.25$$

From equation (*ii*)

$$\sigma_x = \frac{-2812500}{x^2} - 31.25$$

At the inner surface A,

$$\sigma_x\Big)_{\text{at } x=300} = \sigma_{300} = \frac{-2812500}{(300)^2} - 31.25 = -62.5 \text{ N/mm}^2$$

At mid thickness of shell,

$$\sigma_x\Big)_{\text{at } x=400} = \sigma_{400} = \frac{-2812500}{(400)^2} - 31.25 = -48.83 \text{ N/mm}^2$$

At outer surface B,

$$\sigma_x\Big)_{\text{at } x=500} = \sigma_{500} = \frac{-2812500}{(500)^2} - 31.25 = -42.5 \text{ N/mm}^2$$

$$P_x = \frac{-2812500}{x^2} + 31.25$$

$$P_x\Big)_{x=500} = 20 \text{ MPa} (given)$$

$$P_x\Big)_{x=300} = 0$$

$$P_x\Big)_{x=400} = \frac{-2812500}{(400)^2} + 31.25 = 13.67 \text{ N/mm}^2$$

Plot of Stress

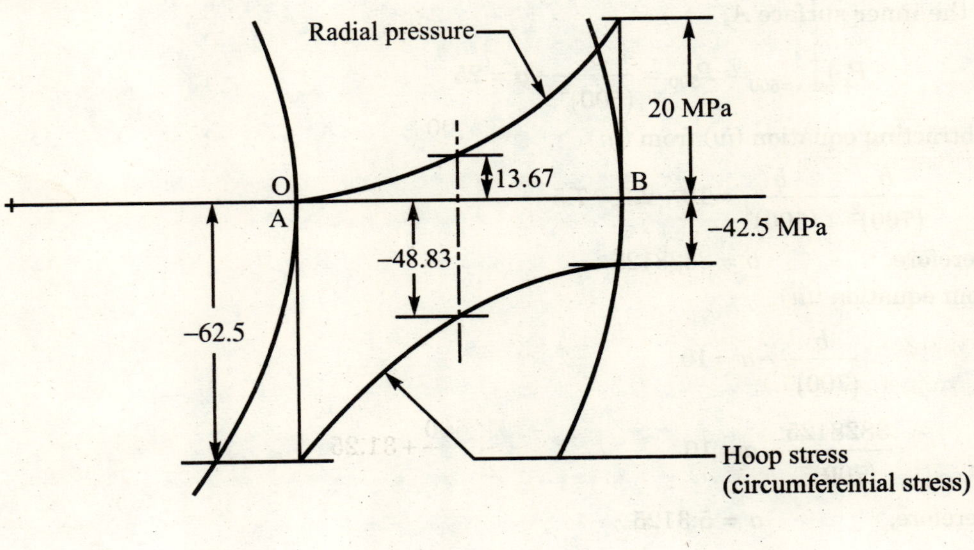

Example 2.22: A thick cylindrical shell 1 metre internal diameter and 200 mm thick is subjected to an internal fluid pressure of 10 N/m² and external fluid pressure of 2.5 N/mm². Find the maximum and minimum intensities of circumferential stress and show the variation along the thickness of shell. Also plot the radial stress along the thickness of shell.

Solution:

Lame's equation for thick cylinders are

$$P_x = \frac{b}{x^2} - a \quad \text{... (i)}$$

And

$$\sigma_x = \frac{b}{x^2} + a \quad \text{... (ii)}$$

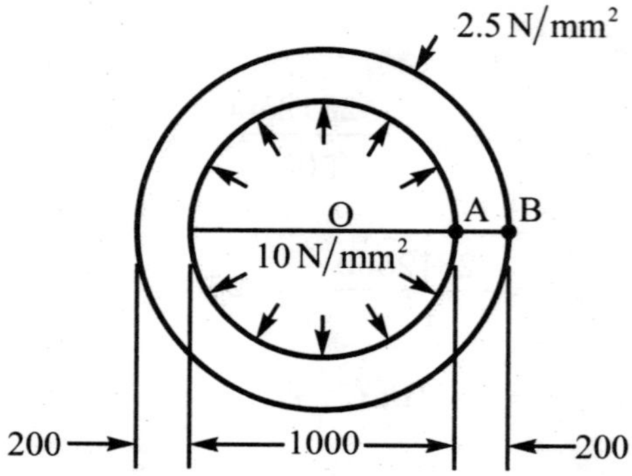

To find constants a and b

At the outer surface *B*,

$$P_x)_{\text{at } x=700} = P_{700} = \frac{b}{(700)^2} - a = 10 \quad \text{... (iii)}$$

At the inner surface *A*,

$$P_x)_{\text{at } x=500} = P_{500} = \frac{b}{(500)^2} - a = 25 \quad \text{... (iv)}$$

Subtracting equation (*iv*) from (*iii*)

$$\frac{b}{(700)^2} - \frac{b}{(500)^2} = 10 - 2.5 = 7.5$$

Therefore, $b = 3828125$

From equation (*iii*)

$$\frac{b}{(700)^2} - a = 10$$

i.e.,

$$\frac{3828125}{(700)^2} - a = 10$$

Therefore, $a = 5.3125$

From equation (*i*)

$$P_x = \frac{3828125}{x^2} - 5.3125$$

From equation (*iii*)

$$\sigma_x = \frac{3828125}{x^2} + 5.3125$$

At the inner surface *A*,

$$\sigma_x\Big)_{\text{at}\, x=500} = \frac{3828128}{(500)^2} + 5.3125 = 20.625 \text{ N/mm}^2$$

At the mid thickness,

$$\sigma_x\Big)_{\text{at}\, x=600} = \frac{3828128}{(600)^2} + 5.3125 = 15.946 \text{ N/mm}^2$$

At the outer surface *B*,

$$\sigma_x\Big)_{\text{at}\, x=700} = \frac{3828128}{(700)^2} + 5.3125 = 13.125 \text{ N/mm}^2$$

Plot of Stress

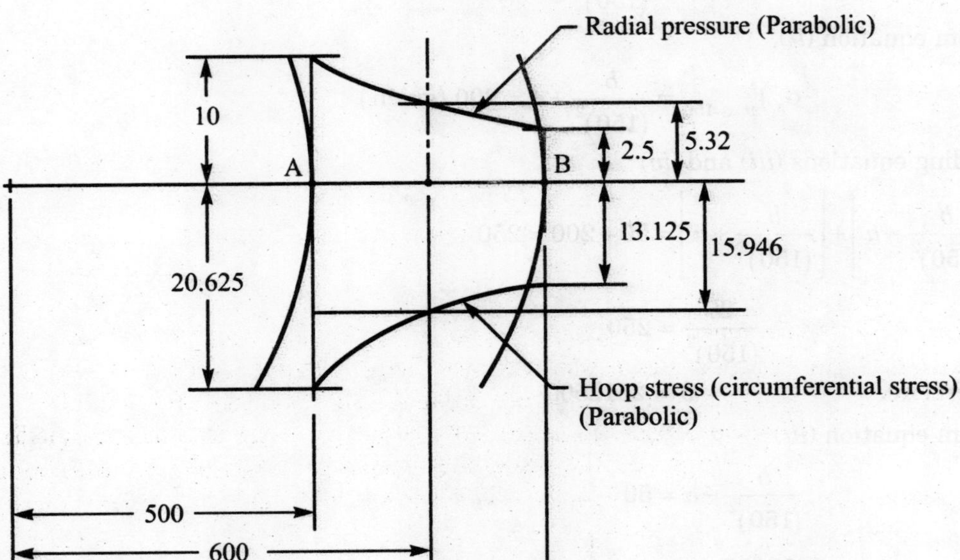

Example 2.23: Calculate the thickness of a cylindrical shell of internal diameter 300 mm required to withstand a fluid pressure of 50 MPa assuming the maximum permissible circumferential stress as 200 MPa. Also plot the stress distribution along the thickness of shell.

Solution:

Lame's equation for thick cylinders are

$$P_x = \frac{b}{x^2} - a \qquad \text{... }(i)$$

And

$$\sigma_x = \frac{b}{x^2} + a \qquad \text{... }(ii)$$

At the inner surface of shell a pressure of 50 MPa is applied.

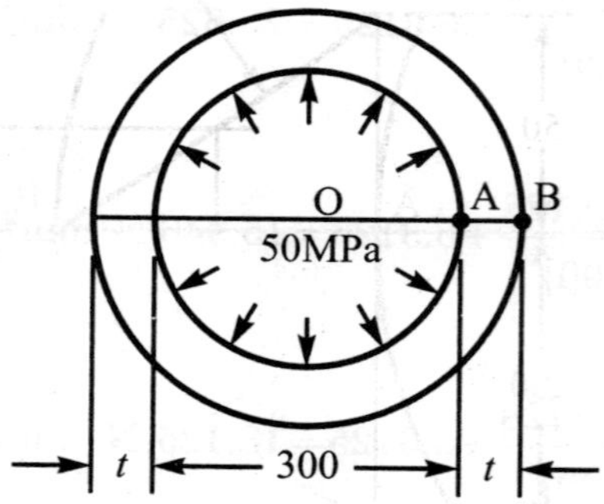

At A,

$$P_x)_{\text{at } x=150} = \frac{b}{(150)^2} - a = 50 \qquad \text{... }(iii)$$

From equation (ii),

$$\sigma_x)_{\text{at } x=150} = \frac{b}{(150)^2} + a = 200 \text{ (given)} \qquad \text{... }(iv)$$

Adding equations (iii) and (iv)

$$\left[\frac{b}{(150)^2} - a\right] + \left[\frac{b}{(150)^2} + a\right] = 50 + 200 = 250$$

$$\frac{2b}{(150)^2} = 250$$

Therefore,

$$b = 2812500$$

From equation (iii)

$$\frac{b}{(150)^2} - a = 50$$

i.e.,

$$\frac{2812500}{(150)^2} - a = 50$$

or

$$a = 75$$

At the outer periphery (surface *i.e.*, at B), no pressure is applied *i.e.*, at B. At $x = (150 + t)$ pressure is 0.

$$P)_{\text{at } B} = P_{(150+t)} = \frac{2812500}{(150+t)^2} - 75 = 0$$

Where, t is the thickness of shell.

Therefore, $t = 43.65$ mm

Plot of Stress

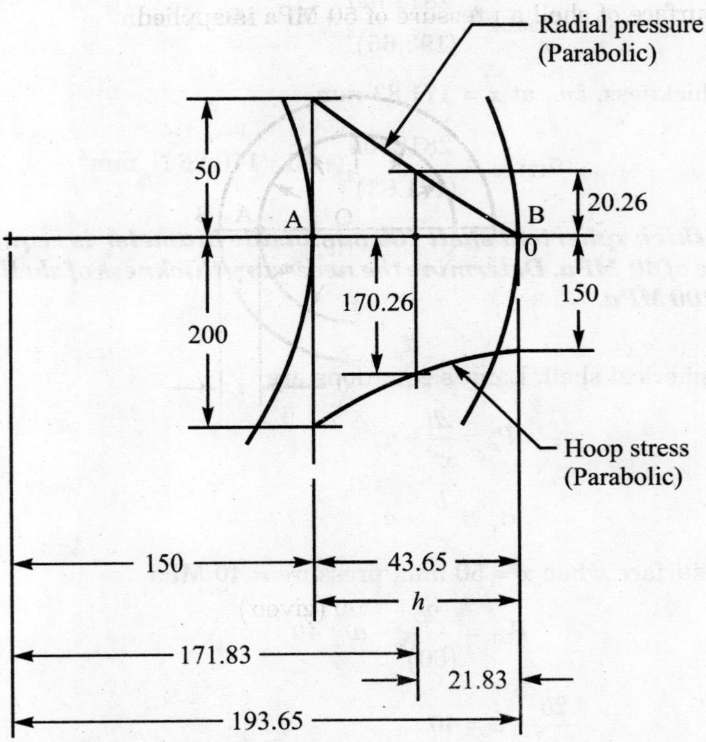

Plot of radial pressure

$$P_x = \frac{2812500}{x^2} - 75$$

At the inner surface, *i.e.*, at $x = 150$,

$$P_{150} = \frac{2812500}{(150)^2} - 75 = 50 \text{ (given)}$$

At the outer surface, *i.e.*, at $x = (150 + 43.65)$,

$$P_{(150+43.65)} = \frac{2812500}{(193.65)^2} - 75 = 0$$

At the mid thickness, *i.e.*, at $x = (150 + 21.83)$, *i.e.*, $x = 171.83$ mm

$$P_{(171.83)} = \frac{2812500}{(171.83)^2} - 75 = 20.26 \text{ N/mm}^2$$

Circumferential stress (Hoop stress)

$$\sigma_x = \frac{b}{x^2} + a = \frac{2812500}{x^2} + 75$$

At the inner surface *i.e.,* at $x = 150$, $\sigma_x = 200$ N/mm^2 (given)

At the outer surface *i.e.,* at $x = 193.65$ mm

$$\sigma_{193.65} = \frac{2812500}{(193.65)^2} + 75 = 150 \text{ N/mm}^2$$

At the mid thickness, *i.e.,* at $x = 171.83$ mm,

$$\sigma_{171.83} = \frac{2812500}{(171.83)^2} + 75 = 170.26 \text{ N/mm}^2$$

Example 2.24: A thick spherical shell 100 mm inside diameter is required to withstand internal pressure of 40 MPa. Determine the necessary thickness of shell if the permissible tensile stress is 100 MPa.

Solution:

For a thick spherical shell, Lame's equations are

$$P_x = \frac{2b}{x^3} - a \qquad \text{... (i)}$$

$$\sigma_x = \frac{b}{x^3} + a \qquad \text{... (ii)}$$

At the inner surface when $x = 50$ mm, pressure = 40 MPa

i.e.,

$$P_{50} = \frac{2b}{(50)^3} - a = 40$$

Therefore,

$$\frac{2b}{50^3} - a = 40 \qquad \text{... (iii)}$$

Stress at inner surface *i.e.,* at $x = 50$ mm, σ_x is maximum

Therefore,

$$\sigma_x = \sigma_{50} = \frac{b}{(50)^3} + a = 100 \qquad \text{... (iv)}$$

Adding equations (*iii*) and (*iv*) yields,

$$\left[\frac{2b}{(50)^3} - a\right] + \left[\frac{b}{(50)^3} + a\right] = 40 + 100$$

i.e.,

$$\frac{3b}{(50)^3} = 140$$

Therefore,

$$b = 5833333.3$$

From equation (*iii*),

$$\frac{2 \times 5833333.3}{(50)^3} - a = 40$$

Therefore, $a = 53.33$

Therefore, equation (*i*) becomes,

$$P_x = \frac{2 \times 5833333.3}{x^3} - 53.33$$

At the outer surface, pressure $p_o = 0$ and $x = (50 + t)$

Therefore, $$P_{(50+t)} = \frac{2 \times 5833333.3}{(50+t)^3} - 53.33 = 0$$

Therefore, $t = 10.255$ mm

Therefore, thickness of shell required = t = 10.255 mm

EXERCISE

1. Calculate the permissible fluid pressure, a cylindrical shell 40 mm thick and 500 mm inside diameter can withstand assuming the permissible stress as 50 N/mm^2.

   [***Ans.***: p = 8 N/mm^2]

2. Determine the thickness of a cylindrical shell of 1 metre diameter to withstand fluid pressure of 10 N/mm^2 assuming the permissible tensile stress of boiler material as 80 N/mm^2.

   [***Ans.***: *Thickness h* = 62.5 /mm]

3. A boiler 1 meter in diameter and made of 10 mm thick plate is subjected to a fluid pressure of 1 N/mm^2. Assuming the permissible tensile stress as 80 N/mm^2, determine the circumferential efficiency.

   [***Ans.***: η = 62.5%]

4. A pipe carrying water is 1 metre in diameter and has a head of 40 metres. Assuming the specific weight of water as 10 kN/m^3 and permissible tensile stress as 2×10^6 N/m^2, calculate the thickness of pipe required.

   [***Ans.***: *Thickness* = 100 mm]

5. A thin cylindrical shell of 1 metre is subjected to an internal pressure of 1 N/mm^2. Find the thickness of the shell if the tensile strength of the plate is 400 N/mm^2 Use factor of safety 4.

   [***Ans.***: *Thickness* = 5 mm]

6. Calculate the increase in volume of a boiler shell 2.4 metre long and 1 metre in diameter when subjected to an internal pressure of 1.6 N/mm^2. The wall thickness is such that the maximum tensile stress is 21.5 N/mm^2 under this pressure.

   [***Ans.***: *Change in volume* = 393.12×10^3 mm^3]

7. Calculate the maximum permissible gas pressure, a spherical tank 1 metre in diameter and 80 mm thick can withstand assuming working stress for the material as 80 N/mm^2.

   [***Ans.***: p = 25.6 N/mm^2]

8. Calculate the change in volume of a spherical shell 1 metre in diameter and 10 mm thick when it is subjected to a fluid pressure of 20 N/mm^2. Use Poisson's ratio = 0.3 and $E = 20 \times 104$ N/mm^2.

   [***Ans.***: *Change in volume* = 2618×10^3 mm^3]

9. A cylindrical steel vessel 500 mm inside diameter and 15 mm thick, 2 metre long (i.e., cylindrical portion) with spherical ends is subjected to an internal pressure of 20 N/mm^2. Calculate the change in volume using $\frac{1}{m}$ = 0.28 and E = 20 × 10^4 N/mm^2.

[***Ans.**: Change in volume* = 1387.548 × 10^3 mm^3]

10. A cylindrical shell with hemispherical ends is 2 metre in diameter and 10 mm thick is subjected to an internal fluid pressure of 25 N/mm^2. Assuming that the strain is same in both cylindrical and hemispherical portion, calculate the thickness of spherical ends. Use μ = 0.3.

[***Ans.**: Thickness* = 4.12 mm]

11. A thick cylindrical pipe 400 mm internal diameter and 100 mm thick is subjected to an internal fluid pressure of 10 N/mm^2. Calculate the maximum and minimum intensities of circumferential stress and plot these along the thickness of pipe.

[***Ans.**: Circumferential stress at the inner side* = 26 N/mm^2
Circumferential stress at the outside = 16 N/mm^2]

12. A thick cylindrical shell 1 metre inner diameter and 200 mm thick is subjected to an internal fluid pressure of 10 N/mm^2 and external fluid pressure of 2.5 N/mm^2. Find the maximum and minimum intensities of circumferential stress and show the variation along the thickness of shell.

[***Ans.**: At the inner fibre, Circumferential stress* = 20.625 N/mm^2
At the outer fibre, Circumferential stress = 13.125 N/mm^2]

13. A thick pipe 500 mm internal diameter and 700 mm external diameter is subjected to an external fluid pressure of 20 N/mm^2. Determine the maximum and minimum hoop stress and plot the values along the thickness of pipe.

[***Ans.**: At the inner fibre, stress* = – 81.67 N/mm^2
At the outer fibre, stress = – 61.67 N/mm^2]

14. A thick spherical shell 800 mm in diameter is required to withstand an internal pressure of 30 N/mm^2. Determine the necessary thickness of shell if the permissible tensile stress is 80 N/mm^2.

[***Ans.**: Thickness* = 7.667 mm]

15. Calculate the thickness of a cylindrical shell of internal diameter 250 mm required to withstand fluid pressure of 50 N/mm^2 assuming the permissible circumferential stress as 180 N/mm^2.

[***Ans.**: Thickness* = 41.3 mm]

CHAPTER

3 Springs

NOTATIONS AND SYMBOLS USED

b = Width of rectangular section of spring, mm.

b' = Width of spring leaves in locomotive springs, mm.

c = Spring index; Ratio $= \dfrac{D}{d}$.

D = Mean diameter of helical spring, mm.

d = Wire diameter, mm.

D_i = Inside diameter of spring, mm.

D_o = Outside diameter of spring, mm.

E = Young's modulus of material of spring, MPa.

F = Axial load on helical spring, N.

= Half the central load in a laminated spring, N.

= Axial load sustained by a concentric spring, N.

F_b = Band load in a laminated spring.

F_f = Load shared by full length leaves, N.

F_g = Load shared by graduated leaves, N.

G = Modulus of rigidity of spring material, MPa.

h = Thickness of leaves used in spring, mm.

= Depth of rectangular section of helical springs, mm.

i = Total number of leaves in laminated springs.

i_g = Number of graduated leaves.

i_f = Number of full length leaves.

k = Wahl's factor.

l = Effective length of laminated spring, mm.

l_f = Free length of coil spring, mm.

l_s = Solid length of coil spring, mm.
p = Pitch of coils in coil spring, mm.
r = Ratio of full length leaves to total number of leaves.
σ_f = Stress in full length leaves, MPa.
σ_g = Stress in graduated leaves, MPa.
σ = Equalized stress in spring leaves, MPa.
σ_b = Bending stress in leaves.
τ = Shear stress in helical springs, MPa.
y = Deflection of helical springs, mm.
= Deflection of locomotive springs, mm.
y_i = Deflection of inner spring in a nested spring, mm.
y_o = Deflection of outer spring in a nested spring, mm.

INTRODUCTION

Springs are machine members designed and constructed to give relatively large elastic deflection under a given load. Spring design involves establishing of relationship between force, torque, deflection and stress. They have many applications in connection with machine design such as cushion impact and shock loading (as in vehicle suspension) to maintain contact between members, measurement of forces (as in weighing scales), etc.

HELICAL SPRINGS

Helical springs are usually made from wire of circular cross-section and sometimes square and rectangular cross-section.

These springs are subjected to both torsional shear stress and transverse shear stress due to load '*F*'. To take into account the curvature effect, the shear stress induced in springs is multiplied by a constant '*K*' called Wahl's factor.

The shear stress induced in a Helical spring is given by

Shear stress $$\tau = \frac{8FDk}{\pi d^3} \qquad \text{... E(20-22)}$$

Where, F = Axial load on spring, *N*.
D = Mean diameter of coil, mm.
d = Wire diameter, mm.
k = Wahl's factor.

$$= \frac{4c-1}{4c-4} + \frac{0.615}{c} \qquad \text{... E(20-23)}$$

$$c = \text{Spring index} = \frac{D}{d} \qquad \text{... E(20-24)}$$

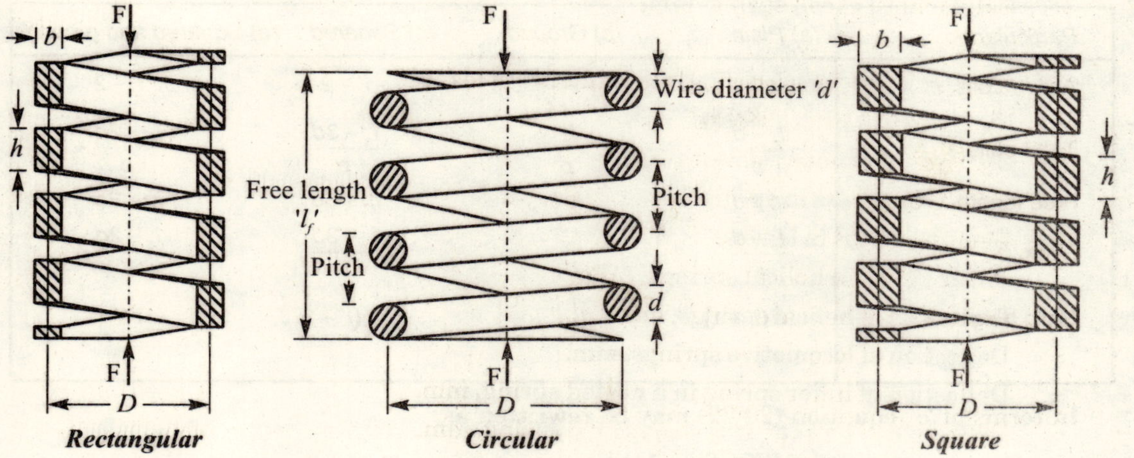

Figure: 3.1

From figure 3.2,

D_o = Outside diameter of coil = $D + d$

D_i = Inside diameter of coil = $D - d$

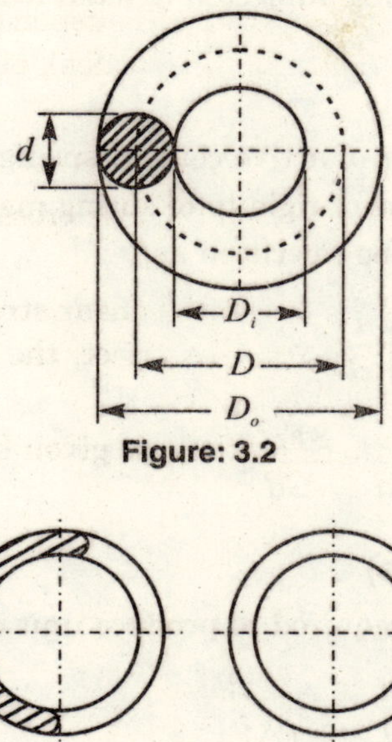

Figure: 3.2

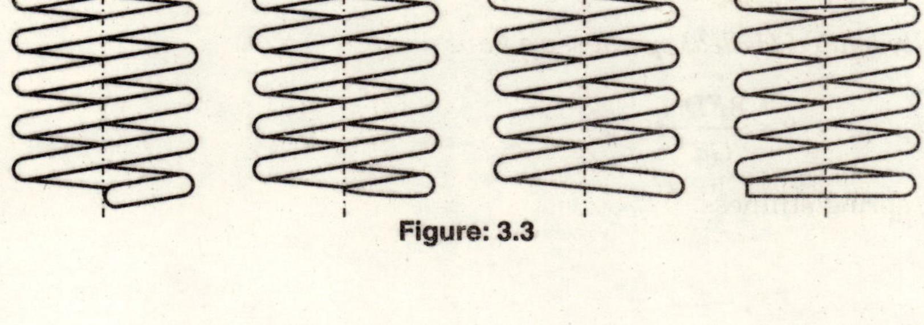

Figure: 3.3

Particulars	(a) Plain	(b) Ground	(c) Squared	(d) Squared and ground
Active coils, i	i'	$i'-\frac{1}{2}$	$i'-2$	$i'-2$
Total coils, i'	$\frac{l_o-d}{p}$	$\frac{l_o}{p}$	$\frac{l_o-3d}{p}$	$\frac{l_o-2d}{p}+2$
Free length, l_o or l_f	$ip+d$	ip	$ip+3d$	$ip+2d$
Pitch, p	$\frac{l_o-d}{i'}$	$\frac{l_o}{i'}$	$\frac{l_o-3d}{i'}$	$\frac{l_o-2d}{i'}$
Solid height, h	$d(i'+1)$	$d\left(i'+\frac{1}{2}\right)$	$d(i'+1)$	$i'd$

In terms of 'c', equation (20-22) may be rewritten as,

$$\tau = \frac{8FK}{\pi}\left(\frac{D}{d}\right)\left(\frac{1}{d^2}\right)$$

$$= \frac{8FK}{\pi}(c)\frac{1}{d^2}, \qquad \text{Where, } \frac{D}{d} = c$$

The deflection 'y' of helical spring subjected to axial load 'F' is given by

Deflection $$y = \frac{8FD^3 i}{Gd^4} \qquad \text{... E(20-29)}$$

Where, i = Number of active coils in spring

G = Modulus of rigidity of spring material. [Refer T(20-14) MDH]

The equation of deflection can be rewritten as,

$$y = \frac{8F}{G}\left(\frac{D}{d}\right)^3 \frac{i}{d}$$

$$= \frac{8F}{G}\left(c^3\right)\frac{i}{d} = \frac{8Fc^3 i}{Gd}$$

Spring Rate (or spring stiffness)

Spring rate is defined as the load required to produce unit deflection or the ratio of load 'F' to deflection 'y'.

$$\text{Spring rate} = \frac{\textit{Load}}{\textit{Deflection}} = \frac{F}{y} \text{ N/mm}$$

Note: *For axially loaded Helical springs, we have*

Deflection, $$y = \frac{8FD^3 i}{Gd^4} \qquad \text{... E(20-29)}$$

Therefore, spring stiffness

$$\frac{F}{y} = \frac{Gd^4}{8D^3 i}$$

$$= \frac{G}{8i}\left(\frac{d}{D}\right)^3 d$$

$$= \frac{G}{8i}\left(\frac{1}{c}\right)^3 d$$

$$= \frac{Gd}{8c^3 i} \quad \text{... E(20-30)}$$

Stiffness of Springs in Series and Parallel Arrangement

(a) Springs in series

Figure 3.4(*a*) shows three coiled springs arranged in series. If k_1, k_2 and k_3 are the stiffness of these springs, then the equivalent spring stiffness K_{eq} is given by,

$$K_{eq} = \frac{1}{\frac{1}{k_1} + \frac{1}{k_2} + \frac{1}{k_3}}$$

In figure 3.4(*b*) is shown the same springs placed in parallel arrangement. The equivalent spring stiffness K_{eq} is given by,

$$K_{eq} = k_1 + k_2 + k_3$$

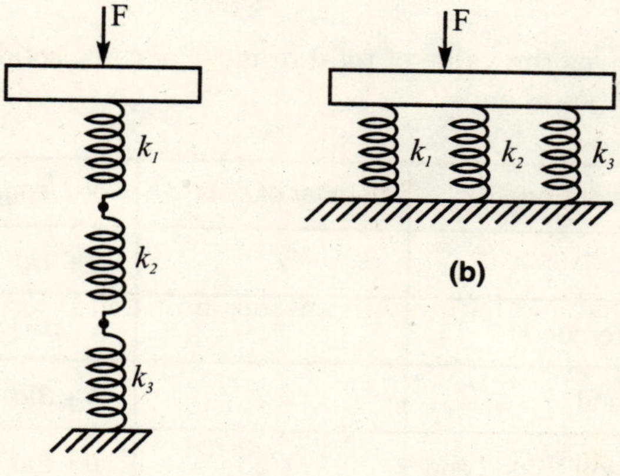

Figure: 3.4

Materials of Springs

Springs are produced from carbon and alloy steels having carbon content 0.5 to 1.1%. Springs upto 100 mm diameter are produced from carbon steels. Alloy steels are used for springs subjected to high stresses and working at elevated temperatures. The elastic properties of steel can be improved by the addition of silicon (upto 2%) and resistance to temperature can be improved by the addition of tungsten (upto 1.2%) and vanadium (upto 0.2%).

The mechanical properties of various springs steels are shown in Table T(20-14 MDH). The fatigue life of spring steels can be improved through polishing and strain hardening of the surface by processes such as Drawing and Shot peening. Copper base alloys are used for springs used in humid and chemical environment and in applications where the effect of magnetic fields is to be avoided. Berylium bronze alloy have superior stable elastic properties, corrosion resistance properties and high electrical conductivity and hence finds its application in electrical industries.

Manufacture of Springs

Springs having spring index $c = \frac{D}{d} > 4$ are produced by winding in cold condition. Springs having $c < 4$ are wound hot. Wire wound either after heat treatment or after cold drawing is subjected to tempering (200°C to 300°C) to stress relieve or it is wound in the annealed state and then hardened or tempered. Piano wire is produced from carbon steel (less than 1% carbon) and is subjected to Isothermal hardening (temperature 900°C) with subsequent conditioning in a bath of molten lead maintained at 500°C. Finally, the wire is drawn to the required sizes.

Springs made from alloy steels are heat treated (oil hardening at 800 to 850°C) followed by tempering at 400°C to 500°C. Berylium Bronze spring are water quenched from 800°C and tempered (250°C to 350°C). Steel springs used for cyclic loads are shot peened after heat treatment. Finally a corrosive coating of zinc or cadmium is provided on the springs.

Spring Ends

Spring ends for Helical springs may be plain, plain and ground, squared, squared and ground as shown in Fig. 3.3.

The following table gives the value of total number of coils, solid length and free length of springs having different types of ends.

Sl. No.	Type of Ends	Number of coils (i)	Solid length	Free length (l_f)
1.	Plain	i	$(i + 1)d$	$ip + d$
2.	Plain and ground	i	id	ip
3.	Squared end	$i + 2$	$(i + 3)d$	$ip + 3d$
4.	Squared and ground end	$i + 2$	$(i + 2)d$	$ip + 2d$

Buckling of Compression Springs

Buckling may occur in compression springs if the free length (l_f) is greater than 4 times mean diameter. *i.e.*, ($l_f > 4D$). If $l_f > 4D$, the spring should be properly guided to avoid buckling.

The critical load that will cause buckling may be approximated as,

$$F_{cr} = k\, l_f\, k_l$$

Where, F_{cr} = Axial load required to produce buckling, N.

k = Spring rate or spring stiffness, N/mm.

l_f = Free length of spring; mm.

k_l = A factor which depends on the ratio $\frac{l_f}{D}$

k_l varies from 0.04 to 0.72 for hinged ends with $\frac{l_f}{D}$, 8 to 1 and 0.19 to 0.72 for $\frac{l_f}{D}$, 8 to 1 respectively for built in ends.

Surging of Springs

Surging may occur in helical springs which are subjected to repetitive loads at a rate closer to the natural frequency of the spring. To avoid surging, the natural frequency of the spring should be at least 20 times the frequency of the applied load.

To avoid surge, the natural frequency of the spring is given by,

$$f = \frac{d}{iD^2}\sqrt{\frac{G}{w}} \qquad \text{... E(20-78)}$$

Where, w = Specific weight of spring material, N/m^3

G = Modulus of rigidity of spring material, N/mm^2

Nomenclature of Helical Spring

Figure 3.5 shows the cross-sectional front view and top view of a helical compression spring. The various terms associated with this spring are as shown.

(a) Wire diameter (d)

This is the diameter of the wire used in forming the spring.

(b) Mean diameter (D)

It is the diameter of the spring measured from the centres of wire normal to the axis of the spring. In terms of wire diameter 'd' and outside diameter 'D_o', the mean diameter

$$D = D_o - \frac{d}{2} - \frac{d}{2} = D_o - d$$

(c) Outside diameter (D_o)

The outside diameter of the spring is the maximum outside diameter of the spring measured normal to the axis.

From figure 3.5,

Outside diameter $D_o = D + \frac{d}{2} + \frac{d}{2} = D + d$

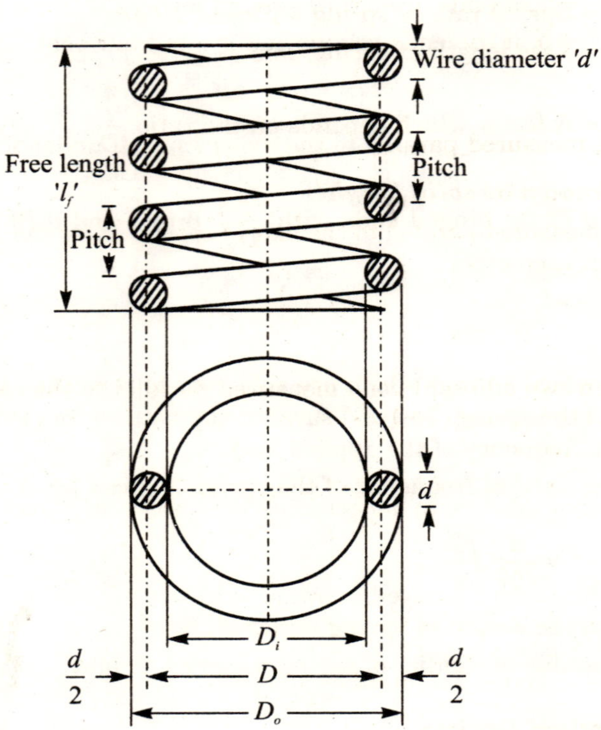

Figure: 3.5

(d) Inside diameter (D_i)

The maximum inside diameter of spring measured normal to the axis of spring is called inside diameter.

Therefore, $$D_i = D - \frac{d}{2} - \frac{d}{2} = D - d$$

(e) Spring index (c)

The ratio of the mean diameter of spring *(D)* to the wire diameter *(d)* is called spring index and is denoted by '*c*'

i.e., $$c = \frac{D}{d}\text{; Usually } c \text{ varies from 6 to 10.}$$

(f) Free length of spring (l_f)

The total length of spring measured parallel to the axis of spring in unloaded position is called free length of spring.

Free length (l_f) $\geq (i + n)d + y + a$ ... E(20-53)

Where, i = Total number of active coils.

n = A factor which depends on type of end of coil.

= 2, if ends are bent before grinding.

= 1, if ends are either ground or bent.

= 0, if the ends are neither ground nor bent.

(g) Compressed length

It is the length of spring, measured parallel to the axis of spring under the action of a load.

(h) Solid length (also known as solid height)

It is the length of spring measured parallel to the axis of spring under the action of load causing the adjacent coils to touch each other.

Solid length $= l_s = id$

(i) Pitch of coils (p)

It is the distance between two adjacent coils measured parallel to the axis from a point on a coil to a similar point on the adjacent coil.

(j) Active coils (i)

It is the number of coils that are free to deflect under the action of a load.

(k) Inactive coils

It is the number of coils rendered inactive by contact with the supports.

(l) Total number of coils

It is the sum of the active and inactive number of coils

Helical Springs of Non-circular Section

For higher load capacity in a given space, the section of helical spring is changed from circular to square or rectangular cross-section.

(a) Spring of square section

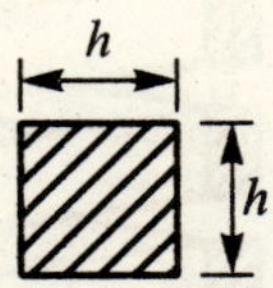

(Square section)

The maximum shear stress τ' induced in a helical spring of square section is given by,

$$\tau' = \frac{2.4\, kFD}{h^3} \qquad \text{... E(20-43)}$$

Deflection,
$$y = \frac{5.66\, iFD^3}{h^4 G} \qquad \text{... E(20-44)}$$

Where, k = Whal's factor $= \dfrac{4c-1}{4c-4} + \dfrac{0.615}{c}$

c = Spring index = $\frac{D}{d} = \frac{D}{b} = \frac{D}{h}$

D = Mean diameter of coils, mm

h = Side of square section , mm

F = Axial load on spring, N

G = Modulus of rigidity of material of spring, N/mm^2

i = Total number of coils in spring

(b) Rectangular section

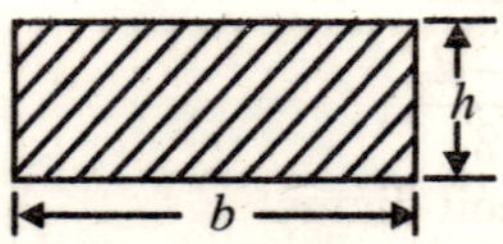

For spring of rectangular section, the maximum shear stress in the spring is given by,

Shear stress $$\tau' = \frac{kFD(1.5h + 0.9b)}{b^2h^2}$$ ... E(24-34a)

$$= \frac{kFD(1.5 + 0.9m)}{m^2h^3}$$ ... E(20-34b)

Where, $m = \frac{b}{h}$; $c = \frac{D}{b}$ *if* $b < h$ ... E(20-38)

$= \frac{D}{h}$ *if* $h < b$

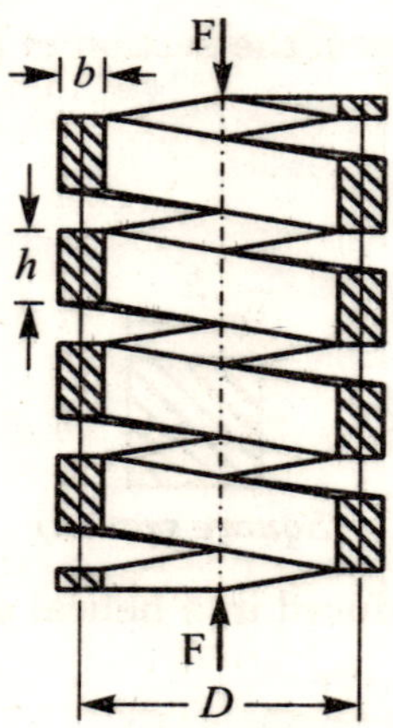

Figure: 3.6

Note: *The longer side of rectangle i.e. 'h' is parallel to the axis of spring and shorter side normal to it.*

The deflection of spring is given by,

$$y = \frac{2.83\, iFD^3\left(b^2 + h^2\right)}{b^3h^3G}$$ ... E(20-39)

Concentric Springs (also called Nested springs or Cluster springs or Composite springs) Refer figure (20-10 MDH)

Composite springs are used for obtaining greater spring force in a given space. Here two or more springs are placed one inside the other such that they have opposite windings. If the springs used are made of same material, then it is preferable to have same spring index so that the shear stress induced in all the springs is the same and no individual spring is over stressed.

The clearance between two adjacent springs will be generally equal to half the difference of the wire diameter.

***i.e.,* if d_1 and d_2 are the wire diameters, then the clearance is given by,**

$$\text{Clearance} = \frac{d_1 - d_2}{2}; \quad \text{where } d_1 > d_2$$

Let D_1, d_1, i_1, G_1 are the mean coil diameter, wire diameter, number of coils and modulus of rigidity of one of the springs used in a nested spring; D_2, d_2, i_2, G_2 are respectively the mean coil diameter, wire diameter, number of coils and modulus of rigidity of the other spring.

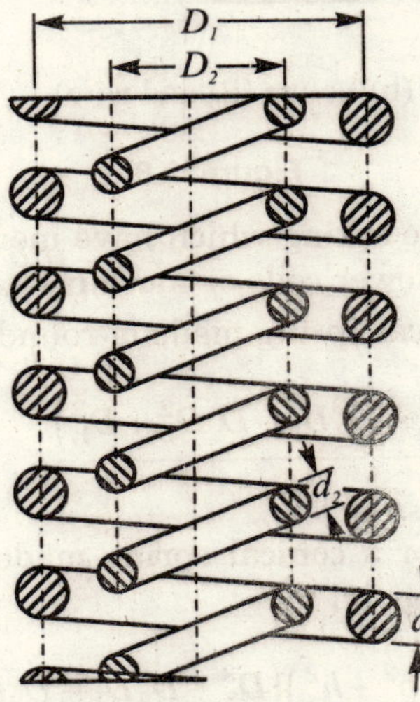

Figure: 3.7

(i) If F_1 and F_2 are the loads shared by the individual springs, and springs are of same length then,

$$\frac{F_1}{F_2} = \left(\frac{D_2}{D_1}\right)^3 \left(\frac{d_1}{d_2}\right)^4 \left(\frac{i_2}{i_1}\right)\left(\frac{G_1}{G_2}\right) \quad \text{... E(20-69)}$$

(ii) The relation between the two springs when they are equally stressed is given by,

$$\frac{F_1}{F_2} = \left(\frac{D_2}{D_1}\right)\left(\frac{d_1}{d_2}\right)^2 \left(\frac{k_1}{k_2}\right) \quad \text{... E(20-70)}$$

(iii) The approximate relation between the sizes of two concentric springs when wound from wire of same material,

$$\frac{F_1}{F_2} = \left(\frac{D_2}{D_1}\right)^{0.75} \left(\frac{d_1}{d_2}\right)^{2.5} \quad \text{... E(20-71)}$$

Note: *If 'F' is the total maximum load on the springs, then*

$$F = F_1 + F_2 \quad \text{... E(20-72)}$$

Conical Springs

Helical springs have linear load deflection characteristics. In some instances it becomes necessary to have non-linear variation of deflection with load. This is achieved by using compact conical springs in which the wire is wound in the form of a cone as shown in Fig. 3.8.

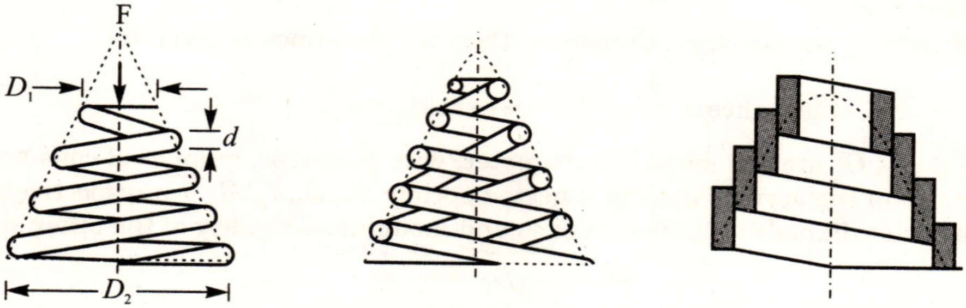

(a) Conical (Round wire) (b) Volute (Round wire) (c) Volute (Rectangular wire)

Figure: 3.8

The larger coils at the bottom of the spring which have more deflection become non-operative at higher loads as they rest on the lower coils or move inside the other in a telescopic manner.

The axial deflection 'y' for conical spring made of round stock is given by,

$$y = \frac{2\,iF\left(D_2^3 + D_2^3 D_1 + D_2 D_1^2 + D_1^3\right)}{d^4 G} \quad \text{... E(20-79)}$$

Similarly axial deflection 'y' for a conical spring made of rectangular stock with radial thickness 'b' and axial diameter 'h' given by,

$$y = \frac{0.71\,iF\left(b^2 + h^2\right)\left(D_2^3 + D_2^2 D_1 + D_2 D_1^2 + D_1^3\right)}{b^3 h^3 G} \quad \text{... E(20-81)}$$

Belleville Springs (Also known as Disc Springs)

Belleville springs are made from tapered washers as shown in figure- 3.9. They may be arranged in series, parallel or a combination of parallel-series as shown in Fig. 3.10.

These springs find application where space limitation requires very high spring rate and compact spring units.

The relation between load 'F' on spring and the corresponding axial deflection 'y' is given by,

$$F = \frac{4Ey}{\left(1-\gamma^2\right) M d_o^2}\left[(h-y)\left(h-\frac{y}{2}\right)t + t^3\right] \quad \text{... E(20-19)}$$

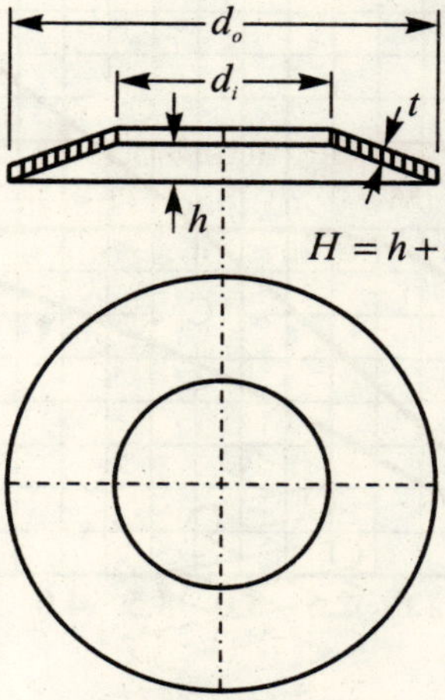

Figure: 3.9

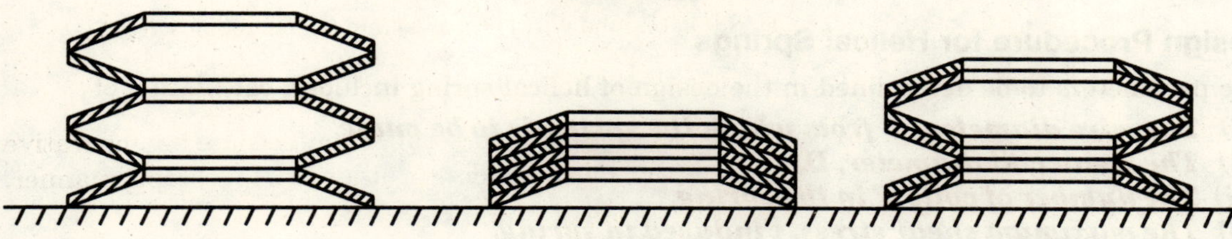

Figure: 3.10

Where, E = Young's modulus of material, N/mm^2
γ = Poisson's ratio
d_o = Outside diameter of disc, mm
d_i = Inside diameter of disc, mm
h = Height of disc or washer, mm
t = Thickness of disc, mm

M is a constant, it depends on $\frac{d_o}{d_i}$ ratio and obtained from figure (20-3 MDH).

The maximum stress induced at the inner edge is given by,

$$\sigma_i = \frac{8Ey}{(1-\gamma^2)d_o^2}\left[C_1\left(h-\frac{y}{2}\right)+C_2 t\right] \quad \text{... E(20-20)}$$

Similarly the maximum stress induced at the outer edge is given by,

$$\sigma_o = \frac{4Ey}{(1-\gamma^2)d_o^2}\left[C_1\left(h-\frac{y}{2}\right)+C_2 t\right] \quad \text{... E(20-21)}$$

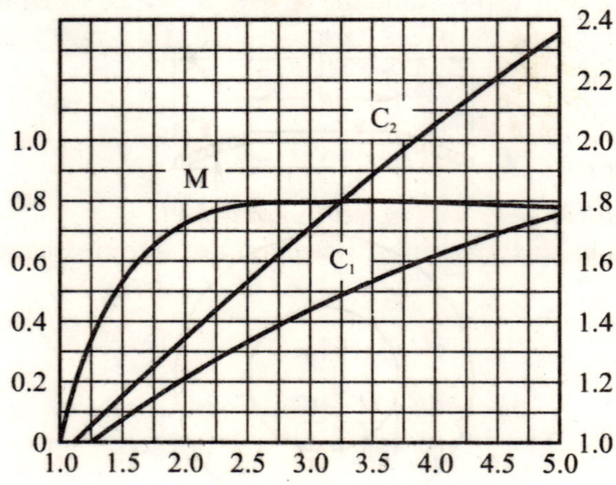

C_1, C_2 and M are obtained from *figure 20-3 MDH* based on $\frac{d_o}{d_i}$ ratio.

Design Procedure for Helical Springs

The parameters to be determined in the design of helical spring includes, calculation of

(i) The wire diameter, d from which the spring is to be made.
(ii) The mean coil diameter, D.
(iii) The number of coils 'i' in the spring.
(iv) The maximum shear stress, τ induced in spring.
(v) The load F the spring can sustain.
(vi) The deflection 'y', the spring undergoes due to load F.

(A) Calculation of wire diameter d and mean diameter of coil D.

The wire diameter '*d*' and coil diameter *D* are calculated by considering maximum shear stress induced in spring due to axial load *F* given by,

$$\tau = \frac{8FDk}{\pi d^3} \quad \text{... E(20-22)}$$

Where, τ = Maximum shear stress induced in spring.

k = Wahl's factor

$$= \frac{4c-1}{4c-4} + \frac{0.615}{c}$$

$$c = \text{Spring index} = \frac{D}{d}$$

Equation E(20-22) can be rewritten as,

$$\tau = \frac{8F}{\pi}\left(\frac{D}{d}\right)\frac{k}{d^2}$$

$$= \frac{8Fck}{\pi d^2}$$

Hence knowing, F, c and τ, the diameter of wire d can be calculated. Knowing 'd', mean diameter of coil 'D', inside diameter of coil D_i and outside diameter D_o are obtained.

Mean diameter of coil $D = cd$

Inside diameter of coil $D_i = D - d$

Outside diameter of coil $D_o = D + d$

(B) Calculation of number of coils 'i' used in spring.

The number of coils in spring and the deflection are obtained using equation,

Deflection, $$y = \frac{8FD^3 i}{Gd^4} \qquad \text{... E(20-29)}$$

$$= \frac{8F}{G}\left(\frac{D}{d}\right)^3 \frac{i}{d}$$

$$= \frac{8Fc^3 i}{Gd}; \qquad \text{Where, } c = \frac{D}{d}$$

Hence knowing load F, deflection y, spring index 'c' and G modulus of rigidity of material used for spring, the number of coils 'i' can be calculated. Few coils, called inactive coils are added to the value of 'i' calculated from the above equation depending on end condition of spring. For example, when the spring ends are squared and ground, two extra leaves are added to 'i'.

i.e., Total number of coils

$$i' = i + 2$$

To derive expressions for stress and deflections of helical spring

Consider a helical spring made of circular wire subjected to load 'F'.

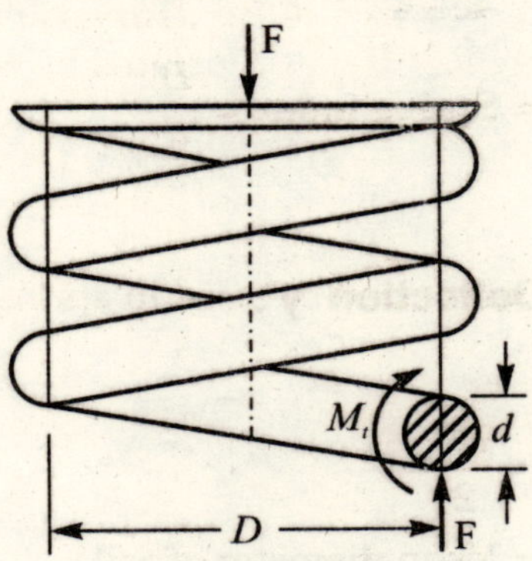

Figure: 3.11

Let, d = Diameter of wire

D = Mean diameter of coil

i = Number of coils in spring

Due to load 'F', the *torque induced* in the spring is,

Torque, $$M_t = F\frac{D}{2} \qquad \text{... (1)}$$

The resisting moment in wire is,

$$M_t = \frac{\pi d^3}{16}\tau \quad \text{... (2)}$$

Note: *Equation (2) is obtained from,*

Shear stress $\tau = \frac{M_t}{Z_t}$ where, $Z_t = \frac{J}{c} = \frac{\pi d^3}{16}$ for torsion.

i.e., $$\tau = \frac{M_t}{\frac{\pi d^3}{16}} = \frac{16 M_t}{\pi d^3} \text{ or } M_t = \frac{\pi d^3}{16}\tau$$

Equating (1) and (2), we get,

$$\frac{FD}{2} = \frac{\pi d^3}{16}\tau$$

Therefore, shear stress

$$\tau = \frac{FD}{2} \times \frac{16}{\pi d^3} = \frac{8FD}{\pi d^3} \quad \text{... (3)}$$

Equation (3) does not take into account the effect of curvature in spring. Considering, the effect of curvature, equation (3) is multiplied by a constant '*k*'.

Therefore shear stress, $$\tau = \frac{8FDk}{\pi d^3} \quad \text{... E(20-22)}$$

Where, k = Whal's factor given by,

$$= \frac{4c-1}{4c-4} + \frac{0.615}{c} \quad \text{... E(20-23)}$$

Where, c = Spring index $= \frac{D}{d}$

Note: *Usually c = 6 to 10.*

Derivation of Expression for Deflection 'y'.

The deflection of spring

$$y = \frac{D\theta}{2} \quad \text{... (4)}$$

Where, D = Mean diameter of coil.

θ = Angle of twist

From equation of torsion,

$$\frac{M_t}{J} = \frac{G\theta}{l} = \frac{\tau}{r},$$

We have, $$\frac{M_t}{J} = \frac{G\theta}{l}$$

or $$\theta = \frac{M_t l}{JG}$$

Where, $$M_t = \frac{FD}{2}$$

l = Length of wire = $i\ (\pi D)$ mm

i = Number of coils in spring

J = Polar moment of inertia = $\frac{\pi d^4}{32}$ mm^4

G = Modulus of rigidity, N/mm^2

Therefore, $$\theta = \frac{\frac{FD}{2} i(\pi D)}{\frac{\pi d^4}{32} G} = \frac{16 FD^2 i}{Gd^4}$$

Substituting the value of θ in equation (4),

Deflection, $$y = \frac{D\theta}{2} = \frac{D}{2}\left(\frac{16 FD^2 i}{Gd^4}\right)$$

i.e., $$y = \frac{8 FD^3 i}{Gd^4} \quad \text{... E(20-29)}$$

Laminated Spring (Locomotive spring or semi-elliptical spring)

A semi-elliptical spring used in automobile consist of a number of leaves (or plates) of equal width and uniform thickness held together by U-clips to sustain a central load 2F.

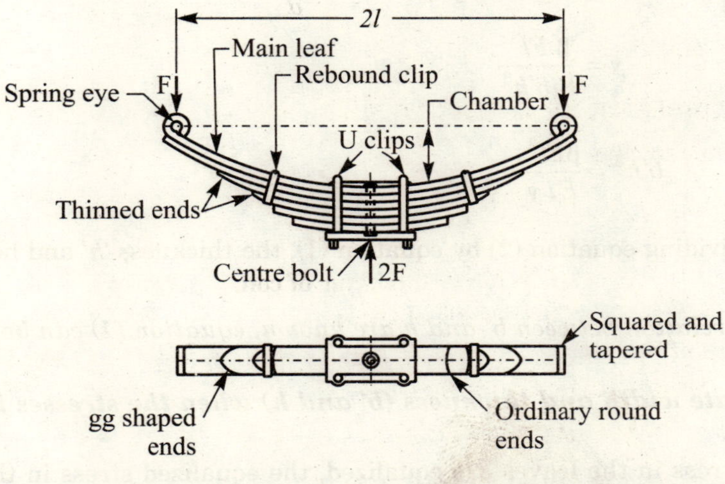

The leaf extending throughout the length of spring is called full length leaf or Master leaf. The ends of the full length leaves are bent to form an eye to support load. For higher capacities, additional full length leaves are added below the main leaf.

Graduated leaves are stacked below full length leaves. Rebound clips are used to hold the leaves together and also to transfer a portion of spring load to graduated leaves. Leaf springs are generally made of Vanadium steel or silicon manganese steel or hardened plain carbon steels.

Design Procedure for Laminated Springs

The design of Laminated springs used in automobile includes calculation of,

(i) ***The width and thickness of leaves (i.e., b′ and h) to sustain a central load 2F.***

(ii) ***The total number of leaves (i) which is the sum of graduated and full length leaves.***

(iii) ***The load shared by graduated leaves (F_g) and load shared by full length leaves (F_f).***

(iv) ***The deflection of spring (y).***

(v) ***The stresses induced in full length and graduated leaves (σ_f, σ_g) when the stresses in the leaves are not equalized.***

(vi) ***The equalized stress (σ) in the leaves when the stresses in the leaves are equalized.***

(A) ***To calculate the width and thickness of leaves (b′ and h) when the stresses are not equalized.***

Note: *When the stresses in the leaves are not equalized use equation E(20-14),*

i.e., The maximum stress in full length leaves given by,

$$\sigma_f = \frac{1.5\,\alpha Fl}{ib'h^2} \qquad \text{... E(20-14)}$$

And obtain

$$b'h^2 = \frac{1.5\,\alpha Fl}{i(\sigma_f)} \qquad \text{... (1)}$$

Use equation of deflection given by,

$$y = \frac{\beta\, Fl^3}{Eib'h^3} \qquad \text{... E(20-15)}$$

And obtain

$$b'h^3 = \frac{\beta Fl^3}{E\,i\,y} \qquad \text{... (2)}$$

Hence, by dividing equation (2) by equation (1), the thickness '*h*' and hence width b' can be computed.

Note: *When the relation between b′ and h are known, equation (1) can be used to calculate b′ and h.*

(B) ***To calculate width and thickness (b′ and h) when the stresses in the leaves are equalized.***

When the stress in the leaves are equalized, the equalized stress in the full length and graduated leaves is given by,

$$\sigma = \frac{\alpha Fl}{ib'h^2} \qquad \text{... E(20-18)}$$

i.e.,
$$b'h^2 = \frac{\alpha\, Fl}{i(\sigma)} \qquad \text{... (3)}$$

The equation of deflection is given by,

$$y = \frac{\beta Fl^3}{Eib'h^3} \qquad \text{... E(20-15)}$$

i.e.,
$$b'h^3 = \frac{\beta Fl^3}{E\,i\,y} \qquad \text{... (4)}$$

Dividing equation (4) by equation (3), thickness *'h'* and hence b' can be calculated.

(C) To calculate the loads shared by graduated leaves and full length leaves (F_g and F_f)

(i) The load shared by graduated leaves in spring is,

$$F_g = \frac{2(1-r)F}{2+r} \qquad \text{... E(20-11)}$$

Where,
$$r = \frac{i_f}{i}, \qquad i = i_f + i_g$$

$$F = \frac{\text{Central load } 2F}{2}$$

(ii) The load shared by full length leaves is given by

$$F_f = \left(\frac{3r}{2+r}\right)F \qquad \text{... E(20-12)}$$

Note:

1. ***The values of constant α, α′, β and β′ can be obtained from Table (20-7 MDH) shown below.***

Table (20-7) MDH

Constant	*Cantilever*	*Simply Supported*
α	$\frac{12}{2+r}$	$\frac{3}{2+r}$
β	$\frac{12}{2+r}$	$\frac{3}{4(2+r)}$
α′	6	1.5
β′	2	$\frac{1}{8}$

2. ***The value of width (b′)and thickness (h)obtained above are rounded off to the standard values using Table (20-4)***

Table (20-4) MDH

Width, mm		Thickness mm					
40.0	75.0	5.00	7.10	10.00	14.00	20.00	28.00
45.0	90.0	5.30	7.50	10.60	15.00	21.20	30.00
50.0	100.0	5.60	8.00	11.20	16.00	22.40	31.50
56.0	125.0	6.00	8.50	11.80	17.00	23.60	33.50
63.0	150.0	6.30	9.00	12.50	18.00	25.00	35.50
		6.70	9.50	13.20	19.00	25.50	37.50

To derive the relation between the stress in the full length leaves and the graduated leaves of a cantilever leaf spring, when the stresses in the leaves are not equalized.

A semi-elliptical leaf spring (or laminated leaf spring) used in an automobile with a central load '2F' can be considered to be equivalent to two cantilever springs subjected to point load 'F' at the end.

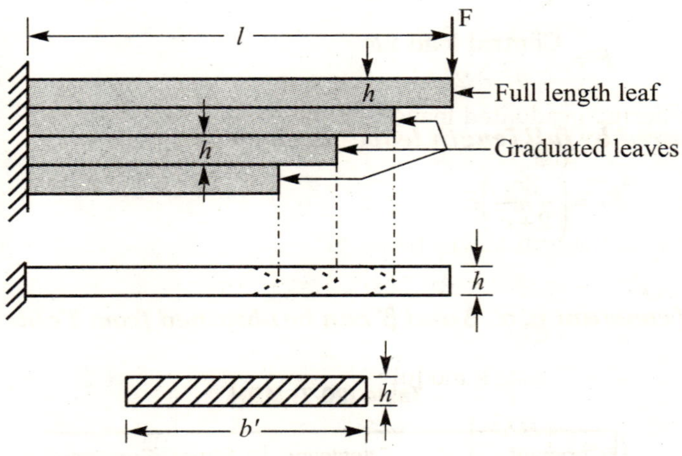

Cross-section of leaves

Note: *It is to be noted that all the leaves (plates) used in the spring have the same width b′ and thickness h.*

Let, i_f = Total number of full length leaves.

i_g = Total number of graduated leaves.

F_f = Load shared by full length leaves.

F_g = Load shared by graduated leaves.

The full length leaves may be considered as cantilever beams of constant depth and graduated leaves as constant strength beams.

Considering the bending stress induced in full length leaves, we have,

$$\sigma_b)_{\text{full length leaves}} = \sigma_f = \frac{M_b}{Z_b}$$

Where, $M_b = F_f l$

$$Z_b = \frac{I}{c}$$

$$I = \frac{b'h^3}{12}; \; c = \frac{h}{2}$$

$$Z_b = \frac{b'h^2}{6}$$

For total number of full length leaves i_f,

$$Z_b = i_f\left(\frac{b'h^2}{6}\right)$$

Therefore, $\sigma_f = \dfrac{F_f l}{i_f\left(\dfrac{b'h^2}{6}\right)}$

$$= \frac{6F_f l}{i_f b'h^2} \quad \text{... (1)}$$

Similarly, considering graduated leaves, the bending stress in graduated leaves is given by,

$$\sigma_g = \frac{6\,F_g l}{i_g b'h^2} \quad \text{... (2)}$$

The deflection in full length leaves (leaves of constant depth) is given by,

$$y_f = \frac{F_f l_f^3}{3\,EI_f} \quad \text{... (3)}$$

Where, E = Young's modulus of material of spring.

But, $I_f = i_f\left(\dfrac{b'h^3}{12}\right)$

Substituting the value of I_f in equation (3),

$$y_f = \frac{F_f l_f^3}{3E\left(i_f\dfrac{b'h^3}{12}\right)}$$

$$= \frac{4\,F_f l_f^3}{E i_f b'h^3} \quad \text{... (4)}$$

The deflection of graduated leaves is given by,

$$y_g = \frac{F_g l_g^3}{2\,EI_g} \qquad \text{... (5)}$$

Where, $$I_g = i_g\left(\frac{b'h^3}{12}\right)$$

Therefore, $$y_g = \frac{F_g l_g^3}{2E\left(i_g \frac{b'h^3}{12}\right)}$$

$$= \frac{6\,F_g l_g^3}{Ei_g b'h^3} \qquad \text{... (6)}$$

Note: *Since the full length leaves are in direct contact with the graduated leaves, both the springs undergo the same deflection.*

i.e., $$y_f = y_g$$

Also, $$l_f = l_g = l$$

Therefore, equating equations (4) and (6), we get,

$$\frac{4\,F_f l^3}{Ei_f b'h^3} = \frac{6\,F_g l^3}{Ei_g b'h^3}$$

Therefore, $$\frac{F_f}{F_g} = \frac{3}{2}\left(\frac{i_f}{i_g}\right) \qquad \text{... (7)}$$

Total load applied at the end of main leaf = Sum of load shared by full length leaves and graduated leaves.

i.e.,

$$F = F_f + F_g$$

$$F = F_f - F_g$$

Where, $$F_g = \frac{2\,i_g F_f}{3\,i_f}$$ from equation (7)

Therefore, $$F_f = F - \frac{2\,i_f F_f}{3\,i_f}$$

Rearranging terms,

$$F_f + \frac{2\,i_g F_f}{3\,i_f} = F$$

$$F_f\left(1 + \frac{2\,i_g}{3\,i_f}\right) = F$$

$$F_f\left(\frac{3\,i_f + 2\,i_g}{3\,i_f}\right) = F$$

i.e., $$F_f = \frac{3\,F\,i_f}{2\,i_g + 3\,i_f} \quad \text{... (8)}$$

Similarly from, $$F_f = F - F_g,$$

$$\frac{3\,Fi_f}{(2\,i_g + 3\,i_f)} = F - F_g$$

i.e., $$F_g = F - \left(\frac{3\,Fi_f}{2\,i_g + 3\,i_f}\right)$$

$$= F\left(1 - \frac{3\,i_f}{2\,i_g + 3\,i_f}\right)$$

$$= F\left(\frac{2\,i_g + 3\,i_f - 3\,i_f}{2\,i_g + 3\,i_f}\right)$$

$$= \frac{2\,Fi_g}{2\,i_g + 3\,i_f} \quad \text{... (9)}$$

Equations (8) and (9) give the load shared by full length and graduated leaves
From equation (1),

i.e., $$\sigma_f = \frac{6\,F_f l}{i_f b' h^2}$$, Substituting the values of F_f,

$$\sigma_f = \frac{6\,l}{i_f b' h^2}\left[\frac{3\,Fi_f}{2\,i_g + 3\,i_f}\right]$$

$$= \frac{18\,Fl}{b' h^2 (2\,i_g + 3\,i_f)} \quad \text{... (10)}$$

Similarly from equation (2),

$$\sigma_g = \frac{6\,F_g l}{i_g b' h^2}$$

$$= \frac{12\,Fl}{b' h^2 (2\,i_g + 3\,i_f)} \quad \text{... (11)}$$

On comparison of equations (10) and (11), we find that the stress in the full length leaves (σ_f) is 1.5 times the stress in the graduated leaves.

Or, in other words, the stress induced in full length leaves is 50% higher than the stress induced in graduated leaves.

Note: *When the stress in the leaves are equalized, the maximum equalized stress in leaves is given by,*

Maximum equalized stress,

$$\sigma = \frac{\alpha' Fl}{i b' h^2} \quad \text{... E(20-18)}$$

Where, $\alpha' = 6$ for cantilever.

i = Total number of leaves = $i_f + i_g$

Equalization of Stress in Spring Leaves

We have seen in the previous equations (10) and (11) that the stress in the full length leaves is 50% greater than that in the graduated leaves. In order to equalize the stresses in the full length and graduated leaves, the full length leaves are given greater radius of curvature [R_1] than that of graduated leaves [R_2]as shown in figure before they are assembled. This difference in radius of full length and graduated leaves results in an initial gap between full length and graduated leaves called *'Nip'*. When the leaves during assembly are tightened, the full leaf spring will have an initial stress opposite to that produced during service loading. The graduated leaves will experience the initial stress of same nature as that produced by normal loading. As a result, the resultant stress in full length leaves with gap will be lesser than that without gap.

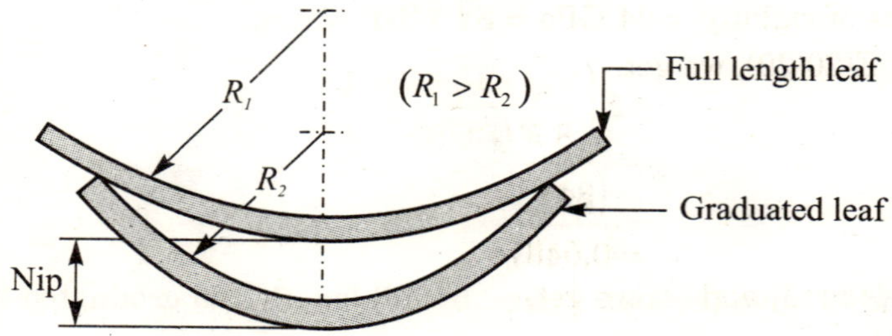

The maximum equalized stress in full length and graduated leaves is given by,

$$\sigma = \frac{\alpha' Fl}{ib'h^2} \qquad \text{... E(20-18)}$$

Where, Constant $\alpha' = 6$

i = Total number of leaves in spring.

$= i_g + i_f$

Example 3.1: A load of 1 kN is dropped axially on a close coiled helical compression spring from a height of 250 mm. The spring has 20 active turns made from 20 mm wire diameter and spring index 8. Determine the deflection and maximum shear stress induced in spring. Use G = 84 GPa.

Solution:

(i) To calculate deflection 'y' of spring.

Load dropped on spring = 1 kN = 1000 N

Total distance including the compression = (y + 250)

Therefore, Work done = 1000 (y + 250) ... (1)

$$\text{Energy stored in spring} = \frac{1}{2}Fy \qquad \text{... (2)}$$

Equating (1) and (2)

$$1000\,(y + 250) = \frac{Fy}{2}$$

i.e.,

$$y = \frac{50 \times 10^4}{(F - 2000)} \qquad \text{... (3)}$$

For helical spring, we have,

Deflection, $$y = \frac{8FD^3 i}{Gd^4}$$ ... E(20-29)

$$= \frac{8F}{G}\left(\frac{D}{d}\right)^3\left(\frac{i}{d}\right)$$

Where, Spring index $= \frac{D}{d} = 8$

i = Number of active turns = 20

d = Wire diameter = 20 mm

G = Modulus of rigidity = 84 GPa = 84×10^3 N/mm²

Substituting in E(20-29), we get,

$$y = \frac{8F(8)^3 20}{(84\times10^3)(20)^4}$$

$$= 0.04876 \text{ F}$$ ... (4)

Equating equations (3) and (4) we get,

$$\frac{50\times10^4}{(F-2000)} = 0.04876F$$

Therefore, F = 3251.37 N

From equation (4), the deflection is

$$y = 0.04876 \text{ F}$$
$$= 0.04876 \; 5 \; 3251.37$$
$$= 158.54 \text{ mm}$$

(ii) To calculate the shear stress 't' induced in spring.

For coiled spring, the shear stress induced is given by,

$$\tau = \frac{8FDk}{\pi d^3} = \frac{8F}{\pi d^2}\left(\frac{D}{d}\right)k$$ ... E(20-22)

Where, F = 3251.37 N; d = 20 mm

$$c = \frac{D}{d} = 8$$

$$k = \frac{4c-1}{4c-4} + \frac{0.615}{c}$$

$$= \frac{4\times8-1}{4\times8-4} + \frac{0.615}{8}$$

$$= 1.184$$

Therefore, $$\tau = \frac{8\times3251.37\times8\times1.184}{\pi\times20^2}$$

$$= 196.06 \text{ N/mm}^2$$

Example 3.2: At the bottom of an elevator shaft, a group of 8 identical springs are set in parallel to absorb the shock of the elevator in case of failure. The elevator weighs 3000 N. Assuming the elevator has a free fall of 1200 mm from rest, determine the maximum stress in each spring if spring is made from 25 mm diameter rod. The spring index is 6 and the number of active turns in each spring is 15. Take G = 80 GPa.

Solution:

(i) To calculate the axial load 'F' on each spring

Weight of elevator = 3000 N.

Number of springs sharing the load = 8.

Therefore, load on each spring $= \frac{3000}{8} = 375$ N

The distance through which load travels (including compression) = $(y + 1200)$

Energy absorbed by each spring $= 375\ (y + 1200)$ ... (1)

Work done $= \frac{1}{2} Fy$ ... (2)

Equating (1) and (2),

$$375\ (y + 1200) = \frac{1}{2} Fy$$

Therefore, $y = \frac{45 \times 10^4}{0.5\ F - 375}$ ... (3)

Now, deflection of coil spring,

$$y = \frac{8\ FD^3 i}{Gd^4} \quad \text{... E(20-29)}$$

$$= \frac{8F}{G} \left(\frac{D}{d}\right)^3 \left(\frac{i}{d}\right)$$

Where, $\frac{D}{d} = c = 6$; $i = 15$, $d = 25$ mm, $G = 80 \times 10^3$ MPa

Therefore, $y = \frac{8\ F\ (6)^3\ 15}{(80 \times 10^3) 25}$

$y = 0.01296$ F ... (4)

Equating (3) and (4)

$$0.1296\ F = \frac{45 \times 10^4}{0.5F - 375}$$

Therefore, $F = 8716.77$ N

(ii) To calculate the shear stress 'τ' induced in each spring.

We have shear stress $\tau = \frac{8FDk}{\pi d^3}$ ... E(20-22)

$$= \frac{8F}{\pi}\left(\frac{D}{d}\right)\frac{k}{d^2}$$

Where, $F = 8716.77$ N

$$k = \text{Wahl's factor} = \frac{4c-1}{4c-4} + \frac{0.615}{c}$$

$$= \frac{4\times6-1}{4\times6-4} + \frac{0.615}{6}$$

$$= 1.2525$$

d = Wire diameter = 25 mm

Substituting the values in equation E(20-22), we get

$$\tau = \frac{8\times8716.77\times6\times1.2525}{\pi(25)^2}$$

$$= 266.9 \text{ N/mm}^2$$

Therefore, shear stress induced in each spring = 266.9 N/mm²

Example 3.3: Design a helical tension spring for a spring loaded safety valve (Rams bottom safety value) to meet the following requirements.

Diameter of valve seat = 70 mm.

Operating pressure (when the valve begins to lift) = 0.70 N/mm²

Maximum pressure (when the valve blows off freely) = 0.75 N/mm²

Lift of valve during change of pressure = 4 mm.

Modulus of rigidity, G = 84 GPa.

Spring Index, c = 6. ***(VTU, July 2007)***

Solution:

Load on the valve when it begins to lift

$$= \frac{\pi}{4}(d_p)^2\, p_1$$

$$= \frac{\pi}{4}(70)^2\times0.7$$

$$= 2693.92 \text{ N}$$

Load on the valve when it blows off freely

$$= \frac{\pi}{4}(d_p)^2\, p_2$$

$$= \frac{\pi}{4}(70)^2\times0.75$$

$$= 2886.34 \text{ N}$$

Therefore, the load F causing deflection

$$= 2693.92 - 2886.34$$

$$= -192.42 \text{ N}$$

(a) To calculate the coil dimensions.

Maximum torque to be resisted by spring is given by,

$$M_t = F_{\max} \frac{D}{2}$$

Where, $F_{\max} = 2886.34$ N

D = Mean diameter of coil = $6d$ (given)

Therefore, $$M_t = 2886.34 \times \frac{6d}{2}$$

$$= 8659\, d$$

But, $$M_t = \frac{\pi d^3}{16} \tau$$

$$8659\, d = \frac{\pi d^3}{16} \times 560$$

$d = 8.9$ mm; Use $d = 9$ mm

Therefore, Mean diameter of coil $D = 6d = 6 \times 9 = 54$ mm

(b) The number of coils 'i' is obtained using deflection equation,

Deflection, $$y = \frac{8\, FD^3 i}{Gd^4} \quad \text{... E(20-29)}$$

Where, F = Axial load on spring = 192.42 N

$\frac{D}{d} = c$ = Spring index = 6

$G = 84$ GPa $= 84 \times 10^3$ MPa

$d = 9$ mm

Therefore, $$y = \frac{8 \times 192.42 \times (6)^3 i}{(84 \times 10^3) 9} = 4 \text{ mm (given)}$$

Therefore, $i = 9.09$; Use $i = 10$ Coils

Example 3.4: A spring loaded safety valve for a boiler is required to blow off at a pressure of 1.5 N/mm². The diameter of valve is 60 mm. Using spring index = 6, initial compression of 25mm, maximum lift of valve = 150 mm, permissible shear stress = 450 MPa, G = 0.84 × 10⁵ MPa, design a suitable compression spring.

Solution:

Load on valve when it just begins to lift

$$= \frac{\pi}{4} (D_i)^2\, p_f$$

$$= \frac{\pi}{4} (60)^2 \times 1.5$$

$$= 4241.2 \text{ N}$$

Note: *The valve is kept tight in its seat against a steam load of 4241.2 N by providing initial compression of 25 mm.*

Therefore, Stiffness of spring $= \dfrac{4241.2}{25} = 169.62$ N/mm

Lift of valve = 15 mm.

Therefore, maximum compression of spring = 25 + 15 = 40 mm

Maximum load on valve when it is fully open

$$= 169.65 \times 40$$

$$= 6786 \text{ N}$$

(i) To calculate coil dimensions

Maximum torque to be resisted by spring is

$$M_t = F_{max} r_m$$

$$= F_{max} \times \frac{D}{2}$$

Where, $F_{max} = 9789$ N

D = Mean diameter of coil = $6d$

Therefore, $M_t = 6789 \times \dfrac{6d}{2}$

$$= 20367d \text{ N-mm}$$

But, $M_t = \dfrac{\pi d^3}{16}\tau$

i.e., $20367d = \dfrac{\pi d^3}{16} \times 450$

$d = 15.18$ mm, Use $d = 16$ mm

Therefore, mean diameter of coil $D = 6d = 6 \times 16 = 96$ mm

(ii) To calculate the number of coils 'i' in spring.

We have deflection of spring given by,

$$y = \frac{8\,FD^3 i}{Gd^4} \quad \text{... E(20-29)}$$

i.e., $i = \dfrac{yGd^4}{8\,FD^3}$

$$i = \left(\frac{y}{F}\right)\left(\frac{G}{8}\right)\left(\frac{d}{D}\right)^3 d$$

Where, $\dfrac{F}{y} = 169.65$ N/mm

$G = 0.84 \times 10^5$ N/mm²

$\dfrac{d}{D} = \dfrac{1}{c} = \dfrac{1}{6}$

d = Wire diameter = 16 mm

Therefore, $$i = \left(\frac{1}{169.65}\right)\left(\frac{0.84\times10^5}{8}\right)\left(\frac{1}{6}\right)^3 \times 16$$

$$= 4.59$$

Use, $i = 5$ Coils

Assuming squared and ground ends for coil, the total number of coils

$$i' = i + 2 = 5 + 2 = 7 \text{ Coils}$$

Example 3.5: Design a close coil helical spring for an engine using the following data,

Length of spring when the valve is open	***= 40 mm.***
Length of spring when the valve is closed	***= 50 mm.***
Load on the spring when the valve is open	***= 400 N.***
Load on the spring when the valve is closed	***= 200 N.***
Maximum inside diameter of spring	***= 28 mm.***
Maximum shear stress in spring	***= 400 MPa.***
Modulus of rigidity for spring material	***= 80 GPa.***

Solution:

(i) To calculate the axial load 'F' on spring

Load on spring when the valve is open = 400 N.

Load on spring when the valve is closed = 200 N.

Therefore, Load F causing deflection = 400 – 200

$$F = 200 \text{ N}$$

Length of spring when valve is open = 40 mm.

Length of spring when the valve is closed = 50 mm.

Therefore, deflection of spring = 50 mm – 40 mm

$$y = 10 \text{ mm}$$

(ii) To calculate the dimensions of coil

Maximum torque resisted by spring is

$$M_t = F_{max} r_{mean}$$

$$= F_{max} \times \frac{D}{2}$$

Where, $F_{max} = 400$ N

D = Mean diameter of coil.

$= D_i + d$

$= 28 + d$

Therefore, $$M_t = 400\left(\frac{28+d}{2}\right)$$

$$= 200\,(28 + d) \quad \ldots (1)$$

But, $$M_t = \frac{\pi d^3}{16}\tau \quad \ldots (2)$$

Equating (1) and (2),

$$200(28+d) = \frac{\pi d^3}{16}\tau$$

$$200(28+d)=\frac{\pi d^3}{16}\times 400$$

$$d = 4.5 \text{ mm}$$

Therefore, mean diameter of coil $D = 28 + d = 32.5$ mm

Outside diameter of coil, $D + d = 32.5 + 4.5 = 37$ mm

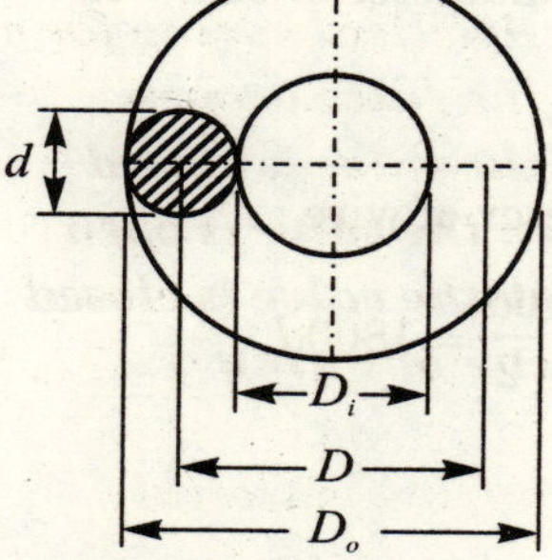

(iii) To calculate the number of coils (turns)

We have deflection of helical spring given by,

$$y = \frac{8\,FD^3 i}{Gd^4} \quad \text{... E(20-29)}$$

Where, $F = 200$ N, $D = 32.5$ mm $d = 4.5$ mm

$G = 80$ GPa $= 80 \times 10^3$ MPa, $y = 10$ mm

Therefore,
$$10 = \frac{8\times 200\times (32.5)^3\, i}{(85\times 10^3)(4.5)^4}$$

$i = 5.97$, Use $i = 6$ Coils (turns)

Assuming squared and ground ends, the total number of coils in spring is

$$i' = i + 2$$
$$= 6 + 2 = 8 \text{ Coils}$$

Example 3.6: The spring used in an automobile engine has to exert 500 N when the valve is closed and 600 N when the valve is open. The displacement of the valve is 5 mm. The engine crank shaft rotates at 800 rpm. Design the spring if permissible stress in the material of the spring is 300 MPa. The ratio of mean coil diameter to wire diameter is 6. The modulus of rigidity of the spring material is 8 × 10⁴ MPa. The ends of the spring are squared and ground. ***(VTU, July 2006)***

Solution:

(i) To calculate the axial load 'F' on spring

The load on the spring when the valve is closed = 500N.

The load on the spring when the valve is open = 600N.

Therefore, the load causing deflection of = 600 N – 500 N

$F = 100$ N

(ii) To calculate the dimensions of coils

Maximum torque the spring has to overcome is

$$M_t = F_{max} r_{mean}$$

$$= F_{max} \times \frac{D}{2}$$

Where, $F_{max} = 600$ N

D = Mean diameter of coil = $6d$

i.e., Spring index, $c = \frac{D}{d} = 6$

d = Diameter of wire

Therefore, $M_t = 600 \times \frac{6d}{2} = 1800d$

But, $M_t = \frac{\pi d^3}{16} \tau_s$

i.e., $1800d = \frac{\pi d^3}{16} \times 300$

i.e., $d = 5.53$ mm

Use $d = 6$ mm, hence mean diameter of coil

$D = 6d$

$= 6 \times 6 = 36$ mm

$D_i = D - d = 36 - 6 = 30$ mm

$D_o = D + d = 36 + 6 = 42$ mm

(iii) To calculate the number of coils 'i' in spring

The deflection of coiled spring (helical spring) is given by,

$$y = \frac{8\,FD^3 i}{Gd^4} \quad \text{... E(20-29)}$$

Where, y = Deflection = 5 mm

F = Axial load on spring = 100 N

$G = 8 \times 10^4$ MPa

Substituting in E(20-29), we get

$$5 = \frac{8 \times 100 \times (36)^3 i}{(8 \times 10^4)(6)^4}$$

Therefore, $i = 13.89$ Use $i = 14$ coils

Since the ends of spring are squared and ground, the total number of coils

$i' = i + 2$

$= 14 + 2 = 16$ Coils

Example 3.7: Design a helical compression spring for a maximum load of 1000 N for a deflection of 25 mm. The maximum permissible shear stress for the spring wire is 420 N/mm^2. Modulus of rigidity is 0.84 × 10^5 N/mm^2 and spring index 6.

(VTU, Dec 07 / Jan 08)

Solution:

(i) To find wire diameter (d) and coil diameter (D)

The shear stress in helical spring is given by,

Shear stress $$\tau = \frac{8\,FDk}{\pi d^3}$$

$$= \frac{8\,F}{\pi}\left(\frac{D}{d}\right)\frac{1}{d^2}k$$

Where, F = Axial load on spring = 1000 N

$$c = \frac{D}{d} = \text{Spring index} = 6$$

k = Wahl's factor

$$= \frac{4c-1}{4c-4} + \frac{0.615}{c}$$

$$= \frac{4\times6-1}{4\times6-4} + \frac{0.615}{6} = 1.2525$$

τ = Shear stress = 420 N/mm^2

Therefore, substituting the values in the equation of τ,

$$420 = \frac{8\times1000}{\pi}(6)\frac{1}{d^2}\times1.2525$$

d = 6.75 mm

Hence mean coil diameter $D = 6d = 6 \times 6.75 = 40.5$ mm

(ii) To find the number of coils (i)

For helical spring, deflection 'y' is given by,

$$y = \frac{8\,FD^3i}{Gd^4}$$

$$= \frac{8\,F}{G}\left(\frac{D}{d}\right)^3\left(\frac{1}{d}\right)i$$

$$25 = \frac{8\times1000}{0.84\times10^5}(6)^3\times\frac{1}{6.75}\times i$$

Therefore, $i = 8.203$

Say, $i = 9$ coils

Assuming squared and ground ends, the total number of coils is

$i' + 2 = 9 + 2 = 11$ coils

Example 3.8: Two helical springs are nested one inside the other to support a load of 500 N. Both springs are made of same material with G = 82.7 × 10³ MPa. The particulars of springs are tabulated below

Particulars	Outer Spring	Inner Spring
D	40 mm	28 mm
d	5 mm	4 mm
i	10	8
Free length	90 mm	78 mm

Determine,
(i) Deflection of each spring.
(ii) Load carried by each spring and
(iii) Shear stress induced in each spring.

Solution:

(i) To calculate the deflection of outer and inner springs [y_o and y_i] and loads carried by outer and inner springs [F_o and F_i].

Let y_o and y_i be the deflections of outer and inner springs.

$$y_i = (y_o - 12), \text{ from figure.}$$

For the outer spring, deflection y_o is given by,

$$y_o = \frac{8 F_o D_o^3 i_o}{G d_o^4}$$

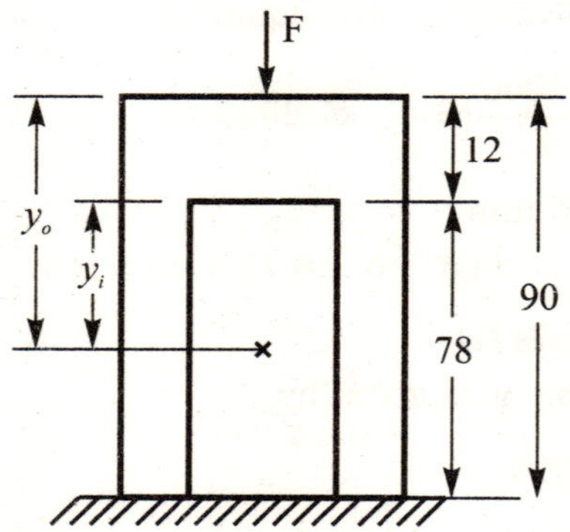

Where, D_o = Medium diameter of outer spring = 40 mm

i_o = Number of active coils in outer spring = 10

G = 8.27 × 10³ N/mm²

d_o = Wire diameter of outer spring = 5 mm

Therefore,
$$y_o = \frac{8F_0 (40)^3 10}{(8.27\times10^3)(5)^4}$$

Therefore, $F_o = 10.0952\, y_o$ ... (1)

Similarly, for the inner spring the deflection y_i is given by,

$$y_i = \frac{8\,F_i D_i^3 i_i}{G d_i^4}$$

$$(y_o - 12) = \frac{8\,F_i\,(28)^3\,8}{\left(82.7\times10^3\right)(4)^4}$$

Therefore, $F_i = 15.07\,(y_o - 12)$ ... (2)

Total load, $F = F_i + F_o = 500$ ... (3)

Substituting the value of F_i and F_o in (3), we get

$15.07\,(y_o - 12) + 10.0952\,y_o = 500$

Therefore, $y_o = 82.51$ mm

i.e., $F_i = 15.07\,(y_o - 12)\;y_i = 82.51 - 12 = 70.51$ mm

For equation (1)

$F_o = 10.0952\,y_o = 10.0952 \times 13.51 = 136.39$ N

$F_i = 15.07\,(y_o - 12)$

$= 500 - 136.39 = 363.61$ N

(ii) To calculate the shear stress induced in springs (τ_i and τ_o)

For the outer spring,

$$\tau_o = \frac{8F_o D_o k_o}{\pi d_o^3}$$

$$= \frac{8\times136.39\times40\times1.184}{\pi\times5^3} = 131.59\ \text{N/mm}^2$$

Where, $k_o = \dfrac{4c-1}{4c-4} + \dfrac{0.615}{c}$; $\quad c = \dfrac{D_o}{d_o} = \dfrac{40}{5} = 8$

$$= \frac{4\times8-1}{4\times8-4} + \frac{0.615}{8} = 1.184$$

For the inner spring,

$$\tau_i = \frac{8\,F_i D_i k_i}{\pi d_i^3}$$

$$= \frac{8\times363.61\times28\times1.213}{\pi\times4^3} = 491.38\ \text{N/mm}^2$$

Where, $k_i = \dfrac{4c-1}{4c-4} + \dfrac{0.615}{c}$; $\quad c = \dfrac{D_i}{d_i} = \dfrac{28}{4} = 7$

$$= \frac{4\times7-1}{4\times7-4} + \frac{0.615}{7} = 1.213$$

Example 3.9: A helical spring is set inside the other, the outer spring having a free length 45 mm greater than the inner spring. The particulars of springs are tabulated below

Particulars	Outer Spring	Inner Spring
Mean coil diameter D	100 mm	75 mm
Wire diameter, d	12 mm	12 mm
Number of coils, i	20	15

Using G = 8 × 10³ MPa, determine the combined spring rate of the two spring after sufficient load has been applied to deflect the outer spring by 75 mm.

Solution:

Let F_o and F_i be the loads required to deflect the outer and inner springs and let y_o and y_i be the corresponding deflection of outer and inner springs.

$$Spring\ rate = \frac{Load}{Deflection}$$

$$Spring\ rate\ of\ outer\ spring = \frac{F_o}{y_o}$$

$$Spring\ rate\ of\ inner\ spring = \frac{F_i}{y_i}$$

Therefore, $$Combined\ spring\ rate = \frac{F_o}{y_o} + \frac{F_i}{y_i} \quad \ldots (1)$$

Here, $y_o = 75$ mm (given)

$y_i = y_o - 45 = 75 - 45 = 30$ mm

(Because free length of outer spring is 45mm greater than inner spring).

To calculate F_o and F_i

We have deflection,

$$y = \frac{8\ FD^3 i}{Gd^4}$$

For outer spring,

$$y_o = \frac{8F_o D_o^3 i_o}{Gd_o^4}$$

Substituting the values,

$$75 = \frac{8F_o (100)^3 \times 20}{(80 \times 10^3)(12)^4}$$

Therefore, $F_o = 777.6$ N

For the inner spring,

$$y_i = \frac{8\ F_i D_i^3 i_i}{Gd_i^4}$$

i.e., $$30 = \frac{8\,F_i\,(75)^3 \times 15}{\left(80\times10^3\right)(12)^4}$$

Therefore, $F_i = 983.04$ N

Substituting the values of F_o, F_i, y_o and y_i in equation (1),

Combined spring rate,

$$= \frac{777.6}{75} + \frac{983.04}{30}$$

$$= 43.136 \text{ N/mm}$$

Example 3.10: One helical spring is set inside the other; the particulars of springs are tabulated as shown

Particulars	Outer Spring	Inner Spring
D	100 mm	80 mm
d	15 mm	12 mm
i	20	15
Free length	75 mm	75 mm

Using G = 8 × 10³ MPa, determine

(i) Load carried by the inner and outer springs taking y_o = 40 mm.

(ii) Shear stress induced in the outer and inner springs.

(iii) Combined spring rate.

Solution:

(i) To calculate the load carried by inner and outer spring [F_o and F_i]

Both the springs have the same free length and hence they undergo the same deflection (compression) due to load F. *i.e.,* $y_o = y_i$

Deflection of outer spring is

$$y_o = \frac{8F_oD_o^3i_o}{Gd_o^4} \qquad \ldots (1)$$

Where, y_o = 40 mm, D_o = 100 mm d_o = 15 mm

G = 80 × 10³ MPa, i_o = 20 turns,

Substituting the values in the equation of deflection,

$$40 = \frac{8F_o\,(100)^3\,20}{\left(80\times10^3\right)(15)^4}$$

Therefore, $F_o = 1012.5$ N

i.e., Load carried by outer spring = 1012.5 N.

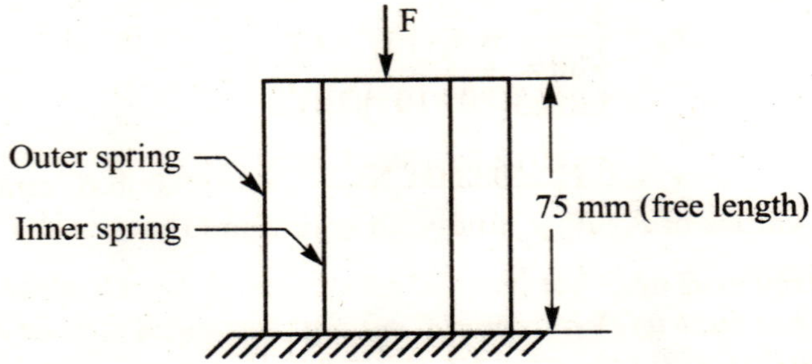

Deflection of inner spring,

$$y_i = \frac{8F_iD_i^3i_i}{Gd_i^4}$$

Where, $y_i = y_o = 40$ mm (data)

$D_i = 80$ mm, $i_i = 15$, $G = 80 \times 10^3$ MPa $d_i = 12$ mm

Therefore, $$40 = \frac{8\,F_i\,(80)^3\,15}{\left(80\times10^3\right)(12)^4}$$

Therefore, $F_i = 1080$ N

i.e. load carried by inner spring = 1080 N.

(ii) To calculate the combined spring rate.

Combined spring rate $= \frac{F_o}{y_o} + \frac{F_i}{y_i}$

$$= \frac{1012.5}{40} + \frac{1080}{40}$$

$= 52.31$ N/mm

(iii) To calculate the shear stress induced in the outer and inner springs Shear stress induced in inner spring is given by,

$$\tau_i = \frac{8F_iD_ik_i}{\pi d_i^3}$$

Where, $$k_i = \frac{4c-1}{4c-4} + \frac{0.615}{c}; \qquad c = \frac{D_i}{d_i} = \frac{80}{12} = 6.67$$

$$= \frac{4\times6.67-1}{4\times6.67-4} + \frac{0.615}{6.67} = 1.2245$$

Therefore, $$\tau_i = \frac{8\times1080\times80\times1.2245}{\pi(12)^3} = 155.91\ \text{N/mm}^2$$

Shear stress induced in outer spring is given by,

$$\tau_o = \frac{8F_oD_ok_o}{\pi d_o^3},$$

Where, $$k_o = \frac{4c-1}{4c-4} + \frac{0.615}{c}; \quad c = \frac{100}{15} = 6.67$$
$$= 1.2245$$

Therefore, $$\tau_o = \frac{8 \times 1012.5 \times 100 \times 1.2245}{\pi (15)^3} = 93.545 \text{ N/mm}^2$$

Example 3.11: The free end of a horizontal constant strength steel cantilever beam is directly over and in contact with a vertical coil spring as shown in figure. The width of beam at the fixed end is 400 mm and its length is 800 mm. The thickness of beam is 15 mm. The coil spring has 10 coils of 15mm diameter. The coil has an outside diameters of 100 mm. Taking G = 79.3 GPa, E = 206.8 GPa, determine,

(i) What force 'Q' if gradually applied to the end of cantilever beam is required to cause a deflection of 30mm.

(ii) What is the bending stress in the beam at a section 400 mm from the fixed point.

(iii) How much of energy is absorbed by coil spring.

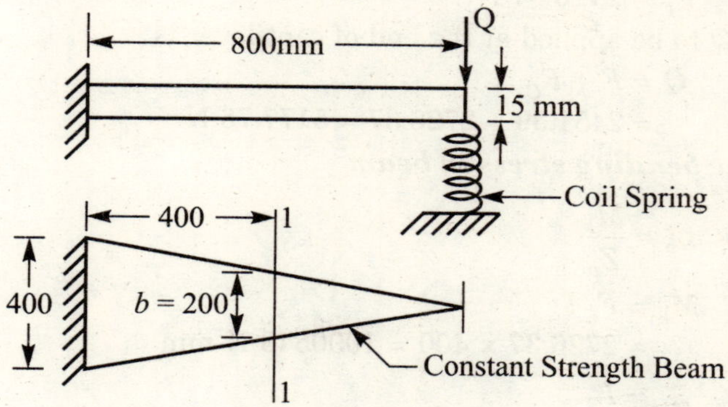

Solution:

(i) To calculate load 'Q' required to deflect the spring by 30 mm.

Since the springs are in contact, they undergo the same deflection.

Therefore, $y_{\text{coil spring}} = y_{\text{cantilever spring}} = 30$ mm (given)

For the coil spring (Helical spring),

$$y_{\text{coil spring}} = \frac{8FD^3 i}{Gd^4} \quad \text{... (1)}$$

Where, $y_{\text{coil spring}} = 30$ mm

D = Mean diameter of coil = $D_o - d = 100 - 15 = 85$ mm

i = Number of active coils = 10

$G = 79.3$ GPa $= 79.3 \times 10^3$ MPa

d = Wire diameter = 15 mm

Substituting the values in equation (1)

$$30 = \frac{8F \times (85)^3 \times 10}{(79.3 \times 10^3)(15)^4}$$

Therefore, $F = 2451.39$ N

Considering constant strength beam, deflection of constant strength beam (*i.e.*, cantilever beam),

$$y_{\text{cantilever}} = \frac{c_2 F_C l^3}{E b h^3} \quad \text{... E(20.2)}$$

Where, $c_2 = 6$, $y_{\text{cantilever}} = 30$ mm

l = Length of cantilever = 800 mm

$E = 206.8 \times 10^3$ N/mm²

b = Maximum width of beam at the fixed end = 400 mm

h = Thickness of beam = 15 mm

Therefore, substituting the values in E(20.2)

$$30 = \frac{6\, F_C\, (800)^3}{(206.8 \times 10^3)(400)(15)^3}$$

Therefore, $F_C = 2726.37$ N

Therefore, Load Q to be applied at the end of cantilever is

$$Q = F + F_C$$

$$= 2451.39 + 2726.37 = 5177.76 \text{ N}$$

(ii) To calculate the bending stress in beam

Bending stress $\sigma_b = \dfrac{M_b}{Z_b}$

Where, $M_b = F_C\, l$

$$= 2726.37 \times 400 = 1090548 \text{ N-mm}$$

$$Z_b = \frac{I}{C}$$

Where, $I = \dfrac{bh^3}{12} = \dfrac{200(15)^3}{12} = 56250 \text{ mm}^4$

$$C = \frac{h}{2} = \frac{15}{2} = 7.5 \text{ mm}$$

Therefore $Z_b = \dfrac{56250}{7.5} = 7500 \text{ mm}^3$

$$\sigma_b = \frac{1090548}{7500} = 145.41 \text{ N/mm}^2$$

(iii) To calculate the energy absorbed by the coil spring

Energy absorbed by the coil spring

$$= \frac{1}{2} Fy$$

$$= \frac{1}{2} \times 2451.39 \times 30$$

$$= 36770.85 \text{ N-mm}$$

Example 3.12: A railway wagon weighing 50 kN moving with a speed of 8km / hour has to be stopped by four buffer springs in which the maximum compression allowed is 220 mm. Find the number of active turns in each spring of mean diameter 150 mm. The diameter of spring wire is 25 mm. Also determine the maximum shear stress in each spring. Take G = 84 GPa. ***(VTU, Dec 06 / Jan 07)***

Solution:

(i) To calculate the maximum axial load (F) on spring.

Kinetic energy of wagon $= \frac{1}{2}mv^2$

$= \frac{1}{2}\left(\frac{w}{g}\right)v^2$

Where, $w = 50 \text{ kN} = 50 \times 10^3 \text{ N}$

$g = 9.81 \text{ m/sec}^2$

$v = 8 \text{ km/hr} = \frac{8\times10^3}{60\times60} \text{ m/sec} = 2.22 \text{ m/sec}$

Therefore, Kinetic energy

$= \frac{1}{2}\left(\frac{50\times10^3}{9.81}\right)(2.22)^2$

$= 12559.633 \text{ N-m}$

$= 12559.633 \times 10^3 \text{ N-mm}$

Given, number of springs $= 4$.

Therefore, energy absorbed by each spring

$= \frac{12559.633\times10^3}{4}$

$= 3140 \times 10^3 \text{ N-mm}$

Work done $= \frac{1}{2}Fy$

Where, F = Axial load on spring, N

y = Deflection of spring = 220 mm

Therefore, work done $= \frac{1}{2}Fy$

$= \frac{1}{2}F\times220 = 110\,F$

Equating energy absorbed to work done,

$3140 \times 10^3 = 110\,F$

Therefore, F, the axial load on each spring = 28545.5N

(ii) To calculate the number of active coils (turns) (i)

We have deflection,

$$y = \frac{8\,FD^3 i}{Gd^4} \quad \text{... E(20-29)}$$

Where, y = Deflection = 220 mm

F = 28545.5 N

D = Mean Diameter of Coil = 150 mm

G = 84 GPa = 84 × 10^3 MPa

d = wire diameter = 25 mm

Therefore, from equation of deflection, E(20-29),

$$220 = \frac{8\times28545.5\times(150)^3 i}{(84\times10^3)\times(25)^4}$$

$$i = 9.366$$

Use i = 10 turns (or coils)

Assuming squared and ground ends, total number of coils 'i' = 10 + 2 = 12 coils.

(iii) To determine the maximum shear stress (τ) in each spring

For a helical spring, the maximum shear stress is given by,

$$\tau = \frac{8FDk}{\pi d^3}$$

Where, F = 28545.5 N

D = 150 mm; d = 25 mm

k = Wahl's factor

$$= \frac{4c-1}{4c-4} + \frac{0.615}{c}$$

Where, $c = \frac{D}{d} = \frac{150}{25} = 6$

Therefore, $k = \frac{4\times6-1}{4\times6-4} + \frac{0.615}{6} = 1.2525$

$$\tau = \frac{8\times28545.5\times150\times1.2525}{\pi(25)^3} = 874 \text{ N/mm}^2$$

Example 3.13: A railway wagon weighing 40 kN and moving with a speed of 10 km/hour has to be stopped by four buffer springs in which the maximum compression allowed is 200 mm. Find the number of turns in each spring of mean diameter 150 mm. The diameter of spring wire is 25 mm. Take G = 82.7 × 10^3 MPa.

(VTU, June / July 08)

Solution:

(i) To calculate the maximum axial load (F) on spring.

Kinetic energy of wagon $= \frac{1}{2}mv^2$

$$= \frac{1}{2}\left(\frac{w}{g}\right)v^2$$

Where, w = 40 kN = 40 × 10^3 N

$$g = 9.81 \text{ m/sec}^2$$

$$v = 10 \text{ m/hr} = \frac{10\times10^3}{60\times60} \text{ m/sec} = 2.778 \text{ m/sec}$$

Therefore, Kinetic energy

$$= \frac{1}{2}\left(\frac{40\times10^3}{9.81}\right)(2.778)^2$$

$$= 15733.5 \text{ N-mm}$$

$$= 15733.5 \times 10^3 \text{ N-mm}$$

Given number of springs = 4.

Therefore, energy absorbed by each spring

$$= \frac{15733.5\times10^3}{4}$$

$$= 3933375 \text{ N-mm}$$

Work done $= \frac{1}{2}Fy$

$$= \frac{1}{2}F \times 200 = 100\,F$$

Equating energy absorbed to work done,

$$3933375 = 100\,F$$

Therefore, F, the axial load on each spring = 39333.75 N

(ii) To calculate the number of active coils (turns) (i)

We have deflection,

$$y = \frac{8\,FD^3 i}{Gd^4} \qquad \text{... E(20-29)}$$

Where,
y = Deflection = 200 mm
F = 39333.75 N
D = Mean diameter of coil = 150 mm
$G = 82.7 \times 10^3$ MPa
d = Wire diameter = 25 mm

Therefore, from equation of deflection

$$200 = \frac{8\times39333.75\times(150)^3\,i}{\left(82.7\times10^3\right)\times(25)^4}$$

$$i = 6.08 \text{ turns}$$

Use $i = 7$ Coils

Assuming squared and ground ends, the total number of coils in spring is

$$i' = i + 2 = 7 + 2 = 9 \text{ coils}$$

Example 3.14: A loaded narrow gauge car weighing 15 kN and moving at a velocity of 1 m/sec is brought to rest by a buffer consisting of 2 Helical steel springs of square section. The mean diameter of coil is 6 times the side of square section. In bringing the car to rest, the springs are to be compressed 100 mm. Taking the shear stress for the material of spring = 350 MPa, determine,

(i) Load on each spring.

(ii) Side of square section and Mean coil diameter.

(iii) Number of active coils. Use G = 82.7 GPa.

Solution:

(i) To calculate the load on each spring (F)

Kinetic energy of car $= \frac{1}{2}mv^2$

$$= \frac{1}{2}\left(\frac{w}{g}\right)v^2$$

Where, $w = 15 \text{ kN} = 15 \times 10^3 \text{ N}$

$g = 9.81 \text{ m/sec}^2$

$v = 1 \text{ m/sec}$

Therefore, kinetic energy

$$= \frac{1}{2}\left(\frac{15\times10^3}{9.81}\right)(1)^2$$

$= 764.53$ N-m

$= 764.53 \times 10^3$ N-mm

Given, number of springs = 2.

Therefore, energy absorbed by each spring

$$= \frac{764.53\times10^3}{2}$$

$= 382.265 \times 10^3$ N-mm

Work done $= \frac{1}{2}Fy$

Where, F = Axial load on spring.

y = Maximum deflection = Compression of spring = 100 mm

Therefore, work done $= \frac{1}{2}Fy$

$$= \frac{1}{2}F\times100 = 50\,F$$

Equating energy absorbed to work done,

$50F = 382.265 \times 10^3$

Therefore, $F = 7645.3$ N

(ii) To calculate the side of square section and mean diameter of coil.

For helical springs of square section, we have

Shear stress, $$\tau = \frac{2.4\, kFD}{h^3} \quad \text{... E(20-43)}$$

Where, $\tau = 350$ MPa

$F = 7645.3$ N

$$k = \frac{4c-1}{4c-4} + \frac{0.615}{c}$$

$$c = \frac{D}{d} = 6 \text{ (given)}$$

Therefore, $$k = \frac{4\times6-1}{4\times6-4} + \frac{0.615}{6} = 1.2525$$

$D = 6h$ (given)

Therefore, substituting in equation E(20-43),

$$350 = \frac{2.4\times1.2525\times7645.3\times6h}{h^3}$$

Therefore, $h = 19.85$ mm

Use $h = 20$ mm = Side of square section

Hence, mean diameter of coil $D = 6h = 6 \times 20 = 120$ mm

(iii) To calculate the number of coils (i)

We have for square section, deflection 'y' is given by,

$$y = \frac{5.66\, i\, FD^3}{h^4 G} \quad \text{... E(20-44)}$$

i.e., $$100 = \frac{5.66\times i\times7645.3\times(120)^3}{(20)^4\times\left(82.7\times10^3\right)}$$

Therefore, $i = 17.69 \approx 18$ coils

Example 3.15: A loaded wagon weighing 15 kN and moving at a velocity of 1 m/sec is to be brought to rest by a buffer consisting of 2 Helical springs of rectangular section with depth = twice width. The mean diameter of coil is 6 times the shorter side of rectangle. In bringing the car to rest, the springs are to be compressed to 100 mm. Using shear stress τ = 350 MPa, determine,

(i) The load on each spring.

(ii) Dimensions of cross-section of each spring and mean diameter of coil.

(iii) The number of coils in each spring. Use G = 82.7 GPa.

Solution:

(i) To calculate the load on each spring (F)

Kinetic energy of wagon $= \frac{1}{2}mv^2$

$$= \frac{1}{2}\left(\frac{w}{g}\right)v^2$$

Where, $w = 15 \text{ kN} = 15 \times 10^3 \text{ N}$

$g = 9.81 \text{ m/sec}^2$

$v = 1 \text{ m/sec}$

Therefore, kinetic energy of wagon

$$= \frac{1}{2}\left(\frac{15\times10^3}{9.81}\right)(1)^2$$

$$= 764.53 \text{ N-m}$$

$$= 764.53 \times 10^3 \text{ N-mm}$$

Number of springs sharing kinetic energy = 2.

Therefore, energy absorbed by each spring

$$= \frac{764.53\times10^3}{2}$$

$$= 382.265 \times 10^3 \text{ N-mm}$$

Work done $= \frac{1}{2}Fy$

Where, F = Maximum axial load on each spring

y = Deflection = 100 mm

Therefore, work done $= \frac{1}{2}F\times100 = 50\ F$

Equating work done to energy absorbed by spring,

$$50\ F = 382.265 \times 10^3$$

Therefore, $F = 7645.3 \text{ N}$

(ii) To calculate the dimensions of cross-section and mean diameter of coil.

For rectangular section helical springs, we have,

Shear stress $$\tau' = \frac{kFD(1.5h+0.9b)}{b^2h^2} \quad \text{... E(25-34a)}$$

Where, $\tau' = 350 \text{ MPa}$

$$k = \frac{4c-1}{4c-4}+\frac{0.615}{c}$$

$$c = \frac{D}{b} = 6 \text{ (given)};\ \text{Therefore } D = 6b$$

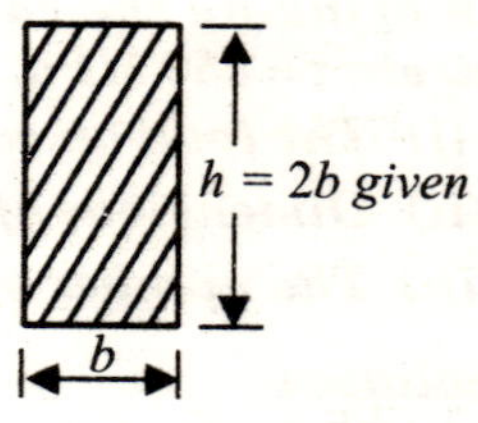

Therefore, $$k = \frac{4\times6-1}{4\times6-4}+\frac{0.615}{6} = 1.2525$$

Therefore, substituting in E(25-34a),

$$350 = \frac{1.2525\times7645.3\times(6b)[1.5\times2b+0.9b]}{b^2(2b)^2}$$

Therefore, $b = 12.65 \text{ mm}$

Depth $h = 2b = 2 \times 12.65 = 25.3$ mm

Mean diameter of coil $D = 6b = 75.9$ mm

(iii) To calculate the number of coils (i)

For rectangular section spring, the deflection 'y' is given by,

$$y = \frac{2.83\, iFD^3 \left(b^2 + h^2\right)}{b^3 h^3 G} \quad \text{... E(20-39)}$$

i.e.,

$$100 = \frac{2.83 \times i \times 7645.3 \times (75.9)^3 \left[12.65^2 + 25.3^2\right]}{(12.65)^3 (25.3)^3 \times 82.7 \times 10^3}$$

Therefore, $i = 36$ coils

Example 3.16: Design a helical compression spring to sustain an axial load that fluctuates between 1.5 kN and 2 kN with an associated deflection of 15mm during fluctuation of load.

Solution:

For fluctuating axial load, the Soderberg's equation is

$$\frac{\tau_a}{\tau_{-1d}} + \frac{\tau_m}{\tau_{yd}} = 1 \quad \text{... E(20-62)}$$

To calculate τ_a, the shear stress amplitude

$$\tau_a = k_w \left(\frac{8D}{\pi d^3}\right)\left(\frac{F_{max} - F_{min}}{2}\right) \quad \text{... E(20-58)}$$

Where, $k_W = k_\tau k_C$

$$k_\tau = 1 + \frac{0.5}{C} \quad \text{... (Given below equation 20-59MDH)}$$

Assuming $\frac{D}{d} = c = 6,$

$$k_\tau = 1 + \frac{0.5}{6} = 1.083$$

For k_C, refer Table (20-15)MDH; k_C is curvature factor.

For, $c = 6$, $k_C = 1.15$

Therefore, $k_w = 1.083 \times 1.15 = 1.2455$

Equation (20-58) may be rewritten as

$$\tau_a = k_w \left(\frac{8}{\pi d^2} \times \frac{D}{d}\right)\left(\frac{F_{max} - F_{min}}{2}\right) \quad \text{... E(20-58)}$$

Where, $\frac{D}{d} = c = 6$ (assumed)

F_{max} = Maximum load on spring = 2 kN = 2000 N

F_{min} = Minimum load on spring = 1.5 kN = 1500 N

Therefore, $$\tau_a = 1.2455\left(\frac{8}{\pi d^2}\times 6\right)\left(\frac{2000-1500}{2}\right)$$

$$\tau_a = \frac{4757.5}{d^2}$$

To calculate τ_m, the mean shear stress

$$\tau_m = k_\tau\left(\frac{8D}{\pi d^3}\right)\left(\frac{F_{max}+F_{min}}{2}\right) \quad \text{... E(20-59)}$$

$$= k_\tau\left(\frac{8}{\pi d^2}\times\frac{D}{d}\right)\left(\frac{F_{max}+F_{min}}{2}\right)$$

$$= 1.083\left(\frac{8}{\pi d^2}\times 6\right)\left(\frac{2000+1500}{2}\right)$$

$$\tau_m = \frac{28957.29}{d^2}$$

To calculate τ_{-1d}, the design endurance shear stress

$$\tau_{-1d} = \frac{\tau_{-1}}{n_{-1d}}$$

Assuming high carbon wire for material of spring (Table 20-10) MDH

$$\sigma_u = 1103 \text{ MPa}$$

Taking, $\tau_{-1} = 0.25\sigma_u$,

$$\tau_{-1} = 0.25 \times 1103 = 275.75 \text{ N/mm}^2$$

Assuming factor of safety = 3,

$$\tau_{-1d} = \frac{275.75}{3} = 91.92 \text{ MPa}$$

To calculate τ_{yd}, the design yield shear stress

$$\tau_{yd} = \frac{\tau_y}{f.o.s}$$

Assuming $\tau_y = 0.6\sigma_y$ in torsion and using

$$\sigma_y = 0.6\ \sigma_u,$$

$$\sigma_y = 0.6 \times 1103 = 661.8 \text{ MPa}$$

Therefore, $\tau_y = 0.6 \times 6618 = 397.1$ MPa

$$\tau_{yd} = \frac{397.1}{3} = 132.36 \text{ MPa}$$

Substituting the values in Soderberg's equation,

$$\frac{\frac{4757.5}{d^2}}{91.92} + \frac{\frac{28957.29}{d^2}}{132.36} = 1$$

i.e., $$\frac{4757.5}{91.92d^2} + \frac{28957.29}{132.36d^2} = 1$$

d = 16.45 mm Use d = 17 mm

Hence, wire diameter d = 17 mm, and mean coil diameter $D = 6d$ = 102 mm

Example 3.17: A helical spring is subjected to axial load varying from 500 N to 900 N. Taking spring index = 6, yield shear stress = 750 MPa, torsional fatigue strength = 350 MPa. Determine the wire diameter and coil diameter based on a factor of safety = 1.5.

Solution:

For fluctuating torsional loads, the Soderberg's equation is

$$\frac{\tau_a}{\tau_{-1d}} + \frac{\tau_m}{\tau_{yd}} = 1 \quad \text{... E(20-62)}$$

To find τ_a, the shear stress amplitude

$$\tau_a = k_w\left(\frac{8D}{\pi d^3}\right)\left(\frac{F_{max} - F_{min}}{2}\right) \quad \text{... E(20-58)}$$

Where, $k_w = k_\tau k_C$ Refer Table (20-7) MDH for k_C

For, $c = 6$, $k_C = 1.15$

$$k_\tau = 1 + \frac{0.5}{c} = 1 + \frac{0.5}{6} = 1.083$$

Therefore, $k_w = 1.083 \times 1.15 = 1.24545$

F_{max} = Maximum load on spring = 900 N

F_{min} = Minimum load on spring = 500 N

Equation (20-58) may be rewritten as

$$\tau_a = k_w\left(\frac{8}{\pi d^2} \times \frac{D}{d}\right)\left(\frac{F_{max} - F_{min}}{2}\right)$$

$$= 1.24545\left[\frac{8}{\pi d^2} \times 6\left(\frac{900 - 500}{2}\right)\right]$$

$$\tau_a = \frac{3805.8}{d^2}$$

To calculate τ_m, the mean shear stress

$$\tau_m = k_\tau\left(\frac{8D}{\pi d^3}\right)\left(\frac{F_{max} + F_{min}}{2}\right) \quad \text{... E(20-59)}$$

$$= k_\tau\left(\frac{8}{\pi d^2} \times \frac{D}{d}\right)\left(\frac{F_{max} + F_{min}}{2}\right)$$

$$= 1.24545\left(\frac{8}{\pi d^2} \times 6\right)\left(\frac{900 + 500}{2}\right)$$

$$\tau_m = \frac{13320.35}{d^2}$$

To calculate τ_{-1d}, the design endurance shear stress

$$\tau_{-1d} = \frac{\tau_{-1}}{factor\ of\ safety}$$

$$= \frac{350}{1.5} = 233.33\ \text{N/mm}^2$$

To calculate τ_{yd}, the design yield shear stress

$$\tau_{yd} = \frac{\tau_y}{factor\ of\ safety}$$

$$= \frac{750}{1.5} = 500\ \text{N/mm}^2$$

Substituting the values in E(20-62), we get

$$\frac{\frac{3805.8}{d^2}}{233.33} + \frac{\frac{13320.35}{d^2}}{500} = 1$$

i.e., $$\frac{3805.5}{233.33\,d^2} + \frac{13320.35}{500\,d^2} = 1$$

i.e., $d = 6.6$ mm

Hence, Mean diameter of coil

$$D = 6d$$
$$= 6 \times 6.6 = 39.6\ \text{mm}$$

Note: *Outside diameter of coil*

$$D_o = D + d$$
$$= 39.6 + 6.6 = 46.2\ \text{mm}$$

Inside diameter of coil

$$D_i = D - d$$
$$= 39.6 - 6.6 = 33\ \text{mm}$$

Example 3.18: A helical spring is subjected to a load varying from 1 kN to 2 kN. Determine the wire diameter and mean coil diameter taking,

Spring index = 6.
Ultimate stress = 1000 MPa.
Yield stress = 700 MPa.
Factor of safety = 3.

Solution:
The shear stress induced in the spring due to varying axial load is obtained from Soderberg's equation given by,

$$\frac{\tau_a}{\tau_{-1d}} + \frac{\tau_m}{\tau_{yd}} \qquad \text{... E(5-64)}$$

Where, τ_a = Shear stress amplitude

$$= \frac{8F_a Dk}{\pi d^3} \qquad \text{... E(20-22)}$$

Where, F_a = Load amplitude = $\dfrac{F_{max} - F_{min}}{2}$

$$F_{max} = 2 \text{ kN} = 2000 \text{ N}$$

$$F_{min} = 1 \text{ kN} = 1000 \text{ N}$$

Therefore, $F_a = \dfrac{2000 - 1000}{2} = 500 \text{ N}$

$\tau_a = \dfrac{8\, F_a D k}{\pi d^3}$ may be rewritten as,

$$\tau_a = \frac{8F_a}{\pi}\left(\frac{D}{d}\right)\frac{1}{d^2}k$$

Where, $\dfrac{D}{d}$ = Spring index = 6(given)

$$k = \text{Wahl's factor} = \frac{4c-1}{4c-4} + \frac{0.615}{c}$$

$$= \frac{4\times 6-1}{4\times 6-4} + \frac{0.615}{6} = 1.2525$$

Therefore, $\tau_a = \dfrac{8\times 500}{\pi}(6)\dfrac{1}{d^2}\times 1.2525$

$$= \frac{9568.4}{d^2}$$

τ_m = Mean shear stress = $\dfrac{8\, F_m D k}{\pi d^3}$

Where, F_m = Mean load = $\dfrac{F_{max} + F_{min}}{2}$

$$= \frac{2000 + 1000}{2} = 1500 \text{ N}$$

$\tau_m = \dfrac{8\, F_m}{\pi d^3}(D)k$; rewritten as

$$= \frac{8F_m}{\pi}\left(\frac{D}{d}\right)\frac{1}{d^2}k,$$

$$= \frac{8\times 1500}{\pi}(6)\frac{1}{d^2}\times 1.2525$$

Therefore, $\tau_m = \dfrac{28705.2}{d^2}$

$$\tau_{-1d} = \frac{\tau_{-1}}{n_{-1d}}$$

Where, $\tau_{-1} = 25\%\sigma_u$

$$= 0.25 \times 1000 = 250 \text{ MPa}$$

$$n_{-1d} = k_{sz}\, k_{sr}\, k_l\, n_{-1a}$$

Where, $k_{sz} = 0.85$

$$k_{sr} = \frac{1}{e_{sr}} \quad \text{... E(5-7)}$$

$$k_l = 0.6$$

$$n_{-1a} = 3$$

Therefore, $n_{-1d} = 0.85 \times \dfrac{1}{e_{sr}} \times 0.6 \times 3$

For torsion, $e'_{sr} = 0.425 + 0.575 e_{sr}$ ... E(5-8)

Referring to figure (5-3MDH), for $\sigma_u = 1000$ MPa,

$$e'_{sr} = 0.86$$

Therefore, $0.86 = 0.425 + 0.575 e_{sr}$

Therefore, $e_{sr} = 0.7565$

Therefore, $n_{-1d} = 0.85 \times \dfrac{1}{0.7565} \times 0.6 \times 3 = 2.0225$

Therefore, $\tau_{-1d} = \dfrac{250}{2.0225} = 123.61 \text{ N/mm}^2$

Finally, $\tau_{yd} = \dfrac{\tau_y}{n_{yd}}$

$$\tau_y = 0.6\sigma_y = 0.6 \times 700 = 420 \text{ MPa}$$

$$n_{yd} = k_{sz} k_{\sigma a} n_{ya} = 0.85 \times 1 \times 3 = 2.55$$

Therefore, $\tau_{yd} = \dfrac{450}{2.55} = 164.71$ MPa

Therefore substituting in Soderberg's equation, we get

$$\frac{\dfrac{9568.4}{d^2}}{123.61} + \frac{\dfrac{28705.2}{d^2}}{164.71} = 1$$

Therefore, $d = 15.86$ mm ; Adopt $d = 16$ mm

Wire diameter $D = 6d$

$$= 6 \times 16 = 96 \text{ mm}$$

Example 3.19: A helical spring made from round wire with squared and ground ends is impacted by an axial load of 5 kN falling through a distance of 250 mm. The spring undergoes a deflection of 200 mm. Using spring index 6, $G = 0.85 \times 10^5$ N/mm^2, shear stress = 4000 MPa, determine

(i) The maximum load on spring.
(ii) The wire diameter, coil diameter.
(iii) The number of coils in spring.

Solution:

(i) To find the maximum load on spring (F)

Note: *The potential energy of falling weight is absorbed by the spring.*

Potential energy (PE) of falling weight is given by

$$PE = w(h+y)$$

Where, w = Weight = 5 kN = 5000 N

h = Height of fall = 250 mm

y = Deflection of spring = 200 mm

Therefore, $PE = 5000(250+200)$ N-mm

Energy absorbed by spring = Work done $= \frac{1}{2}Fy$

$$= \frac{1}{2}F \times 200 = 100F$$

Equating PE and work done

$$5000(450) = 100F$$

Therefore, $F = 22500$ N

Therefore, the maximum load on spring

$$F = 22500 \text{ N} = 22.5 \text{ kN}$$

(ii) To find the wire diameter, d

We have shear stress

$$\tau = \frac{8FDk}{\pi d^3}$$

$$= \frac{8F}{\pi}\left(\frac{D}{d}\right)\left(\frac{1}{d^2}\right)k$$

Where, $\frac{D}{d}$ = Spring index = 6 = c

$$k = \text{Whal's factor} = \frac{4c-1}{4c-4} + \frac{0.615}{c}$$

$$= \frac{4\times6-1}{4\times6-4} + \frac{0.615}{6} = 1.2525$$

Therefore, substituting we get,

$$4000 = \frac{8 \times 22500}{\pi}(6)\frac{1}{d^2} \times 1.2525$$

i.e., $d = 10.375$ mm ; Adopt $d = 11$ mm

From, Spring index $c = \frac{D}{d} = 6,$

Mean coil diameter

$$D = 6d$$
$$= 6 \times 11 = 66 \text{ mm}$$

(iii) To find the number of coils (i)

We have,

Deflection $y = \frac{8FD^3 i}{Gd^4}$

$$= \frac{8F}{G}\left(\frac{D}{d}\right)^3\left(\frac{1}{d}\right)i$$

Where, $y = 200$ mm, $F = 22500$ N, $\frac{D}{d} = c = 6,$ $d = 11$ mm

Substituting in the equation of shear stress we get,

$$200 = \frac{8 \times 22500}{0.85 \times 10^5}(6)^3\left(\frac{1}{11}\right)i$$

Therefore, $i = 4.8096$; say $i = 5$ coils

Adding 2 coils for squared and ground ends, the total number of coils in spring

$$i' = i + 2$$
$$= 5 + 2 = 7 \text{ coils}$$

(iv) Static Loading

When the spring is loaded statically, load $F = 5 \text{ kN} = 5000 \text{ N}$

(a) To find wire and coil diameter.

Shear stress $\tau = \frac{8\,FDk}{\pi d^3}$

$$= \frac{8F}{\pi}\left(\frac{D}{d}\right)\left(\frac{1}{d^2}\right)k$$

Where, $F = 5000$ N, $\frac{D}{d} = 6,$ $k = 1.2525$ for $c = 6$

Therefore, $4000 = \frac{8 \times 5000}{\pi}(6)\left(\frac{1}{d^2}\right)1.2525$

i.e., $d = 4.89$ mm; Adopt $d = 5$ mm

Now, Mean diameter of coil

$$D = 6d$$
$$= 6 \times 5 = 30 \text{ mm}$$

(b) To find the number of coils (i)

We have,

Deflection $$y = \frac{8\,FD^3 i}{Gd^4}$$

$$y = \frac{8F}{G}\left(\frac{D}{d}\right)^3\left(\frac{i}{d}\right)$$

i.e., $$200 = \frac{8\times 5000}{0.85\times 10^5}(6)^3\left(\frac{i}{5}\right)$$

Therefore, number of coils $i = 9.84$ coils; Say $i = 10$ coils

Adding 2 coils for squared and ground ends of spring,

Total number of coils, $i' = i + 2$

$$= 10 + 2 = 12 \text{ coils}$$

Example 3.20: A semi elliptical spring is 1 meter long and is to support a load of 50 kN. The spring has 15 leaves out of which 3 are full length leaves. The width of central band is 100 mm. All the leaves are to be stressed to 400 MPa. The ratio of total depth to width of plates is 3. Taking E = 210 GPa, determine,

(i) The width and thickness of leaves.

(ii) The initial gap that should be provided between full length and graduated leaves before assembly.

(iii) The load exerted on the band after assembly.

Solution:

(i) To calculate the width and thickness of leaves.

Note: *The stresses in the leaves are equalized.*

The maximum equalized stress in leaves is given by,

$$\sigma = \frac{\alpha' Fl}{ib'h^2} \qquad \text{... E(20-18)}$$

Where, $\sigma =$ Equalized stress in leaves = 400 MPa

α', a constant = 6 for cantilever beam ... T(20-7)

Table - 20-7 MDH

Constant	*Cantilever*	*Simply Supported*
α	$\frac{12}{2+r}$	$\frac{3}{2+r}$
β	$\frac{12}{2+r}$	$\frac{3}{4(2+r)}$
α'	6	1.5
β'	2	$\frac{1}{8}$

$$2F = \text{Central load} = 50\text{ kN} = 50\times10^3\text{N}$$

Therefore, $F = 25\times10^3$ N

$$l = \textit{Effective length of leaf} = \frac{\textit{Total length} - \textit{Bandwidth}}{2}$$

$$= \frac{1000-100}{2}$$

$$= 450\text{ mm}$$

i = Total number of leaves in spring = 15

Given, $$\frac{\text{Total depth of leaves}}{\text{Width}} = 3$$

i.e., $$\frac{15h}{b'} = 3 \textit{ i.e.}, b' = 5h$$

Table - 20-4 MDH

Width, mm		*Thickness mm*					
40.0	75.0	5.00	7.10	10.00	14.00	20.00	28.00
45.0	90.0	5.30	7.50	10.60	15.00	21.20	30.00
50.0	100.0	5.60	8.00	11.20	16.00	22.40	31.50
56.0	125.0	6.00	8.50	11.80	17.00	23.60	33.50
63.0	150.0	6.30	9.00	12.50	18.00	25.00	35.50
		6.70	9.50	13.20	19.00	25.50	37.50

Where, h = Thickness of leaves.

b' = Width of leaves.

Substituting the values in E(20-18),

$$400 = \frac{6\left(25\times10^3\right)450}{15(5h)(h)^2}$$

h = 13.1 mm; Adopt h = 13.2 mm ... T(20-4)

Therefore, $b' = 5h = 66$ mm

(ii) To calculate the initial gap (Nip) between leaves before assembly.

The initial gap between full length leaves and graduated leaves is given by,

$$\text{Nip} = \frac{\beta' F l^3}{E i b' h^3} \quad \text{... E(20-16)}$$

Where, β' = Constant = 2 ... T(20-7)

$$E = 210 \times 10^3 \text{ MPa}$$

Therefore, substituting the values in E(20-16).

$$\text{Nip} = \frac{2\left(25 \times 10^3\right)(450)^3}{\left(210 \times 10^3\right)15 \times 66(13.2)^3}$$

$$= 9.5286 \text{ mm}$$

(iii) To calculate the load exerted on band [i.e., F$_b$]

Load exerted on band,

$$F_b = \frac{2i_g\, i_f\, F}{i\left(3i_f + 2i_g\right)}$$

Where, $i_f = 3, \quad i_g = 12$

$$i = i_g + i_f$$

$$= 12 + 3 = 15$$

Therefore, $F_b = \dfrac{2 \times 12 \times 3\left(25 \times 10^3\right)}{15(3 \times 3 + 2 \times 12)} = 3636.36 \text{ N}$

Example 3.21: A semi elliptical laminated spring made of 9 leaves is 1.1 m long between the centres of eye. Two of the leaves extend to the full length of spring. The leaves are held together by a band 80 mm wide. If the spring is to carry a load of 5.4 kN and the permissible stress is 400 MPa, determine the width and thickness of leaves when

(i) Leaves are not stressed initially.

(ii) Leaves are stressed initially. Use E = 210 GPa.

Solution:

Case (i) To calculate the width and thickness when the leaves are not stressed initially.

Note: *When the leaves are not stressed initially, the maximum stress occurs in full length leaves given by*

$$\sigma_f = \frac{1.5\alpha F\, l}{ib'h^2} \qquad \text{... E(20-14)}$$

Where, σ_f = Stress in full length leaves = 400 MPa

$$\alpha = \text{a constant} = \frac{12}{2 + r} \qquad \text{... T(20-7)}$$

Where, $r = \dfrac{i'}{i}$

i' = Number of full length leaves = 2 = i_f

i = Total number of leaves = 9

Therefore, $r = \dfrac{2}{9}$

$$\alpha = \frac{12}{2+r} = \frac{12}{2+\frac{2}{9}} = 5.4$$

Central load, $2F = 5.4 \text{ kN} = 5.4 \times 10^3 \text{ N}$

$$F = 2.7 \times 10^3 \text{ N}$$

Effective length $l = \frac{\text{Total length} - \text{Band width}}{2}$

$$= \frac{1100 - 80}{2} = 510 \text{ mm}$$

Substituting in E(20-14)

$$400 = \frac{1.5(5.4)(2.7 \times 10^3) \times 510}{9(b'h^2)}$$

Therefore, $b'h^2 = 3098.25$ ... (1)

Deflection $y = \frac{\beta F l^3}{E i b' h^3}$ ... E(20-15)

Where, $y =$ Deflection $= 70$ mm

$$\beta = \text{a constant} = \frac{12}{2+r} = \frac{12}{2+\frac{2}{9}} = 5.4$$

$F = 2.7 \times 10^3$ N; $l = 510$ mm

$E = 210 \text{ GPa} = 210 \times 10^3 \text{ MPa}$

Substituting in E(20-15),

$$70 = \frac{5.4(2.7 \times 10^3)(510)^3}{(210 \times 10^3) 9 \times b'h^3}$$

Therefore, $b'h^3 = 14618.68$ ... (2)

Dividing equation (2) by equation (1) yields,

$$\frac{b'h^3}{b'h^2} = \frac{14618.68}{3098.25}$$

$h = 4.72$ mm Say $h = 5$ mm ... T(20-4)

From equation(1),

$$b'h^2 = 3098.25$$

i.e., $b' = \frac{3098.25}{5^2} = 123.93$ mm Adopt $b' = 125$ mm ... T(20-4)

Case (ii) When the leaves are prestressed initially

Maximum equalized stress is given by,

$$\sigma = \frac{\alpha' F l}{i b' h^2} \quad \text{... E(20-18)}$$

For a cantilever $\alpha' = 6$ ... T(20-3)

Stress $\sigma = 400$ MPa

Therefore, substituting in E(20-18),

$$400 = \frac{6 \times 2.7 \times 10^3 \times 510}{9 b' h^2}$$

Therefore, $b'h^2 = 2295$ ... (3)

Also deflection

$$y = \frac{\beta F l^3}{E i b' h^3} \quad \text{... (20-15)}$$

$$70 = \frac{5.4\left(2.7 \times 10^3\right) 510^3}{\left(210 \times 10^3\right) \times 9 \times b' h^3}$$

Therefore, $b'h^3 = 14618.68$ ... (4)

Dividing equation (4) by equation (3)

$$\frac{b'h^3}{b'h^2} = \frac{14618.68}{2295}$$

i.e., $h = 6.37$ Use $h = 6.7$ mm ... T(20-4)

Hence from equation (3),

$$b'h^2 = 2295$$

$$b' = \frac{2295}{h^2}$$

$$= \frac{2295}{(6.7)^2}$$

$$b' = 51.12 \text{ mm}$$

Adopt, $h = 6.7$ mm

$b' = 56$ mm ... T(20-4)

Example 3.22: A locomotive spring has an overall length of 1100 mm and sustains a load of 75 kN at its centre. The spring has 3 full length leaves and 15 graduated leaves with a central band of 100 mm. All the leaves are to be stressed at 0.4 GPa when fully loaded. The ratio of total depth of spring to its width is to be 2. Determine,

(i) The width and thickness of leaves.

(ii) The initial gap between full length and graduated leaves. Use E = 206.8 GPa.

(VTU, Dec 06 / Jan 07)

Solution:

(i) To calculate the width and thickness of leaves

Note: *The stresses in the leaves are equalized.*

The maximum equalized stress in leaves is given by,

$$\sigma = \frac{\alpha' F l}{i b' h^2} \quad \text{... E(20-18)}$$

Where, $\sigma =$ Equalized stress in leaves $= 0.4$ GPa $= 0.4 \times 10^3$ MPa $= 400$ MPa

α', a constant $= 6$ for cantilever beam ... T(20-7)

$2F =$ Central load $= 75$ kN $= 75 \times 10^3$ N

Therefore, $$F = \frac{75 \times 10^3}{2} = 37.5 \times 10^3 \text{ N}$$

Effective length,

$$l = \frac{\text{Total length} - \text{Width of band}}{2}$$

$$= \frac{1100 - 100}{2} = 500 \text{ mm}$$

$i =$ Total number of leaves $= i_f + i_g$

$= 3 + 15 = 18$

Where, $h =$ Thickness of leaf.

$b' =$ Width of leaf.

Given, $$\frac{\text{Total depth of leaves}}{\text{Width}} = 2$$

i.e., $$\frac{18h}{b'} = 2 \text{ i.e., } b' = 9h$$

Substituting the values in E(20-18),

$$400 = \frac{6\left(37.5 \times 10^3\right)500}{18(9h)(h)^2}$$

Therefore, $h = 12.02$ mm; Use $h = 12.5$ mm ... T(20-4)

$b' = 9h$

$= 9 \times 12.5$

$= 112.5$ mm Adopt $b' = 125$ mm ... T(20-4)

(ii) To calculate the initial gap (Nip) between full length and graduated leaves.

The initial gap between full length leaves and graduated leaves is given by,

$$\text{Nip} = \frac{\beta' F l^3}{E i b' h^3} \qquad \text{... E(20-16)}$$

Where, β' = Constant = 2 ... T(20-7)

$E = 206.8 \text{ GPa} = 206.8 \times 10^3 \text{ MPa}$

Therefore, substituting the values in E(20-16).

$$\text{Nip} = \frac{2(37.5 \times 10^3)(500)^3}{(206.8 \times 10^3)18 \times 125(12.5)^3}$$

$$= 10.32 \text{ mm}$$

Example 3.23: Design a truck spring that has 12 number of leaves two of which are full length leaves. The spring supports are 1 m apart and the central band is 70mm wide. The central load is to be 6 kN with a permissible stress of 200 MPa. Determine the thickness, width and deflection of spring leaves if the total depth to width of spring is 3, Use $E = 210 \times 10^3$ MPa. ***(VTU, June / July 2008)***

Solution:

(i) To calculate the width and thickness of leaves.

Assuming that the stresses are equalized in springs, the maximum equalized stress is given by,

$$\sigma = \frac{\alpha' F l}{i b' h^2} \qquad \text{... E(20-18)}$$

Where, σ = 200 MPa

α', a constant = 6 for cantilever beam ... T(20-7)

$2F$ = Central load = 6 kN = 6×10^3 N

Therefore, $F = \dfrac{6 \times 10^3}{2} = 3000$ N

Effective length,

$$l = \frac{\text{Total length} - \text{Width of band}}{2}$$

$$= \frac{1000 - 70}{2} = 465 \text{ mm}$$

i = Total number of leaves = $i_f + i_g$

$12 = 2 + i_g$

Therefore, i_g = 10 leaves

Where, h = Thickness of leaf.

b' = Width of leaf.

Given, $\dfrac{\text{Total depth of leaves}}{\text{Width}} = 3$;

Where, Total depth of leaves $= i \times h$

$= 12h$

i.e., $\frac{12h}{b'} = 3$ i.e., $b' = 4h$

Substituting the values in E(20-18),

$$200 = \frac{6 \times 3000 \times 465}{12\,(4h)\,h^2}$$

Therefore, $h = 6.552$ mm; Use $h = 10$ mm ... T(20-4)

Therefore, $b' = 4h$

$$= 4 \times 10 = 40 \text{ mm}$$

(ii) To calculate the deflection of spring leaves

We have deflection

$$y = \frac{\beta F l^3}{E i b' h^3} \quad \text{... E(20-15)}$$

Where, $\beta = \text{ a constant } = \frac{12}{2+r}$

Where, $r = \frac{i'}{i} = \frac{i_f}{i}$

$$= \frac{2}{12} = \frac{1}{6} = 0.167$$

Therefore, $\beta = \frac{12}{2+0.167} = 5.538$

$$E = 210 \times 10^3 \text{ MPa}$$

Therefore, $y = \frac{5.538 \times 3000 \times (465)^3}{\left(210 \times 10^3\right) 12 \times 40 \times (10)^3}$

$$= 16.57 \text{ mm}$$

Example 3.24: An automobile spring has an overall length of 1100 mm and bandwidth 100 mm sustains a central load of 12 kN. The stress in the heavily loaded leaves is not to exceed 500 MPa and the deflection is to be limited to 60 mm. The width of leaves is to be 20 times the thickness of leaves. Taking E = 206.8 GPa, calculate

(i) Total number of leaves required in the spring.

(ii) The number of graduated leaves required assuming that two leaves in the spring extend to the full length.

(iii) Load shared by full length leaves and graduated leaves.

(iv) Stress induced in the graduated leaves.

Solution:

Note : *The stresses in the leaves are not equalized. Therefore, the maximum stress induced in the full length leaves given by*

$$\sigma_f = \frac{1.5 \alpha F l}{i b' h^2} \quad \text{... E(20-14)}$$

Where, $\sigma_f = 500$ MPa

$$\alpha = \frac{12}{2+r}$$

Where, $r = \frac{i_f}{i}$ ... T(20-7)

Total central load,

$$2F = 12 \text{ kN} = 12 \times 10^3 \text{ 1N}$$

Therefore, $F = \frac{12 \times 10^3}{2}$ N

$$= 6 \times 10^3 \text{N} = 6000 \text{ N}$$

Effective length of leaves,

$$l = \frac{\text{Total length} - \text{Bandwidth}}{2}$$

$$= \frac{1100 - 100}{2} = 500 \text{ mm}$$

Where, i = Total number of leaves in spring.

b' = Width of leaves (plates) = $20h$ (given)

h = Thickness of leaves.

Substituting in E(20-14), we get,

$$500 = \frac{1.5\left(\frac{12}{2+r}\right)6000 \times 500}{i(20h)h^2}$$

i.e., $$i(2+r)h^3 = \frac{1.5 \times 12 \times 6000 \times 500}{20 \times 500}$$

$$= 5400 \qquad \text{... (1)}$$

Considering deflection,

Deflection $y = \frac{\beta F l^3}{E i b' h^3}$ ... E(20-15)

Where, $\beta = \alpha = \left(\frac{12}{2+r}\right)$

$$E = 206.8 \text{ GPa} = 206.8 \times 10^3 \text{ MPa}$$

$$y = 60 \text{ mm}$$

Substituting the value in E(20-15), we get

$$60 = \frac{12 \times 6000 \times (500)^3}{(2+r)(206.8 \times 10^3)\, i\, (20h)h^3}$$

Therefore, $i(2+r)h^4 = \dfrac{12 \times 6000 \times (500)^3}{60 \times (206.8 \times 10^3) \times 20}$

$= 36266.92$ ... (2)

Dividing equation (2) by equation (1), we get,

$$\frac{i(2+r)h^4}{i(2+r)h^3} = \frac{36266.92}{5400}$$

i.e., $h = 6.72$ mm Use $h = 7.1$ mm ... T(20-4)

Width of leaves, $b' = 20h$

$= 20 \times 7.1 = 142$ mm Adopt $b' = 150$ mm ... T(20-4)

From equation (1)

$$i(2+r)h^3 = 5400$$

Where, $r = \dfrac{i_f}{i} = \dfrac{2}{i}$

From equation (1),

$$i\left(2+\frac{2}{i}\right)(7.1)^3 = 5400$$

$$(2i + 2)\,(7.1)^3 = 5400$$

$i = 6.54$ leaves Use $i = 7$ leaves

But, $i = i_f + i_g$

i.e., $7 = 2 + i_g$

Therefore, number of graduated leaves $i_g = 5$

(iii) To calculate the load shared by full length leaves and graduated leaves.

(a) Load shared by full length leaves is given by,

$$F_f = \left(\frac{3r}{2+r}\right)F$$ ... E(20-12)

Where, $r = \dfrac{i_f}{i} = \dfrac{2}{7} = 0.2857$

$F = 6000$ N

Therefore, $F_f = \left(\dfrac{3 \times 0.2857}{2 + 0.2857}\right)6000$

$= 2250$ N

(b) Load shared by graduated leaves is given by,

$$F_g = \frac{2(1-r)}{(2+r)}F$$ ... E(20-11)

$$= \frac{2(1-0.2857)}{(2+0.2857)} \times 6000$$

$$= 3750 \text{ N}$$

Note: *F_g may also be calculated from equation $F_g = F - F_f = 6000 - 2250 = 3750N$.*

(iv) To calculate the stress in graduated leaves

Stress in graduated leaves is given by

$$\sigma_g = \frac{\alpha F l}{i b' h^2} \quad \text{... E(20-13)}$$

Where, $\alpha = \frac{12}{2+r}$; $r = \frac{i_f}{i} = 0.2857$

Therefore, $\alpha = \frac{12}{2+0.2857} = 5.25$

$l = 500$ mm, $i = 7, b' = 140$ mm, $h = 7$ mm

Therefore, $\sigma_g = \frac{5.25 \times 6000 \times 500}{7 \times 140 \times 7^2}$

$$= 327.99 \text{ N/mm}^2 \quad \text{... (A)}$$

Note: *When the stresses in the leaves are not equalized, maximum stress occurs in the full length leaves given by*

$$\sigma_f = \frac{1.5\, \alpha F l}{i b' h^2} \quad \text{... E(20-14)}$$

$$\sigma_g = \frac{\alpha F l}{i b' h^2}$$

Therefore, $\frac{\sigma_f}{\sigma_g} = 1.5$

or, $\sigma_g = \frac{\sigma_f}{1.5} = \frac{500}{1.5} = 333.33 \text{ N/mm}^2$ ... (B)

Note: *The difference in reading (A) and (B) is due to the rounding off of 'r' to 0.2857 instead of its actual value 0.285714285.*

Example 3.25: A Belleville spring made from 5 mm thick steel sheet having outside diameter 150 mm and inside diameter 70 mm. The height of the spring is 10 mm. Using Poisson's ratio g = 0.3, E = 10 × 10 N/mm^2, determine,

(i) The deflection of spring.

(ii) The load the spring can carry.

(iii) Stress at the outer edge.

Limit the maximum stress at the inner edge to 450 N/mm².

Solution:

(i) To find deflection 'y'

The maximum stress at the inner edge is given by,

$$\sigma_i = \frac{4E_y}{(1-\gamma^2)d_0^2}\left[c_i\left(h-\frac{y}{2}\right)+c_2t\right] \qquad \text{... E(20-20)}$$

Where, $\sigma_i = 450\ \text{N/mm}^2$, $E = 2\times10^5\ \text{N/mm}^2$

$\gamma = 0.3$, $h = 10$ mm, $t = 5$ mm

For the given spring, $d_o = 150$ mm, $d_i = 70$ mm

Therefore, $\frac{d_o}{d_i} = \frac{150}{70} = 2.14$

Corresponding to $\frac{d_o}{d_i} = 2.14$, (Referring Fig. 20-3 MDH),

Constants $c_1 = 0.22$, $c_2 = 0.37$, $M = 0.68$

Substituting the values in E(20-20) we get,

$$450 = \frac{4(2\times10^5)y}{(1-0.3^2)150^2}\left[0.22\left(10-\frac{y}{2}\right)+0.37(5)\right]$$

$$= 39.07y[1.1-0.11y+1.85]$$

$$= 42.98y-4.3y^2+72.28y$$

$$= 115.26y-4.3y^2$$

i.e., $4.3y^2-115.26y+450 = 0$

$$y^2-26.8y+104.65 = 0$$

$$y = \frac{26.8\pm\sqrt{(26.8)^2-4\times1\times104.65}}{2}$$

$$y = 22.1\ \text{mm}$$

(ii) The axial load on spring is given by,

$$F = \frac{4Ey}{(1-\gamma^2)Md_o^2}\left[(h-y)\left(h-\frac{y}{2}\right)t+t^3\right] \qquad \text{... E(20-19)}$$

$$= \frac{4(2\times10^5)22.1}{(1-0.3^2)(0.68)150^2}\left[\left(10-\frac{22.1}{2}\right)5+5^3\right]$$

$$= 78063.4\ \text{N}$$

(iii) Stress at the outer edge is given by,

$$\sigma_o = \frac{4Ey}{(1-\gamma^2)d_o^2}\left[c_1\left(h-\frac{y}{2}\right)-c_2t\right] \qquad \text{... E(20-21)}$$

$$= \frac{4(2\times10^5)22.1}{(1-0.3^2)150^2}\left[0.22\left(10-\frac{22.1}{2}\right)-0.37\times5\right]$$

$$= -1796.93 \text{ N/mm}^2$$

EXERCISE

1. Design a helical spring for a spring loaded safety valve using the following data.

   Diameter of valve seat = 60 mm.

   Operating pressure = 0.65 MPa.

   Maximum pressure = 0.7 MPa.

   Lift of valve = 4 mm.

   Modulus of rigidity of spring material, $G = 85\times10^3 \text{ N/mm}^2$.

   Spring index = 6.

2. Design a helical compression spring for a load of 2 kN. The deflection of the spring is 50 mm. The permissible shear stress for spring material is 400 MPa. Use spring index = 6 and modulus of rigidity G = 84 GPa.

3. Two helical springs are nested one inside the other to support a load of 1 kN. The particulars are as shown,

Particulars	*Outer Spring*	*Inner Spring*
Coil diameter	*60 mm*	*40 mm*
Wire diameter	*8 mm*	*6 mm*
Number of coils	*15*	*10*
Free Length	*120 mm*	*90 mm*

   Determine,

   (*i*) Deflection of each spring.

   (*ii*) Load shared by each spring.

   (*iii*) Shear stress induced in springs. Use $G = 80\times10^3$ MPa

4. A composite spring (concentric spring) has the following particulars

Particulars	*Outer Spring*	*Inner Spring*
Mean diameter of coil	*120 mm*	*100 mm*
Wire diameter	*20 mm*	*15 mm*
Number of coils	*25*	*15*

   The outer spring has a free length 50 mm greater than inner spring. Using G = 80 GPa, determine the combined spring rate of springs after sufficient load has been applied to deflect the outer spring by 100 mm.

5. Design a helical compression spring to sustain an axial load fluctuating between 2 kN and 4 kN limiting the deflection to 25 mm.

6. A semi elliptical spring 1000 mm long is used to support a load of 60 kN. The spring has 20 leaves out of which the leaves extend to the full length. The width of central band is 150 mm. The leaves are stressed to 400 MPa. The width of spring (plate) is 10 times thickness of plate. Using $E = 200 \times 10^3$ MPa, determine,
   (*i*) Width and thickness of leaves.
   (*ii*) The nip to be provided between full length and graduated leaves.
   (*iii*) The load shared by full length leaves and graduated leaves.
   (*iv*) The load exerted on band after assembly.
7. Design a locomotive spring to support a load of 10 kN. The spring has 10 leaves out of which two are full length leaves. The spring supports are 1.1 m long and the central band is 100 mm. Using permissible shear stress in spring as 400 MPa, total depth of spring to width as 5, determine the width and thickness of leaves. Use E = 200 GPa.
8. A truck spring having an overall length of 1.1 m long with a central band 100 mm supports a load of 15 kN at its centre. The stress is in the heavily loaded leaves is not to exceed 0.5 GPa and the deflection to be limited to 75 mm. The width of leaves is to be 15 times the thickness of leaves. Using E = 200 GPa, calculate
   (*i*) Total number of leaves required in spring.
   (*ii*) Load shared by full length and graduated leaves.
   (*iii*) The stress induced by the graduated leaves.

CHAPTER

4 Spur and Helical Gears

NOTATIONS AND SYMBOLS USED

a = Centre distance between gear shafts; mm.
b = Face width of Gear, Pinion; mm.
d = Pitch circle diameter; mm.
d_1 = Pitch circle diameter of Pinion; mm.
d_2 = Pitch circle diameter of Gear; mm.
C_w = Wear and lubrication factor.
C_s = Service factor.
C_v = Velocity factor.
E_1 = Young's modulus of material of Pinion; N/mm^2.
E_2 = Young's modulus of material of Gear; N/mm^2
E_0 = Equivalent Young's modulus; N/mm^2
F_d = Dynamic load on Gear teeth; N.
F_i = Incremental load on Gear teeth; N.
F_t = Tangential load on Gear teeth; N.
F_{-1} = Endurance load on Gear teeth.
σ_{-1C} = Fatigue endurance strength.
f = Error in Gear teeth, mm.
F_w = Wear load, N.
h_f = Dedendum of Gear, mm.
h_a = Addendum of Gear, mm.
H_B = Brinell hardness of softer of Gear and Pinion.
i = Transmission ratio.
α = Pressure angle of Gears; Degree.
β = Helix angle of helical Gear; Degree.
m = Module of Gears; mm.
m_n = Normal module; mm.
m_t = Transverse module; mm.
M_t = Torque transmitted by Gears; N-mm.
M_b = Bending moment; N-mm.

n = Speed of Gears; rpm.
n_1 = Speed of Pinion; rpm.
n_2 = Speed of Gear; rpm.
S = Tooth thickness; mm.
P_C = Circular pitch; mm.
Q = Ratio factor.
r_1 = Pitch circle radius of Pinion; mm.
r_2 = Pitch circle radius of Gear; mm.
σ_o = Allowable static stress for Pinion, Gear; N/mm^2.
σ_u = Ultimate tensile stress; N/mm^2
v_m = Mean velocity of Pinion or Gear.
Z = Number of teeth.
Z_1 = Number of teeth on Pinion.
Z_2 = Number of teeth on Gear.
Z_b = Section modulus; mm^3.
Z_V = Virtual number of teeth or formative number of teeth.
Z_{1V} = Virtual number of teeth on Pinion.
Z_{2V} = Virtual number of teeth on Gear.

SPUR GEARS

Spur Gears are used to transmit power between two or more parallel shafts at a constant velocity ratio.

In a spur Gear, the teeth are cut parallel to the axis of Gear. When pair of Gears in mesh rotates, the contact takes place throughout the width of teeth. Hence they are noisy in operation, produce more vibration compared to helical Gears.

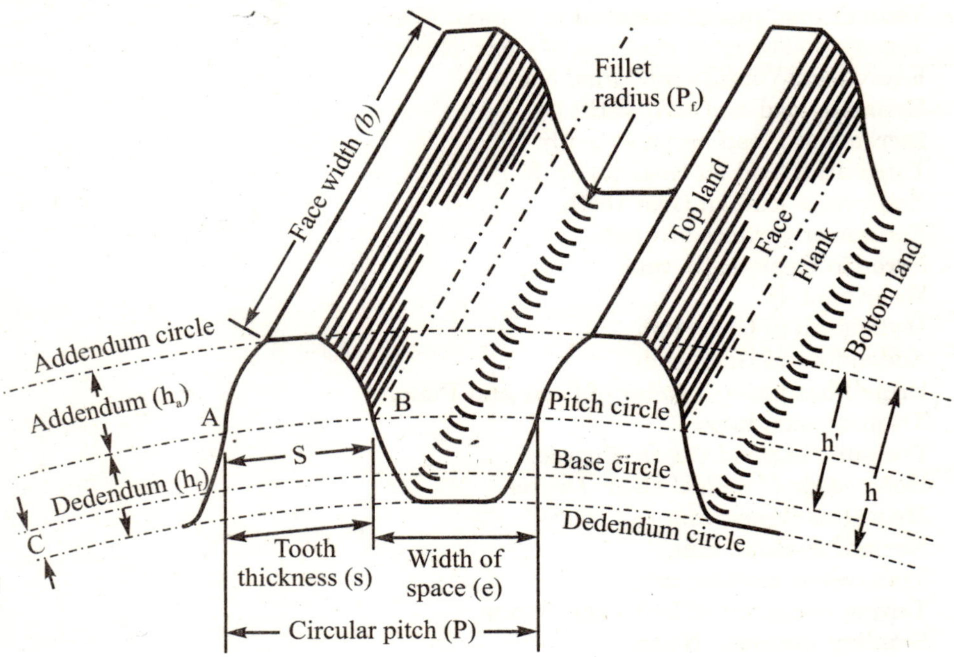

Figure: 4.1

Gear Tooth Terminology (Nomenclature of gear teeth)

(a) ***Top land:*** The top portion of gear tooth at addendum circle is called top land.

(b) ***Bottom land:*** It is the bottom portion of gear between two adjacent teeth.

(c) ***Face:*** The portion of gear tooth above pitch circle parallel to axis is called "Face".

(d) ***Flank:*** The portion of gear tooth between the pitch circle and bottom land parallel to axis is called flank.

(e) ***Tooth width:*** The dimension of gear tooth at the pitch circle measured parallel to its axis is called tooth width and is designated as '*b*'.

Its value varies from $3\pi m$ to $4\pi m$ *i.e.*, $b = 3\pi m \text{ to } 4\pi m$ ... E(2-125)

(f) ***Tooth of thickness:*** It is the dimension of gear tooth measured along pitch circle. It is designated as '*S*' and its value is $S = \dfrac{\pi m}{2}$, where m = module. In figure AB represents tooth thickness.

(g) ***Circular pitch:*** It is the distance between a point on a gear tooth and the corresponding point on the adjacent tooth measured along the pitch circle. It is represented as $P_C = \pi m$.

(h) ***Module:*** The ratio of pitch diameter to the number of teeth in a Gear is called module and is designated by '*m*'. *i.e.*, Module $m = \dfrac{d}{Z}$, where '*d*' is the pitch diameter of Gear and '*Z*' is the number of teeth on Gear.

(i) ***Addendum:*** The radial distance measured from pitch circle to the tip of gear tooth is called addendum. It is designated as h_a. Its value is $h_a = m$.

(j) ***Dedendum:*** It is the radial distance measured from pitch circle to the dedendum circle and is designated as h_f. Its value is $h_f = 1.25\,m$.

(k) ***Whole depth:*** It is the sum of addendum and dedendum

i.e., Whole depth = Addendum + Dedendum

$$= h_a + h_f$$

$$= m + 1.25m = 2.25m \quad \text{...E(2-12)}$$

(l) ***Centre distance:*** The distance between the centres of a pair of gears in mesh is called centre distance. It is represented as '*a*' and is given by

$$a = \frac{d_1}{2} + \frac{d_2}{2}$$

Where, d_1 is the pitch diameter of Pinion $= mZ_1$.
d_2 is the pitch diameter of Gear $= mZ_2$.

i.e., $$a = \frac{mZ_1}{2} + \frac{mZ_2}{2}$$

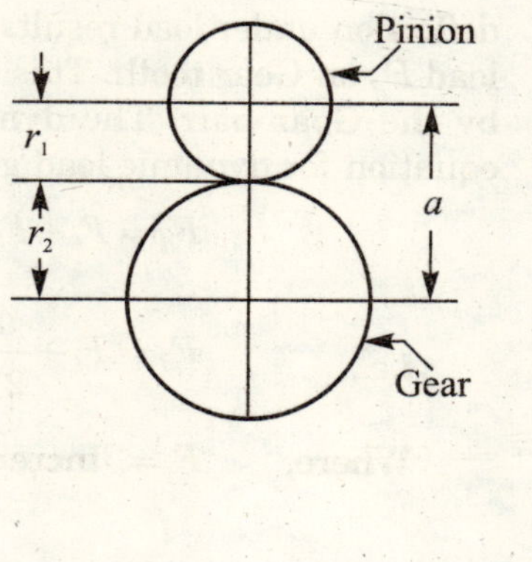

$$= \frac{m}{2}(Z_1 + Z_2)$$

Z_1 and Z_2 are the number of teeth on Pinion and Gear respectively.

(m) ***Clearance:*** The difference between addendum of one Gear and dedendum of mating gear is called clearance.

(n) ***Pitch point:*** The point of tangency of a pair of mating Gears.

(o) ***Backlash:*** The difference between the tooth space and tooth width is known as backlash.

(p) ***Transmission ratio or Angular velocity ratio:*** It is the ratio of angular velocity of Pinion to the angular velocity of Gear.

i.e., Transmission ratio $i = \frac{Z_2}{Z_1} = \frac{d_2}{d_1} = \frac{n_1}{n_2}$

where n_1 and n_2 are the speeds of rotation of Pinion and Gear respectively.

(q) ***Pressure angle:*** It is the angle between the line of action and the common tangent to the pitch circle. The standard pressure angle used on Gears is $14\frac{1}{2}^\circ$ or 20°.

Fundamental Law of Gearing

In order to maintain a constant angular velocity ratio of a pair of Gear, the common normal to the tooth profile at the point of contact must always pass through a fixed point called pitch point.

The involute curve satisfies the law of Gearing and hence most commonly used on Gear tooth profile. Some times a combination of involute and cycloidal curves is used to avoid interference.

Interference : Involute profiles overlap or cut into the mating teeth under certain condition. This can be avoided by taking maximum addendum radius

$$\leq \sqrt{(\text{Radius of base circle radius})^2 + (\text{Centre distance})^2 \sin^2 \alpha}$$

Where, α = Pressure angle $\left(14\frac{1}{2}^\circ \text{ or } 20^\circ\right)$

Buckingham's Equation for Dynamic Tooth Loads

Due to inaccuracies of tooth profile, misalignment in mounting of Gears, spacing and tooth deflection under load results in change in velocity which results in dynamic force called dynamic load F_d on Gear tooth. This dynamic load F_d is greater than the tangential force F_t transmitted by the Gear pair. The dynamic load and tangential force F_t are related by Buckingham's equation for dynamic load given by

$$F_d = F_t + F_i$$

i.e.,
$$F_d = F_t + \frac{21v(F_t + bc)}{21v + \sqrt{F_t + bc}} \quad \text{... E (2-148a)}$$

Where, F_i = Incremental load.

Table - (2-35)

Material, Pinion and Gear	Tooth Form	Error in Action, *f, mm*											
		0.0125		0.025		0.050		0.075		0.100		0.125	
		kgf/mm	*kgf/mm*	*kgf/mm*	*kN/m*	*kgf/mm*	*kN/m*	*kgf/mm*	*kN/m*	*kgf/mm*	*kN/m*	*kgf/mm*	*kN/m*
Cast iron and cast iron	14½°	7.12	69.85	14.24	139.70	28.48	279.40	42.72	419.10	56.96	558.80	71.206	698.50
Steel and cast iron	14½°	9.79	96.04	19.58	192.08	39.16	384.16	58.74	576.34	78.32	768.32	97.90	960.40
Steel and steel	14½°	14.24	139.70	28.48	279.48	56.96	558.80	85.44	838.20	113.92	1117.60	142.40	1397.00
Cast iron and cast iron	20° full depth	7.39	72.50	14.78	145.00	29.56	290.00	44.34	435.00	59.12	580.00	73.90	725.00
Steel and cast iron	20° full depth	10.15	99.57	20.30	192.14	40.60	398.28	60.90	597.42	81.20	796.56	101.50	995.70
Steel and steel	20° full depth	14.78	145.00	29.56	290.00	59.12	580.00	88.68	870.00	118.24	1116.00	147.80	1450.00
Cast iron and cast iron	20° stub	7.65	75.05	15.30	150.10	30.60	300.20	45.90	450.30	61.20	600.40	76.50	750.50
Steel and cast iron	20° stub	10.50	103.01	21.00	206.02	42.00	412.04	63.00	618.06	84.80	824.08	105.00	1030.10
Steel and steel	20° stub	15.30	150.10	30.60	300.20	61.20	600.40	91.80	900.60	122.40	1200.80	153.00	1501.00

$$= \frac{21v(F_t + bc)}{21v + \sqrt{F_t + bc}}$$

$$F_t = \frac{M_t C_s}{r} \text{ newton}$$

C_s = Service factor which depends on severity of service. Its value is generally 1.25 to 2.

b = Face width of Gears, mm.

c = A constant which depends on the material used for Gears, the tooth profile and the degree of accuracy to which Gears are cut. It is obtained from Table (2-35).

$$v = v_m = \text{mean velocity} = \frac{\pi dn}{60} \text{ m/sec}$$

d = Diameter of Gear or Pinion; m.

n = Speed of Pinion or Gear; rpm.

Note: *The dynamic load F_d must be less than the allowable endurance load F_{-1} given by,*

$$F_{-1} < \sigma_0 b y m \pi$$

i.e., $F_d < F_{-1}$

Where σ_o is the allowable static stress in N/mm^2.

Buckingham's Equation for Wear Load

To ensure durability of a pair of Gear, the tooth profile should not have excessive contact stress as determined by wear load F_w given by

$$F_w = d_1 bQK \qquad \text{...E(2-160)}$$

Where, d_1 = Diameter of Pinion; mm.

b = Face width; mm.

$$Q = \text{Ratio factor} = \frac{2Z_2}{Z_2 + Z_1} = \frac{2d_2}{d_2 + d_1} = \frac{2n_1}{n_2 + n_1} \qquad \text{... E(2-162)}$$

Where, Z_1 and Z_2 are the number of teeth on Pinion and Gear.

d_1 and d_2 are the pitch diameters of Pinion and Gear.

n_1 and n_2 are the speeds of rotation (rpm) of Pinion and Gear respectively.

K = Load stress factor. Refer T (2-40)

$$K = \frac{1.43\sigma_{-1C}^2 \sin\alpha}{E_0} \qquad \text{... E(2-161)}$$

E_0 = Equivalent Young's modulus in N/mm^2.

$$= \frac{2E_1E_2}{E_1 + E_2}$$

Where E_1 and E_2 are modulii of elasticity of Pinion and Gear respectively in N/mm^2.

Note: *When materials of Gear and Pinion are same, then* $E_1 = E_2$

And $$E_0 = \frac{2E_1^2}{2E_1} = E_1$$

σ_{-IC} = Fatigue endurance stress of Gear materials N/mm^2.

$$= 2.75H_B - 69 \quad \text{... E(2-168C)}$$

Note: F_w, *the wear load is an allowable load and must be greater than dynamic load* F_d.

i.e., $$F_w = d_1bQK > F_d$$

Derivation of Lewis Equation

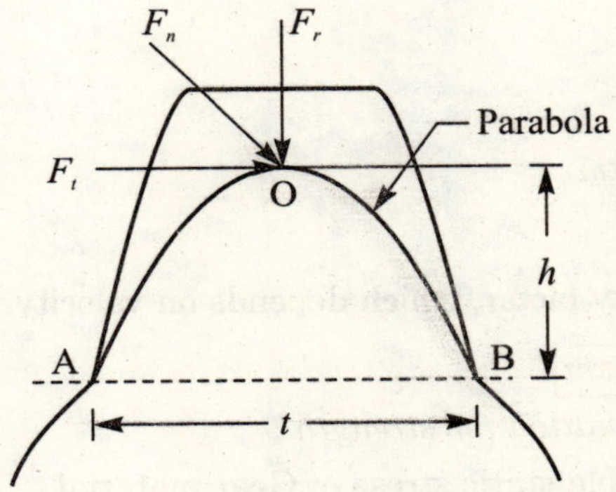

Consider a pair of spur Gears in mesh. At the beginning of action between the Gear pair, the flank of driver tooth makes contact with the tip of driven teeth. Let F_n be the normal tooth load *i.e.,* the load normal to the tooth profile carried by one tooth.

Let F_t and F_r be the horizontal and radial components of F_n. The horizontal load (or tangential force) causes bending stress at the base of tooth AB and the radial load F_r causes compression. The effect of F_r is very small compared to F_t and hence it is neglected.

A parabola AOB shown in figure represents the beam of uniform strength with the weakest section at AB where the parabola is tangential to the tooth profile. The bending stress σ_b in the Gear is given by

$$\sigma_b = \frac{M_b}{Z_b}$$

Where, bending moment $M_b = F_t h$

And section modulus $$Z_b = \frac{I}{C}$$

$$I = \frac{bt^3}{12} \quad \text{and} \quad C = \frac{t}{2};$$

Where, b = Face width of Gear (which is perpendicular to the plane of paper)

Therefore, $Z_b = \frac{I}{C} = \frac{bt^3}{12} \div \frac{t}{2} = \frac{bt^2}{6}$

i.e., $$F_t = \frac{bt^2\sigma_b}{6h} \quad \ldots(1)$$

Multiplying the numerator and denominator of R.H.S. of equation 1 by circular pitch $P_c = \pi m$,

$$F_t = \frac{bt^2\sigma_b(\pi m)}{6h(\pi m)} = \sigma_b b\left(\frac{t^2}{6\pi hm}\right)\pi m$$

The quantity $\left(\frac{t^2}{6\pi hm}\right)$ is a dimensionless quantity called the "Form Factor" represented by 'y'.

i.e., $$y = \frac{t^2}{6\pi hm}$$

Hence, $F_t = \sigma_b b(y)\pi m$

But, $\sigma_b = \sigma_o C_v$

Where, C_v = Velocity factor, which depends on velocity.

Therefore, $$\boxed{F_t = \sigma_o C_v by\pi m} \quad \ldots \text{E(2-91)}$$

E(2-91) is the *"Lewis equation for strength"*.

σ_o = Allowable static stress of Gear material. Refer T(2-16)

Note: *When the value of σ_o is not available in table, use $\sigma_o = \frac{1}{3}\sigma_u$*

In equation (2-91), the tangential force F_t is given by

$$F_t = \frac{M_t}{r}$$

Where, r = Radius of weaker member.

$r = \frac{d_1}{2}$, if Pinion is weaker.

$= \frac{d_2}{2}$, if Gear is weaker.

b = Face width = $3\pi m$ to $4\pi m$ ...E(2-125)

y = Lewis form factor and depends on tooth profile and the number of teeth.

Note: *For standard value of module 'm', Refer T(2-3)*

Design for Largest Number of Teeth

In the design of Gears, the pitch diameter of Gear may be known or unknown. When the diameter of Gears or the centre distance between Gears is known, *design for largest number of teeth is possible.*

Design of Smallest Pitch Diameter

When the diameters are unknown, *design for smallest pitch diameters is possible.*

Design Procedure for Spur Gears

Step I: ***Selection of materials for Gear and Pinion*** ***...(Refer T-2.16MDH)***

While selecting materials for Gear and Pinion, the designer has the option of selecting,

Table - (2-16) MDH

Material	*Static Stress, σ_o*		
	kgf/mm²	*MN/m²*	*MPa*
Ordinary cast iron	5.5	53.955	53.955
Cast iron, about class No. 35	8.5	83.305	83.305
High grade cast iron, about class No. 50	10.5	103.005	103.005
Cast steel, 0.20% C, untreated	14.0	137.340	137.340
Cast steel, 0.20%, heat treated	19.5	191.295	191.295
Bronze, SAE 62	7.0	68.67	68.67
Phosphor gear bronze, SAE 65	8.5	83.385	83.385
Manganese bronze, SAE 43	14.0	137.340	137.340
Aluminum bronze, SAE 68	15.5	152.005	152.005
Forged steel, about SAE 1030	17.5	172.375	172.375
Steel, SAE 1030, heat treated	22.5	220.725	220.725
Steel, SAE 1040, untreated	21.0	206.810	206.810
Alloy steel, case hardened	35.0	343.350	343.350
Cr-Va steel, about SAE 6145, heat treated	52.5	515.035	515.035
Cr-Ni steel, about SAE 3245, heat treated	47.0	461.070	461.070
Rawhide, Farbroil, etc	42.0	412.020	412.020
Laminated phenolic materials (Bakelite, Micarta, Celoron)	42.0	412.020	412.020

Case (i) Same material for Pinion and Gear

Such as cast steel 0.2% C steel heat treated having $\sigma_o = 191.295 \text{ N/mm}^2$, or high grade cast iron with $\sigma_o = 103.005 \text{N/mm}^2$

or

Case (ii) Two different materials for Pinion and Gear

Note: *It is to be noted that while selecting different materials for Gear and Pinion, the material selected for Pinion must be stronger than the material selected for Gear. In other words the material selected for Pinion should possess higher value of static stress σ_o compared to that of Gear.*

Step II: ***Identifying the weaker member of Gear pair***

(*i*) When Gear and Pinion are made of same material, Pinion is the weaker member and the design is based on Pinion.

(*ii*) When Gear and Pinion are made of different materials, the strength factor $(\sigma_o y)$ is computed as shown and the member with smaller value of $(\sigma_o y)$ is taken as the weaker member and the design is based on that member.

Example: Selecting the material of Pinion as cast steel i.e., 0.2% C steel heat treated having $\sigma_o = 191.25\, N/mm^2$ high grade cast iron for Gear for which

$\sigma_o = 103.005\ \text{N/mm}^2$, tabulate as shown below

Member	?o	y	?o y	Remarks
Pinion	191.295	0.097	18.556	Strong
Gear	103.005	0.14488	14.9234	Weak

In the above table, $\sigma_o y)_{gear} = 14.9234 < \sigma_o y)_{pinion} = 18.556$. Hence Gear is the weaker member and the design is based on Gear

In the above computation,

The Lewis form factor 'y' is based on $14\frac{1}{2}^\circ$ involute profile and 16 teeth on Pinion with transmission ratio 4:1. i.e.,

$$y = 0.124 - \frac{0.684}{Z} \qquad \text{... E(2-97)}$$

$$y_1 = y_{\text{pinion}} = 0.124 - \frac{0.684}{16} = 0.097$$

$$y_2 = y_{\text{gear}} = 0.124 - \frac{0.684}{64} = 0.14488$$

Step III: ***Calculation of module (m) of Gears***

Module *'m'* is calculated using the modified Lewis equation given by,

$$m = \frac{F_t}{\sigma_o C_v b y \pi} \qquad \text{... E(2.91)}$$

Where, F_t = Tangential force on weaker member in N

$$= \frac{M_t}{r} C_s$$

M_t = Torque on weaker member in N-mm and is given by

$$= \frac{9550N \times 10^3}{n_1} \text{ N-mm; if Pinion is weaker.}$$

$$= \frac{9550N \times 10^3}{n_2} \text{ N-mm; if Gear is weaker.}$$

Where n_1 and n_2 are the speeds of Pinion and Gear respectively.

N = Power transmitted in kW.

r = Radius of weaker member

$$= \frac{d_2}{2}, \text{ if Gear is weaker.}$$

$$= \frac{d_1}{2}, \text{ if Pinion is weaker.}$$

C_s = Service factor [generally 1.25 to 1.5 is used].

σ_o = Allowable static stress of weaker member.

C_v = Velocity factor. It depends on linear velocity 'v'.

Where, $v = \frac{\pi d n}{60}$; (in general).

$$= \frac{\pi d_1 n_1}{60}, \text{ if Pinion is weaker.}$$

$$= \frac{\pi d_2 n_2}{60}, \text{ if Gear is weaker.}$$

d_1 and d_2 are pitch diameters of Gears [Pinion and Gear] in meter.

Note: $v_{pinion} = v_{gear}$

Based on velocity range, C_v is calculated using equations .... E(2-128) to E(2-134)

Velocity Factors

The velocity factor or Barth's formula for ordinary cut gears running with pitch line velocity up to 7.6 m/sec is given by

$$C_v = \frac{3}{3 + v_m} \text{ for } v_m = 7.5\,\text{m/sec} \quad \text{... E(2-128)}$$

Barth's formula for carefully cut gears

$$C_v = \frac{4.5}{4.5 + v_m} \quad \text{for } v_m \text{ upto } 12.5\,\text{m/sec} \qquad \text{... E(2-129)}$$

Barth's formula for accurately cut and ground metallic gears

$$C_v = \frac{6.1}{6.1 + v_m} \quad \text{for } v_m \text{ from } 6.5\,\text{m/sec to } 20\,\text{m/sec} \qquad \text{... E(2-130)}$$

Barth's formula for hardened steel ground and lapped in precision gears as per AGMA recommendation

$$C_v = \frac{5.55}{5.55 + \sqrt{v_m}} \quad \text{for } v_m \text{ over } 20\,\text{m/sec} \qquad \text{... E(2-131)}$$

Velocity factor or Barth's formula for a commercially hobbed or shaved teeth as per AGMA recommendation

$$C_v = \frac{3.55}{3.55 + \sqrt{v_m}} \qquad \text{... E(2-132)}$$

Velocity factor for non-metallic gears as per AGMA recommendation

$$C_v = \frac{0.75}{1 + v_m} + 0.07625 \qquad \text{... E(2-133)}$$

Another formula for velocity factor for non-metallic gears

$$C_v = \frac{1 + \left(\frac{v_m}{4}\right)}{1 + v_m} \qquad \text{... E(2-134)}$$

Note: *Since C_v is based on velocity 'v' which in turn depends on diameter 'd', its value can be calculated only if diameter is known.*

If diameter is unknown, velocity 'v' and hence C_v cannot be calculated and is retained as C_v in the equation of module.

Face Width 'b'

The face width 'b' of Pinion and Gear is related to module by the equation

$$b = 3\pi m \text{ to } 4\pi m \qquad \text{... E(2-125)}$$

Usually $b = 3.5\pi\text{m} = 10\text{m}$ is adopted.

Lewis Form Factor 'y'

Lewis form factor 'y' depends on

(i) The tooth profile used and

(ii) The number of teeth on Gears.

For Gears with 20° involute profile,

$$y = 0.154 - \frac{0.912}{Z} \qquad \text{... E (2.98)}$$

And $$y = 0.124 - \frac{0.684}{Z} \quad \text{For } 14\tfrac{1}{2}^\circ \text{ involute profile Gears.} \qquad \text{... E(2.97)}$$

Where, Z = Number of teeth.

Note: *It is advisable to select minimum 16 teeth on Pinion.*

Governing Equation of Module

Case 1: When diameter of Gear and Pinion are known or the centre distance between Gears is known.

In the modified Lewis equation used to calculate module, *i.e.*,

$$m = \frac{F_t}{\sigma_o C_v b y \pi} \qquad \text{... E(2-91)}$$

Retain $m = m$ (unknown)

$F_t = M_t \dfrac{C_s}{r}$ it can be calculated since '*r*' is known.

σ_o is selected from table of materials, ... T(2-16)

Since diameters are known, velocity '*v*' and hence C_v can be computed based on velocity range.

b, the face width is chosen as $3.5\pi m$

y, the Lewis form factor is retained as '*y*' since the number of teeth are unknown.

Note: *When diameter of Gears are known, the Designer is to compute the number of teeth 'Z' on Gears and hence, 'y' is retained as 'y'.*

After substitution in Lewis equation, we obtain

$$m^2 y\Big]_{\text{allowable}} = [\text{A known numerical value}] \qquad \text{... (1)}$$

And this equation is taken as the governing equation.

Case 2: Diameter of Gears are unknown

In the modified Lewis equation

$$m = \frac{F_t}{\sigma_o C_v b y \pi} \quad \text{used for calculating module,}$$

Retain $m = m(\text{an unknown parameter})$

$$F_t = \frac{M_t C_s}{r}$$

Where, $M_t = M_t)_{\text{weaker member}}$

Say Pinion is the weaker member for which

$$M_t = \frac{9550 N \times 10^3}{n_1} \text{N-mm}$$

Where n_1 = Speed of rotation of Pinion in rpm.

$$r = \frac{d_1}{2} = \frac{mZ_1}{2}; \quad \text{since } d = mZ$$

Where 'm' is the module.

Therefore,

F_t will be in terms of 'm' i.e., $F_t = \ldots\ldots\ldots \frac{1}{m}$.

σ_o, the value of σ_o is known (or selected from table).

C_v, the velocity factor which depends on velocity 'v', cannot be computed since diameters are unknown. Hence C_v is retained as C_v in the module equation.

b, the face width is taken as $3.5\pi m$ i.e., $b = 3.5\pi m$.

y, the Lewis form factor is calculated by assuming suitable number of teeth on weaker member with minimum 16 teeth on Pinion.

With the substitution of the above values, the controlling equation or governing equation for module reduces to

$$\boxed{m^3 C_v = (\text{A known numerical value})} \qquad \ldots (2)$$

In the design of Gears, say the centre distance or the diameters of Gears are known, then use the controlling equation

$m^2 y) =$ A known numerical value is used to determine 'm', the allowable module by selecting a standard preferred module. ... (Table 2-3)

Table - (2-3) MDH

Module, m (mm)		
0.05	(1.125)	(18)
(0.055)	1.25	20
0.06	(1.375)	(22)
(0.07)	1.5	(24)
0.08	(1.75)	25
(0.09)	2.0	(27)
0.10	(2.25)	(28)
(0.11)	2.5	(30)
0.12	(2.75)	32
(0.14)	3.0	(33)
0.15	(3.25)	(36)
(0.18)	(3.5)	(39)
0.2	(3.75)	40
(0.22)	4.0	(42)

Module, m (mm)		
0.25	(4.5)	(45)
(0.28)	5	50
0.3	(5.5)	(55)
(0.35)	6	60
0.4	(6.5)	(65)
(0.45)	(7)	(70)
0.5	8	(75)
(0.55)	(9)	80
0.6	10	(85)
(0.7)	(11)	(90)
0.8	12	100
(0.9)	(14)	
1.0	16	

Note: *In table (2-3), the values of modules preferred are those values shown without brackets. As far as possible avoid using modules shown in brackets (since they are not preferred).*

Trials to find 'm'

Trial 1: *Select m = 5 mm[selected from table 2-3]*

To find 'y', the Lewis form factor

Assuming Pinion as weaker member,

$$d_1 = mZ_1$$

Since d_1 is known, y_1, the Lewis form factor based on Z_1 can be computed.

Note: *Continue the trials with increasing or decreasing values of standard module till the quantity $\left.m^2 y\right)_{allowable}$ equals the numerical value of the RHS of governing equation of module or less than the numerical value on the RHS of equation.*

Case 2: When diameters are unknown, use

Governing equation,

$$m^3 C_v = \text{A known numerical value}$$

Note: *Since diameters are unknown, $m^3 C_v$ is an induced value.*

Trial 2: *Select m = 5 mm*

To find C_v, the velocity factor

Considering Pinion as weaker member, $d_1 = mZ_1$ can be calculated. Based on d_1, the velocity 'v' is computed using $v = \dfrac{\pi d_1 n_1}{60}$.

Based on velocity determine C_v. Repeat the trials with increasing or decreasing standard values of 'm' till the product, $m^3 C_v$ equals or less than the numerical value on the RHS of controlling equation.

Particulars of Gears

Sl. No	Particulars	Pinion	Gear
1.	Material	Selected from T(2-16)	Selected from T(2-16)
2.	Module, m	m	m
3.	Number of teeth, Z	Z_1	Z_2
4.	Pitch circle diameter, d; $d = mZ$	$d_1 = mZ_1$	$d_2 = mZ_2$
5.	Face width b; $b = 3.5\pi m$	$b = 3.5\pi m$	$b = 3.5\pi m$
6.	Tooth thickness S; $S = \pi m/2$	$S = \dfrac{\pi m}{2}$	$S = \dfrac{\pi m}{2}$
7.	Addendum $h_a = m$	$h_a = m$	$h_a = m$
8.	Dedendum $h_f = 1.25\ m$	$h_f = 1.25\ m$	$h_f = 1.25\ m$

Step IV: ***Check for wear and dynamic loads*** $(F_w$ ***and*** $F_d)$

Wear load F_w is given by,

$$F_w = d_1 bQK > F_d \qquad \text{... E(2-160)}$$

Where F_d is the dynamic load. In equation $F_w = d_1 bQK$,

d_1 = Diameter of Pinion, mm [Irrespective of whether Gear or Pinion is weaker]

b = face width, mm.

$$Q = \text{Ratio factor} = \frac{2Z_2}{Z_2 + Z_1} \qquad \text{... W(2-163)}$$

Z_2 = Number of teeth on Gear.

Z_1 = Number of teeth on Pinion.

$$K = \frac{1.43\sigma^2_{-1C} \sin\alpha}{E_0} \qquad \text{... E(2-161)}$$

E_0 = Equivalent Young's modulus

$$E_0 = \frac{2E_1E_2}{E_1 + E_2} \qquad \text{... E(2-162)}$$

E_1 = Young's modulus of Pinion is N/mm^2.

E_2 = Young's modulus of Gear in N/mm^2.

σ_{-1C} = Fatigue endurance strength of Gear materials in N/mm^2.

$$= 2.75H_B - 69 \qquad \text{... E(2-168C)}$$

H_B = BHN of the softer of two Gears.

Note: *The value of 'K' can also be obtained from T(2-40) based on Gear materials and tooth profile.*

F_d, the dynamic load on Gears

F_d, is calculated using equation,

$$F_d = F_t + \frac{21v(F_t + bc)}{21v + \sqrt{F_t + bc}} \qquad \text{... E(2-148a)}$$

Note: *Constant 'c' is obtained from Table (2-35) based on velocity 'v' and error 'f' Table (2-34) (explained in detail in numerical examples).*

Table - (2-34) MDH

v_m, m/s	Error f, mm	v_m, m/s	Error f, mm	v_m, m/s	Error f, mm
1.25	0.0925	8.75	0.0425	16.25	0.0200
2.50	0.0800	10.00	0.0375	17.25	0.0170
3.75	0.0700	11.25	0.0325	20.00	0.0150
5.00	0.0600	12.50	0.0300	22.50	0.0150
6.25	0.0525	13.75	0.0250	22 and over	0.0125
7.50	0.0475	15.00	0.0225		

Case 1: Hardness of Gears unknown

When hardness of Gears is unknown,

Use, $F_w = d_1 bQK > F_d$ ... E(2-160)

i.e., $d_1 bQK > F_d$

or $K > \dfrac{F_d}{d_1 bQ}$

After obtaining '*K*', refer table (2-40) and obtain the hardness (BHN) of Pinion and Gear.

Case 2: Hardness of Gears known

When hardness of Gears is known,

Calculate '*K*' using equation,

$$K = \frac{1.43\sigma_{-1C}^2 \sin\alpha}{E_0} \quad \text{... E(2.161)}$$

Where $\alpha =$ Pressure angle $\left(14\frac{1}{2}^\circ \text{ or } 20^\circ\right)$ and check whether $F_W > F_d$ for safe design.

Step V: ***Class of Gears (i.e., precision to which Gears are to be cut)***

The class of Gears or the precision to which the Gears are to be cut is based on module, '*m*' and expected error '*f*' and is obtained by referring to Fig. (2.29MDH).

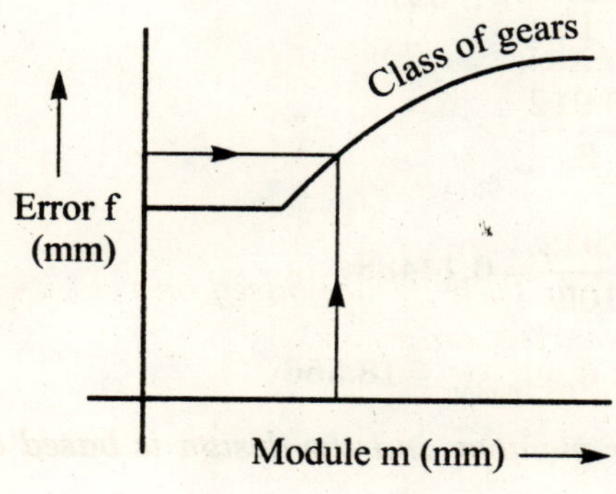

Example 4.1. A cast steel Pinion rotating at 900 rpm is to drive a cast iron Gear at 144 rpm. The teeth are of 20° involute profile and the power transmitted is 20 kW. The number of teeth on Pinion is 16. Design the Gears for smallest pitch diameter.

Solution:

Note: *Since the diameter are unknown, it is possible to design for smallest pitch diameter.*

Step I: *Selection of material:* ***(Refer table 2-16)***

For Pinion, select cast steel 0.2% C heat treated steel for which allowable static stress

$$\sigma_o = 191.295 \text{ N/mm}^2$$

And for Gear select, high grade cast iron for which

$$\sigma_o = 103.005 \text{ N/mm}^2$$

Step II: *To determine the weaker member of Gear pair*

Member	σ_o	*y*	σ_o *y*	*Remarks*
Pinion	191.295	0.097	18.556	Strong
Gear	103.005	0.14488	14.9234	Weak

To determine 'y', the Lewis form factor

For 20° involute profile,

$$y = 0.154 - \frac{0.912}{Z} \quad \text{... E(2-98)}$$

Z_1 = Number of teeth on Pinion = 16.

Z_2 = Number of teeth on Gear $= Z_1 \times$ Transmission ratio

$$= 16 \times \frac{900}{144} = 100$$

$$y_1 = y_{\text{pinion}} = 0.154 - \frac{0.912}{Z_1}$$

$$= 0.154 - \frac{0.912}{16} = 0.097$$

$$y_2 = y_{\text{gear}} = 0.154 - \frac{0.912}{Z_2}$$

$$= 0.154 - \frac{0.912}{100} = 0.14488$$

$$\sigma_o y\big]_{\text{gear}} = 14.9234 < \sigma_o y\big]_{\text{pinion}} = 18.556$$

Hence, Gear is the weaker member and the design is based on Gear.

Step III: ***To calculate module 'm'***

Modified Lewis equation for module *'m'* is given by

$$m = \frac{F_t}{\sigma_o C_v b y \pi} \quad \text{... E(2-91)}$$

Where, m = Module, mm

F_t = Tangential force on weaker member

$$= \frac{M_t}{r} C_s$$

$$M_t = \frac{9550 N \times 10^3}{n}; \text{ N-mm}$$

N = Power transmitted = 20 kW

n = Speed of weaker member = Speed of Gear = 144 rpm.

Therefore, $M_t = \frac{9550 \times 20 \times 10^3}{144}$ N-mm

$= 1326388.89$ N-mm

$r = r_2$ = Radius of Gear

$$= \frac{d_2}{2} = \frac{m Z_2}{2} = \frac{m \times 100}{2} = 50m$$

C_s = Service factor = 1.5(assumed)

Therefore, $F_t = \frac{1326388.85}{50m} \times 1.5$

$$= \frac{39791.67}{m}$$

$\sigma_o = \sigma_o)_{\text{weaker member}} = 103.005 \text{N/mm}^2$

$b = 3\pi m$ *to* $4\pi m$ ... E(2-215)

Say, $b = 3.5\pi m$, a mean value

$y = y_2 = 0.14488$ ('y' of weaker member)

Substituting in E(2-91) we get,

$$m = \frac{39791.67}{m \times 103.005 \times C_v \times 3.5\pi m \times 0.14488\pi}$$

Therefore, $m^3C_v\Big)_{\text{induced}} = 77.23$

To find 'm', the module [Refer table 2-3 for standard module 'm']

Trial 1: Let m = 5 mm

Then, $d_2 = mZ_2$

$= 5 \times 100 = 500$ mm

Velocity, $v_m = \frac{\pi d_2 n_2}{60}$

$= \frac{\pi}{60} \times \frac{500}{1000} \times 144 = 3.77$ m/sec

Velocity factor, $C_v = \frac{4.5}{4.5 + v_m}$ ... E(2-129)

$= \frac{4.5}{4.5 + 3.77} = 0.544$

Therefore, $m^3C_v = 5^3 \times 0.544 = 68 < 77.23$

Trial 2: Let m = 6 mm

Then, $d_2 = mZ_2$

$= 6 \times 100 = 600$ mm

Velocity. $v_m = \frac{\pi d_2 n_2}{60}$

$= \frac{\pi}{60} \times \frac{600}{1000} \times 144 = 4.524$ m/sec

Velocity factor, $C_v = \frac{4.5}{4.5 + V_m}$

$= \frac{4.5}{4.5 + 4.524} = 0.4987$

Therefore, $m^3C_v = 6^3 \times 0.4987 = 107.72 > 77.23$

Therefore, adopt module $m = 6$ mm

Particulars of Gears

Sl. No	Particulars	Pinion	Gear
1.	Material	Cast steel	High grade cast Iron
2.	Module, m	$m = 5$ mm	$m = 5$ mm
3.	Number of teeth, Z	$Z_1 = 16$ teeth	$Z_2 = 100$ teeth
4.	Pitch circle diameter, d; $d = mZ$	$d_1 = mZ_1 = 5\times16 = 80$ mm	$d_2 = mZ_2 = 5\times100 = 500$ mm
5.	Face width b; $b = 3.5\pi m$	$b = 55$ mm	$b = 55$ mm
6.	Tooth thickness S; $S = \pi\ m/2$	$S = \pi\times\frac{5}{2} = 7.85 \approx 8$ mm	$S = 8$ mm
7.	Addendum $h_a = m$	$h_a = 5$ mm	$h_a = 5$ mm
8.	Dedendum $h_f = 1.25$ m	$h_f = 6.25$ m	$h_f = 6.25$ mm

Step IV: ***To check for wear and dynamic load and to determine the hardness of Gears.***

Wear load $F_w = d_1bQK > F_d$ ... E(2-160)

Where, F_w = Wear load, F_d = Dynamic load

d_1 = Diameter of Pinion = 80 mm

b = face width of Gear/Pinion = $3.5\pi m = 3.5\pi\times5 = 55$ mm

$$Q = \text{Ratio factor} = \frac{2Z_2}{Z_2+Z_1} \quad \text{... E(2-163)}$$

$$= \frac{2\times100}{100+16} = 1.724$$

K = Load stress factor

Therefore, $F_W = 80\times55\times1.724\times K = 7585.6K$

To find dynamic load F_d

$$F_d = F_t + \frac{21V\left(F_t+bc\right)}{21V+\sqrt{F_t+bc}} \quad \text{... E(2-148a)}$$

$$F_t = \frac{39791.67}{m}$$

$$= \frac{39791.67}{5} = 7958.334 \text{ N}$$

$$V = v_m = \frac{\pi d_2 n_2}{60}$$

$$= \frac{\pi}{60} \times \frac{500}{1000} \times 144 = 3.77 \text{ m/sec}$$

$$b = 55 \text{ mm} = \frac{55 \text{ mm}}{1000} = 0.055 \text{ m}$$

Calculation of 'C' [Refer tables (2-34) and (2-35)]

From (table-2.34),

Interpolate and get the value of 'f' (error)

For $V_m = 3.75$ m/sec; error $f = 0.0700$ mm

For $V_m = 5.00$ m/sec; error $f = 0.0600$ mm

Therefore, Difference in $V_m = 1.25$ (increases);

Difference in $f = 0.01$ (decreases).

Note: *When V_m increases, f decreases.*

Decrease in $f = \frac{0.01}{1.25} \times (3.77 - 3.75) = 0.00016$ mm

Therefore, $f = 0.07 - 0.00016 = 0.06984$ mm

Now referring table (2-35)

For steel Pinion and cast iron Gear, (20° full depth profile)

For $f = 0.05$ mm; $C = 398.28$ kN/m

For $f = 0.075$ mm; $C = 597.42$ kN/m

Therefore, Difference in $f = 0.025$ mm (increases);

Difference in $C = 199.14$ kN/m (increases)

Note: *'C' increases with increase in 'f'*

$$\text{Increase in } C = \frac{199.14}{0.025}(0.06984 - 0.05)$$

$$= 158.04 \text{ kN/m}$$

$$\text{Therefore, } C = 398.28 + 158.04$$

$$= 556.32 \text{ kN/m} = 556.32 \times 10^3 \text{ N/m}$$

$$F_d = F_t + \frac{21V(F_t + bc)}{21V + \sqrt{F_t + bc}};$$

Becomes, $$F_d = 7958.334 + \frac{21\times 3.77\left(7958.334 + 0.055\times 556.32\times 10^3\right)}{21\times 3.77 + \sqrt{7958.334 + 0.055\times 556.32\times 10^3}}$$

$$= 8009.7 \text{ N}$$

Now equating F_W and F_d,

i.e., $F_W = d_1 bQK > F_d$

$$7585.6K > 8009.7$$

i.e., $K > 1.056$

Referring Table (2-40) for $K > 1.056$ *i.e.,* $K = 1.1174$, the Pinion is to be hardened to 300 BHN and Gear to 250 BHN.

Step V: ***Class of Gears*** ***[Refer figure 2.29 MDH]***

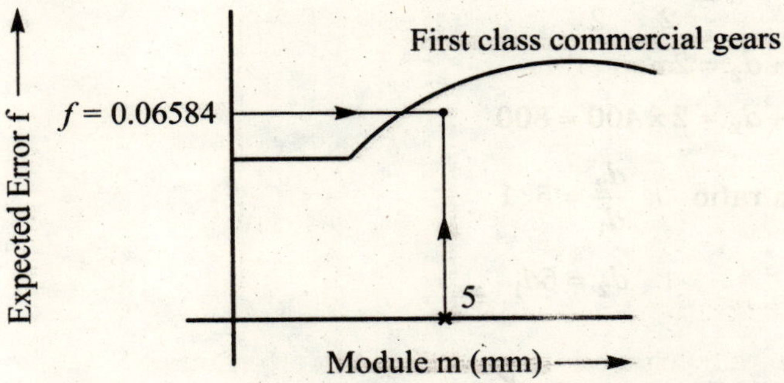

Corresponding to $m = 5$ mm and error $f = 0.06984$, the class of gears is first class commercial gears.

Example 4.2: Design a pair of cast iron Spur Gears to transmit 15 kW at 1440 rpm of the Pinion. The desired transmission ratio is 5 : 1. The centre distance between shafts should be very close to 400 mm.

Solution:

Step I: *Selection of material for Gear and Pinion (Refer Table 2-16)*

Select high grade cast iron for both Pinion and Gear for which $\sigma_o = 103.005 \text{ N/mm}^2$

Step II: *To determine the weaker. member of Gear pair*

Note: *Since Gear and Pinion are made of same material, Pinion is the weaker member and the design is based on Pinion.*

Step III: *To determine module (m).*

Modified Lewis equation for module *'m'* is given by

$$m = \frac{F_t}{\sigma_o C_v b y \pi} \quad \text{... E(2-91)}$$

Where, m = module,

$$F_t = \frac{M_t}{r} C_s$$

$$M_t = \frac{9550\ \text{N} \times 10^3}{n_1} \text{N-mm}$$

$$= \frac{9550 \times 15 \times 10^3}{1440}\ \text{N-mm}$$

$$= 99479.17\ \text{N-mm}$$

Service factor $C_s = 1.5 (\text{assumed})$

To determine 'r', radius of Pinion

Now,

Centre distance $a = r_1 + r_2$

$$a = \frac{d_1}{2} + \frac{d_2}{2}$$

i.e., $d_1 + d_2 = 2a$

$$d_1 + d_2 = 2 \times 400 = 800 \qquad \text{... (1)}$$

Also transmission ratio $\frac{d_2}{d_1} = 5:1$

i.e., $d_2 = 5d_1$ ... (2)

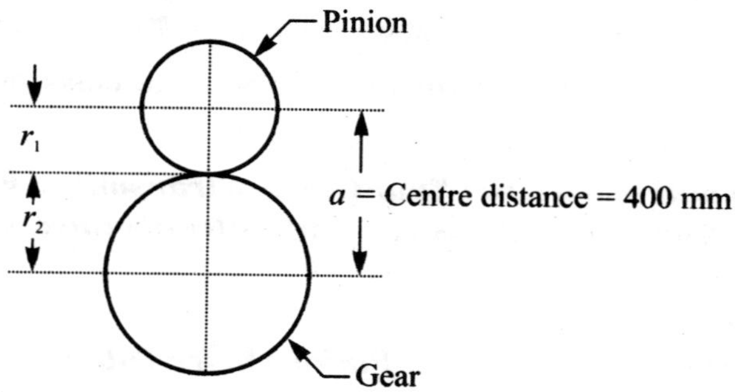

From equations (1) and (2)

$$d_1 + 5d_1 = 800$$

i.e., $d_1 = 133.33$ mm

$$d_2 = 666.67\ \text{mm}$$

Therefore, $r = r_1 = \frac{133.33\ \text{mm}}{2}$

$$= 66.67\ \text{mm}$$

$$F_t = \frac{99479.17 \times 1.5}{\frac{133.33}{2}}$$

$$= 2238.33 \text{ N}$$

$$\sigma_o = \sigma_o)_{\text{pinion}} = 103.005 \text{ N/mm}^2$$

To find C_v, the velocity factor

Mean velocity $\quad V = v_m = \dfrac{\pi d_1 n_1}{60}$

$$= \frac{\pi}{60} \times \frac{133.33}{1000} \times 1440 = 10.05 \text{ m/sec}$$

$$C_v = \frac{4.5}{4.5 + v_m} \qquad \text{... E(2-129)}$$

Therefore, $\quad C_v = \dfrac{4.5}{4.5 + 10.05} = 0.275$

$$b = \text{ face width} = 3\pi m \text{ to } 4\pi m \qquad \text{... E(2-126)}$$

Use $\quad b = 3.5\pi m$

Retain Lewis form factor $y = y$, since the number of teeth are unknown.
Substituting in equation (2-91) we get,

$$m = \frac{2238.33}{103.005 \times 0.275 \times 3.5\pi m y \pi}$$

Therefore, $\quad m^2 y = 0.5719$; $\quad$ ($m^2 y$ is an allowable value).

Trials to find 'm'

Trial 1: Let m = 5 mm

Then, $\quad d_1 = mZ_1$

i.e., $\quad 133.33 = 5Z_1$ or $Z_1 = 26.66 \approx 27$ teeth

Assuming $14\frac{1}{2}^{\circ}$ involute profile,

$$y = 0.124 - \frac{0.684}{Z} \qquad \text{... E(2-97)}$$

$$y_{\text{pinion}} = y_1 = 0.124 - \frac{0.684}{Z_1}$$

$$= 0.124 - \frac{0.684}{27} = 0.097$$

Therefore, $\quad m^2 y = 5^2 \times 0.097 = 2.425 > 0.5719$

Now reduce module 'm' to 2 mm [Refer table 2-3]

Trial 2: Let m = 2mm

Then, $d_1 = mZ_1$

i.e., $133.33 = 2Z_1$

i.e., $Z_1 = 66.67$ say $Z_1 = 67$ teeth

$$y = y_1 = 0.124 - \frac{0.684}{67}$$

$$= 0.1138$$

Therefore, $m^2y = 2^2 \times 0.1138 = 0.4558$

This value is lesser than the allowable value $\left.m^2y\right)_{allowable} = 0.5719$

Adopt m = 2 mm

Particulars of Gears

Sl. No	Particulars	Pinion	Gear
1.	Material	High grade cast Iron	High grade cast Iron
2.	Module, m	m = 2 mm	m = 2 mm
3.	Number of teeth, Z	Z_1 = 67 teeth	Z_2 = 67 × 5 = 335 teeth
4.	Pitch circle diameter, d; $d = mZ$	$d_1 = mZ_1 = 134$ mm	$d_2 = mZ_2 = 134 \times 5 = 670$ mm
5.	Face width b; $b = 3.5\pi m$	b = 22 mm	b = 22 mm
6.	Tooth thickness S; $S = \pi m/2$	S = 3.14 mm	S = 3.14 mm

Check for centre distance

Centre distance $$a = \frac{m(Z_1 + Z_2)}{2}$$ ... E(2-19)

$$a = \frac{2(67 + 335)}{2} = 402 \text{ mm}$$

Which is very close to the required centre distance a = 400 mm and hence the design is safe.

Step IV: *To check for wear and dynamic load and to find the hardness of Gears.*

Wear load $F_W = d_1bQK > F_d$ ... E(2-160)

$F_W = d_1bQK$

Here, $d_1 = 134$ mm, $b = 22$ mm

$$Q = \text{Ratio factor} = \frac{2Z_2}{Z_2 + Z_1}$$ ... E(2-163)

$$= \frac{2 \times 335}{335 + 67} = 1.67$$

Therefore, $F_W = 134 \times 22 \times 1.67 \times K = 4923.16K$

Now, $$F_d = F_t + \frac{21V(F_t + bc)}{21V + \sqrt{F_t + bc}}$$

Where, $$F_t = \frac{M_t}{r} C_s = 559.59 \text{ N}$$

$$V = v_m = \frac{\pi d_1 n_1}{60}$$

$$= \frac{\pi}{60} \times \frac{134}{1000} \times 1440 = 10.1 \text{m/sec}$$

$$b = 22 \text{ mm} = \frac{22}{1000} \text{m} = 0.022 \text{ m}$$

To find 'C ***[Refer table (2-34) and table (2-35)]***

Referring table (2-34),

For $v_m = 10 \text{m/sec}$; Error $f = 0.0375$ mm

For $v_m = 11.25 \text{m/sec}$; Error $f = 0.0325$ mm

Difference in $v_m = 1.25$ m/sec (increases);

Difference in error $f = 0.005$ mm (decreases)

Decrease in $$f = \frac{0.005}{1.25}(10.1 - 10)$$

$$= 0.0004$$

Therefore, $$f = 0.0375 - 0.0004$$

$$= 0.037 \text{ mm}$$

The value of '*f*' lies between 0.025 mm and 0.050 mm. Now refer table (2-35) to obtain '*C*'.

For cast iron Pinion and cast iron Gear, and $14\frac{1}{2}^{\circ}$ involute profile,

For $f = 0.025$ mm; $C = 139.7 \text{kN/m}$

$f = 0.050$ mm; $C = 279.4 \text{kN/m}$

Difference in $f = 0.025$ mm (increases);

Difference in $C = 139.7 \text{kN/m}$ (increases)

Note: *The value of 'C' increases with increase in 'f'.*

Therefore, $$C = \frac{139.7}{0.025}(0.0379 - 0.025) + 139.7$$

$$= 211.79 \text{ kN/m}$$

Therefore, $$F_d = F_t + \frac{21V(F_t + bc)}{21V + \sqrt{F_t + bc}}$$

Where, $F_t = 559.59 \text{N}$

$V = v_m = 10.1 \text{ m/sec}$

$b = 0.022$ m

$C = 211.79$ kN/m $= 211.79 \times 10^3$ N/m

$$F_d = 559.59 + \frac{21 \times 10.1\left(559.59 + 0.022 \times 211.79 \times 10^3\right)}{21 \times 10.1 + \sqrt{559.59 + 0.022 \times 211.79 \times 10^3}}$$

$= 4035.4$ N

From, $F_W > F_d$

$4923.16K > 4035.4$

Therefore, $K > 0.8196$

Referring table (2-40), for $K = 0.8211$, the Pinion is to be hardened to 300 BHN and Gear to 250 BHN.

Step V: ***Class of Gears (refer figure 2-29 MDH)***

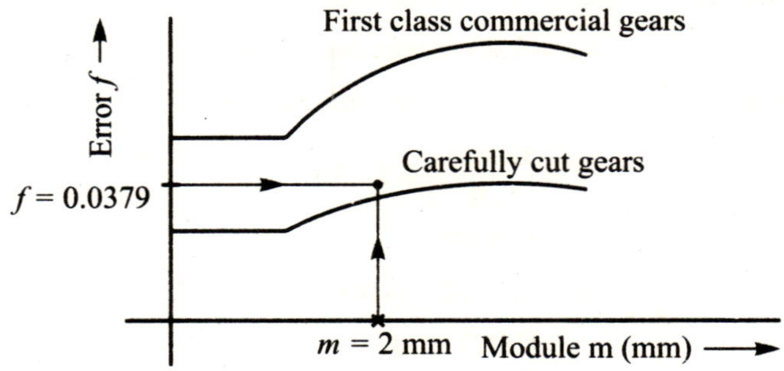

Corresponding to $m = 2$ mm, $f = 0.0379$ mm, the class of Gears is

(a) *First class commercial Gear or*

(b) *Carefully cut Gears since the point of intersection of lines drawn from 'f' and 'm' lie exactly between first class commercial Gear and carefully cut Gears.*

Example 4.3: Design a pair of cast steel Gears to transmit 15 kW at 1440 rpm of the Pinion. The desired transmission ratio is 4 : 1. The teeth have $14\frac{1}{2}^{o}$ involute profile. The diameter of the Pinion is to be restricted to 80 mm. Specify the hardness to which the Gears must be hardened and also the class of Gears. Use face width b = 10 m (m = module). Design for largest number of teeth.

Solution:

Note: Since diameters of Gear and Pinion are known, design for largest number of teeth is possible

Step I: ***Selection of material (Refer Table 2-16)***

For Pinion, select cast steel 0.2%C heat treated for which $\sigma_o = 191.295$ N/mm^2 and for Gear select cast steel 0.2% C, untreated for which $\sigma_o = 137.34$ N/mm^2.

Step II: *To determine the weaker member of Gear pair*

Member	σ_o	*y*	$\sigma_o y$	*Remarks*
Pinion	191.295	0.0898	17.178	Strong
Gear	137.34	0.1155	15.863	Weak

To find 'y', the Lewis form factor

For Gear teeth with $14\frac{1}{2}^{\circ}$ involute profile,

Lewis form factor,

$$y = 0.124 - \frac{0.684}{Z} \quad \text{... E(2-97)}$$

Assuming, $Z_1 = 20$ teeth (use minimum 16 teeth)

$$Z_2 = Z_1 \times \text{Transmission ratio}$$

$$= 20 \times 4 = 80 \text{ teeth}$$

$$y_1 = 0.124 - \frac{0.684}{Z_1}$$

$$= 0.124 - \frac{0.684}{20} = 0.0898$$

$$y_2 = 0.124 - \frac{0.684}{Z_2}$$

$$= 0.124 - \frac{0.684}{80} = 0.1155$$

Note: *Since* $\sigma_o y)_{gear} = 15.863 < \sigma_o y)_{pinion} = 17.178$, *Gear is weaker and hence the design is based on Gear.*

Step III: *To find module 'm'*

Modified Lewis equation for module *'m'* is given by

$$m = \frac{F_t}{\sigma_o C_v b y \pi}$$

Where, $m = \text{module(mm)}$

$$F_t = \frac{M_t C_s}{r} \times 10^3 \text{ N}$$

$$= \frac{\frac{9550 \times 15}{360} \times 1.5 \times 10^3}{160}$$

$$= 3730.47 \text{ N}$$

$$\sigma_o = \sigma_o)_{gear} = 137.34 \text{ N/mm}^2$$

$$n_1 = \text{Speed of Pinion} = 1440 \text{ rpm}$$

Therefore, speed of Gear

$$n_2 = \frac{1440}{4} = 360\,\text{rpm}$$

$$r_1 = \frac{80\text{ mm}}{2} = 40\text{ mm}$$

$$d_1 = 80\text{ mm}$$

$$d_2 = 80 \times 4 = 320\text{ mm}$$

$$r_2 = 160\text{ mm}$$

To find C_v, the velocity factor

Velocity, $$V = \frac{\pi d_2 n_2}{60}$$

$$= \frac{\pi}{60}\left(\frac{320}{1000}\right)360\text{ m/sec} = 6.032\text{ m/sec}$$

Therefore, $$C_v = \frac{4.5}{4.5 + v_m}$$ ... E(2-129)

$$= \frac{4.5}{4.5 + 6.032} = 0.4273$$

Retain 'y' as 'y'

Therefore, substituting in the equation of module, we get,

$$m = \frac{3730.47}{137.34 \times 0.4273 \times 10m \times y \times \pi}$$

Therefore, $$\left.m^2 y\right)_{\text{allowable}} = 2.023$$

Trials to find 'm'

Trial 1: Let m = 5 mm ***[Refer table 2-3]***

Then, $$d_2 = mZ_2$$

$$320 = 5Z_2$$

Therefore, $$Z_2 = 64\text{ teeth}$$

Form, $$y = 0.124 - \frac{0.684}{Z}$$

$$y = y_2 = y_{\text{gear}} = 0.124 - \frac{0.684}{64}$$

$$= 0.1133$$

Therefore, $m^2 y = 5^2 \times 0.1133 = 2.8325 > 2.023$ (not desirable)

Trial 2: Let m = 4 mm

$$d_2 = mZ_2 = 4Z_2$$

Therefore from $320 = 4Z_2$

$$Z_2 = 80 \text{ teeth}$$

$$y = 0.124 - \frac{0.684}{80} = 0.1155$$

Therefore, $m^2y = 4^2 \times 0.1155 = 1.848 < m^2y)_{\text{allowable}} = 2.023$

Adopt $m = 4$ mm.

Particulars of Gears

Sl. No	*Particulars*	*Pinion*	*Gear*
1.	Material	Cast steel 0.2% C heat treated	Cast steel 0.2% C untreated
2.	Module, *m*	*m* = 4 mm	*m* = 4 mm
3.	Number of teeth, *Z*	Z_1= 20 teeth	Z_2= 80 teeth
4.	Pitch circle diameter, *d; d = mZ*	$d_1 = mZ_1 = 80$ mm	$d_2 = mZ_2 = 320$ mm
5.	Face width *b; b = 10 m*	*b* = 40 mm	*b* = 40 mm
6.	Tooth thickness *S; S = πm/2*	*S* = 6.3 mm	*S* = 6.3 mm

Step IV: *To check for wear and dynamic loads and to determine hardness of Gears*

Wear load $F_W = d_1bQK > F_d$ ... E(2-160)

In equation $F_W = d_1bQK$,

$$d_1 = 80 \text{ mm}, b = 40 \text{ mm}$$

$$Q = \text{ Ratio factor} = \frac{2Z_2}{Z_2 + Z_1} \quad \text{... E(2-163)}$$

$$= \frac{2 \times 80}{80 + 20} = 1.6$$

Therefore, $F_W = 80 \times 40 \times 1.6 \times K = 5120K$

Now, $$F_d = F_t + \frac{21V(F_t + bc)}{21V + \sqrt{F_t + bc}} \quad \text{... E(2-148a)}$$

Where, $F_t = 3730.47$ N

$$V = v_m = \frac{\pi d_2 n_2}{60}$$

$$= \frac{\pi}{60} \times \frac{320}{1000} \times 360 = 6.032 \text{ m/sec}$$

$$b = 40 \text{ mm} = \frac{40}{1000} = 0.04 \text{ m}$$

To find 'C' ***[Refer table (2-34) and table (2-35)]***

v_m lies between 5 m/sec and 6.25 m/sec

From table (2-34),

For $v_m = 5 \text{ m/sec};$ Error $f = 0.06$ mm

$v_m = 6.25 \text{ m/sec};$ Error $f = 0.0525$ mm

Difference in $v_m = 1.25$ m/sec (increases)

Difference in error $f = 0.0075$ mm (decreases)

Therefore, $$f = 0.06 - \frac{0.0075 \times (6.032 - 5)}{1.25}$$

$$= 0.05381 \text{ mm}$$

From Table (2-35)

Error 'f' lies between 0.050 and 0.075 mm.

For steel Pinion and steel Gear with $14\frac{1}{2}^{\circ}$ involute profile,

For $f = 0.050$ mm; $C = 558.8$ kN/m

$f = 0.075$ mm; $C = 838.2$ kN/m

Difference in $f = 0.025$ mm (increases);

Difference in $C = 279.4$ kN/m (increases)

Note: *The value of 'C' increases with increase in 'f'.*

Therefore, $$C = 558.8 + \frac{279.4}{0.025}(0.05381 - 0.050)$$

$$= 601.38 \text{ kN/m} = 601.38 \times 10^3 \text{ N/m}$$

Therefore, $$F_d = 3730.47 + \frac{21 \times 6.032 (3730.47 + 0.04 \times 601.38 \times 10^3)}{21 \times 6.032 + \sqrt{3730.47 + 0.04 \times 601.38 \times 10^3}}$$

$$= 3825.19 \text{ N}$$

Equating F_W and F_d,

$$5120K > 3825.19$$

Therefore, $K > 0.747$

Now referring table (2-40), for steel Pinion and steel Gear

For, $K = 1.7727 > 0.747$, the Pinion and Gear are to be hardened to 450 BHN.

Step V: ***Class of Gears (refer figure-2-29 MDH)***

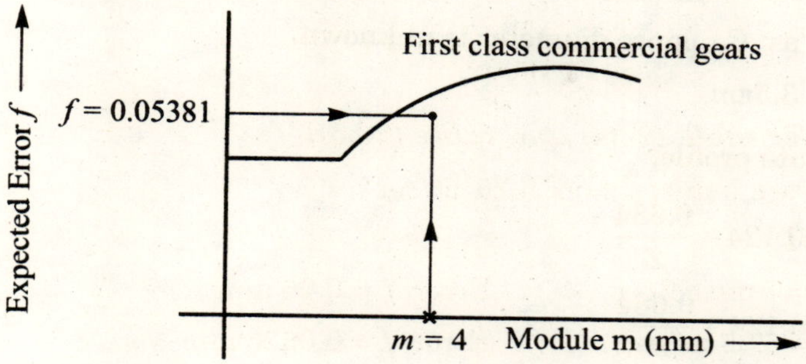

Corresponding to $m = 4$ mm and $f = 0.05381$ mm, the class of *Gears is first class commercial Gears.*

Example 4.4. Design a pair of steel Spur Gears of $14\frac{1}{2}^{\circ}$ involute profile to transmit 20 kW at 1400 rpm of the Pinion. The number of teeth on Pinion and Gear are respectively 25 and 125.

Solution:

Step I: ***Selection of material for Gear and Pinion*** ***(Refer Table 2-16)***

Select cast steel 0.2% C heat treated for both Pinion and Gear for which allowable static stress $\sigma_o = 191.295\ \text{N/mm}^2$.

Step II: ***Determination of weaker member of Gear pair.***

Since Gear and Pinion are of same material, Pinion is the weaker member and the design is based on Pinion.

Step III: ***To find module (m)***

Modified Lewis equation for module '*m*' is given by,

$$m = \frac{F_t}{\sigma_o C_V b y \pi} \qquad \text{... E(2-91)}$$

$$F_t = \frac{M_t}{r} C_S$$

Where, $M_t = M_t)_{\text{weaker member}} = \dfrac{9550 \times 20 \times 10^3}{1400}$

$= 136428.57$ N-mm

Therefore, $F_t = \dfrac{136428.57}{12.5\,\text{m}} \times 1.5$

$= \dfrac{16371.43}{m}$

$r = r_1 = \dfrac{mZ_1}{2}$

$= \dfrac{m \times 25}{2}$

$$\sigma_o = \sigma_o\Big)_{\text{weaker member}} = 191.195 \text{ N/mm}^2$$

Retain C_V as C_V, since diameter is unknown.

$$b = 3.5\pi m \quad \text{... E(2-125)}$$

For $14\frac{1}{2}^o$ involute profile,

$$y = 0.124 - \frac{0.684}{Z} \quad \text{... E(2-97)}$$

$$y_{\text{pinion}} = 0.124 - \frac{0.684}{25}$$

$$= 0.09664$$

Substituting we get,

$$m = \frac{16371.43}{m \times 191.295 \times C_V \times 3.5\pi m \times 0.09664 \times \pi}$$

i.e., $$m_n^3 C_V\Big)_{\text{induced}} = 25.64$$

Trials to find 'm'

Trial 1: Let *m* = 5mm **... Table (2-3)**

From, $d_1 = mZ_1$

$$d_1 = 5 \times 25 = 125 \text{ mm}$$

$$v = v_m = \frac{\pi d_1 n_1}{60}$$

$$= \frac{\pi}{60}\left(\frac{125}{1000}\right)1400 \text{ m/sec}$$

$$= 9.163 \text{ m/sec}$$

$$C_V = \frac{4.5}{4.5 + V_m}$$

$$= \frac{4.5}{4.5 + 9.163}$$

$$= 0.3294$$

Therefore, $m^3 C_V = 5^3 \times 0.3294 = 41.175 > m^3 C_V\Big)_{\text{induced}} = 25.64$

Therefore, adopt m = 5 mm.

$$F_d = 3274.29 + \frac{21 \times 9.163(3274.29 + 0.055 \times 536.45 \times 10^3)}{21 \times 9.163\sqrt{3274.29 + 0.055 \times 536.45 \times 10^3}}$$

$$= 3486.27 \text{ N}$$

Equating F_W and F_d,

$$11481.25K > 3486.27$$

Therefore, $$K > 0.3036$$

Now, referring T(2-40) for steel Pinion and steel Gear with $14\frac{1}{2}^{\circ}$ involute profile, for $K > 0.3036$ (Table value 0.4002), Pinion is to be hardened to 250 BHN and Gear to 150 BHN.

Step V: ***Class of Gears***

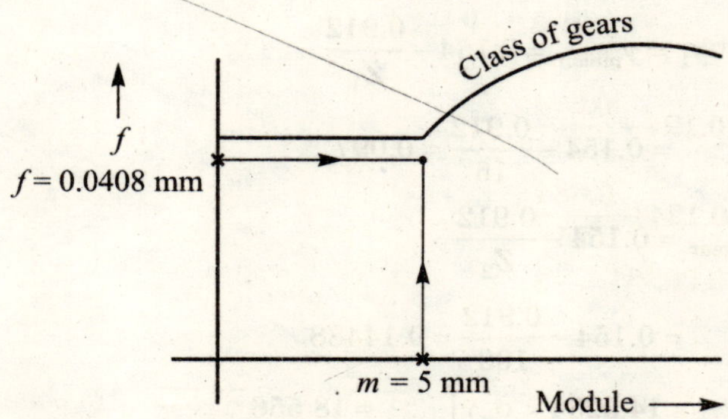

Corresponding to $m = 5$ mm and $f = 0.0408$ mm, the class of *Gears is first class commercial Gears.*

Example 4.5 : A cast steel Pinion rotating at 900 rpm is to drive a cast iron Gear at 144 rpm. The teeth are of 20° involute profile and the power transmitted is 20 kW. The number of teeth on Pinion is 16. The Pinion is to be hardened to 300 BHN and Gear to 250 BHN. Design the gears for smallest pitch diameter.

Solution:

Note: *Since the diameter are unknown, it is possible to design for smallest pitch diameter.*

Step I: ***Selection of material:*** ***(Refer table 2-16)***

For Pinion, select cast steel 0.2% C heat treated steel for which allowable static stress

$$\sigma_o = 191.295 \text{N/mm}^2$$

And for Gear select, high grade cast iron for which

$$\sigma_o = 103.005 \text{N/mm}^2$$

Step II: ***To determine the weaker member of Gear pair***

Member	σ_o	y	$\sigma_o\, y$	Remarks
Pinion	191.295	0.097	18.556	Strong
Gear	103.005	0.14488	14.9234	Weak

To determine 'y', the Lewis form factor

For 20° involute profile,

$$y = 0.154 - \frac{0.912}{Z} \qquad \text{... E(2-98)}$$

Z_1 = Number of teeth on Pinion = 16.

Z_2 = Number of teeth on Gear $= Z_1 \times$ Transmission ratio

$$= 16 \times \frac{900}{144} = 100$$

$$y_1 = y_{pinion} = 0.154 - \frac{0.912}{Z_1}$$

$$= 0.154 - \frac{0.912}{16} = 0.097$$

$$y_2 = y_{gear} = 0.154 - \frac{0.912}{Z_2}$$

$$= 0.154 - \frac{0.912}{100} = 0.14488$$

$$\sigma_o y]_{gear} = 14.9234 < \sigma_o y]_{pinion} = 18.556$$

Hence Gear is the weaker member and the design is based on Gear.

Step III: *To calculate module 'm'*

Modified Lewis equation for module *'m'* is given by

$$m = \frac{F_t}{\sigma_o C_v b y \pi} \qquad \ldots \text{E(2-91)/E(23-91)}$$

Where, m = module, mm

F_t = Tangential force on weaker member

$$= \frac{M_t}{r} C_s$$

$$M_t = \frac{9550N \times 10^3}{n}; \text{ N-mm}$$

N = Power transmitted = 20 kW

n = Speed of weaker member = Speed of Gear = 144 rpm.

Therefore, $M_t = \frac{9550 \times 20 \times 10^3}{144}$ N-mm

$= 1326388.89$ N-mm

$r = r_2$ = Radius of Gear

$$= \frac{d_2}{2} = \frac{mZ_2}{2} = \frac{m \times 100}{2} = 50\text{ m}$$

C_s = Service factor $= 1.5$(assumed)

Therefore, $F_t = \frac{1326388.85}{50\,m} \times 1.5$

$$= \frac{39791.67}{m}$$

$$\sigma_o = \sigma_o\Big)_{\text{weaker member}} = 103.005 \text{ N/mm}^2$$

$$b = 3\pi m \text{ to } 4\pi m \qquad \text{... E(2-215)}$$

Say, $b = 3.5\pi m$

$y = y_2 = 0.14488$ *('y' of weaker member)*

Substituting in E(2-91) we get,

$$m = \frac{39791.67}{m \times 103.005 \times C_v \times 3.5\pi m \times 0.14488\pi}$$

Therefore, $m^3 C_v\Big)_{\text{induced}} = 77.23$

To find 'm', the module [Refer table 2-3 for standard module 'm']

Trial 1: Let *m* = 5 mm

Then, $d_2 = mZ_2$

$$= 5 \times 100 = 500 \text{ mm}$$

Velocity, $v_m = \dfrac{\pi d_2 n_2}{60}$

$$= \frac{\pi}{60} \times \frac{500}{1000} \times 144 = 3.77 \text{ m/sec}$$

Velocity factor, $C_v = \dfrac{4.5}{4.5 + v_m}$ ... E(2-129)

$$= \frac{4.5}{4.5 + 3.77} = 0.544$$

Therefore, $m^3 C_v = 5^3 \times 0.544 = 68 < 77.23$

Trial 2: Let *m* = 6 mm

Then, $d_2 = mZ_2$

$$= 6 \times 100 = 600 \text{ mm}$$

Velocity $v_m = \dfrac{\pi d_2 n_2}{60}$

$$= \frac{\pi}{60} \times \frac{600}{1000} \times 144 = 4.524 \text{ m/sec}$$

Velocity factor, $C_V = \dfrac{4.5}{4.5 + v_m}$

$$= \frac{4.5}{4.5 + 4.524} = 0.4987$$

Therefore, $m^3 C_v = 6^3 \times 0.4987 = 107.72 > 77.23$

Therefore, adopt module $m = 6$ mm

Particulars of Gears

Sl. No	Particulars	Pinion	Gear
1.	Material	Cast steel	High grade cast Iron
2.	Module, m	$m = 5$ mm	$m = 5$ mm
3.	Number of teeth, Z	$Z_1 = 16$ teeth	$Z_2 = 100$ teeth
4.	Pitch circle diameter, d; $d = mZ$	$d_1 = mZ_1 = 5 \times 16 = 80$ mm	$d_2 = mZ_2 = 5 \times 100 = 500$ mm
5.	Face width b; $b = 3.5\pi m$	$b = 55$ mm	$b = 55$ mm
6.	Tooth thickness S; $S = \pi$ m/2	$S = \pi \times \frac{5}{2} = 7.85 \approx 8$ mm	$S = 8$ mm
7.	Addendum h_a = m	$h_a = 5$ mm	$h_a = 5$ mm
8.	Dedendum h_f = 1.25 m	$h_f = 6.25$ m	$h_f = 6.25$ mm

Step IV: *To check for wear and dynamic load and to determine the hardness of Gears.*

Wear load $F_w = d_1 bQK > F_d$ ... E(2-160)

Where, F_W = Wear load

F_d = Dynamic load

d_1 = Diameter of Pinion = 80 mm

b = Face width of Gear/Pinion

$= 3.5\pi m = 3.5\pi \times 5 = 55$ mm

$$Q = \text{Ratio factor} = \frac{2Z_2}{Z_2 + Z_1} \quad \text{... E(2-163)}$$

$$= \frac{2 \times 100}{100 + 16} = 1.724$$

K = Load stress factor

Therefore, $F_W = 80 \times 55 \times 1.724 \times K$

$= 7585.6K$

To find dynamic load F_d

$$F_d = F_t + \frac{21v_m(F_t + bc)}{21v_m + \sqrt{F_t + bc}} \quad \text{... E(2-148a)}$$

$$F_t = \frac{39791.67}{m}$$

$$= \frac{39791.67}{5} = 7958.334 \text{ N}$$

$$v = v_m = \frac{\pi d_2 n_2}{60}$$

$$= \frac{\pi}{60} \times \frac{500}{1000} \times 144 = 3.77 \text{ m/sec}$$

$$b = 55 \text{ mm} = \frac{55 \text{ mm}}{1000} = 0.055 \text{ m}$$

Calculation of 'C' [Refer tables (2-34) and (2-35)]

From (table-2.34),

Interpolate and get the value of '*f*' (error)

For $v_m = 3.75 \text{m/sec};$ Error $f = 0.0700$ mm

$v_m = 5.00 \text{ m/sec};$ Error $f = 0.0600$ mm

Therefore, Difference in $v_m = 1.25$ (increases);

Difference in $f = 0.01$ (decreases).

Note: *When V_m increases, f decreases.*

$$\text{Decrease in } f = \frac{0.01}{1.25} \times (3.77 - 3.75)$$

$$= 0.00016 \text{ mm}$$

$$\text{Therefore}, \ f = 0.07 - 0.00016$$

$$= -0.06984 \text{ mm}$$

Now referring table (2-35)

For steel Pinion and Cast Iron Gear, (20° full depth profile)

For $f = 0.05 \text{mm};$ $C = 398.28 \text{kN/m}$

$f = 0.075 \text{ mm};$ $C = 597.42 \text{kN/m}$

Therefore, Difference in $f = 0.025$ mm (increases);

Difference in $C = 199.14 \text{kN/m}$ (increases)

***Note:* 'C' increases with increase in 'f'**

Increase in $C = \frac{199.14}{0.025}(0.06984 - 0.05)$

$= 158.04$ kN/m

Therefore, $C = 398.28 + 158.04$

$= 556.32$ kN/m $= 556.32 \times 10^3$ N/m

$$F_d = F_t + \frac{21v_m(F_t + bs)}{21v_m + \sqrt{F_t + bs}}\text{; becomes}$$

Becomes, $F_d = 7958.334 + \frac{21 \times 3.77(7958.334 + 0.055 \times 556.32 \times 10^3)}{21 \times 3.77 + \sqrt{7958.334 + 0.055 \times 556.32 \times 10^3}}$

$= 8009.7$ N

We have, $F_W = d_1 bQK$

Where, $K = 1.1174$ for Pinion hardened to 300 BHN and Gear hardened to 250 BHN (Refer Table 2-40).

Therefore, $F_W = 80 \times 55 \times 1.724 \times 1.1174$

$= 8476.15$ N

Therefore, $F_W = 8476.15\text{ N} > F_d = 8009.7\text{ N}$.

Hence the design is safe.

Step V: *Class of Gears* ***[Refer figure 2.29 MDH]***

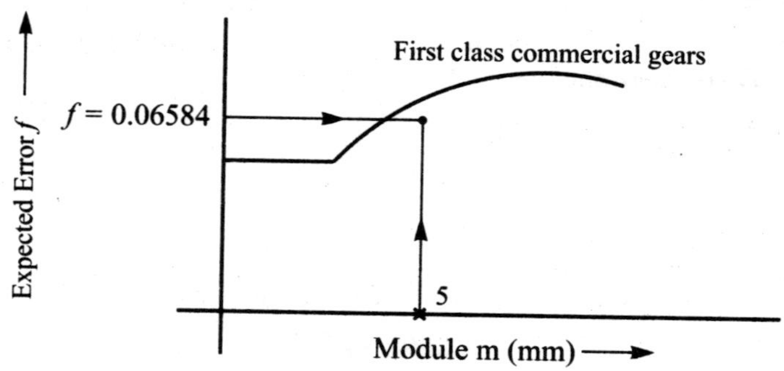

Corresponding to m = 5 mm and error f = 0.06984, the class of gears is first class commercial gears.

EXERCISE

1. A pair of spur Gears is required to transmit 5 kW of power. The Pinion rotates at a speed of 1620 rpm and the gear is required to run at 420 rpm. Determine the least number of teeth on the Gear and Pinion such that velocity ratio does not deviate at all. The tooth form is 20° full depth involute, therefore the number of teeth selected on the Pinion should not be less than the theoretical minimum. The permissible stress in the material of the Gear and the Pinion are 55 MPa and 65 MPa respectively. Design the Gears for beam strength only and determine all the proportions of the gearing. ***(VTU, July 2006)***
2. (*a*) Derive an expression for beam strength of a spur Gear tooth with standard notations. ***(VTU, Dec 06 / Jan 07), (VTU, July 07)***

   (*b*) A pair of spur gears has to transmit 20 kW from a shaft rotating at 1000 rpm to a parallel shaft which is to rotate at 310 rpm. Number of teeth on Pinion is 31 with 20° full depth involute tooth form. The material for Pinion is steel SAE 1040 untreated with allowable static stress 206.81 MPa and the material for gear is cast steel 0.20% C untreated with allowable static stress 137.34 MPa. Determine the module and face width of the Gear pair. Also find the dynamic tooth load on the Gears. Take the service factor as 1.5. ***(VTU, Dec 06 / Jan 07)***
3. Design a pair of spur Gears to transmit 15 kw from a shaft rotating at 1000 rpm to a parallel shaft which is to rotate at 310 rpm. Assume number of teeth on Pinion 31 and 20° full depth tooth form. The material for Pinion is C40 steel untreated and for Gear, cast steel 0.20%C untreated. ***(VTU, July 07)***
4. A cast steel Pinion rotating at 900 rpm is to derive a cast iron gear at 144 rpm. The static design stresses for Pinion and Gear materials are 103 MPa and 55 MPa respectively. The teeth are to have standard 20° stub involute profiles and the maximum power to be transmitted is 25 kW. Design the spur Gears completely and check for the dynamic and wear loads. The gear surfaces are hardened to BHN 250. Use 16 teeth on the Pinion. ***(VTU, Dec 07 / Jan 08)***
5. A machine running at 360 rpm is driven by 12 kW, 1440 rpm motor through a 14 ½ involute Gear. The centre distance between the Gears is 120 mm. The Pinion is made up of heat treated cast steel with allowable stress of 191.2 MPa and of 450 BHN. The Gear is made of untreated cast steel with allowable static stress of 137.3 MPa and BHN of 300. Assuming Gears working 8 hours/day and subjected to light shocks determine the module, face width and number of teeth on each gear. Also check the design for wear. ***(VTU, June / July 08)***

HELICAL GEARS

Helical Gears are used to transmit power between parallel and non-parallel shafts. The teeth are cut in the form of an helix at an angle to the axis called helix angle. In these gears, when a pair of gears mesh, the contact begins at one end of mating Gear and gradually moves along a diagonal line across the width. The number of pairs of teeth in mesh are more compared to spur gear and since there is gradual contact between mating pair, they are less noisy, produce less vibration and are able to transmit more power. Velocity ratios upto 10 : 1 may be obtained in a single step.

A double helical gear is called a Herringbone Gear in which the teeth along width inclined to the axis are cut in the opposite directions as shown in figure below.

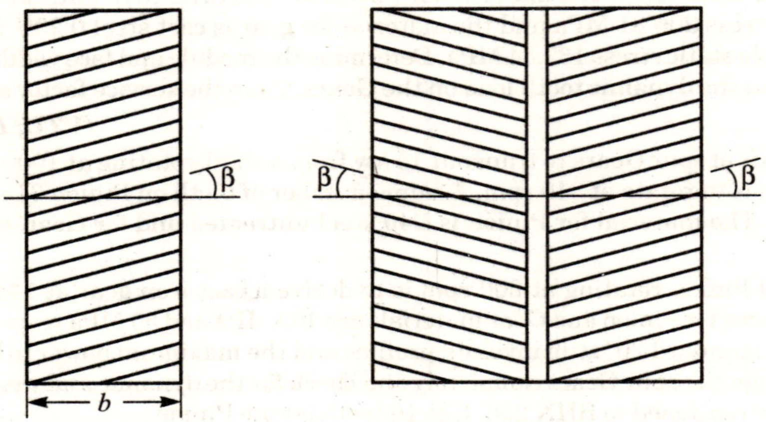

Helical Gear

Double Helical Gear (Herringbone Gear)

Formative Number of Teeth (or Virtual number of teeth)

Formative number of teeth on a helical Gear is defined as the number of teeth that can be produced on a surface of a cylinder having pith radius equal to the radius of curvature at a point at the tip of minor axis of an ellipse obtained by taking section through the helical Gear in plane normal to the tooth at that point.

Formative number of teeth

$$Z_V = \frac{Z}{\cos^3 \beta}$$

where, Z_V = Virtual number of teeth or formative number of teeth.

Z = Actual number of teeth.

β = Helix angle (which usually ranges from 10° to 45°)

Design Procedure for Helical Gears

Step I: ***Selection of material for Gear and Pinion*** ***(Refer Table 2-57) MDH***

Table - (2-57) MDH

Material	Elastic Limit σ_e			Allowable Static Stress, σ_o		
	kgf/mm²	MN/m²	MPa	kgf/mm²	MN/m²	MPa
Cast iron, ordinary	8.44	82.80	82.80	2.81	27.57	27.57
Cast iron, better grade	11.25	110.36	110.36	3.16	31.00	31.00
Laminated phenolic materials	7.03	69.66	69.66	2.81	27.57	27.57
Bronze, SAE 65	16.88	165.59	165.59	4.22	41.40	41.40
Cast steel ASTM class B medium	24.61	240.82	240.75	5.27	51.70	51.70
0.40 to 0.5 per cent carbon steel, non-treated	28.12	275.86	275.86	7.03	69.66	69.66
0.40 to 0.5 per cent carbon steel, heat treated	35.15	344.57	344.57	8.79	86.03	86.03
High carbon or alloy steels, heat treated	42.19	413.88	413.88	10.55	103.50	103.50

Select same or different materials for Gear and Pinion, such as cast steel for which allowable static stress $\sigma_o = 51.7 \text{N/mm}^2$. If the materials are different, then the material chosen for Pinion should possess higher value of σ_o than that of Gear.

Step II: ***To determine weaker member of Gear pair***

(*a*) If Gear and Pinion are made of same material, Pinion is the weaker member and the design is to be based on Pinion.

(*b*) If Gear and Pinion are made of different materials such as Pinion made of 0.4 to 0.5% carbon steel (heat treated) for which $\sigma_o = 86.03 \text{ N/mm}^2$ and Gear made of 0.4 to 0.5% carbon steel (untreated) for which $\sigma_o = 69.66 \text{N/mm}^2$, then the strength factor $(\sigma_o y)$ is calculated as shown below.

Note: *The Lewis form factor 'y' is based on Z_V, the formative number of teeth or virtual member of teeth given by*

$$Z_V = \frac{Z}{\cos^3 \beta} \quad \text{... E(2-285)}$$

Where, β = Helix angle of gear; Degree.

Where, $Z_{1V} = \dfrac{Z_1}{\cos^3 \beta}$ for Pinion.

$Z_{2V} = \dfrac{Z_2}{\cos^3 \beta}$ for Gear, assume $\beta = 10°$ to $45°$.

Z_1 and Z_2 are the actual number of teeth on Pinion and Gear respectively.

Member	σ_o	y	$\sigma_o y$	Remarks
Pinion	86.03	0.112	9.6354	Strong
Gear	69.66	0.12099	8.4282	Weak

Note: *'y' shown in the above table is based on $Z_1 = 20$ and $Z_2 = 80$ teeth with $14\frac{1}{2}^\circ$ involute profile,*

Lewis form factor, $y = 0.124 - \dfrac{0.684}{Z}$ ... E(2-97)

Where, $Z = Z_V$

In the above table, the strength factor,

$$\sigma_o y)_{\text{gear}} = 8.4282 < \sigma_o y)_{\text{pinion}} = 9.6354$$

Hence, Gear is weaker and the design is based on Gear.

Step III: *Calculation of module (m) of Gears*

The modified Lewis equation for module is given by

$$m_t = \sqrt[3]{\frac{2M_t C_W}{\lambda Z \sigma_o (\pi y) C_V}}; \quad \text{Where } Y = \pi y \qquad \text{... E(2-287b)}$$

Where, m_t = Transverse module = $\dfrac{m_n}{\cos\beta}$ ... E(2-212)

m_n = Normal module, mm

Substituting $m_t = \dfrac{m_n}{\cos\beta}$ and cubing both sides of equation (2-287b) we get,

$$\left(\frac{m_n}{\cos\beta}\right)^3 = \frac{2M_t C_W}{\lambda Z \sigma_o (\pi y) C_V}$$

Case 1: When diameters of Gears are known or centre distance between shafts is known,

In the above equation, *i.e.,* E(2-287b),

$$m_n = m_n$$

$$M_t = \frac{9550 N \times 10^3}{n_1}, \text{ if Pinion is weaker.}$$

$$= \frac{9550 N \times 10^3}{n_2}, \text{ if Gear is weaker.}$$

Where, n_1 and n_2 are the speeds of Pinion and Gear respectively.

N = Power transmitted in kW.

C_W = Wear and lubrication factor ... T(2-56)

Table - (2-56) MDH

Nature of Lubrication	C_W
For enclosed gears continuously lubricated with oil of proper viscosity and character	1.15
For scant lubricated but regular, frequent inspection	1.25
For indifferent lubrication	1.35

$\lambda = 10$, (Varies from 4 to 12).

Z = Number of teeth on weaker member = Z_1, if Pinion is weaker.

= Z_2, if Gear is weaker.

$\sigma_o = \sigma_o)_{\text{weaker member}}$

y = Lewis form factor based on Z_V, the virtual member of teeth.

C_V = Velocity factor. It depends on velocity 'v' and is given by

$$v = \frac{\pi d_1 n_1}{60}, \text{ if Pinion is weaker.}$$

$$= \frac{\pi d_2 n_2}{60}, \text{ if Gear is weaker.}$$

With the substitution of the above values, the modified Lewis equation reduces to

$$m_n^2 y = \text{A known numerical value} \qquad \text{... (1)}$$

Note: *When diameter of Gears or the centre distance of Gears is known, $m_n^2 y$ is an allowable value.*

Case 2: When diameters are unknown

$$M_t = \frac{9550 N \times 10^3}{n_1} \text{ N-mm, when Pinion is weaker.}$$

$$= \frac{9550 N \times 10^3}{n_2} \text{ N-mm, when Gear is weaker.}$$

C_V is retained as C_V, since velocity is unknown.

With the substitution of the values,

$$m_n^3 C_V = \text{A known numerical value is obtained.} \qquad \text{... (2)}$$

Note: *When diameter of Gears are unknown, $m_n^3 C_V$ is an induced value.*

(a) Module (m) when diameter is known

The governing equation $m_n^2 y$ = A known numerical value

Trials to find m_n

Let $m_n = 5$ mm (Table 2-3)

$$d_1 = \frac{m_n Z_1}{\cos\beta}, \text{ if Pinion is weaker.}$$

$$d_2 = \frac{m_n Z_2}{\cos\beta}, \text{ if Gear is weaker.}$$

Since diameters are known, Z_1 or Z_2 is obtained from d_1 or d_2
Based on Z_1 or Z_2, Z_V is calculated using equation

$$Z_V = \frac{Z}{\cos^3\beta}$$

'y' is calculated based on Z_V.

Continue trials till the quantity $m_n^2 y$ equals the numerical value of RHS of $m_n^2 y$ or it is lesser than the numerical value.

Particulars of Gears

Sl. No	*Particulars*	*Pinion*	*Gear*
1.	Material	Selected from T(2-57)	Selected from T(2-57)
2.	Module, m_n	m_n	m_n
3.	Number of teeth, Z	Z_1	Z_2
4.	Pitch circle diameter, d	$d_1 = \frac{m_n Z_1}{\cos\beta}$	$d_2 = \frac{m_n Z_2}{\cos\beta}$
5.	Face width $b = \frac{1.15\pi m_n}{\cos\beta \tan\beta}$	b	b

Step IV: ***To check for wear and dynamic loads and to determine the hardness of Gears.***

Wear load $F_W = \frac{d_1 b Q K}{\cos^2\beta} > F_d$ ... E(2-298)

Where, d_1 = Pitch circle diameter of Pinion, mm.

b = Face width of Gears, mm

Q = Ratio factor $= \frac{2Z_2}{Z_2 + Z_1}$

Z_1 = Number of teeth on Pinion.

Z_2 = Number of teeth on Gear.

β = Helix angle.

F_d, the dynamic load is calculated from equation,

$$F_d = F_t + \frac{21V\left(F_t + bc\cos^2\beta\right)\cos\beta}{21V + \sqrt{\left(F_t + bc\cos^2\beta\right)}} \quad \text{... E(2-297)}$$

Constant 'C' is obtained from T(2-35), and based on velocity 'v' and error 'f' obtained from T(2-34)

Case 1: When hardness of Gears is unknown

Use, $$F_W = \frac{d_1 bQK}{\cos^2\beta} > F_d$$

i.e., $$K \geq \frac{F_W\cos^2\beta}{d_1 bQ} \quad \text{... E(2-298)}$$

Based on 'K', refer table (2-40) and obtain the hardness of Pinion and Gear.

Case 2: When hardness of Gears is known,

Use K = Load stress factor, obtained from,

$$K = \frac{1.43\sigma_{-1C}^2 \sin\alpha}{E_o} \quad \text{... E(2-161)}$$

Where, σ_{-1C} = Fatigue endurance strength in N/mm^2..

$= 2.75H_B - 69$ ... E(2-168C)

H_B = Brinell hardness number of softer of the two Gears.

α = Pressure angle of Gears $\left(14\frac{1}{2}^\circ \text{ or } 20^\circ\right)$

Based on 'K', F_w and F_d are calculated and checked wether $F_w > F_d$

Example 4.6: A pair of helical Gears is to transmit 15 kW. The teeth are 20° stub form and have a helix angle of 45°. The Pinion has pitch diameter of 80 mm and operates at 10,000 rpm. The Gear has 320 mm pitch circle diameter. The Gears are made of cast steel. Design the Gears completely.

Solution:

Step I: ***Selection of material*** ***(Refer Table 2-57)***

Select cast steel for both Pinion and Gear for which the allowable static stress

$\sigma_o = 51.7\,\text{N/mm}^2$

Step II: ***To decide weaker member of Gear pair***

Since Gear and Pinion are made of same material, Pinion is the weaker member and the design is based on Pinion.

Step III: ***To calculate module*** **(m_n)**

Modified Lewis equation for module is given by

$$m_t = \sqrt[3]{\frac{2M_t C_W}{\lambda Z \sigma_o Y C_V}} \quad \text{... E(2-287b)}$$

Where, m_t = Transverse module = $\dfrac{m_n}{\cos\beta}$ ... E(2-212)

m_n = Normal module

Substituting $m_t = \dfrac{m_n}{\cos\beta}$ and cubing both sides of E(2-287b),

Therefore, $\left(\dfrac{m_n}{\cos\beta}\right)^3 = \dfrac{2M_t C_W}{\lambda Z \sigma_o (\pi y) C_V}$; $Y = \pi y$

β = Helix angle = 45°

$$M_t = M_t)_{\text{weaker member}} = \frac{9550N \times 10^3}{n} \text{ N-mm}$$

$$= \frac{9550 \times 15 \times 10^3}{10000} = 14{,}325 \text{ N-mm}$$

C_W = Wear and lubrication factor (Refer Table 2-56)

Note: *For enclosed Gears continuously lubricated with oil of proper viscosity,*

$C_W = 1.15$; ... *T(2-56)*

- $\lambda = \dfrac{b}{m_t} = 4$ to 12, say $\lambda = 10$

$Z = Z_1$ = Number of teeth on Pinion.

To find Z_1,

We have, $d = \dfrac{mZ}{\cos\beta}$ ... E(2-218)

i.e., $d_1 = \dfrac{m_n Z_1}{\cos\beta}$

$80 = \dfrac{m_n Z_1}{\cos 45}$ *i.e.,* $Z_1 = \dfrac{56.57}{m_n}$

Retain $y = y$ (since number of teeth unknown).

To find C_V, the velocity factor

$$V_m = v = \frac{\pi d_1 n_1}{60}$$

$$= \frac{\pi}{60} \times \frac{80}{1000} \times 10000 = 41.89 \text{ m/sec}$$

Therefore, $C_V = \frac{5.55}{5.55 + \sqrt{V_m}}$ ... E(2-289b)

$$= \frac{5.55}{5.55 + \sqrt{41.89}}$$

$$= 0.4616$$

Substituting in Lewis equation we get

$$\left(\frac{m_n}{\cos\beta}\right)^3 = \frac{2 \times 14325 \times 1.15}{10 \times \frac{56.57}{m_n} \times 51.7 \times \pi \times 0.4616 \times y}$$

$$m_n^2 y = \frac{2 \times 14325 \times 1.15 \cos 45°}{10 \times 56.57 \times 51.7 \times 0.4616 \times \pi}$$

$$m_n^2 y\Big)_{\text{allowable}} = 0.5493$$

$m_n^2 y$ is an allowable value since diameter of Gears are known.

To find module (m_n)

Trial 1: Let m_n = 5 mm

From, $d_1 = \frac{m_n Z_1}{\cos\beta}$ ... E(2-227)

$$80 = \frac{5Z_1}{\cos 45°}; \quad Z_1 = 11.31 \approx 12 \text{ teeth}$$

To find 'y', the Lewis form factor

Note: *For helical Gears, 'y' is based on Z_V, the virtual number of teeth.*

For 20° stub profile,

$y = 0.170 - \frac{0.95}{Z_{1V}}$ ... E(2-99)

Where, Z_{1V} = Number of virtual teeth on Pinion.

$Z_V = \frac{Z}{\cos^3\beta} \qquad \therefore Z_{1V} = \frac{Z_1}{\cos^3\beta}$ ... E(2-285)

i.e., $$Z_{1V} = \frac{12}{\cos^3 45} = 33.94 \approx 34 \text{ teeth}$$

$$y = 0.170 - \frac{0.95}{34}$$

$$= 0.14206$$

i.e., $m_n^2 y = (5)^2 \times (0.14206) = 3.5515 > m_n^2 y)_{\text{allowable}} = 0.5493$

Hence reduce m_n

Trial 2: Let m_n = 2 mm

From, $d_1 = \frac{m_n Z_1}{\cos\beta}$ ... E(2-227)

$$80 = \frac{2Z_1}{\cos 45}; \qquad Z_1 = 28.29 \approx 29 \text{ teeth}$$

$$Z_{1V} = \frac{Z_1}{\cos^3\beta}$$

$$= \frac{29}{\cos^3 45°} = 82.02 \approx 82 \text{ teeth}$$

Therefore, $y = 0.17 - \frac{0.95}{82}$

$$= 0.1584$$

$$m_n^2 y = (2)^2 \times (0.1584) = 0.6336 > m_n^2 y)_{\text{allowable}} = 0.5493$$

Further reduce m_n

Trial 3: Let m_n = 1.5 mm

$$d_1 = \frac{m_n Z_1}{\cos\beta}$$ ... E(2-227)

i.e., $80 = \frac{1.5Z_1}{\cos 45}; \qquad Z_1 = 38 \text{ teeth}$

Therefore, $Z_{1V} = \frac{Z_1}{\cos^3\beta}$

$$= \frac{38}{\cos^3 45°} = 107.48 \approx 108 \text{ teeth}$$

$$y = 0.17 - \frac{0.95}{108}$$

$$= 0.1612$$

$$m_n^2 y = (1.5)^2 \times (0.1612) = 0.3627 < m_n^2 y)_{\text{allowable}} = 0.5493$$

Therefore, adopt m_n = 1.5 mm

Particulars of Gears

Sl. No	Particulars	Pinion	Gear
1.	Material	Cast Steel	Cast Steel
2.	Module, m_n	$m_n = 1.5$ mm	$m_n = 1.5$ mm
3.	Number of teeth, Z	$Z_1 = 38$ teeth	$Z_2 = 3 \times 84 = 142$
4.	Pitch circle diameter, d	$d_1 = 80$ mm	$d_2 = 320$ mm
5.	Face width, b	$b = \dfrac{1.15\pi m_n}{\cos\beta \tan\beta} = \dfrac{1.15\pi \times 1.5}{\cos 45° \times \tan 45°} = 8$ mm	$b = 8$ mm

Step IV: ***To check for wear and dynamic load and to determine hardness of Gears***

Wear load $$F_W = \frac{d_1 b Q K}{\cos^2\beta} > F_d \qquad \text{... E(2-298)}$$

$$d_1 = 80 \text{ mm}, b = \text{ face width} = 8 \text{ mm}$$

$$Q = \text{Ratio factor} = \frac{2d_2}{d_2 + d_1}$$

$$= \frac{2 \times 320}{320 + 80} = 1.6$$

$$\cos^2\beta = \cos^2 45° = 0.5$$

Therefore, $F_W = 80 \times 8 \times 1.6K = 1024K$

Dynamic load $$F_d = F_t + \frac{21V\left(F_t + bc\cos^2\beta\right)\cos\beta}{21V + \sqrt{\left(F_t + bc\cos^2\beta\right)}}$$

Where, $V = v_m = 41.89$ m/sec

$$F_t = \frac{M_t C_s}{r_1}$$

$$= \frac{14325 \times 1.5}{40} = 537.19 \text{ N}$$

$$b = 8 \text{ mm} = \frac{8}{1000} = 0.008 \text{ m}$$

To find 'C' ***[Refer Table (2-34) and Table (2-35)***

From Table (2-34), for $v_m = 22$ m/sec and above error $f = 0.0125$ mm

From Table (2-35), for steel Pinion and steel Gear (20° stub)

$$f = 0.0125 \text{ mm}, c = 1501 \text{ kN/m} = 1501 \times 10^3 \text{ N/m}$$

Therefore,

$$F_d = 537.19 + \frac{21 \times 41.49\left(537.19 + 0.008 \times 1501 \times 10^3 \times 0.5\right)}{21 \times 41.89 + \sqrt{537.19 + 0.008 \times 1501 \times 10^3 \times 0.5}} \times 0.7071$$

$$F_d = 4438.92 \text{ N}$$

Now, $F_W \geq F_d$

i.e., $1024\,K > 4438.92$ *i.e.,* $k > 4.335$

Now referring table (2-40), for steel Pinion, steel Gear of 20° stub form, for $K = 4.9521 > 4.335$, the Pinion and Gear are to be hardened to 500 BHN.

Step V: ***Class of Gears***

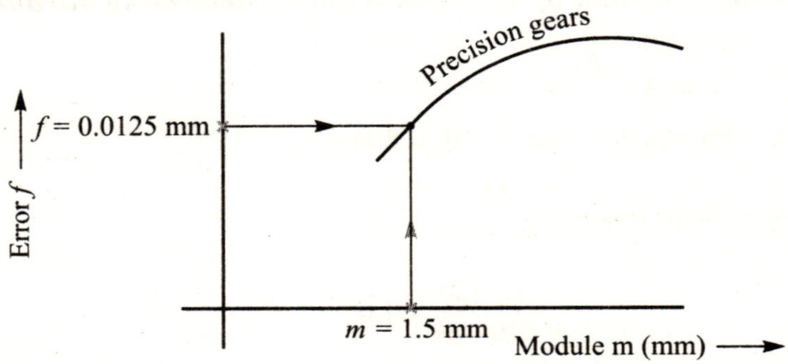

Figure: 2.29 MDH

Note: *Corresponding to m_n = 1.5 mm and error f = 0.0125 mm, the Gears are to be precision cut.*

Example 4.7: A pair of steel helical Gears for parallel shafts is to transmit 15 kW at 2400 rpm of Pinion. Both Gears are made of same material having a design static stress of 105 N/mm². The transmission ratio is to be 4:1. The teeth are 20° stub involute in the normal plane with helix angle not greater than 25°. The minimum number of teeth to be used on either Gears is 28. Design the Gears completely.

Solution:

Step I: ***Selection of material*** ***(Refer Table 2-57)***

Materials of Gear and Pinion having σ_o closer to 105 N/mm^2 are high carbon steels (or alloy steels).

Step II: ***To decide the weaker member of Gear pair***

Since Pinion and Gear are made of same material, Pinion is the weaker member and the design is based on Pinion.

Step III: ***To find module m_n***

Modified Lewis equation for module is

$$m_t = \sqrt[3]{\frac{2M_t C_W}{\lambda Z \sigma_o Y C_V}} \qquad \text{... E(2-287b)}$$

Where, $$m_t = \frac{m_n}{\cos\beta}$$ ... E(2-212)

Substituting $m_t = \dfrac{m_n}{\cos\beta}$ and cubing both sides of E(2-287b) we get,

$$\left(\frac{m_n}{\cos\beta}\right)^3 = \frac{2M_tC_W}{\lambda Z\sigma_o(\pi y)C_V}; \qquad Y = \pi\times y$$

i.e., $$m_n^3C_V = \frac{2M_tC_W\cos^3\beta}{\lambda Z\sigma_o(\pi y)}$$

Where, $$M_t = M_t)_{\text{pinion}} = \frac{9550N\times10^3}{n}$$

$$= 59687.5 \text{ N-mm}$$

$C_W =$ Wear and lubrication factor (Refer Table 2-56)

For completely enclosed Gears lubricated with oil of proper viscosity, $C_W = 1.15$

$$\cos^2\beta = \cos^2 25° = 0.8214, \ \lambda = 10$$

To find Z, the number of teeth on Gear and Pinion

$$Z_1 = 28 \text{ (given)}$$

Therefore, $$Z_2 = Z_1\times\text{Transmission ratio}$$

$$= 28\times4 = 112 \text{ teeth}$$

$$\sigma_o = 105 \text{ N/mm}^2$$

To find 'y', the Lewis form factor

Note: *'y' is based on virtual number of teeth or formative number of teeth* Z_V.

For 20° stub profile,

$$y = 0.17 - \frac{0.95}{Z}$$ ... E(2-99)

Where, $$Z = Z_{1V} = \frac{Z_1}{\cos^3\beta}$$ ... E(2-285)

$$= \frac{28}{\cos^3 25°} = 37.62 \approx 38$$

$$y_{\text{pinion}} = 0.17 - \frac{0.95}{38}$$

$$= 0.145$$

Therefore, $$m_n^3C_V = \frac{2\times59687.5\times1.15\times0.7444}{10\times28\times105\times\pi\times0.145}$$

$$= 7.63$$

Note: *Since diameters are unknown,* $m_n^3C_V$ *is an induced value.*

To determine module m_n

Trial 1: Let m_n = 3 mm **(Table 2-3)**

$$d_1 = \frac{m_n Z_1}{\cos\beta}$$

$$= \frac{3\times 28}{\cos 25^\circ} = 92.68 \text{ mm}$$

$$v_m = V_1 = \frac{\pi d_1 n_1}{60}$$

$$= \frac{\pi}{60}\times\frac{92.68\times 2400}{1000} = 11.65 \text{ m/sec}$$

Therefore, $C_V = \dfrac{4.5}{4.5+v_m}$ ... E(2-288)

$$= \frac{4.5}{4.5+11.65} = 0.2786$$

Therefore, $m_n^3 C_V = (3)^3 \times (0.2786) = 7.72 \approx m_n^3 C_V\big)_{\text{induced value}}$

Hence adopt m_n = 3 mm

Particulars of Gears

Sl. No	*Particulars*	*Pinion*	*Gear*
1.	Material	High Carbon Steel	High Carbon Steel
2.	Module, m_n	m_n = 3 mm	m_n = 3 mm
3.	Number of teeth, Z	Z_1 = 28 teeth	Z_2 = 112 teeth
4.	Pitch circle diameter, d	$d_1 = \frac{m_n Z_1}{\cos\beta} = \frac{3\times 28}{\cos 25} = 92.68$ mm	d_2 = 320 mm
5.	Face width, b $b = \frac{1.15\pi m_n}{\cos\beta\tan\beta}$	b = 26 mm	b = 26 mm

Step IV: ***To check wear and dynamic loads and to determine the hardness of Gears.***

Wear load $F_W = \dfrac{d_1 b Q K}{\cos^2\beta} > F_d$ ... E(2-298)

Where, d_1 = 82.68 mm, b = face width = 26 mm

$$Q = \text{Ratio factor} = \frac{2Z_2}{Z_2+Z_1}$$

$$= \frac{2d_2}{d_2+d_1}$$

$$= \frac{2\times 112}{112+28} = 1.6$$

$$\cos^2\beta = \cos^2 25° = 0.8214$$

Therefore, $F_W = 92.68 \times 26 \times 1.6 \times K$

$$= 3855.49K$$

Dynamic load $$F_d = F_t + \frac{21V\left(F_t + bc\cos^2\beta\right)\cos\beta}{21V + \sqrt{\left(F_t + bc\cos^2\beta\right)}} \quad \text{... E(2-297a)}$$

Where, $$F_t = \frac{M_t C_s}{r_1}$$

$$= \frac{59687.5 \times 1.5}{\frac{92.68}{2}} = 1932.05 \text{ N}$$

$$V = v_m = 11.65 \text{ m/sec}$$

$$b = 26 \text{ mm} = \frac{26}{1000}\text{ m} = 0.026\text{ m}$$

$$\cos\beta = \cos 25° = 0.906$$

To find 'C' ***[Refer Table (2-34) and Table (2-35)***

We have velocity $v_m = 11.65$ m/sec .

This v_m lies between 11.25 m/sec and 12.5 m/sec (Table 2-34)

For, $v_m = 11.25$ m/sec; Error $f = 0.0325$ mm

$v_m = 12.51$ m/sec; Error $f = 0.0300$ mm

Therefore, Difference in $v_m = 1.25$ (increases) and

Difference in $f = 0.0025$ mm (decreases)

Note: *Error 'f' decreases with increase in velocity* V_m

Therefore, $v_m = 11.65$ m/sec ,

$$f = 0.0325 - \frac{0.0025}{1.25} \times (11.65 - 11.25)$$

$$f = 0.0317 \text{ mm}$$

To find 'C' ***(Refer Table 2-35)***

For steel Pinion and steel Gear with 20° stub profile and error lying between 0.025 mm and 0.05 mm, we have

For $f = 0.025$ mm ; $C = 300.2$ kN/m

$f = 0.05$ mm ; $C = 600.4$ kN/m

Therefore, Difference in $f = 0.025$ mm (increases) and

Difference in $C = 300.2$ kN/m (increases).

Note: *The value of 'C' increases with increase in error 'f'*

Therefore, corresponding to error

$$f = 0.0317 \text{ mm},$$

$$C = 300.2 + \frac{300.2}{0.025} \times (0.037 - 0.025)$$

$$= 444.296 \text{ kN/m} = 444.296 \times 10^3 \text{ N/m}$$

$$F_d = 1932.05 + \frac{21 \times 11.65 (1932.05 + 0.026 \times 444.296 \times 10^3 \times 0.8214)}{21 \times 11.65 + \sqrt{1932.05 + 0.026 \times 444.296 \times 10^3 \times 0.8214}} \times 0.906$$

$$= 9133.44 \text{ N}$$

i.e., $3855.49K \geq 9133.44$

Therefore, $k \geq \frac{9133.44}{3855.49}$

i.e., $K \geq 2.369$

To find hardness of Gears ***(Refer Table 2-40)***

For steel Pinion and steel Gear having $20°$ stub teeth, and $K = 2.4211 (i.e., > 2.369)$, the Gear and Pinion are to be hardened to 450 BHN.

Step V: *Class of Gears*

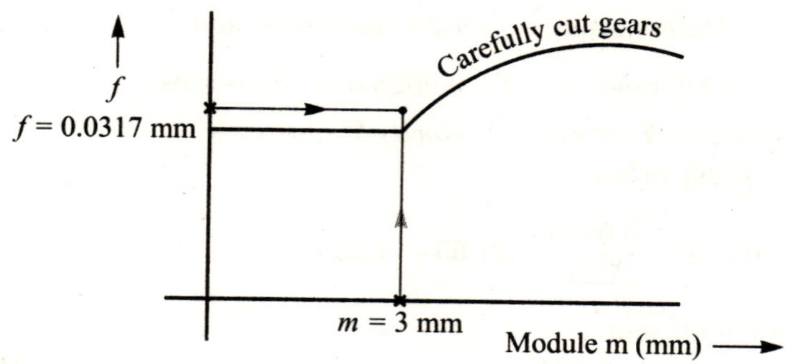

Figure: 2.29 MDH

Referring figure (2-29 MDH), corresponding to module $m_n = 3$ mm and error $f = 0.0317$, *the class of Gears is carefully cut Gears.*

Example 4.8: Design a pair of steel Helical Gears of $14\frac{1}{2}°$ involute profile having helix angle 45° to transmit 20 kW at 1440 rpm of Pinion. The centre distance between Gears is to be closer to 400 mm. The desired transmission ratio is 4:1.

Solution:

Step I: ***Selection of materials*** ***(Refer Table 2-57)***

Select 0.4 to 0.5% carbon steel (heat treated) for Pinion for which allowable static stress $\sigma_o = 86.03 \text{N/mm}^2$ and 0.4 to 0.5% carbon steel (untreated) for Gear for which $\sigma_o = 69.66 \text{N/mm}^2$.

Step II: ***To determine the weaker member of Gear pair***

Member	σ_o	y	$\sigma_o y$	*Remarks*
Pinion	86.03	0.112	9.6354	Strong
Gear	69.66	0.12099	8.4282	Weak

To find 'y', the Lewis form factor

For $14\frac{1}{2}°$ involute profile,

$$y = 0.124 - \frac{0.684}{Z} \quad \text{... E(2-97)}$$

Assume, $Z_1 = 20$ *(arbitrarily chosen with not less than 15 teeth on Pinion).*

$Z_2 = 20 \times 4 = 80$ teeth

For Pinion,

$$Z_{1V} = \frac{Z_1}{\cos^3 \beta} \quad \text{... E(2-285)}$$

$$= \frac{20}{\cos^3 \beta}$$

$$= \frac{20}{\cos^3 45°} = 56.57 = 57 \text{ teeth}$$

$$Z_{2V} = \frac{Z_2}{\cos^3 \beta}$$

$$= \frac{80}{\cos^3 45°} = 227 \text{ teeth}$$

$$y_{\text{pinion}} = y_1 = 0.124 - \frac{0.684}{Z_{1V}}$$

$$= 0.124 - \frac{0.684}{57} = 0.112$$

$$y_{\text{gear}} = y_2 = 0.124 - \frac{0.684}{Z_{2V}}$$

$$= 0.124 - \frac{0.684}{227} = 0.12099$$

Since $\sigma_o y)_{gear} = 8.4282 < \sigma_o y)_{pinion} = 9.6354$, Gear is weaker and hence the design is based on Gear.

Step III: *To determine module, m_n*

We have modified Lewis equation for module given by

$$m_t = \sqrt[3]{\frac{2M_t C_W}{\lambda Z \sigma_o Y C_V}} \quad \text{... E(2-287b)}$$

Here, $$m_t = \frac{m_n}{\cos\beta} \quad \text{... E(2-212)}$$

Substituting $m_t = \dfrac{m_n}{\cos\beta}$ and cubing both sides of E(2-287b) we get,

$$\left(\frac{m_n}{\cos\beta}\right)^3 = \frac{2M_t C_W}{\lambda Z \sigma_o (\pi y) C_V}$$

Where, $\cos\beta = \cos 45° = 0.7071$

$$M_t)_{gear} = \frac{9550\ N}{n} 10^3$$

$$n = n_2 = \text{Speed of Gear} = \frac{\text{Speed of Pinion}}{\text{Transmission ratio}}$$

$$= \frac{1440}{4} = 360 \text{ rpm}$$

$$M_t)_{gear} = \frac{9550 \times 20 \times 10^3}{360}$$

$$= 530555.56 \text{ N-mm}$$

$C_W =$ Wear and lubrication factor.

For completely enclosed Gears lubricated with oil of proper viscosity, $C_W = 1.15$

$$\lambda = 10, Z = Z_2$$

To find Z_2

$$d_2 = \frac{m_n Z_2}{\cos\beta}$$

To find d_1 and d_2, the diameters of Pinion and Gear

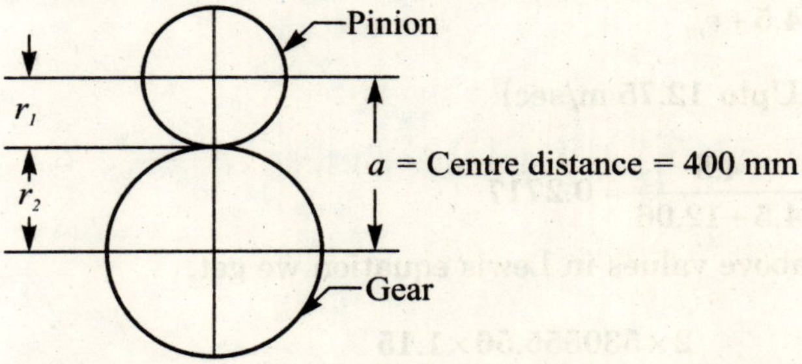

Centre distance $a = r_1 + r_2$

$$a = \frac{d_1}{2} + \frac{d_2}{2}$$

i.e., $d_1 + d_2 = 2a = 2 \times 400 = 800$ ... (1)

Also, transmission ratio

$$i = \frac{d_2}{d_1} = 4$$

Therefore, $d_2 = 4d_1$ ... (2)

From equation 1,

$$d_1 + 4d_1 = 800$$

Therefore, $d_1 = 160$ mm and $d_2 = 640$ mm

From, $d_2 = \dfrac{m_n Z_2}{\cos\beta}$

i.e.,
$$Z_2 = \frac{d_2 \cos\beta}{m_n}$$

$$= \frac{640 \times \cos 45°}{m_n}$$

$$= \frac{452.55}{m_n}$$

$\sigma_o = \sigma_o)_{gear} = 69.66 \text{N/mm}^2$ since Gear is weaker.

Retain y as y; because the number of teeth on Gear is unknown.

To find C_V, the velocity factor

$$V = v_m = V_2 = \frac{\pi d_2 n_2}{60}$$

$$= \frac{\pi}{60}\left(\frac{640}{1000}\right)360$$

$$= 12.06 \text{ m/sec}$$

Therefore, $C_V = \dfrac{4.5}{4.5 + v_m}$ ... E(2-288)

$(v_m = \text{Upto } 12.75 \text{ m/sec})$

Therefore, $C_V = \dfrac{4.5}{4.5 + 12.06} = 0.2717$

Substituting the above values in Lewis equation we get,

$$\left(\frac{m_n}{0.7071}\right)^3 = \frac{2 \times 530555.56 \times 1.15}{10 \times \dfrac{452.55}{m_n} \times 69.66 \times \pi \times y \times 0.2717}$$

Therefore, $\left.m_n^2 y\right)_{\text{allowable}} = 1.602$

Note: *When diameters are known, $m_n^2 y$ is an allowable value.*

To find m_n ***(Refer Table 2-3 for standard value of m_n)***

Trial 1: Let m_n = 4 mm

$d_2 = \dfrac{m_n Z_2}{\cos\beta}$ *i.e.,* $640 = \dfrac{4Z_2}{\cos 45°}$

Therefore, $Z_2 = 113.13 \approx 114$ teeth

$$Z_{2V} = \frac{Z_2}{\cos^3 \beta}$$

$$= \frac{114}{\cos^3 45°} = 322.44 \approx 323 \text{ teeth}$$

Therefore, $y_2 = 0.124 - \dfrac{0.684}{Z_{2V}}$

$$y_2 = 0.124 - \frac{0.684}{323} = 0.1219$$

And $m_n^2 y = 14^2 \times 0.1219 = 1.9504 > \left.m_n^2 y\right)_{\text{allowable}}$

Hence reduce m_n

Trial 2: Let m_n = 3 mm

$d_2 = \dfrac{m_n Z}{\cos\beta}$ *i.e.,* $640 = \dfrac{3Z_2}{\cos 45°}$

Therefore, $Z_2 = 150.9 \approx 151$ teeth

$$Z_{2V} = \frac{Z_2}{\cos^3 \beta}$$

$$= \frac{151}{\cos^3 45°} = 427 \text{ teeth}$$

$$y = y_2 = 0.124 - \frac{0.684}{Z_{2V}}$$

$$= 0.124 - \frac{0.684}{427} = 0.1224$$

Therefore, $m_n^2 y = 3^2 \times 0.1224 = 1.1016 < m_n^2 y\Big)_{\text{allowable}} = 1.602$

Therefore, adopt $m_n = 3$ mm

Particulars of Gears

Sl. No	Particulars	Pinion	Gear
1.	Material	Carbon Steel (Heat treated)	Carbon Steel (Untreated)
2.	Module, m_n	$m_n = 3$ mm	$m_n = 3$ mm
3.	Number of teeth, Z	$Z_1 = 38$ teeth	$Z_2 = 151$
4.	Pitch circle diameter, d	$d_1 = 160$ mm	$d_2 = 640$ mm
5.	Face width, b	$b = \frac{1.15\pi m_n}{\cos\beta \tan\beta} = 22$ mm	$b = 22$ mm

Step IV: *To check for wear and dynamic loads and to determine the hardness of Gears.*

Wear load $$F_W = \frac{d_1 bQK}{\cos^2\beta} > F_d \qquad \text{... E(2-298)}$$

Where, $d_1 = 160$ mm, $b = 22$ mm

$$Q = \text{Ratio factor} = \frac{2d_2}{d_2 + d_1}$$

$$= \frac{2 \times 640}{640 + 160} = 1.6$$

Therefore, $F_W = 160 \times 22 \times 1.6 \times K = 5632K$

Dynamic load $$F_d = F_t + \frac{21V\left(F_t + bc\cos^2\beta\right)\cos\beta}{21V + \sqrt{\left(F_t + bc\cos^2\beta\right)}} \qquad \text{... E(2-297a)}$$

$$F_t = \frac{M_t C_s}{r_1}$$

$$= \frac{530555.56}{\frac{640}{2}} \times 1.5 = 2486.98 \text{ N}$$

$$V = v_m = 12.06 \text{ m/sec}$$

$$b = 22 \text{ mm} = \frac{22}{1000} \text{ m} = 0.022 \text{ m}$$

To find 'C' ***[Refer Table (2-34) and Table (2-35)***

We have velocity $v_m = 12.06$ m/sec. (Refer Table 2-34)

This value of v_m lies between 11.25 m/sec and 12.5 m/sec

For, $v_m = 11.25$ m/sec; Error $f = 0.0325$ mm

$v_m = 12.5$ m/sec; Error $f = 0.0300$ mm

Therefore, Difference in $v_m = 1.25$ (increases) and

Difference in $f = 0.0025$ mm (decreases)

Note: *Error 'f' decreases with increase in velocity* V_m

Therefore, $v_m = 12.06$ m/sec,

$$\text{Error} \quad f = 0.0325 - \frac{0.0025}{1.25} \times (12.06 - 11.25)$$

$$f = 0.0309 \text{ mm}$$

To find 'C' ***(Refer Table 2-35)***

Error $f = 0.0309$ mm and this value lies between 0.025 mm and 0.05 mm.

For steel Pinion and steel Gear of $f = 0.0309$ mm $14\frac{1}{2}^\circ$ involute profile,

For $f = 0.025$ mm ; $C = 279.48$ kN/m

$f = 0.05$ mm ; $C = 558.84$ kN/m

Therefore, Difference in $f = 0.05$ mm (increases) and

Difference in $C = 279.4$ kN/m (increases).

Note: *The value of 'C' increases with increase in error 'f'*

Therefore, error $f = 0.0309$ mm,

$$C = 279.48 + \frac{279.4}{0.025} \times (0.0309 - 0.025)$$

$$C = 345.42 \text{ kN/m} = 345.42 \times 10^3 \text{ N/m}$$

Therefore,

$$F_d = 2486.98 + \frac{21 \times 12.06\left(2486.98 + 0.022 \times 345.42 \times 10^3 \times 0.5\right) \times 0.7071}{21 \times 12.06 + \sqrt{2486.98 + 0.022 \times 345.42 \times 10^3 \times 0.5}}$$

$$F_d = 4533.11 \text{ N}$$

Equating F_W and F_d

$$5632\,K > 4533.11$$

Therefore, $k > 0.8045$

Referring Table (2-40), for $K = 1.7727$ (*i.e.*, > 0.8045), the Pinion and Gear are to be hardened to 450 BHN.

Step V: ***Class of Gears*** ***(Refer Table 2.29 MDH)***

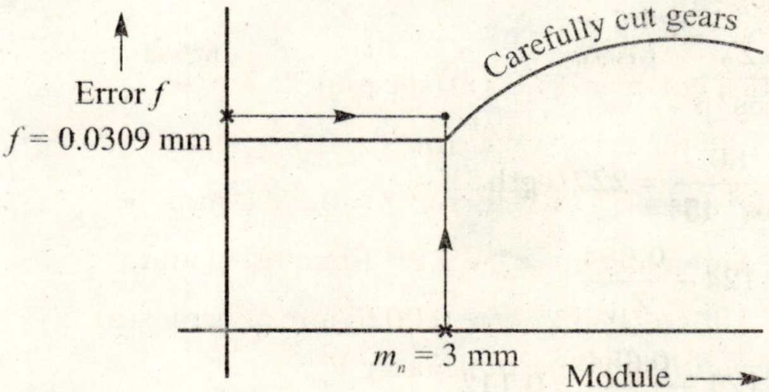

Corresponding to $m_n = 3$ mm and error $f = 0.0309$ mm , *the class of Gears recommended is carefully cut Gears.*

Example 4.9: Design a pair of steel helical Gears of $14\frac{1}{2}^\circ$ ***involute profile having helix angle 45° to transmit 20 kW at 1440 rpm of Pinion. The centre distance between Gears to be closer to 400mm. The desired transmission ratio = 4:1. The gears are hardened to 450 BHN.***

Solution:

Step I: ***Selection of materials*** ***(Refer Table 2-57)***

Select 0.4 to 0.5% carbon steel (heat treated) for Pinion for which allowable static stress $\sigma_o = 86.03$ N/mm^2 and 0.4 to 0.5% carbon steel (untreated) for Gear for which $\sigma_o = 69.66$ N/mm^2 .

Step II: ***To determine the weaker member of Gear pair***

Member	σ_o	*y*	$\sigma_o y$	*Remarks*
Pinion	86.03	0.112	9.6354	Strong
Gear	69.66	0.12099	8.4282	Weak

To find 'y', the Lewis form factor

For gear teeth with $14\frac{1}{2}^\circ$ involute profile,

$$y = 0.124 - \frac{0.684}{Z} \quad \ldots \text{E(2-97)}$$

Assume, $Z_1 = 20$ (arbitrarily chosen with not less than 15 teeth on Pinion).

$Z_2 = 20 \times 4 = 80$ teeth

For Pinion,
$$Z_{1V} = \frac{Z_1}{\cos^3 \beta} \quad \ldots \text{E(2-285)}$$

$$= \frac{20}{\cos^3 \beta}$$

$$= \frac{20}{\cos^3 45} = 56.57 = 57\,\text{teeth}$$

$$Z_{2V} = \frac{Z_2}{\cos^3 \beta}$$

$$= \frac{80}{\cos^3 45°} = 227\,\text{teeth}$$

$$y_{\text{pinion}} = y_1 = 0.124 - \frac{0.684}{Z_{1V}}$$

$$= 0.124 - \frac{0.684}{57} = 0.112$$

$$y_{\text{gear}} = y_2 = 0.124 - \frac{0.684}{Z_{2V}}$$

$$= 0.124 - \frac{0.684}{227} = 0.12099$$

Since $\sigma_o y)_{\text{gear}} = 8.4282 < \sigma_o y)_{\text{pinion}} = 9.6354$ Gear is weaker and hence the design is based on Gear.

Step III: *To determine module, m_n*

We have modified Lewis equation for module given by

$$m_t = \sqrt[3]{\frac{2M_t C_W}{\lambda Z \sigma_o Y C_V}} \quad \text{... E(2-287b)}$$

Here, $$m_t = \frac{m_n}{\cos \beta} \quad \text{... E(2-212)}$$

Substituting $m_t = \frac{m_n}{\cos \beta}$ and cubing both sides of E(2-287b) we get,

$$\left(\frac{m_n}{\cos\beta}\right)^3 = \frac{2M_t C_W}{\lambda Z \sigma_o (\pi y) C_V}$$

Where, $\cos\beta = \cos 45° = 0.7071$

$$M_t)_{\text{gear}} = \frac{9550N}{n} \times 10^3$$

$$n = n_2 = \text{Speed of Gear} = \frac{\text{Speed of Pinion}}{\text{Transmission ratio}}$$

$$= \frac{1440}{4} = 360 \text{ rpm}$$

$$M_t)_{\text{gear}} = \frac{9550 \times 20 \times 10^3}{360}$$

$$= 530555.56 \text{ N-mm}$$

$C_W =$ Wear and lubrication factor.

For completely enclosed Gears lubricated with oil of proper viscosity, $C_W = 1.15$

$$\lambda = 10, Z = Z_2$$

To find Z_2

$$d_2 = \frac{m_n Z_2}{\cos\beta}$$

To find d_1 and d_2, the diameters of Pinion and Gear

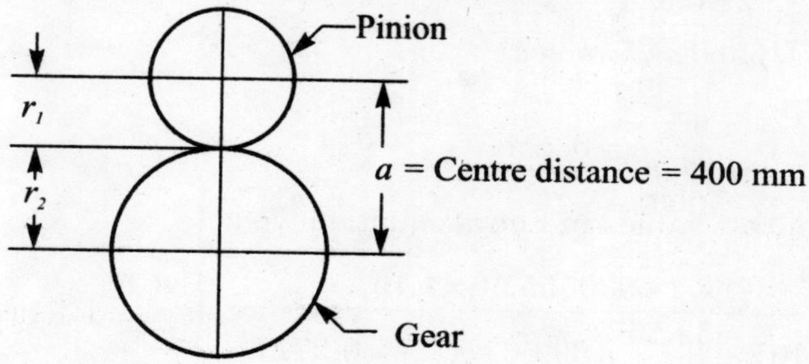

Centre distance $a = r_1 + r_2$

$$= \frac{d_1}{2} + \frac{d_2}{2}$$

i.e., $d_1 + d_2 = 2a = 2 \times 400 = 800$ ... (1)

Also transmission ratio

$$i = \frac{d_2}{d_1} = 4$$

Therefore, $d_2 = 4d_1$ ... (2)

From equation (1),

$$d_1 + 4d_1 = 800$$

Therefore, $d_1 = 160$ mm and $d_2 = 640$ mm

From, $d_2 = \frac{m_n Z_2}{\cos\beta}$

i.e.,

$$Z_2 = \frac{d_2 \cos\beta}{m_n}$$

$$= \frac{640 \times \cos 45°}{m_n}$$

$$= \frac{452.55}{m_n}$$

$\sigma_o = \sigma_o)_{gear} = 69.66\,\text{N/mm}^2$ since Gear is weaker.

Retain y as y; because the number of teeth on Gear is unknown.

To find C_V, the velocity factor

$$V = v_m = V_2 = \frac{\pi d_2 n_2}{60}$$

$$= \frac{\pi}{60}\left(\frac{640}{1000}\right)360$$

$$= 12.06 \text{ m/sec}$$

Therefore, $C_V = \dfrac{4.5}{4.5 + v_m}$ ... E(2-288)

$(v_m = \text{Upto } 12.75 \text{ m/sec})$

Therefore, $C_V = \dfrac{4.5}{4.5 + 12.06} = 0.2717$

Substituting the above values in Lewis equation we get,

$$\left(\frac{m_n}{0.7071}\right)^3 = \frac{2 \times 530555.56 \times 1.15}{10 \times \dfrac{452.55}{m_n} \times 69.66 \times \pi \times y \times 0.2717}$$

Therefore, $m_n^2 y)_{\text{allowable}} = 1.602$

***Note:** When diameters are known, $m_n^2 y$ is an allowable value.*

To find m_n ***(Refer Table 2-3 for standard value of m_n)***

Trial 1: Let m_n = 4 mm

$$d_2 = \frac{m_n Z_2}{\cos\beta} \quad i.e., \quad 640 = \frac{4Z_2}{\cos 45°}$$

Therefore, $Z_2 = 113.13 \approx 114$ teeth

$$Z_{2V} = \frac{Z_2}{\cos^3 \beta}$$

$$= \frac{114}{\cos^3 45°} = 322.44 \approx 323$$

Therefore, $y_2 = 0.124 - \dfrac{0.684}{Z_{2V}}$

$$= 0.124 - \frac{0.684}{323} = 0.1219$$

And $m_n^2 y = 4^2 \times 0.1219 = 1.9504 > m_n^2 y)_{\text{allowable}}$

Hence reduce m_n

Trial 2: Let m_n = 3 mm

$$d_2 = \frac{m_n Z_2}{\cos\beta} \quad i.e., \quad 640 = \frac{3Z_2}{\cos 45°}$$

Therefore, $Z_2 = 150.9 \approx 151$ teeth

$$Z_{2V} = \frac{Z_2}{\cos^3 \beta}$$

$$= \frac{151}{\cos^3 45°} = 427 \text{ teeth}$$

$$y = y_2 = 0.124 - \frac{0.684}{Z_{2V}}$$

$$= 0.124 - \frac{0.684}{427} = 0.1224$$

Therefore, $m_n^2 y = 3^2 \times 0.1224 = 1.1016 < m_n^2 y\Big)_{\text{allowable}} = 1.602$

Therefore, adopt $m_n = 3$ mm

Particulars of Gears

Sl. No	Particulars	Pinion	
1.	Material	Carbon Steel (Heat treated)	Carbon Steel (Untreated)
2.	Module, m_n	$m_n = 3$ mm	$m_n = 3$ mm
3.	Number of teeth, Z	$Z_1 = 38$ teeth	$Z_2 = 151$
4.	Pitch circle diameter, d	$d_1 = 160$ mm	$d_2 = 640$ mm
5.	Face width, b	$b = \frac{1.15\pi m_n}{\cos\beta \tan\beta} = 22$ mm	$b = 22$ mm

Step IV: *To check for wear and dynamic loads and to determine the hardness of Gears.*

Wear load $F_W = \dfrac{d_1 b Q K}{\cos^2 \beta} > F_d$ ... E(2-298)

Where, $d_1 = 160$ mm, $b = 22$ mm

$$Q = \text{Ratio factor} = \frac{2d_2}{d_2 + d_1}$$

$$= \frac{2 \times 640}{640 + 160} = 1.6$$

Therefore, $F_W = 160 \times 22 \times 1.6 \times K = 5632K$

Dynamic load $F_d = F_t + \dfrac{21V\left(F_t + bc\cos^2\beta\right)\cos\beta}{21V + \sqrt{\left(F_t + bc\cos^2\beta\right)}}$ ... E(2-297a)

$$F_t = \frac{M_t C_s}{r_1}$$

$$= \frac{530555.56}{\frac{640}{2}} \times 1.5 = 2486.98$$

$$V = v_m = 12.06 \text{ m/sec}$$

$$b = 22 \text{ mm} = \frac{22}{1000} \text{m} = 0.022 \text{ m}$$

To find 'C' **[Refer Table (2-34) and Table (2-35)**

We have velocity $v_m = 12.06$ m/sec. **(Refer Table 2-34)**

This value v_m lies between 11.25 m/sec and 12.5 m/sec

For, $v_m = 11.25$ m/sec; Error $f = 0.0325$ mm

$v_m = 12.5$ m/sec; Error $f = 0.0300$ mm

Therefore, Difference in $v_m = 1.25$ (increases) and

Difference in $f = 0.0025$ mm (decreases)

Note: *Error 'f' decreases with increase in velocity* V_m

Therefore, $V_m = 12.06$ m/sec,

Error $$f = 0.0325 - \frac{0.0025}{1.25} \times (12.06 - 11.25)$$

$$f = 0.0309 \text{ mm}$$

To find 'C' **(Refer Table 2-35)**

Error $f = 0.0309$ mm and this value lies between 0.025 mm and 0.05 mm.

For steel Pinion and steel Gear of $f = 0.0309$ mm $14\frac{1}{2}^\circ$ involute profile,

For $f = 0.025$ mm ; $C = 279.48$ kN/m

$f = 0.05$ mm ; $C = 558.84$ kN/m

Therefore, Difference in $f = 0.025$ mm (increases) and

Difference in $C = 279.4$ kN/m (increases).

Note: *The value of 'C' increases with increase in error 'f'*

Therefore, error $f = 0.0309$ mm,

$$C = 279.48 + \frac{279.4}{0.025} \times (0.0309 - 0.025)$$

$$= 345.42 \text{ kN/m} = 345.42 \times 10^3 \text{ N/m}$$

Therefore,

$$F_d = 2486.98 + \frac{21 \times 12.06\left(2486.98 + 0.022 \times 345.42 \times 10^3 \times 0.5\right) \times 0.7071}{21 \times 12.06 + \sqrt{2486.98 + 0.022 \times 345.42 \times 10^3 \times 0.5}}$$

$$F_d = 4533.11 \text{ N}$$

$$F_W = 5632K$$

Obtain *'k'* based on BHN of Gear and Pinion from Table (2-40)

i.e., $K = 1.7727$

Therefore, $F_W = 5632 \times 1.7727$

$= 9983.85 \text{ N} > F_d = 4553.11 \text{ N}$

Hence the design is safe.

Step V: *Class of Gears* ***(Refer Table 2.29 MDH)***

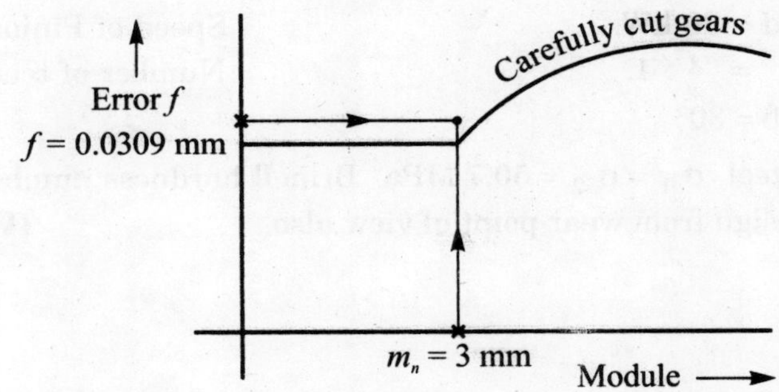

Corresponding to $m_n = 3$ mm and error $f = 0.0309$ mm, *the class of Gears recommended is carefully cut Gears.*

EXERCISE

1. A pair of herringbone Gears is used to transmit 50 kW power. The Pinion rotates at 2800 rpm. The number of teeth on the Pinion and Gear are 21 and 109, respectively. The tooth form 20° full depth involute and the helix angle 25°. The material for the Gear is cast steel with a hardness of 150 BHN and for the Pinion is steel. The wear and lubrication factor may be taken as 1.15. The normal module employed for the Gears is 4 mm and the face width of the gears is 20 times the normal module. Determine the required hardness for the Pinion for continuous operation of the drive. Also recommend the class of Gears.

(VTU, July 2006)

2. A pair of carefully cut helical Gears for a turbine has a transmission ratio of 10 : 1. The teeth are 20° stub involute in the normal plane. Pinion has 25 teeth and rotates at 5000 rpm. Material for Pinion and Gear is 0.4% carbon steel untreated with allowable static stress of 69.66 MPa. Helix angle = 30°. Power transmitted = 90 kW. Service factor = 1.25. Wear

and lubrication factor = 1.25. Determine the module in normal plane and face width of the gears. Suggest suitable surface hardness for the gear pair.

(VTU, Dec 06 / Jan 07)

3. (*a*) Explain formative number of teeth in helical Gears. ***(VTU, July 07)***

   (*b*) A pair of helical gears are to transmit 16 kW. The teeth are 20° stub in diametral plane and have a helix angle of 45°. The Pinion runs at 10000 rpm and has 80 mm pitch diameter. The gear has 320 mm pitch diameter. If the gears are made of cast steel having allowable static strength of 100 MPa, determine module and face width from static strength considerations and check the gears for wear, given $\sigma_{es} = 618$ MPa .

(VTU, July 07)

4. A pair of helical Gears with a 23° helix angle is to transmit 2.5 kW at 10000 rpm of the Pinion. The velocity ratio is 4 : 1. Both Gears are to be made of hardened steel with an allowable stress of 100 MPa for each gear. The gears are 20° stub and the pinion is to have 24 teeth. Design the gears and determine the required BHN.

(VTU, Dec 07 / Jan 08)

5. Design a pair of steel helical Gear from the following data:

   Power transmitted = 30 kW. Speed of Pinion = 1500 rpm.

   Velocity ratio = 4 : 1. Number of teeth on Pinion = 24.

   Helix angle $\beta = 30°$

   Static stress for steel $\sigma_{o1} = \sigma_{o2} = 50.7$ MPa. Brinell hardness number for gear material = 350. Check the design from wear point of view also. ***(VTU, June / July 08)***

CHAPTER

5 Bevel and Worm Gears

INTRODUCTION

Bevel Gears are used to connect and to transmit power between two intersecting shafts, intersecting at 90°, less than 90° or more than 90° (but less than 180°). When the angle between the intersecting shafts is 90°, we call the Gear pair as right angled Bevel Gears. A pair of equal sized right angle Bevel Gears are called "Mitre Gears". When the angle between intersecting shafts is less than 90°, the pair is called "Acute angle Bevel Gears or external Bevel Gears". When the pitch cone angle is more than 90° (but less than 180°), the Gears are called "Internal Bevel Gears or obtuse angle Bevel Gears".

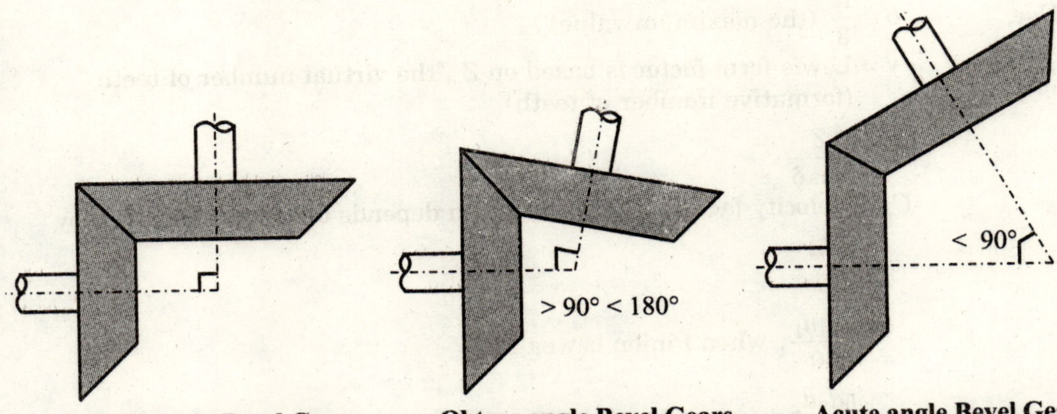

Right angle Bevel Gears (or Crown Gears)

Obtuse angle Bevel Gears (or Internal Bevel Gears)

Acute angle Bevel Gears (or External Bevel Gears)

Figure: 5.1

The sum of pitch angle of two mating Bevel Gears equals the angle between the intersecting shafts.

i.e., $\Sigma = \delta_1 + \delta_2$

Bevel Gears may be,

(*i*) Straight tooth Bevel Gears or

(*ii*) Spiral tooth Bevel Gears.

"Straight tooth Bevel Gears" have straight teeth converging at the apex of pitch cone. Spiral tooth Bevel Gears have curved tooth cut on conical blank. These gears have smoother tooth engagement than those of straight tooth Bevel Gears.

Modified Lewis Equation for Module

Module '*m*' is obtained from Modified Lewis equation

$$F_t = \sigma_o C_v bYm\left(\frac{R-b}{R}\right) \quad \text{... E(2-426)}$$

$$= \sigma_o C_v b(\pi y)m\left(\frac{R-b}{R}\right); \text{ because } Y = \pi y$$

$$R = \text{Cone distance} = \frac{m}{2}\sqrt{Z_1^2 + Z_2^2}$$

$$= \frac{1}{2}\sqrt{d_1^{\ 2} + d_2^{\ 2}} \quad \text{... E(2-414)}$$

b = Face width of Gear and has a value between $\frac{R}{4}$ and $\frac{R}{3}$.

i.e., $$\frac{R}{4} \le b \le \frac{R}{3} \quad \text{...E(2-423)}$$

Use, $b = \frac{R}{3}$ (the maximum value)

y = Lewis form factor is based on Z_v, the virtual number of teeth (formative number of teeth)

$$Z_v = \frac{Z}{\cos\delta}$$

C_v = Velocity factor, a constant which depends on velocity 'v' given by

$$v = \frac{\pi dn}{60}$$

$$= \frac{\pi d_1 n_1}{60}, \text{ when Pinion is weaker}$$

$$= \frac{\pi d_2 n_2}{60} \text{ m/sec, when Gear is weaker}$$

For Pinion, $$Z_{1v} = \frac{Z_1}{\cos\delta_1}$$

For Gear, $$Z_{2v} = \frac{Z_2}{\cos\delta_2}$$

Where Z_1 and Z_2 are the actual number of teeth on Pinion and Gear respectively. δ_1 and δ_2 are semi cone angles of Pinion and Gear.

Note: *δ_1 and δ_2 are obtained based on transmission ratio given by,*

Transmission ratio, $$i = \frac{1}{\tan\delta_1} = \tan\delta_2 = \frac{Z_2}{Z_1}$$ ... E(2-393)

For right angle Bevel Gears,

$$\sum = \text{Sum of angle} = \delta_1 + \delta_2 = 90°$$

For acute angle Bevel Gears,

$$\tan\delta_1 = \frac{\sin\Sigma}{\frac{Z_2}{Z_1} + \cos\Sigma}$$ ... E(2-400)

For obtuse angle Bevel Gears,

$$\tan\delta_1 = \frac{\sin(180° - \Sigma)}{\frac{Z_2}{Z_1} - \cos(180° - \Sigma)}$$ ... E(2-404)

Modified Buckingham's Equation for Dynamic Load

According to Buckingham, the modified equation for dynamic load is given by,

$$F_d = F_t + F_i$$

$$F_d = F_t + \frac{21v_m(F_t + bc)}{21v_m + \sqrt{F_t + bc}}$$ ... E(2-440a)

Where, F_t = Tangential load, N

F_d = Dynamic load, N

F_i = Incremental load, N

$v = v_m$ = Mean velocity = $\frac{\pi dn}{60}$ m/sec

b = Face width of Gear, metre

C = A constant which depends on tooth profile, the materials of gears and the error, obtained from T(2-40).

Wear load, F_w

The limiting wear load for Bevel Gears is given by,

$$F_w = \frac{d_1 bQK}{\cos\delta_1} > F_d$$ ... E(2-441a)

Where, F_w = Wear load, N

d_1 = Pitch diameter of Pinion, mm

b = Face width of Gears = 8 × Module

Q = Ratio factor

δ_1 = Semi cone angle or pitch angle of Pinion.

Note: *Q is based on virtual number of teeth (or formative number of teeth) and is given by,*

$$Q = \frac{2Z_{2v}}{Z_{2v} + Z_{1v}}$$

Where, Z_{1v} = Formative number of teeth on Pinion

Z_{2v} = Formative number of teeth on Gear

Endurance load:
The limiting endurance load is given by,

$$F_{-1} = \sigma_o bYm\left(\frac{R-b}{R}\right)$$

Where, $Y = \pi y$

$$F_{-1} = \sigma_o b(\pi y)m\left(\frac{R-b}{R}\right)$$

Note: *The wear load F_w and endurance load F_{-1} are permissible values (or allowable values) and must be more than the dynamic load F_d,*

i.e., $F_w \geq F_d$ and

$F_{-1} \geq F_d$

Design Procedure for Bevel Gears

Step I: *Selection of materials* ***(Refer Table 2-16)***

The Materials of Gear and Pinion are selected from T(2-16). The materials selected may be same for Gear and Pinion or may be different.

Note: *When different materials are selected for Pinion and Gear, care is to be taken to select a stronger material for Pinion than that of Gear i.e., the material of Pinion should have higher value of static stress σ_o than that of Gear.*

Table - (2-16) MDH

Material	*Static Stress, σ_o*		
	kgf/mm²	*MN/m²*	*MPa*
Ordinary cast iron	5.5	53.955	53.955
Cast iron, about class No. 35	8.5	83.305	83.305
High grade cast iron, about class No. 50	10.5	103.005	103.005
Cast steel, 0.20% C, untreated	14.0	137.340	137.340
Cast steel, 0.20%, heat treated	19.5	191.295	191.295
Bronze, SAE 62	7.0	68.67	68.67
Phosphor gear bronze, SAE 65	8.5	83.385	83.385
Manganese bronze, SAE 43	14.0	137.340	137.340
Aluminum bronze, SAE 68	15.5	152.005	152.005
Forged steel, about SAE 1030	17.5	172.375	172.375
Steel, SAE 1030, heat treated	22.5	220.725	220.725
Steel, SAE 1040, untreated	21.0	206.810	206.810
Alloy steel, case hardened	35.0	343.350	343.350
Cr-Va steel, about SAE 6145, heat treated	52.5	515.035	515.035
Cr-Ni steel, about SAE 3245, heat treated	47.0	461.070	461.070
Rawhide, Farbroil, etc.	42.0	412.020	412.020
Laminated phenolic materials (Bakelite, Micarta, Celoron)	42.0	412.020	412.020

Step II: ***To decide the weaker member of Gear pair***

(*i*) When Pinion and Gear are of same material, Pinion is the weaker member and the design is based on Pinion.

(*ii*) When Pinion and Gear are of different materials, the strength factor $\sigma_o y$ is calculated for Gear and Pinion and the member for which the product $\sigma_o y$ is smaller is considered as the weaker member.

Member	σ_o	*y*	$\sigma_o\, y$	*Remarks*
Pinion	191.295	0.09426	18.03	Strong
Gear	103.005	0.12024	12.39	Weak

Note: *In the above tabulation, Material selected for Pinion is cast steel 0.2% C heat treated for which* $\sigma_o = 191.295\ N/mm^2$

Material of Gear is high grade cast iron for which,

$$\sigma_o = 103.005\ \text{N/mm}^2$$

Lewis form factor *y* is based on virtual or formative number of teeth and the tooth profile is based on $14\frac{1}{2}^\circ$ pressure angle.

For $14\frac{1}{2}^\circ$ involute profile,

$$y = 0.124 - \frac{0.684}{Z} \qquad \text{... E(2-97)}$$

Where, $Z = Z_{1v}$ = Virtual number of teeth

For Pinion, $$Z_{1v} = \frac{Z_1}{\cos\delta_1} \qquad \text{... E(2-418)}$$

For Gear, $$Z_{2v} = \frac{Z_2}{\cos\delta_2} \qquad \text{... E(2-419)}$$

δ_1 and δ_2 are the semi cone angles of Pinion and Gear.

For Bevel Gears,

Transmission ratio, $$i = \tan\delta_2 = \frac{1}{\tan\delta_1} \qquad \text{... E(2-393)}$$

$$i = \frac{n_1}{n_2} = \frac{\text{Speed of Pinion}}{\text{Speed of Gear}}$$

For right angle Bevel Gears, $\delta_1 + \delta_2 = 90^\circ$.

Note: **(*a*)** *For acute angle Bevel Gears, use*

$$\tan\delta_1 = \frac{\sin\Sigma}{\frac{Z_2}{Z_1}+\cos\Sigma} \qquad \text{... E(2-400)}$$

(*b*) *For obtuse angle Bevel Gears, use*

$$\tan\delta_1 = \frac{\sin(180-\Sigma)}{\frac{Z_2}{Z_1}-\cos(180-\Sigma)} \qquad \text{... E(2-404)}$$

Where, $\Sigma = \delta_1 + \delta_2$

Hence, knowing transmission ratio, δ_1 and δ_2, Z_{1v} and Z_{2v} can be computed.

Step III: *Calculation of module 'm'*

For Bevel Gears, the module *'m'* is obtained from modified Lewis equation,

$$F_t = \sigma_o C_v b Y m\left(\frac{R-b}{R}\right) \qquad \text{... E(2-426a)}$$

Case 1: When diameters of Gears are known

In equation (2-426a),

$$F_t = \frac{M_t\,C_s}{r}$$

Where, $M_t = \dfrac{9550N\times10^3}{n_1}$ N-mm, when Pinion is weaker.

C_s = Service factor = 1.25 to 1.5 generally

r = Radius of weaker member.

$= \dfrac{d_1}{2}$, when Pinion is weaker

$= \dfrac{d_2}{2}$, when Gear is weaker.

C_v = Velocity factor. It depends on velocity. Since velocity is known, C_v can be calculated.

b = Face width = 8m (assumed)

$Y = \pi y$, where y is Lewis form factor.

Taking, $b = \dfrac{R}{3}$, $R = 3b$.

Hence, $\dfrac{R-b}{R} = \dfrac{3b-b}{3b} = \dfrac{2}{3}$

Substituting the above values in Lewis equation,

$m^2 y$ = A known numerical value is obtained.

Note: *$m_n^2 y$ is an allowable value since diameters are known.*

Case 2: When diameters of Gears are unknown

From $F_t = \sigma_o C_v bYm\left(\frac{R-b}{R}\right)$,

$$F_t = \frac{M_t C_s}{r}$$

$$M_t = \frac{9550N \times 10^3}{n_1}, \text{ When Pinion is weaker.}$$

$$= \frac{9550N \times 10^3}{n_2}, \text{ When Gear is weaker.}$$

$$r = \frac{d_1}{2} = \frac{mZ_1}{2}, \text{ When Pinion is weaker.}$$

$$= \frac{d_2}{2} = \frac{mZ_2}{2}, \text{ When Gear is weaker.}$$

Hence F_t is obtained is terms of *'m'*

$\sigma_o = \sigma_o$) weaker member to be used.

C_v = Velocity factor. It depends on velocity *'v'*. Since diameters are unknown, retain C_v as C_v.

Note: *When diameters are unknown, use*

$Z_1 = 16$ (Minimum 15 teeth)

$Z_2 = Z_1 \times$ Transmission ratio

'y' is based on Z_v, the virtual number of teeth.

Using, $b = \frac{R}{3}$; $R = 3b$

$$\frac{R-b}{R} = \frac{3b-b}{3b} = \frac{2}{3}$$

Substituting the above values in Lewis equation, we obtain the *"Governing equation of module"*

$m^3 C_v$ = A known numerical value.

Note : *Since diameters are unknown, $m^3 C_V$ is an induced value.*

Trials to find m, the module

1. ***When diameters are known***

When diameters of Gear and Pinion are known, use the "Governing equation",

$m^2 y)_{\text{allowable}}$ = A known numerical value.

Trial 1: ***Select standard value of module m from T(2-3)***

Table - (2-3) MDH

Module, m (mm)		
0.05	(1.125)	(18)
(0.055)	1.25	20
0.06	(1.375)	(22)
(0.07)	1.5	(24)
0.08	(1.75)	25
(0.09)	2.0	(27)
0.10	(2.25)	(28)
(0.11)	2.5	(30)
0.12	(2.75)	32
(0.14)	3.0	(33)
0.15	(3.25)	(36)
(0.18)	(3.5)	(39)
0.2	(3.75)	40
(0.22)	4.0	(42)

Module, m (mm)		
0.25	(4.5)	(45)
(0.28)	5	50
0.3	(5.5)	(55)
(0.35)	6	60
0.4	(6.5)	(65)
(0.45)	(7)	(70)
0.5	8	(75)
(0.55)	(9)	80
0.6	10	(85)
(0.7)	(11)	(90)
0.8	12	100
(0.9)	(14)	
1.0	16	

Say, $m = 5$ mm

Then, $d_1 = mZ_1$ (when Pinion is weaker)

Since d_1 is known, Z_1 can be calculated.

Based on Z_1, Z_{1v} can be computed (as explained earlier), based on Z_{1v}, y_{pinion} is calculated.

The trials are continued with varying values of standard module till the product m^2y in the Governing equation equals the numerical value on the RHS of equation or less than the numerical value. The value *'m'* for which m^2y equals the numerical value on the RHS of Governing equation or lesser than the numerical value on the RHS of equation is selected for Gears.

2. *When diameter of Gears are unknown*

When diameters are unknown, the governing equation,

m^3C_v = A known numerical value is used to compute module *'m'*.

Assuming Pinion as weaker member and based on number of teeth on Pinion (assumed), the pitch circle diameter d_1 is calculated from,

$$d_1 = mZ_1$$

Based on d_1, the velocity $v_1 = \dfrac{\pi d_1 n_1}{60}$ is computed. Finally based on *'v'*, the velocity factor C_v is calculated.

Trials are continued till the product, m^3C_v equals the numerical value on the RHS of governing equation.

The value *'m'* corresponding to m^3C_v equaling the numerical value on the governing equation is selected as the required module *'m'*.

Particulars of Gears

Sl. No	Particulars	Pinion	Gear
1.	Material	Selected from T(2-16)	Selected from T(2-16)
2.	Module, m	m	m
3.	Number of teeth, Z	Z_1	Z_2
4.	Pitch circle diameter, d	$d_1 = mZ_1$	$d_2 = mZ_2$
5.	Face width, $b = 8$ m	$b = 8$ m	$b = 8$ m
6.	Semi cone angle δ	δ_1	δ_2

Step IV: *Check for wear and dynamic load*

Wear load, $$F_w = \frac{d_1 bQK}{\cos\delta_1} \quad \text{... E(2-441a)}$$

Note:* *'Q' is based on Z_v and is given by,

$$Q = \frac{2Z_{2v}}{Z_{2v} + Z_{1v}}$$

For safe design, $F_w > F_d$

F_d = Dynamic load and is given by,

$$F_d = F_t + \frac{21v_m(F_t + bc)}{21v_m + \sqrt{F_t + bc}} \quad \text{... E(2-440a)}$$

Where, F_t = Tangential load on weaker member

$$v_m = v_1 = \frac{\pi d_1 n_1}{60}; \quad v_2 = \frac{\pi d_2 n_2}{60}$$

b = Face width of Gear

Constant 'C' is obtained using tables T(2-34) and T(2-35)

Case 1: When the hardness of Gears is unknown

When hardness of Gears is unknown,

Use, $$F_w = \frac{d_1 bQK}{\cos\delta_1} > F_d$$

i.e., $$k > \frac{F_w \cos\delta_1}{d_1 bQ}$$

Knowing 'K', use T(2-40) and obtain Hardness of Pinion and Gear.

Case 2: When hardness of Gears is known

When hardness of Gears is known, Calculate F_w, the wear load using equation

1. $$F_w = \frac{d_1 bQK}{\cos\delta_1}$$

Where, $$K = \frac{1.43\sigma^2_{-1c} \sin\alpha}{E_0} \quad \text{... E(2-161)}$$

$$E_0 = \frac{2E_1 E_2}{E_1 + E_2} \quad \text{... E(2-162)}$$

E_1 = Young's modulus of Pinion, N/mm^2

E_2 = Young's modulus of Gear, N/mm^2

σ_{-1c} = Fatigue endurance strength of Gear materials

$$\sigma_{-1c} = 2.75 H_B - 69 \quad \text{... E(2-168c)}$$

H_B = BHN of softer of two Gears

2. ***Dynamic load F_d is obtained from E(2-440a)***
   If $F_w > F_d$, the design is safe.
   If F_w is not greater than F_d, redesign the Gears by selecting stronger materials.

Step V: ***Class of Gears***

The class of Gears or precision to which Gears must be cut is obtained from Fig. 2.29 MDH, based on module *'m'* and error *'f'*.

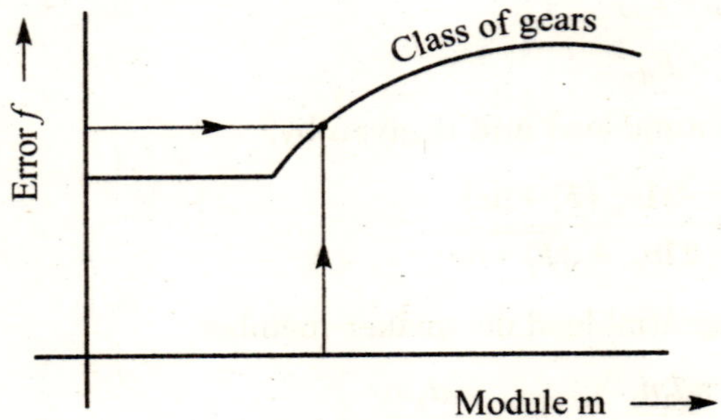

Example 5.1: Design a pair of right angle Bevel Gears to transmit 10 kW at 1200 rpm of Pinion. The Gear is to run at 420 rpm. The Pinion is made of steel and Gear is of cast iron. The number of teeth on Pinion is 21 and teeth are of 14.5° involute profile.

Solution:

Step I: ***Selection of materials*** ***(Refer T(2-16))***

For Pinion, select cast steel 0.2%C heat treated for which the allowable static stress,

$$\sigma_o = 191.295 \text{ N/mm}^2$$

For Gear, select high grade cast Iron for which,

$$\sigma_o = 103.005 \text{ N/mm}^2$$

Step II: ***To decide the weaker member of Gear pair***

Member	σ_o	y	$\sigma_o y$	Remarks
Pinion	191.295	0.09426	18.03	Strong
Gear	103.005	0.12024	12.39	Weak

Note: *Since materials selected for Pinion and Gear are different, the above table is formed to determine the weaker member of Gear pair.*

To find 'y', the Lewis from factor

For Bevel Gears, 'y' is based on virtual number of teeth Z_v..

For Pinion, $$Z_{1v} = \frac{Z_1}{\cos\delta_1} \quad \text{... E(2-418)}$$

For Gear, $$Z_{2v} = \frac{Z_2}{\cos\delta_2} \quad \text{... E(2-419)}$$

To find δ_1 and δ_2 (semi cone angles of Pinion and Gear)

For Bevel Gears, transmission ratio 'i' is given by,

$$i = \tan\delta_2 = \frac{1}{\tan\delta_1} \quad \text{... E(2-393)}$$

Where, $$i = \frac{n_1}{n_2}$$

$$= \frac{1200}{420} = 2.857$$

i.e., $$i = 2.857 = \tan\delta_2 \quad \text{... from E(2-393)}$$

Therefore, $$\delta_2 = 70.71 \text{ and}$$

$$\delta_1 = 90 - \delta_2 = 90 - 70.71° = 19.29°$$

[Because for right angled Bevel Gears, sum of angles $\sum = \delta_1 + \delta_2 = 90°$]

Now, $$Z_{1v} = \frac{Z_1}{\cos\delta_1}$$

$$= \frac{21}{\cos 19.29°} = 22.24 \text{ teeth} \approx 23 \text{ teeth}$$

$$Z_{2v} = \frac{Z_2}{\cos\delta_2}$$

$$= \frac{21 \times 2.857}{\cos 70.71} = 181.62 \text{ teeth} \approx 182 \text{ teeth}$$

For Gears with $14\frac{1}{2}°$ involute profile,

$$y = 0.124 - \frac{0684}{Z} \quad \text{... E(2-97)}$$

Where, $$Z = Z_v$$

Now, $$y_{\text{Pinion}} = y_1 = 0.124 - \frac{0.684}{23} = 0.096426$$

$$y_{\text{Gear}} = y_2 = 0.124 - \frac{0.684}{182} = 0.12024$$

From Table formed,

$$\sigma_o y)_{Gear} = 12.39 < \sigma_o y)_{Pinion} = 18.03$$

Therefore, Gear is the weaker member and hence the design is based on Gear

Step III: ***To determine module (m)***

For Bevel Gears, the modified Lewis equation is given by,

$$F_t = \sigma_o C_v b Y m \left[\frac{R-b}{R}\right] \quad \text{... E(2-426a)}$$

Where,
$$F_t = \frac{M_t C_s}{r}$$

$$M_t = \frac{9550 \times 10}{420} \times 10^3$$

$$= 227380.95 \text{ N-mm}$$

$$C_s = 1.5 \text{ (assumed)}$$

$$r = r_2$$

$$= \frac{d_2}{2} = \frac{mZ_2}{2}$$

$$= \frac{m}{2}\left(21 \times \frac{1200}{420}\right) = 30 \text{ m}$$

Therefore,
$$F_t = \frac{227380.95 \times 1.5}{30 \text{ m}}$$

$$= \frac{11369.05}{\text{m}}$$

$$\sigma_o = \sigma_o)_{Gear} = 103.005 \text{N/mm}^2$$

C_v is retained as C_v since diameters are unknown.

$$b = \text{Face width} = 8m$$

$$Y = \pi y$$

Cone distance R is obtained from equation,

$$\frac{R}{4} \le b \le \frac{R}{3} \quad \text{... E(2-423)}$$

Use, $b = \frac{R}{3}$, $R = 3b$

Therefore,
$$\frac{R-b}{R} = \frac{3b-b}{3b} = \frac{2}{3}$$

Substituting the values in equation (2-286),

$$\frac{11369.05}{m} = 103.005 C_v (8m) \pi \times \frac{2}{3} \times 0.12024 \times m$$

Therefore,
$$m^3 C_v = 54.78$$

***Note:** Since diameters are unknown, m^3C_v is an induced value.*

Trials to find 'm'

Trial 1: Let m = 4 mm

$$d_2 = mZ_2 = 4Z_2$$

Where, $$Z_2 = Z_1 \frac{n_1}{n_2}$$

$$= 21 \times \frac{1200}{420} = 60 \text{ teeth}$$

Therefore, $$d_2 = 4 \times 60 = 240 \text{ mm}$$

Velocity, $$v_m = v_2 = \frac{\pi d_2 n_2}{60}$$

$$= \frac{\pi}{60}\left(\frac{240}{1000}\right)420 = 5.28 \text{ m/sec}$$

Velocity factor, $$C_v = \frac{4.5}{4.5 + v_m}$$

$$= \frac{4.5}{4.5 + 5.28} = 0.4601$$

Therefore, $$m^3C_v = (4)^3 \times 0.4601 = 29.45 < m^3C_v)_{\text{induced}} = 54.78$$

Therefore, increase the value of module *'m'*

Trial 2: Let, m = 6 mm

$$d_2 = 5 \times 60 = 300 \text{ mm}$$

Velocity, $$v_m = v_2 = \frac{\pi d_2 n_2}{60}$$

$$= \frac{\pi}{60}\left(\frac{300}{1000}\right)420 = 6.57 \text{ m/sec}$$

$$C_v = \frac{4.5}{4.5 + v_m}$$

$$= \frac{4.5}{4.5 + 6.57} = 0.4055$$

$$m^3C_v = (5)^3 \times 0.4055 = 50.68 < m^3C_v)_{\text{induced}} = 54.78$$

Further increase the value *'m'*.

Trial 3: Let, m = 6 mm

$$d_2 = 6 \times 60 = 360 \text{ mm}$$

Velocity, $$v_m = v_2 = \frac{\pi d_2 n_2}{60}$$

$$= \frac{\pi}{60}\left(\frac{360}{1000}\right)420 = 7.92 \text{ m/sec}$$

$$C_v = \frac{4.5}{4.5 + v_m}$$

$$= \frac{4.5}{4.5 + 7.92} = 0.3624$$

$$m^3 C_v = (6)^3 \times 0.3624 = 78.82 > 54.78$$

Therefore, Adopt m = 6 mm

Particulars of Gears

Sl. No	Particulars	Pinion	Gear
1.	Material	Cast Steel, Heat Treated	High Grade Cast Iron
2.	Module, m	6 mm	6 mm
3.	Number of teeth, Z	$Z_1 = 21$	$Z_2 = 21 \times \frac{1200}{420} = 60$
4.	Pitch circle diameter, d	$d_1 = mZ_1 = 6 \times 21 = 126$ mm	$d_2 = mZ_2 = 6 \times 60 = 360$ mm
5.	Face width, $b = 8$ m	$b = 8$ m $= 8 \times 6 = 48$ mm	$b = 48$ mm
6.	Semi cone angle δ	$\delta_1 = 19.29°$	$\delta_2 = 70.71°$

Step IV: ***To check for wear and dynamic loads and to find the hardness of Gears.***

Wear load $$F_w = \frac{d_1 b Q K}{\cos\delta_1} > F_d \qquad \text{... E(2-441a)}$$

$$d_1 = 126 \text{ mm}; \; b = 48 \text{ mm}$$

$$Q = \frac{2Z_{2v}}{Z_{2v} + Z_{1v}}$$

$$= \frac{2 \times 182}{182 + 23} = 1.776$$

Note: *For Bevel Gears, 'Q' is based on virtual number of teeth or formative number of teeth*

Therefore, $$F_w = \frac{126 \times 48 \times 1.776K}{\cos 19.29}$$

$$= 11380.15\text{N}$$

Dynamic load, $$F_d = F_t + \frac{21v_m(F_t + bc)}{21v_m + \sqrt{F_t + bc}} \qquad \text{... E(2-400a)}$$

Where, $F_t = \dfrac{11369.05}{m}$

$$= \frac{11369.05}{6} = 1894.84 \text{ N}$$

$$v = v_m = 7.92 \text{ m/sec}$$

$$b = 48 \text{ mm} = \frac{48}{1000} \text{m} = 0.048 \text{ m}$$

To find 'C' ***(Refer T(2-34) and T(2-35)***

Velocity $v_m = 7.92$ m/sec and lies between,

$v_m = 7.75$ m/sec and 10 m/sec

For, $v_m = 8.75$ m/sec; Error $f = 0.0425$ mm

$v_m = 10.0$ m/sec; Error $f = 0.0375$ mm

Therefore, Difference in $v_m = 1.25$ m/sec (increases);

Difference in $f = 0.005$ mm (decreases)

Note: *'f' decreases with increase in v_m*

Therefore, Error $f = 0.0425 \text{ mm} - \dfrac{0.005}{1.25}(8.75 - 7.92)$

$$f = 0.0392 \text{ mm}$$

Note: *This value of 'f' lies between 0.025 mm and 0.05 mm and for steel Pinion and cast iron Gear and $14\frac{1}{2}°$ involute profile, from T(2-35)*

For $f = 0.025$ mm; $C = 192.08$ kN/m

$f = 0.05$ mm; $C = 384.16$ kN/m

Therefore, Difference in $f = 0.025$ mm (increases);

Difference in $C = 192.08$ kN/m (increases)

Note: *'C' increases with increase in 'f'.*

Therefore, $C = 192.08 + \dfrac{192.08}{0.025}[0.0392 - 0.025]$

$$= 301.18 \text{ kN/m}$$

$$= 301.18 \times 10^3 \text{ N/m}$$

$$F_d = 1894.84 + \frac{21 \times 7.92\left(1894.84 + 0.048 \times 301.18 \times 10^3\right)}{21 \times 7.92 + \sqrt{1894.84 + 0.048 \times 301.18 \times 10^3}}$$

$$F_d = 1930.17 \text{ N}$$

Equating F_w and F_d

$$11380.15 > 1930.17$$

$$K > 0.1696$$

Referring T(2-40) for steel Pinion and cast iron Gear with $14\frac{1}{2}°$ involute profile, for K = 0.3031, Pinion and Gear are to be hardened to more than 150 BHN.

Step V: ***Class of Gears (Refer figure 2.29)***

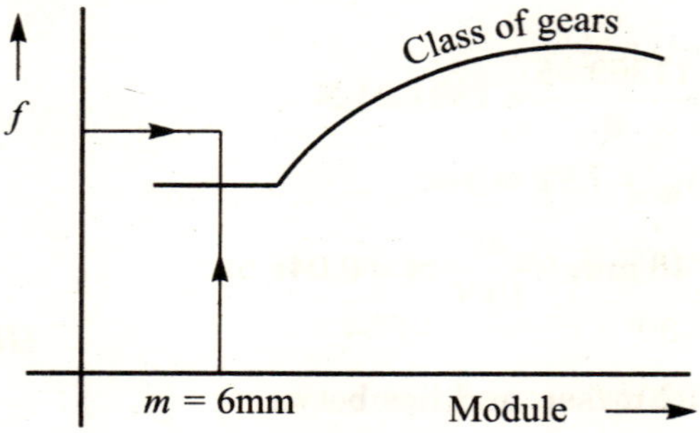

Figure: 2.29

Corresponding to $m = 6$ mm and $f = 0.0392$ mm, *the class Gears is "Carefully Cut Gears"*

Example 5.2: The vertical spindle of a drilling machine is driven by a right angle Bevel speed reducer. The Gear is made of cast iron $\left(\sigma_o = 56\ N/mm^2\right)$ and the Pinion is made of cast steel $\left(\sigma_o = 140\ N/mm^2\right)$. The transmission ratio is 4. The Pinion shaft receives 2 kW at 600 rpm. The Pinion diameter is to be closer to 100 mm. The teeth are 20° full depth involute form, Design the Gears completely.

Solution:

Step I: ***Selection of material***

Given, Pinion is of cast steel for which allowable static stress $\sigma_o = 140\ \text{N/mm}^2$

Gear is of cast iron for which $\sigma_o = 56\ \text{N/mm}^2$

Step II: ***To identify the weaker member of Gear pair***

Since Gear and Pinion are made of different materials, the following table is to be formed to determine the weaker member of Gear pair.

Member	σ_o	*y*	$\sigma_o\, y$	*Remarks*
Pinion	140	0.1106	15.484	Strong
Gear	56	0.15124	8.47	Weak

To find y, the Lewis .form factor,

For 20° involute profile,

$$y - 0.154 - \frac{0.192}{Z} \qquad \text{... E(2-98)}$$

Note: *y is based on Z_V, the virtual number of teeth,*

To determine Z_V, the formative or virtual number of teeth

For Pinion, $$Z_{1v} = \frac{Z_1}{\cos \delta_1} \qquad \text{... E(2-418)}$$

For Gear, $$Z_{2v} = \frac{Z_2}{\cos \delta_2} \qquad \text{... E(2-419)}$$

To determine δ_1 and δ_2 (semi-cone angles of Pinion Gear)

Transmission ratio, $i = \tan\delta_2 = \dfrac{1}{\tan\delta_1}$ ... E(2-393)

Here, $i = 4$

Therefore, $i = 4 = \tan\delta_2$ *i.e.*, $\delta_2 = 75.96°$ and

$$\delta_1 = 90 - \delta_2 \left[\text{Because } \delta_1 + \delta_2 = 90°\right]$$

$$\delta_1 = 90° - 75.96° = 14.04°$$

$$Z_1 = 20 \text{ (assumed)}$$

Therefore, $Z_{1v} = \dfrac{Z_1}{\cos\delta_1}$

$$= \frac{20}{\cos 14.04} = 20.61 \approx 21 \text{ teeth}$$

$$Z_{2v} = \frac{Z_2}{\cos\delta_2}$$

$$= \frac{80}{\cos 75.96} = 329.76 \approx 330 \text{ teeth}$$

Therefore, $y_1 = y_{\text{Pinion}} = 0.154 - \dfrac{0.192}{Z_{1v}}$

$$= 0.154 - \frac{0.912}{21} = 0.1106$$

$$y_2 = y_{\text{Gear}} = 0.154 - \frac{0.192}{Z_{2v}}$$

$$= 0.154 - \frac{0.912}{330} = 0.15124$$

$$\sigma_o y)_{\text{Gear}} = 8.47 < \sigma_o y)_{\text{Pinion}} = 15.484$$

Therefore, Gear is weaker and the design based on Gear

Step III: *To determine module 'm'*

We have for Bevel Gears, the tangential load given by,

$$F_t = \sigma_o C_v b(\pi y) m \left[\frac{R-b}{R}\right]$$ ... E(2-286)

Where, $F_t = \dfrac{M_t C_s}{r}$

Where, $r = r_2 = \dfrac{100 \times 4}{2}$

$$= \frac{400}{2} \qquad \left[\text{Because } d_2 = 4d_1\right]$$

Since, $$n_2 = \frac{n_1}{4}$$

$$= \frac{600}{4} = 150 \text{ rpm}$$

$$M_t = \frac{9550 \text{ N} \times 10^3}{n} = \frac{9550 \times 2 \times 10^3}{150}$$

Therefore, $$F_t = \frac{9550 \times 2 \times 1.5 \times 10^3}{150 \times 200} = 9550 \text{ N}$$

$$\sigma_o = \sigma_o)_{\text{Gear}} = 56 \text{ N/mm}^2$$

To find C_v

$$v = v_m = \frac{\pi d_2 n_2}{60}$$

$$= \frac{\pi}{60} \times \frac{400}{1000} \times \frac{600}{4} = 3.14 \text{ m/sec}$$

$$C_v = \frac{3}{3 + v_m} \text{ for } v_m < 7.5 \text{m/sec} \qquad \text{... E(2-428)}$$

Therefore, $$C_v = \frac{3}{3 + 3.1415} = 0.4885$$

$$b = 8m \text{ (assumed)}$$

$y = y$ (Because number of teeth unknown) and Retain, 'm' as 'm'

Assuming, $$b = \frac{R}{3}, R = 3b$$

Therefore, $$\left(\frac{R - b}{R}\right) = \frac{3b - b}{3b} = \frac{2}{3}$$

$$9550 = 56 \times 0.4885 \times 8m \times (\pi y) m \left(\frac{2}{3}\right)$$

Therefore, $m^2 y)_{\text{allowable}} = 2.084$

To determine 'm', the module

Trial 1: Let $m = 5$ mm

$$d_2 = mZ_2$$

i.e., $400 = 5Z_2$ *i.e.,* $Z_2 = 80$ teeth

$$Z_{2v} = \frac{Z_2}{\cos \delta_2}$$

$$= \frac{80}{\cos 75.96} = 330 \text{ teeth}$$

Therefore, $y_{Gear} = 0.154 - \frac{0.912}{330} = 0.15$

Therefore, $m^2y = 5^2 \times 0.15 = 3.75 > m^2y)_{allowable} = 2.084$

Therefore, reduce the value of '*m*'

Trial 2: Let *m* = 4 mm

$$d_2 = mZ_2;\quad 400 = 4Z_2 \quad i.e.,\quad Z_2 = 100 \text{ teeth}$$

$$Z_{2v} = \frac{Z_2}{\cos\delta_2}$$

$$= \frac{100}{\cos 75.96} = 412.2 \text{ teeth} \approx 413 \text{ teeth}$$

$$y_2 = 0.154 - \frac{0.912}{413} = 0.1518$$

Therefore, $m^2y = 5^2 \times 0.1518 = 2.42 > m^2y)_{allowable} = 2.084$

Further reduce the value of '*m*'.

Trial III: Let *m* = 3 mm.

$$d_2 = mZ_2$$

i.e., $400 = Z_2 \quad i.e.,\quad Z_2 = 133.33 \approx 134 \text{ teeth}$

$$Z_{2v} = \frac{Z_2}{\cos\delta_2}$$

$$= \frac{134}{\cos 75.96} = 552.35 \approx 553 \text{ teeth}$$

$$y_2 = 0.154 - \frac{0.912}{553} = 0.1524$$

Therefore, $m^2y = 3^2 \times 0.1524 = 1.368 < m^2y)_{allowable} = 2.084$

Therefore, Adopt $m = 3$ mm

Particulars of Gear and Pinion

Sl. No	Particulars	Pinion	Gear
1.	Material	Cast Steel	Cast Iron
2.	Module, m	3 mm	3 mm
3.	Number of teeth, Z	$=\left(\frac{Z_2}{i}\right)=\left(\frac{Z_2}{4}\right)=34$	134 Teeth
4.	Pitch circle diameter, d	$d_1 = mZ_1 = 102$ mm	$d_2 = mZ_2 = 402$ mm
5.	Face width, $b = 8$ m	$b = 24$ mm	$b = 24$ mm
6.	Semi-cone angle δ	$\delta_1 = 14.04°$	$\delta_2 = 75.96°$

Step IV: ***To check for wear and dynamic load and to determine the hardness of Gears.***

Wear load, $$F_w = \frac{d_1 bQK}{\cos\delta_1} > F_d$$ ... E(2-298)

Where, $d_1 = 102$ mm; $b = 24$ mm

$$Q = \frac{2Z_{2v}}{Z_{2v} + Z_{1v}}$$

$$= \frac{2 \times 553}{553 + 35} = 1.88$$

Therefore, $F_w = 102 \times 24 \times 1.88 \times K = 4602.24K$

$$F_d = F_t + \frac{21v_m (F_t + bc)}{21v_m + \sqrt{F_t + bc}}$$ ... E(2-440a)

Where, $F_t = 955\text{N}$

$$v_m = \frac{\pi d_2 n_2}{60}$$

$$= \frac{\pi}{60} \times \frac{402}{1000} \times 150 = 3.157\,\text{m/sec}$$

$$b = 24 \text{ mm} = \frac{24}{1000} = 0.024 \text{ m}$$

To find 'c' ***[Refer Tables (2-34) and (2.35)]***

We have velocity $v_m = 3.157$ m/sec which lies between 2.5 m/sec and 3.75 m/sec, (Table 2-34)

For, v_m = 2.5 m/sec; Error f = 0.08 mm

v_m = 3.75 m/sec; Error f = 0.07 mm

Therefore, Difference in v_m = 1.25 m/sec (increases);

Difference in f = 0.001 mm (decreases)

Note: *'f' decreases with increase in* v_m

Therefore, $v_m = 3.157$ m/sec ,

$$f = 0.08 - \frac{0.01}{1.25} \times (3.157 - 2.5) = 0.0747 \text{ mm}$$

This error lies between error 0.05 and 0.075 (Refer Table 2-35)

For steel Pinion and cast iron Gear of $14\frac{1}{2}^\circ$ involute profile,

For, $f = 0.05$ mm; $C = 384.16\,\text{kN/m}$

$f = 0.075$ mm; $C = 576.34\,\text{kN/m}$

Therefore, Difference in $f = 0.025$ mm (increases);

Difference in $C = 192.18\,\text{kN/m}$ (increases)

***Note:* 'C' increases with increase in value of 'f'.**

Therefore, $f = 0.0747$ mm

$$C = 384.6 + \frac{192.18}{0.025} \times [0.0747 - 0.05]$$

$$= 574.03 \text{ kN/m}$$

$$= 574.03 \times 10^3 \text{ N/m}$$

Therefore, $$F_d = 955 + \frac{21 \times 3.157 (955 + 0.024 \times 574.03 \times 10^3)}{21 \times 3.157 + \sqrt{955 + 0.024 \times 574.03 \times 10^3}}$$

$$= 6159.15 \text{ N}$$

Equating F_w and F_d,

$$4602.2K > 6159.15$$

Therefore, $K > 1.3383$

Referring to Table (2-40), For steel Pinion, cast iron Gear with $14\frac{1}{2}^\circ$ involute profile, corresponding to $K = 1.3862 (> 1.3527)$, the Pinion and Gear are to be hardened to 350 BHN.

Step V: *Class of Gear*

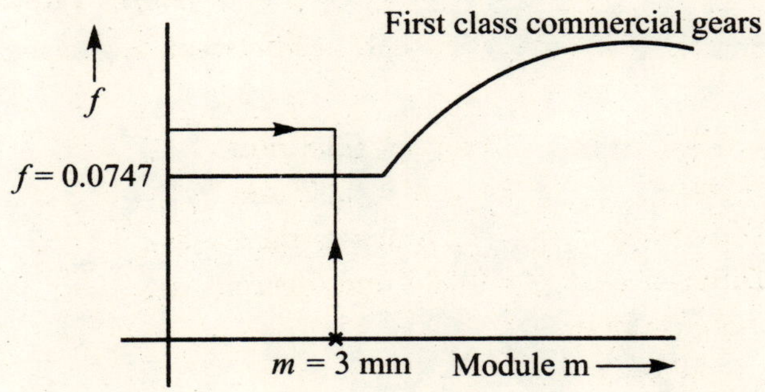

Figure: 2.29

Corresponding to $m = 3$ mm and $f = 0.0747$ mm, *the class of Gears suggested is "First class commercial Gears".*

EXERCISE

1. A pair of straight bevel Gears transmits 15 kW at 1250 rpm of 120 mm diameter Pinion. The speed reduction is 3.5. Use 14.5° involute tooth system. The angle between the shaft axis is 90°. The Pinion is made of case hardened alloy steel with allowable static stress 343.34 MPa and Gear is cast steel of 0.20% C heat treated with allowable static stress 191.295 MPa. Determine module, face width, number of teeth on Pinion and Gear. Suggest suitable surface hardness for the Gear pair. Take service factor as 1.5 and assume the teeth are generated.

   (VTU, Dec 06 / Jan 07)

2. A pair of 20° full depth involute teeth bevel Gears connect two shafts at right angles having velocity ratio 3 : 1. The Gear is made of cast steel, 0.20% untreated and the Pinion material is of steel, C30 heat treated. The Pinion has 20 number of teeth and transmits 40 kW at 750 rpm. Determine,

   (*i*) Module.

   (*ii*) Face width.

   (*iii*) Pitch diameters.

   Assume width of Gear face as one third of the length of pitch cone. ***(VTU, July 07)***

3. A pair of straight tooth bevel Gears at right angles is to transmit 15 kW at 1200 rpm of the Pinion. The diameter of the Pinion is 80 mm and the velocity ratio is 3 : 5. The tooth form is 14½° . Both the Pinion and Gear are cast iron with allowable stress of 55 MN/m^2. Determine module from the stand point of dynamic load and wear load.

   (VTU, June / July 08)

WORM GEARS

INTRODUCTION

Worm Gears are used to connect non-parallel, non-intersecting shafts usually at right angles to each other. A worm Gear drive (called worm set) consists of a worm and a worm wheel (or worm Gear) as shown in Fig.

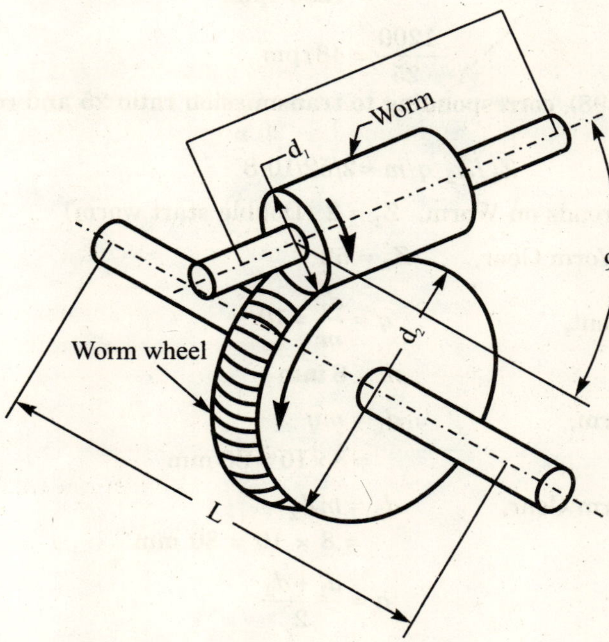

A worm can be considered as a helical Gear with a helix angle so large that a single tooth embraces around its circumference. The worm is analogous to a screw thread and worm wheel (*i.e.,* worm Gear) is analogous to a nut.

Worms are generally single threaded and result in transmission ratio as large as the number of teeth on worm Gear. On account of this, worm sets are compact compared to other Gears such as spur and helical Gears (for the same velocity ratio) in which transmission ratio is usually of the range 10 : 1. Worm sets are available in the range 1 : 1 to 360 : 1 with the usual range 3 : 1 to 100 : 1.

Worm sets having transmission ratio above 30 : 1 usually have a single threaded worm whereas those having the ratio less than 30 use double or triple start worm. Another greater advantage of worm drive is their ability to self lock.

The major disadvantages of worm Gears drive are:

(*i*) Low efficiency and low power transmitting capacity compared to spur, bevel and helical Gear.

(*ii*) Worm sets are costly since worm gear is generally made of phosphor bronze.

(*iii*) The amount of heat generated is high compared to the conventional spur, bevel and helical Gear drives.

DESIGN OF WORM GEARS

Example 5.3: Design a worm gear drive to transmit 5 kW at 1200 rpm. The speed ratio is to be 25 and the centre distance 250 mm.

Solution:

Step I: ***To select module, number of teeth and pitch diameters of worm and worm Gear.***

For the given drive, speed ratio $i = 25$

Speed of Worm $= 1200$ rpm.

Speed of Worm Gear $\dfrac{1200}{25} = 48\,\text{rpm}.$

Referring to Table (2-98), corresponding to transmission ratio 25 and centre distance 250 mm, the quantity,

$$Z_1/Z_2/q/m = 2/52/10/8$$

i.e., the number of threads on Worm, $Z_1 = 2$ (Double start worm)

Number of teeth on Worm Gear, $Z_2 = 52$

The diametral coefficient, $q = \dfrac{d_1}{m} = 10$

Module $m = 8$ mm

Pitch diameter of Worm, $d_1 = mq$

$$= 8 \times 10 = 80 \text{ mm}$$

Pitch diameter of Worm Gear, $d_2 = mZ_2$

$$= 8 \times 10 = 80 \text{ mm}$$

Centre distance , $a = \dfrac{d_1 + d_2}{2}$

$$= \frac{80 + 416}{2} = 248 \text{ mm}$$

We have speed ratio, $i = 25$

But, $$i = \frac{\pi d_2}{P_Z} \quad \text{... E(2-502)}$$

i.e., $$25 = \frac{\pi \times 416}{P_Z}$$

Therefore, lead $$P_Z = \frac{\pi \times 416}{25} = 52.28 \text{ mm}$$

$$\tan \gamma = \frac{P_Z}{\pi d_1} \quad \text{... E(2-527)}$$

Lead angle $$\gamma = \tan^{-1}\left(\frac{52.28}{\pi \times 80}\right) = 0.208$$

$$= \tan^{-1}(0.208) = 11.75°$$

Table - (2-98)

Centre Distance \ Transmission Ratio	5.0	7.5	10.0	12.5	15.0
25	2/10/(11)/2.5	1/7/(18)/2	---	---	1/15/(18)/1.5
31.5	4/21/(11)/2	2/15/(11)/2.5	2/21/(11)/2	1/13/(18)/2	1/15/(11)/2.5
40	4/21/(11)/2.5	---	2/21/(11)/2.5	---	1/16/16/2.5
50	6/29/(11)/2.5	4/29/(11)/2.5	4/38/(11)/2	---	2/29/(11)/2.5
63	6/31/(11)/3	4/31/(11)/3	4/31/(11)/2.5	4/51/(11)/2	2/31/(11)/3
80	6/29/(11)/4	4/30/(10)/4	4/42/(11)/3	4/53/(11)/2.5	2/30/10/4
100	6/29/(11)/5	4/30/10/5	4/40/10/4	4/49/(18)/3	2/30/10/5
125	6/32/(10)/6	4/31/10/6	4/40/10/5	4/52/10/4	2/31/10/6
160	6/31/(9)/8	4/30/10/8	4/43/10/6	4/54/10/5	2/30/10/8
200	8/39/(11)/8	4/30/10/10	4/40/10/8	---	2/30/10/10
250	8/39/(11)/10	---	4/40/10/10	4/52/8/8	---
315	8/41/(11)/12	4/30/(9)/16	4/43/(9)/12	2/53/(10)/10	2/30/(9)/6
400	8/39/(11)/16	4/31/(9)/20	4/41/(9)/16	---	2/31/(9)/2
500	8/39/(11)/20	---	4/41/(9)/20	4/53/(9)/16	---

Centre Distance \ Transmission Ratio	20.0	25.0	30.0	40.0	50.0	60.0
25	1/21/(18)/1.25	---	1/33/16/1	---	---	---
31.5	1/20/(11)/2	1/26/16/1.5	1/32/(18)/1.25	---	1/48/16/1	---
40	1/21/(11)/2.5	---	1/29/(11)/2	---	---	1/62/16/1
50	2/38/(11)/2	---	1/29/(11)/2.5	1/38/(11)/2	---	1/62/(18)/1.25
63	2/39/(11)/2.5	2/51/(11)/2	1/31/(11)/3	1/39/(11)/2.5	1/51/(11)/2	---
80	2/42/(11)/3	2/53/(11)/2.5	1/30/10/4	1/42/(11)/3	1/53/(11)/2.5	1/62/(18)/2
100	2/40/10/4	2/54/(11)/3	1/30/10/5	1/40/10/4	1/55/(11)/3	1/64/16/2.5
125	2/40/10/5	2/52/10/4	1/31/10/6	1/40/10/5	1/52/10/4	---
160	---	2/54/10/5	1/30/10/8	---	1/54/10/5	1/62/(18)/4
200	2/40/10/8	---	1/30/10/10	1/40/10/8	---	---
250	2/40/10/10	2/52/10/8	---	1/40/10/10	1/52/10/8	---
315	---	2/53/10/10	1/30/(9)/16	---	1/53/10/10	1/16/(18)/8
400	2/41/(9)/16	---	1/31/(9)/20	1/41/(9)/16	1/49/(18)/12	1/58/(9)/12
500	2/41/(9)/20	1/53/(9)/16	---	1/41/(9)/20	1/53/(9)/16	---

Step II: ***To find width of worm***

The Lewis equation for permissible tangential load on Worm Gear tooth is

$$F_t = \sigma_o mbY C_V \qquad \text{... E(2-593)}$$

Where, $$F_t = \frac{M_t C_S}{r}$$

$$M_t = \frac{9500N \times 10^3}{n_2} \text{ N-mm}$$

$$= \frac{9550 \times 5 \times 10^3}{48} = 994791.67 \text{ N-mm}$$

$$r = \frac{d_2}{2}$$

$$= \frac{416}{2} = 208 \text{mm}$$

Assuming $C_S = 1.25$, tangential load F_t on Worm Gear (or worm wheel) is,

$$F_t = \frac{994791.67 \times 1.25}{208}$$

$$= 5978.32 \text{N}$$

To find C_V, the velocity factor

Velocity, $$v = \frac{\pi d_2 n_2}{60}$$

$$= \frac{\pi}{60} \times \frac{416}{1000} \times 48 = 1.045 \text{ m/sec}$$

Therefore,

Velocity factor $$C_V = \frac{6}{6 + v_m} \qquad \text{... E(2-542b)}$$

$$= \frac{6}{6 + 1.045} = 0.8517$$

Selecting phosphor bronze as material of Worm Gear, the allowable static stress

$$\sigma_o = 103.5 \text{ MPa} \qquad \text{... T(2-106)}$$

$$Y = \pi y \qquad \text{... E(2-541b)}$$

'y' is obtained from T(2-105)

Table - (2-106) MDH

Material	σ_o		
	kgf/mm²	MN/m²	MPa
Ordinary cast iron	7.03	69.00	69.00
High grade cast iron or semi steel	10.55	103.50	103.50
Bakelite, Textolite, Raw Hide, etc.	4.22	41.40	41.40
Leaded gun metal, SAE 63	5.62	55.13	55.13
Manganese bronze, SAE 43	14.06	137.90	137.90
Phosphor bronze, SAE 65	10.55	103.50	103.50

Table - (2-105) MDH

Normal Pressure Angle, degrees	Form Factor 'y'
14 ½	0.100
20	0.125
25	0.150
30	0.175

Assuming pressure angle as $14\frac{1}{2}^\circ$, $y = 0.1$

$$Y = \pi \times 0.1$$
$$= 0.314$$

Substituting these values in E(2-593),

$$5978.32 = 103.5 \times 8b(0.314)0.8517$$

i.e., $b = 26.99$ mm say $b = 27$ mm

Face width $b \le 0.75 d_1'$ for $Z_1 = 1$ to 3 ... E(2-538a)

Where, $d_1' =$ Pitch diameter of worm = 80 mm

Therefore, $b \le 0.75 \times 80$

$b \le 60$ mm

Use, $b = 50$ mm [Value lying between 27 and 60 mm]

Step III: ***To calculate wear and dynamic load***

Wear load $F_W = d_2 b K$ ... E(2-557)

Where, $d_2 =$ Pitch diameter of Gear = 416 mm

$b =$ Face width of Gear = 50 mm

$K =$ Load stress factor ... T(2-111)

Table - (2-111) MDH

Material		Load Stress Factor, K					
		y = 0° –10°		y = 10° – 25°		y = 25° and up	
Worm	Gear	MPa	kgf/mm²	MPa	kgf/mm²	MPa	kgf/mm²
Steel, 250 H_B	Phosphor bronze	0.414	0.042	0.517	0.052	0.621	0.063
Hardened steel	Phosphor bronze	0.552	0.056	0.690	0.070	0.827	0.084
Hardened steel	Chilled phosphor bronze	0.827	0.084	1.034	0.106	1.241	0.127
Hardened steel	Antimony bronze	0.827	0.084	1.034	0.106	1.241	0.127
Cast iron	Phosphor bronze	1.034	0.106	1.290	0.132	1.551	0.158

From T(2-111)MDH, corresponding to Worm made of hardened steel, Gear of phosphor bronze and lead angle $\gamma = 11.75°$,

$$K = 0.69$$

Therefore, $F_w = 416 \times 50 \times 0.69 = 14352 \text{ N}$

The dynamic load F_d is given by,

$$F_d = F_t C_V$$

$$= 5878.3 \times 0.8517 = 5091.72 \text{ N}$$

$$F_w = 14352 \text{ N} > F_d = 5091.72 \text{ N}$$

Hence the design is safe.

Step IV: *To calculate the efficiency of Gear drive*

Assuming that the Worm drives the Worm Gear,

$$\text{Efficiency } \eta = \frac{\tan\gamma(\cos\alpha_n \cos\gamma - \mu \sin\gamma)}{\cos\alpha_n \sin\gamma + \mu\cos\gamma} \quad \text{... E(2-587)}$$

Where, $\gamma = 11.75°$ and $\alpha = \alpha_n = 14\frac{1}{2}°$

Coefficient of friction μ depends on rubbing velocity v_r

For the given drive,

Rubbing velocity,

$$v_r = \frac{\pi d_1 n_1'}{\cos\gamma} \quad \text{... E(2-544b)}$$

$$= \pi\left(\frac{80}{1000}\right)\left(\frac{1200}{60}\right)\left(\frac{1}{\cos 11.75}\right)$$

$$= 5.134 \text{ m/sec}$$

$$\mu = 0.025 + \frac{v_r}{305} \qquad \text{... E(2-543b)}$$

(For $2.75 < v_r < 20$ m/sec),

Therefore, $$\mu = 0.025 + \frac{5.134}{305} = 0.0418$$

Therefore, $$\eta = \frac{\tan 11.75\left(\cos 14\frac{1}{2}\cos 11.75 - 0.0418\sin 11.75\right)}{\cos 14\frac{1}{2}\sin 11.75 + 0.0418\cos 11.75}$$

$$= \frac{0.19538}{0.2381}$$

$$= 0.8207 = 82.07\%$$

Heat dissipation from Worm Gears

(a) *Heat generated,*

$$H_g = \frac{\mu F_n v_r}{1000} \qquad \text{... E(2-576a)}$$

Where, $\mu = 0.0418$

$$F_n = \text{Normal force} \approx \frac{2M_{t2}}{d_2 \cos\gamma \cos\alpha} \qquad \text{... E(2-546)}$$

$$F_n \approx \frac{2 \times 994791.7}{416 \times \cos 11.75 \times \cos 14\frac{1}{2}}$$

$$\approx 5045.73 \text{ N}$$

Therefore, $$H_g = \frac{0.0418 \times 5045.73 \times 5.134}{1000}$$

$$= 1.0828 \text{ kW}$$

(b) *Heat dissipated H_d*

$$H_d = \frac{h_{cr} A}{1000}\left(t_g - t_a\right)$$

Where, $$A = 14.4(a)^{1.7} \qquad \text{... E(2-577)}$$

a = Centre distance between gears

= 248 mm = 0.248 m

Therefore, $$A = 14.4(0.248)^{1.7} = 1.3456 \text{ m}^2$$

Corresponding to $A = 1.3456 \text{ m}^2$, referring figure (2-73),

h_{cr} = Coefficient of heat transfer

$\approx 300 \text{ w/m}^2\text{K}$

Assuming $\left(t_g - t_a\right) = 25°\,C$,

$$H_d = \frac{300(1.3456)25}{1000}$$

$$= 10.092 \text{ kW}$$

$$H_d = 10.092 \text{ kW} > H_g = 1.0526 \text{ kW}$$

Hence the design is safe.

Example 5.4. A hardened steel Worm at 1250 rpm transmits power to a phosphor bronze Gear with a transmission ratio of 20:1. The centre distance is 200 mm. Determine the input power capacity.

Solution:

Speed of Worm $n_1 = 1250 \text{ rpm}$

Speed of Worm Gear $n_2 = \frac{1250}{i} = \frac{1250}{20} = 62.5 \text{ rpm}$

Step I: ***To find number of teeth, module and diameter of Worm and Worm Gear***

Corresponding to centre distance 200 mm and transmission ratio 20 : 1, the quantity

$$Z_1/Z_2/q/m = 2/40/10/8 \quad \text{... T(2-98)}$$

Table - (2-103)

Number of Starts, Z_1	Face width, b
1	$0.75d_1$
2 or 3	$0.75d_1$
4	$0.67d_1$

i.e., Number of threads on Worm , Z_1 = 2 (*i.e.*, double start)

Number of threads on Worm Gear, Z_2 = 40

Diametral coefficient, $q = \frac{d_1}{m} = 10$

Diameter of Worm, $d_1 = qm$

$$= 10 \times 8 = 80 \text{ mm}$$

Centre distance, $a = \frac{d_1 + d_2}{2}$

i.e., $200 = \frac{80 + d_2}{2}$

Therefore, $d_2 = 320$ mm

Note: *d_2 can also be obtained from equation*

$$d_2 = mZ_2$$

$$= 8 \times 40 = 320 \text{mm}$$

To find the input power capacity (N)

$$M_t = \frac{9550N \times 10^3}{n}$$

Therefore, $$N = \frac{M_t n}{9550 \times 10^3} \text{ kW}$$

Where, n = Speed of worm gear = 62.5 rpm

To find M_t, the torque transmitted

$$\left.M_t\right)_{\text{Gear}} = M_{t2} = F_t r$$

$$= F_t \frac{d_2}{2}$$

Therefore, $$F_t = \frac{2M_{t2}}{d_2} \quad \text{... (1)}$$

Where, $$F_t = \sigma_o b m \pi y C_V \quad \text{... E(2-539)}$$

$$\sigma_o = 103.5 \text{ MPa for phosphor bronze gear} \quad \text{... T(2-106)}$$

$$b \le 0.75 d_i \text{ (for } Z_1 = 1 \text{ to } 3) \quad \text{... E(2-538a)}$$

$$b \le 0.75 \times 80 = 60 \text{ mm}$$

Say, $$b = 50 \text{ mm}$$

Assuming pressure angle $14\frac{1}{2}^\circ$, $y = 0.1$ ... T(2-105)

Velocity, $$v = \frac{\pi d_2 n_2}{60}$$

$$= \frac{\pi}{60}\left(\frac{320}{1000}\right)62.5 = 1.047 \text{ m/sec}$$

Velocity factor, $$C_V = \frac{6}{6 + v_m}$$

$$= \frac{6}{6 + 1.047} = 0.8514$$

Therefore, $$F_t = 103.5 \times 50 \times 8 \times \pi \times 0.1 \times 0.8514$$

$$= 11073.47 \text{ N} \quad \text{... (2)}$$

Equating (1) and (2),

$$\frac{2M_{t2}}{d_2} = 11073.47$$

i.e., $$M_{t2} = \frac{11073.47 d_2}{2}$$

$$= \frac{11073.47 \times 320}{2}$$

$$= 1771755.2 \text{ N-mm}$$

Therefore, $$N = \frac{1771755.2 \times 62.5}{9550 \times 10^3} \text{ kW}$$

$$N = 11.595 \text{ kW}$$

Example 5.5: Design a Worm Gear drive to transmit 20 kW from a shaft running at 2000 rpm to another shaft to be run at 80 rpm.

Solution:

Step I: ***Selection of material (Refer T-2.106)***

Select hardened steel for Worm and phosphor bronze SAE65 as material of Gear for which the allowable static stress $\sigma_o = 103.5 \text{ N/mm}^2$

Step II: ***To find the number of teeth, module and pitch diameter of Worm and Worm Gear***

For the given drive,

Speed ratio $$i = \frac{n_1}{n_2}$$

$$= \frac{2000}{80} = 25$$

Centre distance $$a = 8\left[(i+5)\text{N}\right]^{0.588}$$

Note: *According to AGMA recommendations minimum and maximum values of pitch diameter of worm is*

$$\frac{(a)^{0.875}}{3} \le d_2 \le \frac{(a)^{0.875}}{1.6}$$

According to Dudley,

$$d_2 = \frac{(a)^{0.875}}{2.2}$$

Therefore, $$a = 8\left[(25+5)20\right]^{0.588}$$

$$= 344.07 \text{ mm}$$

Use, $$a = 315 \text{ mm}$$

Corresponding to $a = 315$ mm and transmission ratio = 25, the quantity

$$Z_1/Z_2/q/m = 2/53/10/10 \qquad \text{... T(2-98)}$$

i.e., The number of threads on Worm, $Z_1 = 2$

Number of threads on Gear, $Z_2 = 53$

Diametral coefficient, $$q = \frac{d_1}{m}$$

$$d_1 = qm$$

$$= 10 \times 10 = 100 \text{ mm}$$

And $d_2 = mZ_2$

$$= 10 \times 53 = 530 \text{ mm}$$

Speed ratio $i = 25$

$$i = \frac{\pi d_2}{P_Z} \quad \text{... E(2-502)}$$

Therefore,

Lead $P_Z = \dfrac{\pi d_2}{25}$

$$= \frac{\pi \times 530}{25} = 66.6 \text{ mm}$$

Lead angle $\gamma = \tan^{-1}\left(\dfrac{P_Z}{\pi d_1}\right)$ ... E(2-527)

$$= \tan^{-1}\left(\frac{66.6}{\pi \times 100}\right) = 11.97°$$

Step III: *To check for wear and dynamic load*

Tangential load $F_t = \sigma_o m b Y C_V$ ... E(2-593)

Where, $F_t = \dfrac{M_t C_S}{r}$

$$M_t = \frac{9500 \text{ N} \times 10^3}{n_2} \text{ N-mm}$$

$$= \frac{9550 \times 20 \times 10^3}{80}$$

$$= 2387500 \text{ N-mm}$$

Service factor $C_S = 1.25$,

$$r = r_2 = \frac{d_2}{2} = \frac{530}{2} = 265 \text{ mm}$$

Therefore, $F_t = \dfrac{2387500 \times 1.25}{265} = 11261.8 \text{ N}$

To find C_v, the velocity factor

Velocity, $v = \dfrac{\pi d_2 n_2}{60}$

$$= \frac{\pi}{60} \times \frac{530}{1000} \times 80 = 2.22 \text{ m/sec}$$

$$C_V = \frac{6}{6 + v_m}$$

$$= \frac{6}{6 + 2.22} = 0.73$$

$$Y = \pi y$$

$$= \pi \times 0.1 = 0.314$$

Substituting in equation (2-593),

$$11261.8 = 103.5 \times 10 \times 0.73 \times 0.314 \times b$$

i.e., $b = 47.46$ mm say $b = 48$ mm

Note: *Face width 'b' is also given by*

$$b \le 0.75 d_1' \qquad \text{for } (Z_1 = 1 \text{ to } 3) \qquad \text{... E(2-538a)}$$

$$\le 0.75 \times 100$$

$$= 75 \text{ mm}$$

Say $b = 60$ mm (an average value)

Step IV: ***To calculate wear and dynamic load***

Wear load $F_W = d_2 b K$ ... E(2-557)

Where, d_2 = Pitch diameter of Gear = 530 mm

b = Face width of Gear = 60 mm

For K = Load stress factor, refer T(2-111)

For hardened steel Worm, phosphor bronze Gear and lead angle $\gamma = 11.97°$,

$$K = 0.69$$

Therefore, $F_w = 530 \times 60 \times 0.69 = 21942$ N

The dynamic load F_d is given by,

$$F_d = F_t C_V$$

$$F_d = 11261.8 \times 0.73 = 8221.11 \text{ N}$$

$$F_w = 21942 > F_d = 8221.11 \text{ N}$$

Hence the design is safe.

Step V: ***To calculate the efficiency*** **(η)** ***of gear drive***

Assuming that the Worm drives the Worm Gear,

Efficiency, $$\eta = \frac{\tan\gamma(\cos\alpha_n \cos\gamma - \mu\sin\gamma)}{\cos\alpha_n \sin\gamma + \mu\cos\gamma} \qquad \text{... E(2-587)}$$

Here μ, the coefficient of friction depends on rubbing velocity v_r given by

$$v_r = \frac{\pi d_1 n_1'}{\cos\gamma} \qquad \text{... E(2-544b)}$$

Where, $$n_1' = \frac{n_1}{60}$$

$$= \frac{2000}{60} = 33.33 \text{ rpm}$$

Therefore, $v_r = \pi\left(\frac{100}{1000}\right)\frac{33.33}{\cos 11.97}$

$= 10.71 \text{ m/sec}$

$$\mu = 0.025 + \frac{v_r}{305} \qquad \text{... E(2-543b)}$$

$= 0.025 + \frac{10.71}{305}$

$= 0.0601$

Therefore, $$\eta = \frac{\tan 11.97\left(\cos 14\frac{1}{2}\cos 11.97 - 0.0601 \sin 11.97\right)}{\cos 14\frac{1}{2}\ \sin 11.97 + 0.0601\cos 11.97}$$

$\eta = 0.7632 = 76.32\%$

Step VI: ***Heat dissipation from Worm Gears***

(a) Heat generated, H_g

The heat generated, $$H_g = \frac{\mu F_n v_r}{1000} \qquad \text{... E(2-576a)}$$

Where, $\mu = 0.0601$

$$F_n = \text{Normal force} \approx \frac{2M_{t2}}{d_2 \cos\gamma \cos\alpha} \qquad \text{... E(2-545)}$$

$$F_n \approx \frac{2\times 2387500}{530\times\cos 11.97\times\cos 14\frac{1}{2}}$$

$= 9512.69 \text{ N}$

$$H_g = \frac{\mu F_n v_r}{1000}$$

$= \frac{0.0601\times 9512.69\times 10.71}{1000}$

$= 6.123 \text{ kW}$

(b) Heat dissipated H_d

$$H_d = \frac{h_{cr}A}{1000}\left(t_g - t_a\right) \qquad \text{... E(2-577)}$$

Where, $A = 14.4\times(a)^{1.7}$

a = Centre distance between Gears

= 315 mm = 0.315 m

Therefore, $A = 14.4(0.315)^{1.7}$

$= 2.0206 \text{ m}^2$

Corresponding to $A = 2.0206\ \text{m}^2$, referring figure (2-73 MDH),

$$h_{cr} = \text{Coefficient of heat transfer} = 300\ \text{w/m}^2\text{k}$$

Assuming $(t_a - t_g) = 25°C$, From E(2-577),

$$H_d = \frac{300 \times (1.3456) \times 25}{1000}$$

$$= 15.15\ \text{kW}$$

Therefore, $H_d = 15.15\ \text{kW} > H_g = 6.123\ \text{kW}$; Hence no cooling is required.

Hence the design is safe.

EXERCISE

1. Determine the proportions of a worm gear drive to transmit 15 kW power from a motor shaft rotating at 2800 rpm. The wheel shaft rotates at 240 rpm. The gear is made from phosphor bronze with permissible strength of 82.4 MPa and hardness 100 BHN, while the worm is made from hardened steel. Determine
   (*a*) The efficiency of the drive.
   (*b*) Whether the drive requires cooling. ***(VTU, July 2006)***
2. Design a worm gear drive for a speed of 500 rpm of the worm transmitting 20 kW. The velocity ratio is 25:1. The material of the gear is phosphorus bronze and the worm is hardened steel. Determine the efficiency of the drive also.

(VTU, Dec 07 / Jan 08)

CHAPTER 6

Brakes and Clutches

NOTATIONS AND SYMBOLS USED

a_1 = Width of flat belt; mm.

α = Semi cone angle of cone; Degree.

b = Width of lever; mm.

= Width of friction lining; mm.

d = Diameter of shaft; mm.

= Diameter of handle (lever) used in brakes; mm.

d_p = Diameter of pin; mm.

D_1 = Minimum diameter of disc in a plate clutch; mm.

= Minimum diameter of cone in cone clutch; mm.

D_2 = Maximum diameter of disc in a plate clutch; mm.

= Maximum diameter of cone in cone clutch; mm.

D_m = Mean diameter of disc in a plate clutch; mm.

= Mean diameter of cone in a cone clutch; mm.

h = Thickness of lever; mm.

i = Total number of discs in a disc clutch.

i_1 = Number of discs on the driver shaft.

i_2 = Number of discs on the driven shaft.

F_a = Axial load required to engage clutch; N.

θ = Angle of wrap of band on drum; Degree.

2θ = Angle extended by a block (shoe) in a block brake; Degree.

μ = Coefficient of friction.

σ_b = Bending stress in lever; MPa.

l = Length of lever in brakes; mm.

= Length of shoe in a block brake; mm.

T_1 = Maximum belt tension in belt; N.

= Maximum tension in band; N.

T_2 = Minimum belt tension in belt; N.
= Minimum tension in band; N.
P = Effort required to operate brake; N.

INTRODUCTION

Clutches and brakes are the mechanical devices that provide the connection (frictional, mechanical, and electrical) between the driver and driven members. In a clutch both the connected elements rotate, whereas in a brake one element rotates while the other is fixed. Hence a clutch provides an uninterrupted connection between the members such as in the crank shaft of an automobile engine and the input shaft.

A brake provides an uninterrupted connection to rotating members where one is fixed, the other rotates such as the wheel of an automobile and its chassis.

Clutches and brakes are extensively used in production machinery not just in vehicle application where they are required to stop motion. Clutches help in starting a high inertia load with a smaller electric motor than would otherwise be required if it were directly connected.

(I) Brakes

(a) Simple band brake:

In a simple band brake, one end of band (which is made of steel or leather and usually of rectangular section) is attached to the fulcrum 0 and the other end is attached at a distance 'a' from the fulcrum on the lever. The angle of lap of the band on the surface of brake drum is θ. The radius of brake drum is 'r' and the length of lever (measured from fulcrum) is 'l'.

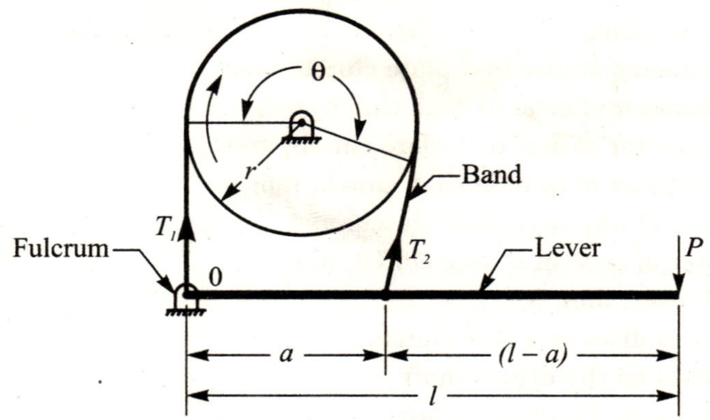

Figure: 6.1

Analysis of Simple Band Brake

Case 1: Analysis for clockwise rotation of drum

Consider the drum rotating in the clockwise direction as shown in Fig. 6.1. The band tensions T_1 and T_2 act as shown. Let 'P' be the effort applied to operate the brake. Taking moments about the fulcrum 0, and equating clockwise moments to anticlockwise moments,

$$Pl = T_2 a$$

Therefore, $$P = \frac{T_2 a}{l} \quad \text{...(1)}$$

To find T_1 and T_2

The ratio of band tensions, $$\frac{T_1}{T_2} = e^{\mu\theta} \quad \text{... (2)}$$

Torque $$M_t = (T_1 - T_2)r \quad \text{... (3)}$$

Knowing '*N*', the power absorbed, M_t can be calculated using equation,

$$M_t = \frac{9550 N \times 10^3}{n} \text{N-mm}$$

Now using equations (2) and (3), T_1 and T_2 are calculated. Finally knowing the values of T_1 and T_2, the effort '*P*' required to operate the brake is computed using equation (1).

Case 2: Analysis for counter clockwise rotation of drum

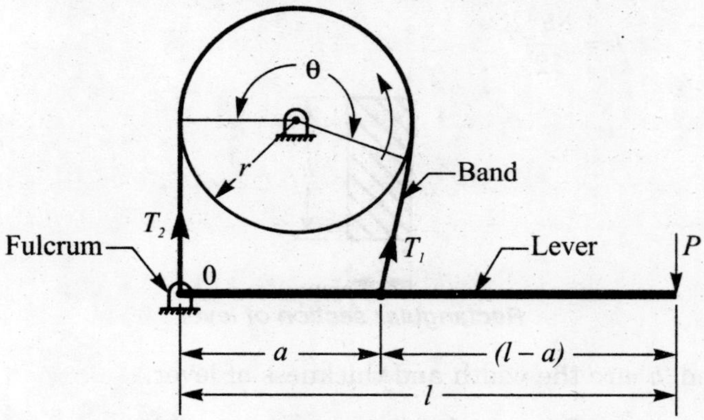

Figure: 6.2

When the drum rotates in the counter clockwise direction, the tensions T_1 and T_2 act as shown in Fig. 6.2. Taking moments about 0,

$$Pl = T_1 a$$

Note: *The band is assumed to be normal to lever.*

$$P = T_1 \frac{a}{l} \quad \text{... (4)}$$

From equations (1) and (4), we find that the effort required to operate the brake is minimum for the clockwise rotation of drum because

$$P_{\text{clockwise rotation}} = T_2 \frac{a}{l} < P_{\text{counter clockwise rotation}} = T_1 \frac{a}{l}$$

Because $T_2 < T_1$ and $\frac{a}{l}$ is a constant for a given brake.

Design of Brake Lever (or Handle)

The brake lever is generally made of rectangular or circular cross-section.

Note: *The dimensions of cross-section are obtained by considering the bending stress due to maximum load given by,*

$$P_{max} = P = T_1 \frac{a}{l}$$

i.e., The lever is to be designed for maximum load required to operate brake.

Now bending stress in lever is given by,

$$\sigma_b = \frac{M_b}{Z_b}$$

Where, M_b = Bending moment = $P_{max}(l - a)$, N-mm

$$Z_b = \frac{I}{C}$$

For rectangular section,

$$I = \frac{bh^3}{12}$$

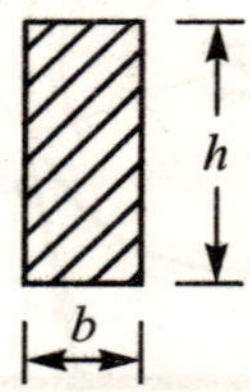

Rectangular section of lever

where, 'b' and 'h' are the width and thickness of lever.

$$C = \frac{\text{Depth}}{2} = \frac{h}{2}$$

Therefore, $Z_b = \frac{I}{C}$ becomes $= \frac{bh^3}{12} \div \frac{h}{2} = \frac{bh^2}{6}$

For circular cross-section lever, with 'd' as diameter of lever,

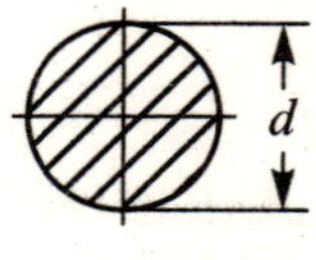

Circular section of lever

$$I = \frac{\pi d^4}{64}$$

$$C = \frac{d}{2}$$

Therefore, $$Z_b = \frac{I}{C} = \frac{\pi d^4}{64} \div \frac{d}{2} = \frac{\pi d^3}{32}$$

Knowing the material of lever or the bending stress of the material of lever, the dimensions of cross-section (b and h or d) can be computed.

Design of Band

The band is subjected to tensile load T_1 and hence the tensile stress induced in the band is given by,

$$\sigma_{tensile} = \frac{T_1}{\text{Area of cross-section of band}}$$

Where, Area of cross-section = $a_1 t$

a_1 = Width of band, mm.

t = Thickness of band, mm.

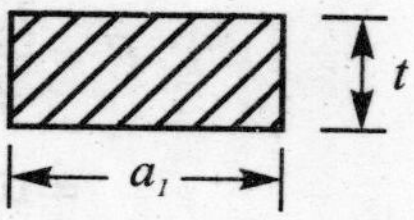

Hence, knowing the tensile strength of band, maximum tension T_1 in band, and width or thickness, the other dimension (width or thickness) can be calculated.

Example 6.1: ***In a simple band brake used on a brake drum of 600 mm diameter, one end of the band is attached to the fulcrum while the other end is attached to the lever at a distance of 600 mm from the fulcrum on the lever which is 1200 mm long. The brake is used to absorb 10 kW at 1000 rpm of drum. Taking coefficient of friction between drum and band as 0.3, determine,***

(i) The minimum effort required to operate the brake and the direction of rotation for minimum effort.

(ii) The area of cross-section of band assuming 40C8 (i.e. C40) as material of lever. Use a factor of safety 4.

(iii) The dimensions of rectangular cross-section of lever taking depth equal to thrice width and material of lever same as that of band.

Solution:

(i) To find the minimum effort required to operate the brake

(a) Consider the clockwise rotation of drum

The tensions T_1 and T_2 act as shown in Fig. 6.3. Taking moments of load 'P' and tensions T_1 and T_2 about 0, the fulcrum,

$$P \times 1200 = T_2 \times 600$$

Therefore, $$P = T_2 \times \frac{600}{1200} = \frac{T_2}{2} \quad \text{... (1)}$$

To find T_1 and T_2

Ratio of band tensions,

$$\frac{T_1}{T_2} = e^{\mu\theta} = e^{0.3 \times 180° \times \frac{\pi}{180}} = 2.57$$

Here, $\theta = 180°$, because, $a = d$ = Diameter of brake drum = 600 mm

Therefore, $$T_1 = 2.57T_2 \qquad ...(2)$$

Also, Torque $$M_t = (T_1 - T_2)r$$

i.e., $$\frac{9550 \times 10 \times 10^3}{1000} = (2.57T_2 - T_2)\frac{600}{2}$$

Therefore, $$T_2 = 202.76 \text{ N}$$

$$T_1 = 521.1 \text{ N}$$

Hence, from equation-(1)

$$P = \frac{T_2}{2}$$

$$= 101.38 \text{ N}$$

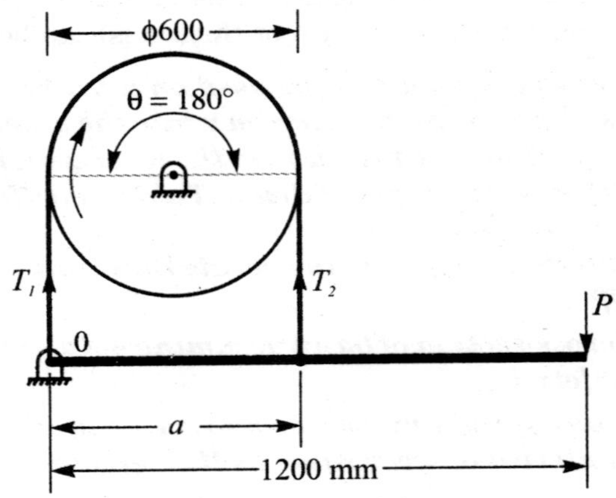

Figure: 6.3

(b) Consider the counter clockwise rotation of drum

The tensions T_1 and T_2 act as shown in Fig. 6.4. Taking moments about 0,

$$P \times 1200 = T_1 \times 600$$

Note: *The tensions T_1 and T_2 remain the same for a given brake drum irrespective of the direction of rotation of drum.*

Therefore, $$P = T_1 \times \frac{600}{1200}$$

$$= \frac{T_1}{2} = 260.55 \text{ N}$$

From the above analysis we find that the effort 'P' required to operate brake is minimum for the clockwise rotation of drum and its value is $P_{min} = 101.38$ N

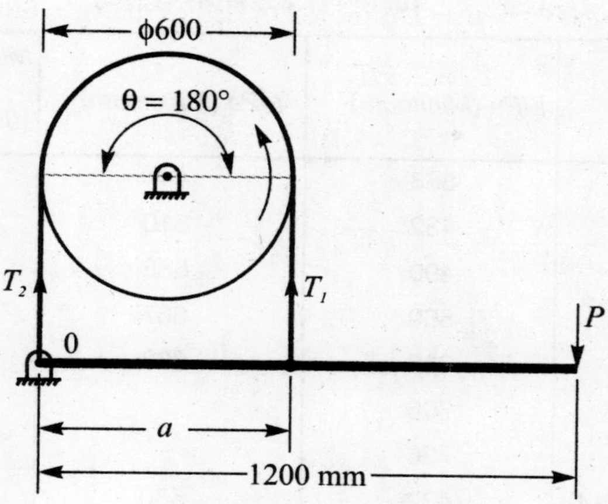

Figure: 6.4

(ii) To determine the dimensions of cross-section of band required.

The band is subjected to tensile load T_1 and hence the tensile stress induced in the band is given by,

$$\sigma_t = \frac{T_1}{\text{Area of cross-section}}$$

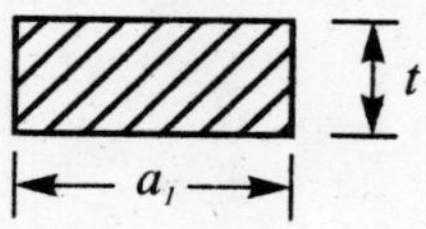

i.e., Area of cross-section of band $a_1 t = \dfrac{T_1}{\sigma_t}$

Where, $T_1 = 521.1$ N

For 40C8 steel, $\sigma_{ut} = 600$ MPa ... T(1-25)

Assuming $\sigma_y = 0.6\sigma_{ut}$, $\sigma_y = 360$ MPa

$$\sigma_{tensile} = \frac{\sigma_y}{\text{Factor of safety}}$$

$$= \frac{360}{4} = 90 \text{ N/mm}^2$$

Therefore, Area of cross-section

$$a_1 t = \frac{T_1}{\sigma_t}$$

$$= \frac{521.1}{90} = 5.79 \text{ mm}^2$$

Table - (1.25) MDH

Steel Designation	MPa (Minimum)	MPa (Maximum)	Minimum elongation (gauge length $=5.65\sqrt{a^*}$),%
14 C 4 (C 14)**	363	441	26
20 C 8 (C 20)	432	510	24
30 C 8 (C 30)	490	588	21
40 C 8 (C 40)	569	667	18
45 C 8 (C 45)	618	696	15
55 C 8 (C 55 Mn 75)	706		13
65 C 6 (C 65)	736		10
14 C 14 S 14 (14 Mn 1 S 14)	432	530	22
11 C 10 S 25 (13 S 25)	363	481	23

*Note** = Steel designations in parentheses are old designations, a* = Area of cross-section*

(iii) Design of lever

The lever is to be designed for maximum load P_{max}. The bending stress in lever is given by,

$$\sigma_b = \frac{M_b}{Z_b}$$

Where,

$$\sigma_b = 90 \text{ N/mm}^2$$

$$M_b = P_{max}(1200-600)$$

$$= 260.55(600) = 156330 \text{ N-mm}$$

$$Z_b = \frac{I}{C} = \frac{bh^2}{6} \quad \text{Where, } h = 3b$$

Therefore,

$$Z_b = \frac{b}{6}(3b)^2 = 1.5b^3$$

Now from,

$$\sigma_b = \frac{M_b}{Z_b},$$

$$90 = \frac{156330}{1.5b^3}$$

Therefore, Width of lever, $b = 10.5$ mm

Depth of lever, $h = 3b = 3 \times 10.5 = 31.5$ mm

Differential Band Brake

In a differential band brake, one end of the band is attached to point 'A' on the extension of lever at a distance 'a' from fulcrum and the other end is attached at 'B' on fulcrum at a distance 'b' from fulcrum on the other side of it (effort side). Let 'r' be the radius of brake drum and θ be the angle of lap of band on drum.

(a) Consider clockwise rotation of drum

Taking moment of load 'P' and tensions T_1 and T_2 about 0, the fulcrum,

$$Pl + T_1 a = T_2 b$$

i.e., $$P = \frac{T_2 b - T_1 a}{l} \quad \text{... (1)}$$

Where, $$\frac{T_1}{T_2} = e^{\mu\theta} \quad \text{... (2)}$$

And Torque $$M_t = (T_1 - T_2) r \quad \text{... (3)}$$

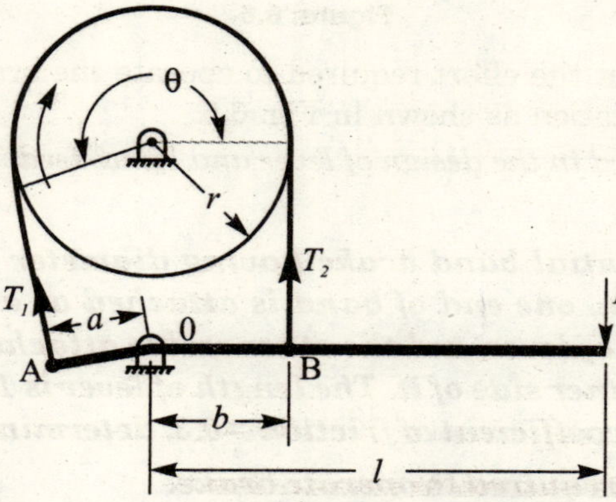

Figure: 6.5

Knowing 'N', the power absorbed, M_t is calculated from equation

$$M_t = 9550 \frac{N}{n} \times 10^3 \text{ N-mm}$$

Using equations (2) and (3), the band tensions T_1 and T_2 are calculated. Finally, the effort 'P' is calculated using equation (1)

(b) Counter clockwise rotation of drum

For counter clockwise rotation, the tensions T_1 and T_2 act as shown in figure-6.6.

Taking moments about 0,

$$Pl + T_2 a = T_1 b$$

Therefore, $$P = \frac{T_1 b - T_2 a}{l}$$

From equations (1) and (3), we find that for a given value of 'a' and 'b',

$$\frac{T_2 b - T_1 a}{l} < \frac{T_1 b - T_2 a}{l}$$

Because $T_1 > T_2$ and $b > a$

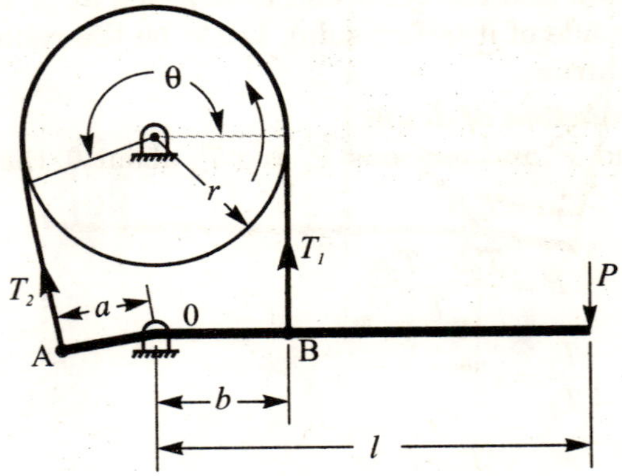

Figure: 6.6

Hence, we conclude that the effort required to operate the brake is minimum when it is rotating in the clockwise rotation as shown in Fig. 6.6.

Note: *The procedure followed in the design of lever and band used is identical to that of simple band brake.*

Example 6.2. In a differential band brake having diameter of drum 600 mm used to absorb 25 kW at 1000 rpm, one end of band is attached at a distance of 25 mm from fulcrum on the extension of lever and the other end is attached at a distance of 50mm from the fulcrum on the other side of it. The length of lever is 1.2 m. Taking angle of lap of band on drum as 210°, coefficient of friction = 0.3, determine,

(i) The minimum effort required to operate brake.

(ii) The width of steel band required taking thickness, as 2 mm and limiting the stress in band to 80 MPa.

(iii) The dimensions of rectangular section of lever with depth of section 2.5 times width and permissible bending stress in lever 75 MPa.

Solution:

(i) To find the minimum effort (P_{min}) required to operate the brake.

(a) Consider the clockwise rotation of drum.

The tensions T_1 and T_2 acts as shown in Fig. 6.7. Taking moment about 0, the fulcrum,

$$P \times 1200 + T_1 \times 25 = T_2 \times 50$$

Therefore,
$$P = \frac{50T_2 - 25T_1}{1200} \quad \text{... (1)}$$

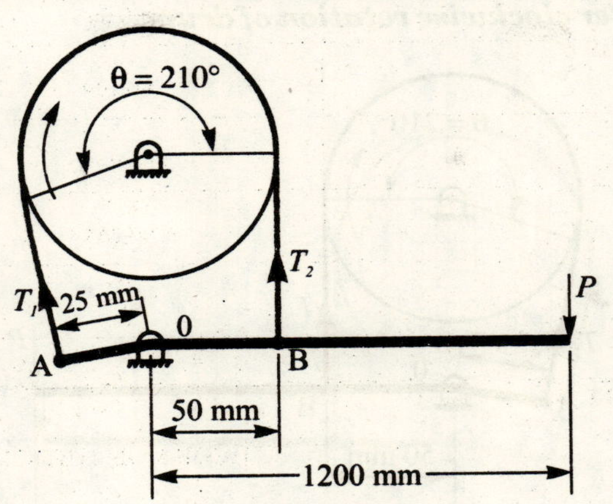

Figure: 6.7

To find T_1 and T_2

Ratio of band tensions

$$\frac{T_1}{T_2} = e^{\mu\theta} = e^{0.3 \times 210 \times \frac{\pi}{180}} = 3$$

i.e., $T_1 = 3\,T_2$ ... (2)

Also Torque M_t is given by,

$$M_t = \frac{9550 N \times 10^3}{n}$$

$$= \frac{9550 \times 25 \times 10^3}{1000} = 238750 \text{ N-mm}$$

But, $M_t = (T_1 - T_2) r$

i.e., $238750 = (3T_2 - T_2)\frac{600}{2}$

Therefore, $T_2 = 795.83$ N

$T_1 = 3\,T_2$

$= 2387.5$ N

Hence, $$P = \frac{50 \times 795.83 - 25 \times 2387.5}{1200}$$

$= -16.58$ N

(b) Consider counter clockwise rotation of drum.

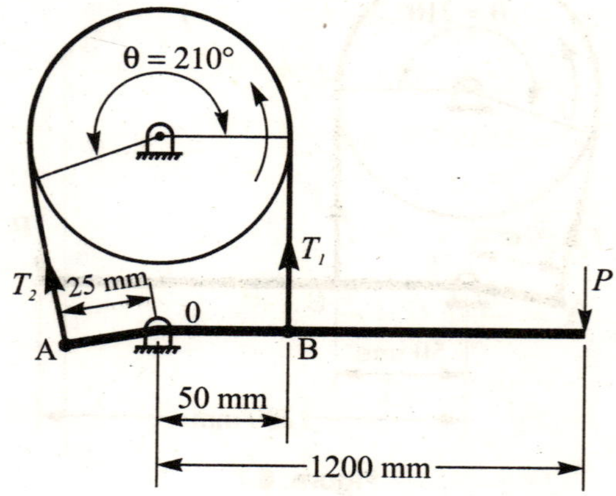

Figure: 6.8

The tensions T_1 and T_2 act as shown in Fig. 6.8. Taking moment about 0, the fulcrum,

$$P \times 1200 + T_2 \times 25 = T_1 \times 50$$

Therefore, $$P = \frac{50T_1 - 25T_2}{1200} \quad \dots (3)$$

Substituting the values of T_1 and T_2,

$$P = 82.9 \text{ N}$$

Therefore, minimum effort (P_{min}) required to operate the brake is 16.58 N and it is minimum for clockwise rotation of drum.

Note: *P_{min} is negative and hence 'P' be applied in the opposite direction i.e., the upward direction.*

(ii) To determine width of band required (i.e., a_1)

The band is subjected to tensile load T_1 and hence the tensile stress in the band is given by,

$$\sigma_t = \frac{T_1}{\text{Area of cross-section}}$$

$$= \frac{T_1}{a_1 t}$$

Where, $\sigma_t = 80$ MPa (given)

t = Thickness of band = 2 mm

Therefore, $$80 = \frac{2387.5}{a_1 \times 2}$$

Width of band, $a_1 = 14.92$ mm

(iii) To find the dimensions of cross-section of lever

The lever is subjected to bending and hence the bending stress in the lever is given by

$$\sigma_b = \frac{M_b}{Z_b}$$

Where, $\sigma_b = 75$ MPa (given)

$$M_b = P_{max}(1200-50)$$
$$= 82.9(1200-50)$$
$$= 95335 \text{ N-mm}$$

$$Z_b = \frac{I}{C}$$

Where, $I = \frac{bh^3}{12};\ C = \frac{h}{2}$

Therefore, $Z_b = \frac{bh^2}{6} = \frac{b}{6}(2.5b)^2$; because $h = 2.5b$

$$= 1.0417b^3$$

Therefore, substituting in $\sigma_b = \frac{M_b}{Z_b}$ we get,

$$75 = \frac{95335}{1.0417b^3}$$

Therefore, width of lever $b = 10.67$ mm

Depth of lever $h = 2.5b = 26.68$ mm

Example 6.3: The drum of a band brake of a crane is 300 mm in diameter. The crane barrel is 350 mm. The angle of contact is 280° and $\mu = 0.25$. The brake lever is arranged as shown in figure-6.9. Calculate the force 'F' required to support a load of 10 kN on the rope round the barrel.

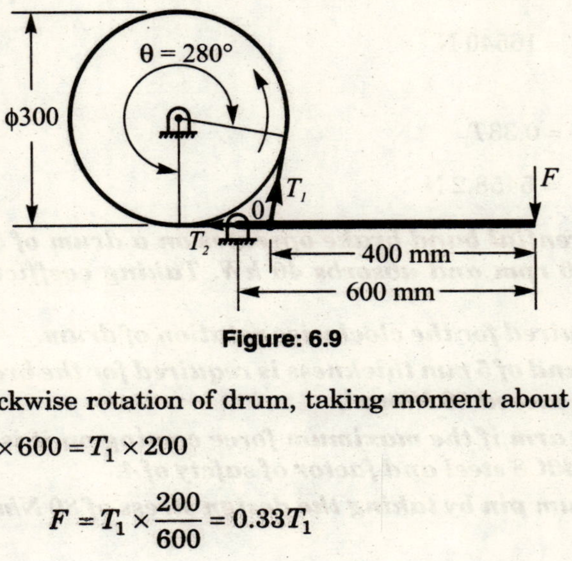

Figure: 6.9

Solution:

For the counter clockwise rotation of drum, taking moment about the fulcrum 0,

$$F \times 600 = T_1 \times 200$$

Therefore, $F = T_1 \times \frac{200}{600} = 0.33T_1$ ... (1)

To find T_1 and T_2

Ratio of band tensions

$$\frac{T_1}{T_2} = e^{\mu\theta} = e^{0.25 \times 250 \times \frac{\pi}{180}} = 3.39$$

i.e., $T_1 = 3.39 T_2$ ... (2)

Considering the crane barrel shown in figure below,

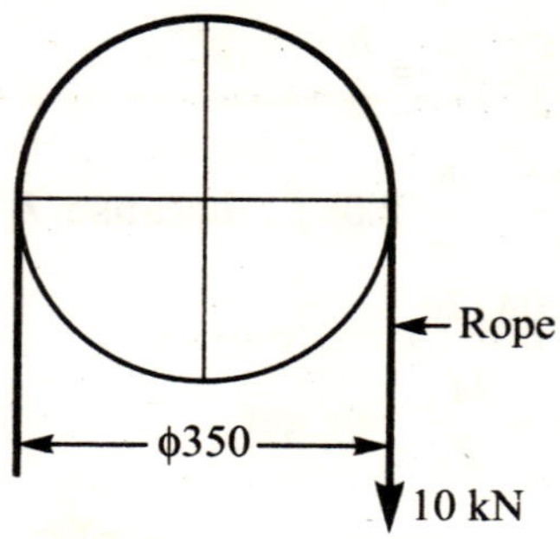

Torque $M_t = (10 \times 10^3) \frac{350}{2}$

$= 1750 \times 10^3$ N-mm

But $M_t = (T_1 - T_2) r$

$$1750 \times 10^3 = (3.39 T_2 - T_2) \frac{300}{2}$$

Therefore, $T_2 = 4880$ N

$T_1 = 16540$ N

From equation (1)

$F = 0.33 T_1$

$= 5458.2$ N

Example 6.4: A differential band brake operates on a drum of 500 mm diameter. The drum operates at 300 rpm and absorbs 40 kW. Taking coefficient of friction = 0.25. Determine

(i) The force 'F' required for the clockwise rotation of drum.

(ii) What width of band of 5 mm thickness is required for the brake if the tensile stress in band is not to exceed 60 N/mm².

(iii) Design the lever arm if the maximum force coming on it is twice the force calculated in (i). Use 40C8 steel and factor of safety of 4.

(iv) Design the fulcrum pin by taking the design stress of 80 N/mm² in shear.

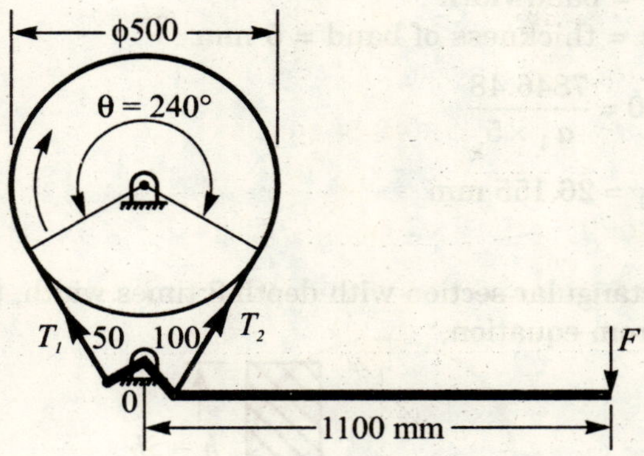

Figure: 6.10

Solution:

(i) To find F, the force required to operate brake

Taking moments about 0, For the clockwise rotation of drum,

$$(F \times 1100) + (T_1 \times 50) = T_2 \times 100$$

Therefore, $$F = \frac{100T_2 - 50T_1}{1100}$$

To find T_1 and T_2

$$\frac{T_1}{T_2} = e^{\mu\theta} = e^{0.25 \times 240 \times \frac{\pi}{180}} = 2.85$$

Therefore, $$T_1 = 2.85T_2$$

Also, Torque $$M_t = (T_1 - T_2)r$$

$$\frac{9550N}{n} \times 10^3 = (2.85T_2 - T_2)\frac{500}{2}$$

i.e., $$\frac{9550 \times 40 \times 10^3}{300} = 1.85T_2 \times \frac{500}{2}$$

Therefore, $$T_2 = 2753.15 \text{ N}$$

$$T_1 = 7846.48 \text{ N}$$

$$F = \frac{(100 \times 2753.15) - (50 \times 7846.48)}{1100}$$

$$= -106.37 \text{ N}$$

(ii) To find band width (a_1)

Note: *The band is subjected to tensile load and hence the tensile stress induced in band is given by,*

$$\sigma_t = \frac{T_1}{a_1 t}$$

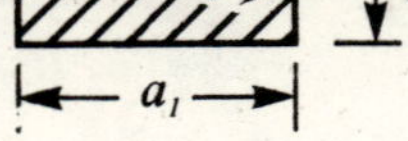

Where, b = bandwidth

h = thickness of band = 5 mm.

Therefore,
$$60 = \frac{7846.48}{a_1 \times 5}$$

$$a_1 = 26.155 \text{ mm}$$

(iii) To design lever

Assuming lever of rectangular section with depth 3 times width, the bending stress induced in lever is obtained from equation,

$$\sigma_b = \frac{M_b}{Z_b}$$

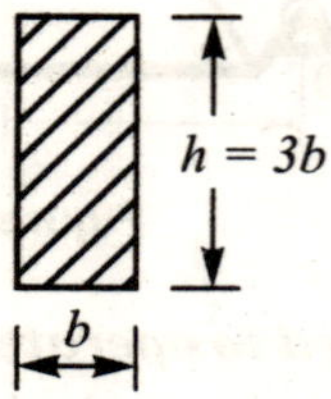

Where, $M_b = P_{max}(1100 - 100)$ (Assuming the dimension 100 mm normal to lever).

From data,
$$F_{max} = 2F$$
$$= 2 \times 106.37$$
$$= 212.74 \text{ N}$$

Therefore,
$$M_b = 212.74 \times 1000 \text{ N-mm}$$
$$= 212740 \text{ N-mm}$$

$$Z_b = \frac{I}{C}$$
$$= \frac{bh^2}{6} = \frac{b(3b)^2}{6} = 1.5b^3$$
$$\sigma_b = \frac{M_b}{Z_b}$$

For 40C8 material,

$$\sigma_{ut} = 600 \text{ MPa} \qquad \text{... T(1.25)}$$

Assuming,
$$\sigma_y = 0.6\sigma_{ut},$$
$$\sigma_y = 0.6 \times 600 = 360 \text{ MPa}$$

$$\sigma_{permissible} = \frac{\sigma_y}{\textit{Factor of safety}}$$
$$= \frac{360}{5} = 72 \text{ N/mm}^2$$

From,
$$\sigma_b = \frac{M_b}{Z_b},$$

Therefore, $72 = \dfrac{212740}{1.5b^3}$

Therefore, $b = 12.54$ mm

$h = 3b$

$h = 37.62$ mm

(iv) Design of fulcrum pin

The fulcrum Pin is under double shear and hence the shear stress induced in Pin is

Shear stress, $\tau = \dfrac{F}{2\left(\dfrac{\pi d_p^2}{4}\right)}$

Where, $F = F_{max}$ on lever.

$= 2 \times 106.37$ N (data)

Therefore, $80 = \dfrac{2 \times 106.37 \times 4}{2\pi d_p^2}$

Diameter of fulcrum Pin $d_p = 1.3$ mm

Example 6.5: A differential band brake is arranged as shown in figure-6.11 to absorb 20 kW at 300 rpm. Determine

(i) The force 'F' for clockwise rotation of drum.

(ii) What is the width of band required if the stress in band is not to exceed 60 N/mm². The thickness of band may be taken as 2 mm. Use $\mu = 0.3$.

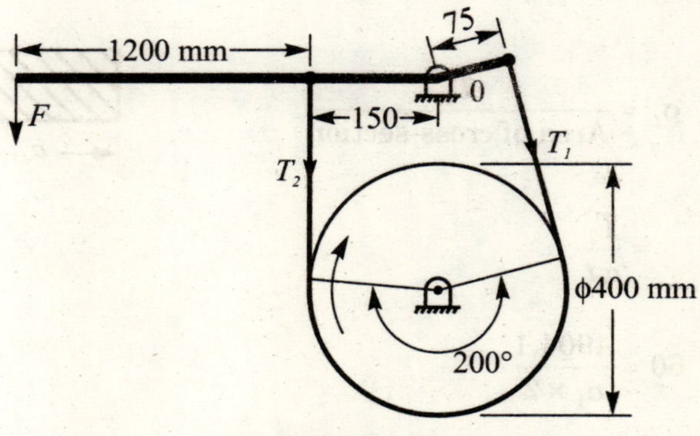

Figure: 6.11

Solution:

For the clockwise rotation of drum, the tensions T_1 and T_2 act as shown in Fig. 6.11. Taking moments about 0, the fulcrum

$$T_1 \times 75 = T_2 \times 150 + F\,(1200 + 150)$$

Therefore, $$F = \frac{(T_1 \times 75) - (T_2 \times 150)}{1350} \quad \text{... (1)}$$

(i) To find T_1 and T_2

Ratio of band tensions,

$$\frac{T_1}{T_2} = e^{\mu\theta} = e^{0.3 \times 200 \times \frac{\pi}{180}} = 2.85$$

i.e., $$T_1 = 2.85T_2$$

Torque, $$M_t = \frac{9550 \text{ N} \times 10^3}{n} \text{ N-mm}$$

$$= \frac{9550 \times 20 \times 10^3}{300}$$

$$= 636666.67 \text{ N-mm}$$

But, $$M_t = (T_1 - T_2)r$$

$$636666.67 = (2.85T_2 - T_2)\frac{400}{2}$$

Therefore, $$T_2 = 1720.72 \text{ N}$$

and $$T_1 = 4904.1 \text{ N}$$

Therefore force, $$F = \frac{75T_1 - 150T_2}{1350}$$

$$= 81.26 \text{ N}$$

(ii) To find width of band, 'a_1'

The band is subjected to tensile load T_1 and hence the tensile stress induced in the band is given by,

$$\sigma_t = \frac{T_1}{\text{Area of cross-section}}$$

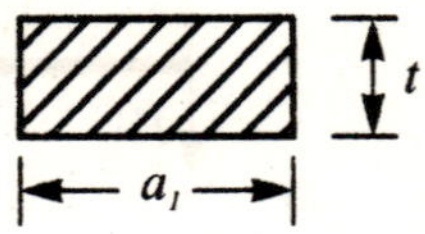

$$= \frac{T_1}{a_1 t}$$

$$60 = \frac{4904.1}{a_1 \times 2}$$

Therefore, $$a_1 = 40.87 \text{ mm}$$

Example 6.6: A differential band brake shown in figure 6.12 is mounted on a shaft of diameter 1000 mm. The rope of rope drum carries 15 kN. Determine

(i) The force 'F' for counter clockwise rotation of drum.

(ii) What is the width of band required if the stress in band is not to exceed 55 N/mm². The thickness of band may be taken as 2.5 mm. Use $\mu = 0.3$.

Solution:

For the counter clockwise rotation of drum, the band tension T_1 and T_2 act as shown in Fig. 6.12.

(i) *To find force 'F'*

Taking moment about 0, the fulcrum,

$$F\,(400+400)+T_2\,(100)=T_1\,(400)$$

i.e.,
$$(F\times 800)+(T_2\times 100)=400T_1$$

$$8F+T_2=4T_1$$

$$F=\frac{4T_1-T_2}{8} \qquad \ldots (1)$$

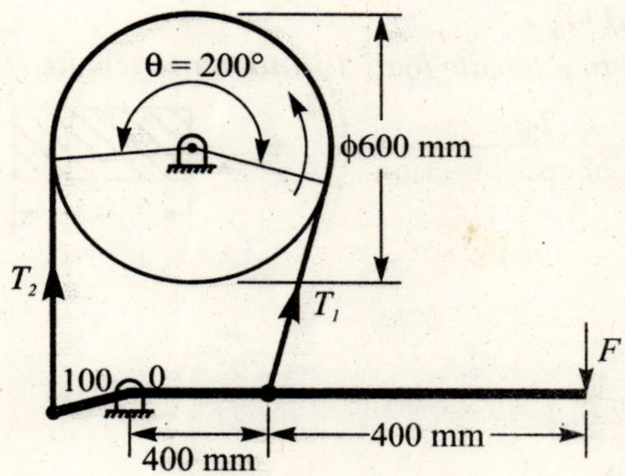

Figure: 6.12

To find T_1 and T_2

$$\frac{T_1}{T_2}=e^{\mu\theta}=e^{0.3\times 200\times \frac{\pi}{180}}=2.85$$

i.e.,
$$T_1=2.85T_2$$

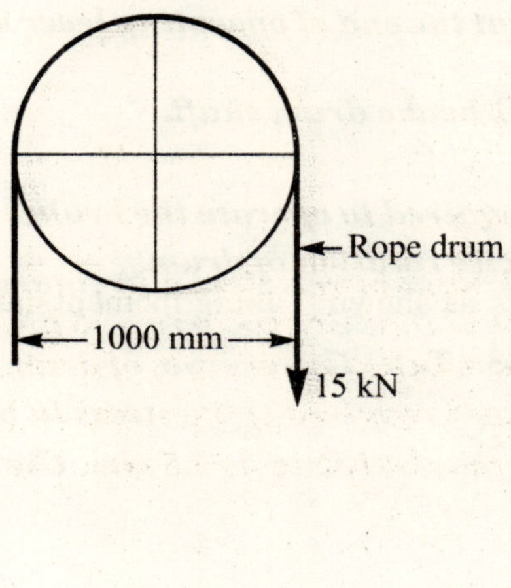

Torque $$M_t = \left(15\times10^3\right)\frac{1000}{2}$$

$$= 7.5\times10^6 \text{ N-mm}$$

But $$M_t = (T_1 - T_2)r$$

$$7.5\times10^6 = (2.85T_2 - T_2)\frac{600}{2}$$

Therefore, $$T_2 = 13513.5 \text{ N},$$

and $$T_1 = 38513.5 \text{ N}$$

(ii) To find width of band 'a_1'

Note: *The band is subjected to a tensile load T_1 and hence tensile stress in band is given by*

$$\sigma_t = \frac{T_1}{\text{Area of cross-section}}$$

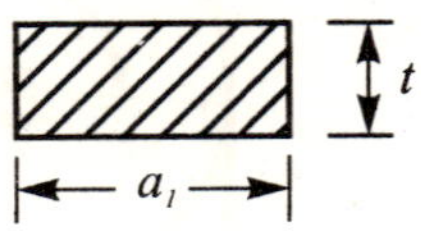

$$= \frac{T_1}{a_1 t}$$

$$= \frac{38512.6}{a_1 t}$$

i.e., $$55 = \frac{38512.6}{a_1\times2.5}$$

Therefore, $a_1 = 280.1$ mm

Example 6.7: A differential band brake shown in figure - 6.13 operates on a drum of diameter 600 mm. The band is 3.2 mm × 100 mm and the coefficient of friction is 0.22. Determine,

(i) The least force required at the end of operating lever when the band is subjected to a stress of 55 N/mm².

(ii) The torque applied to the brake drum shaft. ***(VTU, Dec 06 / Jan 07)***

Solution:

(i) To find the least force required to operate the brake.

Case (a): Consider the clockwise rotation of drum.

The tensions T_1 and T_2 acts as shown. Taking moments about the fulcrum 0,

$$F\times225 + T_1\times38 = T_2\times127$$

Therefore, $$F = \frac{127T_2 - 38T_1}{225} \quad \ldots (1)$$

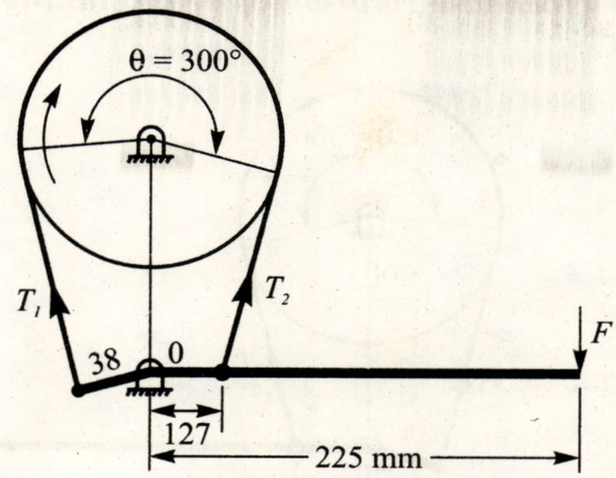

Figure: 6.13

To find tensions T_1 and T_2

Ratio of band tensions,

$$\frac{T_1}{T_2} = e^{\mu\theta} = e^{0.22 \times 300 \times \frac{\pi}{180}} = 3.1643$$

Therefore, $T_1 = 3.1643 T_2$ ... (2)

The band is subjected to tension and hence the tensile stress in band is given by

$$\sigma_t = \frac{T_1}{\text{Area of cross-section of band}}$$

Therefore, $T_1 = \sigma_t \times \text{Area of cross-section of band}$

$$= 55 \times (3.2 \times 100) = 17600 \text{ N}$$

From, $T_1 = 3.1643 T_2$

i.e., $T_2 = \frac{T_1}{3.1643}$

$$= \frac{17600}{3.1643} = 5562 \text{ N}$$

Therefore '*F*', the effort required for the clockwise rotation of drum is

$$F = \frac{127 T_2 - 38 T_1}{225}$$

$$F_{\text{clockwise}} = 167 \text{ N}$$

Case (b): For the counter clockwise rotation of drum, taking moments about 0, the fulcrum,

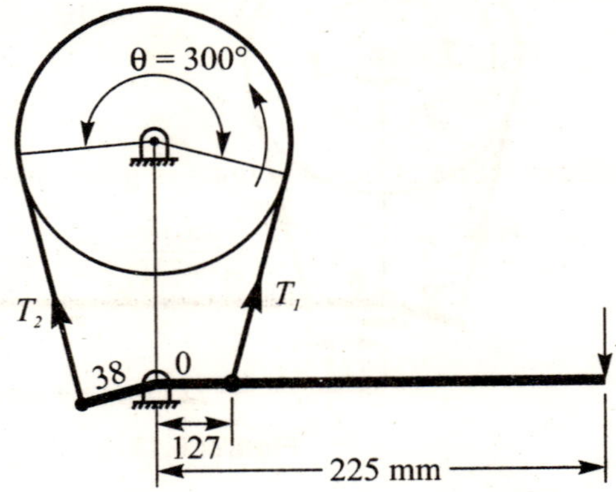

$$F \times 225 + T_2 \times 38 = T_1 \times 127$$

Therefore,
$$F = \frac{127T_1 - 38T_2}{225}$$

$$F_{\text{counter clockwise}} = 8994.9 \text{ N}$$

Therefore, the minimum effort required to operate brake

$$= F_{\min} = F_{\text{clockwise}} = 167 \text{ N}$$

(ii) To find torque applied to brake drum shaft.

Torque,
$$M_t = (T_1 - T_2) r_{\text{drum}}$$

$$= (17600 - 5562)\frac{600}{2}$$

$$= 3611400 \text{ N-mm}$$

Example 6.8: A band brake shown in figure - 6.14 uses a v-belt. The pitch diameter of the V-grooved pulley is 400 mm. The groove angle is 45° and the coefficient of friction is 0.3. Determine the power rating. ***(VTU, Dec 07 / Jan 08)***

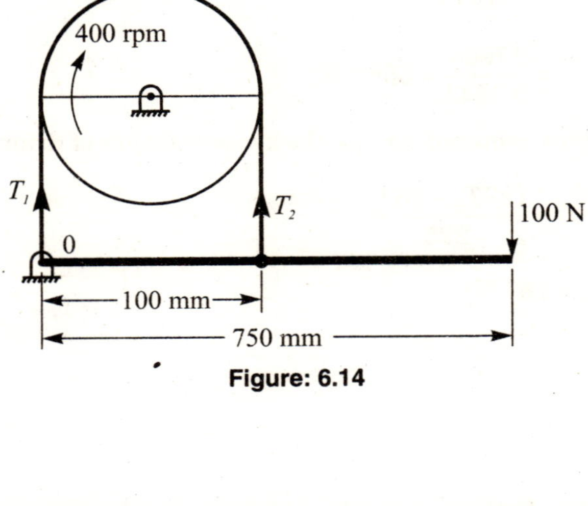

Figure: 6.14

Solution:

Taking moment about fulcrum, 0

$$100 \times 750 = T_2 \times 400$$

Therefore, $T_2 = 187.5$ N

For V-grooved pulleys, ratio of belt tensions is given by

$$\frac{T_1}{T_2} = e^{\frac{\mu\theta}{\sin\alpha}} = e^{\frac{0.3\times180}{\sin 22.5}\times\frac{\pi}{180}} = 11.74$$

Therefore, $T_1 = 11.74T_2$

$= 2201.25$

Torque, $$M_t = \frac{9550N \times 10^3}{n}$$

i.e., $$402750 = \frac{9550N \times 10^3}{400}$$

Therefore, Power rating $N = 16.869$ kW

Design of Block Brake

(a) Design of single block brake

Figure 6.15 shows a single shoe brake or single block brake pressing against a brake drum of diameter $2r$ subtending angle 2θ at the drum centre 0. For the clockwise rotation of drum, let N' be the normal reaction on shoe and $\mu N'$ the tangential force acting at the periphery of drum. Taking moments of the forces about fulcrum 0′,

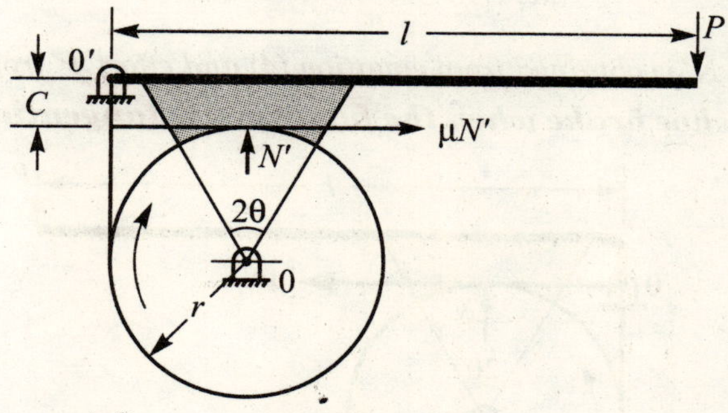

Figure: 6.15

$$Pl = N'r + (\mu N')C$$

Therefore, $$P = \frac{N'r + \mu N'C}{l} \quad \text{... (1)}$$

Also Torque $$M_t = (\mu N')r \quad \text{... (2)}$$

Where, $$M_t = \frac{9550\,N \times 10^3}{n} \text{ N-mm}$$

Knowing 'N', the power absorbed, the normal reaction N' on the shoe can be determined using equation (2). The effort 'P' required to operate brake is then determined from equation (1).

Note: *For the counter clockwise rotation of drum, the tangential force acts in the opposite direction as shown in figure-6.16*

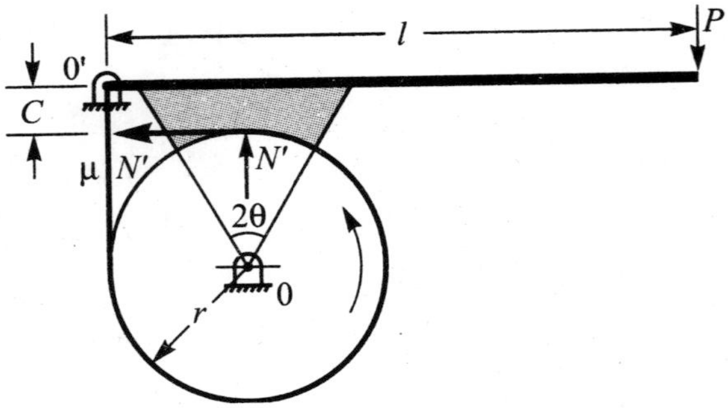

Figure: 6.16

Taking moments about 0′, the fulcrum,

$$Pl + (\mu N')C = N'r$$

Therefore, $$P = \frac{N'r - \mu N'C}{l} \quad \text{... (3)}$$

Torque $$M_t = (\mu N')r \quad \text{... (4)}$$

Where, $$M_t = \frac{9550N \times 10^3}{n} \text{ N-mm}$$

Note: *Normal reaction N' is obtained from equation (4) and effort 'P' from equation (3).*

(b) Design of single shoe brake when the fulcrum 0 is tangential to the drum surface.

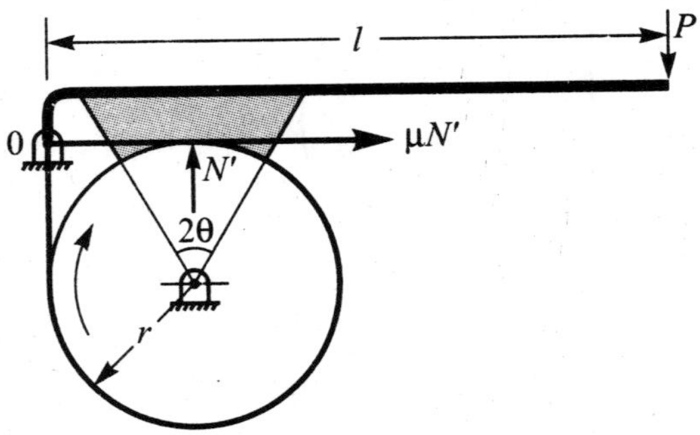

Figure: 6.17

Figure 6.17 shows a single shoe brake rotating in the clockwise direction in which the centre of fulcrum 0′ is tangential to the drum surface. Taking moments about 0′,

$$Pl = N'r$$

Therefore, $$P = \frac{N'r}{l} \quad \text{... (1)}$$

Note: *For the counter clockwise rotation of drum, μN′ acts as shown in figure-6.17.*

Taking moments about 0′,

$$Pl = N'r$$

Therefore, $$P = \frac{N'r}{l} \quad \text{... (2)}$$

Note: *From (1) and (2), we find that the direction of rotation has no effect on 'P', the effort required to operate brake, when the fulcrum is tangential to the drum surface.*

(c) Design of single shoe brake when the fulcrum is below the tangent to drum surface.

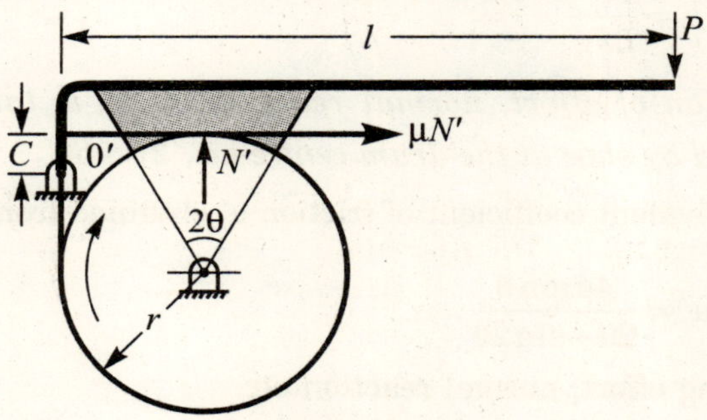

Figure: 6.18

Figure 6.18 shows a single shoe brake in which the fulcrum is below the tangent to the drum surface. Taking moments about 0′,

$$Pl + (\mu N')C = N'r$$

Therefore, $$P = \frac{N'r - (\mu N')C}{l} \quad \text{... (3)}$$

Also Torque $$M_t = \frac{9550N}{n} \times 10^3 = (\mu N')r \quad \text{... (4)}$$

Use equation (4), power 'N' is calculated. Then equation (3) is used to determine the effort 'P' required to operate the brake.

For the clockwise rotation of drum, the tangential force μN′acts in the opposite direction and by taking moments about 0′,

$$Pl = (\mu N')c + N'r$$

i.e., $$P = \frac{\mu N'c + N'r}{l} \quad \text{... (5)}$$

From equations (4) and (5) we find that the effort required to operate brake is minimum for the clockwise rotation of drum.

To determine the dimensions of shoe: (i.e., length of shoe 'L' and width of shoe 'b')

(i) Length of shoe L = r (2θ)

Where, r = radius of drum and 2θ is the angle subtended by block at the drum centre.

(ii) Width of shoe 'b'

The width of shoe (normal to plane of paper) is determined by considering the bearing pressure P_b.

$$\text{Bearing pressure, } P_b = \frac{\text{Bearing load}}{\text{Projected area of bearing}}$$

$$= \frac{\text{Normal reaction } N'}{Lb}$$

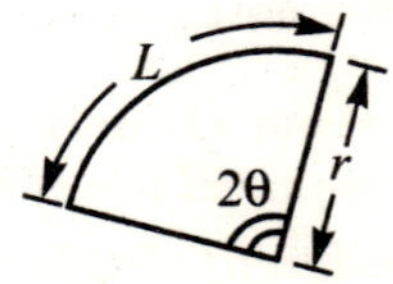

Therefore, $$b = \frac{N'}{LP_b}$$

Note: *In the computation of effort, normal reaction etc, μ is taken equal to μ when the angle 2θ subtended by shoe at the drum centre i.e., 2θ ≤ 60°.*

If $2\theta > 60°$, the equivalent coefficient of friction μ′ obtained from equation

$$\mu' = \frac{4\mu \sin\theta}{2\theta + \sin 2\theta} \quad \text{... (1)}$$

Is used for computing effort, normal reaction etc.

Example 6.9: For the single shoe brake shown in figure-6.19, determine

(i) The normal reaction on shoe.

(ii) The tangential force.

(iii) The effort required to operate the brake to absorb 10 kW at 1000 rpm. Use coefficient of friction = 0.3.

(iv) Rate at which heat is generated.

(v) The dimensions of shoe taking bearing pressure = 0.05 N/mm²

Solution:

For the clockwise rotation drum, the normal reaction N' and tangential force $\mu' N'$ act as shown.

(i) To find the normal force N′ on shoe

Torque $$M_t = \mu' N' r \; (2\theta > 60°)$$

$$M_t = \frac{9550 \times 10 \times 10^3}{1000} \text{N-mm}$$

$$= 95500 \text{N-mm}$$

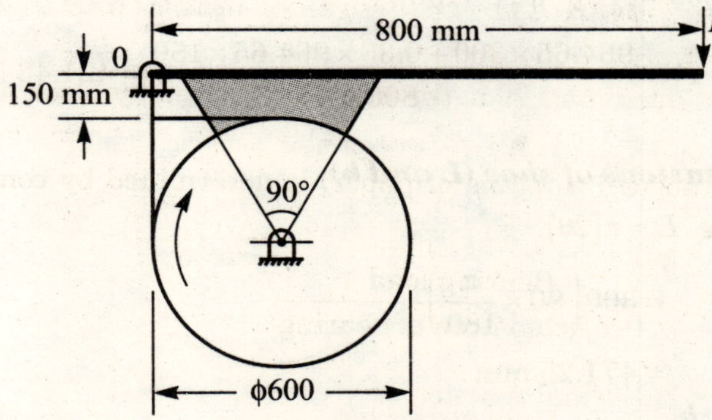

Figure: 6.19

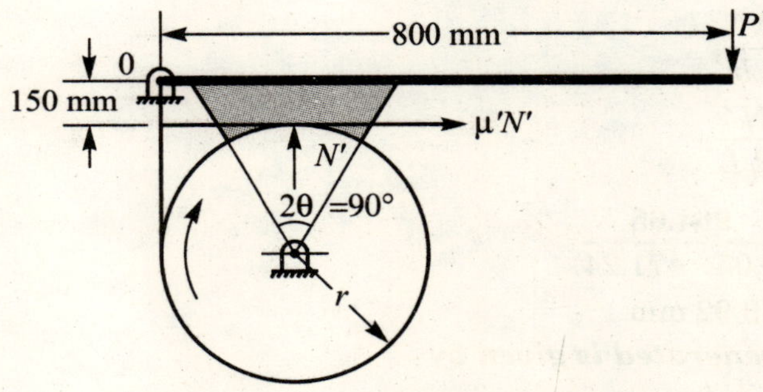

Figure: 6.20

Note: *Since the angle subtended by shoe at the drum centre* $2\theta = 80° > 60°$,

The equivalent coefficient of friction μ' is calculated using equation,

$$\mu' = \frac{4\mu \sin\theta}{2\theta + \sin 2\theta}$$

$$= \frac{4 \times 0.3 \sin 45°}{\left(90 \times \frac{\pi}{180}\right) + \sin 90°} = 0.33$$

Therefore, from $\qquad M_t = \mu' N' r$,

$$95500 = 0.33 N' \frac{600}{2}$$

Hence, $\qquad N' = 964.65$ newton

(ii) To find the tangential force

The tangential force $= \mu' N'$

$= 0.33 \times 964.65$ N

$= 318.33$ N

(iii) To find the effort required to operate brake

Taking moments about 0, the fulcrum

$$P \times 800 = N'r + \mu' N'(150)$$

i.e.,
$$P = \frac{964.65 \times 300 + 0.33 \times 964.65 \times 150}{800} = 421.43 \text{ N}$$

(iv) To find the dimensions of shoe (L and b)

(a) Length of shoe $L = r(2\theta)$

$$= 300\left(90 \times \frac{\pi}{180}\right)$$

$$= 471.25 \text{ mm}$$

(b) Width of shoe, b

From bearing pressure ,

$$P_b = \frac{N'}{Lb},$$

$$b = \frac{N'}{P_b L}$$

$$= \frac{964.65}{0.05 \times 471.24}$$

Width of shoe, $b = 40.92$ mm

(v) Rate at which heat is generated is given by

$$H_g = \mu' N' v$$

$$= 0.33 \times 964.65 \times \left(\pi \times \frac{300 \times 1000}{1000 \times 60}\right)$$

$$= 5000 \text{ N-m/sec}$$

$$= 5000 \text{ J/sec}$$

Example 6.10: The diameter of the drum of a single block brake shown in figure - 6.21 is 200 mm and the angle of contact is 90°. If an operating force of 700 N is applied at the end of a lever and the coefficient of friction between the drum and the lining is 0.35, determine the torque that may be transmitted by the block brake. (VTU, July 2007)

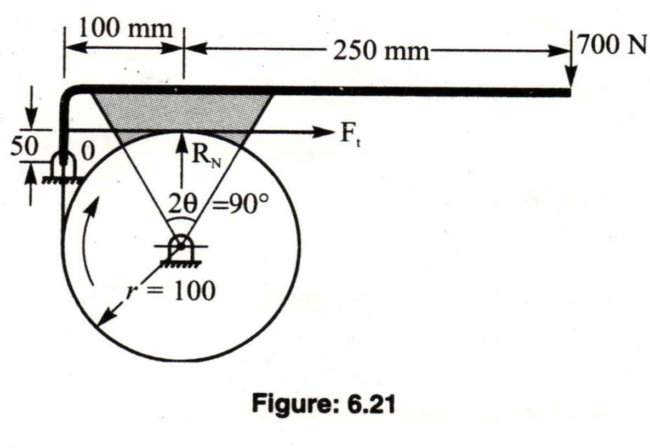

Figure: 6.21

Solution:

To determine the torque transmitted by the block brake

Torque, $M_t = F_t r$

$= F_t \times 100$

To find M_t

Note: *The equivalent coefficient of friction μ' is given by,*

$$\mu' = \frac{4\mu \sin\theta}{2\theta + \sin 2\theta}; \text{ (because } 2\theta = 90° > 60°)$$

Where, $\mu = 0.35$

Therefore,
$$\mu' = \frac{4 \times 0.35 \sin 45°}{\left(90° \times \frac{\pi}{180}\right) + \sin 90°} = 0.385$$

Taking moments about the fulcrum 0,

$$700(250 + 100) + F_t\,(50) = R_N\,(100)$$

i.e.,
$$F_t = \frac{100R_N - 700 \times 350}{50}$$

$$= 2R_N - 4900 \qquad \ldots (1)$$

But $F_t = \mu' R_N$

$= 0.385R_N$

Substituting in equation (1),

$$0.385R_N = 2R_N - 4900$$

$$1.615R_N = 4900$$

Therefore,
$$R_N = \frac{4900}{1.615} = 3034.1 \text{ N}$$

$$F_t = \mu' R_N = 0.385 \times 3034.1 = 1168.13 \text{ N}$$

And Torque $M_t = F_t r$

$= 1168.13 \times 100 = 116813$ N-mm

$= 11.6813 \times 10^4$ N-mm

Design of Double Shoe Brake (or Double block brake)

Figure 6.22 shows a Double shoe brake having brake drum of radius '*r*' operated by spring force '*S*'. Let N_L and N_R be the normal reactions on left and right shoes respectively.

Let μN_L and μN_R are the corresponding tangential forces at the left and right shoes.

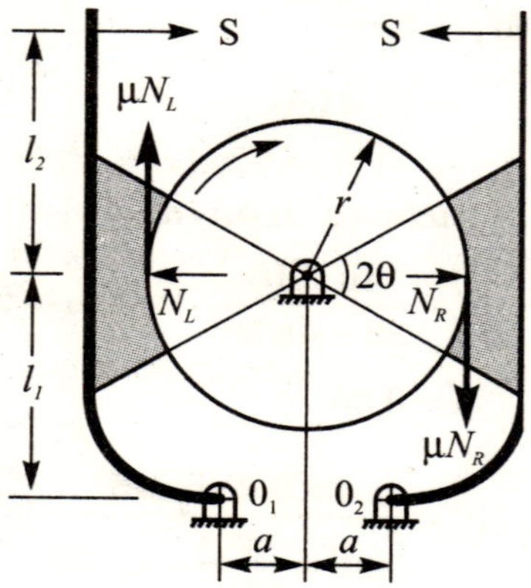

Figure: 6.22

Considering the left shoe and taking moments about the fulcrum 0_1,

$$S(l_1 + l_2) + \mu N_L (r - a) = N_L l_1$$

i.e.,
$$N_L l_1 - \mu N_L (r - a) = S(l_1 + l_2)$$

$$N_L [l_1 - \mu(r - a)] = S(l_1 + l_2)$$

i.e.,
$$N_L = \frac{S(l_1 + l_2)}{l_1 - \mu(r - a)} \quad \ldots (1)$$

Similarly considering the right shoe and taking moments about 0_2,

i.e.,
$$\mu N_R (r - a) + N_R l_1 = S(l_1 + l_2)$$

i.e.,
$$N_R [\mu (r - a) + l_1] = S(l_1 + l_2)$$

i.e.,
$$N_R = \frac{S(l_1 + l_2)}{\mu(r - a) + l_1} \quad \ldots (2)$$

Now Torque $M_t = \mu N' r$ ... (3)

Where, $N' = N_L + N_R$

When $2\theta \leq 60°$

Torque $M_t = \mu' N' r$

$= \mu' (N_L + N_R) r$ ... (4)

Where, $2\theta > 60°$

Using equations (1) to (4), the spring force '*S*' required to operate brake can be calculated.

To determine the dimensions of shoe (length 'L' and width 'b')

(a) Length of shoe, L = r(2θ)

(b) Width of shoe 'b' is obtained from the consideration of bearing pressure given by,
Bearing pressure ,

$$P_b = \frac{\text{Bearing load}}{\text{Projected area of shoe}}$$

$$= \frac{N_L \text{ or } N_R \text{ (Whichever is maximum)}}{Lb}$$

Note: *From equations (1) and (2), for the clockwise rotation of drum, the value of N_L is more compared to that of N_R.*

When the drum rotates in the counter clockwise direction, N_L and N_R, μN_L and μN_R act as shown in Fig. 6.23. Considering the left shoe and taking moments about 0_1,

$$S(l_1 + l_2) = N_L l_1 + \mu N_L (r - a)$$

i.e.,

$$N_L = \frac{S(l_1 + l_2)}{l_1 + \mu(r - a)} \quad \text{... (5)}$$

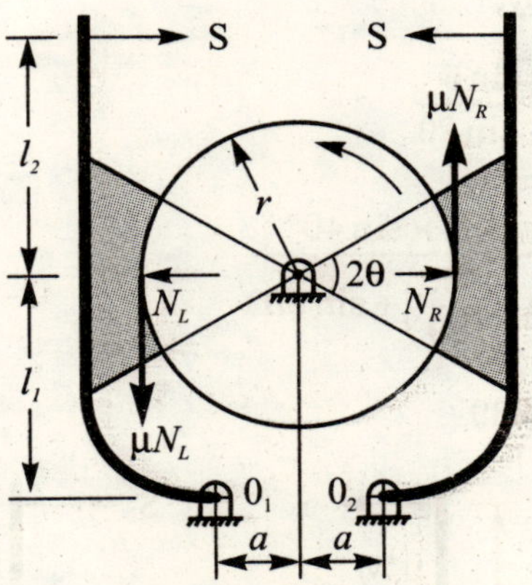

Figure: 6.23

Similarly considering right shoe and taking moments about 0_2,

$$S(l_1 + l_2) + \mu N_R (r - a) = N_R l_1$$

Therefore,

$$N_R = \frac{S(l_1 + l_2)}{l_1 - \mu(r - a)} \quad \text{... (6)}$$

Note: *From equations (1) to (4), we see that the values of N_L and N_R get interchanged, when the direction of rotation is reversed.*

Example 6.11: For the double shoe brake shown in figure-6.24, determine

(a) The spring force 'S' required if 10 kW is absorbed at 1000 rpm.

(b) The dimensions of shoe taking bearing pressure = 0.05 N/mm^2. Use coefficient of friction between drum and shoe = 0.3.

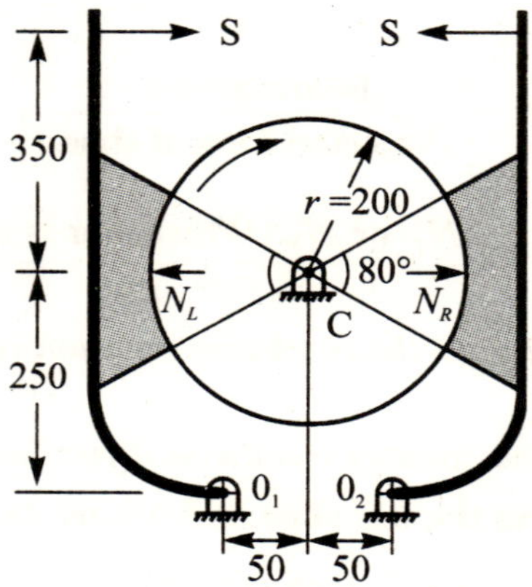

Figure: 6.24

Solution:

The angle subtended by shoe at the drum centre 'C' is $2\theta = 80° > 60°$. Hence the equivalent coefficient of friction μ' is given by,

$$\mu' = \frac{4\mu \sin\theta}{2\theta + \sin 2\theta}$$

$$= \frac{4 \times 0.3 \times \sin 40°}{\left(80 \times \frac{\pi}{180}\right) + \sin 80°}$$

$$= 0.3239$$

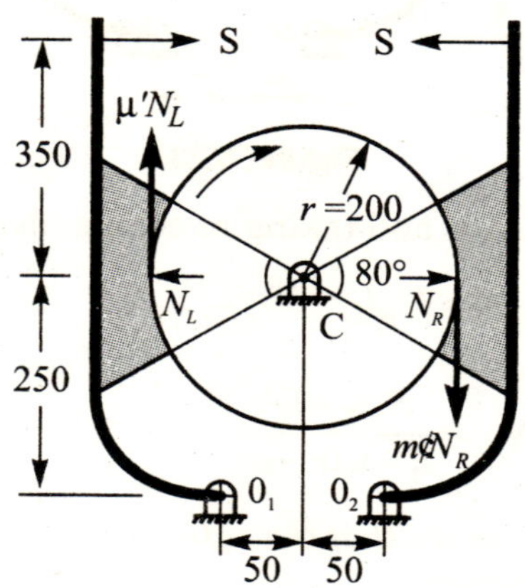

Figure: 6.25

(a) To determine 'S', the spring force required to operate brake.

Considering left shoe and taking moments of forces about fulcrum 0_1,

$$S(250+350)+\mu' N_L(200-50)=N_L(250)$$

i.e., $$S(600)+0.3239N_L(150)=N_L(250)$$

Therefore, $$N_L = 2.979S \qquad \text{... (1)}$$

Similarly, considering right shoe and taking moment about fulcrum 0_2,

$$S(250+350)=\mu' N_R(200-50)+N_R(250)$$

$$S(600)=0.3239N_R(150)+N_R(250)$$

i.e., $$N_R = 2.0095S$$

Torque, $$M_t = \mu' N' r$$

Where, $$N' = (N_L + N_R)$$

i.e., $$9550\times\frac{10}{1000}\times 10^3 = 0.3239(N_L+N_R)200$$

$$N_L + N_R = 2.979S + 2.0095S$$
$$= 4.9885S$$

From, $$M_t = \mu' N' r,$$

$$95500 = 0.3239(4.9885S)200$$

$$S = 295.52 \text{ N}$$

i.e., Spring force '*S*' required to operate brake = 295.52 N.

(b) To determine the dimensions of shoe (i.e., L and b)

(i) Length of shoe L = r (2θ)

$$= 200\left(80\times\frac{\pi}{180}\right)$$

$$= 279.25 \text{ mm}$$

(ii) Width of shoe 'b' is obtained from bearing pressure P_b given by,

$$P_b = \frac{\text{Bearing load}}{\text{Projected area of shoe}}$$

$$= \frac{N_L \text{ or } N_R \text{ (Whichever is maximum)}}{Lb}$$

Here, $$P_b = 0.05 \text{ N/mm}^2$$

$$N_L = 2.978S > N_R = 2.0095S$$

$$N_L = 2.978S$$
$$= 2.978 \times 295.52$$
$$= 880.35 \text{ newton}$$

Therefore, $$0.05 = \frac{880.35}{279.25b}$$

Therefore, width of shoe **$b = 63.05$ mm**

Example 6.12: In a double block brake, an effort of 300 N is used to operate the brake having drum diameter 500 mm, the blocks subtend an angle of 90° at the drum centre. Determine,

(a) The loads on the left and right shoes.

(b) The power absorbed by brake at 1000 rpm taking $\mu = 0.25$

(c) The bearing pressure induced in shoe taking width of shoe as 50 mm.

Solution:

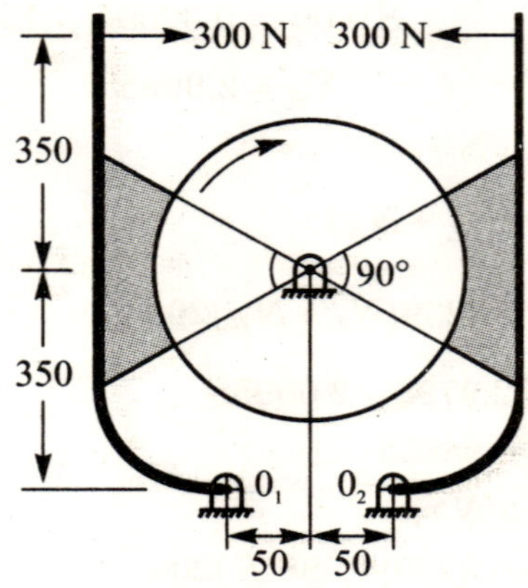

Figure: 6.26

The angle subtended by shoe at the drum centre is $2\theta = 90° > 60°$. Therefore, the equivalent coefficient of friction μ' is given by,

$$\mu' = \frac{4\mu \sin\theta}{2\theta + \sin 2\theta}$$

$$= \frac{4 \times 0.25 \times \sin 90°}{\left(90 \times \frac{\pi}{180}\right) + \sin 90°}$$

$$= 0.3889$$

(a) To calculate loads on left and right shoes $(N_L$ and $N_R)$

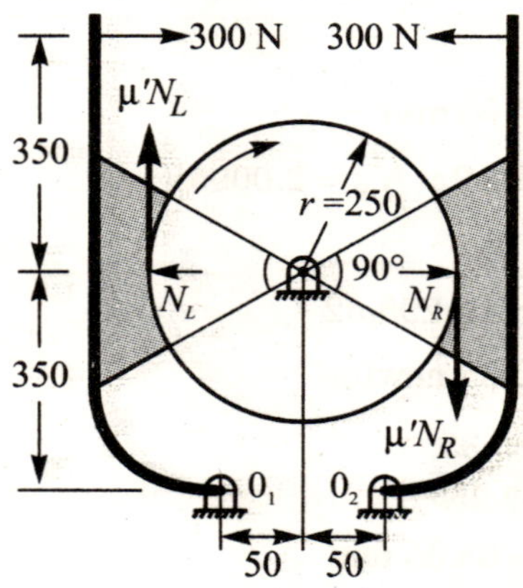

Figure: 6.27

Considering left shoe and taking moment about 0_1,

$$300(700)+\mu' N_L(250-50)=N_L\times 350$$

i.e.,

$$300\times 700+0.3889\times N_L(200)=N_L\times 350$$

$$N_L=771.43\text{ N}$$

i.e., Load on left shoe = N_L = 771.43 N

Considering right shoe and taking moments about the fulcrum 0_2,

$$300(350+350)=\mu' N_R(250-50)+N_R(350)$$

$$300(700)=0.3889\times N_R\times 200+N_R(350)$$

Therefore, $N_R=490.91\text{ N}$

i.e., Load on right shoe, $N_R=490.91\text{ N}$

(b) *To determine the power absorbed by brake.*

Torque $M_t=\mu' N' r$

$$=\mu'(N_L+N_R)r$$

$$=0.3889(771.43+490.91)250$$

$$=122731\text{ N-mm}$$

But, $$M_t=\frac{9550\times \text{Power absorbed}\times 10^3}{n}$$

$$122731=\frac{9550\times \text{Power absorbed}\times 10^3}{1000}$$

Power absorbed = 12.85 kW.

(c) *To determine the bearing pressure induced in shoe*

Bearing pressure,

$$P_b=\frac{\text{Bearing load}}{\text{Projected area of shoe}}$$

$$=\frac{N_L}{Lb};$$

Note: $N_L=771.43N>N_R=490.91\text{ N}$

(Bearing load is N_L or N_R whichever is maximum)

L = Length of shoe = $r(2\theta)$

$$=250\left(90\times\frac{\pi}{180}\right)=392.7\text{ mm}$$

$$b = \text{Shoe width} = 50 \text{ mm(given)}$$

Therefore, $$P_b = \frac{771.43}{392.7 \times 50} = 0.0393 \text{N/mm}^2$$

Therefore, bearing pressure induced in shoe is 0.0393N/mm^2

Design Procedure for Disc Clutch (or Plate Clutch)

Step I: ***To determine the dimensions of plate (or disc) (i.e., to find D_2, D_1, b and h).***

Where, D_1 = Minimum diameter of plate.

D_2 = Maximum diameter of plate.

b = Width of friction lining

$$= \frac{D_2 - D_1}{2}$$

h = Thickness of disc (Usually 1 to 3 mm)

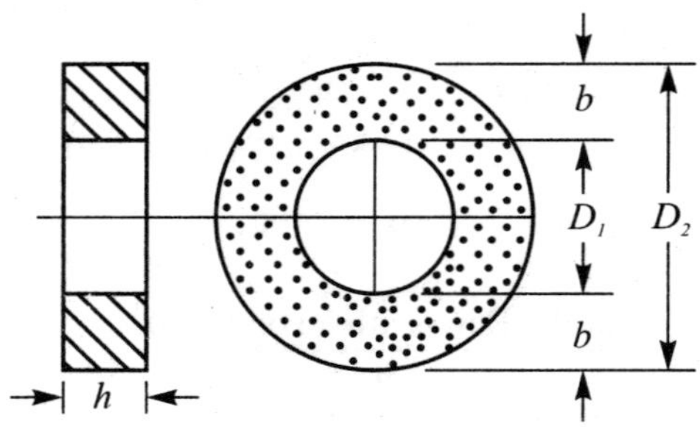

Design Procedure

When diameters D_1 and D_2 are unknown,

Calculate the shaft diameter *'d'* by selecting suitable material for shaft such as 40C8 and a factor of safety, using the formula

$$M_t = \frac{\pi d^3}{16} \eta \tau_s$$

Where, η = Keyway factor = 0.75(usual value).

M_t is obtained from formula,

$$M_t = \frac{9550 \text{N} \times 10^3}{n} \text{N-mm}$$

N = Power transmitted in kW.

n = Speed of rotation in rpm.

Knowing, *'d'*, obtain D_1, the minimum diameter of plate using,

$$D_1 = 4d \quad \text{... E(19-91)}$$

Then D_2 is obtained from equation,

$$D_2 = 2.5 \text{ to } 3.6D_1 \quad \text{... E(19-90)}$$

Step II: ***To find 'p', the pressure between contact surfaces***

'p' is obtained from equation,

$$M_t = \frac{1}{2}\mu F_a D_m i \quad \text{... E(19-84)}$$

Where, μ = Coefficient of friction (usually 0.2 to 0.3).

D_m = Mean diameter of plate.

$$= \left(\frac{D_2 + D_1}{2}\right) \text{ according to uniform wear theory.} \quad \text{... E(19-85b)}$$

$$= \frac{2}{3}\left(\frac{D_2^3 - D_1^3}{D_2^2 - D_1^2}\right) \text{ according to uniform pressure theory} \quad \text{... E(19-85a)}$$

i = Number of friction surfaces (always an even number)

= 2; for a single plate clutch, since both sides of plate are effective.

$= (i_1 + i_2) - 1$; for a multiple plate clutch. ... E(19-93)

Where, i_1 = Number of discs on the driver shaft.

$$= \frac{i}{2} \quad \text{... E(19-94)}$$

i_2 = Number of discs on the driven shaft.

$$= \frac{i}{2} + 1 \quad \text{... E(19-95)}$$

Note: *Total number of discs on the driven shaft is one more than that on driver shaft.*

Step III: ***To find F_a, the axial force required to engage clutch.***

$$F_a = \frac{1}{2}\pi p D_1 (D_2 - D_1) \quad \text{... E(19-83)}$$

Design Procedure for Cone Clutch

Step I: ***To determine the dimensions of cone (i.e. D_1, D_2, and b).***

This step involves, the calculation of

(i) D_1, *the minimum diameter of cone.*

(ii) D_2, *the maximum diameter of cone and*

(iii) *b, the width of friction lining.*

From triangle *ABC*,

$$\sin\alpha = \frac{AB}{AC} = \frac{\frac{D_2 - D_1}{2}}{b}$$

i.e., $D_2 - D_1 = 2b \sin \alpha$ ... (1)

Where, α = Semi-cone angle of cone; Degree.

$= 12\frac{1}{2}^\circ$;for cone clutches faced with leather, asbestos and or cork.

$= 14^\circ$; For clutches faced with wood.

Note: *When 'b', the width of friction lining is not given,*

Use, $q = \frac{D_m}{b} = 6$ ... E(19-81)

The mean diameter of cone D_m

$$D_m = \frac{D_2 + D_1}{2}; \textit{ for uniform wear.}$$

$$D_m = \frac{2}{3}\left(\frac{D_2^3 - D_1^3}{D_2^2 - D_1^2}\right); \textit{ for uniform pressure.}$$

i.e., $D_2 + D_1 = 2D_m$ ... (2)

Obtain D_1 and D_2 using equations (1) and (2).

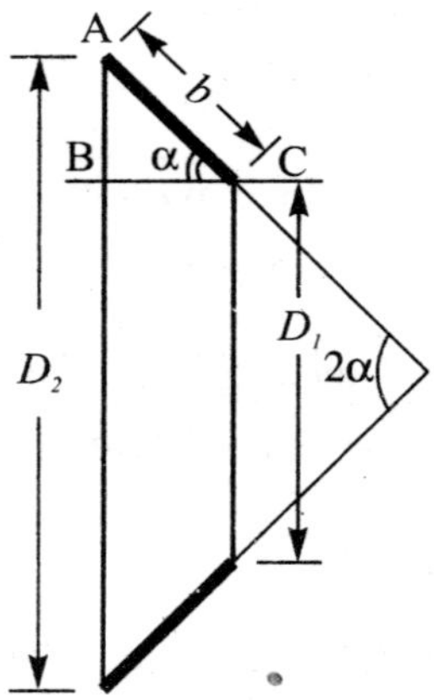

Step II: ***To find F_a, the axial force required to engage clutch.***

F_a is obtained from equation,

$$M_t = \frac{\mu F_a D_m}{2 \sin \alpha}$$ ... E(19-78)

Step III: ***To find 'p', the normal pressure on cone.***

'p' is obtained from equation,

$$F_a = \pi D_m p b \sin \alpha$$ ... E(19-75)

Example 6.13: Design a single plate clutch required to transmit 20 kW at 1200 rpm taking coefficient of friction 0.25. Assume uniform wear.

Solution:

(a) To find shaft diameter 'd'

The torque transmitted by clutch is given by,

$$M_t = \frac{9550N \times 10^3}{n} \text{ N-mm}$$

Where, N = Power transmitted in kW = 20 kW

n = Speed in rpm = 1200

Therefore, $M_t = \frac{9550 \times 20 \times 10^3}{1200}$

$= 159.17 \times 10^3$ N-mm

'd' is obtained from equation,

$$M_t = \frac{\pi d^3}{16} \eta \tau_s$$

Where, η = Keyway factor = 0.75(assumed)

To find the shear stress (τ_s) of shaft material

Assuming 40C8 as the material of shaft, from Table (1-25), $\sigma_{ut} = 600 \text{ N/mm}^2$

Assuming $\sigma_y = 0.6\sigma_{ut}$,

$\sigma_y = 0.6 \times 300 = 360 \text{ N/mm}^2$

Now, $\tau_y = \frac{\sigma_y}{2}$

$= \frac{360}{2} = 180 \text{ N/mm}^2$ and

$$\tau_s = \frac{\tau_y}{\text{Factor of safety}}$$

$= \frac{180}{3} = 60 \text{ N/mm}^2$ (Assuming factor of safety = 3).

From, $M_t = \frac{\pi d^3}{16} \eta \tau_s$

i.e., $159.17 \times 10^3 = \frac{\pi d^3}{16} \times 0.75 \times 60$

$d = 26.21$

Adopt d = 30 mm *(standard size)*.

(b) *To find the dimensions of disc (or plate)*

(i) *The maximum diameter D_2 of disc is given by,*

$$D_2 = 2.5 \text{ to } 3.6D_1 \quad \text{... E(19-90)}$$

Say, $D_2 = 3D_1$

Where, D_1 = Minimum diameter of disc.

$$= 4d \quad \text{... E(19-91)}$$

$$= 120 \text{ mm}$$

Therefore, $D_2 = 3D_1$

$$= 3 \times 120 = 360 \text{ mm}$$

(ii) *To find 'b', the radial width of friction lining.*

From figure, radial width of friction lining

$$b = \frac{D_2 - D_1}{2}$$

$$= \frac{360 - 120}{2} = 120 \text{ mm}$$

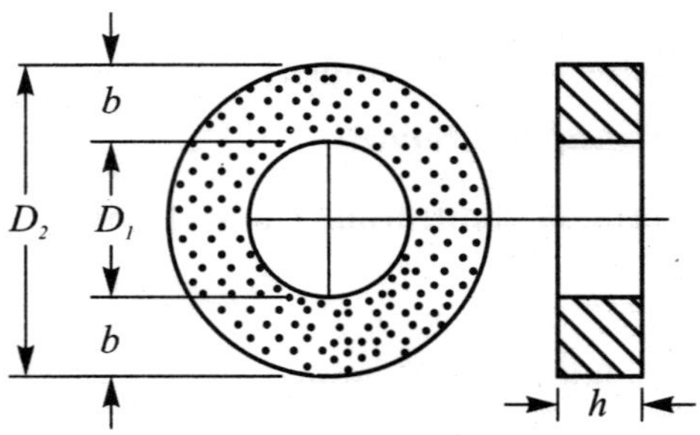

(iii) *Thickness of disc (h)*

Thickness of disc, $h = 1$ to 3 mm ... E(19-92)

Say $h = 2$ mm

(c) *To find the pressure (p) between contact surfaces.*

The torque transmitted by clutch is given by,

$$M_t = \frac{1}{2}\mu F_a D_m i \quad \text{... E(19-84)}$$

Where, μ = Coefficient of friction = 0.25

$$M_t = 159.17 \times 10^3 \text{ N-mm}$$

For uniform wear, D_m = Mean diameter of disc

$$D_m = \frac{D_2 + D_1}{2} \quad \text{... E(19-85b)}$$

$$= \frac{360+120}{2} = 240 \text{ mm}$$

i = Number of friction surfaces.

= 2 for a single plate clutch since both sides of the disc are effective.

Substituting the values in E(19-84),

$$159.17 \times 10^3 = \frac{1}{2} \times 0.25 \times F_a \times 240 \times 2$$

Therefore, F_a = Axial force required to engage clutch.

$$= 2.653 \times 10^3 \text{ N}$$

To find 'p', the pressure between contact surfaces,

$$F_a = \frac{1}{2}\pi p D_1 (D_2 - D_1) \qquad \text{... E(19-83)}$$

i.e., $$2.653 \times 10^3 = \frac{1}{2}\pi p \times 120(360-120)$$

Therefore, $p = 0.0586$ MPa

Example 6.14: Determine the power transmitted by a single plate clutch at 1200 rpm where the inside and outside diameters of disc are 100 mm and 300 mm respectively. Use coefficient of friction = 0.25 and the permissible pressure of 0.06 MPa. Assume uniform pressure.

Solution:

We have torque transmitted $M_t = \dfrac{9550 \text{ N} \times 10^3}{n}$

Where, N = Power transmitted in kW.

n = Speed of rotation = 1200 rpm

Torque, $$M_t = \frac{1}{2}\mu F_a D_m i \qquad \text{... E(19-84)}$$

Where, μ = Coefficient of friction = 0.25

D_m = Mean diameter of disc

$$= \frac{2}{3}\left[\frac{D_2^3 - D_1^3}{D_2^2 - D_1^2}\right]; \text{ for uniform pressure.} \qquad \text{... E(19-85a)}$$

$$= \frac{2}{3}\left[\frac{300^3 - 100^3}{300^2 - 100^2}\right] = 216.67 \text{ mm}$$

i = Number of friction surfaces.

= 2; for a single plate clutch since both sides of the disc are effective.

$$159.17 \times 10^3 = \frac{1}{2} \times 0.25 \times F_a \times 240 \times 2$$

F_a = Axial force required to engage clutch.

$$= \frac{1}{2}\pi p D_1 (D_2 - D_1) \quad \text{... E(19-83)}$$

$$= \frac{1}{2}\pi \times 0.06 \times 100(300 - 100)$$

$$= 1884.6 \text{ N}$$

Now, $M_t = \frac{1}{2}\mu F_a D_m i$; becomes

$$= \frac{1}{2} \times 0.25 \times 1884.6 \times 216.67 \times 2$$

$$= 102103.57 \text{ N-mm}$$

But, $M_t = \dfrac{9550 \text{ N} \times 10^3}{n}$

$$102103.57 = \frac{9550 \text{N} \times 10^3}{1200}$$

Therefore, Power transmitted, N = 12.83 kW

Example 6.15: A multi disc clutch (or multiple plate clutch) is required to transmit 25 kW at 1400 rpm. The maximum and minimum diameters of discs are 300 mm and 100 mm respectively. Assuming coefficient of friction as 0.2, pressure between contact surfaces = 0.08 MPa. Determine,

(i) The axial force required to engage clutch.

(ii) The number of friction surfaces and

(iii) The number of discs on the driver and driven shafts.

Assume uniform wear.

Solution:

(i) To find the axial force (F_a) required to engage clutch.

$$F_a = \frac{1}{2}\pi p D_1 (D_2 - D_1) \quad \text{... E(19-83)}$$

Where, p = Permissible pressure = 0.08 MPa

D_1 = Minimum diameter of disc = 100 mm

D_2 = Maximum diameter of disc = 300 mm

Therefore, $F_a = \frac{1}{2}\pi \times 0.08 \times 100(300 - 100)$

$$= 2513.27 \text{ N}$$

(ii) To find the number of friction surfaces, (i)

For a multiple plate clutch,

$$i = (i_1 + i_2) - 1 \quad \text{... E(19-93)}$$

Where, i_1 = Number of discs on the driver shaft.

$$= \frac{i}{2} \quad \text{... E(19-94)}$$

i_2 = Number of discs on the driven shaft.

$$= \frac{i}{2} + 1 \quad \text{... E(19-95)}$$

The torque transmitted by clutch is given by,

$$M_t = \frac{9550N \times 10^3}{n}$$

$$= \frac{9550 \times 25 \times 10^3}{1400} \text{ N-mm}$$

$$= 170535.71 \text{ N-mm}$$

But, $M_t = \frac{1}{2}\mu F_a D_m i$ ... E(19-84)

Therefore, $170535.71 = \frac{1}{2} \times 0.2 \times 2513.27 \times D_m i$

But, D_m = Mean diameter of disc.

$$= \frac{D_2 + D_1}{2} \text{ for uniform wear} \quad \text{... E(19-85b)}$$

$$= \frac{300 + 100}{2} = 200 \text{ mm}$$

From equation, E(19-84)

$$170535.71 = \frac{1}{2} \times 0.2 \times 2513.27 \times 200i$$

$$i = 3.392$$

Say $i = 4$ *(always an even number).*

Therefore, Number of discs on the driver shaft

$$i_1 = \frac{i}{2} = \frac{4}{2} = 2$$

Number of discs on the driven shaft

$$i_2 = \frac{i}{2} + 1 = \frac{4}{2} + 1 = 3$$

Example 6.16: A multiple plate clutch having 5 discs on the driving shaft and 6 on the driven shaft has maximum diameter of friction surfaces = 350 mm. Assuming μ = 0.25 and permissible pressure = 0.1 MPa, determine,

*(i) **The axial force required to engage the clutch.***
*(ii) **The power transmitted at 1400 rpm.***
Assume uniform pressure.

Solution:

*(i) **To find the axial force (F_a) required to engage clutch.***

For disc clutches,

$$F_a = \frac{1}{2}\pi p D_1 (D_2 - D_1) \qquad \text{... E(19-83)}$$

Where, p = Permissible pressure = 0.1 MPa

D_1 = Minimum diameter of disc.

D_2 = Maximum diameter of disc = 350 mm (given)

Assuming, $D_1 = \frac{D_2}{3}$, ... E(19-90)

$$= \frac{350}{3} = 116.67 \text{ mm}$$

Therefore, $F_a = \frac{1}{2}\pi \times 0.1 \times 116.67(350 - 116.67)$

$$= 4276.12 \text{ N}$$

*(ii) **To find the power transmitted, (N)***

Torque transmitted by a disc clutch is given by,

$$M_t = \frac{1}{2}\mu F_a D_m i \qquad \text{... E(19-84)}$$

Where, μ = Coefficient of friction = 0.25

For uniform pressure, mean diameter is given by

$$D_m = \frac{2}{3}\left[\frac{D_2^3 - D_1^3}{D_2^2 - D_1^2}\right] \qquad \text{... E(19-85a)}$$

$$= \frac{2}{3}\left[\frac{350^3 - 116.67^3}{350^2 - 116.67^2}\right] = 252.78 \text{ mm}$$

i = Number of friction surfaces.

$$= (i_1 + i_2) - 1 \qquad \text{... E(19-93)}$$

Where, i_1 = Number of discs on driver shaft = 5

i_2 = Number of discs on driven shaft = 6

Therefore, $i = (5 + 6) - 1 = 10$

Substituting in E(19-84), yields

$$M_t = \frac{1}{2} \times 0.25 \times 4276.12 \times 252.75 \times 10$$

$= 1351147$ N-mm

But, $M_t = \dfrac{9550N \times 10^3}{n}$

$1351147 = \dfrac{9550 \times N \times 10^3}{1400}$

$N = 198.07$ kW

The power transmitted by clutch is 198.07 kW.

Example 6.17: A multi disc clutch is required to transmit 200 kW at 1400 rpm. The inside and outside diameters of disc are 120 mm and 360 mm respectively. Assuming m = and uniform wear, determine,

(i) The axial force required to engage clutch assuming pressure between contact surfaces = 0.08 MPa.

(ii) The number of discs on the driver and driven shafts.

Solution:

(i) To find the axial force (F_a) required to engage clutch

For a disc clutch,

$$F_a = \frac{1}{2}\pi p D_1 (D_2 - D_1) \quad \text{... E(19-83)}$$

Where, p = Permissible pressure = 0.08 MPa

D_1 = Minimum diameter of disc = 120 mm

D_2 = Maximum diameter of disc = 360 mm

Therefore, $F_a = \dfrac{1}{2}\pi \times 0.08 \times 120(360 - 120)$

$= 3619.11$ N

(ii) To find the number of friction surfaces, 'i'

Torque $M_t = \dfrac{9550N \times 10^3}{n}$

$= \dfrac{9550 \times 200 \times 10^3}{1400}$

$= 1364285.71$ N-mm

For a disc clutch, torque M_t is given by,

$$M_t = \frac{1}{2}\mu F_a D_m i \quad \text{... E(19-84)}$$

Where, $\mu = 0.25$,

$$D_m = \frac{1}{2}(D_2 + D_1) \text{ for uniform wear} \quad \text{... E(19-85b)}$$

$$= \frac{1}{2}(360 + 120) = 240 \text{ mm}$$

Therefore, $1364285.71 = \frac{1}{2} \times 0.2 \times 3619.11 \times 240 \times i$

Therefore, $i = 12.565$

Use, $i = 14$ *(always an even number).*

(iii) To find the number of discs on the driver and driven shafts

Number of discs on the driver shaft

$$i_1 = \frac{i}{2} \quad \text{... E(19-94)}$$

$$= \frac{14}{2} = 7 \text{ discs}$$

Number of discs on the driven shaft

$$i_2 = \frac{i}{2} + 1 \quad \text{... E(19-95)}$$

$$= \frac{14}{2} + 1 = 8 \text{ discs}$$

Example 6.18: In a multiple plate clutch used to transmit 200 kW at 1400 rpm, 8 discs are used on driving shaft and 9 discs on the driven shaft. Assuming uniform wear and coefficient of friction = 0.25, determine the pressure between contact surfaces. Limit the maximum diameter of discs to 400 mm.

Solution:

Torque $M_t = \frac{9550N \times 10^3}{n}$

$$= \frac{9550 \times 200 \times 10^3}{1400}$$

$$= 1364285.71 \text{ N-mm}$$

For a disc clutch,

$$M_t = \frac{1}{2}\mu F_a D_m i \quad \text{... E(19-84)}$$

Where, $\mu = 0.25$

F_a = Axial force required to engage clutch.

i = Number of friction surfaces

$= (i_1 + i_2) - 1$

$$= (8+9)-1 = 16$$

$$D_m = \text{Mean diameter of disc}$$

$$= \frac{1}{2}(D_2 + D_1) \text{ for uniform wear} \qquad \text{... E(19-85b)}$$

$$D_2 = \text{Maximum diameter of disc}$$

$$= 400 \text{ mm(given)}$$

$$D_1 = \text{Minimum diameter of disc}$$

$$= \frac{D_2}{3} \qquad \text{... E(19-90)}$$

$$= \frac{400}{3} = 133.33 \text{ mm}$$

Therefore, $D_m = \frac{1}{2}(400 + 133.33) = 266.67$ mm

Substituting in equation E(19-84),

$$1364285.71 = \frac{1}{2} \times 0.25 \times F_a \times 266.67 \times 16$$

Therefore, $F_a = 2558$ N

To find the pressure (p) between contact surfaces

$$F_a = \frac{1}{2}\pi p D_1 (D_2 - D_1) \qquad \text{... E(19-83)}$$

$$2558 = \frac{1}{2}\pi p \times 133.33(400 - 133.33)$$

$$p = 0.0458 \text{ N/mm}^2$$

Therefore, Pressure between contact surfaces of clutch $= 0.0458 \text{ N/mm}^2$

Example 6.19: A multiple plate clutch with steel on bronze is to transmit 8 kW at 1440 rpm. The inner diameter of contact is 80 mm and the outer diameter of contact is 140 mm. The clutch operates in oil with expected coefficient of friction of 0.1 and allowable pressure of 0.35 MPa. Assuming uniform wear determine the number of steel and bronze plates required. ***(VTU, Dec 06 / Jan 07)***

Solution:

The torque transmitted by clutch, M_t is given by

$$= \frac{9550N \times 10^3}{n}$$

$$= \frac{9550 \times 8 \times 10^3}{1440}$$

$$= 53055.56 \text{ N-mm}$$

The axial force (F_a) required to engage clutch is given by,

$$F_a = \frac{1}{2}\pi p D_1 (D_2 - D_1) \quad \text{... E(19-83)}$$

Where, p = Pressure between contact surfaces = 0.35 MPa

D_1 = Inner diameter of contact = 80 mm

D_2 = Outer diameter of contact = 140 mm

Therefore, $F_a = \frac{1}{2}\pi \times 0.35 \times 80(140 - 80)$

$= 2638.94$ N

To find the number of friction surfaces.

We have, $M_t = \frac{1}{2}\mu F_a D_m i$ ... E(19-84)

Where, μ = Coefficient of friction = 0.1

D_m = Mean diameter of disc

$= \left(\frac{D_2 + D_1}{2}\right)$ for uniform wear.

$= \left(\frac{140 + 80}{2}\right) = 110$ mm

Therefore, substituting in equation E(19-84)

$$53055.56 = \frac{1}{2} \times 0.1 \times 2638.94 \times 110 \times i$$

i, the number of friction surfaces = 3.655

Say, i = 4 *(an even number).*

Number of discs on driver shaft

$$i_1 = \frac{i}{2} = \frac{4}{2} = 2$$

Number of discs on the driven shaft

$$i_2 = \frac{i}{2} + 1 = \frac{4}{2} + 1 = 3$$

Example 6.20: A single plate clutch with both sides effective is required to transmit 25 kW at 1600 rpm. The outer diameter of the plate is limited to 0.3 m and the intensity of pressure is not to exceed 0.07 MPa. Assuming uniform wear and the coefficient of friction 0.3, determine the inner diameter of plate and the axial force necessary to engage the clutch. ***(VTU, June / July 2008)***

Solution:

The torque transmitted by plate clutch is

$$M_t = \frac{9550N \times 10^3}{n}$$

$$= \frac{9550 \times 25 \times 10^3}{1600}$$

$$= 149218.75 \text{ N-mm}$$

But, $M_t = \frac{1}{2}\mu F_a D_m i$

Where, μ = Coefficient of friction = 0.3

i = Number of friction surfaces = 2 (for single plate clutch)

i.e., $149218.75 = \frac{1}{2} \times 0.3 F_a D_m \times 2$

$$F_a D_m = 497395.83 \quad \text{... (1)}$$

For a plate clutch, the axial force (F_a) required to engage the clutch is

$$F_a = \frac{1}{2}\pi p D_1 (D_2 - D_1)$$

$$= \frac{1}{2}\pi \times 0.07 \times D_1 (300 - D_1)$$

$$= 0.10996 D_1 (300 - D_1)$$

Substituting the value of F_a in equation (1),

$$0.10996 D_1 (300 - D_1)\left[\frac{D_2 + D_1}{2}\right] = 497395.83$$

i.e., $0.10996 D_1 (300 - D_1)\left[\frac{300 + D_1}{2}\right] = 497395.83$

$$D_1 (300 - D_1)(300 + D_1) = 9046850.31$$

i.e., $D_1\left(300^2 - D_1^2\right) = 9046850.31$

i.e., $90000 D_1 - D_1^3 = 9046850.3$

By trail and error,

$D_1 = 121.7$ mm (minimum diameter of plate).

Now the axial force (F_a) required to engage the clutch is

$$F_a = 0.10996 D_1 (300 - D_1)$$

$$= 0.10996 \times 121.7 (300 - 121.7)$$

$$= 2386.03 \text{ N}$$

Example 6.21: An engine developing 50 kW at 1000 rpm is fitted with a cone clutch. The cone has a face angle of 12.5° and width of face is one fourth of mean diameter of friction lining. If the normal intensity of pressure between the contact surfaces is not to exceed 0.1 N/mm², assuming uniform wear criterion and taking μ = 0.2 calculate the dimensions of clutch. ***(VTU, July 2007)***

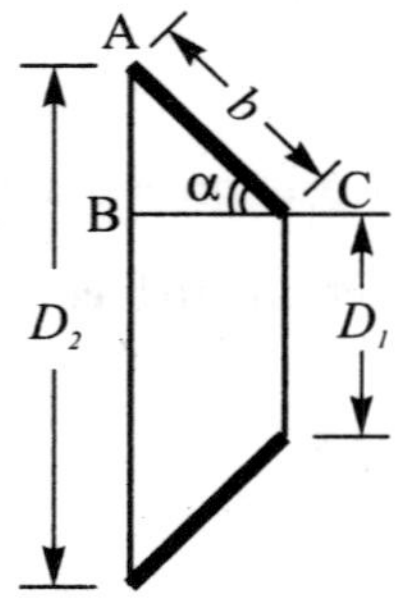

Solution:

To find the dimensions of cone (D_1, D_2, and b)

Mean diameter of cone,

$$D_m = \frac{D_2 + D_1}{2} \text{ as per uniform wear criterion.}$$

Therefore, $D_2 + D_1 = 2D_m$ ... (1)

Where, $b = \frac{1}{4}$ (Mean diameter of friction lining)

$$b = \frac{1}{4} D_m$$

i.e., $b = \frac{D_m}{4}$ or $D_m = 4b$ ... (2)

Torque transmitted by cone clutch is given by,

$$M_t = \frac{9550 N \times 10^3}{n}$$

$$= \frac{9550 \times 50 \times 10^3}{1000}$$

$$= 477500 \text{ N-mm}$$

But, $M_t = \frac{\mu F_a D_m}{2 \sin \alpha}$

i.e., $477500 = \frac{0.2 F_a D_m}{2 \sin 12.5}$

Therefore, $F_a D_m = 1033499.16$ ... (3)

But the axial force F_a required to engage the clutch is

$$F_a = \pi D_m p b \sin \alpha$$

i.e., $$\frac{1033499.16}{D_m} = \pi D_m \times 0.1 \times b \sin 12.5$$

Therefore, $D_m^2 b = 15199297.07$

But $D_m = 4b$ from equation 2

Therefore, $(4b)^2 b = 15199297.07$

$$b = 98.3 \text{ mm}$$

Therefore, $D_m = 4b = 393.2$ mm

Hence, $$D_2 + D_1 = 2D_m = 786.4 \quad \text{... (4)}$$

$$D_2 - D_1 = 2b \sin\alpha = 42.55 \quad \text{... (5)}$$

Solving equations (4) and (5),

$$D_2 = 414.5 \text{ mm}$$

$$D_1 = 371.94 \text{ mm}$$

Therefore, the dimensions of cone are

Maximum diameter, $D_2 = 414.5$ mm

Minimum diameter, $D_1 = 371.94$ mm

Width of face, $b = 98.3$ mm

Example 6.22: A cone clutch is required to transmit 20 kW at 1400 rpm. Limiting the mean diameter of cone to 300 mm, determine,

(i) The dimensions of cone using face width = 60 mm.

(ii) The axial force required to engage clutch assuming coefficient of friction $\mu = 0.25$ and

(iii) Normal pressure on cone.

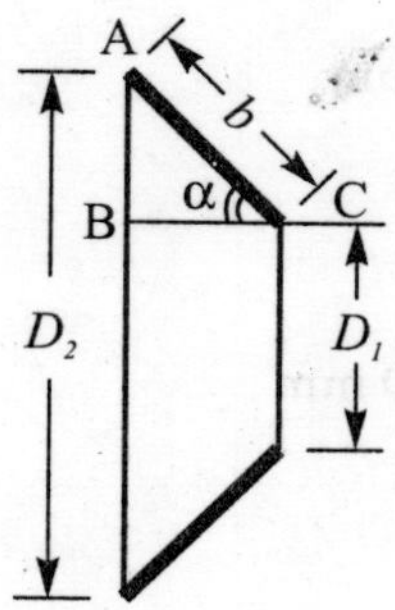

Solution:

(i) To find the dimensions of cone (D_1, D_2 and b).

Given, mean diameter of cone $D_m = 300$ mm

Assuming uniform wear,

$$D_m = \frac{1}{2}(D_2 + D_1) = 300 \text{ mm}$$

or, $D_2 + D_1 = 600$ ... (1)

From figure,

$$\sin\alpha = \frac{AB}{AC}$$

$$= \frac{\frac{D_2 - D_1}{2}}{b}$$

$$= \frac{D_2 - D_1}{2b}$$

or, $D_2 - D_1 = 2b\sin\alpha$

Where, $\alpha = 12\frac{1}{2}^\circ$ for cone clutches faced with leather, asbestos or cork.

$b = 60$ mm

Therefore, $D_2 - D_1 = 2b\sin\alpha$

$= 25.97$ ... (2)

Solving equations (1) and (2)

$D_2 = 312.99$ mm

$D_1 = 287.01$ mm

(ii) To find the axial force (F_a) required to engage clutch

Torque, $$M_t = \frac{9550N \times 10^3}{n}$$

$$= \frac{9550 \times 20 \times 10^3}{1400}$$

$= 136428.57$ N-mm

For a cone clutch,

$$M_t = \frac{\mu F_a D_m}{2\sin\alpha}$$ ... E(19-78)

Where, $\mu = 0.25,\ D_m = 300$ mm

Therefore, $136428.57 = \dfrac{0.25F_a \times 300}{2\sin 12.5}$

$F_a = 787.43$ N

(iii) To find 'p', the normal pressure on cone

For a cone clutch,

$F_a = \pi D_m pb\sin\alpha$ ... E(19-75)

i.e., $787.43 = \pi \times 300 \times p \times 60\sin 12.5$

$p = 0.0643\text{N/mm}^2$

Example 6.23: Design a cone clutch to transmit 20 kW at 1400 rpm. The mean diameter of cone is 400 mm. The design must include

(i) The dimensions of cone.

(ii) The axial force required to engage clutch assuming $\mu = 0.3$ and

(iii) The normal pressure on cone.

Solution:

(i) To find the dimensions of cone (D_1, D_2 and b)

The mean diameter of cone

$$D_m = \frac{D_2 + D_1}{2}$$

i.e., $$D_2 + D_1 = 2D_m = 2 \times 400 = 800 \quad \text{... (1)}$$

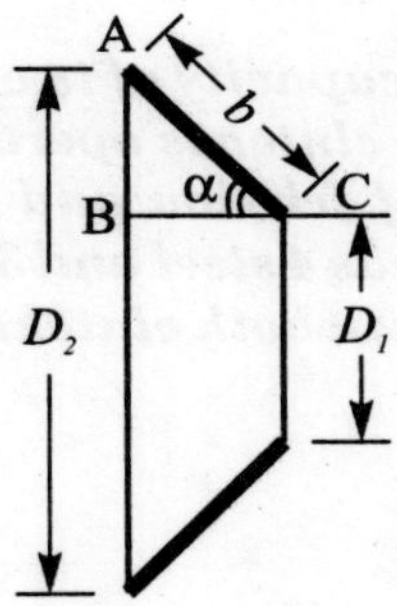

From figure,

$$\sin\alpha = \frac{D_2 - D_1}{2b}$$

i.e., $$D_2 - D_1 = 2b\sin\alpha$$

Assuming, $$q = \frac{D_m}{b} = 6; \text{ (since } b \text{ is unknown)} \quad \text{... E(19-81)}$$

Face width $$b = \frac{D_m}{6} = \frac{400}{6} = 66.67 \text{ mm}$$

Therefore, $$D_2 - D_1 = 2b\sin\alpha$$
$$= 28.86 \quad \text{... (2)}$$

From equations (1) and (2)

D_2 = *Maximum diameter of cone* = 414.43 mm

D_1 = *Minimum diameter of cone* = 385.57 mm

(ii) To find the axial force (F_a) required to engage clutch

Torque $$M_t = \frac{9550N \times 10^3}{n}$$

$$= \frac{9550 \times 20 \times 10^3}{1400}$$

$$= 136428.57 \text{ N-mm}$$

But, $$M_t = \frac{\mu F_a D_m}{2\sin\alpha}$$ ... E(19-78)

i.e., $$136428.57 = \frac{0.3F_a \times 400}{2\sin 12.5}$$

$$F_a = 492.14 \text{ N}$$

(iii) To find 'p', the normal pressure on cone

Axial force $$F_a = \pi D_m pb \sin\alpha$$

i.e., $$492.14 = \pi \times 400 \times p \times 66.67 \sin 12.5$$

$$p = 0.027 \text{ N/mm}^2$$

Example 6.24: Compare the power capacity of two clutches, one a multiple disc clutch and the other, a cone clutch. Both clutches operate at the same speed, both have the same diameter, same coefficient of friction and same axial force is exerted in both clutches. The multiple disc clutch has 4 steel and 3 bronze discs. The total cone angle of clutch is 20°. Assume uniform wear in both clutches.

Solution:

It is required to find the ratio of

$$\frac{N_{\text{cone clutch}}}{N_{\text{disc clutch}}} \text{ or } \frac{M_t)_{\text{cone clutch}}}{M_t)_{\text{disc clutch}}}$$

$$M_t)_{\text{cone clutch}} = \frac{\mu F_a D_m}{2\sin\alpha}$$ ... E(19-78)

$$M_t)_{\text{disc clutch}} = \frac{\mu F_a D_m i}{2}$$ ... E(19-84)

Where, $$i = (i_1 + i_2) - 1 = (3+4) - 1 = 6$$

$$M_t)_{\text{disc clutch}} = \frac{\mu F_a D_m \times 6}{2} = 3\mu F_a D_m$$

Therefore, $$\frac{M_t)_{\text{cone clutch}}}{M_t)_{\text{disc clutch}}} = \frac{\frac{\mu F_a D_m}{2\sin\alpha}}{3\mu F_a D_m} = 0.9598$$

(Where, $2\alpha = 20°$)

$$M_t)_{\text{cone clutch}} = 0.9598 M_t)_{\text{disc clutch}}$$

Therefore,

Power capacity of cone clutch = 0.9598 × *Power capacity of disc clutch*

i.e., $$N)_{\text{cone clutch}} = 0.9598 N)_{\text{disc clutch}}$$

Example 6.25: A cone clutch with face angle 12.5° is to transmit 7.5 kW at 900 rpm. The width of face is half the mean radius and the normal pressure between the contact faces is not to exceed $0.09\ MN/m^2$. Assuming uniform wear and the coefficient of friction between contact faces as 0.2, determine the main dimensions of cone and the axial force required to engage the clutch. ***(VTU, Dec 07 / Jan 08)***

Solution:

To determine the main dimensions of cone (D_1, D_2 and b).

Assuming uniform wear,

Mean diameter of cone D_m is given by,

$$D_m = \frac{D_2 + D_1}{2}$$

i.e., $D_2 + D_1 = 2D_m$ ... (1)

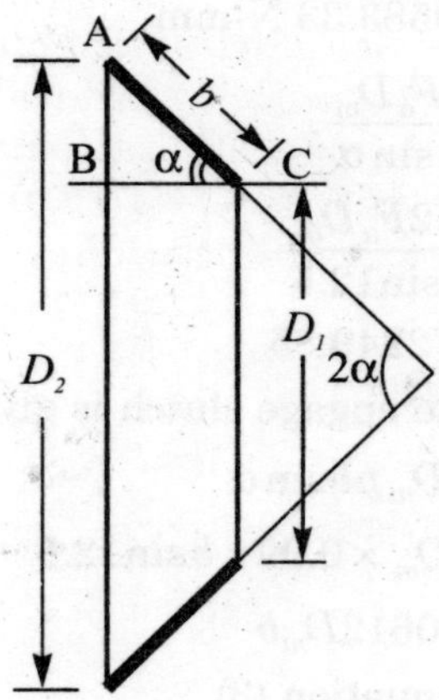

For triangle ABC,

$$\sin\alpha = \frac{AB}{AC}$$

Where, $AB = \dfrac{D_2 - D_1}{2}$ and $AC = b$

Therefore, $$\sin\alpha = \frac{D_2 - D_1}{2b}$$

i.e., $D_2 - D_1 = 2b\sin\alpha$ ... (2)

But face width $b = \dfrac{1}{2}$ mean radius (data)

$$b = \frac{1}{2}\left(\frac{D_m}{2}\right)$$

$$= \frac{1}{4}\left(\frac{D_2 + D_1}{2}\right)$$

$$= \frac{D_2 + D_1}{8}$$

Therefore, $D_2 + D_1 = 8b$

Hence, $b = \frac{D_2 + D_1}{8}$

α = Semi cone angle = 12.5°

The torque transmitted by the cone clutch is

$$M_t = \frac{9550N \times 10^3}{n}$$

$$= \frac{9550 \times 7.5 \times 10^3}{900}$$

$$= 79583.33 \text{ N-mm}$$

But, $M_t = \frac{\mu F_a D_m}{2 \sin \alpha}$

i.e., $79583.33 = \frac{0.2 F_a D_m}{2 \sin 12.5}$

Therefore, $F_a D_m = 172249.85$ ... (3)

But the axial force F_a required to engage clutch is given by

$$F_a = \pi D_m p b \sin \alpha$$

$$= \pi D_m \times 0.09 \times b \sin 12.5$$

$$= 0.0612 D_m b$$

Substituting the value of F_a in equation (3)

$$(0.0612 D_m b) D_m = 172249.85$$

$$D_m^2 b = 2814540$$

$$\left(\frac{D_1 + D_2}{2}\right)^2 \left(\frac{D_2 + D_1}{8}\right) = 2814540$$

Therefore, $D_2 + D_1 = 355.78$

Also $D_2 + D_1 = 8b$

Therefore, $8b = 355.78$

$$b = 44.47 \text{ mm}$$

Now, $D_2 - D_1 = 2b \sin \alpha$

$$= 2 \times 44.47 \times \sin 12.5$$

$$= 19.25$$

From $D_2 + D_1 = 8b = 355.78$ ... (4)

And $D_2 - D_1 = 19.25$ ... (5)

From (4) and (5)

$$D_2 = 187.52 \text{ mm}$$

$$D_1 = 168.27 \text{ mm}$$

Therefore, $$D_m = \frac{D_2 + D_1}{2} = 177.9 \text{ mm}$$

The axial force required to engage clutch is given by

$$F_a = 0.0612 D_m b$$
$$= 0.0612 \times 177.9 \times 44.47$$
$$= 484.17 \text{ N}$$

EXERCISE

1. Figure shows a single block brake used to absorb a torque of 95500 N-mm. Determine
   (*a*) The normal reaction on shoe taking coefficient of friction between drum and shoe = 0.3.
   (*b*) The bearing pressure on shoe taking width of shoe = 200 mm.
   (*c*) The effort required to operate brake.

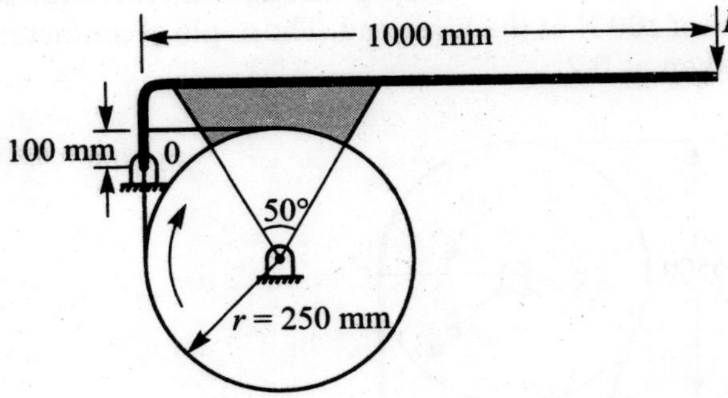

Answers:

(*a*) Normal reaction on shoe = 1273.33 N.

(*b*) Bearing pressure on shoe = 0.0292N/mm^2.

(*c*) Effort (*P*) required to operate brake = 261.03 N.

2. A single shoe brake, shown in figure is used on a brake drum of diameter 500 mm to absorb 10 kW at 1000 rpm. Determine,
   (*a*) The normal reaction on shoe taking coefficient of friction $\mu = 0.3$
   (*b*) The effort required to operate the brake for the clockwise rotation of drum.
   (*c*) The dimensions of shoe limiting the bearing pressure to 0.04 N/mm^2.

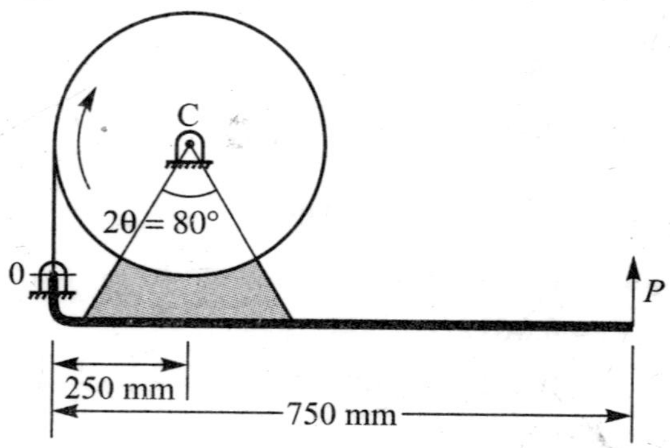

Answers:

(*a*) Normal reaction on shoe = 1179.4 N.

(*b*) Effort for clockwise rotation of drum P = 393.13 N.

(*c*) (*i*) Width of shoe = 84.47 mm.

(*ii*) Length of shoe = 249.07 mm.

3. A simple band brake has one end passing through the lever fulcrum. Determine the torque capacity for a force of 100 N at the lever end. The angle of contact is 210° and the coefficient of friction may be taken as 0.2.

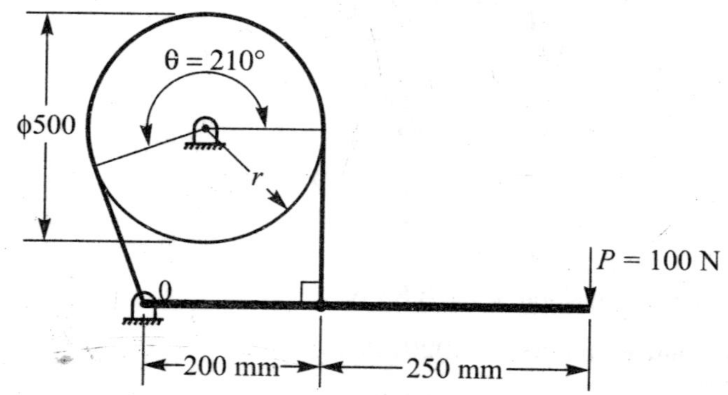

Answer:

Torque capacity = 60750 N-mm.

4. A simple band brake of drum diameter 650 mm has a band passing over it with an angle of contact 225°. While one end is connected to the fulcrum, the other end is connected to the fulcrum at a distance of 400mm from the fulcrum. The brake lever is 1000 mm long and is to absorb 15 kW at 720 rpm. Design the brake lever of rectangular cross-section assuming depth to be thrice the width.

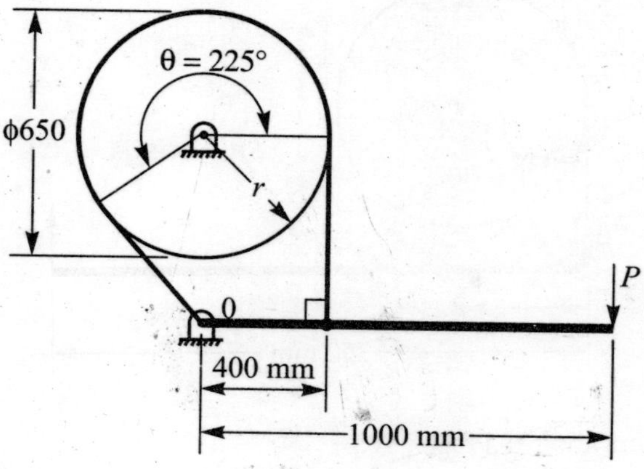

Answers:

Width of lever = 12.09 mm.

Depth of lever = 36.27 mm.

5. A multiple disc clutch is required to transmit 30 kW at 1440 rpm. The maximum diameter of disc is to be limited to 400 mm. Taking coefficient of friction = 0.25, pressure between contact surfaces = 0.09 MPa, calculate,
   (*i*) The axial force required to engage clutch.
   (*ii*) The number of friction surfaces and
   (*iii*) The number of discs on driver and driven shafts.
   Assume uniform wear.
6. A multiple clutch with 6 discs on the driver shaft and 7 on the driven shaft has maximum diameter restricted to 400 mm. Assuming $\mu = 0.22$ and permissible pressure of 0.09 MPa, determine,
   (*i*) The axial force required to engage clutch.
   (*ii*) The power transmitted at 1440 rpm.
   Assume uniform pressure.
7. A cone clutch is to be designed to transmit 25 kW at 1400 rpm. Limiting the mean diameter of cone to 450 mm, determine,
   (*i*) The dimensions of cone.
   (*ii*) The axial force required to engage clutch using $\mu = 0.25$ and
   (*iii*) The normal pressure on cone.

CHAPTER

7 Lubrication and Bearings

NOTATIONS AND SYMBOLS USED

A = Effective surface area of bearing housing; m^2.
B = Width of ball bearing; mm.
c = Diametral clearance; mm.
d = Diameter of journal; mm.
= Diameter of shaft; mm.
F_a = Axial load (thrust load) in ball bearing; N.
F_r = Radial load in ball bearing; N.
h_{min} = Minimum film thickness; mm.
H_g = Heat generated in journal bearing; Watts.
H_d = Heat dissipated from journal bearing; Watts.
l = Length of bearing; mm.
L_n = Life of bearing (in millions of revolutions).
n = Speed of journal; rpm.
n' = Speed of journal; rps.
η = Viscosity of oil in Pas (Pascal seconds).
η_1 = Absolute viscosity in cP (Centipoise).
K_a = A constant used in journal bearing.
μ = Coefficient of friction.
ψ = Ratio of diametral clearance to diameter of journal $= \frac{c}{d}$.
t_b = Temperature of bearing; °C.
t_a = Ambient temperature; °C.
t_o = Oil temperature; °C.
r = Fillet radius in ball bearing; mm.
δ = Minimum thickness variable; mm.

INTRODUCTION

By definition, any two parts which have relative motion constitute a bearing regardless their shape and configuration. The supporting member is called a bearing.

In a journal bearing the shaft that rotates in a housing is called a journal whereas the supporting member is called a bearing. Similarly in a thrust bearing, such as a collar bearing the load on the shaft acts along the axis.

In a ball bearing (also called antifriction bearing), the bearings are subjected to both radial and axial loads (thrust loads).

Bearing are used to support rotating shafts over small or large distances and help in providing stability and smooth running of shaft.

Design Procedure for Journal Bearing

The following are the steps generally followed while designing a journal bearing.

Step I: *Calculation of the length and diameter of journal.*

(a) When the application of journal bearing is known, refer T(24-2) and obtain bearing modulus S".

For example, for the main bearings used in the rotor of a generator,

Bearing modulus,

$$S'' = \eta \frac{n'}{P}$$

$$= 483.5 \times 10^{-9} \quad \ldots (1)$$

Where, $\eta = 10^{-3} \eta_1$

η = Absolute viscosity in Pascal seconds (Pas).

η_1 = Viscosity of oil in cP.

P = Pressure in bearing

$$= \frac{w}{Ld} \text{N/m}^2$$

Where, w = Load sustained by bearing in Newton.

L = Length of journal in metre.

d = Diameter of journal in metre.

From equation (1) knowing, n' and P, the viscosity can be calculated.

Table - (24-2) MDH

Machinery	Bearing	Maximum Pressure, P (MPa)	Diameter clearance ratio $\psi = \frac{c}{d}$	Ratio $\frac{L}{d}$	Viscosity η_1 (cP)	Viscosity η (Pas × 10^{-3})	Bearing modulus (minimum) $S'' = \frac{\eta_1 n}{P}$ Metric units × 10^2	Bearing modulus (minimum) $S'' = \frac{\eta_1 n}{P}$ SI units × 10^{-9}
Automobile and aircraft engines	Main	5.50 - 11.70	---	0.8 - 1.8	7	7	213.0	36.3
	Crankpin	10.40 - 24.40	---	0.7 - 1.4	to	to	142.0	24.2
	Wristpin	15.00 - 34.80	---	1.5 - 2.2	8	8	114.0	19.3
Gas and oil engines (four-stroke	Main	4.85 - 8.35	0.001	0.6 - 2.0	20	20	285.0	48.4
	Crankpin	4.80 - 12.40	< 0.001	0.6 - 1.5	to	to	142.0	24.2
	Wristpin	12.40 - 15.20	< 0.001	1.5 - 2.0	65	65	71.0	12.1
Gas and oil engines (two-stroke	Main	3.24 - 5.50	0.001	0.6 - 2.0	20	20	356.0	60.4
	Crankpin	6.85 - 10.49	< 0.001	0.6 - 1.5	to	to	171.0	29.0
	Wristpin	8.35 - 12.50	< 0.001	1.5 - 2.0	65	65	142.0	24.2
Marine steam engines	Main	3.42	< 0.001	0.7 - 1.5	30	30	285.0	48.4
	Crankpin	4.14	< 0.001	0.7 - 1.2	40	40	213.0	36.3
	Wristpin	10.40	< 0.001	1.2 - 1.7	30	30	141.0	24.2
Stationary slow-speed steam engines	Main	2.75	< 0.001	1.0 - 2.0	60	60	285.0	48.4
	Crankpin	10.40	< 0.001	0.9 - 1.3	80	80	85.0	14.5
	Wristpin	12.50	< 0.001	1.2 - 1.5	60	60	71.0	12.1
Stationary high-speed steam engines	Main	1.66	< 0.001	1.5 - 3.0	15	15	356.0	60.4
	Crankpin	4.14	< 0.001	0.9 - 1.5	30	30	85.0	14.5
	Wristpin	12.50	< 0.001	1.3 - 1.7	25	25	71.0	12.1
Steam locomotives	Driving axle	3.72	0.001	1.6 - 1.8	100	100	427.0	72.5
	Crankpin	13.70	< 0.001	0.7 - 1.1	40	40	71.0	12.1
	Wristpin	27.60	< 0.001	0.8 - 1.3	30	30	71.0	12.1
Reciprocating pumps and compressors	Main	1.66	< 0.001	1.0 - 2.2	30	30	427.0	72.5
	Crankpin	4.14	< 0.001	0.9 - 1.7	to	to	285.0	48.4
	Wristpin	6.85	< 0.001	1.5 - 2.0	80	80	142.0	24.2
Railway cars, Steam turbines, Generators, Motors, Centrifugal pumps	Axle	3.42	0.001	1.8 - 2.0	100	100	711.0	120.9
	Main	0.69 - 1.87	0.001	1.0 - 2.0	2.16	2.16	1422.0	241.8
	Rotor	0.69 - 1.37	0.0013	1.0 - 2.0	25	25	2845.0	483.5
Gyroscope	Rotor	5.90	0.0013		30	30	782.0	133.0
Transmission shafting	Light, fixed	0.17	0.001	2.0 - 3.0	25	25	1422.0	241.8
	Self-aligning	1.04	0.001	2.5 - 4.0	to	to	427.0	72.5
	Heavy	1.04	0.001	2.0 - 3.0	60	60	427.0	72.5
Cotton mill	Spindle	0.0069	0.005		2	2	142220.0	24177.6
Machine tools	Main	2.06	0.001	1.0 - 1.4	40	40	517.5	96.7
Punching and shearing machine	Main	27.80	0.001	1.0 - 2.0	100	100	---	---
	Crankpin	55.60	0.001	1.0 - 2.0	100	100	---	---
Rolling mills	Main	20.60	0.0015	1.1 - 1.5	50	50	142.0	24.2

(b) The minimum value of S″ can also be obtained for various combination of journal bearing materials by referring to Table T(24-7).

For example, for hardened and ground steel journal with Babbit bearing, bearing modulus,

$$S'' = 48.5 \times 10^{-9}$$

Table - (24-7)

Shaft	*Bearing*	*Bearing modulus*	
		$S ?? \frac{?_1 n}{P}$ *Metric*	$S ?? \frac{?_1 n?}{P}$ *SI* $\times 10^{-9}$
Hardened and ground steel	Babbit	28500	48.5
Machined, soft steel	Babbit	36000	61.2
Hardened and ground steel	Plastic bronze	42700	72.6
Machined, soft steel	Plastic bronze	35800	60.9
Hardened and ground steel	Rigid bronze	56900	96.7
Machined, soft steel	Rigid bronze	71100	120.8

Step II: *Calculation of coefficient of friction (μ)*

Coefficient of friction is calculated using McKee's equation given by

$$\mu = K_a\left(\eta\frac{n'}{P}\right)\left(\frac{1}{\psi}\right)10^{-10} + \Delta\mu \qquad \text{... E(24-22)}$$

Where, $K_a = \text{a constant} = 1.95 \times 10^{11}$

(For full journal bearing; $\beta = 360°$)

$$\eta = 10^{-3}\eta_1 \qquad \text{... E(24-2a)}$$

$n' =$ Speed in revolutions per second

$= \frac{n}{60}$

$n =$ Speed of rotation in rpm

$P =$ Pressure in bearing

$= \frac{w}{Ld}; \text{N/m}^2$

$w =$ Load on bearing in Newton.

$L =$ Length of journal in metre.

$d =$ Diameter of journal in metre.

$$\psi = \frac{c}{d}$$

Where, $c =$ Diametral clearance; mm.

Note: *Usually* $\psi = \left(\frac{1}{1000}\right)$ *i.e.,* $\frac{1}{\psi} = 1000$

$\Delta\mu$ = Correction factor for end leakage.

$= 0.002$ for $\frac{L}{d}$ ranging from 0.75 to 2.8

Note: Other equations used to calculate m

1. $\mu)_{Petroffs} = \frac{2\pi^2 \eta n'}{P}\left(\frac{1}{\psi}\right)$ ... E(24-21)

2. $\mu]_{\text{Raimondi and Boyd curve}}$ may be used to obtain 'μ', the coefficient of friction. It is to be noted that Raimondi and Boyd curves are used to determine 'μ' for a square bearing only.

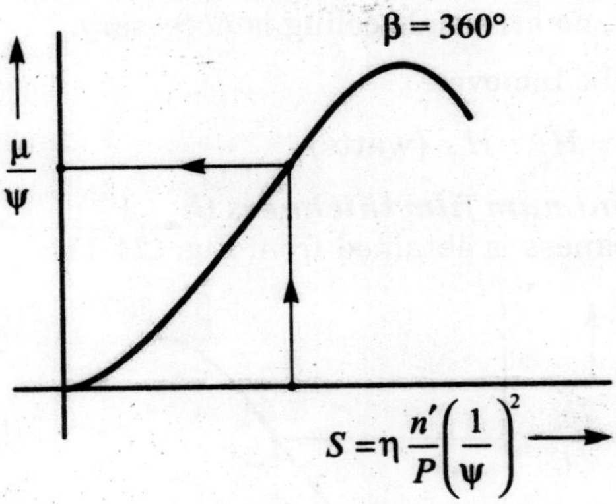

Step III: *Calculation of heat generated* (H_g) ***in bearing (or heat lost due to friction)***

The heat generated in bearing is given by,

$$H_g = \mu w v;\text{(watts)} \quad \text{... E(24-72a)}$$

Where,

w = Load on bearing; N.

v = Velocity of journal; m/sec

$= \frac{\pi d n}{60}$ m/sec

Note: $w = PLd$

Step IV: *Calculation of heat dissipated* (H_d) ***from bearing***

The heat dissipated from bearing is given by

$$H_d = CA(t_b - t_a)\text{ (watts)} \quad \text{... E(24-77)}$$

Where,

C = Combined coefficient of radiation and correction.

A = Effective sufrace area of bearing housing.

$= 25dL;\ m^2$

t_b = Temperature of bearing housing; °C.

t_a = Ambient temperature; °C.

Note: *Other equations for H_d, such as Pederson's equation is given by*

$$H_d = \frac{(18+\Delta T)^2 Ld}{K}$$

Where, $\Delta T = (t_b - t_a)$

$$= \frac{1}{2}(t_o - t_a) \text{ may also be used for calculating } H_d.$$

Step V: ***Check for artificial cooling.***

Artificial cooling is to be provided when the heat generated in bearing is more than the heat dissipated from bearing.

i.e., Artificial cooling is provided when $H_g > H_d$

If $H_d = H_g$ or $H_g < H_d$, no artificial cooling is necessary.

The quantity of heat to be removed

$$= H_g - H_d \text{ (watts)}$$

Step VI: ***Calculation of minimum film thickness (h_{min})***

Minimum film thickness is obtained from Fig. (24-11)

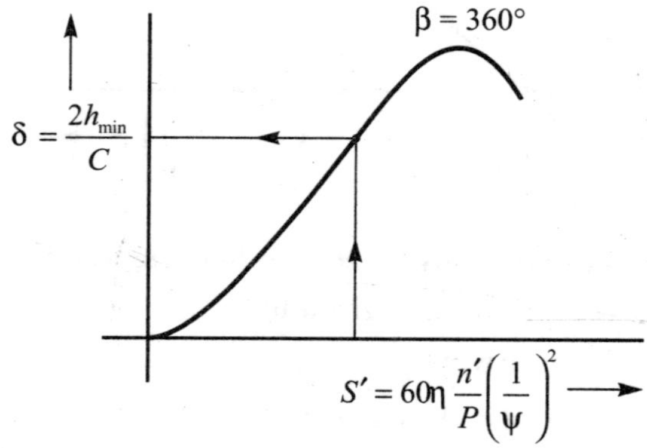

Knowing bearing modulus

$$S' = 60\eta \frac{n'}{P}\left(\frac{1}{\psi}\right)^2$$

Minimum thickness variable $\delta = \frac{2h_{\min}}{c}$ is obtained.

Knowing δ, $h_{\min}$ is obtained from,

$$h_{\min} = \frac{c\delta}{2}$$

Step VII: ***Calculation of Sommerfeld number (or bearing characteristics number)***

Sommerfeld number is obtained from equation,

$$S = \eta \frac{n'}{P}\left(\frac{1}{\psi}\right)^2$$

Note: *Sommerfeld number is a dimensionless quantity.*

Step VIII: *Calculation of equilibrium temperature (t_{eq})*

Equilibrium temperature is the temperature of oil at which the heat generated in bearing equals heat dissipated from bearing.

Procedure to obtain equilibrium temperature

(*i*) Obtain the viscosity of the given oil (lubricant) for various values of temperature range (Say 60° to 100° C).

(*ii*) Calculate coefficient of friction for each of the above temperature (Say 60°, 70°, 80° and 90° C).

(*iii*) Calculate the heat generated and heat dissipated, for the above values of t_o.

(*iv*) Plot the variation of H_g and H_d versus temperature t_o.

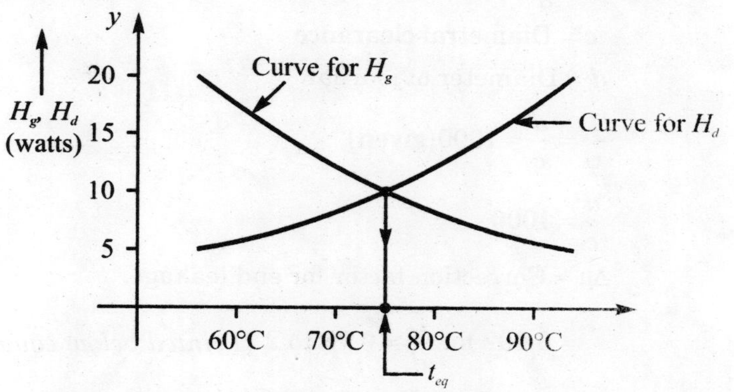

(*v*) Draw a vertical line from the point of intersection of curves of H_g and H_d to intersect X-axis at t_{eq} to obtain equilibrium temperature.

Example 7.1: A 75 mm journal bearing of diameter 75 mm supports a load of 12 kN on a journal running at 1800 rpm. Assuming $\frac{d}{c}$ ratio 1000 and an oil having viscosity of 10 cP at the operating temperature, determine,

1. ***(a) Coefficient of friction using McKee's equation.***
   (b) Coefficient of friction using Petroff's equation.
   (c) Coefficient of friction using Raimondi and Boyd Curve.
2. ***The amount of heat generated using coefficient of friction obtained by McKee's equation.***
3. ***Determine the probable surface temperature of bearing assuming that the heat generated is all dissipated in still air at 21°C.***

Solution:

1. ***(a) To find coefficient of friction (μ) using McKee's equation.***
   McKee's equation for coefficient of friction is given by,

$$\mu]_{\text{McKee's}} = K_a\left(\eta\frac{n'}{P}\right)\left(\frac{1}{\psi}\right)10^{-10} + \Delta\mu \qquad \text{... E(24-22)}$$

Where, $K_a = 1.95\times10^{11}$; a constant for a full journal bearing with $\beta = 360°$.

$$\eta = 10^{-3}\eta_1 \qquad \text{... E(24-2a)}$$

η is in Pas (Pascal seconds)

η_1 = Viscosity in centipoise = 10 cP

Therefore, from E(24-2a),

$$\eta = 10^{-3}\times10 = 10^{-2}\text{Pas}$$

$$n' = \text{Speed in rps} = \frac{n}{60}$$

$$= \frac{1800}{60} = 30 \text{ rps}$$

$$\psi = \frac{c}{d}$$

Where, c = Diametral clearance

d = Diameter of journal

$$\frac{1}{\psi} = \frac{d}{c} = 1000(\text{given})$$

***Note:** Generally,* $\frac{d}{c} = 1000$

$\Delta\mu$ = Correction factor for end leakage.

$= 0.002$ for $\frac{L}{d} = 0.75$ to 2 *[Printed below equation 24-22a]*

Therefore, $$\mu]_{\text{McKee's}} = 1.95\times10^{11}\left[\frac{10^{-2}\times30}{21.33\times10^5}\right]1000\times10^{-10} + 0.002$$

$$P = \text{Bearing pressure} = \frac{w}{Ld};\ w = 12\text{ kN} = 12\times10^3\text{N}$$

$$= \frac{12\times10^3}{\left(\frac{75}{1000}\right)\left(\frac{75}{1000}\right)} = 21.33\times10^5\text{ N/m}^2$$

Therefore, $\mu]_{\text{McKee's}} = 0.004742$

1. *(b) To find coefficient of friction using Petroff's equation*

$$\mu]_{\text{Petroff's}} = 2\pi^2\eta\frac{n'}{P}\left(\frac{1}{\psi}\right) \qquad \text{... E(24-21)}$$

$$= \frac{2\pi^2\times10^{-2}\times30}{21.33\times10^5}(1000)$$

$$= 0.002776$$

***Note:** Petroff's equation does not consider the effect of end leakage.*

1. (c) *To find coefficient of friction using Raimondi and Boyd Curve*

***Note:** Applicable only for square bearings in which $\frac{L}{d} = 1$*

Here, $L = 75$ mm; $d = 75$ mm

Therefore, $\frac{L}{d} = 1$

For the given bearing,

Bearing characteristic number 'S' is given by,

$$S = \eta \frac{n'}{P}\left(\frac{1}{\psi^2}\right)$$

$$= \frac{10^{-2} \times 30}{21.33 \times 10^5}(1000)^2 = 0.1406$$

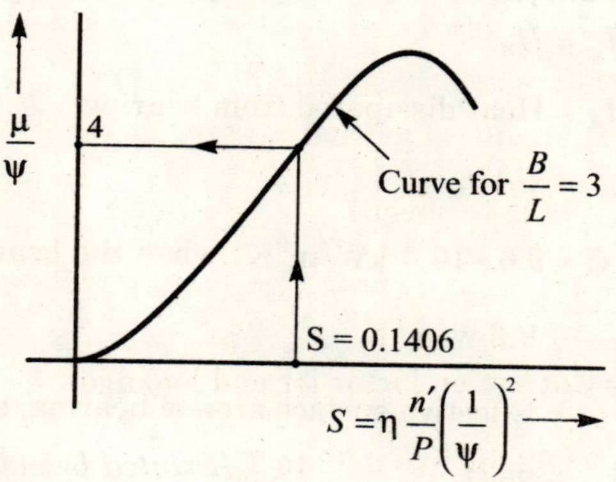

To find ratio $\frac{B}{L}$

B = Length of bearing in the direction of rotation.

$$= \frac{\pi d \beta^\circ}{360} = \pi \times 75 \times \frac{360^\circ}{360} = 75\pi \quad \text{... E(24-19)}$$

L = Length of bearing = 75 mm

Therefore, $\frac{B}{L} = \frac{75\pi}{75} = \pi = 3.14$

Corresponding to S = 0.1406 and $\frac{B}{L} = 3.14 (\approx 3)$,

From figure (24-19-MDH),

$$\frac{\mu}{\psi} = 4$$

Therefore, $\mu = 4\psi$

$$= 4 \times 0.001 = 0.004$$

$$\mu]_{\text{Raimondi and Boyd}} = 0.004$$

2. *To find heat generated in bearing (H_g) based on $\mu]_{McKee's}$*

$$H_g = \mu w v \qquad \text{... E(24-72a)}$$

$$= \mu]_{McKee's}\, wv$$

Where, $$v = \frac{\pi d n}{60}$$

$$= \frac{\pi}{60} \times \frac{75}{1000} \times 1800 = 7.069 \text{ m/sec}$$

Therefore, $$H_g = 0.04742 \times \left(12 \times 10^3\right) \times 7.069$$

$$= 402.25 \text{ watts}$$

3. *To find the probable surface temperature of bearing (t_b)*

Given, $$H_g = H_d$$

Where, H_d = Heat dissipated from bearing

$$= CA\left(t_b - t_a\right) \qquad \text{... E(24-77)}$$

$C = 9.6 \times 10^{-3}$ kW/m²K; when the bearing is located in still air.

$$= 9.6 \text{ w/m}^2\text{K}$$

A = Effective surface area of bearing; m^2

$$= 25dL$$

Where, d and L are in metre.

Therefore, $$H_d = 9.6 \times \left(25 \times \frac{75}{1000} \times \frac{75}{1000}\right)\left(t_b - 21\right)$$

$$= 1.35\left(t_b - 21\right)$$

Equating, H_g and H_d we get,

$$402.25 = 1.35\left(t_b - 21\right)$$

Therefore, t_b = Temperature of bearing surface; °C

$$= 318.96\,°\text{C}$$

***Example 7.2:* A Journal bearing 75mm long supports a load of 7335 N on a 50 mm diameter journal running at 750 rpm. The diametral clearance is 0.06825 mm. What should be the viscosity of oil in cP if the temperature of bearing surface is to be limited to 77°C when in still air at 21°C. Assume that the heat generated is all dissipated ?**

Solution:

As per data, $H_g = H_d$

Where, $$\mu = K_a\left(\eta\frac{n'}{P}\right)\left(\frac{1}{\psi}\right)10^{-10} + \Delta\mu \qquad \text{... E(24-22)}$$

Where, $K_a = 1.95\times10^{11}$; for $\beta = 360°$ (full journal bearing)

$$\eta = 10^{-3}\eta_1 \text{ Pas}$$

$$n' = \frac{n}{60} = \frac{750}{60} = 12.5 \text{ rps}$$

$$P = \text{Bearing pressure} = \frac{w}{Ld};\ w = 7335 \text{ N}$$

$$L = 75 \text{ mm};\ d = 50 \text{ mm}$$

$$= \frac{7335}{\left(\frac{75}{1000}\right)\left(\frac{50}{1000}\right)} = 19.56\times10^5 \text{ N/m}^2$$

$$\psi = \frac{c}{d} = \frac{0.06825}{50} = 0.001365$$

Therefore, $$\frac{1}{\psi} = 732.6$$

$$\Delta\mu = 0.002$$

Therefore, $$\mu = 1.95\times10^{11}\left(\frac{10^{-3}\eta\times12.5}{19.56\times10^5}\right)732.6\times10^{-10} + 0.002$$

$$= 0.00009129\eta_1 + 0.002$$

Now $H_g = \mu w v$

Where, $w = 7335$ N;

$$v = \frac{\pi d n}{60} = \frac{\pi}{60}\times\frac{50}{1000}\times750 = 1.9635 \text{ m/sec}$$

Therefore, $$H_g = (0.00009129\,\eta_1 + 0.002)7335\times1.9635$$

$$= (0.00009219\,\eta_1 + 0.002)14402.273 \text{ watts}$$

Heat dissipated from bearing is given by,

$$H_d = CA(t_b - t_a) \qquad \text{... E(24-77)}$$

$$C = 9.6\,\text{W}^2/\text{m}^2\text{K}$$

$$A = 25dL$$

$$= 25 \times \frac{75}{1000} \times \frac{50}{1000} = 0.09375\ \text{m}^2$$

$$(t_b - t_a) = (77 - 21) = 56°\text{C}$$

Equating H_g and H_d we get,

$$(0.00009219\eta_1 + 0.002)(14402.273) = 9.6 \times 0.09375 \times 56$$

Therefore, $\eta_1 = 16.425$ cP

Example 7.3: A Journal bearing 150 mm in diameter, 225 mm long supports a load of 8900 N at 1200 rpm. If the radial clearance is 0.075 mm and the bearing wastes 1495 watts in friction, what is the viscosity of oil in cP at the operating temperature.

Solution:

The heat generated $H_g = \mu w v$

Where, $H_g = 1495$ watts (From data)

The coefficient of friction

$$\mu = K_a \left(\eta \frac{n'}{P}\right)\left(\frac{1}{\psi}\right) 10^{-10} + \Delta\mu \qquad \text{... E(24-22)}$$

$$K_a = 1.95 \times 10^{11}; \qquad \eta = 10^{-3}\eta_1$$

Where, η_1 is in cP

$$n' = \frac{n}{60}$$

$$= \frac{1200}{60} = 20\ \text{rps}$$

Pressure $$P = \frac{w}{Ld}$$

$$= \frac{8900}{\left(\frac{225}{1000}\right)\left(\frac{150}{1000}\right)} = 2.637 \times 10^5\ \text{N/m}^2$$

$$\psi = \frac{c}{d}; \quad c = \text{diametral clearance}$$

$$= \frac{2 \times \text{ Radial clearance}}{d}$$

$$= \frac{2 \times 0.075}{150} = 0.001$$

Therefore, $$v = \frac{\pi d n}{60}$$

$$= \frac{\pi}{60} \times \left(\frac{150}{1000}\right) 1200 = 9.4248 \text{ m/sec}$$

$\Delta\mu$ = Correction factor for end leakage = 0.002

Equating H_g and H_d we get,

$$1495 = \left[\left(1.95 \times 10^{11}\right)\left(\frac{10^{-3}\eta_1 \times 20}{2.637 \times 10^5}\right)(1000) \times 10^{-10} + 0.002\right] wv$$

i.e., $$1495 = (0.001479\eta_1 + 0.002) 8900 \times 9.4248$$

Therefore, Viscosity of oil

$$\eta_1 = 10.698 \text{ cP}$$

Example 7.4: A full Journal bearing 100 mm in diameter and 150 mm long supports a radial load of 5350 N. The speed of shaft is 500 rpm. The room temperature is 32.2°C and the surface of bearing is to be limited to 62.78°C. Select a suitable oil to satisfy the above requirement if the bearing is well ventilated and no artificial cooling is used.

Assume $\frac{d}{c} = 1000$.

Solution:

Since no artificial cooling is used,

$$H_g = H_d$$

i.e., Heat generated = Heat dissipated.

$$H_g = \mu w v$$

Where, $$\mu = K_a\left(\eta \frac{n'}{P}\right)\left(\frac{1}{\psi}\right) 10^{-10} + \Delta\mu \qquad \text{... E(24-22)}$$

$$K_a = 1.95 \times 10^{11}$$

$$\eta = 10^{-3}\eta_1$$

$$n' = \frac{n}{60}$$

$$= \frac{500}{60} = 12.5 \text{ rps}$$

Where, $$\psi = \frac{c}{d}$$

Therefore, $$\frac{1}{\psi} = \frac{d}{c} = 1000 \text{ (given)}$$

Bearing pressure, $P = \dfrac{w}{Ld}$

$$= \frac{5350}{\left(\frac{150}{1000}\right)\left(\frac{100}{1000}\right)} = 3.57\times10^5 \text{ N/m}^2$$

Therefore, $\mu = \left(1.95\times10^{11}\right)\left(\dfrac{10^{-3}\eta_1\times12.5}{3.57\times10^5}\right)(1000)\times10^{-10} + 0.002$

$$= 0.0006834\eta_1 + 0.002$$

And $H_g = (0.0006834\eta_1 + 0.002)5350\times\left[\dfrac{\pi}{60}\times\left(\dfrac{100}{1000}\right)500\right]$

$$= (0.0006834\eta_1 + 0.002)14006.27$$

Heat dissipated, $H_d = CA(t_b - t_a)$

Where, $C = 9.6\times10^{-3} \text{ kW/m}^2\text{K} = 9.6 \text{ W/m}^2\text{K}$

$$A = 25dL$$

$$= 25\times\left(\frac{100}{1000}\right)\times\left(\frac{150}{1000}\right)$$

$$(t_b - t_a) = (62.78 - 32.2) = 30.58°\text{C}$$

Therefore, $H_d = (9.6)\left(25\times\dfrac{100}{1000}\times\dfrac{150}{1000}\right)\times30.58$

$$= 110 \text{ watts}$$

But, $H_g = H_d$

i.e., $(0.0006834\eta_1 + 0.002)14006.27 = 110$

or, $\eta_1 = 8.57 \text{ cP}$

That is, Viscosity of oil required is

$$\eta_1 = 8.57 \text{ Centipose}$$

Example 7.5 A full Journal bearing $(\beta = 360°)$ having a diameter 75 mm and length 125 mm supporting a load of 20 kN runs at 1000 rpm. The temperature of bearing surface is not to exceed 76.7°C and room temperature 37.8°C. The oil used has a viscosity of 10CP at 115.6°C. Determine the amount of artificial cooling required by means of external cooler.

Solution:

Given, $L = 125$ mm, $d = 75$ mm, Load $w = 20$ kN $= 20 \times 10^3$ N

$n = 1000$ rpm, $t_b = 76.7°C$, $t_a = 37.8°C$

Viscosity $\eta_1 = 10 \text{ cP} = 10 \times 10^{-3} \text{ Pas} = 10^{-2} \text{ Pas}$

The heat generated,

$$H_g = \mu w v \text{ watts}$$

Where,
$$\mu = K_a \left(\eta \frac{n'}{P}\right)\left(\frac{1}{\psi}\right) 10^{-10} + \Delta\mu \qquad \text{... E(24-22)}$$

$$K_a = 1.95 \times 10^{11}$$

$$\eta = 10^{-2} \text{ Pas}$$

$$n' = \frac{n}{60}$$

$$= \frac{1000}{60} = 16.67 \text{ rps}$$

Pressure
$$P = \frac{w}{Ld}$$

$$= \frac{20 \times 10^3}{\left(\frac{125}{1000}\right)\left(\frac{75}{1000}\right)} = 21.33 \times 10^5 \text{ N/m}^2$$

Where,
$$\psi = \frac{c}{d}$$

Therefore,
$$\frac{1}{\psi} = \frac{d}{c} = 1000 \text{ (assumed)}$$

$$\Delta\mu = 0.002$$

Therefore,
$$\mu = \left(1.95 \times 10^{11}\right)\left[\frac{10^{-2} \times 16.67}{21.33 \times 10^5}\right] 1000 \times 10^{-10} + 0.002$$

$$= 0.003524$$

Velocity,
$$v = \frac{\pi d n}{60}$$

$$= \frac{\pi}{60} \times \frac{75}{1000} \times 1000 = 3.927 \text{ m/sec}$$

Therefore,
$$H_g = 0.003524 \times 20 \times 10^3 \times 3.927$$

$$= 276.775 \text{ watts}$$

The heat dissipated from bearing is given by,

$$H_d = CA\left(t_b - t_a\right) \qquad \text{... E(24-77)}$$

Where, $C = 9.6\ \text{W/m}^2\text{K}$

$$A = 25dL$$

$$= 25 \times \frac{75}{1000} \times \frac{125}{1000}\ \text{m}^2$$

$$(t_b - t_a) = (76.7°\text{C} - 37.8°\text{C}) = 38.9°\text{C}$$

Therefore,

$$H_d = (9.6)\left(25 \times \frac{75}{1000} \times \frac{125}{1000}\right)(38.9)$$

$$= 87.525 \text{ watts}$$

$H_g > H_d$, and hence artificial cooling is to be provided.

The amount of heat to be removed

$$= H_g - H_d$$

$$= (276.775 - 87.525) \text{ watts}$$

$$= 189.28 \text{ watts}$$

$$= 189.28\ \text{J/sec} = 11.355\ \text{KJ/min}$$

Example 7.6: A bronze backed Babbit bearing and a hardened steel journal is used to support a load of 4.5 kN at 600 rpm. Abundant oil is supplied by means of oiling rings. Assuming temperature of oil = 80°C, determine,

(i) The length and diameter of bearing.

(ii) The coefficient of friction using McKee's equation.

(iii) The heat generated.

(iv) The heat dissipated (based on projected area of bearing).

(v) Sommerfeld number.

Solution:

(i) To find the length and diameter of bearing (i.e., 'L' and 'd')

For hardened steel journal and Babbit bearing,

Bearing modulus,

$$S'' = \eta\frac{n'}{P} = 48.5 \times 10^{-9} \qquad \text{... T(24-7)}$$

$$n' = \frac{n}{60}$$

$$= \frac{600}{60} = 10 \text{ rps}$$

$$\eta = 10^{-3}\eta_1$$

Where, η_1 is in cP

Table- 24-1 MDH: Specific gravity of oils at 15.5°C

No.	Oil Characteristics	$\gamma_{15.5}$
A	Turbine oil, ring-oiled bearing	0.8877
B	Turbine oil, ring-oiled bearing, SAE 10	0.8894
C	All year automobile-oil, SAE 20	0.9036
D	Ring-oiled bearing oil, high speed machinery	0.9346
E	Automobile oil, SAE 20	0.9254
F	Automobile oil, SAE 30	0.9263
G	Automobile oil, SAE 40, medium-speed machinery	0.9275
H	Aeroplane oil 100, SAE 60	0.8927
I	Transmission oil, SAE 110, spur and bevel gears	0.9328
J	Gear oil, slow speed worm gears	0.9153
K	Transmission oil, SAE 60, slow-speed gears	0.9365

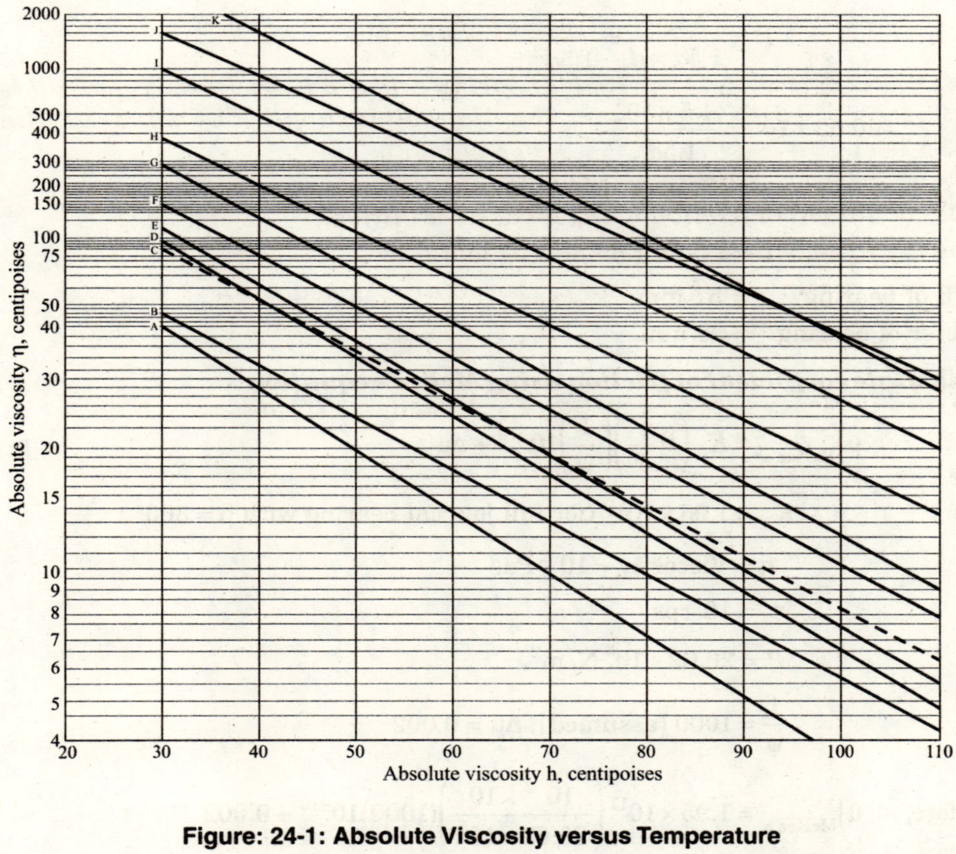

Figure: 24-1: Absolute Viscosity versus Temperature

Referring T(24-1), for ring oiled bearing use curve D. Referring Figure (24-2), for curve D and oil at $t_o = 80°C$

$$\eta_1 = 10 \text{ cP}$$

Therefore, $\eta = 10^{-3}\eta_1$

$$= 10^{-3} \times 10 = 10^{-2} \text{ Pas}$$

From, $S'' = \eta\dfrac{n'}{P} = 48.5 \times 10^{-9}$,

$$= \frac{10^{-2} \times 10}{P} = 48.5 \times 10^{-9}$$

Therefore, $P = \dfrac{10^{-2} \times 10}{48.5 \times 10^{-9}} = 20.62 \times 10^5 \text{ N/m}^2$

But, Pressure $P = \dfrac{w}{Ld}$

Assuming, $\dfrac{L}{d} = 1.5$,

$$P = \frac{w}{1.5d \times d} = \frac{w}{1.5d^2}$$

i.e., $20.62 \times 10^5 = \dfrac{4.5 \times 10^3}{1.5d^2}$

Therefore, $d = 0.038 \text{ m} = 38 \text{ mm}$

$$L = 1.5d = 1.5 \times 38 = 57 \text{ mm}$$

Length of bearing = 57 mm.
Diameter of bearing = 38 mm.

(ii) To calculate coefficient of friction using McKee's equation

$$\mu]_{\text{McKee's}} = K_a\left(\eta\frac{n'}{P}\right)\left(\frac{1}{\psi}\right)10^{-10} + \Delta\mu \qquad \text{... E(24-22)}$$

Where, $K_a = 1.95 \times 10^{11}$ (for full journal bearing with $\beta = 360°$).

$$\eta = \text{Viscosity} = 10^{-2} \text{ Pas}$$

$$n' = 10 \text{ rps}$$

$$P = 20.62 \times 10^5 \text{ N/m}^2$$

$$\frac{1}{\psi} = 1000 \text{ (assumed)};\ \Delta\mu = 0.002$$

Therefore, $\mu]_{\text{McKee's}} = 1.95 \times 10^{11}\left(\dfrac{10^{-2} \times 10}{20.62 \times 10^5}\right)(1000)10^{-10} + 0.002$

$$= 0.002946$$

(iii) To calculate the heat generated in bearing (H_g)

Heat generated in bearing is given by,

$$H_g = \mu w v$$

Where, $\mu = 0.002946$

w = Load on bearing $= 4.5\times10^3$ N

$$v = \frac{\pi d n}{60}$$

$$= \frac{\pi}{60}\left(\frac{38}{1000}\right)600 = 1.1938 \text{ m/sec}$$

Therefore, $H_g = 0.002946\times\left(4.5\times10^3\right)\times1.1938$

$= 15.83$ watts

(iv) To calculate heat dissipated from bearing (H_d)

Heat dissipated $H_d = CA\left(t_b - t_a\right)$

Where, $C = 9.6 \text{ w/m}^2\text{K}$

$A = 25dL$

$$= 25\left(\frac{38}{1000}\right)\left(\frac{57}{1000}\right) = 0.05415 \text{ m}^2$$

$$\left(t_b - t_a\right) = \frac{1}{2}\left(t_o - t_a\right)$$

$$= \frac{1}{2}(80 - 25) = 27.5$$

Therefore, $H_d = 9.6\times0.05415\times27.5$

$= 14.296$ watts

(v) To calculate Sommerfeld number 'S' (or bearing characteristic number)

$$S = \eta\frac{n'}{P}\left(\frac{1}{\psi}\right)^2$$

$$= \left(48.5\times10^{-9}\right)(1000)^2$$

$$= 0.0485$$

Example 7.7: A full journal bearing having 90 mm diameter and 150 mm long has a radial load resulting in pressure of 2 MPa per unit projected area. The speed of shaft is 500 rpm. The bearing operates in SAE 20 oil at 50°C. Calculate,

(i) The minimum film thickness.

(ii) Heat lost due to friction, and check

(iii) Whether artificial cooling is required. ***(VTU, July / August 2005)***

Solution:

(i) To calculate the minimum film thickness (h_{min})

Referring figure (24-11 MDH),

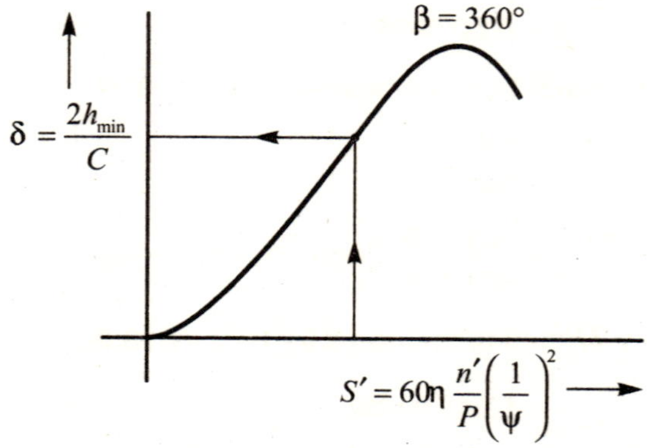

$$S' = 60\eta \frac{n'}{P}\left(\frac{1}{\psi^2}\right)$$

Where, $\eta = 10^{-3}\eta_1$ and η_1 is obtained from figure $(24-2MDH)$

For SAE 20 oil (Table 24-1); use curve E. At 50°C, for curve E, $\eta_1 = 36$ cP

Therefore, $\eta = 36 \times 10^{-3}$ Pas

$$n' = \frac{n}{60}$$

$$= \frac{500}{60} = 8.33 \text{ rps}$$

$$P = \frac{w}{Ld}$$

Therefore, $w = PLd$

$$= 2 \times 150 \times 90 = 27000 \text{ N}$$

$$P = 2 \text{ MPa} = \frac{2N}{\text{mm}^2} = 2 \times 10^6 \text{ N/m}^2$$

Therefore, $S' = 60 \times \left(36 \times 10^{-3}\right) \times \frac{8.33}{2 \times 10^6} \times (1000)^2$

$$= 8.9964$$

Corresponding to $S' = 8.9964$,

$\delta =$ Minimum film thickness variable $= 0.9$

But, $\delta = \frac{2h_{min}}{c}$

i.e., $h_{min} = \frac{\delta c}{2}$

Where, $c = \psi d$

$= 0.001 \times 90 = 0.09$ mm

Therefore, $h_{min} = \dfrac{0.9 \times 0.09}{2} = 0.0405$ mm

(ii) Heat lost due to friction (H_g)

$$H_g = \mu w v$$

Where, $$\mu = K_a\left(\eta\frac{n'}{P}\right)\left(\frac{1}{\psi}\right)10^{-10} + \Delta\mu \quad \text{... E(24-22)}$$

$$K_a = 1.95 \times 10^{11}; \qquad \eta = 10^{-3}\eta_1 = 10^{-3} \times 36 \text{ Pas}$$

$$P = 2 \times 10^6 \text{ N/m}^2; \qquad \frac{1}{\psi} = 1000$$

Therefore $$\mu = 1.95 \times 10^{11}\left(\frac{36 \times 10^{-3} \times 8.33}{2 \times 10^6}\right) \times 1000 \times 10^{-10} + 0.002$$

$$= 0.004924$$

Therefore, $$H_g = \mu w v$$

$$= 0.004924(27000)\left[\frac{\pi}{60} \times \frac{90}{1000} \times 500\right]$$

$$= 313.25 \text{ watts} = 18795.08 \text{ J/min}$$

(iii) To check for artificial cooling

$$H_d = CA(t_b - t_a)$$

$$= 9.6(25dL)(12.5)$$

$$= 9.6\left(25 \times \frac{90}{1000} \times \frac{150}{1000}\right)12.5$$

$$= 40.5 \text{ watts}$$

$H_g > H_d$ and hence artificial cooling is to be provided.

Example 7.8: A 75mm long journal bearing of diameter 75 mm supports a radial load of 12 kN at shaft speed of 1800 rpm. Assume ratio of diameter to diametral clearance as 1000. The viscosity of oil is 0.01 Pas at the operating temperature. Determine,

(i) Sommerfeld number.

(ii) μ based on McKee's equation.

(iii) Amount of heat generated. ***(VTU, July / August 2004)***

Solution:

(i) To calculate Sommerfeld number (S).

Sommerfeld number,

$$S = \eta \frac{n'}{P}\left(\frac{1}{\psi^2}\right)$$

Where, $\eta = 0.01$ Pas

$$n' = \frac{1800}{60} = 30 \text{ rps}$$

Bearing pressure,

$$P = \frac{w}{Ld}; \quad w = 12 \text{ kN} = 12 \times 10^3 \text{N}, \quad L = d = 75 \text{ mm}$$

$$= \frac{12 \times 10^3}{\left(\frac{75}{1000}\right)\left(\frac{75}{1000}\right)} = 21.33 \times 10^5 \text{ N/m}^2$$

Where, $\psi = \dfrac{c}{d}$

$$\frac{d}{c} = 1000 \text{ (given)}$$

Therefore, $S = \dfrac{0.01 \times 30}{21.33 \times 10^5}(1000)^2 = 0.1406$

(ii) To find coefficient of friction using McKee's equation.

$$\mu]_{\text{McKee's}} = K_a \left(\eta \frac{n'}{P}\right)\left(\frac{1}{\psi}\right) 10^{-10} + \Delta\mu \qquad \text{... E(24-22)}$$

$$K_a = 1.95 \times 10^{11} \text{ for full journal bearing.}$$

Therefore, $\mu]_{\text{McKee's}} = 1.95 \times 10^{11}\left(\dfrac{0.01 \times 30}{21.33 \times 10^5}\right)(1000) \times 10^{-10} + 0.002$

$$= 0.004742$$

(iii) To find H_g, the heat generated in bearing.

$$H_g = \mu w v$$

$$= 0.004741\left(12 \times 10^3\right)\left[\frac{\pi}{60} \times \frac{75}{1000} \times 1800\right]$$

$$= 402.23 \text{ watts}$$

Example 7.9: Design a Journal bearing for a rotary compressor for operation at a speed of 1500 rpm. The bearing is to sustain a load of 4500 N and the diameter of main shaft is 50 mm. Determine,

(i) Length of bearing bush.

(ii) Viscosity of oil to be used and hence suggest a suitable oil.

(iii) The coefficient of friction.

(iv) The heat generated.

(v) The heat dissipating capacity.

(vi) The amount of heat to be removed by artificial cooling.

(vii) Sommerfeld number. ***(VTU, Jan / Feb 2005)***

Solution:

(i) To calculate length of bearing bush (i.e. L)

Referring Table (24-2), for main bearing of rotary compressor,

Ratio $\frac{L}{d} = 1.0 \text{ to } 2.2$

Say, $\frac{L}{d} = 1.5$

Therefore, $L = 1.5d$

$$= 1.5 \times 50 = 75 \text{ mm}$$

(ii) To calculate the viscosity of oil (η)

From Table (24-2) MDH,

Bearing modulus $S'' = \eta \frac{n'}{P} = 72.5 \times 10^{-9}$

Where, $n' = \frac{n}{60}$

$$= \frac{1500}{60} = 25 \text{ rps}$$

$$P = \frac{w}{Ld}$$

$$= \frac{4500}{\left(\frac{75}{1000}\right)\left(\frac{75}{1000}\right)} = 12 \times 10^5 \text{ N/m}^2$$

$$\eta = 10^{-3}\eta_1$$

Therefore, from $S'' = \eta \frac{n'}{P}$,

$$72.5 \times 10^{-9} = \left(10^{-3}\eta_1\right)\frac{25}{12 \times 10^5}$$

$$\eta_1 = 3.48 \text{ cP}$$

Assume $t_o = 80°\text{C}$ and refer Table (24-3) MDH

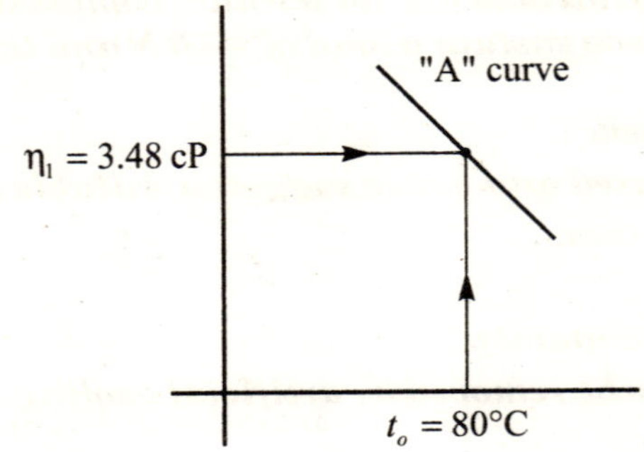

Corresponding to $\eta_1 = 3.48$ cP and $t_o = 80°C$, we obtain curve '*A*' and referring Table (24-1), we use turbine oil ring oiled bearing.

(iii) To calculate the coefficient of friction **(μ)**

$$\mu = K_a\left(\eta\frac{n'}{P}\right)\left(\frac{1}{\psi}\right)10^{-10} + \Delta\mu \qquad \text{... E(24-22)}$$

$$= 1.95\times10^{11}\left(\frac{3.48\times10^{-3}\times25}{12\times10^{5}}\right)(1000)\times10^{-10} + 0.002$$

$$= 0.003414$$

(iv) To find the heat generated in bearing **(H_g)**

Heat generated $H_g = \mu wv$

$$= 0.003414\times4500\times\left(\frac{\pi}{60}\times\frac{50}{1000}\times1500\right)$$

$$= 60.33 \text{ watts}$$

(v) To find the heat dissipated from bearing **(H_d)**

Heat dissipated $H_d = CA(t_b - t_a)$

Where, $C = 9.6\times10^{-3}$ kW/m²k

$= 9.6$ W/m²k

$A = 25dL$

$$= 25\left(\frac{50}{1000}\right)\left(\frac{75}{1000}\right)$$

$$= 0.09375 \text{ m}^2$$

We have $(t_b - t_a) = \frac{1}{2}(t_o - t_a)$

$$= \frac{1}{2}(80 - 25) = 27.5°C$$

Therefore, $H_d = 9.6\times0.09375\times27.5$

$= 24.75$ watts

(vi) To check for artificial cooling

$$H_g = 60.33\,W > H_d = 24.75\,W$$

Therefore, artificial cooling is to be provided.

Rate at which heat is to be removed is $= H_g - H_d$

$$= 60.33 - 24.75$$

$$= 35.58 \text{ watts}$$

$$= 35.58 \text{ J/sec} = 2134.8 \text{ J/min}$$

(vii) To calculate Sommerfeld number (S)

Sommerfeld number $S = \eta \dfrac{n'}{P}\left(\dfrac{1}{\psi}\right)^2$

$$= \frac{(3.48\times10^{-3})25}{12\times10^5}\times(1000)^2$$

$$= 0.0725$$

Design Procedure of Ball Bearings

General steps followed while designing ball bearings

Step I: *Calculation of life of bearing (L_n)*

L_n of bearing is based on,

(i) The number of years of use.

(ii) It's frequency of use and

(iii) *Speed of rotation of bearing/shaft.*

For example, if a bearing is to be used for 3 years at 10 hours/day and the speed of shaft is 1200 rpm, then

$$L_n = 3 \text{ years at } 10 \text{ hours/day; Speed} = 1200 \text{ rpm}$$

$$= 3\times365\times10\times1200 \text{ revolutions}$$

$$= 788.4 \text{ Millions of revolution } (M.O.R.)$$

$$= L_n)_{\text{required}}$$

Step II: *Selection of bearing*

Case A: When diameter of shaft / bearing (d) is known

For example if diameter $d = 50$ mm is known,

(i) 50BC02 bearing (SKF 6210 bearing).

(ii) 50BC03 bearing (SKF 6310 bearing) and

(iii) 50BC03 bearing (SKF 6410 bearing) are tried in order and the bearing which has a life $L_n \geq L_n)_{\text{required}}$ (calculated from step 1) is selected.

Trials to find suitable bearing

Trial 1: ***For 50BC02 bearing***

Static capacity $C_o = 23200\,\text{N}$

Dynamic capacity $C = 35100$ N

For ball bearings,

$$L_n = \left(\frac{C}{P}\right)^3 \quad \text{... E(24-189)}$$

P = Equivalent load (equivalent of axial and radial loads)

$= XF_r + YF_a$

F_r = Radial load on bearing; N

F_a = Axial load or thrust load on bearing; N

X and Y are constants ... T(24-51)

To obtain X and Y

For 50BC02 bearing,

Assuming $F_a = 2000$ N and $F_r = 3000$ N as the loads to be sustained, then

$$\frac{F_a}{F_r} = \frac{2000}{3000} = 0.67$$

Also,

$$\frac{F_a}{C_0} = \frac{2000}{23200} = 0.086$$

The nearest value of $\frac{F_a}{C_0}$ from T(24-51) is $\frac{F_a}{C_0} = 0.084$ for which constant $e = 0.28$

Now comparing $\frac{F_a}{F_r}$ with e,

$$\frac{F_a}{F_r} = 0.67 > e = 0.28$$

Therefore, $X = 0.56$ and $Y = 1.55$

Note: $If\ \frac{F_a}{F_r} < e$, *use* $X = 1$ *and* $Y = 0$

The value of P obtained above is to be multiplied by service factor $C_s = 1.25$ for light shock, 1.50 for medium shock and 1.75 to 2 for heavy shock.

Therefore, $P = 4780C_s$

$= 4780 \times 1.25$ (assuming light shock)

$= 5975$ N

Table 24-51MDH: Factors X and Y for radial ball bearings

Bearing Type		'Relative axial load'*		Single-row bearings $\frac{F_a}{F_r} \le e$		Single-row bearings $\frac{F_a}{F_r} \ge e$		Double-row bearings $\frac{F_a}{F_r} \le e$		Double-row bearings $\frac{F_a}{F_r} \ge e$		*e*
				X	Y	X	Y	X	Y	X	Y	
Radial contact groove ball bearings		$\frac{F_a}{C_{or}}$	$\frac{F_a}{iZD_w^2}$									
		0.014	0.172				2.30				2.30	0.19
		0.028	0.345				1.99				1.99	0.22
		0.056	0.689				1.71				1.71	0.26
		0.084	1.30				1.55				1.55	0.28
		0.11	1.38	1	0	0.56	1.45	1	0	0.56	1.45	0.30
		0.17	2.07				1.31				1.31	0.34
		0.28	3.45				1.15				1.15	0.38
		0.42	5.17				1.04				1.04	0.42
		0.56	6.89				1.00				1.00	0.44
Angular contact groove ball bearings	α	$\frac{iF_a}{C_{or}}$	$\frac{F_a}{ZD_w^2}$									
	5°	0.014	0.172			For this type use the *X*, *Y* and *e* values applicable to single contact groove ball bearings			2.78		3.74	0.23
		0.028	0.345						2.40		3.23	0.26
		0.056	0.689						2.07		2.78	0.30
		0.085	1.03						1.87		2.52	0.34
		0.11	1.38	1	0			1	1.75	0.78	2.36	0.86
		0.17	2.07						1.58		2.13	0.40
		0.28	3.45						1.39		1.87	0.45
		0.42	5.17						1.26		1.69	0.50
		0.56	6.89						1.21		1.63	0.52
	10°	0.014	0.172				1.88		2.18		3.06	0.29
		0.029	0.345				1.71		1.98		2.78	0.32
		0.057	0.689				1.52		1.76		2.47	0.36
		0.086	1.03				1.41		1.63		2.29	0.38
		0.11	1.38	1	0	0.46	1.34	1	1.55	0.75	2.18	0.40
		0.17	2.07				1.23		1.42		2.00	0.44
		0.29	3.45				1.10		1.27		1.79	0.49
		0.43	5.17				1.01		1.17		1.64	0.54
		0.57	6.89				1.00		1.16		1.63	0.54
	15°	0.015	0.172				1.47		1.65		2.39	0.38
		0.029	0.345				1.40		1.57		2.28	0.40
		0.058	0.689				1.30		1.40		2.11	0.43
		0.087	1.03				1.23		1.38		2.00	0.46
		0.12	1.38	1	0	0.46	1.19	1	1.34	0.72	1.93	0.47
		0.17	2.07				1.12		1.26		1.82	0.50
		0.29	3.45				1.02		1.14		1.66	0.55
		0.44	5.17				1.00		1.12		1.63	0.56
		0.58	6.89				1.00		1.12		1.63	0.56
	20°	-	-			0.43	1.00		1.09	0.70	1.63	0.07
	25°	-	-			0.41	0.87		0.92	0.67	1.41	0.68
	30°	-	-			0.39	0.76		0.78	0.63	1.24	0.80
				1	0			1				
	35°	-	-			0.37	0.66		0.66	0.60	1.07	0.95
	40°	-	-			0.35	0.57		0.55	0.57	0.93	1.14
	45°	-	-			0.33	0.50		0.47	0.54	0.81	1.34
Self-aligning ball bearings				1	0	0.40	0.4 cotα	1	0.42 cotα	0.65	0.65 cotα	15 tanα
Single row radial contact separable ball bearings (magnetic bearings)				1	0	0.5	2.5	-	-	-	-	0.2

* Permissible maximum value depends on bearing design

For 50BC02 bearing using,

$$L_n = \left(\frac{C}{P}\right)^3,$$

$$= \left(\frac{35100}{5975}\right)^3 = 202.73\ M.O.R.$$

This value of $L_n < L_n)_{\text{required}} = 788.4\ M.O.R.$ and hence the bearing is not suitable and next trial is made.

Trial 2: ***Try 50BC03 bearing for which***

Static capacity $C_0 = 38000$ N

Dynamic capacity $C = 618000$ N

Now, $$\frac{F_a}{C_0} = \frac{2000}{38000} = 0.053$$

The nearest value of $\frac{F_a}{C_0}$ from T(24-51) is $\frac{F_a}{C_0} = 0.056$ for which $e = 0.26$

Comparing $\frac{F_a}{F_r}$ with e,

$$\frac{F_a}{F_r} = 0.67 > e = 0.26$$

Therefore, $$X = 0.56 \text{ and } Y = 1.71$$

$$P = (XF_r + YF_a)C_s$$

$$= (0.56 \times 3000 + 1.71 \times 2000)1.25$$

$$= 6375 \text{ N}$$

Now, $$L_n = \left(\frac{C}{P}\right)^3$$

$$= \left(\frac{618000}{6375}\right)^3 = 911.01\ M.O.R.$$

This value of $L_n = 911.01\ M.O.R > L_n)_{\text{required}} = 788.4\ M.O.R$, hence the bearing is suitable.

Hence select 50BC03 bearing (SKF 6310) for which

$d = 50$ mm

$D = 110$ mm

B = Width of bearing = 27 mm

r = Fillet radius = 2 mm

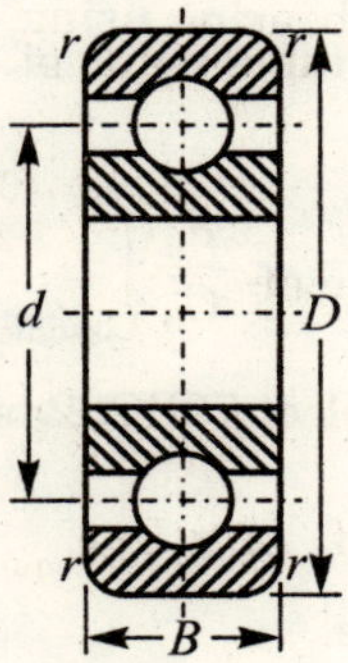

Case B: When diameter of shaft is not known

When diameter of shaft is not known, assume a suitable value of $\frac{F_a}{C_0}$ from Table (24-51).

Say $\frac{F_a}{C_0} = 0.056$ for which $e = 0.26$

From data, $\frac{F_a}{F_r} = \frac{2000}{3000} = 0.67$

Comparing $\frac{F_a}{F_r}$ with e

$$\frac{F_a}{F_r} = 0.67 > e = 0.26$$

Therefore, $X = 0.56$ and $Y = 1.71$

$$P = (XF_r + YF_a)C_s$$

$$= (0.56 \times 3000 + 1.71 \times 2000)1.25$$

$$= 6375 \text{ N}$$

From, $L_n = \left(\frac{C}{P}\right)^3$,

$$C^3 = P^3 L_n$$

$$C = P\sqrt[3]{L_n}$$

$$= 6375\sqrt[3]{788.4}$$

$$= 58892.83 \text{ N}$$

Corresponding to $C = 60{,}500$ N, (equal to or > C, calculated above) $C_0 = 45{,}000$ N

... T(24-60)

Now, $\left.\frac{F_a}{C_0}\right)_{\text{actual}} = \frac{3000}{45000} = 0.067$

The nearest table value of $\frac{F_a}{C_0} = 0.056$ for which $e = 0.26$

i.e., the value of $\left.\frac{F_a}{C_0}\right)_{\text{assumed}}$ is same as $\left.\frac{F_a}{C_0}\right)_{\text{calculated}}$

Therefore, select 70BC02 bearing for which

$d = 70$ mm

$D = 125$ mm

$B =$ Width of bearing = 24 mm

$r =$ Fillet radius = 1.5 mm

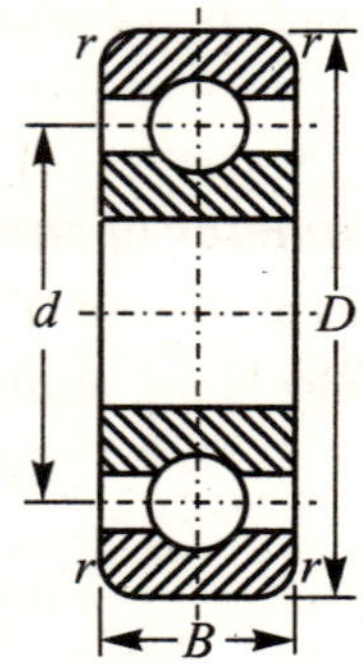

Example 7.10: Select suitable SKF ball bearings to carry a radial load of 3000 N and thrust load of 2000 N. The service imposes light shock and the bearings will be in use for 3 years at 10 hours/day. The speed of shaft is 1200 rpm. Based on strength, the shaft diameter is 50 mm.

Solution:

Step I: ***Calculation of life of bearing (L_n)***

Life of bearing, $(L_n) = 3$ years at 10 hours/day; speed = 1200 rpm

$$= 3 \times 365 \times 10 \times 60 \times 1200 \text{ Revolutions}$$

$$= 788.4 \text{ (millions of revolutions)}$$

Step II: ***Selection of bearing (SKF bearing)***

Note: *Since the diameter of shaft is known to be 50 mm based on strength, try,*

SKF 6210 or 50BC02 bearing,

SKF 6310 bearing, and

SKF 6410 bearing, in ascending order,

Calculate life, L_n of each bearing and finally select a bearing which has an expected life equal to or more than L_n calculated in step (1).

Trials to find suitable bearings

Trial 1: ***Try SKF 6210 bearing (i.e., 50BC02 bearing)***

For 50BC02 bearing, we have,

Static capacity $C_0 = 23200$ N and

Dynamic capacity $C = 35100$ N ... (T24-60)

For Ball bearings we have,

$$L_n = \left(\frac{C}{P}\right)^3 \qquad \text{... E (24-189)}$$

Where, L_n = Life of bearing in millions of revolutions.

P = Equivalent load (*i.e.*, equivalent of axial and radial loads)

$$= XF_r + YF_a \qquad \text{... E (24-190)}$$

F_r = Radial load on bearing = 3000 N

F_a = Axial load or thrust load = 2000 N

Note: *For the values of 'X' and 'Y' refer Table (24-51)*

For ball bearings being analysed,

$$\frac{F_a}{C_0} = \frac{2000\,\text{N}}{23200} = 0.086$$

The nearest Table value of $\frac{F_a}{C_0}$ is 0.084 for which constant $e = 0.28$.

Also, for the given bearing ,

$$\frac{F_a}{F_r} = \frac{2000\text{ N}}{3000\text{ N}} = 0.67$$

Comparing $\frac{F_a}{F_r}$ with 'e', we find,

$$\frac{F_a}{F_r} = 0.067 > e = 0.28$$

Therefore, $X = 0.56$ and $Y = 1.55$

$$P = 0.56 \times 3000 + 1.55 \times 2000 = 4780\,\text{N}$$

Note: *The value of P calculated above is to be multiplied by service factor, 1.25 for Light shock, 1.5 for Medium shock, and 1.75 to 2 for heavy shock.*

Therefore, considering light shock,

$$P = 4780 \times 1.25 = 5975\text{ N}$$

For Ball bearing 50BC02,

$$L_n = \left(\frac{C}{P}\right)^3$$

$$= \left(\frac{35100}{5975}\right)^3 = 202.73\ M.O.R.$$

This value of L_n is less than $L_n)_{\text{required}}$ *i.e.*, 788.4 *M.O.R.* Hence this bearing is not suitable.

Trial 2: *Try SKF 6310 bearing (i.e. 50BC03 bearing)*

For 50BC03 bearing, Referring to Table (24-61),

Static capacity $C_0 = 38000$ N

Dynamic capacity $C = 618000$ N

$$\frac{F_a}{C_0} = \frac{2000\,\text{N}}{38000\,\text{N}} = 0.053$$

The nearest value of $\frac{F_a}{C_0}$ from table is $\frac{F_a}{C_0} = 0.056$ for which $e = 0.26$

Now, $\frac{F_a}{F_r} = \frac{2000N}{3000N} = 0.67$

[which is a constant value for a given bearing]

Comparing, $\frac{F_a}{F_r}$ with 'e', we observe that,

$$\frac{F_a}{F_r} = 0.67 > e = 0.26$$

Therefore, from Table (24-51),

$$X = 0.56 \text{ and } Y = 1.71$$

$$P = [(0.56 \times 3000) + (1.171 \times 2000)]1.25$$

(Considering service factor $C_s = 1.25$),

$$P = 6375 \text{ N}$$

From $L_n = \left(\frac{C}{P}\right)^3$, we get

$$L_n = \left(\frac{61800}{6375}\right)^3 = 911.01\ M.O.R.$$

This value L_n *i.e.*, 911.01 $M.O.R. > L_n)_{\text{required}} = 788.4\ M.O.R.$

Hence select SKF 6310 bearing (*i.e.*, 50BC03 bearing). Referring Table (24-61), the dimensions of bearing are,

$d = 50$ mm

$D = 110$ mm

B = Width of bearing = 27 mm

r = Fillet radius = 2 mm

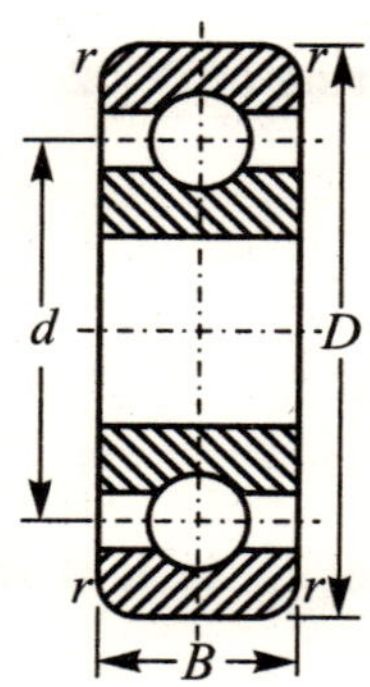

Table 24-61MDH: Deep groove ball bearings

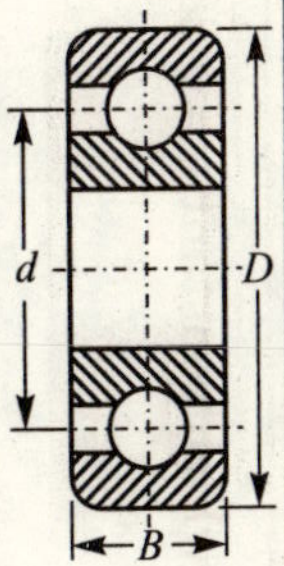

Bearing No.				Dimensions, mm				Factor			Basic load rating capacity				Fatigue load limit, F_u	Kinematically permissible speed, n	Mass kg
IS		FAG	SKF	d	D	B	r	$\frac{F_a}{C_0}$	Y	e	Static, C_0		Dynamic, C				
New No.	Old No.										FAG kN	SKF N	FAG kN	SKF N	N	rpm	
10	10BC03	6300	6300	10	30	11	0.6	.025	2.0	0.22	3.45	3400	8.15	8060	413	56000	0.058
12	12BC03	6301	6301	12	37	12	1.0	.04	1.8	0.24	4.15	4150	9.65	9750	176	53000	0.062
15	15BC03	6302	6302	15	42	13	1.0	.07	1.6	.27	5.40	5400	11.40	11400	228	43000	0.087
17	17BC03	6303	6303	17	47	14	1.0	.13	1.4	.31	6.55	6550	13.40	13500	275	39000	0.116
20	20BC03	6304	04	20	52	15	1.1	.25	1.2	.37	7.80	7800	16.00	15900	335	34000	0.153
25	25BC03	6305	05	25	62	17	1.1	.05	1.0	.44	11.40	11600	22.40	22500	490	28000	0.237
30	30BC03	6306	06	30	72	19	1.1				16.30	16000	29.00	28100	670	24000	0.355
35	35BC03	6307	07	35	80	21	1.5				19.00	19000	33.50	33200	815	20000	0.472
40	40BC03	6308	08	40	90	23	1.5				25.00	24000	42.50	41000	1020	18000	0.639
45	45BC03	6309	09	45	100	25	1.5				32.00	31500	53.00	52700	1340	16000	0.853
50	50BC03	6310	6310	50	110	27	2				38.00	38000	62.00	61800	1600	14000	1.090
55	55BC03	6311	11	55	120	29	2				47.00	45000	76.50	71500	1900	13000	1.400
60	60BC03	6312	12	60	130	31	2.1				52.00	52000	81.50	81900	2200	12000	1.750
65	65BC03	6313	13	65	140	33	2.1				60.00	60000	93.00	92300	2500	11000	2.140
70	70BC03	6314	14	70	150	35	2.1				68.00	68000	104.00	104000	2750	10000	2.610
75	75BC03	6315	15	75	160	37	2.1				76.50	76500	114.00	114000	3000	9500	3.180
80	80BC03	6316	16	80	170	39	2.1				86.50	86500	122.00	124000	3250	9000	3.800
85	85BC03	6317	17	85	180	41	3.0				88.00	96500	125.00	133000	3550	8000	4.350
90	90BC03	6318	18	90	190	43	3.0				102.00	10800	134.00	143000	3800	8000	5.430
95	95BC03	6319	19	95	200	45	3.0				112.00	118000	143.00	153000	4150	7500	6.230
100	100BC03	6320	20	100	215	47	3.0				134.00	140000	163.00	174000	4750	7000	7.670
105	105BC03	6321	21	105	225	49	3.0				146.00	153000	173.00	182000	5100	6700	8.700
110	110BC03	6322	22	110	240	50	3.0				166.00	180000	190.00	203000	5700	6300	10.300
120	120BC03	6324	24	120	260	55	3.0				190.00	186000	212.00	208000	5700	6000	12.800

Example 7.11: Select suitable SKF deep groove single row ball bearings to sustain a radial load 2 kN and axial load of 3 kN. The service imposes medium shock and the bearings will be in use for 2 years at 10 hours/day. The speed of shaft is 1000 rpm. Based on strength, the shaft diameter is 60 mm.

Solution:

Step 1: Calculation of life of bearing (L_n)

$$L_n = 2 \text{ years at } 10\,\text{hours/day; speed} = 1000 \text{ rpm}$$

$$= 2 \times 365 \times 10 \times 60 \times 1000 \text{ Revolutions}$$

$$= 438\ M.O.R.$$

Step 2: Selection of bearing (SKF bearing)

Since the shaft diameter is given, equal to 60 mm *i.e.*, $d = 60$ mm , Try

SKF 6212, (*i.e.*, 60BC02 bearing)

SKF 6312, and

SKF 6412 bearing, in ascending order.

Select one of the above bearings which has a life L_n equal to or more than $L_n)_{\text{required}} = 438\ M.O.R.$

Trials to find suitable bearing

Trial 1: ***Try SKF 6212 bearing (i.e. 60BC02 bearing)***

For 60BC02 bearing,

Static capacity $\quad C_0 = 32500$ N ,

Dynamic capacity $\quad C = 47500$ N ... T (24-60)

Also, For Ball bearings,

$$L_n = \left(\frac{C}{P}\right)^3 \qquad \text{... E (24-189)}$$

Where, L_n = Life of bearing in $M.O.R.$

P = Equivalent load (Equivalent of F_a and F_r)

$$= XF_r + YF_a \qquad \text{... E (24-190)}$$

F_r = Radial load = 2 kN = 2000 N

F_a = Axial load or Thrust load = 3 kN = 3000 N

To find 'X' and 'Y' [Refer Table (24-51)]

For the ball bearing being analysed,

$$\frac{F_a}{C_0} = 0.084 \text{ for which constant } e = 0.28$$

Also, $\dfrac{F_a}{F_r} = \dfrac{3000\text{ N}}{2000\text{ N}} = 1.5$

Comparing $\dfrac{F_a}{F_r}$ with 'e', we find

$$\frac{F_a}{F_r} = 1.5 > e = 0.28$$

Therefore, $X = 0.56$ and $Y = 1.55$

Now, $P = (XF_r + YF_a)C_s$

$= (0.56 \times 2000 + 1.55 \times 3000)1.5; [C_s = 1.5 \text{ for medium shock}]$

$= 8655\text{ N}$

$L_n = \left(\dfrac{C}{P}\right)^3$ becomes

$$= \left(\frac{47500}{8655}\right)^3 = 165.3\,M.O.R < L_n)_{\text{required}} = 438\,M.O.R.$$

Hence this bearing is not suitable.

Trial 2: *Try SKF 6312 bearing (i.e. 60BC03 bearing)*

For 60BC03 bearing,

Static capacity $C_0 = 52000\text{ N}$,

Dynamic capacity $C = 81900\text{ N}$ ... T(24-61)

Also, $\dfrac{F_a}{C_0} = \dfrac{2000\text{N}}{38000\text{N}} = 0.053$

Referring T(24-51), the nearest value of $\dfrac{F_a}{C_0}$ from table is $\dfrac{F_a}{C_0} = 0.056$ for which $e = 0.26$

Comparing $\dfrac{F_a}{F_r}$ with e

$$\frac{F_a}{F_r} = 1.5 > e = 0.26$$

Therefore, $X = 0.56$ and $Y = 1.71$

$P = (XF_r + YF_a)C_s$ becomes

$= [(0.56 \times 2000) + (1.71 \times 3000)]1.5$

$= 9375\text{ N}$

Therefore, $L_n = \left(\dfrac{C}{P}\right)^3 = \left(\dfrac{81900}{9375}\right)^3 = 666.71\,M.O.R > L_n)_{\text{required}} = 438\,M.O.R.$

Therefore, select SKF 6312 bearing (*i.e.,* 60BC03 bearing) which has the dimensions.

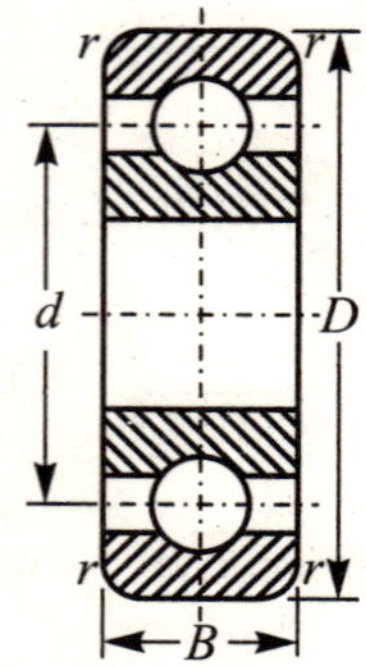

$d = 60$ mm

$D = 130$ mm

B = Width of bearing = 31 mm

r = Fillet radius = 2.1 mm

Example 7.12: A single row ball bearing is to carry an axial load of 2 kN and radial of 3 kN. The service imposes light shock and the bearing will be in use for 3 years at 10 hours/day. Taking speed of shaft equal to 1200 rpm, select suitable medium series SKF ball bearing.

Solution:

Step I: ***Calculation of Life of bearing (L_n)***

Life of bearing,

$$L_n = 3 \text{ years at } 10 \text{ hours/day; speed} = 1200 \text{ rpm}$$

$$= \frac{3 \times 365 \times 10 \times 60 \times 1200}{10^6} \text{ millions of revolutions}$$

$$= 788.4 \; M.O.R.$$

Step II: Selection of bearing (SKF bearing)

Note: *In this Problem, since the shaft diameter is not known. Assume $\frac{F_a}{C_0}$ at random from Table(24-51) MDH and arrive at the actual value of $\frac{F_a}{C_0}$.*

Assuming, $\frac{F_a}{C_0} = 0.056$; we find $e = 0.26$ ... T (24-51)

For the given bearing,

$$\frac{F_a}{F_r} = \frac{2000 \text{ N}}{3000 \text{ N}} = 0.67 \text{ (a constant for a given bearing)}$$

Comparing $\frac{F_a}{F_r}$ with e, we find,

$$\frac{F_a}{F_r} = 0.67 > e = 0.26$$

Therefore, $X = 0.56$ and $Y = 1.71$

Hence, $P = (XF_r + YF_a)C_s$ becomes

$$= [(0.56 \times 3000 + 1.71 \times 2000)]1.25 \text{ (assuming light shock)}$$

$$= 6375 \text{ N}$$

From, $$L_n = \left(\frac{C}{P}\right)^3 \quad \text{... E (24-189)}$$

$$C^3 = P^3 L_n$$

$$= (6375)^3 \times 788.4$$

Therefore, $C = 58592.83$ N

Referring medium series (03series) ball bearings, from T(24-61), corresponding to $C = 61800$ N , $C_0 = 38000$ N

$$\left.\frac{F_a}{C_0}\right]_{actual} = \frac{2000 \text{ N}}{38000 \text{ N}} = 0.0526$$

The nearest value of $\frac{F_a}{C_0}$ from table (24-51) is $\frac{F_a}{C_0} = 0.056$

Hence the assumption $\frac{F_a}{C_0} = 0.056$ is valid and referring to Table (24-61), select SKF 6310 bearing.

For SKF 6310 bearing, the dimensions of bearing are,

$d = 50$ mm
$D = 110$ mm
B = Width of bearing = 27 mm
r = Fillet radius = 27 mm

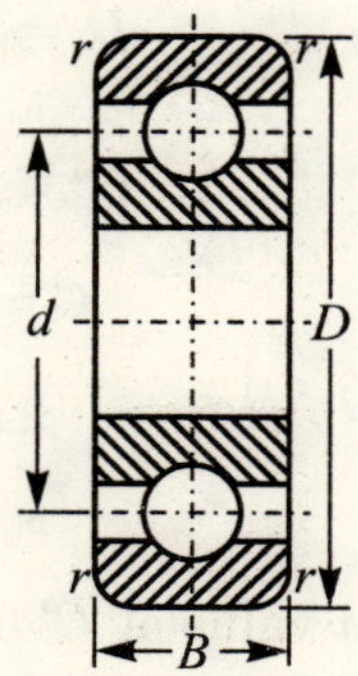

Example 7.13: Select suitable light series deep groove SKF ball bearing to sustain radial load of 2 kN and axial load of 3 kN. The service imposes medium shock and the bearings are to be in use for 2 years at 50 hours/week. The speed of shaft is 1200 rpm.

Solution:

Step I: *Calculation of Life of bearing (L_n)*

$$L_n = 2 \text{ years at } 50 \text{ hours/week; speed} = 1200 \text{ rpm}$$

(Note: 1 year has 52 weeks)

$$= \frac{2 \times 52 \times 50 \times 60 \times 1200}{10^6} M.O.R.$$

$$= 374.4 \; M.O.R.$$

Step II: ***Selection of bearing (SKF Bearing)***

Note: *Since diameter of shaft is unknown, select* $\frac{F_a}{C_0}$ *at random from Table (24-51)*

Assuming $\frac{F_a}{C_0} = 0.056,\ e = 0.26$

For the given bearing ,

$$\frac{F_a}{F_r} = \frac{3000\text{ N}}{2000\text{ N}} = 1.5$$

Comparing $\frac{F_a}{F_r}$ with 'e', $\frac{F_a}{F_r} = 1.5 > e = 0.26$

Therefore, $X = 0.56, Y = 1.71$

Now, $P = (XF_r + YF_a)C_s$

$$= [(0.56 \times 3000 + 1.71 \times 2000)]1.5 \quad [C_s = 1.5 \text{ for medium shock}]$$

$$= 9375 \text{ N}$$

From $L_n = \left(\frac{C}{P}\right)^3$

$$C^3 = P^3 L_n$$

i.e., $C = P\sqrt[3]{L_n}$

$$= 9375 \times \sqrt[3]{374.4}$$

$$= 67569.37 \text{ N}$$

The nearest value of 'C' from T(24-60) i.e. light series bearings, is $C = 70200$ N for which $C_0 = 55000$ N

Now, $\left.\frac{F_a}{C_0}\right)_{\text{actual}} = \frac{3000}{55000} = 0.0545$

The nearest table value of $\frac{F_a}{C_0} = 0.056$ for which $e = 0.26$

Note: *The assumed value of* $\frac{F_a}{C_0} = 0.056$ *is same as the actual value* $\frac{F_a}{C_0}$

Therefore, referring Table (24-60), Select SKF 6216 bearing (*i.e.,* 80BC03 bearing) whose dimensions are,

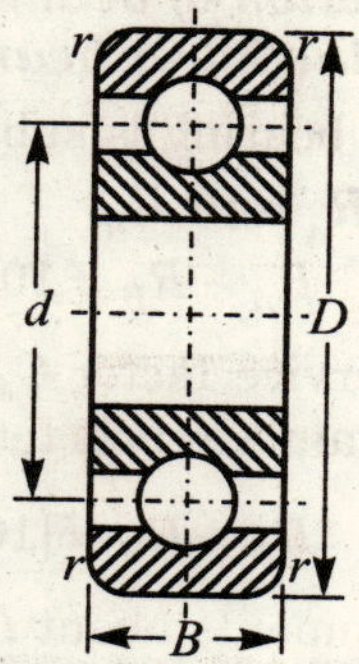

$d = 80$ mm

$D = 140$ mm

B = Width of bearing = 26 mm

r = Fillet radius = 2.0 mm

Example 7.14: Select suitable deep groove SKF ball bearings for the upper and lower bearings of a vertical shaft shown in figure driven by a V-belt. It has been determined that the resultant force $(T_1 + T_2)$ acting on shaft is 10 kN. There is an axial thrust of 2 kN which is taken by lower bearings only. Base the design on steady loading and a life of 10000 hours. The minimum shaft diameter at the lower bearing based on strength is 40 mm. The shaft speed is 300 rpm.

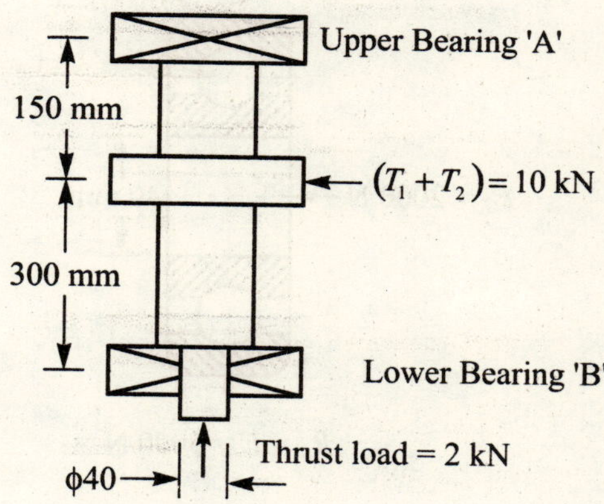

Solution:

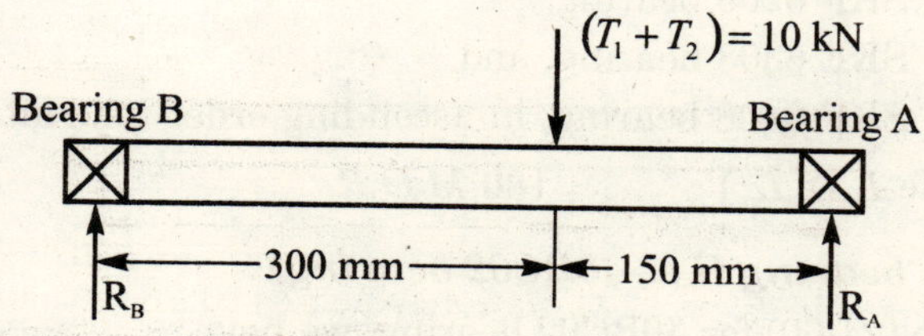

Step I: ***Calculation of Life of bearing (L_n)***

$$L_n = 10000 \text{ hours; Speed of shaft} = 300 \text{ rpm}$$

$$= \frac{10000 \times 60 \times 3000}{10^6} M.O.R.$$

$$= 180 \; M.O.R.$$

Step II: ***Selection of bearings***

(a) Consider the lower bearing 'B'

The lower bearing is subjected to thrust load of 2 kN and radial load R_B

To calculate R_A and R_B

$$R_A + R_B = 10 \text{ kN} = T_1 + T_2$$

Taking service factor $C_s = 1.5$ to take into account belt vibrations and additional force necessary to maintain belt tension,

$$R_A + R_B = \left(10 \times 10^3\right)1.5 = 15 \times 10^3 \quad \ldots (1)$$

Taking moments about B,

$$R_A \times 450 = (T_1 + T_2)300 = \left(15 \times 10^3\right)$$

Therefore, $R_A = \dfrac{15 \times 10^3 \times 300}{450} = 10000 \text{ N}$

From (1), $R_B = 5000 \text{ N} = F_r$

Load on bearing B

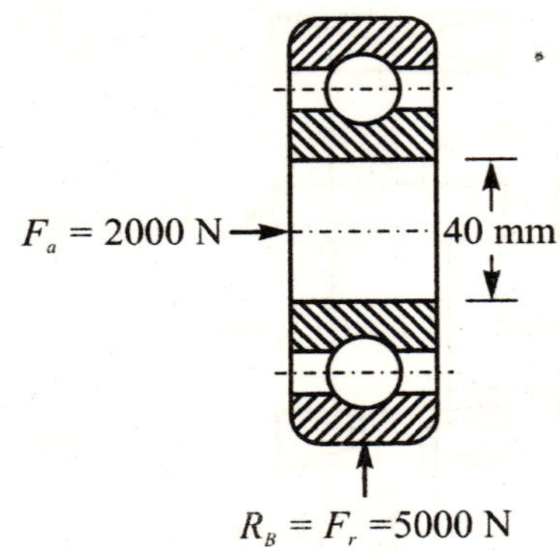

Design of bearing 'B'

Note: *The diameter of lower bearing is known and is equal to 40 mm.*

Therefore, try SKF 6208 bearing,
SKF 6308 bearing, and
SKF 6408 bearing, in ascending order (one after other) and select that bearing which has a life $L_n \geq L_n)_{\text{required}} = 180 \; M.O.R.$

Trial 1: ***Try SKF 6208 bearing (i.e., 40BC02 bearing)***

Referring Table (24-60) for 40BC02 bearing, we have

Static Capacity $C_0 = 19000$ N

Dynamic Capacity $C = 307000$ N

For the given bearing,

$$\frac{F_a}{C_0} = \frac{2000 \text{ N}}{19000 \text{ N}} = 0.105$$

Referring T(24-51), the nearest value of $\frac{F_a}{C_0}$ from table is $\frac{F_a}{C_0} = 0.11$ for which $e = 0.30$

Now, $\frac{F_a}{F_r} = \frac{2000 \text{ N}}{5000 \text{ N}} = 0.4$

Comparing $\frac{F_a}{F_r}$ with 'e',

$$\frac{F_a}{F_r} = 0.4 > e = 0.30$$

Therefore, $X = 0.56$ and $Y = 1.45$

Therefore,
$$P = (XF_r + YF_a)$$
$$= (0.56 \times 5000 + 1.45 \times 2000)$$
$$= 5700 \text{ N}$$

Now
$$L_n = \left(\frac{C}{P}\right)^3 = \left(\frac{30700}{5700}\right)^3 = 156.24 \; M.O.R.$$

Which is less than $L_n)_{\text{required}} = 180 \; M.O.R.$. Hence this bearing 40BC02 is not suitable

Trial 2: *Try 40BC03 bearing,*

Referring Table (24-61), for 40BC03,

Static capacity, $C_0 = 24000$ N

Dynamic capacity, $C = 41000$ N

Now, $\frac{F_a}{C_0} = \frac{2000 \text{ N}}{24000 \text{ N}} = 0.083$

The nearest Table value of $\frac{F_a}{C_0} = 0.084$ for which $e = 0.28$.

Comparing $\frac{F_a}{F_r}$ with 'e',

$$\frac{F_a}{F_r} = 0.4 > e = 0.28$$

Therefore, $X = 0.56, Y = 1.55$

$$P = XF_r + YF_a$$
$$= (0.56 \times 5000 + 1.55 \times 2000) = 5900 \text{ N}$$

Now,
$$L_n = \left(\frac{C}{P}\right)^3$$
$$= \left(\frac{41000}{5900}\right)^3 = 335.58 \; M.O.R. > L_n)_{\text{required}} = 180 \; M.O.R.$$

Therefore, select SKF 6408 bearing (*i.e.*, 40BC03 bearing) which has dimensions as shown

$d = 40$ mm

$D = 90$ mm

B = Width of bearing = 23 mm

r = Fillet radius = 1.5 mm

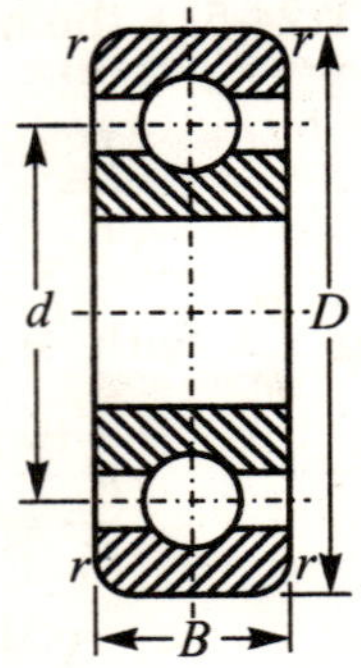

Design of bearing A

The upper bearing A is subjected to only load R_A

i.e., $$F_r = R_A = 10000 \text{ N}$$

Note: *Since no axial load acts on this bearing,*

$$P = F_r = R_A = 10000 \text{ N}$$

Assuming medium series ball bearing,

$$L_n = \left(\frac{C}{P}\right)^3$$

$$C = P\sqrt[3]{L_n}$$

$$= 10000 \times \sqrt[3]{180} = 56462.16 \text{ N}$$

Corresponding to $C = 61800$ N from Table (24-61) MDH medium series ball bearing, choose SKF 6310 bearing (*i.e.*, 50BC03 bearing).

For 50BC03 bearing,

$d = 50$ mm

$D = 110$ mm

B = Width of bearing = 27 mm

r = Fillet radius = 2 mm

Example 7.15: The thrust on the propeller shaft of a marine engine is taken up by 10 collars having internal and external diameters 600 mm and 800 mm respectively. The speed of shaft is 100 rpm. Taking coefficient of friction as 0.04, bearing pressure on collars as 0.5 N/mm². Determine,

(i) The total thrust on collars and

(ii) The power absorbed in overcoming friction using

(a) Uniform pressure theory and

(b) Uniform wear theory.

Solution:

Case (a): *Uniform Pressure Theory*

W, the total thrust on collars is obtained from equation,

$$P = \frac{W}{i \times 0.784\left(d_1^2 - d_2^2\right)} \quad \text{... E(24-120)}$$

Where,

P = Bearing pressure = 0.5 N/mm^2

d_1 = Maximum diameter of collars = 800 mm

d_2 = Minimum diameter of collars = 600 mm

i = Number of collars = 10

Therefore, substituting in equation E(24-120), yields,

$$0.5 = \frac{W}{10 \times 0.784\left(800^2 - 600^2\right)}$$

Therefore, $W = 1097600 \text{ N} = 10.976 \times 10^5 \text{N}$

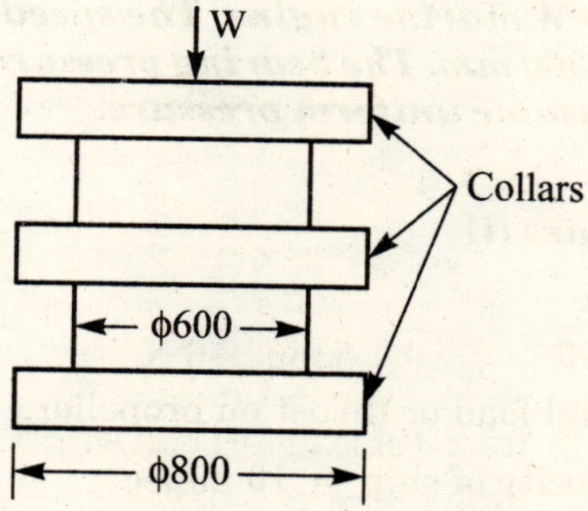

(ii) To find power absorbed in overcoming friction

For uniform intensity of pressure, the total friction moment of frictional torque is given by,

$$M_t = \frac{1}{3}\mu W\left[\frac{d_1^3 - d_2^3}{d_1^2 - d_2^2}\right] \quad \text{... E(24-122)}$$

$$= \frac{1}{3} \times 0.04\left(10.976 \times 10^5\right)\left[\frac{800^3 - 600^3}{800^2 - 600^2}\right]$$

$$= 15.471 \times 10^6 \text{ N-mm}$$

But, $$M_t = \frac{9550N \times 10^3}{n}$$

i.e., $$15.471 \times 10^6 = \frac{9500 \times N \times 10^3}{100}$$

$$N = 162 \text{ kW}$$

Case (b): Uniform Wear Theory

For uniform wear, the total frictional torque is given by,

$$M_t = \mu W\left(\frac{d_1 + d_2}{4}\right) \quad \text{... E(24-123b)}$$

$$= 0.04 \times 10.976 \times 10^5 \left(\frac{800 + 600}{4}\right)$$

$$= 15.37 \times 10^6 \text{ N-mm}$$

But, $$M_t = \frac{9550N \times 10^3}{n}$$

i.e., $$15.37 \times 10^6 = \frac{9550N \times 10^3}{100}$$

Therefore, $$N = 160.905 \text{ kW}$$

Example 7.16: Determine the number of collars and power of a multi collar thrust bearing for the propeller shaft of a 600 kW marine engine. The speed of shaft is 200 mm and the maximum diameter of collar is 300 mm. The bearing pressure is not to exceed 0.5 N/mm². The speed of ship is 10 m/sec. Assume uniform pressure.

Solution:

(i) To find the number of collars (i)

We have power $$N = \frac{Wv}{1000} \quad \text{... (1)}$$

Where, W = Axial load or thrust on propeller.

v = Velocity of ship = 10 m/sec

Substituting (1)

Therefore, $$600 = \frac{W \times 10}{1000}$$

i.e., $$W = 600 \times 10^2 \text{ newton}$$

But, $$W = ip \times 0.784\left(d_1^2 - d_2^2\right) \quad \text{... E(24-120)}$$

i.e., $$600 \times 10^2 = i \times 0.5 \times 0.784\left(300^2 - 200^2\right)$$

$$i = 3.06$$

Use, $$i = 4 \text{ collars}$$

(ii) To find the frictional torque, M_t.

For uniform wear,

$$M_t = \mu W\left(\frac{d_1 + d_2}{4}\right) \quad \text{... E(24-123b)}$$

Where, μ = Coefficient of friction

$$= 83.8\frac{v^{0.5}}{P^{0.67}} \quad \text{... E(24-125)}$$

v is in m/sec and obtained from

$$v = \frac{\pi dn}{60}$$

$$d = \frac{d_1 + d_2}{2}$$

$$= \frac{300+200}{2} = 250 \text{ mm} = 0.25 \text{ m}$$

Therefore, $v = \frac{\pi}{60} \times 0.25 \times 250$

$$= 3.2725 \text{ m/sec}$$

$$P = \text{Pressure} = 0.5 \text{N/mm}^2 = 0.5 \times 10^6 \text{ N/m}^2$$

Therefore, $\mu = \frac{83.8 \times (3.2725)^{0.5}}{\left(0.5 \times 10^6\right)^{0.67}}$

$$= 0.023$$

Frictional torque M_t is

$$M_t = \mu W\left(\frac{d_1 + d_2}{4}\right)$$

$$= 0.023\left(600 \times 10^2\right)\left[\frac{300+200}{4}\right]$$

$$= 1.725 \times 10^5 \text{ N-mm}$$

Friction power is obtained from equation

$$M_t = \frac{9550 \times \text{Power} \times 10^3}{n}$$

i.e., $1.725 \times 10^5 = \frac{9550 \times \text{Power} \times 10^3}{250}$

Therefore, Friction power = 4.516 kW.

Example 7.17: Determine the number of thrust collars required to sustain a load of 50 kN on a shaft 100 mm diameter when the allowable bearing pressure is 0.5 N/mm². If $\mu = 0.03$ and the shaft rotates at 250 rpm, determine the power absorbed in friction.

Solution:

(i) To find the number of collars (i)

Bearing pressure,

$$P = \frac{W}{i \times 0.784\left(d_1^2 - d_2^2\right)} \quad \text{... E(24-120)}$$

Where, $P = 0.5 \text{ N/mm}^2$.

i = Number of collars.

W = Thrust load on collars $= 50 \text{ kN} = 50 \times 10^3 \text{N}$

d_1 = Maximum diameter of collar.

d_2 = Minimum diameter of collar.

= Diameter of shaft = 100 mm

Assuming, $d_1 = 1.5d,$

$$d_1 = 1.5 \times 100 = 150 \text{ mm}$$

Therefore, from E(24-120),

$$0.5 = \frac{50 \times 10^3}{i \times 0.784 \times (150^2 - 100^2)}$$

$$i = 10.204$$

Use, $i = 11$ Collars

(ii) To find the power absorbed in friction

Torque $M_t = \mu W\left(\frac{d_1 + d_2}{4}\right)$ ... E(24-123b)

(Assuming uniform wear theory)

$$M_t = 0.03(50 \times 10^3)\left(\frac{150 + 100}{4}\right)$$

$$= 93750 \text{ N-mm}$$

But, $M_t = \frac{9550N \times 10^3}{n}$

i.e., $93750 = \frac{9550N \times 10^3}{250}$

Therefore, $N = 2.454 \text{ kW}$

EXERCISE

1. A 100 mm journal bearing of length 100 mm supports a load of 15 kN on a journal running at 1800 rpm. Assuming $\frac{d}{c} = 1000$ and an oil having viscosity of 15 cP at the operating temperature, determine,

   (*a*) (*i*) Coefficient of friction using McKee's equation.

   (*ii*) Coefficient of friction using Petroff's equation.

   (*iii*) Coefficient of friction using Raimondi and Boyd curve.

   (*b*) The amount of heat generated using coefficient of friction obtained from

   (*i*) McKee's equation.

   (*ii*) Petroff's equation.

2. A journal bearing 175 mm in diameter, 250 mm long supports a load of 10 kN at 1400 rpm. If the diametral clearance is 0.2 mm and the bearing wastes 2000 watts in friction, determine the viscosity of oil in cP at the operating temperature.

3. A journal bearing 100 mm long supports a load of 10 kN on a 75 mm diameter journal running at 1000 rpm. The diameteral clearance is 0.08 mm. What is the viscosity of oil in cP if the temperature of bearing surface is to be limited to 80°C when in still air at 25°C. Assume that the heat generated is all dissipated.

4. A rigid bronze bearing and a hardened and ground steel journal is used to support a load of 5 kN at 600 rpm. Abundant oil is supplied by means of oiling rings. Assuming temperature of oil 80°C, determine,

   (*i*) The length and diameter of bearing.

   (*ii*) The coefficient of friction using McKee's equation.

   (*iii*) The heat generated.

   (*iv*) The heat dissipated based on projected area of bearing.

   (*v*) Sommerfeld number.

5. A full journal bearing 100 mm in diameter and 150 mm long supports a load of 30 kN. The speed of shaft is 600 rpm. The bearing operates in SAE 20 oil at 70°C. Calculate,

   (*i*) The minimum film thickness.

   (*ii*) Heat lost due to friction.

   (*iii*) Check whether artificial cooling is required.

6. Select suitable SKF ball bearing to sustain radial load of 4 kN and axial load of 3 kN. The service imposes medium shock and the bearings will be in use for 4 years at 10 hours / day. The speed of the shaft is 1200 rpm. Based on strength, the shaft diameter is 60mm.

7. A single row ball bearing is to carry an axial load of 3 kN and radial load of 4 kN. The service imposes medium shock and the bearings will be in use for 3 years at 8 hours/day. Select suitable medium service ball bearings.

8. Select suitable deep groove SKF ball bearings for the upper and lower bearings of a vertical shaft shown in figure driven by a V-belt. It is determined that the resultant stress ($T_1 + T_2$) acting on shaft is 15 kN. There is an axial thrust of 3 kN taken by lower bearing only.

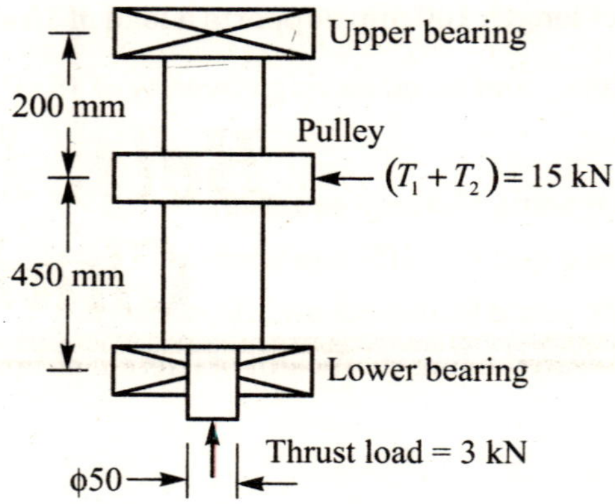

Base the design on steady loading and a life of 15,000 hours.

CHAPTER

8

Belt, Rope and Chain Drives

NOTATIONS AND SYMBOLS USED

A = Area of cross-section of wire rope, mm^2.

a_1 = Width of flat belt; mm. Width of ball bearing; mm.

C = Centre distance between pulleys, chains; mm.

C_p = Centre distance in pitches; mm.

C_{max} = Maximum centre distance; mm.

C_{min} = Minimum centre distance; mm.

D = Diameter of larger pulley; mm.

d = Diameter of smaller pulley; mm.

d_e = Equivalent pitch diameter; mm.

d_p = Diameter of small pulley; mm.

d_w = Wire diameter; mm.

F_a = Correction factor for industrial service.

= Allowable chain pull; N.

F_b = Small diameter factor.

F_c = Correction factor for length of belt.

F_d = Correction factor for angle of lap.

F_θ = Chain pull; N.

F_u = Ultimate load; N.

i = Number of chains in a chain drive.

= Number of ropes in a rope drive.

= Number of V-belts.

K = A constant used in flat belt drive.

K_l = Load factor.

K_s = Service factor.

L = Length of chain; mm.

= Length of flat belt; mm.

L_p = Length of chain in pitches; mm.
N = Power transmitted in kilowatts.
n_1 = Speed of sprocket Pinion; rpm.
= Speed of smaller pulley; rpm.
n_2 = Speed of sprocket Gear; rpm.
= Speed of larger pulley; rpm.
P = Pitch of chain; mm.
P_b = Bending load in rope; N.
= Bearing pressure in block brake; N/mm^2.
θ = Angle of lap of belt; Degree.
θ_S = Angle of lap on small pulley; Degree.
θ_L = Angle of lap on large pulley; Degree.
T_1 = Maximum tension in belt; N.
T_2 = Minimum tension in belt; N.
T_C = Centrifugal tension; N/mm^2.
t = Thickness of V-belt; mm.
= Thickness of flat belt; mm.
v = Velocity of chain; m/sec.
w = Density of belt material; N/m^3.
Z_1 = Number of teeth on sprocket Pinion.
Z_2 = Number of teeth on sprocket Gear.

INTRODUCTION

Flat and *V*-belts (also called *V-V* belts) are used to transmit power between parallel shafts separated by large centre distance where it is not necessary to maintain exact speed ratio between the shafts.

Open and Cross Belt Drives

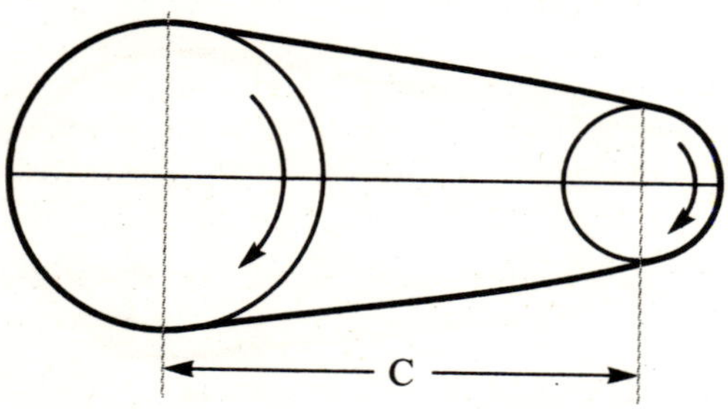

Open Belt Drive

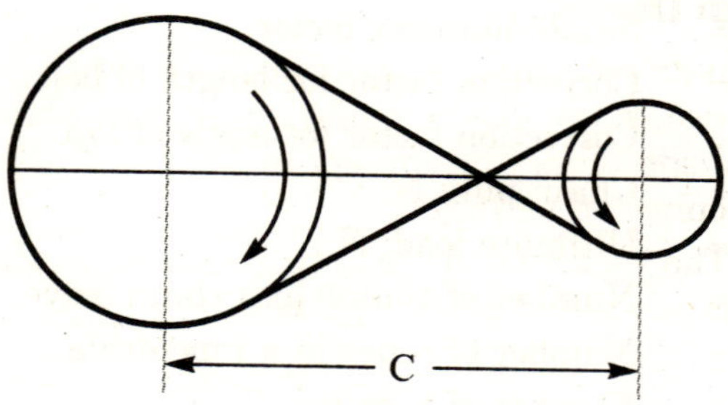

Cross Belt Drive

In an open belt drive, both driver and driven pulleys rotate in the same direction whereas in a cross belt drive, the pulleys rotate in the opposite direction as shown. The belt in cross belt drive is subjected to more wear and tear because of rubbing of belt and hence cross belt drive is used for transmission of small power between parallel shafts at slow speeds.

Belt Design

Belt design involves selection of proper size of belt to transmit the required power or calculation of power transmitted knowing the cross-section of belt (flat or V-belt).

The power transmitted by a belt is a function of the effective belt tension (T_1-T_2) and the velocity of belt. Further it depends on the coefficient of friction μ, the angle of lap on the pulley θ and groove angle in case of V-belt and rope drives.

Power transmitted is given by,

$$N = \frac{(T_1 - T_2)v}{1000} \text{ kW}$$

Where, T_1 and T_2 are the belt tensions on the high tension side and slack side, in 'N',

v = velocity of belt = $\pi d n_1 = \pi D n_2$

Where, 'd' and 'D' are the diameters of small and large pulleys and n_1 and n_2 are the respective speeds of pulleys.

Note: *v is in m/sec*

Velocity ratio,

We have, v = velocity of belt

$$= \pi d n_1 = \pi D n_2$$

i.e.,

$$d n_1 = D n_2$$

or

$$\frac{D}{d} = \frac{n_1}{n_2}$$

The ratio, $\frac{D}{d} = \frac{n_1}{n_2}$ is called velocity ratio.

It is to be noted that velocity ratio is > 1, because D > d and $n_1 > n_2$.

Considering belt thickness, 't',

Velocity ratio $= \frac{D+t}{d+t}$

Chain Drives

Chain drivers are used to transmit power between parallel shafts separated by a small centre distance where exact speed ratio is to be maintained between the shafts. The toothed wheels, called sprockets (the smaller sprocket is called Sprocket Pinion and the larger Sprocket Gear) are connected by chain.

The velocity of drive is based on the pitch of chain 'p' and number of teeth Z_1 on the Pinion and is calculated using equation,

$$v = p\frac{z_1 n_1}{60} \quad \text{... E(21-105)}$$

Where, n_1 = speed of sprocket pinion.

Z_1 = number of teeth on Pinion

The pitch of chain 'p' is obtained from equation,

$$p \le 25\left(\frac{900}{n_1}\right)^{\frac{2}{3}} \quad \text{... E(21-160a)}$$

The number of teeth Z_1 on Pinion depends on the Transmission ratio given by,
Transmission ratio,

$$\frac{n_1}{n_2} = \frac{Z_2}{Z_1} = \frac{d_2}{d_1}$$

Where,
Z_2 = Number of teeth on sprocket Gear
Z_1 = Number of teeth on sprocket Pinion
d_2 = Pitch circle diameter of sprocket Gear
d_1 = Pitch circle diameter of sprocket Pinion

Derivation of Expression for Length of Belt

(a) Open belt drive.

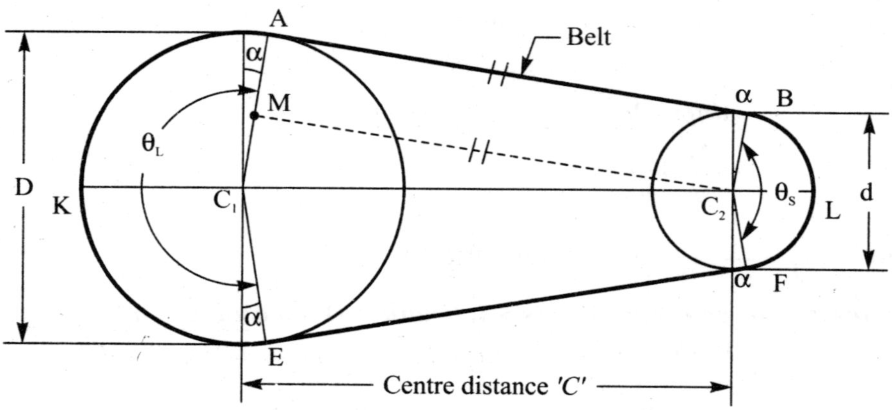

Consider an open belt drive connecting pulleys of diameters '*D*' and '*d*' separated by a centre distance $C_1C_2 = C$.

Let θ_L and θ_s be the angle of lap of belt on the large and small pulleys respectively. The length of belt required for the open belt drive from figure is,

$$L = \text{Length of the arc } AKE + \text{Length of the arc } BLF + 2 \text{ Length } AB \quad \text{... (1)}$$

Where,

Length of arc, $AKE = \frac{D}{2}\theta_L$

$$= \frac{D}{2}(180 + 2\alpha)\text{; because arc length } s = r\theta.$$

Length of arc,

$$BLF = \frac{d}{2}\theta_s$$

$$= \frac{d}{2}(180 - 2\alpha)$$

Length of Portion, $AB =$ Length of C_2M (because C_2M is parallel to AB)

From, right angle triangle C_1C_2M,

$$C_1M = C_1A - AM$$

Where, $C_1A = \frac{D}{2}$, $AM = C_2B = \frac{d}{2}$

Therefore, $C_1M = \frac{D}{2} - \frac{d}{2} = \frac{D-d}{2}$

For right angle triangle C_1C_2M,

$$(C_2M)^2 = (C_1C_2)^2 - (C_1M)^2$$

$$= C^2 - \left(\frac{D-d}{2}\right)^2 = \frac{4C^2 - (D-d)^2}{4}; \quad \text{Since } C_1C_2 = C$$

i.e., $C_2M = \frac{\sqrt{4C^2 - (D-d)^2}}{2} = AB$

Therefore, from (1) length of belt,

$$L = \frac{D}{2}(180 + 2\alpha) + \frac{d}{2}(180 - 2\alpha) + 2\left[\frac{\sqrt{4C^2 - (D-d)^2}}{2}\right]$$

$$= \frac{1}{2}\left[D(180 + 2\alpha) + d(180 - 2\alpha)\right] + \sqrt{4C^2 + (D-d)^2}$$

$$= \frac{1}{2}\left[D(\theta_L) + d(\theta_s)\right] + \sqrt{4C^2 - (D-d)^2} \quad \text{...E(21-7)}$$

Where, $\theta_L =$ Angle of lap on large pulley

$$= 180 + 2\alpha$$

$$= 180 + 2\sin^{-1}\left(\frac{D-d}{2C}\right)$$

$$= \pi + 2\sin^{-1}\left(\frac{D-d}{2C}\right) \quad \text{... E(21-10a)}$$

Similarly, $\theta_S =$ Angle of lap on small pulley is,

$$= 180 - 2\alpha$$

$$= 180 - 2\sin^{-1}\left(\frac{D-d}{2C}\right) \quad \text{... E(21-10b)}$$

(b) Derivation of length of belt required for cross belt drive

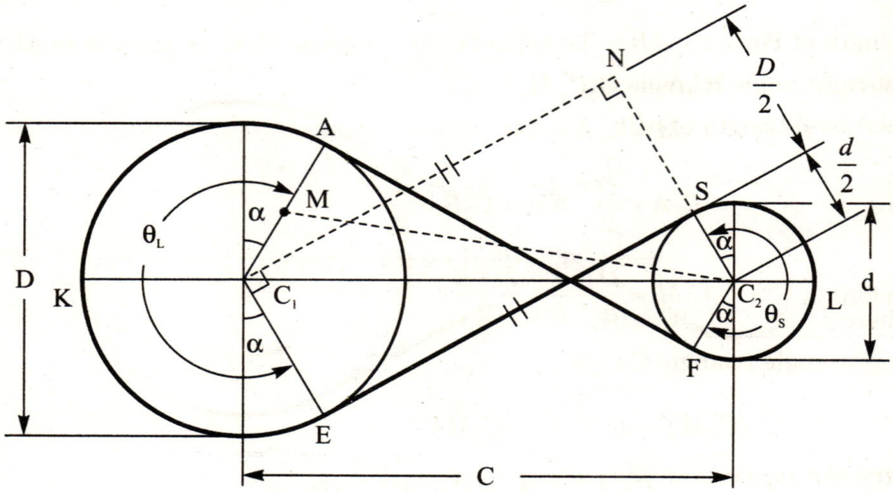

For a cross belt drive connecting pulleys of diameter 'D' and 'd' separated by centre distance $C_1C_2 = C$, let the angle lap on large pulley θ_L = Angle lap on small pulley = $\theta_S = 180 + 2\alpha$

Therefore, length of belt 'L' is given by,

$$L = \text{Length of arc } AKE + \text{ Length of arc } SLF + 2(\text{Length } SE)$$

Note: $EM = AF$

Where,

Length of arc, $\quad AKE = \frac{D}{2}(180 + 2\alpha)$

$$= \frac{D}{2}(\theta_L)$$

Length of arc, $\quad SLF = \frac{d}{2}(180 + 2\alpha)$

$$= \frac{d}{2}(\theta_S)$$

Length SE = Length C_1N

From the right angle triangle C_1C_2N

$$(C_1N)^2 = (C_1C_2)^2 - (C_2N)^2$$

$$= C^2 - \left(\frac{D+d}{2}\right)^2$$

$$\left[\text{Here, } C_2N = C_2S + SN = \frac{d}{2} + \frac{D}{2} = \frac{D+d}{2}\right]$$

$$(C_1N)^2 = \frac{4C^2 - (D+d)^2}{4}$$

i.e., $$C_1N = \frac{\sqrt{4C^2 - (D+d)^2}}{2}$$

Hence , $$2C_1N = \sqrt{4C^2 - (D+d)^2}$$

Therefore, Length of belt,

$$= \frac{D}{2}(\theta_L) + \frac{d}{2}(\theta_S) + \sqrt{4C^2 - (D+d)^2}$$

$$= \frac{1}{2}(D\theta_L + d\theta_S) + \sqrt{4C^2 - (D+d)^2} \quad \text{... E(21-8)}$$

Where , $$\theta_L = \theta_S = (180 + 2\alpha)$$

$$= \pi + 2\sin^{-1}\left(\frac{D+d}{2C}\right) \quad \text{... E(21-10C)}$$

To derive the expression for ratio of belt tensions $\frac{T_1}{T_2}$

Consider a flat belt wound on a pulley. Let θ be the angle of lap of belt on the pulley, and T_1 and T_2 be the tensions on the tight and slack side of belt at the instant of belt slipping on the pulley surface $(T_1 > T_2)$.

Now consider an elemental strip *ECF* of belt subtending angle δθ at the centre of pulley, *O*. $(T + \delta T)$ and *T* are the tensions at '*F*' and '*E*' respectively. Let *N* and μN be the normal force and frictional force on the elemental strip respectively,

Resolving the forces along the horizontal direction *CX*,

$$(T + \delta T)\cos\frac{\delta\theta}{2} = T\cos\frac{\delta\theta}{2} + \mu N$$

$$\mu N = T\cos\frac{\delta\theta}{2} + \delta T\cos\frac{\delta\theta}{2} - T\cos\frac{\delta\theta}{2}$$

$$= \delta T\cos\frac{\delta\theta}{2}$$

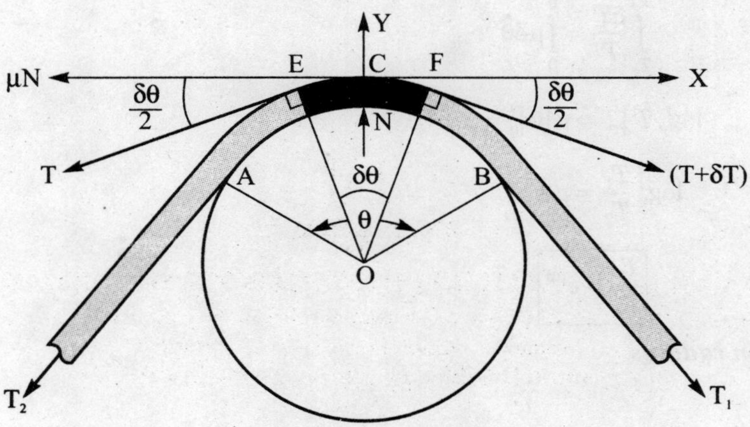

Note: *Since* $\frac{\delta\theta}{2}$ *is a small quantity,* $\cos\frac{\delta\theta}{2}$ *may be taken equal to 1.*

Therefore, $\mu N = \delta T$ ... (1)

Similarly, resolving the forces in the direction of CY

$$N = (T + \delta T)\sin\frac{\delta\theta}{2} + T\sin\frac{\delta\theta}{2}$$

$$= T\sin\frac{\delta\theta}{2} + \delta T\sin\frac{\delta\theta}{2} + T\sin\frac{\delta\theta}{2}$$

$$= 2T\sin\frac{\delta\theta}{2} + \delta T\sin\frac{\delta\theta}{2}$$

For small values of $\frac{\delta\theta}{2}, \sin\frac{\delta\theta}{2} = \frac{\delta\theta}{2}$

Therefore, $N = 2T\frac{\delta\theta}{2} + \delta T\frac{\delta\theta}{2}$

$$= T\delta\theta + \delta T\frac{\delta\theta}{2}$$

Note: *Since* δT *and* $\delta\theta$ *are small quantities, the product* $\delta T\frac{\delta\theta}{2}$ *may be neglected.*

Therefore, $N = T\delta\theta$ ... (2)

From expressions (1) and (2),

$$\frac{\delta T}{T\delta\theta} = \frac{\mu N}{N}$$

i.e., $\frac{\delta T}{T} = \mu\delta\theta$

Integrating we get

$$\int_{T_2}^{T_1}\frac{\delta T}{T} = \int_0^{\theta}\mu\delta\theta$$

$$\log_e T\big]_{T_2}^{T_1} = \mu[\theta]_0^{\theta} = \mu\theta$$

Therefore, $\log_e\frac{T_1}{T_2} = \mu\theta$

or $\boxed{\frac{T_1}{T_2} = e^{\mu\theta}}$ ... E(21-1)

Note: *Here* θ *is in radians.*

Derivation of Expression for the Ratio of Belt Tensions for Grooved Pulley and Rope Drives

Consider a *V*-belt drive connecting sheaves of diameters '*D*' and '*d*' with groove angle 2α . Let T_1 and T_2 be the tensions on the high tension side and slack side respectively, and let '*N*' be the normal reaction on an elemental strip of belt subtending angle $\delta\theta$ at '*O*' the centre of grooved pulley (sheave).

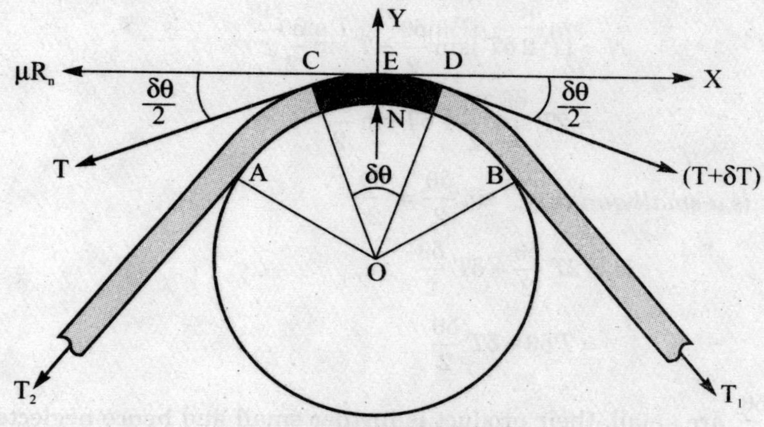

Figure: 1

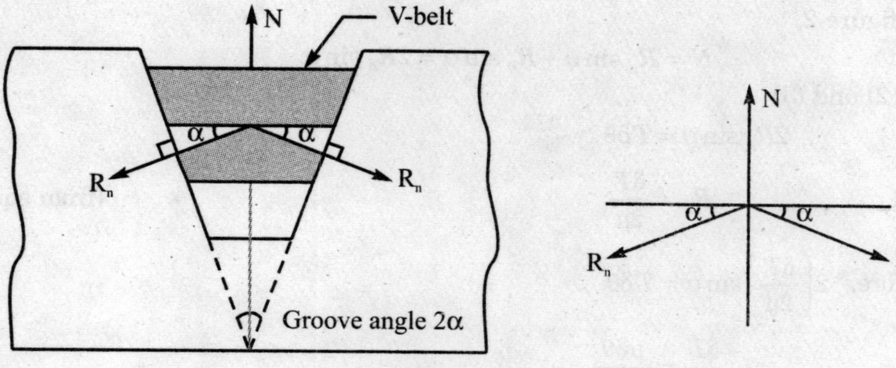

Figure: 2

Let R_n be the normal reaction exerted by belt on pulley at the two sides of belt as shown. From figure-1, resolving forces in the horizontal and vertical directions, we have

In the horizontal direction,

$$(T + \delta T)\cos\frac{\delta\theta}{2} = T\cos\frac{\delta\theta}{2} + \mu R_n$$

i.e.,

$$\mu R_n = (T + \delta T)\cos\frac{\delta\theta}{2} - T\cos\frac{\delta\theta}{2}$$

$$= \delta T\cos\frac{\delta\theta}{2}$$

Note: $\frac{\delta\theta}{2}$ *is a small quantity, and hence* $\cos\frac{\delta\theta}{2} = 1$

Therefore, $\mu R_n = \delta T$

Note: *Since two sides of V-belt (or rope) are in contact with sheave,*

The total frictional force $= 2\mu R_n$

Therefore, $2\mu R_n = \delta T$ ... (1)

Similarly, in the vertical direction, we have,

$$N = (T + \delta T)\sin\frac{\delta\theta}{2} + T\sin\frac{\delta\theta}{2}$$

$$= 2T\sin\frac{\delta\theta}{2} + \delta T\sin\frac{\delta\theta}{2}$$

Note: *Since* $\frac{\delta\theta}{2}$ *is a small quantity,* $\sin\frac{\delta\theta}{2} = \frac{\delta\theta}{2}$

Therefore, $N = 2T\frac{\delta\theta}{2} + \delta T\frac{\delta\theta}{2}$

$$= T\delta\theta + \delta T\frac{\delta\theta}{2}$$

δT and $\frac{\delta\theta}{2}$ are small, their product is further small and hence neglected.

Therefore, $N = T\delta\theta$ .... (2)

From figure 2,

$$N = R_n \sin\alpha + R_n \sin\alpha = 2R_n \sin\alpha \quad \text{... (3)}$$

From (2) and (3)

$$2R_n \sin\alpha = T\delta\theta$$

But, $R_n = \frac{\delta T}{2\mu}$ (from equation (1))

Therefore, $2\left(\frac{\delta T}{2\mu}\right)\sin\alpha = T\delta\theta$

i.e., $\frac{\delta T}{T} = \frac{\mu\delta\theta}{\sin\alpha}$

Integrating we get,

$$\int_{T_2}^{T_1}\frac{\delta T}{T} = \int_0^{\theta}\frac{\mu\delta\theta}{\sin\alpha}$$

i.e., $\log_e T\Big]_{T_2}^{T_1} = \frac{\mu}{\sin\alpha}\theta\Big]_0^{\theta}$

$$\log_e\frac{T_1}{T_2} = \frac{\mu\theta}{\sin\alpha}$$

$$\frac{T_1}{T_2} = e^{\frac{\mu\theta}{\sin\alpha}}$$

$\frac{T_1}{T_2} = e^{\frac{\mu\theta}{\sin\alpha}}$ is the required expression for the ratio of belt tensions for *V*-belt drive and rope drives having groove angle 2α.

Centrifugal Tension in Belt and Rope Drives

When a belt moves on a flat pulley, or a sheave (grooved pulley), because of its mass, it is subjected to a centrifugal force which tends to lift the belt or rope from the pulley rim thereby reducing the power transmitted and also produces additional tension in belt known as centrifugal tension T_C. The effect of T_C is negligible at low speeds but at high speeds (more than 750 m/min), its effect is very important and has to be taken into account.

Derivation of Expression for Centrifugal Tension T_c

Consider an elemental strip of belt strip of belt *AB* subtending an angle $\delta\theta$ at the centre of pulley of radius '*r*'. Let '*m*' be the mass of belt per unit length of belt and T_C be the centrifugal tension in belt due to centrifugal force F_C.

Now length of portion $AB = r\delta\theta$

Mass of $AB = m(r\delta\theta) = mr\delta\theta$

The centrifugal force in belt $= \frac{Mv^2}{r}$; where, M = Total mass of belt

Substituting we get,

Centrifugal force $F_C = \frac{(mr\delta\theta)v^2}{r} = mv^2\delta\theta$ ...(1)

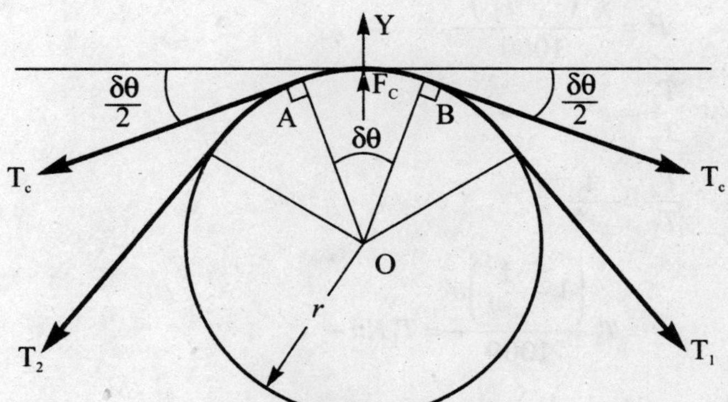

Resolving the centrifugal tension T_C in the horizontal and vertical directions and equating the sum of vertical components to F_C we get,

$$F_C = T_C \sin\frac{\delta\theta}{2} + T_C \sin\frac{\delta\theta}{2}$$

$$= 2T_C \sin\frac{\delta\theta}{2}$$

Since, $\frac{\delta\theta}{2}$ is small; $\sin\frac{\delta\theta}{2} = \frac{\delta\theta}{2}$

Therefore, $F_C = 2T_C \frac{\delta\theta}{2}$

$$= T_C \delta\theta \quad \text{... (2)}$$

Equating (1) and (2) we get,

$$mv^2 \delta\theta = T_c \delta\theta$$

$$\boxed{T_c = mv^2}$$

Therefore, the maximum tension on high tension side (tight side) including centrifugal tension $= T_1 + T_C$

Similarly tension on slack side (less tension side) $= T_2 + T_C$

Condition for Maximum Power Transmitted

We know that, power transmitted by a belt or rope drive is given by,

Power $P = \frac{(T_1 - T_2)v}{1000}$ kW

Where, T_1 and T_2 are belt tensions in Newton,

v = Velocity of belt in m/sec

Now, '*P*' can be rewritten as,

$$P = \frac{T_1\left(1 - \frac{T_2}{T_1}\right)v}{1000}$$

We have, $\frac{T_1}{T_2} = e^{\mu\theta}$

$$\frac{T_2}{T_1} = \frac{1}{e^{\mu\theta}}$$

$$P = T_1 \frac{\left(1 - \frac{1}{e^{\mu\theta}}\right)v}{1000} = T_1 K v$$

Where, $K = \frac{\left(1 - \frac{1}{e^{\mu\theta}}\right)}{1000}$ a constant for a given ratio of belt tensions.

We have, $T = T_1 + T_C$ including centrifugal tension

or, $$T_1 = T - T_C = \left(T - wv^2\right)$$

Therefore, $$P = \left(T - wv^2\right)Kv$$

$$= \left(Tv - wv^3\right)K$$

The power transmitted is maximum when

$$\frac{d}{dv}(P) = 0$$

i.e., $$\frac{d}{dv}\left[\left(Tv - wv^3\right)K\right] = 0$$

$$K\frac{d}{dv}\left[Tv - wv^3\right] = 0$$

$$K\left[T - 3wv^2\right] = 0$$

$K \neq 0$ and hence $T - 3wv^2 = 0$

i.e., $$T = 3wv^2 = 3T_C$$

Because, $$T_C = wv^2$$

Hence power transmitted in belt is maximum when the maximum tension in belt $= T_{max} = 3T_C$ ***or maximum tension is three times the centrifugal tension.***

Hence, $$\boxed{T_{max} = 3T_C}$$

Design procedure for Flat Belts

Design of flat belt includes calculation of the dimensions of rectangular cross-section of belt, or the power that can be transmitted by the belt chosen.

The area of cross-section of (rectangular section) flat belt is given by,

$$a_1 t = \frac{1000N}{Kv\left(\sigma_d - \frac{wv^2}{g} \times 10^{-6}\right)} \qquad \text{... E(21-6a)}$$

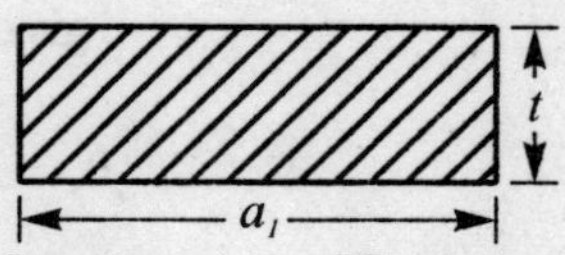

Cross-section of flat belt

Where, a_1 = Width of belt in mm

t = Thickness of belt in mm

N = Power transmitted in kW.

σ_d = Design stress for belt material in N/mm^2. When tension T_1 in belt and dimensions of cross-section of belt are known, $\sigma_d = \frac{T_1}{a_1 t}$

w = Density of belt material in N/m^3

v = Velocity of belt in m/sec

Note: 1. *When thickness of belt is known, use*

$$v = \frac{\pi(d_1 + t)n_1}{60} \text{ m/sec}$$

Where, d_1 = Diameter of small pulley in metre

t = Thickness of belt in metre

n_1 = Speed of small pulley in rpm

Also, $$v = \frac{\pi(d_2 + t)n_2}{60} \text{ m/sec}$$

Where, d_2 = Diameter of larger pulley in metre

n_2 = Speed of larger pulley in metre

$g = 9.8066 \text{ m/sec}^2$

Use velocity 'v' of pulley governing the design.

2. ***When thickness of belt is unknown,***

Use, $$v = \frac{\pi d_1 n_1}{60} = \frac{\pi d_2 n_2}{60} \text{ m/sec}$$

To find 'K'

Constant, $$K = \frac{e^{\mu\theta} - 1}{e^{\mu\theta}}$$

'K' is based on $e^{\mu\theta}$ of pulley governing design.

$$e^{\mu\theta}\Big]_{\text{small pulley}} = e^{\mu_s \theta_s}$$

Where, μ_s = coefficient of friction between small pulley and the belt

θ_s = Angle of contact on small pulley in radians. Angle of lap on small pulley given by,

$$\theta_s = \pi - 2\sin^{-1}\left(\frac{D-d}{2c}\right) \quad \text{... E (21-10b)}$$

Where, $(\pi = 180°)$

D = Diameter of larger pulley, in metre

d = Diameter of small pulley, in metre

c = Centre distance between pulleys, in metre

$$e^{\mu\theta}\Big]_{\text{larger pulley}} = e^{\mu_L \theta_L}$$

Where, μ_L = Coefficient of friction between larger pulley and belt.

θ_L = Angle of contact on large pulley in radians, given by

$$\theta_L = \pi - 2\sin^{-1}\left(\frac{D-d}{2c}\right) \qquad \text{... E(21-10a)}$$

(Where, $\pi = 180°$)

If $\left.e^{\mu\theta}\right)_{\text{small pulley}} < \left.e^{\mu\theta}\right)_{\text{large pulley}}$, small pulley governs design and 'K' is obtained from equation,

$$K = \frac{\left.e^{\mu\theta}\right)_{\text{small pulley}} - 1}{\left.e^{\mu\theta}\right)_{\text{small pulley}}} = \frac{e^{\mu_S\theta_S} - 1}{e^{\mu_S\theta_S}}$$

If $\left.e^{\mu\theta}\right)_{\text{large pulley}} < \left.e^{\mu\theta}\right)_{\text{small pulley}}$, large pulley governs design and 'K' is obtained from equation,

$$K = \frac{e^{\mu_L\theta_L} - 1}{e^{\mu_L\theta_L}}$$

It is to be noted that,

(*a*) In an open belt drive, $\theta_L > \theta_S$ and if both pulleys, driver and the driven are of same material, $e^{\mu\theta_S} < e^{\mu\theta_L}$ and small pulley governs the design and hence 'K' is based on $e^{\mu\theta}$ of small pulley.

(*b*) In a cross belt drive, $\theta_L = \theta_S = \pi + 2\sin^{-1}\left(\frac{D-d}{2c}\right)$. When pulleys are of same material $\mu_L = \mu_S$, 'K' is based on $e^{\mu\theta}$ of large or small pulley.

Example 8.1: Following are the details of a flat belt drive connecting a motor and a fan. The belt is 3 mm thick and has a density of 10 kN/m³. The allowable tensile stress in belt material is 2 MPa. Calculate the width of belt if power transmitted is 8 kW.

Particulars	Motor	Fan
Pulley diameter	400 mm	1600 mm
Angle of lap	3.78 radians	3.78 radians
Coefficient of friction	0.3	0.25
Speed of rotation	700 rpm	175 rpm

(VTU, Feb-2002)

Solution:

The area of cross-section of flat belt is given by

$$a_1 t = \frac{1000N}{Kv\left(\sigma_d - \frac{wv^2}{g}\times 10^{-6}\right)} \qquad \text{... E(21-6a)}$$

Where, a_1 = Width of belt in mm.

t = Thickness of belt in mm = 3 mm.

N = Power transmitted in kW = 8 kW.

v = Velocity of belt

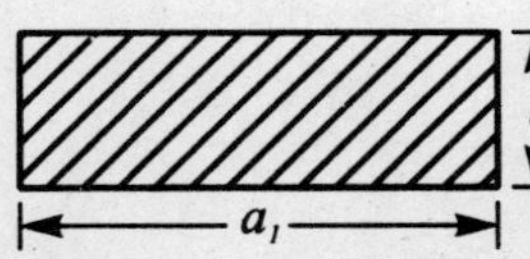

Cross-section of flat belt

$$v = \frac{\pi(d_1 + t)}{60} n_1, \text{m/sec}$$

$$= \frac{\pi}{60}\left(\frac{400+3}{1000}\right)700 = 14.77\,\text{m/sec}$$

σ_d = Design stress for belt material = 2 MPa

w = Density of belt material in N/m^3

$= 10\ kN/m^3 = 10 \times 10^3\ N/m^3$

$g = 9.8066\ m/sec^2$

To find 'K'

$$K = \frac{e^{\mu\theta} - 1}{e^{\mu\theta}}$$

$$\left.e^{\mu\theta}\right)_{\text{motor pulley}} = e^{0.3\times3.78} = 3.1081$$

$$\left.e^{\mu\theta}\right)_{\text{fan pulley}} = e^{0.25\times3.78} = 2.5728$$

***Note:** 'K' is based on smaller of the above two values of $e^{\mu\theta}$. Hence fan pulley governs design.*

Therefore, $e^{\mu\theta} = 2.5728$

Therefore, $K = \frac{2.5728 - 1}{2.5728} = 0.6113$

Substituting the values in equation (21-6a),

$$a_1 \times 3 = \frac{1000 \times 8}{0.6113 \times 14.77\left[2 - \frac{10\times10^3 \times (14.77)^2 \times 10^{-6}}{9.8066}\right]}$$

Width of belt required $a_1 = 166.17$ mm

Adopt standard width $a_1 = 180$ mm ... Table (21-8)

Table - (21-8) MDH

Nominal belt width × 10^{-3}m
25, 32, 40, 50, 63
71, 80, 90, 100, 112, 125
140, 160, 180, 200, 224, 250
280, 315, 355, 400, 450, 500

Example 8.2: An electric motor is to drive an exhaust fan. A flat leather belt is used in the drive

Particulars	*Motor Pulley*	*Fan Pulley*
Diameter	300 mm	1200 mm
Contact angle	2.5 radians	3.78 radians
Coefficient of friction	0.3	0.25
Speed	900 rpm	
Power transmitted	22 kW	

The thickness of belt is 6.25 mm and the maximum permissible stress in belt is 2.1 MPa. The belt weighs 9.708 kN/m³.

(a) Which pulley governs the design.
(b) What is the width of belt required.

Solution:

We have,

$$\left.e^{\mu\theta}\right)_{\text{motor pulley}} = e^{0.3\times3.5} = 2.117$$

$$\left.e^{\mu\theta}\right)_{\text{fan pulley}} = e^{0.25\times3.78} = 2.5728$$

$$\left.e^{\mu\theta}\right)_{\text{motor pulley}} < \left.e^{\mu\theta}\right)_{\text{fan pulley}}$$

Hence motor pulley governs design.

To find the width of belt a_1 required

Area of cross-section of flat belt is given by,

$$a_1 t = \frac{1000\text{ N}}{Kv\left(\sigma_d - \frac{wv^2}{g}\times10^{-6}\right)} \quad \text{... E(21-6a)}$$

Where, a_1 = Width of belt in mm.

t = Thickness of belt in mm = 6.25 mm.

N = Power transmitted in kW = 22 kW.

v = Velocity of belt

$$v = \frac{\pi(d_1+t)}{60}n_1 \text{ in m/sec}$$

$$= \frac{\pi}{60}\left(\frac{300+6.25}{1000}\right)900 = 14.43\text{ m/sec}$$

σ_d = Design stress for belt material = 2.1 MPa

w = Density of belt material in N/m³

$= 9.708\text{ kN/m}^3 = 9708\text{ N/m}^3$

$g = 9.8066\text{ m/sec}^2$

To find 'K'

Constant, $$K = \frac{e^{\mu\theta} - 1}{e^{\mu\theta}}$$

***Note:** 'K' is based on $e^{\mu\theta}$ of governing pulley. Here motor pulley governs design.*

Therefore, $$K = \frac{2.117 - 1}{2.117} = 0.5276$$

Substituting the values, we get

$$a_1 \times 6.25 = \frac{1000 \times 22}{0.5276 \times 14.43 \left[2.1 - \frac{9708 \times (14.43)^2 \times 10^{-6}}{9.8066} \right]}$$

Therefore, width of belt required, $a_1 = 244$ mm

Adopt standard width $a_1 = 250$ mm ... Table (21-8)

Example 8.3: An electric motor drives a compressor by means of a flat leather belt. The following data are known

Particulars	*Motor Pulley*	*Fan Pulley*
Diameter	250 mm	1500 mm
Angle of wrap	4 radians	3.5 radians
Coefficient of friction	0.25	0.3
Speed	1200 rpm	

The cross-section of belt is 200 mm × 6.25 mm. The belt weighs $9.708\, kN/m^3$. If the maximum allowable belt tension is 2700N, determine the power transmitted.

Solution:

The area of cross-section of flat belt is given by

$$a_1 t = \frac{1000N}{Kv\left(\sigma_d - \frac{wv^2}{g} \times 10^{-6}\right)} \quad \text{... E(21-6a)}$$

Where, a_1 = Width of belt in mm = 200 mm

t = Thickness of belt in mm = 6.25 mm

N = Power transmitted in kW

v = Velocity of belt

$$v = \frac{\pi(d_1 + t)}{60} n_1, \text{m/sec}$$

$$= \frac{\pi}{60}\left(\frac{250+6.25}{1000}\right)1200 = 16.1\,\text{m/sec}$$

$$\sigma_d = \frac{T_1}{\text{Area of cross-section of belt}}$$

$$= \frac{2700}{200\times 6.25} = 2.16\,\text{N/mm}^2 = 2.16\ \text{MPa}$$

$$w = \text{Density of belt material in N/m}^3$$

$$= 9.708\,\text{kN/m}^3 = 9708\,\text{N/m}^3$$

$$g = 9.8066\ \text{m/sec}^2$$

To find 'K'

Constant, $$K = \frac{e^{\mu\theta}-1}{e^{\mu\theta}}$$

$$\left.e^{\mu\theta}\right)_{\text{motor pulley}} = e^{0.25\times 4} = 2.7183$$

$$\left.e^{\mu\theta}\right)_{\text{compressor pulley}} = e^{0.3\times 3.5} = e^{1.05} = 2.8577$$

$$\left.e^{\mu\theta}\right)_{\text{motor pulley}} < \left.e^{\mu\theta}\right)_{\text{compressor pulley}}$$

Therefore, $$K = \frac{\left.e^{\mu\theta}\right)_{\text{motor pulley}} - 1}{\left.e^{\mu\theta}\right)_{\text{motor pulley}}}$$

$$= \frac{2.7183-1}{2.7183} = 0.6321$$

Substituting the values in E(21-6a) we get,

$$200\times 6.25 = \frac{1000\ N}{0.6321\times 16.1\left[2.16 - \frac{9708\times(16.1)^2\times 10^{-6}}{9.8066}\right]}$$

Therefore, $N = 24.21$ kW

Hence, power transmitted, $N = 24.21$ kW

Example 8.4: An open belt drive delivers 15 kW when the motor pulley which is 300 mm in diameter runs at 1750 rpm. The belt is 150 mm wide and 10 mm thick. The belt weighs $9.708\,kN/m^3$. The driven pulley which is 1200 mm in diameter has an angle of contact of 200°. What is the maximum stress in the belt assuming the coefficient of friction for both pulleys equal to 0.3 ?

Solution:

The area of cross-section of flat belt is given by

$$a_1 t = \frac{1000\,N}{Kv\left(\sigma_d - \frac{wv^2}{g}\times 10^{-6}\right)} \quad \text{... E(21-6a)}$$

Where, a_1 = Width of belt in mm = 150 mm

t = Thickness of belt in mm = 10 mm

N = Power transmitted in kW=15 kW

v = Velocity of belt

$$v = \frac{\pi(d_1 + t)}{60} n_1, \text{m/sec}$$

$$= \frac{\pi}{60}\left(\frac{300+10}{1000}\right)1750 = 28.41 \text{m/sec}$$

σ_d = Design stress for belt material in N/mm^2

w = Density of belt material in N/m^3

$= 9.708 \text{kN/m}^3 = 9708 \text{N/m}^3$

$g = 9.8066 \text{m/sec}^2$

To find 'K'

Note: *Since angle of contact on driver pulley (motor pulley) is unknown, K is based on* $\left.e^{\mu\theta}\right)_{driven\ pulley}$

$$\left.e^{\mu\theta}\right)_{\text{driven pulley}} = e^{0.3 \times 200 \times \frac{\pi}{180^\circ}} = 2.85$$

Therefore,
$$K = \frac{e^{\mu\theta} - 1}{e^{\mu\theta}} = \frac{2.85 - 1}{2.85} = 0.649$$

Substituting in E(21-6a) we get,

$$150 \times 10 = \frac{1000 \times 15}{0.649 \times 28.41\left(\sigma_d - \frac{9708 \times (28.41)^2}{9.8066} \times 10^{-6}\right)}$$

i.e.,
$$\left[\sigma_d - \frac{9708(28.41)^2}{9.8066} \times 10^{-6}\right] = \frac{1000 \times 15}{150 \times 10 \times 0.649 \times 28.41}$$

$$\sigma_d - 0.799 = 0.5424$$

$$\sigma_d = 1.3414 \text{N/mm}^2$$

Therefore, stress induced in belt = 1.3414 N/mm^2

Example 8.5: A leather belt is to transmit 22 kW from a 250 mm diameter driver pulley running at 1200 rpm to a 600 mm diameter steel pulley. The coefficient of friction between the steel pulley and belt is 0.3 and that between the driver and belt is 0.4. The centre distance between shafts is 1.8 meter. Assuming the maximum allowable working stress in the belt as 1.75N/mm^2, and the belt weighs 9.708kN/m^3. Decide which of the following belts would be more suitable, a belt having 8mm thickness or a belt having 12.5 mm thickness. Determine the width of belt required.

Solution:

(a) To select suitable thickness of belt (8 mm or 12.5 mm)

Note: *A flat belt having a higher ratio of* $\frac{d}{t}$ *is preferred for a greater belt life.*

For belt having thickness $t = 8$ mm, $\frac{d}{t} = \frac{250}{8} = 31.25$

Similarly, for belt having thickness, $t = 12.5$ mm, $\frac{d}{t} = \frac{250}{12.5} = 20$

Therefore, it is preferable to have belt thickness $t = 8$ mm *in the drive.*

(b) Calculation of width of belt

For flat belt, area of cross-section is given by

$$a_1 t = \frac{1000N}{Kv\left(\sigma_d - \frac{wv^2}{g}\times 10^{-6}\right)} \qquad \text{... E(21-6a)}$$

Where, a_1 = Width of belt in mm

t = Thickness of belt in mm = 8 mm

N = Power transmitted in kW = 22 kW

σ_d = Design stress for belt material = 1.75 N/mm^2

w = Density of belt material in N/m^3

= 9.708 kN/m^3 = 9708 N/m^3

g = 9.8066 m/sec^2

To find 'v'

For the driver pulley,

$$v = \frac{\pi(d+t)}{60} n_1$$

$$= \frac{\pi}{60}\left(\frac{250+8}{1000}\right)1200 \text{ m/sec}$$

For the driven pulley,

$$v = \frac{\pi(D+t)}{60} n_2$$

$$= \frac{\pi}{60}\left(\frac{600+8}{1000}\right)500 = 15.92 \text{ m/sec}$$

$$n_2 = \frac{d}{D} n_1$$

$$n_2 = \frac{250}{600}\times 1200 = 500 \text{ rpm}$$

$$\theta)_{\text{small pulley}} = \pi - 2\sin^{-1}\left(\frac{D-d}{2c}\right)$$

$$= 180 - 2\sin^{-1}\left(\frac{600-250}{2\times1800}\right) = 168.48°$$

$$\theta)_{\text{large pulley}} = \pi + 2\sin^{-1}\left(\frac{D-d}{2c}\right)$$

$$= 180 + 2\sin^{-1}\left(\frac{600-250}{2\times1800}\right) = 191.52°$$

$$e^{\mu\theta}\Big)_{\text{driver pulley}} = e^{0.4\times168.48\times\frac{\pi}{180}} = 3.242$$

$$e^{\mu\theta}\Big)_{\text{driven pulley}} = e^{0.3\times191.52\times\frac{\pi}{180}} = 2.726$$

Therefore, $e^{\mu\theta}\Big)_{\text{driven pulley}} < e^{\mu\theta}\Big)_{\text{driver pulley}}$

Therefore, driven pulley governs the design.

Therefore, $K = \dfrac{e^{\mu\theta}-1}{e^{\mu\theta}} = \dfrac{2.726-1}{2.726} = 0.6332$

$$v = \frac{\pi(D+t)}{60} n_2$$

$$= \frac{\pi}{60}\left(\frac{600+8}{1000}\right)500 = 15.92 \text{ m/sec}$$

Substituting in E(21-6a) we get,

$$a_1 \times 8 = \frac{1000\times22}{0.6332\times15.92\left[1.75 - \dfrac{9708\times(15.92)^2\times10^{-6}}{9.8066}\right]}$$

Therefore, $a_1 = 181.97$ mm

Adopt standard width, $a_1 = 200$ mm ... T(21-8)

Example 8.6: A transmission shaft rotating at 500 rpm drives a milling machine which requires 3.75 kW at 750 rpm. A 300mm diameter cast iron pulley is located on the transmission shaft. A belt of 5 mm thick weighing 9.708 kN/m³ is used. The allowable stress in belt is 2.1 N/mm². The pulleys rotate in the opposite directions. The centre distance between shafts is 750 mm and the coefficient of friction is 0.3 for both the pulleys. Determine,

(a) The diameter of the smaller pulley.

(b) The stress on the slack side.

(c) Area of cross-section of belt required.

(d) The width of belt required.

Solution:

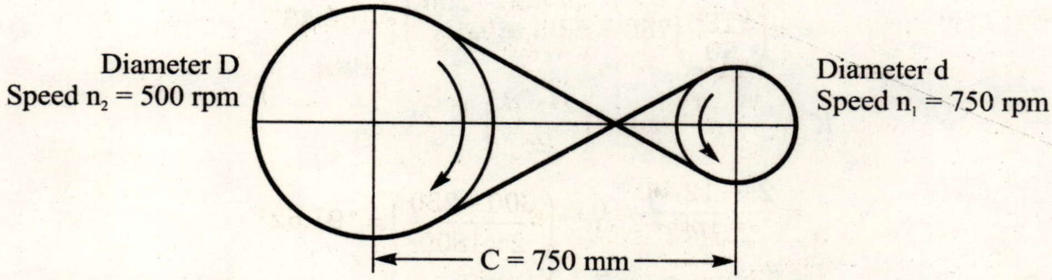

(a) To find diameter of smaller pulley (d)

$$\text{Speed ratio} = \frac{n_1}{n_2} = \frac{D}{d}$$

i.e.,
$$d = D\frac{n_2}{n_1}$$

$$= 300 \times \frac{500}{750} = 200 \text{ mm}$$

i.e., Diameter of small pulley is 200 mm.

(b) To find stress on the slack side.

Note: *For the given cross belt drive,* $\frac{T_1}{T_2} = e^{\mu\theta}$ *and is same at the driver and driven pulleys.*

$$\theta = \theta_S = \theta_L = \pi + 2\sin^{-1}\left(\frac{D-d}{2c}\right)$$

$$= 180 + 2\sin^{-1}\left(\frac{300-200}{2\times 750}\right) = 187.65°$$

Therefore,
$$\frac{T_1}{T_2} = e^{\mu\theta} = e^{0.3\times 187.65\times\frac{\pi}{180}} = 2.6712$$

Therefore,
$$T_2 = \frac{T_1}{2.6712}$$

Where,
$$T_1 = (a_1 t)\sigma_d$$
$$= (a_1 \times 5)2.1$$

Therefore,
$$T_1 = 10.5a_1$$

(c) Area of cross-section of belt is given by

$$a_1 t = \frac{1000\text{ N}}{Kv\left(\sigma_d - \frac{wv^2}{g}\times 10^{-6}\right)} \quad \text{... E(21-6a)}$$

Therefore,
$$a_1 = \frac{1000\text{N}}{Kvt\left(\sigma_d - \frac{wv^2}{g}\times 10^{-6}\right)}$$

Where, N = Power transmitted in kW = 3.75 kW

$$v = \pi\left(\frac{d+t}{60}\right)750 = 8.05 \text{ m/sec}$$

$$K = \frac{e^{\mu\theta}-1}{e^{\mu\theta}}$$

$$= \frac{2.6712-1}{2.6712} = 0.6256$$

Where, $t = 5 \text{ mm}; \; \sigma_d = 2.1 \text{ N/mm}^2$

$$w = 9.708 \text{ kN/m}^3 = 9708 \text{ N/m}^3$$

$$g = 9.8066 \text{ m/sec}^2$$

Therefore,
$$a_1 = \frac{1000\times 3.72}{0.6256\times 8.05\times 5\left[2.1-\dfrac{9708\times(8.05)^2\times 10^{-6}}{9.8066}\right]} = 73.15 \text{ mm}$$

Adopt, $a_1 = 76$ mm (standard size) ... T (21-7)

From, $\dfrac{T_1}{T_2} = 2.6712,$

$$T_2 = \frac{T_1}{2.6712}$$

$$= \frac{10.5a_1}{2.6712} = \frac{10.5\times 76}{2.6712} = 298.74 \text{ N}$$

Therefore, stress on slack side

$$= \frac{T_2}{a_1 t} = \frac{298.74}{76\times 5} = 0.786 \text{ N/mm}^2$$

Design Procedure for V-belts

General Steps followed in Designing V-belts

Step I: *Selection of cross-section of belt such as A, B, C, D or E section (also called size of belt)*

The cross-section of belt selected for the drive depends on d_e, the equivalent pitch diameter is given by

$$d_e = d_p F_b \qquad \text{... E(21-35)}$$

Where, $d_p = d$ = Diameter of small grooved pulley (or small sheave) in mm.

F_b = Small diameter factor (refer table 22-35 MDH)

F_b depends on speed ratio, given by

$$\text{Speed ratio} = \frac{n_1}{n_2} = \frac{D}{d}$$

Where, 'D' and 'd' are the diameters of large and small sheaves (pulleys with grooved periphery).

n_1 and n_2 are the speeds of small and large grooved pulleys (or sheaves).

Note: *Speed ratio > 1*

Based on d_e, select the cross-section of belt such as *A, B, C, D* or *E* section. Also obtain width '*w*' and thickness '*t*' of belt by referring to Table (21-23.)

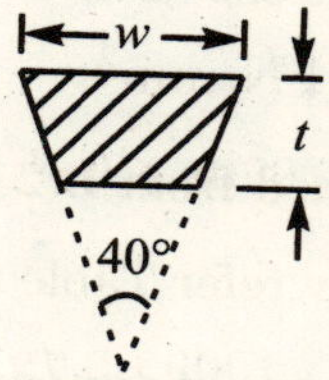

Step II: *Calculation of number of V-belts (i)*

Number of belts is obtained from,

$$i = \frac{NF_a}{N^* F_c F_d} \quad \text{... E(21-36)}$$

Where, N = Drive power in kW.

N^* = Power transmitted by each V-belt selected.

For example, N^* for 'B' section is given by

$$N^* = V\left(\frac{0.79}{V^{0.09}} - \frac{51.33}{d_e} - \frac{1.31v^2}{10^4}\right) \quad \text{... E(21-31)}$$

To calculate factors F_a, F_d and F_c

(i) F_a is called correction factor for industrial service ***(Refer table 21-28)***

F_a depends on the severity of service such as light duty, medium duty etc (depending on application of *V*-belts) and also the hours of service such as 8-10 hours/day service, etc.

(ii) F_c is called correction factor for belt length ***(Refer table 22-27)***

F_c depends on nominal inside length of belt and cross-section of belt. The length of belt is calculated using the formula

$$L = 2c + \frac{\pi}{2}(D+d) + \frac{(D-d)^2}{4c} \quad \text{... E(21-38)}$$

Where '*c*' is the centre distance between pulleys in mm.

Note:

(i) When exact centre distance 'c' between pulleys is given use equation (21-38) and obtain 'L'.

(ii) When approximate centre distance is given, calculate maximum and minimum centre distances given by

$$C_{max} = \textit{Maximum centre distance} = 2(D+d) \quad \text{... E(21-40)}$$

$$C_{min} = \textit{Minimum centre distance} = 0.55(D+d)+t \quad \text{... E(21-41)}$$

Where, 't' is thickness of V-belt obtained from Table (21-23).

After calculating C_{max} and C_{min}, choose an average value of $c = \dfrac{C_{max}+C_{min}}{2}$ and use in equation of 'L'.

Corresponding to value of 'L' obtained from E(21-38), obtain the nearest nominal inside length of belt using Table (21-29). Finally refer Table (22-27) and obtain F_c.

(iii) F_d is called correction factor for arc of contact ***(Refer table 22-26)***

F_d depends on θ_S, the arc of contact on small pulley is given by,

$$\theta_S = \pi - 2\sin^{-1}\left(\frac{D-d}{2C}\right) \quad \text{... E(21-10b)}$$

Where, $(\pi = 180°)$

After calculating F_a, F_c and F_d, obtain i, the number of V-belts required.

Note: *The correct centre distance between pulleys is obtained from E(21-39) given by*

$$\text{Correct centre distance, } C = \frac{L}{4} - \frac{\pi(D+d)}{8} + \sqrt{\left\{\frac{L}{4} - \frac{\pi(D+d)}{8}\right\}^2 - \frac{(D-d)^2}{8}} \quad \text{... E(21-39)}$$

Example 8.7: Select a v-belt drive to transmit 8 kW from a shaft running at 1000 rpm to a parallel shaft to be run at 400 rpm. Limit the pitch diameter of smaller pulley (smaller sheave) to 150 mm. ***(VTU, Jan / Feb 2003)***

Solution:

Step I: *Selection of cross-section of belt (A, B, C, D or E section).*

The cross-section of belt depends on the equivalent pitch diameter d_e is given by,

$$d_e = d_p F_b \quad \text{... E(21-35)}$$

Where, $d_p = d =$ Diameter of smaller pulley (smaller sheave) = 150 mm.

$F_b =$ Small diameter factor.

Note: *F_b depends on speed ratio.*

For the given drive,

$$\text{Speed ratio} = \frac{n_1}{n_2} = \frac{D}{d}$$

Where, n_1 = Speed of small pulley = 1000 rpm

n_2 = Speed of large pulley = 400 rpm

Therefore, Speed ratio $= \dfrac{1000}{400} = 2.5$

Referring to Table (22-25)MDH, for speed ratio = 2.5,

Small diameter factor, $F_b = 1.14$

Therefore, $d_e = 150 \times 1.14 = 169.5$ mm

For, $d_e = 169.5$ mm, we select *'B'* cross-section belt for which

$$N^* = V\left(\frac{0.79}{V^{0.09}} - \frac{51.33}{d_e} - \frac{1.31v^2}{10^4}\right) \quad \text{... E(21-31)}$$

Also width of belt $= w = 17$ mm, Thickness, $t = 11$ mm from Table (21-33)

Where, N^* = Maximum power in kW

v = Velocity in m/sec

$$= \frac{\pi d_1 n_1}{60} = \frac{\pi}{60} \times \left(\frac{150}{1000}\right) \times 1000 = 7.854 \text{ m/sec}$$

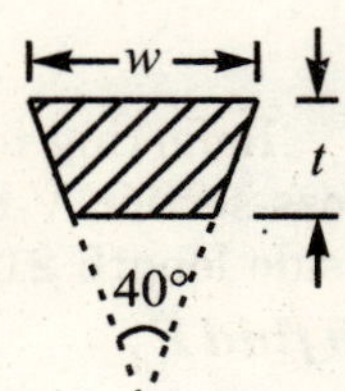

d_e = Equivalent diameter in mm.

Therefore, $$N^* = 7.854\left[\frac{0.79}{(7.854)^{0.09}} - \frac{51.33}{169.5} - \frac{1.31(7.854)^2}{10^4}\right]$$

$$N^* = 2.713 \text{ kW}$$

Step II: *Calculation of number of belts (i)*

Number of belts, $$i = \frac{NF_a}{N^* F_c F_d} \quad \text{... E(21-36)}$$

Where, N = Drive power in kW = 8 kW

F_a = *Correction factor for industrial service (Refer T 21-28)*

It depends on the severity of service and the type of driver and driven machinery. Assuming medium duty and 10-16 hours per day service, $F_a = 1.2$

F_c = *Correction factor for belt length (Refer T 22-27)*

It depends on nominal inside length and cross section of belt. For the drive under consideration, nominal pitch length of belt, 'L' is given by,

$$L = 2c + \frac{\pi}{2}(D+d) + \frac{(D-d)^2}{4c} \qquad \text{... E(21-38)}$$

Where, 'c' is the centre distance between pulleys.

To find 'C'

Maximum centre distance,

$$C_{max} = 2(D+d) \qquad \text{... E(21-40)}$$

Where, $d = 150$ mm, and $D = d\frac{n_1}{n_2}\eta$ ... E(21-37)

$$D = 150 \times \frac{1000}{400} \times 1 = 375 \text{ mm}$$

Therefore, $C_{max} = 2(375+150)$

$= 1050$ mm

Also, $C_{min} = 0.55(D+d)+t$ ... E(21-41)

$= 0.55(375+150)+11 = 299.75$ mm

Say $c = 700$ mm (Average value of C_{max} and C_{min}).

Therefore, $L = 2\times 700 + \frac{\pi}{2}(375+150) + \frac{(375-150)^2}{4\times 700}$

$= 2242.75$ mm

Referring to table T(21-29), corresponding to nearest nominal pitch length 2202 mm, and cross-section V-belt, nominal inside length = 2159 mm. Now referring to T(22-27) for nominal inside length 2159 mm and 'B' cross-section, we get $F_c = 0.99$

To find F_d ***(Refer T 22-26)***

F_d = Correction factor for arc of contact.

Note: *F_d depends on θ_S, the angle of contact for the small pulley.*

For the given drive,

$$\theta_S = \pi - 2\sin^{-1}\left(\frac{D-d}{2C}\right) \qquad \text{... E(21-10b)}$$

$$= 180° - 2\sin^{-1}\left(\frac{375-150}{2\times 700}\right) = 161.5°$$

Corresponding to $\theta_S = 163°$, $F_d = 0.96$

Therefore,

Number of belts, $i = \frac{8\times 1.2}{2.713\times 0.99\times 0.96} = 3.723$

Use , $i = 4$ belts.

The correct centre distance 'C' is given by,

$$C=\frac{L}{4}-\frac{\pi(D+d)}{8}+\sqrt{\left\{\frac{L}{4}-\frac{\pi(D+d)}{8}\right\}^2-\frac{(D-d)^2}{8}} \quad \text{.... E(21-39)}$$

$$=\frac{2242.75}{4}-\frac{\pi}{8}(375+150)+\sqrt{\left\{\frac{2242.75}{4}-\frac{\pi}{8}(375+150)\right\}^2-\frac{(375-150)^2}{8}}$$

$$C = 700 \text{ mm}$$

Example 8.8: A 30 kW, 1200 rpm motor is to drive an air compressor through the medium of V-belting. The mean diameter of the motor and compressor pulley are respectively 250 mm and 750 mm. The shaft centre distance is 1.5 meter. Determine the size and number of V-belts required for the drive.

Solution:

Step I: ***Selection of cross-section of belt (A, B, C, D or E section).***

The cross-section of V-belt is based on the equivalent pitch diameter d_e is given by,

$$d_e = d_p F_b \quad \text{... E(21-35)}$$

Where, $d_p = d =$ Diameter of smaller pulley (smaller sheave) = 250 mm.

F_b = Small diameter factor. It depends on speed ratio.

For the given drive,

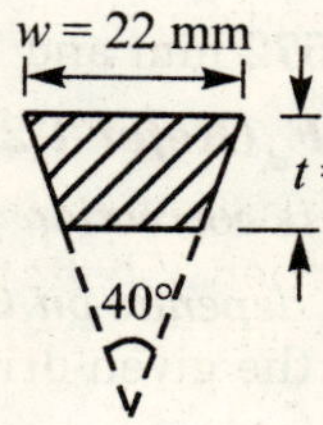

Speed ratio $=\frac{n_1}{n_2}=\frac{D}{d}=\frac{750}{250}=3$

Referring to Table (22-25), for speed ratio = 3,

Small diameter factor, $F_b = 1.14$

Therefore, $d_e = 250 \times 1.14 = 285$ mm

For, $d_e = 285$ mm, select '*C*' section for *V*-belt

w = Width = 22 mm, t = 14 mm ... T(21-23)

$$N^* = V\left(\frac{0.79}{V^{0.09}}-\frac{143.27}{d_e}-\frac{2.34v^2}{10^4}\right) \quad \text{... E(21-32)}$$

Where, v = Velocity in m/sec

$$=\frac{\pi d_1 n_1}{60}=\frac{\pi}{60}\left(\frac{250}{1000}\right)1200 = 15.71 \text{ m/sec}$$

$d_e = 285$ mm

Therefore,

$$N^* = 15.71\left[\frac{1.47}{(15.71)^{0.09}}-\frac{143.27}{285}-\frac{2.34(15.71)^2}{10^4}\right]$$

$$= 9.218 \text{ kW}$$

Step II: ***Calculation of number of belts (i)***

Number of belts is obtained from,

$$i = \frac{NF_a}{N^* F_c F_d} \qquad \text{... E(21-36)}$$

Where, N = Drive power in kW = 30 kW

F_a *is correction factor for industrial service (Refer T 21-28)*

Assuming 10-16 hours per day service, for heavy duty $F_a = 1.3$

To find F_c

F_c *is correction factor for belt length (Refer T 22-27)*

For the given drive, nominal length of belt , *'L'* is given by,

$$L = 2c + \frac{\pi}{2}(D+d) + \frac{(D-d)^2}{4c} \qquad \text{... E(21-38)}$$

Where, $c = 1.5$ m = 1500 mm, $D = 750$ mm $d = 250$ mm

Therefore,

$$L = 2\times1500 + \frac{\pi}{2}(750+250) + \frac{(750-250)^2}{4\times1500}$$

$$= 4612.47 \text{ mm}$$

The nearest nominal inside length from (T 21-29) is 4572 mm. Now referring (T22-27), for length 4572 mm and *'C'* cross-section, $F_c = 1.05$

To find F_d (Refer T 22-26)

F_d *is correction factor for arc of contact .*

Note: *F_d depends on θ_S, the angle of contact for the small pulley.*

For the given drive,

$$\theta_S = \pi - 2\sin^{-1}\left(\frac{D-d}{2C}\right) \qquad \text{... E(21-10b)}$$

$$= 180° - 2\sin^{-1}\left(\frac{750-250}{2\times1500}\right) = 160.81°$$

For $\theta_S = 160°$, $F_d = 0.95$

Therefore,

Number of belts $i = \dfrac{30\times1.3}{9.218\times1.05\times0.95} = 4.24$

Use , $i = 5$ belts.

Example 8.9: Select a V-V belt drive to transmit 10 kW of power from a pulley of diameter 150 mm mounted on an electric motor running at 720 rpm to another pulley mounted on a compressor to be run at 200 rpm. The service is heavy duty varying from 10 to 14 hours per day. The centre distance between centres of pulleys is 300 mm.

Solution:

Step I: ***Selection of cross section of belt (A, B, C, D or E section).***

The cross-section of V-belt is based on the equivalent pitch diameter d_e is given by,

$$d_e = d_p F_b \qquad \text{... E(21-35)}$$

Where, $d_p = d =$ Diameter of smaller pulley (smaller sheave) = 150 mm.

F_b = Small diameter factor, it depends on speed ratio (Refer table 22-25).

For the given drive, speed ratio

$$= \frac{n_1}{n_2} = \frac{D}{d} = \frac{720}{200} = 3.6$$

Referring to Table (22-25)MDH,

$$F_b = 1.14$$

Therefore, $d_e = 150 \times 1.14 = 171$ mm

For, $d_e = 171$ mm, select *'B'* cross-section of *V*-belt

With width, $w = 17$ mm, and thickness $t = 11$ mm ... T(21-23)

$$N^* = V\left(\frac{0.79}{V^{0.09}} - \frac{143.27}{d_e} - \frac{2.34v^2}{10^4}\right) \qquad \text{... E(21-31)}$$

Where, v = Velocity in m/sec

$$= \frac{\pi d_1 n_1}{60} = \frac{\pi}{60}\left(\frac{150}{1000}\right)720 = 5.655 \text{ m/sec}$$

$$d_e = 171 \text{ mm}$$

Therefore,

$$N^* = 5.655\left[\frac{0.79}{(5.655)^{0.09}} - \frac{51.33}{171} - \frac{1.31(5.655)^2}{10^4}\right]$$

$$N^* = 2.1 \text{ kW}$$

Step II: *Calculation of number of belts (i)*

Number of belts, $i = \dfrac{NF_a}{N^* F_c F_d}$ ... E(21-36)

Where, N = Drive power in kW = 10 kW

$$N^* = 2.1 \text{ kW}$$

To find F_a, F_c, and F_d

F_a is correction factor for industrial service (Refer T 21-28)

It depends on severity of service and the type of driver and driven machinery. For the driver (motor), driven machinery, compressor and heavy duty 10-14 hours per day service,

$$F_a = 1.3$$

F_c is correction factor for belt length (Refer T 22-27)

F_c depends on the nominal inside length of belt and the cross-section.

For the drive being analysed, the nominal pitch length

$$L = 2c + \frac{\pi}{2}(D+d) + \frac{(D-d)^2}{4c} \quad \text{... E(21-38)}$$

Where, 'c' is the centre distance between pulleys in mm = 300 mm.

$d =$ Diameter of small pulley = 150 mm

$$D = \text{Diameter of large pulley} = \frac{n_1}{n_2} d\eta \quad \text{... E(21-37)}$$

Assuming $\eta = 100\%$

$$D = \frac{720}{200} \times 150 \times 1 = 540 \text{ mm}$$

Therefore,

$$L = 2 \times 300 + \frac{\pi}{2}(540+150) + \frac{(540-150)^2}{4 \times 300}$$

$$= 1180.27 \text{ mm}$$

The nearest table value of L = 1212 mm, from (T 21-29) for 'B' section and the corresponding value of nominal belt length = 1168 mm. Now referring to Table (T 22-27), for nominal belt length = 1168 mm and 'B' cross-section belt, $F_c = 0.87$

F_d is correction factor for arc of contact (Refer table 22-26)

F_d depends on θ_S, the angle of contact on small pulley given by,

$$\theta_S = \pi - 2\sin^{-1}\left(\frac{D-d}{2C}\right) \quad \text{... E(21-10b)}$$

$$= 180° - 2\sin^{-1}\left(\frac{540-150}{2 \times 300}\right) = 98.92°$$

From Table (22-26), corresponding to $\theta_S = 99°$, $F_d = 0.73$

Therefore,

Number of belts $$i = \frac{10 \times 1.3}{2.1 \times 0.87 \times 0.73} = 9.747$$

Use, $i = 10$ belts.

Example 8.10: 5 kW of power is to be transmitted at 1440 rpm to a 400 rpm blower fan airconditioning unit. Select suitable type and number of V-belts.

Solution:

Step I: *Selection of cross-section of belt (A, B, C, D or E section).*

The cross-section of belt selected depends on d_e, the equivalent pitch diameter is given by,

$$d_e = d_p F_b \quad \text{... E(21-35)}$$

Where, $d_p = d =$ Diameter of smaller pulley (smaller sheave) = 150 mm.

To find 'd'

Note: *Since power transmitted is 5 kW we can select 'B' cross-section belt (for which power rating is 0.22 to 5.44 kW) or 'C' cross-section (for which power rating is 0.37 to 11.99 kW)* ... *T(21-24)*

Select 'B' cross-section,

From table T(22-31), first preferred diameter $d = 140$ mm

F_b = Small diameter factor. It depends on speed ratio (Refer Table 22-35)

For the given drive, speed ratio

$$= \frac{n_1}{n_2} = \frac{D}{d} = \frac{1440}{400} = 3.6$$

Therefore, $F_b = 1.14$ and $d_e = 140 \times 1.14 = 159.6$ mm

Note: *The cross-section 'B' selected is OK since* $\boldsymbol{d_e = 159.6}$ **mm < 175 mm** *(Maximum permitted value).*

Step II: *Calculation of number of belts (i)*

Number of belts,

$$i = \frac{NF_a}{N^* F_c F_d} \quad \text{... E(21-36)}$$

Where, N = Drive power in kW = 5 kW

N^* = Power rating of 'B' cross-section belt selected

$$N^* = V\left(\frac{0.79}{V^{0.09}} - \frac{143.27}{d_e} - \frac{2.34v^2}{10^4}\right) \quad \text{... E(21-31)}$$

Where, $v = \frac{\pi d_1 n_1}{60}$

$$= \frac{\pi}{60}\left(\frac{140}{1000}\right)1440 = 10.56 \text{ m/sec}$$

Therefore, $$N^* = 10.56\left[\frac{0.79}{(10.56)^{0.09}} - \frac{51.33}{159.6} - \frac{1.31(10.56)^2}{10^4}\right]$$

$= 3.198$ kW

To find F_a, F_c, and F_d

F_a *is correction factor for industrial service (Refer T 21-28)*

For blowers assuming 10 to 16 hours per day service, $F_a = 1.1$

F_c *is correction factor for belt length (Refer T 22-27)*

F_c depends on the nominal inside length of belt and the cross-section of belt.

(Refer Table 22-27)

The length of belt, $$L = 2c + \frac{\pi}{2}(D + d) + \frac{(D-d)^2}{4c} \quad \text{... E(21-38)}$$

Where, 'c' is the centre distance.

To find 'C'

We have maximum centre distance,

$$C_{max} = 2(D+d) \quad \text{... E(21-40)}$$

Where, $$D = \frac{n_1}{n_2} d\eta \quad \text{... E(21-37)}$$

$$= \frac{1440}{400} \times 140 \times 1 = 504 \text{ mm}$$

Therefore, $$C_{max} = 2(504+140) = 1288 \text{ mm}$$

Also, C_{min} = Minimum centre distance

$$= 0.55(D+d)+t \quad \text{... E(21-41)}$$

For *'B'* section belt, width $w = 17$ mm and thickness $t = 11$ mm (Table 21-23)

Therefore, $$C_{min} = 0.55(504+140)+11 = 365.2 \text{ mm}$$

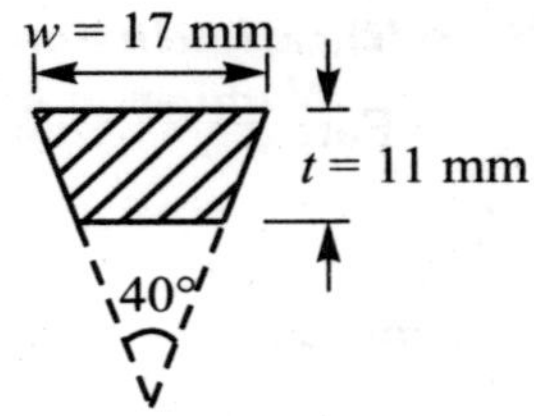

Therefore,

Centre distance *'c'* lies between 365.2 mm and 1288 mm.

Say c = 800 mm (an average value).

Therefore, $$L = 2\times 800 + \frac{\pi}{2}(504+140) + \frac{(504-140)^2}{4\times 800}$$

$$= 2653 \text{ mm}$$

The nearest table value of $L = 2710$ mm for which nominal inside length of belt = 2667 mm (Table T 21-29). Corresponding to the above length, $F_c = 1.04$ (Table 22-27)

To find F_d ***(Refer T 22-26)***

F_d = Correction factor for arc of contact. (Refer Table 22-26)

F_d = depends on θ_S, the angle of contact on small pulley given by,

$$\theta_S = \pi - 2\sin^{-1}\left(\frac{D-d}{2C}\right) \quad \text{... E(21-10b)}$$

$$= 180° - 2\sin^{-1}\left(\frac{504-140}{2\times 800}\right) = 153.7°$$

Corresponding to $\theta_S = 154°$, $F_d = 0.93$

Therefore,

Number of belts $$i = \frac{5\times 1.1}{3.198\times 1.04\times 0.93} = 1.778$$

Use , number of belts $i = 2$

Example 8.11: A 50 kW, 1440 rpm motor is required to drive an air compressor through the medium of V-belting. The diameter of motor and compressor pulleys are respectively 250 mm and 800 mm. The approximate centre distance between shafts is 1.5 m. Select suitable V-belts. ***(VTU, July / August 2002)***

Solution:

Step I: *Selection of cross-section of belt (A, B, C, D or E section).*

The cross-section of V-belt depends on the equivalent pitch diameter d_e is given by,

$$d_e = d_p F_b \qquad \text{... E(21-35)}$$

Where, $d_p = d =$ Diameter of small pulley (small sheave) = 250 mm.

$F_b =$ Small diameter factor (Refer table 22-25)

Note: *F_b depends on the speed ratio.*

For the given belt drive, speed ratio

$$= \frac{n_1}{n_2} = \frac{D}{d} = \frac{800}{250} = 3.2$$

Referring to Table (22-25), $F_b = 1.14$

Therefore, $d_e = 250 \times 1.14 = 285$ mm

For, $d_e = 285$ mm, *select 'C' cross-section V-belt* for which

$$N^* = V\left(\frac{1.47}{V^{0.09}} - \frac{143.27}{d_e} - \frac{2.34v^2}{10^4}\right) \qquad \text{... E(21-32)}$$

Where, $v =$ Velocity in m/sec

$$= \frac{\pi d_1 n_1}{60} = \frac{\pi}{60}\left(\frac{250}{1000}\right)1440 = 18.85 \text{ m/sec}$$

Therefore,

$$N^* = 18.85\left[\frac{1.47}{(18.85)^{0.09}} - \frac{143.27}{285} - \frac{2.34(18.85)^2}{10^4}\right]$$

$$= 18.76 \text{ kW}$$

Step II: *Calculation of number of belts (i)*

$$\textit{Number of belts } i = \frac{NF_a}{N^* F_c F_d} \qquad \text{... E(21-36)}$$

Where, $N =$ Drive power in kW = 50 kW

To find F_a, F_c and F_4

F_a is correction factor for industrial service (Refer T 21-28)

Assuming heavy duty service 10 to 16 hours per day service, $F_a = 1.3$

F_c is correction factor for belt length (Refer T 22-27)

F_c depends on the nominal inside length of belt and the cross-section.

For the given drive, length of belt

$$L = 2c + \frac{\pi}{2}(D + d) + \frac{(D-d)^2}{4c} \qquad \text{... E(21-38)}$$

Where, *'c'* is the centre distance between pulleys in mm .

$d =$ Diameter of small pulley = 250 mm

$D =$ Diameter of large pulley = 800 mm

To find 'C', the centre distance between shafts

Maximum centre distance,

$$C_{max} = 2(D+d) \quad \text{... E(21-40)}$$

$$= 2(800+250) = 2100 \text{ mm}$$

Also, C_{min} = Minimum centre distance

$$= 0.55(D+d)+t \quad \text{... E(21-41)}$$

For 'C' section belt, referring Table(21-23), Width $w = 22$ mm and thickness $t = 14$ mm

Therefore, $C_{min} = 0.55(800+250)+14 = 591.5$ mm

Assuming $C = 1300$ mm (An average value of C_{max} and C_{min})

Therefore,

$$L = 2\times1300 + \frac{\pi}{2}(800+250) + \frac{(800-250)^2}{4\times1300}$$

$$= 4307.51 \text{ mm}$$

Corresponding to the nearest table value of $L = 4450$ mm for which nominal inside length of belt of 'C' section is 4394 mm (Table T 21-29).

Now referring to Table (22-27), corresponding to the nominal inside length of 4394 mm and 'C' section, $F_c = 1.04$.

To find F_d ***(Refer T 22-26)***

F_d is the correction factor for arc of contact ***(Refer Table 22-26)***

F_d depends on θ_S, the angle of contact on small pulley given by,

$$\theta_S = \pi - 2\sin^{-1}\left(\frac{D-d}{2C}\right) \quad \text{... E(21-10b)}$$

$$= 180° - 2\sin^{-1}\left(\frac{800-250}{2\times1300}\right) = 155.57° \approx 157°$$

Therefore, $F_d = 0.94$

Substituting we get,

$$i = \frac{50\times1.3}{18.76\times1.04\times0.94} = 3.54$$

Use , *number of belts* $i = 4$

The correct centre distance 'C' is given by,

$$C = \frac{L}{4} - \frac{\pi(D+d)}{8} + \sqrt{\left\{\frac{L}{4} - \frac{\pi(D+d)}{8}\right\}^2 - \frac{(D-d)^2}{8}}$$

$$= \frac{4450}{4} - \frac{\pi}{8}(250+800) + \sqrt{\left\{\frac{4450}{4} - \frac{\pi}{8}(800+250)\right\}^2 - \frac{(800-250)^2}{8}}$$

$$= 1372.8 \text{ mm}$$

Example 8.12: A V-belt is arranged between two shafts whose centres are 850 mm apart. The driving pulley has 300 mm effective diameter and is to be supplied with 80 kW at 960 rpm. The follower is to run at 450 rpm. Determine the number of belts required using the following data.

(i) Area of cross section of belt = 400 mm²

(ii) Density of belt = 1000 kg/m³

(iii) Safe working tensile stress = 2.1 N/mm²

(iv) Coefficient of friction = 0.27

(v) Groove angle = 40°.

Solution:

Power transmitted by each belt

$$= \frac{(T_1 - T_2)v}{1000} \text{ kW}$$

$$\frac{D}{d} = \frac{n_1}{n_2} = \text{speed ratio} = \frac{960}{450}$$

Therefore, $D = \left(\frac{960}{450}\right)d$

$$= \frac{960}{450} \times 300 = 640 \text{ mm}$$

(Assuming no slip of belt)

Angle of wrap on small pulley is

$$\theta_S = \pi - 2\sin^{-1}\left(\frac{D-d}{2C}\right)$$

$$= 180 - 2\sin^{-1}\left(\frac{640-300}{2\times 850}\right)$$

$$= 156.92°$$

Therefore, angle of wrap on large pulley is

$$\theta_L = \pi + 2\sin^{-1}\left(\frac{D-d}{2C}\right) = 203.08°$$

For large pulley,

$$e^{\frac{\mu\theta_L}{\sin\alpha}} = e^{\frac{\mu\theta_L}{\sin 20}} = e^{\frac{0.27\times 203.08}{\sin 20}\times\frac{\pi}{180}} = 16.412; \qquad 2\alpha = 40°$$

For small pulley,

$$e^{\frac{\mu\theta_S}{\sin 20}} = e^{\frac{0.27\times 156.92}{\sin 20}\times\frac{\pi}{180}} = 8.689$$

$$e^{\frac{\mu\theta_S}{\sin 20}} < e^{\frac{\mu\theta_L}{\sin 20}}$$

Hence small pulley governs the design.

Considering centrifugal tension, T_C

$$\frac{T_1 - T_C}{T_2 - T_C} = e^{\frac{\mu\theta_S}{\sin 20}} = 8.689$$

Where, T_1 = Area of cross section of belt × Permissible stress in belt

$$= 400 \times 2.1 \text{ N}$$

$$= 840 \text{ N}$$

Note: *If 'm' is in kg/m^3*

$$T_C = (\text{Area}) \times mv^2 \times 10^{-6}$$

$$= 400 \times 1000 \times (15.08)^2 \times 10^{-6}$$

$$= 90.96 \text{ N}$$

$$v = \frac{\pi d n_1}{60}$$

$$= \frac{\pi}{60}\left(\frac{300}{1000}\right)960 = 15.08 \text{ m/sec}$$

Therefore, $\dfrac{T_1 - T_C}{T_2 - T_C} = 8.689$

$$\frac{840 - 90.96}{T_2 - 90.96} = 8.689$$

Therefore, $T_2 = 177.1655$ N

Therefore power transmitted/belt

$$= \frac{(T_1 - T_2)v}{1000} \text{ kW}$$

$$= \frac{(840 - 90.96)15.08}{1000}$$

$$= 11.2955 \text{ kW}$$

Total power to be transmitted = 80 kW.

Power transmitted by each belt = 11.2955 kW.

Therefore, number of V-belts required $= \dfrac{80}{11.2955} = 7.08$

Use number of belts $i = 8$.

Example 8.13. Determine the percentage increase in power transmitted made possible in changing over from a flat belt to a V-belt drive. The diameter of the flat pulley is same as the pitch diameter of the grooved pulley. The pulley rotates at the same speed as the grooved pulley. The coefficient of friction of both the belts is the same and equal to 0.3. The groove angle of V-belt pulley is 60°. The belts are made of same material and have the same area of cross-section. The angle of wrap on each pulley is 150°.

Solution:

Power transmitted by a flat belt/V-belt in terms of tensions T_1 and T_2 is given by,

$$\text{Power} = \frac{(T_1 - T_2)v}{1000} \text{ kW}$$

For a flat belt drive, $\dfrac{T_1}{T_2}$ = Ratio of belt tensions $= e^{\mu\theta}$

Where, μ = Coefficient of friction = 0.3

θ = Angle of wrap = 150°

Therefore, $\dfrac{T_1}{T_2} = e^{\mu\theta} = e^{0.3\times 150\times\frac{\pi}{180}} = 2.1933$

Similarly for a *V*-belt drive,

$$\frac{T_1}{T_2} = e^{\mu\theta/\sin\alpha}$$

Where, 2α = Groove angle = 60°

Therefore, $\alpha = 30°$

$\mu = 0.3, \theta = 150°$ (same as that of flat belt)

Therefore, $\dfrac{T_1}{T_2} = e^{\mu\theta/\sin\alpha} = e^{\frac{0.3\times 150}{\sin 30}\times\frac{\pi}{180}} = 4.81$

Power transmitted by *V*-belt

$$P_{V\text{-belt}} = \frac{(T_1 - T_2)v}{1000} \text{ kW}$$

$$= \frac{T_1\left(1 - \frac{T_2}{T_1}\right)v}{1000}$$

Where, $\dfrac{T_2}{T_1} = \dfrac{1}{4.81}$

$$P_{V\text{-belt}} = \frac{T_1\left(1 - \frac{1}{4.81}\right)v}{1000} = \frac{0.792 T_1 v}{1000} \quad \ldots (1)$$

Similarly $\quad P_{\text{flat belt}} = \dfrac{(T_1 - T_2)v}{1000}$

$$= T_1\left(1 - \frac{T_2}{T_1}\right)\frac{v}{1000}$$

Where, $$\frac{T_2}{T_1} = \frac{1}{2.1933}$$

Therefore, $$P_{\text{flat belt}} = T_1(0.5441)\frac{v}{1000}$$

$$= \frac{0.5441 T_1 v}{1000} \quad \text{... (2)}$$

Note:

(i) Since both the pulleys have same diameter and speeds are same, their velocities are same

$$V]_{\text{flat belt}} = V]_{v\text{-belt}}$$

(ii) The materials of both the pulleys is the same and also they have same cross sectional area

Hence, $$T_1]_{\text{flat belt}} = T_1]_{v\text{-belt}}$$

With the above information,

$$\frac{P_{v\text{-belt}}}{P_{\text{flat belt}}} = \frac{\dfrac{0.792\, T_1\, v}{1000}}{\dfrac{0.5441\, T_1\, v}{1000}}$$

$$= \frac{0.792}{0.5441} = 1.455$$

Therefore, $$P_{v\text{-belt}} = 1.455\, P_{\text{flat belt}}$$

i.e., The power transmitted by V-belt is 45.5% higher than the power transmitted by flat belt for the given data.

Design Procedure for Roller Chain Drive

Following steps are generally followed while designing a roller chain drive

Step I: *Calculation of 'p', pitch of chain and chain size (also called chain number)*

The required pitch of chain for roller chains is obtained from equation

$$p \leq 25\left(\frac{900}{n_1}\right)^{\frac{2}{3}} \quad \text{... E(21-106a)}$$

Where, p = Pitch of chain in meter.

n_1 = Speed of small sprocket (toothed wheel) called sprocket Pinion in rpm.

The value of *'p'* obtained form E(21-106a) is rounded off to the standard pitch by referring to Table(21-64) and the corresponding chain number such as 208*A*, 208*B* etc. is obtained.

Table - (21-64) MDH

Chain Number	Pitch P, mm	Roller diameter Max D, mm	Width between inner plates, W Min, mm	Bearing in Diameter Max D_p, mm	Bush Bore, Min d_b, mm	Chain Path Depth Max H_c, mm	Plate Depth, H Min, mm	Crank linked dimensions, Max X, mm	Width over Inner Link Min W, mm	Width between Outer Plates, Max, mm	Width over Bearing pin, Min A, mm	Additional Width for Joint Fastener, Max B, mm	Measuring load		Braking load, Min	
													N	kgf	kN	kgf
208A	25.40	7.92	7.95	3.96	4.01	12.33	12.07	6.9	11.18	11.31	17.8	3.9	127.5	13	13.8	1410
208B	25.40	8.51	7.75	4.45	4.50	12.07	11.81	6.9	11.30	11.43	17.0	3.9	127.5	13	17.9	1820
210A	31.70	10.16	9.53	5.08	5.13	15.35	15.09	8.4	13.84	13.97	21.8	4.1	196.1	20	21.8	2220
210B	31.75	10.16	9.65	5.08	5.13	14.99	14.73	8.4	13.28	13.41	19.6	4.1	196.1	20	22.3	2270
212A	38.10	11.91	12.70	5.94	5.99	18.34	18.08	9.9	17.75	17.88	26.9	4.6	284.4	29	31.2	3180
212B	38.10	12.07	11.68	5.72	5.77	16.39	16.13	9.9	13.62	15.76	22.7	4.6	284.4	29	28.9	2950
216A	50.80	15.88	15.88	7.92	7.97	24.39	24.13	13.0	22.61	22.74	33.5	5.4	500.2	51	55.6	5670
219B	50.80	15.88	17.02	8.28	8.33	21.34	21.08	13.0	25.45	25.58	36.1	5.4	500.1	51	42.3	4310
220A	63.50	19.05	19.05	9.53	9.58	30.48	30.18	16.0	27.46	27.59	41.1	6.1	774.7	79	86.8	8850
220B	63.50	19.05	19.56	10.19	10.24	26.68	26.42	16.0	29.01	29.14	43.2	6.1	774.7	79	64.5	6580
224A	76.20	22.23	25.40	11.10	11.15	36.55	36.20	19.1	35.46	35.59	50.8	6.6	1108.2	113	124.5	12700
224B	76.20	25.40	25.40	14.63	14.68	33.73	33.40	19.1	37.92	38.05	53.4	6.6	1108.2	113	97.9	9980
228B	88.90	27.94	30.99	15.90	15.95	36.46	37.08	21.3	46.58	46.71	65.1	7.4	1510.2	164	129.1	13160
232B	101.60	29.21	30.99	17.81	17.86	42.72	42.29	24.4	45.57	45.70	64.7	7.9	2000.6	204	169.1	17240

Step II: ***Calculation of number of teeth on sprockets [Z_1 and Z_2] and pitch diameter of sprockets [d_1 and d_2].***

(a) To find Z_1 and Z_2, the number of teeth on sprocket Pinion and sprocket Gear.

Note: *The number of teeth on sprocket Pinion (the smaller toothed wheel) depends on the transmission ratio given by*

$$\text{Transmission ratio} = \frac{n_1}{n_2}$$

Where, n_1 and n_2 are speeds of rotation of sprocket Pinion and Gear respectively.

Note: *Transmission ratio* ≥ 1

Knowing transmission ratio, the range of teeth on sprocket Pinion is obtained from Table (21-60).

Table - (21-60) MDH

Transmission Ratio	i	1-2	2-3	3-4	4-5	5-7
Number of Teeth	Z_1	13-27	27-25	26-23	23-21	21-17

Example 8.14: For transmission ratio 4.286, the number of teeth on sprocket Pinion Z_1 = 23 to 21 . Obtain Z_2 for every value of Z_1 as shown in table.

Note: *From the table, select Z_2 which is a whole number or a number very close to a whole number so that the transmission ratio obtained from the combination of Z_1 and Z_2 is very close to the required value (i.e. 4.286 in the above example).*

Sl. No	Z_1	Z_2
1.	When $Z_1 = 21$	$Z_2 = Z_1 \times$ Transmission ratio = 21 × 4.286 = 90.006
2.	22	94.292
3.	23	98.578

(b) Calculation of pitch diameter of sprockets $(d_1$ and $d_2)$

In general, pitch diameter of sprockets is given by

$$d = \frac{p}{\sin\left(\frac{180}{Z}\right)} \qquad \text{... E(21-126)}$$

Therefore, pitch diameter of sprocket Pinion is

$$d_1 = \frac{p}{\sin\left(\frac{180}{Z_1}\right)}$$

Similarly, pitch diameter of sprocket Gear is

$$d_2 = \frac{p}{\sin\left(\frac{180}{Z_2}\right)}$$

Step III: *Calculation of Length of chain (L)*

The length of chain, '*L*' is obtained from equation

$$L = pL_P \qquad \text{... E(21-125)}$$

Where, p = Pitch of chain in mm.

L_P = Chain length in pitches and is given by

$$= 2C_P \cos\alpha + \left(\frac{Z_1 + Z_2}{2}\right) + \alpha\left(\frac{Z_2 - Z_1}{180}\right) \qquad \text{... E(21-122)}$$

Where, $C_P = \frac{C}{p}$

C_P = Centre distance in pitches, (a number).

C = Centre distance between sprockets, mm.

$$\alpha = \sin^{-1}\left(\frac{d_2 - d_1}{2C}\right)$$

Note: *To find C*

(*i*) When exact centre distance between sprockets is known, use the given value of '*C*' in equation $C_p = \frac{C}{p}$.

(ii) When centre distance is unknown, calculate minimum and maximum centre distances given by,

Minimum centre distance $C_{\min} = K_{\min} C'$ ... E(21-120)

Where, $$C' = \frac{d_1 + d_2}{2}$$

Constant $K_{\min}$ depends on transmission ratio (Refer table 21-63)

Table - (21-63) MDH

Transmission Ratio, 'i'	*Minimum Centre Distance Constant, K_{min}*
3	$1 + \frac{30 \text{ to } 50}{c'}$
3 – 4	1.2
4 – 5	1.3
5 – 6	1.4
6 – 7	1.5

Maximum centre distance, $C_{\max} = 80p$ ... E(21-121)

Use $$C = \frac{C_{\max} + C_{\min}}{2} \text{ (an average value)}$$

(iii) The value of L_P obtained from E(21-122) is rounded off to the next even number.

Note: *The length of chain 'L' is based on even value of L_P.*

(iii) Calculation of number of chains 'i' (or number of strands)

The number of chains $$i = \frac{F_\theta}{F_a}$$ ... E(21-118)

Where, F_θ = Chain pull in Newton and is obtained from equation

$$N = \frac{F_\theta v}{1000 K_l K_s}$$ ... E(21-115a)

i.e., $$F_\theta = \frac{1000 N K_l K_s}{v}$$

Where, v = Velocity of chain in m/sec and is given by

$$v = p\frac{Z_1 n_1}{60}$$ ... E(21-105)

Table 21-64: Extended pitch transmission roller chain dimensions. Measuring loads and breaking loads

Chain Number	Pitch, P, mm	Roller diameter Max D_r, mm	Width between Inner Plates, W Min, mm	Bearing in Diameter Max D_p, mm	Bush Bore, Min d_b, mm	Chain Path Depth, Max H_c, mm	Plate Depth, H Min, mm	Crank Linked Dimension, Max X, mm	Width Over Inner Link Min W, mm	Width Between Outer Plates, Max, mm	Width Over Bearing Pin, Min A, mm	Addition Width for Joint Fastener, Max B, mm	Measuring Load		Breaking Load, Min	
													N	kgf	N	kgf
208A	25.40	7.92	7.95	3.96	4.01	12.33	12.07	6.9	11.18	11.31	17.8	3.9	127.5	13	13.8	1410
208B	25.40	8.51	7.75	4.45	4.50	12.07	11.81	6.9	11.30	11.43	17.0	3.9	127.5	13	17.9	1820
210A	31.70	10.16	9.53	5.08	5.13	15.35	15.09	8.4	13.84	13.97	21.8	4.1	196.1	20	21.8	2220
210B	31.75	10.16	9.65	5.08	5.13	14.99	14.73	8.4	13.28	13.41	19.6	4.1	196.1	20	22.3	2270
212A	38.10	11.91	12.70	5.94	5.99	18.34	18.08	9.9	17.75	17.88	26.9	4.6	284.4	29	31.2	3180
212B	38.10	12.07	11.68	5.72	5.77	16.39	16.13	9.9	13.62	15.76	22.7	4.6	284.4	29	28.9	2950
216A	50.80	15.88	15.88	7.92	7.97	24.39	24.13	13.0	22.61	22.74	33.5	5.4	500.2	51	55.6	5670
219B	50.80	15.88	17.02	8.28	8.33	21.34	21.08	13.0	25.45	25.58	36.1	5.4	500.1	51	42.3	4310
220A	63.50	19.05	19.05	9.53	9.58	30.48	30.18	16.0	27.46	27.59	41.1	6.1	774.7	79	86.8	8850
220B	63.50	19.05	19.56	10.19	10.24	26.68	26.42	16.0	29.01	29.14	43.2	6.1	774.7	79	64.5	6580
224A	76.20	22.23	25.40	11.10	11.15	36.55	36.20	19.1	35.46	35.59	50.8	6.6	1108.2	113	124.5	12700
224B	76.20	25.40	25.40	14.63	14.68	33.73	33.40	19.1	37.92	38.05	53.4	6.6	1108.2	113	97.9	9980
228B	88.90	47.94	30.99	15.90	15.95	36.46	37.08	21.3	46.58	46.71	65.1	7.4	1510.2	164	129.1	13160
232B	101.60	29.21	30.99	17.81	17.86	42.72	42.29	24.4	45.57	45.70	64.7	7.9	2000.6	204	169.1	17240

p = Pitch of chain in metre

Z_1 = Number of teeth on sprocket Pinion

n_1 = Speed of sprocket Pinion in rpm

N = Power transmitted in kW

K_l = Load factor = 1.1 to 1.5

K_s = Service factor (Refer table 21-61)

Now, F_a = Allowable pull in chain in N

$$= \frac{F_u}{n_0} \quad \text{... E(21-113)}$$

Where, F_u = Ultimate load for the chain under consideration (Refer Table 21-64)

n_0 = Working factor of safety = 5

Finally 'i' is obtained by dividing F_θ by F_a

i.e., $$i = \frac{F_\theta}{F_a}$$

Example 8.15: Select suitable roller chain drive to transmit 10 kW from a shaft running at 1500 rpm to another shaft to be run at 350 rpm.

Solution:

Step I: ***Calculation of pitch of chain 'p' and size of chain (or chain number)***

For roller chain, $$p \leq 25\left(\frac{900}{n_1}\right)^{\frac{2}{3}} \quad \text{... E(21-106a)}$$

Where, n_1 = Speed of sprocket Pinion in rpm = 1500.

p = Pitch of chain in mm.

Therefore, $$p \leq 25\left(\frac{900}{1500}\right)^{\frac{2}{3}}$$

$$p \leq 17.75 \text{ mm}$$

Referring Table (21-64), select standard pitch p = 25.4 mm and the corresponding *chain number is* 208*A or* 208*B*.

Step II: ***Calculation of diameters of sprockets (d_1 and d_2) and number of teeth on sprockets (Z_1 and Z_2).***

Note: *In general, pitch diameter of sprockets is given by*

$$d = \frac{p}{\sin\left(\frac{180}{Z}\right)} \quad \text{... E(21-126)}$$

Pitch diameter of sprocket Pinion

$$d_1 = \frac{p}{\sin\left(\frac{180}{Z_1}\right)}$$

Pitch diameter of sprocket Gear

$$d_2 = \frac{p}{\sin\left(\frac{180}{Z_2}\right)}$$

To find Z_1 and Z_2

Note: *The number of teeth on sprocket pinion depends on transmission ratio 'i'*

For the gear drive,

$$\textit{Transmission ratio} = \frac{1500}{350} = 4.286$$

For transmission ratio 4 to 5, referring Table (21-60), the number of teeth on sprocket Pinion $Z_1 = 23 \text{ to } 21$

Sl. No	Z_1	Z_2
1.	When Z_1= 21	$Z_2 = Z_1 \times$ Transmission ratio = 21× 4.286 = 90.006
2.	22	94.292
3.	23	98.578

Note: *From the combination of Z_1 and Z_2, select Z_2 such that it gives a transmission ratio $\left(\frac{Z_2}{Z_1}\right)$ which is very close to the required value i.e. 4.286.*

Say Z_1 = 21 teeth and Z_2 = 90 teeth.

With the above values selected, we get

Transmission ratio $= \frac{Z_2}{Z_1} = \frac{90}{21} = 4.2857$ which is very close to the required ratio 4.286.

Hence the selection of Z_1 and Z_2 is correct and the number of teeth Z_1 and Z_2 selected for sprocket Pinion and Gear are suitable.

Therefore,

$$d_1 = \frac{25.4}{\sin\left(\frac{180}{21}\right)} = 170.42 \text{ mm}$$

$$d_2 = \frac{25.4}{\sin\left(\frac{180}{90}\right)} = 727.8 \text{ mm}$$

Step III: *Calculation of length of chain 'L'*

Length of chain in pitches

$$L_p = 2C_P \cos\alpha + \left(\frac{Z_1 + Z_2}{2}\right) + \alpha\left(\frac{Z_2 - Z_1}{180}\right) \quad \text{... E(21-122)}$$

Where, $C_P = \frac{C}{p}$ = Centre distance in pitches

To find 'C', the centre distance

(a) Minimum centre distance $C_{\min} = K_{\min} C'$ ***... E(21-120)***

Where, $C' = \frac{d_1 + d_2}{2} = \frac{170.42 + 727.8}{2} = 449.11$ mm

Factor $K_{\min}$ *depends on transmission ratio* (Refer table 21-63)

For transmission ratio 4.286, $K_{\min} = 1.3$ ... T(21-63)

Therefore, minimum centre distance,

$$C_{\min} = 1.3 \times 449.11 \text{ mm} = 583.843 \text{ mm}$$

(b) Maximum centre distance, C_{max}

$$C_{\max} = 80p \quad \text{... E(21-121)}$$

$$= 80 \times 25.4 \text{ mm} = 2032 \text{ mm}$$

Take C = 1250 mm (an average value of $C_{\max}$ and $C_{\min}$)

Therefore, $C_P = \frac{C}{p}$

$$= \frac{1250}{25.4} = 49.21$$

$$\alpha = \sin^{-1}\left(\frac{d_2 - d_1}{2C}\right)$$

$$= \sin^{-1}\left(\frac{727.8 - 170.42}{2 \times 1250}\right) = 12.88°$$

Therefore, $L_P = 2 \times 49.21 \times \cos 12.88 + \left(\frac{21 + 90}{2}\right) + 12.88\left(\frac{90 - 21}{180}\right)$

$$= 156.377$$

Say $L_P = 158$ (an even number).

Therefore, Length of chain

$$L = pL_P \quad \text{... E(21-125)}$$

$$= 25.4 \times 158 = 4013.2 \text{ mm}$$

Step IV: *Calculation of number of strands (i) or number of chain*

Number of chains $i = \frac{F_\theta}{F_a}$ ... E(21-118)

Where, F_θ is chain pull in Newton and is obtained from

$$N = \frac{F_\theta v}{1000 K_l K_s} \qquad \text{... E(21-115a)}$$

i.e.,
$$F_\theta = \frac{1000 N K_l K_s}{v}$$

Where, v = Velocity of chain in m/sec

$$v = \frac{p Z_1 n_1}{60} \qquad \text{... E(21-105)}$$

$$= \left(\frac{25.4}{1000}\right) 21 \times \frac{1500}{60} = 13.34 \text{ m/sec}$$

K_l = Load factor = 1.1 to 1.5 say $K_l = 1.3$

K_s = Service factor ... Table 21-61

Assuming medium shock and 8 to 10 hours per day service, $K_s = 1.2$ to 1.9.

Say $K_s = 1.5$

N = Power in kW = 10 kW

Therefore,
$$F_\theta = \frac{1000 \times 10 \times 1.3 \times 1.5}{13.34} \text{N} = 1461.77 \text{ N}$$

Also F_a = Allowable pull in chain in N

$$F_a = \frac{F_u}{n_0} \qquad \text{... E(21-113)}$$

Where, F_u = Ultimate load ... Table (21-64)

Assuming 208*B* chain,

F_u = Ultimate load or breaking load

$= 17.9 \text{ kN} = 17.9 \times 10^3 \text{N}$

n_0 = Working factor of safety = 5 (say)

Therefore,
$$F_a = \frac{F_u}{n_0}$$

$$= \frac{17.9 \times 10^3}{5} = 3.58 \times 10^3 \text{N}$$

Therefore, number of strands in chain

$$i = \frac{F_\theta}{F_a}$$

$$= \frac{1461.77}{3.580 \times 10^3} = 1$$

Example 8.16: A roller chain is to be designed to transmit 5 kW from a shaft running at 600 rpm to another shaft to run at 750 rpm. Determine
(a) Pitch of chain and chain number.
(b) Number of teeth on sprockets.
(c) Pitch diameters of sprockets.
(d) Shortest centre distance between them.
(e) Number of chains required.

Solution:

(a) To calculate pitch of chain and chain number

For roller chain,

$$p \leq 25\left(\frac{900}{n_1}\right)^{\frac{2}{3}}; \; n_1 = 750 \text{ rpm} \quad \text{... E(21-106a)}$$

$$\leq 25\left(\frac{900}{750}\right)^{\frac{2}{3}} \leq 28.25 \text{ mm}$$

Where, n_1 = Speed of sprocket pinion = 750 rpm.

Referring to Table (21-64), select pitch p = 25.4 mm and the corresponding *chain number 208A or 208B. Say 208B chain.*

(b) To calculate number of teeth on sprockets (Z_1 and Z_2).

The number of teeth on sprocket Pinion depends on transmission ratio. For the chain drive under consideration,

$$\textit{Transmission ratio } \frac{n_1}{n_2} = \frac{750}{600} = 1.25$$

For the transmission ratio 1.25, referring to Table (21-60), the number of teeth Z_1 on sprocket pinion is 30 to 27.

Sl. No	Z_1	Z_2
1.	When Z_1 = 27	$Z_2 = Z_1 \times$ Transmission ratio = 27 × 1.25 = 33.75
2.	28	35
3.	29	36.25
4.	30	37.5

Therefore, select Z_1 = 28 teeth and Z_2 = 35 teeth since both Z_1 and Z_2 are whole numbers.

(c) To calculate pitch diameter of sprockets (d_1 and d_2).

Pitch diameter of sprocket Pinion

$$d_1 = \frac{p}{\sin\left(\frac{180}{Z_1}\right)}$$

$$= \frac{25.4}{\sin\left(\frac{180}{28}\right)} = 226.86 \text{ mm}$$

Pitch diameter of sprocket Gear

$$d_2 = \frac{p}{\sin\left(\frac{180}{Z_2}\right)}$$

$$= \frac{25.4}{\sin\left(\frac{180}{35}\right)} = 283.36 \text{ mm}$$

(d) To calculate shortest centre distance between sprocket centres (i.e. C)

Minimum centre distance,

$$C_{\min} = K_{\min} C' \qquad \text{... E(21-120)}$$

Where, $$C' = \frac{d_1 + d_2}{2}$$

$$= \frac{226.86 + 283.36}{2} = 255.11 \text{ mm}$$

$$K_{\min} = 1 + \frac{40}{C'}$$

$$= 1 + \frac{40}{255.11} = 1.156$$

Therefore, $$C_{\min} = 1.156 \times 255.11$$

$$= 294.907 \text{ mm}$$

(e) To calculate number of chains required ***... T(21-62)***

Number of strands $$i = \frac{F_\theta}{F_a} \qquad \text{... E(21-118)}$$

Where, F_θ is chain pull in Newton and is obtained from

$$N = \frac{F_\theta v}{1000 K_l K_s} \qquad \text{... E(21-115a)}$$

i.e., $$F_\theta = \frac{1000 N K_l K_s}{v}$$

Where, v = Velocity of chain in m/sec

$$v = \frac{p Z_1 n_1}{60} \qquad \text{... E(21-105)}$$

$$= \left(\frac{25.4}{1000}\right) \frac{28 \times 750}{60} = 8.89 \text{ m/sec}$$

K_l = Load factor = 1.3

K_s = Service factor = 1 for 1 to 10 hours per day service.

Therefore, $F_\theta = \dfrac{1000 \times 5 \times 1.3 \times 1}{8.89}$ N = 731.16 N

Also, F_a = Allowable pull in chain in Newton

$$F_a = \frac{F_u}{n_0} \quad \text{... E(21-113)}$$

Where, F_u = Ultimate strength of chain (Refer Table 21-64)

For 208B chain $F_u = 17.9 \text{ kN} = 17.9 \times 10^3 \text{ N}$

n_0 = Working factor of safety = 5 (assumed)

Then, $F_a = \dfrac{F_u}{n_0}$

$$= \frac{17.9 \times 10^3}{5} = 3.58 \times 10^3 \text{N}$$

Therefore, number of strands in chain

$$i = \frac{F_\theta}{F_a}$$

$$= \frac{731.16}{3.58 \times 10^3} = 1$$

Example 8.17: Design a roller chain to transmit 200 kW from an engine to a generator. The speeds of generator and engine are respectively 500 rpm and 90 rpm.

Solution:

Step I: ***Calculation of pitch of chain 'p' and size of chain.***

$$\text{Pitch} \quad p \le 25\left(\frac{900}{n_1}\right)^{\frac{2}{3}} \quad \text{... E(21-106a)}$$

Where, n_1 = Speed of sprocket Pinion = 500 rpm.

Therefore, $p \le 25\left(\dfrac{900}{500}\right)^{\frac{2}{3}}$

$p \le 37.07$ mm

Referring Table (21-64), select pitch $p = 31.75$ mm and *the corresponding chain number is* 210 *B*.

Step II: ***Calculation of number of teeth (Z_1 and Z_2) and pitch diameters of sprockets (d_1 and d_2).***

(Z_1, the number of teeth on sprocket pinion depends on transmission ratio).

For the given drive,

$$\textit{Transmission ratio} = \frac{n_1}{n_2} = \frac{500}{90} = 5.55$$

Referring Table (21-60), for transmission ratio 5.55, $Z_1 = 17$ to 21

Sl. No	Z_1	Z_2
1.	When $Z_1 = 17$	$Z_2 = Z_1 \times$ Transmission ratio = 17 × 5.55 = 94.35
2.	18	99.9
3.	19	105.45
4.	20	111
5.	21	116.55

Select $Z_1 = 20$ *and* $Z_2 = 111$ *teeth (both* Z_1 *and* Z_2 *are whole numbers)*

Pitch diameter of sprocket Pinion

$$d_1 = \frac{p}{\sin\left(\frac{180}{Z_1}\right)}$$

$$= \frac{31.75}{\sin\left(\frac{180}{20}\right)} = 202.93 \text{ mm}$$

Pitch diameter of sprocket Gear

$$d_2 = \frac{p}{\sin\left(\frac{180}{Z_2}\right)}$$

$$= \frac{31.75}{\sin\left(\frac{180}{111}\right)} = 1121.95 \text{ mm}$$

Step III: *Calculation of length of chain 'L'*

Length of chain $L = pL_P$ ... E(21-125)

Where, L_p = Length of chain in pitches given by

$$L_p = 2C_P \cos\alpha + \left(\frac{Z_1 + Z_2}{2}\right) + \alpha\left(\frac{Z_2 - Z_1}{180}\right) \quad \text{... E(21-122)}$$

Where, C_P = Centre distance in pitches = $\frac{C}{p}$

C = Centre distance

C_{min} = Minimum centre distance

$C_{min} = K_{min} C'$ ... E(21-120)

Where, $$C' = \frac{d_1 + d_2}{2}$$

$$= \frac{202.96 + 1121.95}{2} = 662.46 \text{ mm}$$

Factor K_{min} depends on transmission ratio (Refer table 21-63)

For transmission ratio 5.55,

$$K_{min} = 1.4$$

Therefore $$C_{min} = 1.4 \times 662.46 = 927.4 \text{ mm}$$

Also, $$C_{max} = \text{Maximum centre distance} = 80p$$

$$= 80 \times 31.75 = 2540 \text{ mm}$$

Take C = 1800 mm *(an average value lying between* C_{max} and C_{min}*)*

Therefore, $$C_P = \frac{C}{p}$$

$$= \frac{1800}{31.75} = 56.69$$

$$\alpha = \sin^{-1}\left(\frac{d_2 - d_1}{2C}\right)$$

$$= \sin^{-1}\left(\frac{1121.95 - 202.96}{2 \times 1800}\right) = 14.79°$$

Therefore, $$L_P = 2 \times 56.69 \times \cos 14.79 + \left(\frac{111 + 20}{2}\right) + 14.798\left(\frac{111 - 20}{180}\right)$$

$$= 182.59$$

Say $L_P = 184$ (an even number).

Therefore, Length of chain

$$L = pL_P \quad \text{... E(21-125)}$$

$$= 31.75 \times 184 = 5842 \text{ mm}$$

Step IV: ***To calculate the number of strands (i)***

Number of strands $$i = \frac{F_\theta}{F_a} \quad \text{... E(21-118)}$$

Where, F_θ is chain pull in Newton and is obtained from equation

$$N = \frac{F_\theta v}{1000 K_l K_s} \quad \text{... E(21-115a)}$$

Therefore, $$F_\theta = \frac{1000 N K_l K_s}{v}$$

Where, $N =$ Power in kW = 200 kW

$K_l =$ Load factor = 1.1 to 1.5 say $K_l = 1.3$

$K_s =$ Service factor = 1 for 10 hours per day service.

$v =$ Velocity of chain in m/sec

$$v = \frac{pZ_1 n_1}{60} \quad \text{... E(21-105)}$$

$$= \left(\frac{3.75}{1000}\right) \times \frac{20 \times 500}{60} = 5.29\,\text{m/sec}$$

Therefore, $F_\theta = \dfrac{1000 \times 200 \times 1.3 \times 1}{5.29}$ N

$= 49149.34$ N

Also $F_a =$ Allowable pull in chain in N

$$F_a = \frac{F_u}{n_0} \quad \text{... E(21-113)}$$

Where, $F_u =$ Ultimate load (Refer Table 21-64)

Selecting 210B chain,

$F_u =$ Ultimate load or breaking load

$= 22.3 \times 10^3$ N

$n_0 =$ Working factor of safety = 5 (assumed)

Therefore, $F_a = \dfrac{F_u}{n_0}$

$$= \frac{22.3 \times 10^3}{5} = 4.46 \times 10^3\,\text{N}$$

Therefore, the number of strands in chain

$$i = \frac{F_\theta}{F_a}$$

$$= \frac{49149.34}{4.46 \times 10^3} = 11 \text{ Strands}$$

Example 8.18: A compressor is to be actuated by a 15 kW electric motor running at 970 rpm and the speed of compressor is 330 rpm. The minimum centre distance should be 600 mm. Select suitable roller chain.

Solution:

Step I: ***Calculation of pitch 'p' and size of chain (or chain number)***

For roller chain,

Pitch, $$p \le 25\left(\frac{900}{n_1}\right)^{\frac{2}{3}} \quad \text{... E(21-106a)}$$

Where, p = pitch of chain in mm.

n_1 = Speed of smaller sprocket = 970 rpm.

Therefore,
$$p \le 25\left(\frac{900}{970}\right)^{\frac{2}{3}}$$
$$\le 23.78 \text{ mm}$$

Referring Table (21-64), select pitch p = 25.4 mm *and the corresponding chain number is 208A or 208B. Say chain number 208A.*

Step II: *Calculation of number of teeth on sprockets (Z_1 and Z_2) and pitch diameters of sprockets (d_1 and d_2).*

(a) *Calculation of number of teeth on sprockets (Z_1 and Z_2).*

The number of teeth on sprocket Pinion Z_1 depends on transmission ratio.

For the given drive,

$$\textit{Transmission ratio} = \frac{n_1}{n_2} = \frac{970}{330} = 2.94$$

Referring Table (21-60), for transmission ratio 2.94, the number of teeth on sprocket Pinion is $Z_1 = 27$ to 25.

Sl. No	Z_1	Z_2
1.	When $Z_1 = 25$	$Z_2 = Z_1 \times$ Transmission ratio = 25 × 2.94 = 73.5
2.	26	76.44
3.	27	79.38 ≈ 80

Therefore select $Z_1 = 27$ and $Z_2 = 80$ teeth.

Note: *With the above values of Z_1 and Z_2, the transmission ratio*

$$= \frac{Z_2}{Z_1} = \frac{80}{27} = 2.96$$

(b) *To find pitch diameters of sprockets (d_1 and d_2)*

Pitch diameter of sprocket Pinion

$$d_1 = \frac{p}{\sin\left(\frac{180}{Z_1}\right)}$$

$$= \frac{25.4}{\sin\left(\frac{180}{27}\right)} = 218.79 \text{ mm}$$

Pitch diameter of sprocket Gear

$$d_2 = \frac{p}{\sin\left(\frac{180}{Z_2}\right)}$$

$$= \frac{25.4}{\sin\left(\frac{180}{80}\right)} = 646.97 \text{ mm}$$

Step III: ***Calculation of length of chain 'L'***

Length of chain $L = pL_P$ ... E(21-125)

Where, $L_P =$ Length of chain in pitches given by

$$L_P = 2C_P \cos\alpha + \left(\frac{Z_1 + Z_2}{2}\right) + \alpha\left(\frac{Z_2 - Z_1}{180}\right) \quad \text{... E(21-122)}$$

Where, $C_P =$ Centre distance in pitches $= \frac{C}{p} = \frac{600}{25.4} = 23.2$

$$\alpha = \sin^{-1}\left(\frac{d_2 - d_1}{2C}\right)$$

$$= \sin^{-1}\left(\frac{646.97 - 218.79}{2 \times 600}\right) = 20.9°$$

Therefore, $L_P = 2 \times 23.62 \times \cos 20.9 + \left(\frac{27 + 80}{2}\right) + 20.9\left(\frac{80 - 27}{180}\right)$

$$= 103.78$$

Use $L_P = 104$ (an even number).

Therefore, Length of chain

$$L = pL_P \quad \text{... E(21-125)}$$

$$= 25.4 \times 104 = 2641.6 \text{ mm}$$

Step IV: ***To calculate number of strands (i)***

Number of strands $i = \frac{F_\theta}{F_a}$ ... E(21-118)

Where, F_θ is chain pull in Newton and is obtained from equation

$$N = \frac{F_\theta v}{1000 K_l K_s} \quad \text{... E(21-115a)}$$

Therefore, $F_\theta = \frac{1000 N K_l K_s}{v}$

Where, $N =$ Power in kW = 15 kW

$v =$ Velocity of chain in m/sec

$$v = \frac{p Z_1 n_1}{60} \quad \text{... E(21-105)}$$

$$= \left(\frac{25.4}{1000}\right) \times \frac{27 \times 970}{60} = 11.09 \text{ m/sec}$$

K_l = Load factor = 1.1 to 1.5 say $K_l = 1.3$

K_s = Service factor = 1 for 10 hours per day service.

Therefore, $F_\theta = \dfrac{1000 \times 15 \times 1.3 \times 1}{11.09} \text{N} = 1758.34 \text{ N}$

Also F_a = Allowable pull in chain in N

$$F_a = \frac{F_u}{n_0} \quad \text{... E(21-113)}$$

For 208A chain,

F_u = 13.8 kN ; Refer Table (21-64)

n_0 = Working factor of safety = 5 (assumed)

Therefore, $F_a = \dfrac{F_u}{n_0}$

$$= \frac{13.8 \times 10^3}{5} = 2.76 \times 10^3 \text{ N}$$

Number of chains,

$$i = \frac{F_\theta}{F_a}$$

$$= \frac{1758.34}{2.76 \times 10^3} = 1$$

Example 8.19: Design a roller chain to transmit 50 kW at a speed of 720 rpm. The driven machinery is to run at 250 rpm.

Solution:

Step I: *Calculation of pitch of chain 'p' and size of chain (or chain number)*

For roller chain,

Pitch, $p \le 25\left(\dfrac{900}{n_1}\right)^{\frac{2}{3}}$ ... E(21-106a)

Where, p = pitch of chain in mm.

n_1 = Speed of sprocket Pinion = 720 rpm.

Therefore, $p \le 25\left(\dfrac{900}{720}\right)^{\frac{2}{3}}$

≤ 29.03 mm

Referring Table(21-64), select pitch p = 25.4 mm *and the corresponding chain number is 208A or 208B. Use chain number 208A.*

Step I: *Calculation of number of teeth on sprockets [Z_1 and Z_2] and pitch diameters of sprockets [d_1 and d_2].*

(a) *Calculation of number of teeth on sprockets [Z_1 and Z_2].*

The number of teeth on sprocket pinion Z_1 depends on transmission ratio.

For the given drive,

$$\text{Transmission ratio} = \frac{n_1}{n_2} = \frac{720}{250} = 2.88$$

Referring Table (21-60), for transmission ratio is 2.88, the number of teeth $Z_1 = 27$ to 25

Sl. No	Z_1	Z_2
1.	When $Z_1 = 25$	$Z_2 = Z_1 \times$ Transmission ratio = 25 × 2.88 = 72
2.	26	74.88
3.	27	77.66

Therefore, select $Z_1 = 25$ and $Z_2 = 72$ teeth *(whole numbers)*

(b) *To find pitch diameters of sprockets [d_1 and d_2]*

Pitch diameter of sprocket Pinion

$$d_1 = \frac{p}{\sin\left(\frac{180}{Z_1}\right)}$$

$$= \frac{25.4}{\sin\left(\frac{180}{25}\right)} = 202.66 \text{ mm}$$

Pitch diameter of sprocket Gear

$$d_2 = \frac{p}{\sin\left(\frac{180}{Z_2}\right)}$$

$$= \frac{25.4}{\sin\left(\frac{180}{72}\right)} = 582.31 \text{ mm}$$

Step III: *Calculation of length of chain 'L'*

Length of chain $L = pL_P$ ... E(21-125)

Where, L_P = Length of chain in pitches given by

$$L_P = 2C_P \cos\alpha + \left(\frac{Z_1 + Z_2}{2}\right) + \alpha\left(\frac{Z_2 - Z_1}{180}\right) \quad \text{... E(21-122)}$$

Where, C_P = Centre distance in pitches $= \frac{C}{p}$

To find 'C', the centre distance between sprocket shafts

Minimum centre distance,

$$C_{min} = K_{min} C' \quad \text{... E(21-120)}$$

Where, $C' = \dfrac{d_1 + d_2}{2}$

$$= \frac{202.66 + 582.31}{2} = 392.5 \text{ mm}$$

$$K_{min} = 1 + \frac{40}{C'}$$

$$= 1 + \frac{40}{392.5} = 1.102$$

Therefore, $C_{min} = 1.102 \times 392.5 = 432.5$ mm

Maximum centre distance

$$C_{max} = 80p \quad \text{... E (21-121)}$$

$$= 80 \times 25.4 = 2032 \text{ mm}$$

Therefore use $C = 1250$ mm (average value)

Now, $C_p = \dfrac{C}{p}$

$$= \frac{1250}{25.4} = 49.21$$

$$L_p = 2C_p \cos\alpha + \left(\frac{Z_1 + Z_2}{2}\right) + \alpha\left(\frac{Z_2 - Z_1}{180}\right)$$

$$C_p = 49.21$$

$$\alpha = \sin^{-1}\left(\frac{d_2 - d_1}{2C}\right)$$

$$= \sin^{-1}\left(\frac{582.31 - 202.66}{2 \times 1250}\right) = 8.73$$

Therefore, $L_p = 2 \times 49.21 + \left(\dfrac{25 + 72}{2}\right) + 8.73\left(\dfrac{72 - 25}{180}\right)$

$$= 149.19 \approx 150$$

Length of chain,

$$L = pL_p$$

$$= 25.4 \times 150 = 3810 \text{ mm}$$

To calculate the number of chains 'i'

$$i = \frac{F_\theta}{F_a}$$

Where, $F_\theta = \dfrac{1000NK_lK_s}{v}$

$$v = \frac{pZ_1n_1}{60}$$

$$= \left(\frac{25.4}{1000}\right)\frac{25\times 720}{60} = 7.62\,\text{m/sec}$$

Where, K_l = Load factor = 1.3

K_s = Service factor = 1

Therefore, $F_\theta = \dfrac{1000\times 50\times 1.3\times 1}{7.62}$

$$= 8552.63\text{ N}$$

F_a = Allowable chain pull = $\dfrac{F_u}{\eta_0}$

Where, F_u = Ultimate chain pull

For 208A chain,

$$F_u = 13.8\text{ kN} = 13.8\times 10^3\text{N}$$

η_0 = Factor of safety = 5(assumed)

Therefore, $F_a = \dfrac{13.8\times 10^3}{5} = 2760\text{ N}$

$$i = \frac{F_\theta}{F_a}$$

$$= \frac{8552.63}{2760} = 3.098$$

Use, $i = 4$ Chains

Example 8.20: Select a suitable wire rope for a vertical mine hoist to lift 12 MN of ore in each 8 hours shift from a depth of 600 meters. Assume a two compartment shaft with the hoisting skips in balance. Use the following data:

(i) Maximum velocity of rope = 10 m/sec

(ii) Acceleration and retardation period = 10 seconds each.

(iii) Rest period of 10 seconds from loading an unloading.

(iv) Weight of skip = 0.6 times load capacity.

Solution:

Step I: *To calculate the distances covered during acceleration, full speed and deceleration.*

(i) Distance covered during acceleration (S_1)

v = Velocity of rope = 10 m/sec

t_1 is the time taken for acceleration = 10 secs.

Therefore,

Acceleration $a = \frac{v}{t} = \frac{10}{10} = 1.0 \text{ m/sec}^2$ (from $v = u + at$ when $u = 0$, because it starts from rest).

From, $S = ut + \frac{1}{2}at^2$; taking $u = 0$,

$$S = \frac{1}{2}at^2$$

Therefore, $S_1 = \frac{1}{2}at_1^2$

$$= \frac{1}{2} \times 1 \times (10)^2 = 50 \text{ m}$$

(ii) Distance covered during deceleration (S_2)

Distance covered during deceleration = 50 m. (Since the time taken for acceleration and deceleration is the same).

(iii) Distance covered during full speed (S_3)

S_3 = Total distance (*i.e.*, depth of mine) – Distance covered during acceleration – Distance covered during deceleration.

$$S_3 = 600 \text{ m} - 50 \text{ m} - 50 \text{ m} = 500 \text{ m}$$

And, time required to cover 500 m $= \frac{500}{10} = 50$ secs

Step II: *Calculation of time / trip*

(*a*) *Acceleration period* = 10 *secs.*
(*b*) *Full speed period* = 50 *secs.*
(*c*) *Deceleration period* = 10 *secs.*
(*d*) *Time for loading and unloading* = 10 *secs.*

Therefore, total time / trip = 80 secs (Sum of $a + b + c + d$).

Calculation of Capacity of Skip

Number of trips made in 8 hours shift

$$= \frac{8 \times 3600}{80} = 360 \text{ trips}$$

Quantity of ore to be lifted in one shift = 12 MN = 12×10^6 N

P_{ore} = Quantity of ore lifted/trip (or capacity of skip)

$$= \frac{12 \times 10^6}{360} = 33{,}333.33 \text{ N}$$

$P_s =$ Weight of skip.

$P_s = 0.6 \times \text{Capacity of skip (given)}$

$= 0.6 \times 33{,}333.33 = 20{,}000$ N

Therefore, total load to be lifted $= 33{,}333.33 + 20{,}000 = 53{,}333.33$ N

Step III: ***Selection of wire rope*** ***(Refer Table 21-47)***

Select 6×19 wire rope, the most commonly used wire rope for the mine hoist for which the recommended sheave diameter $D = 60$ to $100d$. Say sheave diameter $D = 80d$.

Where, d = Diameter of wire.

Table - (21-47) MDH

Type of Service	*Rope Construction*	*Sheave Diameter, cm*	
		Recommended	*Minimum*
Haulage Rope:	6 × 7	72d	42d
Mine Haulage			
Factory-yard Haulage			
Inclined Planes			
Tramways			
Power Transmission			
Guy Wires			
Standard Hoisting Rope:	6 × 19	45d	30d
(Most commonly used rope)		60 – 100d	
Mine Hoists			
Quarries			
Ore Docks			
Cargo Hoists			
Car Pullers			
Cranes			
Derricks		20 – 30d	
Tramways			
Well Drilling			
Elevators			
Guy Wires			
Extra-Flexible Hosting Rope:	8 × 19	31d	21d
Special Flexible Hosting Rope:	6 × 37	27d	18d
Steel-mill Laples			
Cranes			
High Speed Elevators			

From Table (21-48), factor of safety to be used in designing wire rope for hoists, for mine hoists based on depth of mine 700 m is 6.

Table - (21-48) MDH

Rope Application	*Factory of Safety*		
(a) From Indian Standards	100 or other Figure Laid Down by the Statutory Authority		
	Class 1**	Class 2 & 3*	Class 4*
Mining Ropes Wire ropes used on the cranes and other hoisting equipment Fixed Guys Unreeved rope bridless of jib cranes or ancillary appliances, such as lifting beams Ropes which are straight between terminal fittings	3 - 5	4.0	4.5
Hoisting, luffing and reeved bridle systems of inherently flexible cranes (for example, mobile crawler tower, guy, derrick, stiffleg derrick) where jibs are supported by ropes or where equivalent shock absorbing devices are incorporated in jib supports	4.0	4.5	5.5
Cranes and hoists in general hoists blocks	4.5	5.0	6.0
(b) From Other Sources			
Mine Shafts: Depths -			
to 152 m	8		
305 to 660 m	7		
610 to 916 m	6		
Over 915 m	5		
Haulage Ropes	6		
Small electric and air hoists	7		
Hot ladle cranes	8		
Slings	8		

Note: *The rope is subjected to severity of stress such as*

(i) Tensile stress due to load being lifted.

(ii) Bending load when it passes over sheave.

(iii) Torsional load when ore is being lifted.

To take into account the complexity of stress, the factor of safety selected from table is doubled. Therefore, use factor of safety = 2 × 6 = 12

Hence, the wire to be designed for a load of

$$53{,}333.33 \times 12 = 639999.96 \text{ N} = 0.639999 \text{ MN}$$

Referring Table (21-46), for 6×19 wire rope.

Ultimate strength $F_u = 500.8d^2$

Table - (21-46) MDH

Rope Construction	Ultimate Strength, F_u		Weight		Wire Diameter d_w, mm	Area A, mm^2	Recommended Sheave Diameter, mm	
	MN	kgf	KN/m	kgf/m			Average	Minimum
6 × 19	$500.8d^2$*	$51.07d^2$	$36.3d^2$*	$0.0037d^2$	0.063d	$0.38d^2$	45d	30d
6 × 37	$473.1d^2$*	$48.24d^2$	$35.3d^2$*	$0.0036d^2$	0.045d	$0.38d^2$	27d	18d
8 × 19	$431.3d^2$*	$43.98d^2$	$34.3d^2$*	$0.0035d^2$	0.050d	$0.35d^2$	31d	21d
6 × 7	$473.0d^2$*	$48.24d^2$	$32.4d^2$*	$0.0033d^2$	0.106d	$0.38d^2$	72d	42d

*SI Units: * d = Diameter of rope, m   Customary Metric Units: d = Diameter of rope, mm*

Where, 'd' is the diameter of rope in m and F_u is in MN.

Wire diameter, $d_w = 0.063d$

Area of wire, $A = 0.38d^2$

Weight/meter of rope $= 36.3d^2$

Equating F_u to 0.639999

$$500.8d^2 = 0.639999$$

Therefore, $d = 36$ mm

With the above value of d,

Wire diameter, $d_w = 0.063d = 2.268$ mm

Area of wire, $A = 0.38d^2 = 492.48 \text{ mm}^2$

Weight of rope $= P_{rope} = 36.3d^2$ kN/m

Length of rope = Depth of mine = 700 m.

Therefore, P_{rope} = Weight of rope/m × Length of rope (*i.e.,* depth of mine)

$$= 36.3d^2 \times 700 \text{ kN}$$

$$= 36.3(0.036)^2\, 700 \text{ kN}$$

$$= 32931.36 \text{ N}$$

Bending load, $P_b = \dfrac{KAd_w}{D}$ ... E(21-63b)

Where, K = Modulus of elasticity of rope = 82728.5 N/mm^2

Therefore, $P_b = \dfrac{82728.5 \times 492.48 \times 2.268}{80 \times 36}$

$$= 32084.43 \text{ N}$$

Load due to acceleration

$$= \left(P_{skip} + P_{ore} + P_{rope}\right)\frac{a}{g}$$

$$= (20000 + 33333.33 + 32931.36)\frac{1.2}{9.8066}$$

$$= 10555.91 \text{ N}$$

Example 8.21: Select suitable wire rope for the elevator of a building 200 m high. The weight of elevator cage is 10 kN and that of passengers is 12 kN. The rope velocity is 5m/sec. Select suitable wire rope for the elevator. The full speed is to be attained in 10 secs.

Solution:

Selection of wire size

Select 6 × 19 wire rope (the most commonly used wire rope) ... T (21-47)

Weight of cage $= P_C = 10 \text{ kN} = 10{,}000 \text{ N}$

Weight of passengers $= P_P = 12 \text{ kN} = 12{,}000 \text{ N}$

Total load on rope $= P_C + P_P = 10{,}000 + 12{,}000 = 22{,}000 \text{ N}$

The height of building = 200 m.

Factor of safety = 7.5 (approximate) for height 200 m ... T(21-48)

This factor is to be doubled to take into account the severity and complexity of stress. Therefore, use factor of safety $= 7.5 \times 2 = 15$

The rope is to be designed for $15 \times 22000 = 330000 \text{ N} = 0.33 \text{ MN}$

For 6 × 19 wire rope, referring Table (21-46), the ultimate load $F_u = 500.8d^2$. Where, F_u *is in MN and 'd' is in metre.*

Equating F_u to 0.33 MN,

$$500.8d^2 = 0.33$$

Therefore, $d = 0.02566 \text{ m}$

Say, $d = 26 \text{ mm}$.

Again from T(21-46),

Wire diameter, $d_w = 0.063d = 1.64 \text{ mm}$

Area of cross-section, $A = 0.38d^2 = 256.88 \text{ mm}^2$

Sheave diameter, $= 80d = 2080 \text{ mm}$

Weight of rope/m $= 36.3d^2 \text{ kN/m}$

Height of building = 200 m

(i) Weight of rope,

$$P_{rope} = 36.3d^2 \times 200$$

$$= 36.3\left(\frac{26}{1000}\right)^2 \times 200 \text{ kN}$$

$$= 4907.76 \text{ N}$$

(ii) Bending load

$$P_b = \frac{KAd_w}{D} \qquad \text{...E(21-63b)}$$

Where, $K = 82728.5 \text{N/mm}^2$

$A = 256.88 \text{ mm}^2$

$d_w = 1.64 \text{ mm}$

$D = 2080 \text{ mm}$

Therefore, $$P_b = \frac{82728.5 \times 256.88 \times 1.64}{2080} \text{N}$$

$= 16,755.83 \text{ N}$

(iii) Load due to acceleration P_a

$$P_{\text{acceleration}} = \left(P_{\text{cage}} + P_{\text{passenger}} + P_{\text{rope}}\right)\frac{a}{g}$$

Where, $a = \frac{v}{t} = \frac{5}{10} = 0.5 \text{ m/sec}^2$

$g = 9.8066 \text{ m/sec}^2$

$$P_{\text{acceleration}} = (10000 + 12000 + 4907.76) \times \frac{0.5}{9.8066}$$

$= 1371.92 \text{ N}$

Check for factor of safety

(i) Load during starting $= 2\left(P_{\text{cage}} + P_{\text{passenger}} + P_{\text{rope}}\right)$

(Assuming no slack in rope)

$= 2(10000 + 12000 + 4907.76)$

$= 53815.52 \text{ N}$

Effective load during starting $= P_{\text{starting}} + P_b$

$= 53815.52 + 16755.83 \text{ N}$

$= 70571.35 \text{ N}$

(ii) Load on rope during acceleration

$= P_{\text{cage}} + P_{\text{passenger}} + P_{\text{rope}} + P_b + P_{\text{acceleration}}$

$= 1000 + 12000 + 4907.76 + 16755.83 + 1371.92$

$= 44035.51 \text{ N}$

(iii) Load during uniform velocity

$= P_{\text{cage}} + P_{\text{passenger}} + P_{\text{rope}} + P_b$

$= 10000 + 12000 + 4907.76 + 16755.83$

$= 42633.59 \text{ N}$

From the above analysis we find that maximum load in rope occurs during starting and its value is 70571.35 N.

$$F_u = 500.8d^2 \text{ MN}$$

Where, F_u is in MN, d is in m

$$F_u = 500.8\left(\frac{26}{1000}\right)^2 \text{ MN}$$

$$= 0.338541 \text{ MN} = 338540.8 \text{ N}$$

Hence the maximum load in rope = 70571.35 N $\ll F_u$ = 338540.8 N and hence the wire selected is safe.

Example 8.22: Calculate the rope diameter of a 6 × 19 wire rope to lift a load of 10 kN of debris from a well 60.25 m deep. The weight of bucket is 5 kN and it is to be lifted at a maximum speed of 150 m/min which is attained in 1 sec. There is no slack in the rope. The sheave diameter is 60 times the rope diameter. The average tensile strength of rope = 590 d^2N where 'd' is the diameter of rope. Factor of safety = 5. Young's modulus for rope is 80.8×10^3 MPa. ***(VTU, Feb 2002)***

Solution:

To find the size of wire (d)

Weight of bucket $P_{bucket} = 5 \text{ kN} = 5000 \text{ N}$

Weight of debris to be lifted $P_{load} = 10 \text{ kN} = 10000 \text{ N}$

Total load on rope

$$= P_{bucket} + P_{load}$$

$$= 5000 + 10000 = 15000 \text{ N}$$

Depth of well = length of rope = 60.25m

Factor of safety = 5

Note: *The factor of safety is doubled to take into account, the complexity of stress induced in rope.*

Therefore, the factor of safety is 2 × 5 = 10

i.e., the rope is to be designed for 10×15000 N = 150000 N = 0.15 MN

For 6 × 19 wire rope,

$$F_u = 500.8d^2$$

Equating F_u to 0.15 MN,

$$500.8d^2 = 0.15$$

$$d = 0.01731 \text{ m} = 17.31 \text{ mm} = 18 \text{ mm}$$

Referring Table (21-46)

For 6 × 19 wire rope,

$$d_w = \text{Diameter of wire } = 0.063d$$

$$= 0.063 \times 18 \text{ mm} = 1.134 \text{ mm}$$

Sheave diameter, $D = 60 \text{ to } 100d = 60d\,(\text{given})$

$$= 60 \times 18 = 1080 \text{ mm}$$

$$A = 0.38d^2$$

$$= 0.38 \times (18)^2 = 123.12 \text{ mm}^2$$

Weight/metre of rope = $36.3d^2$

Calculation of Various loads on rope

(a) $P_{\text{rope}} = \textit{Weight of rope/m} \times \textit{Length of rope (i.e., depth of well)}$

$$P_{\text{rope}} = 36.3d^2 \times 60.25 \text{ kN}$$

$$= 36.3\left(\frac{18}{1000}\right)^2 \times 60.25$$

$$= 0.7086123 \text{ kN}$$

$$= 708.6123 \text{ N}$$

(b) $P_b = \textit{Load due to bending}$

$$P_b = \frac{KAd_w}{D} \qquad \text{... E(21-63b)}$$

$$= \frac{80.8 \times 10^3 \times 123.12 \times 1.134}{1080} \text{ N}$$

$$= 10445.5 \text{ N}$$

Where, K = Young's modulus of rope $= 80.8 \times 10^3$ MPa

A = Area of rope $= 123.12 \text{ mm}^2$

d_w = Wire diameter = 1.134 mm

D = Sheave diameter = 1080 mm

(c) $P_{\text{acceleration}} = \left(P_{\text{bucket}} + P_{\text{load}} + P_{rope}\right)\dfrac{a}{g}$

Where, $a = \dfrac{v}{t} = \dfrac{150/60}{1} = 2.5 \text{ m/sec}^2$; [Since $u = 0$]

Therefore, $P_{\text{acceleration}} = (5000 \text{ N} + 10000 + 708.61)$

$$= 4004.6 \text{ N}$$

Check for factor of safety

(i) Load during starting

$$P_{\text{start}} = 2\left(P_{\text{cage}} + P_{\text{load}} + P_{\text{rope}}\right)$$

$$= 2(5000 + 10000 + 708.6123)$$

$$= 31417.22 \text{ N}$$

Effective load during starting

$$= P_{start} + P_b$$

$$= 31417.22 + 10445.5$$

$$= 41862.72 \text{ N}$$

(ii) Load on rope during acceleration

$$= P_{bucket} + P_{load} + P_{rope} + P_b + P_{acceleration}$$

$$= 5000 + 10000 + 708.6123 + 10445.5 + 4004.6$$

$$= 30158.71 \text{ N}$$

(iii) Load during uniform velocity

$$= P_{bucket} + P_{load} + P_{rope} + P_{bending}$$

$$= 5000 + 10000 + 708.6123 + 10445.5$$

$$= 26154.11 \text{ N}$$

Therefore, from the above analysis it is clear that the maximum load occurs during starting and its value is = 4186.72 N

For 6 × 19 wire rope of 18 mm diameter,

$$F_u = 500.8d^2 \text{ MN}$$

$$F_u = 500.8\left(\frac{18}{1000}\right)^2$$

$$F_u = 0.16226 \text{ MN} = 162259.2 \text{ N}$$

Therefore, maximum load on rope = F_u and hence the wire selected is safe.

Example 8.23: Select suitable size of wire rope to lift the cage of a vertical mine hoist 100 m deep. The cage weighs 5 kN and has to lift 15kN of ore at a speed of 120 m/min. The maximum speed is attained in one second. (VTU, July / August 2002)

Solution:

For mine hoist, select 6 × 19 *wire rope (the most commonly used wire rope)* ... T(21-47)

$$P_c = \text{Weight of cage} = 5 \text{ kN}$$

$$P_l = \text{Weight to be lifted} = 15 \text{ kN}$$

Therefore total weight on rope

$$= P_c + P_l$$

$$= 5 + 15 = 20 \text{ kN} = 20 \times 10^3 \text{ N}$$

For 6 × 19 wire rope, referring Table (21-46) we have,

Ultimate load, $F_u = 500.8d^2$

Where, F_u = Ultimate load in MN.

d = Diameter of rope in metre.

To find F_u, the ultimate load

For depth of mine = 100 m, factor of safety is 8 ... T(21-48)

To take into account the complexity of stresses in rope, the above factor of safety is doubled.

Therefore, use factor of safety = 8 × 2 = 16

i.e., the rope is to be designed for 16×20 kN

$$= 320 \text{ kN} = 320 \times 10^3 \text{N} = 0.32 \text{ MN}$$

Equating $F_u = 0.32$ MN to $500.8d^2$, we get,

$$d = 0.0253 \text{ m} ; \text{ say } d = 26 \text{ mm}$$

Therefore, diameter of rope = 26 mm. Referring Table (21-46), the other dimensions of wire are

Wire diameter $d_w = 0.063d = 1.64$ mm

Sheave diameter $D = 60$ to $100d$; say $D = 80d$

$$= 80 \times 26 = 2080 \text{ mm}$$

Area of wire $A = 0.38d^2 = 0.38 \times (26)^2 = 256.88 \text{ mm}^2$

Weight of rope / m $= 36.3d^2$ kN/m

Depth of mine = 100 m = *Length of rope.*

(a) *Total weight on rope*

$$P_{\text{rope}} = \text{Weight of rope/metre} \times \text{Depth of mine}$$

$$= 36.3\left(\frac{26}{1000}\right)^2 \text{kN} \times 100 \text{ m}$$

$$= 2454 \text{ N}$$

(b) *Bending load*

$$P_b = \frac{KAd_w}{D} \quad \text{... E(21-63b)}$$

Where K = Young's modulus of material of wire = 82728.5N/mm^2

$$P_b = \frac{82728.5 \times 256.88 \times 1.64}{2080} \text{N}$$

$$= 16755.83 \text{ N}$$

(c) *Load due to acceleration*

$$P_{\text{acceleration}} = \left(P_{\text{cage}} + P_{\text{load}} + P_{\text{rope}}\right)\frac{a}{g}$$

Where, $a = \frac{v}{t}$ from $v = u + at$ when $u = 0$

$$v = 120 \text{m/min} = \frac{120}{60} \text{m/sec} = 2 \text{m/sec}$$

$$a = \frac{2}{1} = 2\,\text{m/sec}^2$$

$$g = 9.8066\,\text{m/sec}^2$$

Therefore, load due to acceleration

$$P_{\text{acceleration}} = (5000 + 15000 + 2454)\frac{2}{9.8066}$$

$$= 4579.36 \text{ N}$$

Check for factor of safety

(i) Load during starting

$$P_{\text{start}} = 2\left(P_{\text{cage}} + P_{\text{load}} + P_{\text{rope}}\right) \text{ (assuming no slack in rope)}$$

$$= 2(5000 + 15000 + 2454)$$

$$= 44908 \text{ N}$$

Effective load during starting

$$= P_{\text{start}} + P_b$$

$$= 44908 + 16755.83$$

$$= 61663.83 \text{ N}$$

(ii) Load on rope during acceleration

$$= P_{\text{cage}} + P_{\text{load}} + P_{\text{rope}} + P_b + P_{\text{acceleration}}$$

$$= 5000 + 15000 + 2454 + 16755.83 + 4579.36$$

$$= 43789.19 \text{ N}$$

(iii) Load during uniform velocity

$$= P_{\text{cage}} + P_{\text{load}} + P_{\text{rope}} + P_b$$

$$= 5000 + 15000 + 2454 + 16755.83$$

$$= 39209.83 \text{ N}$$

Therefore, from the above analysis we find that the load on the rope is maximum during starting and is equal to 61663.83 N.

F_u, Ultimate load for 6 × 19 wire rope is

$$F_u = 500.8d^2$$

i.e.,

$$F_u = 500.8\left(\frac{26}{1000}\right)^2 \text{ MN}$$

$$= 0.3385408 \text{ MN} = 338540.8 \text{ N}$$

Therefore, maximum load induced in rope = 61663.8 N hence the wire size selected is safe.

Example 8.24: Design a wire rope to lift 9 MN of ore in each 8 hour shift from a depth of 600 m. The maximum velocity of rope is 12 m/sec and acceleration and retardation period of 15 seconds each. Take rest period of 10 seconds for loading and unloading. The weight of skip is 0.6 time the load capacity.

Solution:

(i) *To calculate the distance covered during acceleration, full speed and declaration.*

We have, $v = u + at$; $u = 0$ since it starts from rest.

Velocity $v = at$,

Here velocity $= 12$ m/sec

Time required for acceleration = 15 sec

Therefore, $a = \frac{v}{t} = \frac{12}{15} = 0.8 \text{ m/sec}^2$

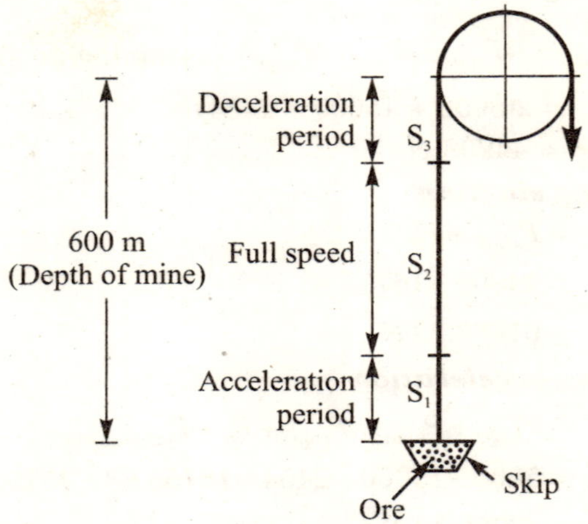

Let S_1, S_2 and S_3 be the distances covered during acceleration, full speed and deceleration.

$$S_1 = \frac{1}{2}at_1^2$$

$$= \frac{1}{2} \times 0.8 \times 15^2 = 90 \text{ m}$$

$$S_2 = \frac{1}{2}at_2^2$$

$$= \frac{1}{2} \times 0.8 \times 15^2 = 90 \text{ m}$$

Therefore, $S_3 = 600 - (S_1 + S_2)$

$$= 600 - (90 + 90) = 420 \text{ m}$$

Time required for full speed $= \frac{S_3}{v} = \frac{420}{12} = 35$ secs

(ii) *To calculate time required / trip*

Time for acceleration	= 15 secs
Time during full speed (Uniform speed)	= 35 secs
Time during deceleration	= 15 secs
Time for loading and unloading	= 10 secs
Therefore, Total time/trip	= 75 secs

Number of trips made in 8 hr shift

$$= \frac{8 \times 60 \times 60}{75} = 384$$

Quantity of ore lifted in 8 hrs = 9 MN = 9×10^6 N

Therefore, the quantity of ore lifted/trip = Capacity of skip

$$P_{\text{ore}} = \frac{9 \times 10^6}{384} = 23437.5 \text{ N}$$

Therefore, Weight of skip = 0.6 times load capacity

$$P_{\text{skip}} = 0.6 \times 23437.5 = 14062.5 \text{ N}$$

Therefore total load to be lifted

$$= P_{\text{ore}} + P_{\text{skip}}$$

$$= 23437.5 + 14062.5 = 37500 \text{ N}$$

(iii) *Selection of wire rope*

A 6 × 19 wire rope is the most commonly used rope for hoisting purpose.

(Table 21-47). Here 6 represents number of strands and 19 represents for number of wires in each strand.

(iv) *To find rope diameter 'd'*

Referring Table (21-46), for 6 × 19 wire rope,

The ultimate strength $F_u = 500.8d^2$ *Where, d is in mm.*

Wire diameter $d_w = 0.063d$

Area of rope $A = 0.38d^2$

Weight of rope $= 36.3d^2$ kN/m

$$F_u = \text{Total load} \times \text{factor of safety}$$

Referring T(21-48), for depth of 600m, factor of safety = 7.

Therefore, $(3500) \times 7 = 500.8d^2$

$$d = 22.89 \text{ mm}; \text{ say } d = 23 \text{ mm}$$

$$d_w = \text{Wire diameter}$$

$$= 0.063 \times 23 = 1.449 \text{ mm}$$

Area of cross-section $A = 0.38d^2$

$$= 0.38 \times 23^2 = 201.02 \text{ mm}^2$$

To calculate various loads on rope

(i) Bending load (P_b)

$$P_b = \frac{KAd_w}{D} \qquad \text{... E(21.63b)}$$

Where, K = Modulus of elasticity of rope = 82728.5N/mm^2

D = Sheave diameter = 60 to $100d$

Say $D = 80d = 80 \times 23 = 1840$ mm

Therefore, $P_b = \dfrac{82728.5 \times 201.02 \times 1.449}{1840} = 13096.19$ N

(ii) Load due to acceleration (P_a)

$$P_a = \left[P_{\text{rope}} + P_{\text{ore}} + P_{\text{skip}}\right]\frac{a}{g}$$

Where, P_{rope} = Weight of rope/m × Length of rope (*i.e.*, Depth of mine)

$$= 36.3dK^2 \text{ kN/m} \times 600$$

$$= 396.3 \times 10^3 \times \left(\frac{23}{1000}\right)^2 \times 600$$

$$= 11521.62 \text{ N}$$

Therefore, $P_a = \left[11521.62 + (37500)\right] \times \dfrac{0.8}{9.81}$

$$= 3997.69 \text{ N}$$

(iii) Impact load during starting (P_s)

$$P_s = 2\left[\left(P_{\text{ore}} + P_{\text{skip}}\right) + P_a\right]$$

$$= 2\left[(37500) + 3997.69\right]$$

$$= 82995.36 \text{ N}$$

Example 8.25: Select a wire rope to lift a load of 10 kN through 200 m. The desired velocity is of 20 m/min is to be achieved while travelling through a distance of 10 m.
(VTU, Feb 2005)

Solution:

Step I: ***Selection of wire rope***

A 6 × 19 wire rope is selected as it is the most commonly used wire ropes for hoisting purpose.

Step II: ***To find rope diameter of rope 'd'***

For 6 × 19 wire rope, from T(21-46),

$F_u = 500.8d^2$; 'd' is in metre.

Wire diameter $d_w = 0.063d$

Area of rope $A = 0.38d^2$

Weight of rope $= 36.3d^2$ kN/m

Ultimate load F_u = Total load × Factor of safety ;

$$\text{Load} = 10\text{ KN} = 10\times10^3\text{N} = 10^{-2}\text{MN}$$

From T (21-48) for depth h = 200 m, factor of safety = 8.

Therefore, $(10)^{-2}\times 8 = 500.8d^2$

$$d = 12.6 \text{ mm}$$

Adopt $d = 13$ mm

$$d_w = 0.063d = 0.063\times13 = 0.819 \text{ mm}$$

Area of cross-section

$$A = 0.38d^2 = 0.38(13)^2 = 64.22 \text{ mm}^2$$

Step III: *To calculate various loads on rope*

(i) Bending load (P_b)

$$P_b = \frac{KAd_w}{D} \qquad \text{... E(21.63b)}$$

Where $K = 82728.5\text{N/mm}^2$

D = Sheave diameter = 60 to 100d

Use $D = 80d = 80\times13 = 1040$ mm

Therefore, $P_b = \dfrac{82728.5\times0.819\times64.22}{1040}\text{ N} = 4183.85\text{ N}$

(ii) Load due to acceleration (P_a)

$$P_a = \left[P_{\text{rope}} + P_{\text{load}}\right]\frac{a}{g}$$

Where, P_{rope} = Weight of rope/m × Length of rope

$= 36.3d^2$ kN/m × Depth of mine

$$= 396.3\times10^3\times\left(\frac{13}{1000}\right)^2\times200$$

$= 1226.94$ N

Therefore, $P_a = \left(1226.94 + 10\times10^3\right)\dfrac{a}{g}$

$$v = at \text{ i.e., } \frac{20}{60}\text{ m/sec}$$

i.e., $at = 0.333$ m/sec

$$S = \frac{1}{2}at^2$$

i.e.,
$$10 = \frac{1}{2}(at)t$$

$$10 = \frac{1}{2}(0.333)t$$

Therefore,
$$t = \frac{20}{0.333}\text{ sec} = 66.67\text{ sec}$$

$$P_a = \left(1226.94 + 10 \times 10^3\right)\frac{0.333}{9.81} = 381.1\text{ N}$$

EXERCISE

1. Select a V-V belt drive to transmit 10 kW from a shaft running at 1200 rpm to another shaft running at 400 rpm. The diameter of smaller pulley is to be limited to 175 mm.
2. A 40 kW, 1440 rpm motor is required to drive an air compressor through the medium V-belt. The diameter of motor and compressor pulleys are respectively 200 mm and 700 mm. The centre distance between pulleys is 1.4 m. Select suitable V-belt drive.
3. Select suitable roller chain to transmit 15 kW from a shaft running at 1800 rpm to another shaft to be run at 400 rpm.
4. A roller chain is to be designed to transmit 7.5 kW from a shaft running at 500 rpm to another shaft running at 900 rpm. Determine,
   (*i*) Pitch of chain and its chain number.
   (*ii*) Number of teeth on sprockets.
   (*iii*) Pitch diameter of sprockets.
   (*iv*) Shortest centre distance between them.
   (*v*) Number of chains required.
5. Design a roller chain to transmit 60 kW at a speed of 800 rpm, the driven machinery is to run at 300 rpm.
6. Select suitable wire rope for a vertical mine hoist to lift 15 MN of ore in 8 hours shift from a depth of 800 meters. Assume a two compartment shaft with the hoisting skips in balance. Use the following data
   (*i*) Maximum velocity of rope = 15 m/sec.
   (*ii*) Acceleration and deceleration period = 10 secs each.
   (*iii*) Rest period of 12 secs for loading and unloading.
   (*iv*) Weight of skip = 0.5 times load capacity.
7. Select suitable size of wire rope to lift the cage of a vertical mine hoist 150 m deep. The cage weighs 7 kN and has to lift 20 kN at a speed of 150 m/min. The maximum speed is attained in one second.
8. Select a wire rope to lift a load of 15 kN through 250 m. The desired velocity of 25 m/min is to be obtained through a distance of 10 meters.